EARLY WRITINGS

OF

BISHOP HOOPER.

EARLY WRITINGS

OF

JOHN HOOPER, D.D.

LORD BISHOP OF GLOUCESTER AND WORCESTER,

MARTYR, 1555.

COMPRISING

THE DECLARATION OF CHRIST AND HIS OFFICE.
ANSWER TO BISHOP GARDINER.
TEN COMMANDMENTS.
SERMONS ON JONAS.
FUNERAL SERMON.

EDITED FOR

The Parker Society,

BY THE

REV. SAMUEL CARR, M.A.

RECTOR OF EVERSDEN, VICAR OF ST PETER'S, COLCHESTER,
LATE FELLOW OF QUEENS' COLLEGE, CAMBRIDGE.

WIPF & STOCK · Eugene, Oregon

Wipf and Stock Publishers
199 W 8th Ave, Suite 3
Eugene, OR 97401

The Early Writings of John Hooper, D. D.,
Lord Bishop of Gloucester and Worcester, Martyr, 1555
Comprising The Declaration of Christ and His Office,
Answers to Bishop Gardiner, Ten Commandments, Sermons on Jonas,
Funeral Sermon.
By Hooper, John
ISBN 13: 978-1-60608-434-2
Publication date 12/9/2009
Previously published by Cambridge University Press, 1843

CONTENTS.

	PAGE
A Declaration of Christ and his Office.	1
Answer to the Bishop of Winchester's Book.	97
A Declaration of the Ten Holy Commandments of Almighty God	249
An Oversight and Deliberation upon the holy Prophet Jonas	431
A Funeral Sermon upon Revelation xiv. 13.	561

[HOOPER.]

BIOGRAPHICAL NOTICE

OF

BISHOP HOOPER.

JOHN HOOPER was born in Somersetshire, about the close of the fifteenth century. His name is usually spelt Hoper, or Houper, by himself and his contemporaries. He studied at Oxford, probably in Merton College, and subsequently embraced the monastic life. After the dissolution of the monasteries, and when the Act of the Six Articles was in force, he withdrew to the continent, where he was kindly received at Zurich by Bullinger. He remained abroad till the accession of King Edward VI. In 1548 he returned to England, and residing in London, preached continually to large congregations, taking also an active part in the proceedings of that period.

In May, 1550, he was nominated to the bishopric of Gloucester, but was not consecrated till the next year. This delay was owing to his objections to an oath by the saints, and to some of the vestments formerly worn by the Romish prelates, and then retained. The former point was conceded; but the dispute respecting the habits went so far, that Hooper was for a short time confined in the Fleet. This matter being at last arranged by his yielding in a great measure to what was required, he entered upon his diocese, to which that of Worcester was afterwards added, and discharged the duties of the episcopal office in a most exemplary manner.

On the accession of Queen Mary, Hooper was one of the first who were brought into trouble. He was committed to the Fleet in September, 1553, on a false allegation of being indebted to the Queen, and was treated with much severity. The particulars are related by himself in one of his letters.

When popery was fully restored, Hooper was among the earliest sufferers, as he had predicted would be the case. Gardiner treated him with unrelenting severity. He was condemned in January, 1555, taken to Gloucester, and burned near to his own cathedral on the 9th of February. His cruel sufferings, augmented by the barbarous orders of his persecutors, are fully related by Foxe.

Bishop Hooper appears to have taken an active part in the reformation during the reign of King Edward VI.; and although for a time at variance with Cranmer and Ridley on the question respecting habits, a perfect reconciliation afterwards took place, and he was an inmate with the former at Lambeth, when visiting London.

No life of Bishop Hooper has yet appeared as a separate work: materials had been collected for a fuller biographical notice for this volume, when the Editor's attention was called to some letters of this reformer, transcribed from originals in the Archives at Zurich. As these letters supply important additional information respecting the writer, and it is probable that the researches at Zurich and elsewhere in Switzerland, now in progress in behalf of the Parker Society, may give yet further particulars; the Editor is unwilling to delay the publication of the present volume, now completed at the press, and therefore gives the preceding very brief sketch, hoping that a more detailed memoir, with fuller statements, may appear with the remaining portion of the author's writings. Of the pieces included in this publication it is unnecessary to say any thing in addition to the preliminary notices: it is evident from the remarks of contemporary writers, that they had considerable influence in their day.

The subjoined list of Bishop Hooper's writings, from the Bibliotheca of Bishop Tanner, will shew what remain to be printed. His letters mention two treatises sent to Zurich a short time before his martyrdom. Hitherto these have been sought for in vain; but the researches above alluded to being still in progress, it is possible they may yet be found.

November, 1843.

The following is the list of Bishop Hooper's works, as given by Bishop Tanner in his Bibliotheca Britanico-Hibernica.

HOOPERUS (JOHANNES) patria Somersetensis in academia Oxon. et, ut A. Wood videtur, in collegio Merton. in studiis humanioribus institutus. Emenso philosophiæ curriculo, monachi Cisterciensis habitum assumpsit, quem mox abjecit, et Londinum se contulit, ubi lectione quorundam Lutheri librorum amplectendam doctrinam reformatam invitabatur. Circa annum MDXXXIX. metu sex articulorum solum vertit, et usque ad Henrici VIII. mortem per Galliam, Hiberniam, et Helvetiam vagari coactus est. Regnante Edwardo in patriam rediit, et A. MDXLIX. unus accusatorum Bonneri fuit. Fox. i. edit. p. 700, et capellanus ducis Somerset. Strype in *Vita Cranmer.* p. 219. Anno MDL. episcopus Glocestrensis designatus est; accepto etiam A. MDLII. (regis dono) Wigorniensi multo opulentiori episcopatu, quem simul cum Glocestrensi per dispensationem regiam quæ *Commenda* vocatur, tenuit. Maria regnum auspicante Londinum accersitus est, ubi 28 Jan. MDLIV. Stephanus Gardiner, episcopus Winton. ei duos objecit articulos, unum de matrimonio clericorum, alterum de divortio, (vid. Ric. Smith librum De cœlibatu) deinde in carcerem compactus, et tandem hæreseos damnatus, igni traditus est, Glocestriæ, 9 Febr. MDLV. Inter doctos sui seculi viros in primis annis philologia simul et philosophia clarus, senex autem theologia et patrum lectione non minus insignis habebatur. Erat ecclesiæ Romanæ infensissimus, matri Anglicanæ autem non per omnia amicus: utpote qui puritanis favebat, et ritibus ecclesiæ, saltem, quod ad vestes sacras spectat, se non conformem præstabat. Scripsit Anglice, *Answer to the bishop of Winchester's book, entit.*

A detection of the devil's sophistry, wherewith he robbeth the unlearned of the true belief in the sacrament of the altar. Pr. "Youre booke, my lorde, intytlid." Zurich, MDXLVII. 4to. *A declaration of Christ and his office.* Ded. to Edw. duke of Somerset. 8 Dec. MDXLVII. Pr. "The godlye pretence." Zurich, MDXLVII. 8vo. recus. cum correctionibus Christoph. Rosdell... 12mo. *Lesson of the incarnation of Christ.* Pr. pr. "Seyng we be even so apointed." Lond. MDXLIX. 8vo. *Sermons on Jonas before the king and council in Lent.* MDL. Pr. ded. regi Edw. VI. "Amonge other most noble and." Lond. MDL. et MDLIX. 8vo. *Answers to certain queries concerning the abuses of the mass.* Burnet, *Hist. reform.* vol. II. num. 25. *A godly confession and protestation of the christian faith, wherein is declared what a Christian man is bound to believe of God, his king, his neighbour and himself.* ded. K. Edw. VI. and parliament. "The wyse man Cicero most." Pr. lib. "I beleve accordynge to the holi." Lond. MDL. 8vo. *Homily to be read in the time of the pestilence, and a most present remedy for the same*... MDLIII. 4to. *Various letters written in prison.* X. in Fox. *Acts et monum. of the church.* A. MDLV. pp. 1507, 1511, etc. III. in Strype, in *Vita Cranmer.* append. p. 133, seq. *to the prisoners in the counter*, dat. 4 Jan. MDLIV. extat ad finem *Apologiæ* i. *about the story of his recanting*, dat. 20 Febr. MDLIV. MS. Eman. Cantabr. *Exhortation to patience sent to his wife Anne.* Pr. "Our Saviour Jesus Christ." Fox, p. 1513. *Certain sentences written in prison.* Lond. MDLIX. 8vo. *Speech at his death. An apology against the untrue and slanderous report made of him, that he should be a maintainer and encourager of such that cursed queen Mary.* Pr. "It is the use and fashion of all." Lond. MDLXII. 8vo. Quibus adduntur epistolæ nonnullæ scriptæ in carcere. *Comfortable expositions on the* 23. 62. 73. *et* 77. *psalms.* Lond. MDLXXX. 4to. *Exposition on Psal.* XXIII. Pr. "To the faithful in the city of London." Pr. "Your fayth and hope of." Lond. MDLXII.

tempore reg. Mariæ. *Annotations on the* 13. *chapt. to the Romans.* Pr. ded. decano, cancellario, archidiacono, etc. diœc. Glocestr. " If the dangers and perils." Worcester, MDLI. Lond. MDLXXXIII. 12mo. *Twelve lectures upon the creed.* Lond. MDLXXXI. 8vo. *Confession of the Christian faith, containing* 100 *articles according to the order of the creed of the apostles.* Pr. " I believe in one God." . . . . MDL. Lond. MDLXXXI. 8vo. A. MDLXXXIV. annectebantur Johannis Baker *Lecturis super symbolum apostolorum. Declaration of the ten holy commandments of Almighty God.* cap. 19. Pr. " I commende here unto thy charitie." . . . MDXLVIII. Lond. MDL. et MDLXXXVIII. 8vo. *Articulos* 50, *Injunctiones* 31, *et Examinationes, etc. in visitatione diœc. Glocestr.* Strype in *Vita Cranmer.* p. 216. *Concionem funebrem habitam.* 14 Januar. MDXLIX. in *Revel.* XIV. 13. I heard a voice, etc. Pr. " The death of a man's frendis." Lond. MDXLIX. in 12mo. recus. per Tho. Purfote . . . 8vo. His addidit Baleus. *Varias conciones,* lib. I. *An fides celari possit,* lib. I. *De perseverantia Christianorum,* lib. I. *Vitandos esse pseudoprophetas,* lib. I. *Ad Vigornienses et Glocestrenses,* lib. I. *Contra abominationes missæ,* lib. I. *Adversus concionem Jacobi Brokes,* lib. I. *Contra mendacia Thomæ Martin,* lib. I. *In psalmum, Levavi oculos meos,* lib. I. *Super orationem Dominicam,* lib. I. *Fidelis uxoris officia,* lib. I. *De triplici hominis statu,* lib. I. *Contra Buceri calumniatorem,* lib. I. *De re eucharistica,* lib. I. *De vera et falsa doctrina,* lib. I. *Contra obtrectatores divini verbi,* lib. I. *Ad Londinensis antichristi articulos,* lib. I. *Contra primatum Romani episcopi,* lib. I. *Exhortationes ad Christianos,* lib. I. Latine etiam ex carcere scripsit *Epistolam ad episcopos, decanos, archidiaconos et cæteros cleri ordines.* A. MDLIV. Pr. " Non vos latet viri doctissimi." Fox, p. 2135. *De pseudo-doctrina fugienda,* lib. I. " Adversarius humani generis." *Ad parliamentum contra neotericos,* lib. I. " Quanquam viri illustrissimi." *Pro doctrina cœnæ Dominicæ,* lib. I. " Ne cuiquam vestrum fratres." *Contra corporalem præsentiam,* lib. I. " Secundus liber in quo neoterici." *Ad Glocestrios et Vigornios,* epist. I. " Per duos annos et aliquot." *Ad cardinalem Polum,* epist. I. " Non eo animo, vir ornatissime." *Ad Cicestrensem episcopum,* epist. I. " Pii et boni viri, præsul amplissime." *Epistolam I. Lat. Calvino.* dat. 3 Sept. MDLII. edit. per Colomesium, Lond. MDCXCIV. 12mo. p. 288. Epistolas II. Fox, p. 1482. *Transtulit in Anglic. Tertulliani ad uxorem* lib. II. *De electione mariti et uxoris.* Lond. MDL. 8vo. Bal. VIII. 86. Athen. Oxon. I. 91. seqq. Godwin, p. 590. Fox, p. 1502.

A DECLARATION

OF

CHRIST AND HIS OFFICE.

[HOOPER.]

A Declaracion

of Christe and of his

offyce compylyd by Jo-

han Hoper Anno

1547.

Matth. 7.

Hic est filius meus dilectus, in quo mihi bene cōplacuit, ipsum audite.

[Title-page of the First Edition.]

A Godlie and pro-
fitable treatise contei-
nyng a declaration of
Christ and his
Office.

compiled 1547 by the reverend father, and faithfull Minister of Christe, and constant martyre in the truthe Maister Jhon Hoper: and newly corrected, and purged by the Godlie industrie of C. R. from a multitude of grosse faultes, where withall it was pestered, through the corruption of the print, and great unskilfulnesse of the Printer, beyng a mā of an other Nation.

Matt. vii.

This is my beloved Sonne in whō I am well pleased, heare hym.

℃ Imprinted at London for John Perrin, and are to be sold at his shop in Paules Churchyard, at the Signe of the Aungell.

[*Title-page of the Second Edition.*]

[THE first edition of this treatise, printed at Zurich, 1547, by persons ignorant of the English language, is so full of typographical errors, as oftentimes to obscure the sense[1]. About thirty-five years afterwards another edition was printed by Christopher Rosdell, who professed to correct these errors (see the title on the preceding page,) and translated the Latin quotations. He also prefixed a dedication to Edward Seymour, Earl of Hertford, son of Edward Seymour, Duke of Somerset, the Protector and Uncle of King Edward VI., to whom Bishop Hooper had inscribed the first edition.

These two editions have been carefully collated on the present occasion: the text of that of 1547 has been uniformly retained, corrected only as to the literal and typographical errors by comparison with Rosdell's.

The marginal notes are supplied from the latter source; and Rosdell's translations and principal alterations are appended, distinguished by the initial R.

For the other notes the Editor is responsible.

[1] The following specimen of the first sentence of the Zurich edition will give some idea, though only an imperfect one, of the difficulty arising from what Rosdell terms "the multitude of gross faults wherewithal it was pestered." His own edition was also very far from being correct.

For asmouche as all mightye God of his infinit mercye and Goddenys preparyd Ameanes wherby Adame and his posterite might be restoryd agayne unto there Originall iustite and perfection boothe of body and soule and to lyne eternally unto the sa me end that they were creatyd for to blysse and magnifie for euer the immortall and lyuyng God. it is thoffice of euery trew Christiane before all other studies, trauelles and paynes that he shall susteyne for the tyme of this brieffe and miserable lief to applye hymselfe with all diligeteforseand labor to know perfetlye this meanes ordeynid by God for our saluation and the thingonsknowen diligently with hart &c. &c.]

[THE EPISTLE DEDICATORY OF THE ENGLISH
EDITION, 1582.]

¶ To the right ho-
nourable Edward Seymour
Earl of Hertford, and Lord
Beauchamp: Christopher Rosdell wisheth health, with
increase of godliness
honour and
wealth.

IF either Hippocrates (right honourable) for sending certain of his scholars into divers cities of Græcia to help them, when they began to be visited with great mortality through a dangerous and grievous sickness, merited at the hands of the Græcians the honour of Hercules; or Aristides deserved at the hands of the Athenians so great things as after his departure were recompensed to his posterity, for a reward of that he had sustained in the wars of the Persians, to defend and save their city; with how great praise is master Hooper to be extolled of us? And how great rewards have his merits won at our hands, who hath done more for his country than Hippocrates for Græcia, and sustained more for the defence of the gospel, than Aristides for the defence of Athens? For when a most dangerous and pernicious disease, not of the body but of the soul, (I mean heresy, superstition, and idolatry,) had not invaded (as the plague in Græcia) certain cities, but (as the clouds in the sky) overspread the whole land; he did not only send others, but also most diligently went himself to wash the impure and unclean lepers, not in the waters of Jordan, but in the liv- ing and pure fountain of the gospel of Jesus Christ; where-

Sabel. Lib. vii. cap. 1.

[2] Reg. v.

of many yet remaining can testify and bear witness. And when the uncircumcised Philistines, the wild boar out of the wood, and the wild beasts of the field, yea, when that beast John speaketh of in the Revelation, with an infinite brood of his worshippers, for the sins of the people had prevailed in this commonwealth, and began to defile the holy temple of the Lord, and to make Hierusalem an heap of stones; he, for the health and safety of the Lord's inheritance, did not only with Aristides sustain and suffer many hard things, but also was another Sampson fighting against the Romish Philistines, and in the end, rather than he would worship the beast, he chose to be cast into their hot fiery furnace, wherein for righteousness' sake, like unto Polycarpus, with singular courage, wonderful patience and constancy, he yielded his soul into the hands of the eternal Father, and deserved the name of an holy and constant martyr. In whom the scripture was truly verified, which saith, "The world shall hate you, persecute you, and some of you shall they kill and put to death for my name's sake." "Whoso will be my disciple, let him take up his cross and follow me." "All that will live godly in Christ Jesus, shall suffer persecution." And "through many afflictions we must enter into the kingdom of God." Therefore this is not more old than it is a true saying,

Psal. lxxx.

Apoc. xiii.

Psal. lxxix.

[1] *Euseb. Lib. iii. cap. 4.*

Matt. x.
Luke xxi.
John xiii.
2 Tim. iii.
Acts xiv.

> "*Sanguine mundata est ecclesia, sanguine cœpit,*
> *Sanguine succrevit, sanguine finis erit*[2]."

Yet to the great comfort and consolation of all those that suffer for Christ's sake, it is said: "Right precious and dear in the sight of the Lord is the death of his saints." "Whosoever shall lose his life for my sake, and the gospel's, shall

Psal. cxvi.

Mark viii.

[1] The reference appears to be wrong. The martyrdom of Polycarp, as related by Eusebius, is in Lib. iv. cap. xv. Euseb. Op. Moguntiæ. 1672. Tom. i. p. 128.]

[2] The church was cleansed by blood, it commenced in blood, it has increased through blood, and its termination will be with blood.]

save it." "It is a true saying, If we die with him, we shall also live with him: If we suffer with him, we shall also reign with him; if we deny him, he will also deny us." Therefore "blessed are the dead which die in the Lord; even so, saith the Spirit." But because, right honourable, as these places of holy scripture do most plainly teach us, and as Saint Augustine[3] hath truly said, "It is not the death, but the cause for the which one dieth, that maketh a martyr;" not every one that suffereth, but he that suffereth for righteousness' sake, deserveth the praise of martyrdom: the Lord himself was crucified with thieves, yet there was great diversity and difference between the causes of their suffering, as one of the thieves confessed, reproving the other and saying, "We receive things worthy of that we have done, but this man hath done nothing amiss:" and as Apollinaris saith, "Where the verity and truth of Christ is not, there is no martyrdom:" therefore, that the cause which this good man so valiantly defended, and doctrine which he so diligently preached and finally sealed with his blood, might appear and be seen to all posterities; he left the tenor and effect thereof (to the great benefit of God's church in all ages to come) in writing, as by certain books extant at this day is to be seen. Amongst the which there is none doth more plainly shew forth the cause he maintained, and quarrel wherein he died, than this little treatise, entituled, A True Declaration of Christ and his Office. Wherein the principal points of christian religion are so sententiously handled, and Christ and his office so lively described, that nothing can be more clear to the eye, or more melodious and sweet to the ear of the godly Christian. Yet, alas! right honourable, as that famous river Hypanis,

2 Tim. ii.

Rev. xiv.

Aug. Ep. v. ad Bonif. eques. digni virum.

Luke xxiii.

[3 Jam enim nescio quoties disputando et scribendo monstravimus non eos posse habere martyrum mortem, quia christianorum non habent vitam, cum martyrem non faciat pœna sed causa. Aug. Op. Basil. (Frobenii) 1541. Ep. 61, ad Dulcetium, Tom. II. col. 310. A.]

Vitruvius, Lib. viii. cap. 3.

the prince of rivers amongst the Scythians, which in itself is most pure and sweet, by running through the bitter pool Exampeus, or it come to the sea, is infected, and made bitter, and altogether unlike unto itself[1]; whereupon Solinus saith, *Qui in principiis eum norunt, prædicant, qui in fine experti sunt, execrantur*[2]: so this godly and profitable tract, in itself most pure and pleasant, by passing through the press of an unskilful printer at Zurich in Germany, or it came to be published in the sea of this world, was so infected and corrupted, not with small and petty scapes, but with gross and palpable faults, not here and there, but in every leaf, in every page, and almost in every line, that it might truly be said, Either this is not master Hooper's work, or else, *quam dissimilis sui prodit*[3]. So that Apelles had not so great cause to bewail his Venus, nor Protogenes to beweep his Hialysum, daubed and piteously mortered, than he had to lament his book so greatly corrupted. And that which is most of all to be lamented, it hath remained in this pickle, and continued in this rust, by the space of thirty and five years, or thereabout, and was not unlike to have remained therein for ever, if, at the earnest petitions of a certain godly Christian, I had not taken this labour upon me. Whereunto, as the petitions of the godly, the desire of profiting the church of Christ, and care to salve the wounded and martyred work of so good a man, did not a little on the one side move and persuade me; so the tediousness of the thing (wherein methought I saw an idea of the pestered stable of Augea) did greatly on the other side terrify and dissuade me. But

[1 Varenius's account is: Parvulus rivus, dictus Exampeus, amarus admodum, reddit Hypanem fluvium cui influit amarum. Var. Geog. Lib. i. cap. xvii. prop. x.]

[2 They who knew it at its source praise it, they who have made trial of it at its termination execrate it.]

[3 How unlike himself does he come forth!]

when I called to mind that old saying[4], *Labor improbus* Virgil. *omnia vincit*, and considered withal, how great labour we ought to sustain for the glory of God and benefit of our brethren, all delays and excuses laid apart, yea, and all other business for the present time set aside; as Abraham wholly gave himself to deliver his cousin Loth out of the bondage and captivity of the Assyrians, and to reduce not only him, but also his substance to their former state of freedom and liberty; so I employed my whole power, travail, and study, to bring again this treasure of our christian brother, from that servitude and bondage it sustained by the German printer, unto his native liberty and freedom; providing also that the allegations and testimonies alleged out of the holy scripture or fathers, for confirmation of any matter, (which in the first edition were all in Latin,) might now, for the use and benefit of the simple reader, come forth in English. All which things when I had accomplished, and (though not in such perfect and absolute manner as I wished, yet in such sort as I could) brought to an end, I began to think with myself, to whom chiefly and principally I should dedicate this my labour, whatsoever it is. And your most honourable lordship came to my remembrance, as the only man to whom this Treatise doth by right and just title appertain. For notwithstanding I may seem (being a man not only altogether unknown, but also unworthy to write unto so noble a personage) very bold in coming so familiarly unto your honour, yet there were divers urgent causes and great reasons, which induced me hereunto. As, that when I had diligently weighed and considered with myself, to whom the author hereof did dedicate this his travail, when he first published and set it forth, methought I was sufficiently instructed to whom I

^{Gen. xiv.} ^{Joseph[5].} ^{Antiq.} ^{Lib. i. cap. 3.}

[4 Virg. Georg. II. v. 145. "Great labour overcomes all difficulties."]
[5 The reference should be Joseph. Op. Lib. I. cap. x. (p. 31. Amst. 1726.)]

should present the same, being newly furbished. And when I bethought of that rare affability and singular humanity, which all men report to have been evermore in your honour, towards the favourers of true religion, I was not only confirmed against all fear, but also emboldened to offer this small gift unto your honour, as a testimony of my good will towards the same. And although my gift is of no such price, that it should be offered unto so great a man; yet I doubt not but your honour will respect more the mind of the giver, than the dignity or excellency of the thing that is given; not so much for the example of Artaxerxis, king of Persia, receiving a handful of water in good part of the poor Persian, as for the example of Christ, (in whom only you rejoice,) who esteemed more of the poor widow's mite, than of all the rich gifts which the richer sort of their superfluity did cast into the treasury. For it is an old saying, χαρίτων θυμὸς ἄριστος[1]. Nothing doubting therefore but your most honourable lordship, through that special humanity and clemency which always hath appeared in you, will accept this simple gift with the same mind wherewith it is offered unto you, I beseech the everlasting Father, in the name of his Son our Saviour Jesus Christ, to preserve you and yours in health, wealth, godliness, and honour, long to continue in this world, and after this life to give unto you the blessing of eternal felicity in his rich and most glorious kingdom. Amen.

Mark xii.

Your most honorable lordship's

to command, in the Lord,

CHRISTOFER ROSDELL.

[[1] The intention is the best of gifts.]

ORIGINAL DEDICATION.

To the most noble and victorious prince Edward, duke of Somerset, earl of Hertford, viscount Beauchamp, lord Seymour, governor of the person of the king's majesty, and protector of all his realms, his lieutenant-general of all his armies, both by land and by sea, treasurer and earl-marshal of England, governor of the isles of Guernsey and Jersey, and knight of the most noble order of the garter, Johan Hoper wisheth grace and peace, with long and gracious life in the living God, through Christ Jesus our only Saviour.

THE godly pretence and consideration of your warfare of late into Scotland, most gracious and victorious prince, and the just occasion given by your enemies to use the force of your most mighty and virtuous army, the Lord hath so magnified with prosperous and victorious success, that it seemeth not only a victory[2] most noble, worthy perpetual memory, but also to be esteemed as a singular favour and merciful benediction of God given from heaven, who accustometh many times unto such a godly-pretenced purpose to annex and add an external sign and testimony of his good will, that the world should not only acknowledge him to be the God of battle, and say, "This thing is done by the Lord, and is wonderful in our eyes," but also remember that thus the Lord useth to bless such as feareth his name, both in war and in peace. And as every godly and good

[[2] The battle of Pinkey, Sept. 10, 1547, in which, it was said, 14,000 Scots were slain, and 1,500 taken prisoners. See Burnet's Hist. Reform.]

man doth praise the divine majesty of God, for his inestimable favour and grace in this heavenly victory; so he is to be called upon always hereafter to follow your grace with like aid and consolation, that the thing godly begun may take a gracious and blessed success, the old amity and friendship restored, that God by the creation of the world appointed to be in that one realm and island, divided from all the world by imparking of the sea, by natural descent of parentage and blood, one in language and speech, in form and proportion of personage one, one in manner and condition of living; and the occasion of all discord and hatred banished, that the good Scottish-Englishman may confess and do the same at home that he doth in foreign and strange countries, calling an Englishman always his countryman, and studious to do him pleasure before any other nation of the world. The breach of this divine and natural friendship is the very work of the devil by his wicked members, that hath not taught Scotland only disobedience unto her natural and lawful prince and superior power, the king's majesty of England[1], but also the contempt of Christ and his most holy word: through all the world their iniquity and malice is fulfilled, and God's mercy sufficiently declared; for seeing they will not repent, he revengeth their injustice with his most dreadful ire, not only extenuating their force and diminishing their strength, but also infatuateth and turneth into foolishness their most prudent and circumspect counsels. As it appeared in this battle, where as God used your grace as a means, to your immortal renown, to obtain a glorious and celestial victory against his enemies and yours, that were not only match and equal in force with your army, but also treble, or at the least double, as strangers report,

[[1] The war with Scotland originated in Henry the eighth's claim of homage from the kings of Scotland to the English crown. See Burnet's Hist. Reform.]

in number at the first onset. A gracious and good beginning at the first brunt of your grace's godly vocation unto so high honour, not only to defend the king's majesty's most noble person and the realm, but also to better and perfect the crown, if God will, in reconciling the unnatural and ungodly hatred between two members of one body, which of right and office should be as the right hand and the left, in peace and amity to resist and withstand the force of all strange and foreign assaults and violence. And as this victory and triumph is to be rejoiced at, so the end why God gave it is most diligently to be considered; who giveth the upper hand in the world to godly princes, because his afflicted church should have some place to rest itself in, and the kingdom of God to be amplified in truth and verity: the effect thereof must be followed, that as well the ministry of the church be enriched with the word of God, as the civil kingdom with worldly honour, as I am assured your most noble grace right well knoweth. Notwithstanding, because the right of every just and lawful heir is half lost, and more, when his title and claim is unknown, I have written this little book, containing what Christ is, and what his Office is, that every godly man may put to his helping hand to restore him again unto his kingdom; and dedicated the same unto your noble grace, unto whom God hath not only committed the defence of a politic and civil realm, but also the defence of his dear Son's right, Jesus Christ in the church, who hath sustained open and manifest wrong this many years, as it appeareth by his evidence and writings, the gospel sealed with his precious blood. And whereas I cannot make his cause and right as plain as it meriteth, nor as it is decent for him that would offer and prefer any matter to so prudent and mighty a prince, my good will and diligence is accepted of God in Christ, I doubt not, though it be very little that I can do; and trust likewise, that for the merits of this simple and manifest verity, your grace will pardon my bold enterprise, and accept this poor work in good and gracious part: and then it shall appear your most noble puissance to be conjoined with like clemency and mercy, the which virtue of all other causeth man most to resemble the Almighty God, that made not only all things for his mercy's sake, but likewise with mercy overcame himself, and his rigorous justice also; that the defaults of mortal man might find solace in Jesus Christ his only Son, who preserve the king his highness, your most noble grace, with all the council and the whole realm, to the glory of God! Amen.

Tiguri, 8 Decembris, 1547.

Your grace's most
Humble Orator,
JOHN HOPER.

A TREATISE

OF

CHRIST AND HIS OFFICE.

THE FIRST CHAPTER.

FORASMUCH as Almighty God, of his infinite mercy and goodness, prepared a means whereby Adam and his posterity might be restored again unto their original justice[1] and perfection, both of body and soul, and to live eternally unto the same end that they were created for, to bless and magnify for ever the immortal and living God; it is the office of every true Christian, before all other studies, travails, and pains, that he shall sustain for the time of this brief and miserable life, to apply himself with all diligent force[2] and labour, to know perfectly this means, ordained by God for our salvation; and, the thing once known, diligently with heart, soul, and mind, to follow the means, until such time as the effect and end be obtained, wherefore the means was appointed. The means was shewed unto Adam at his first and original transgression, the seed of a woman[3], which should break the head of the serpent, destroy the kingdom of the devil, and restore Adam, and as many as knew and believed in this seed, unto life everlasting. And as the sin of Adam, the only occasion of all man's misery, was derived into all his posterity, and made [it][4] subject unto death and the ire of God for ever; so was this seed from the beginning a very true and sufficient remedy to as many as believed; and God, for his promise' sake, quit and delivered man from the right and claim of the devil, and by mercy restored the place,

God hath prepared a means for the restoration of man.

The office of every Christian.

When and to whom were first revealed the means of man's salvation.

As Adam's sin was derived into all his posterity to make them the children of wrath, so Christ's righteousness is derived into all the faithful, to make them the children of grace.

[1] Righteousness. R.
[2] Diligence, force. R.
[3] That the seed of the woman should break. R.
[4] (it) supplied from R.

<small>The consideration of the greatness of God's mercy and the sin of man.</small>
that was by malice and contempt lost. He that would consider diligently these two things, the sin of Adam, and the mercy of God, should find himself far unable to express, or sufficiently think, the greatness of the one or of the other, <small>All man's consolation resteth in the abundance of God's grace.</small> when they are so far passing the reason and understanding of man. All the solace and joy of Adam's posterity consisteth solely and only in this, Rom. v. *Ubi abundavit delictum, superabundavit et gratia*[1]. The benefits and merits of this <small>The merits of Christ are of greater power to save, than the world, the flesh, and the devil, to condemn.</small> seed aboundeth and is more available before the judgment of God, than sin, the flesh, the devil, and the world. This treasure and inestimable riches must be perfectly known of every person that will be saved. It is only in Christ, and in the knowledge of him, what he is, and what is his office.

THE SECOND CHAPTER,

Containeth what Christ is.

<small>The proposition of this book. What Christ is.</small>
HE is the Son of the living God and perpetual virgin Mary; both God and man, the true Messias, promised unto man from the beginning of his fall: whom St John calleth the Word of eternal essence and divine majesty, saying, *In principio erat Sermo, et Sermo erat apud Deum, et Sermo erat Deus*[2]. Joan. i. Saint Paul, ad Coloss. capite i. calleth him "the image of God, &c." unto the Hebrews, cap. i., "the brightness of God." The creed of Nice calleth him *Lumen de lumine*[3], the natural Son of God, in whom dwelleth the fountain of all divinity naturally, as Paul saith, Col. ii., *In eo inhabitat plenitudo divinitatis corporaliter*[4]; meaning, that <small>How the faithful are the sons of God.</small> he is not the Son of God by adoption or acceptation into grace, as Abraham, David, and other holy saints; but naturally the Son of God, equal with the Father in all things, as John

---

[1] Where sin abounded, grace abounded much more. R.

[2] In the beginning was the Word, and the Word was with God, and the Word was God. R.

[3] Light of light. R.

[4] In him dwelt the fulness of the Godhead bodily. R.

saith, *Vidimus gloriam ejus tanquam unigeniti a Patre*[5]. Cap. i. So doth Saint John prove him in all his writings to be the very true and everlasting God, and not, as Ebion and Cerinthus said, that he was but very man only: he was made mortal man, as John saith, *Et Sermo ille caro factus est*[6], Cap. i., to save the damned man from immortal death, and to be a mediator and intercessor unto God for man. Matt. xi. John iii. Esay xi.

_{The heresy of Ebion and Cerinthus.}

This scripture doth not only teach us the knowledge of salvation, but doth comfort us against all the assaults, subtilties, and crafts of the devil, that God would of his inestimable love rather suffer his only Son to die for the world, than all the world should perish: remaining always, as he was, very God immortal, received the thing he was not, the mortal nature and true flesh of man, in the which he died, as Peter saith, 1 Pet. iv. Irenæus, p. 185, hath these godly words[7]: *Christus fuit crucifixus et mortuus, quiescente Verbo, ut crucifigi et mori possit*[8]. The divine nature of Christ was not rent, nor torn, nor killed; but it obeyed the will of the Father. It gave place unto the displeasure and ire of God, that the body of Christ might die. Being always equal with his Father, he could, if he had executed his divine power, have delivered his[9] body from the tyranny of the Jews.

_{The great love of God. Christ in receiving man's nature left not his Deity. Christ suffered not according to his Deity.}

These words of Irenæus doth wonderfully declare unto us what Christ is, and agreeth with Paul, Phil. ii. *Qui cum in forma Dei esset, non rapinam arbitratus est ut esset æqualis Deo, sed semetipsum inanivit, forma servi sumpta*[10]. Seeing he was sent into the world to suffer this most cruel death and passion, he would do nothing that should be contrary

---

[5] And we saw the glory of him as the glory of the only-begotten of the Father. R.

[6] And the Word was made flesh. R.

[[7] Ἡσυχάζοντος μὲν τοῦ λόγου ἐν τῷ πειράζεσθαι καὶ σταυροῦσθαι καὶ ἀποθνήσκειν. Iren. Op. Par. 1710, Lib. III. contra Hær. cap. xix. 3.]

[8] Christ was crucified and dead, the Word giving place that he might be crucified and die. R.

[[9] This, ed. 1547: his, R.]

[10] Who, being in the form of God, thought it no robbery to be equal with God: but he made himself of no reputation, and took on him the form of a servant. R.

unto his vocation; but, with patience praying for his enemies, submitted himself unto the ignominy and contempt of the cross, suffering pains innumerable without grudge or murmur against the holy will of his Father: his godhead hiding itself until the third day, when it restored the soul again unto the body, and caused it to rise with great triumph and glory, Rom. i. Matt. xxviii. John xx. Luke xxiv. Mark xvi. repeating the doctrine that before his death he preached unto the world, that he was both king and lord, high bishop and priest, both of heaven and of earth: *Data est mihi omnis potestas in cœlo et in terra: Euntes ergo docete omnes gentes, &c*¹. Matt. xxviii.

Christ raised his body by the power of his Godhead.

He that before was most vile and contemptible in the sight of the world, now by right and just title acclaimeth the dominion and empire of all the world. How mighty a prince he is, the creation of the world and the preservation thereof declareth. How merciful towards them that repent, we know by daily experience in ourselves, and by the example of other, Adam, David, Manasse, and Peter. How cruel² and rigorous for sin, the punishment that we suffer and the calamities of this world declareth, specially the death of his most innocent body. How immortal his ire is against such as repent not, Saul, Pharao, Judas, with other, declare. How mighty and fearful a Lord this is, our Saviour Jesus Christ, read his title and style, Naum i. where the prophet threateneth the destruction of Nineve and the whole kingdom of the Assyrians. As the princes of the world use to declare in their letters patent, of what power, force, and strength they be of, and the names of the realms and dominions that they have under their protection and governance, to fear³ their enemies, that they make no resistance, nor move not the peace of so mighty a prince: so such a title giveth the prophet unto God, to fear³ the city of Nineve and kingdom of the Assyrians, saying, *Quid cogitatis contra Dominum? Ipse consummationem facit, nec consurgit vice altera tribulatio*⁴. This is the style of the God omnipotent, our

Christ's might is declared by the creation and preservation of the world, his mercy by experience in ourselves and examples in others. God a severe punisher of sin. God's ire immortal against the impenitent.

The prophet giveth to the Lord.

---

¹ All power is given me in heaven and in earth: go therefore, and teach all nations, &c. R.
² Severe. R.   ³ [Fear, frighten.]
⁴ What do ye imagine against the Lord? He will make an utter destruction: affliction shall not rise up the second time. R.

Saviour Jesus Christ, in whose name all powers bow their knees in heaven, in earth, and in hell. Philip. ii.

CAPUT III.
[THE THIRD CHAPTER.]

Now that the scripture hath taught us to know, that Christ is both God and man, I will briefly entreat of his office: first, of his priesthood; then, of his kingdom and reign over his church till the world's end; then, for ever, in solace with his elect, in perpetual mercy and favour; with such as contemn in this world his holy commandment and pleasure, in severe justice and immortal hatred and ire for ever. John iii. *[Of the office of Christ.]*

Saint Paul, in the epistle to the Hebrews, proveth him to be the priest, called by God unto that function and office of the high bishop: *Christus non glorificavit seipsum ut fieret Pontifex, sed is qui dixerat ei, Filius meus es tu, ego hodie genui te. Et alibi, Tu es sacerdos in æternum, secundum ordinem Melchisedek*[5]. Caput v. By whose obedience unto the cross he gave everlasting health to as many as obeyed him, and in all things executed the very true office of a bishop, to whom it appertained to teach the people; which was the chiefest part of the bishop's office, and most diligently and straitly commanded by God. As all the books of Moses and the prophets teach, and Christ commanded Peter, John xx. Paul all the bishops and priests of his time. Acts xx. *[Of Christ's priesthood. The first part of the office of a bishop is to teach.]*

Of Christ's authority and preaching, Moses and Stephen, Acts vii. Deut. xviii. saith thus: *Prophetam suscitabit vobis Deus vester e fratribus vestris similem mei, illum audietis*[6]. He that will not hearken unto his voice, shall be as none of the people of God. This authority to preach the Father gave unto him in the hearing of the apostles, Matt. iii. xvii., *[He that will not hearken to the voice of Christ shall be none of the people of God.]*

[5] Christ took not to himself this honour to be made the high priest; but he that said unto him, Thou art my Son, this day begat I thee. And in another place, Thou art a priest for ever after the order of Melchisedec. R.

[6] Your God will raise up unto you a prophet of your brethren: Him shall ye hear. R.

and bound his church to receive his doctrine, saying, This is my dear beloved Son, in whom I delight, hear him. He taught the will of his Father unto the world, and how they might be saved from death infernal, John xvii. vi. Matt. xi. v. vi. vii. so that they repented and believed the gospel. Matt. iii. Mark x.; left nothing untaught, but, as a good doctor, manifested unto his audience all things necessary for the health of man: as the woman confessed, John iv. *Messias cum venerit docebit nos omnia*[1]. He preached not only himself, but sent his apostles and disciples to manifest unto the world, that the acceptable time of grace was come, and the sacrifice for sin born into the world, Matt. x. John x. And after his resurrection he gave them commandment to preach, and likewise what they should preach: *Ite in universum mundum, et prædicate quæ ego præcepi vobis, evangelium omni creaturæ*[2]. Matt. xxviii. The which doctrine Luke thus expoundeth: *Pœnitentiam ac remissionem peccatorum in omnes gentes in nomine meo, initio facto ab Hierosolymis*[3]. Luke xxiv. In his name, to say, in the knowledge and faith of his merits, they should preach repentance and remission of sin unto all the world: as they did most sincerely and plainly, without all glosses or additions of their own invention, and were as testimonies[4] of the truth, and not the authors thereof. Acts i. John i.

So doth Paul teach with gravity[5] and manifest words, what is to be judged of himself and all other ministers: *Deus erat in Christo, inquit, mundum reconcilians sibi, non imputans ei peccata sua, et posuit in nobis sermonem reconciliationis. Itaque nomine Christi legatione fungimur, tanquam Deo hortante vos per nos, rogamus pro Christo reconciliemini Deo*[6].

---

[1] The Messias, when he cometh, shall teach us all things. R.

[2] Go into all the world, and preach those things I have commanded you, the gospel, to every creature. R.

[3] Repentance and remission of sins to all nations in my name, beginning at Hierusalem. R.

[4] Witnesses. R.   [5] Grave. R.

[6] For God was in Christ, and reconciled the world to himself, not imputing their sins unto them; and hath committed to us the word of reconciliation. Now then are we ambassadors for Christ, as though God did beseech through us: we pray you in Christ's stead, that ye be reconciled to God. R.

Always in their doctrine they taught the thing, that Christ first taught, and God's holy Spirit inspired them. Gal. i. 2 Cor. iii. Holy apostles never took upon them to be Christ's vicar in the earth, nor to be his lieutenant; but said, *Sic nos æstimet homo, ut ministros Christi ac dispensatores mysteriorum Dei*[7]. 1 Cor. iv. In the same epistle he bindeth the Corinthians to follow him in nothing but whereas he followed Christ, cap. xi. *Imitatores mei estote, sicut et ego Christi*[8]. They ministered not in the church, as though Christ were absent, although his most glorious body was departed corporally into the heavens above; but as Christ present, that always governeth his church with his Spirit of truth, as he promised, Matt. xxviii. *Ecce ego vobiscum sum usque ad consummationem seculi*[9]. *The apostles took not upon them to be Christ's vicar. How far the ministers are to be followed. Christ being bodily absent is spiritually present with his church.*

In the absence of his body, he hath commended the protection and governance of his church unto the Holy Ghost, the same God, and one God with the Father and his divine nature: whose divine puissance and power overmatcheth the force of the devil, so that hell itself cannot take one of Christ's flock out of God's protection. John x. And this defence dureth not for a day, nor year[10], but shall demour[11] for ever, till this[12] church be glorified at the resurrection of the flesh. John xv. *The power of the Spirit of Christ. The continuance thereof.*

It was no little pain that Christ suffered in washing away the sins of this church: therefore he will not commit the defence thereof unto man. It is no less glory to defend and keep the thing won by force, than it is by force to obtain the victory. Adam, Abel, Abraham, Moses, nor Aaron, could not win this church out of the devil's tyranny: no more can they defend it, delivered. For although by imputation of Christ's justice[13] these men and all other faithfuls be delivered from the tyranny of the devil and condemnation of the law: yet had and hath the devil his very friends dwelling within the nature of man, corrupt[14] as long as he liveth; the *As Christ in his own person hath redeemed his church, so he doth defend it. Abraham and all the faithful saved by the imputation of Christ's righteousness.*

---

[7] Let a man so esteem us, as the ministers of Christ, and stewards of the secrets of God. R.

[8] Be ye followers of me, as I am of Christ. R.

[9] Behold, I am with you unto the end of the world. R.

[10 Here, ed. 1547.]   [11] Endure. R.   [12] His. R.

[13] Righteousness. R.   [14] Corrupt man. R.

concupiscence and rebellion of man's nature, who ceaseth nor day nor night to betray man again to the devil, except with the motion of true penitence[1] this concupiscence be kept under in fear and faith; which two virtues be so infirm in man, that be he never so perfect, yet falleth he from God sometime, as Abraham, Isaac, Jacob, Moses, and Aaron. Isa. xliii. Num. xix. Therefore he keepeth the defence and governance of the church only and solely himself, in whom the devil hath not a jot of right. Though the apostles were instructed in all truth, and left the same written unto his church; yet were they ministers, servants, testimonies[2], and preachers of this verity, and not Christ's vicars in earth and lieutenant to keep the keys of heaven, hell, and purgatory; but only appointed to approve the thing to be good, that God's laws commanded, and that to be ill, that the word of God condemned.

Seeing that Christ doth govern his church always by his holy Spirit, and bindeth all the ministers thereof unto the sole word of God, what abomination is this, that any bishop of Rome, Hierusalem, Antioche, or elsewhere, should acclaim to be Christ's vicar in the earth, and take upon him to make any laws in the church of God to bind the conscience of man, beside the word of God; and, in placing of their superstition and idolatry, put the word of God out of his place! By what law, by whom, or where hath any this title given unto him, to be God's vicar and lieutenant upon the earth?

Moses[3], the best prince that ever was and most godly governor of the people, and[4] Aaron, that fidele[5] high priest and preacher of God's word, never usurped this title, to be as a second Christ and master over men's conscience. If godly Moses and his brother Aaron never acclaimed this title in the earth, doubtless it is a foul and detestable arrogancy, that these ungodly bishops of Rome attribute unto themselves to be the heads of Christ's church, the more to be lamented. He[6] that considereth their life, and conferreth it with the scripture, will judge by the authority

---

[1] Repentance. R.
[2] Witnesses. R.
[3 Moses and Aaron, 1547.]
[4] Supplied from R.
[5] Faithful. R.
[6] Because he. R.

thereof, that they were not for these many years worthy to be accounted any members of God's church, but the members of the devil and the first-begotten of antichrist.

Thus is true[7], the see of Rome is not only a tyranny and pestilence of body and soul, but the nest of all abomination. God give him grace and all his successors to leave their abomination, and to come unto the light of God's word! This beast is preached unto the people to be a man that cannot err, his authority to be above God and his laws, and to be the prince upon the earth of all princes: but God will judge him as he is, a murderer of both body and soul, and punish the princes of the world, that uphold his abomination. The see of Rome a tyranny of body and soul.

Moses and Aaron, by the testimony of the scripture, never taught, but that they received of God, and at the last both they offended, Num. xx.: insomuch that God gave sentence against them, that none of them both should enter into the land of promise for their arrogancy and pride. The text saith, "Because ye were unfaithful unto me." This false belief was of no doubt[8] they had in the power of God; for the miracle was done, as God said: but that they attributed too much unto their own power, and said, *Audite rebelles, num de petra ista nos educemus vobis aquas*[9]? For the changing of the *third* person in this sentence into the *first*, the ire of God pronounced sentence of death against these two very godly ministers of his word. They sinned, because they said not, "Hear, ye rebellious, cannot Jehovah, the Omnipotent, give ye water of this stone?" And is this first-begotten of antichrist, the bishop of Rome, without sin, that changeth not only the person in a sentence, but the whole sentence, yea, the whole law of God and of man? So that he reigneth in the conscience above the law of God, and will save him that God hath damned, and damn him that God hath saved; yet [this] person and man of sin cannot err! But he that spared not to kill[10] good Moses and Aaron for the abuse of the word of God, will not favour this wicked man, nor none of his holy doctors, at the terrible day of judgment. Moses and Aaron fell.

---

[7] This is most true. R.   [8] Not of any doubt. R.
[9] Hear, ye rebellious, shall we bring you water out of this rock? R.
[10] To kill, omitted in R.

Naum, the prophet, doth give God a wonderful name, which the Latin nor the Greek cannot properly express without circumlocution, Noter hu leobau[1], *quasi injuriarum memoriam retinens, et ulciscendi occasionem expectans*[2]. He is the God that writeth all these blasphemies in his book of remembrance; and when he hath shewed his mercy sufficiently, he revengeth the ill that man thinketh is forgotten. It is of his superabundant mercy that he throweth not suddenly fire upon the world for sin; and not that he is asleep, or cannot do it. Right well judged Valerius Maximus[3], better than now the most part of christian men: *Lento quidem gradu ad vindictam sui procedit divina ira; sed gravitate supplicii tarditatem compensabit*[4].

<small>God is slow in coming to vengeance, yet he recompenseth the slackness with the severity of the punishment when it cometh.</small>

Because God hath given this light unto my countrymen, which be all persuaded, (or else God send them to be persuaded!) that the bishop of Rome nor none other is Christ's vicar upon the earth; it is no need to use any long or copious oration: it is so plain that it needeth no probation; the very properties of antichrist, I mean of Christ's great and principal enemy, is so openly known to all men, that are not blinded with the smoke of Rome, that they know him to be the beast that John describeth in the Apocalypse, as well as the logician knoweth that *risibilitate distinguitur homo a ceteris animantibus*[5].

<small>The knowledge of Christ's continual presence in the church admitteth no general vicar.</small>

This knowledge of Christ's supremacy and continual presence in the church admitteth no lieutenant nor general vicar. Likewise it admitteth not the decrees and laws of men, brought into the church contrary unto the word and scripture of God, which is only sufficient to teach all verity and truth for the salvation of man, as it shall appear in this chapter following.

[[1] נוטר הוא לאיביו Nah. i. 2.]

[2] As though he should say, keeping the remembrance of injuries, and expecting an occasion of revengement. R.

[[3] Val. Max. Op. Leidæ, 1726, Lib. I. cap. i. De religione, p. 35.]

[4] The wrath of God goeth forth slowly unto revengement, but yet with the grievousness of the punishment he recompenseth his slackness. R.

[5] By the faculty of laughing man is distinguished from other living creatures. R.

CAPUT IV.
[THE FOURTH CHAPTER.]

CHRIST, the only light of the world, sent from his Father, and born[6] mortal man, according unto the scripture, began to teach the word of God purely and sincerely unto the world, and chose ministers and apostles convenient for the expedition thereof; and approved to be the very Messias by God the Father, Matt. iii. xvii. John v. taught his disciples the truth by the only law, written by Moses and the prophets, and not by unwritten verities. And in all controversies and doubtful questions he answered his contraries[7] by the word of God. In that wonderful temptation of the devil, Matt. iv. by collation of the places of scripture he killed the devil with his own sword, (falsely and in a wrong sentence alleging the word of God,) by the word of God godly applied.

Christ confirmeth his doctrine by the testimony of the law.

When his disciples were reprehended by the Pharisees, as breakers of the sabbath, Matt. xii. he excused their fact by the law, *Non legistis quid fecerit David et qui cum eo erant*[8]*?* So likewise, Matt. xv. xix. in all controversies he made the law judge between his enemies and him. When he was desired to teach a young man the way to heaven, and to come to everlasting life, he said, *In lege quid scriptum est? Quomodo legis*[9]*?* Matt. xxii. Likewise the Saducees, that denied the resurrection of the dead: *Erratis, inquit, nescientes scripturas et verbum Dei*[10]. The rich man in hell, that was so desirous that his brothers[11] living in the earth might have knowledge and warning to beware they were not damned in time to come, would gladly have warned them himself for a more surety, Luke xvi. that the message should be done. Abraham answered, *Habent Mosen et prophetas; audient illos*[12]. The scripture teacheth what

---

[6] Born, omitted in R.

[7] His contraries, 1547. To their objections. R.

[8] Have you not read what David did, and they [which] were with him? R.

[9] What is written in the law? How readest thou? R.

[10] You err (said he), not knowing the scriptures and the word of God. R.

[11] Brethren. R.

[12] They have Moses and the prophets, let them hear them. R.

The scripture teacheth what Christ is, what man is, and what heaven and hell is.

heaven, hell, and what man is, and what Christ is: therefore Christ sendeth us thither. John v. *Scrutamini, inquit, scripturas*[1].

Again, being required in a civil matter concerning tribute and obedience unto the princes of the world, Matt. xxii. he said, *Reddite quæ sunt Cæsaris Cæsari, et quæ sunt Dei Deo*. "Give unto the emperor that that is due unto the emperor, and unto God that that is due unto God." And under the name of the emperor he understandeth all superior powers appointed over the people by God, and would to give[2] due honour unto them both, as Paul teacheth. Rom. xiii. 1 Pet. ii.

Wherein God's law differeth from man's law.

This law teacheth man sufficiently, as well what he is bound to do unto God, as unto the princes of the world. Nothing can be desired necessary for man, but in this law it is prescribed: of what degree, vocation, or calling soever he be, his duty is shewed unto him in the scripture. And in this it differeth from man's laws, because it is absolute, perfect, and never to be changed; nothing added unto it, nor taken from it. And the church of Christ, the more it was and is burdened with man's laws, the farther it is from the true and sincere verity of God's word. The more man presumeth and taketh authority to interpretate the scripture after his own brain and subtle wit, and not as the verity of [the][3] text requireth, the more he dishonoureth the scripture, and blasphemeth God, the author thereof.

The office of a good minister.

It is the office of a good man to teach the church as Christ taught, to revoke all errors, and such as err, unto the fold of Christ only by the word of Christ. For the

The water runneth purest at the fountain's head.

water at the fountain's head is more wholesome and pure, than when it is carried abroad in rotten pipes or stinking ditches. I had rather follow the shadow of Christ, than the body of all general councils or doctors since the death of

The devil never ceaseth to assault the truth.

Christ. The devil never slept, but always by his ministers attempted to destroy the verity of Christ's religion, and clean to put out the light of truth, which was perfect in Christ's time and in the time of the apostles. None since that time

---

[1] Search the scriptures, saith he. R.
[2] Have given. R.
[3] Supplied from R.

so pure. Saint Hierome, *in vita Malchi*[4], saith, that his time was darkness in the respect of the apostles' time. <small>The truth darkened in the time of Jerome.</small>

The antiquity of the world doth darken the verity of God's word; as Varro[5] saith truth, *Vetustatem multa depravare, multa etiam tollere. Et, Tertium sæculum, inquit, non videt eum hominem quem vidit primum*[6]. The truth of God's verity, the more it is used, practised, and taught after the wisdom of man, the more is the glory and perfection thereof darkened. It is the contrary in all human arts, as Cicero saith[7]: *In humanis nihil simul inventum et perfectum fuit, usuque et exercitatione factum sit; ut hoc præstantiores artes quædam fuerint, quo longius ab origine sua et inventoribus essent deductæ*[8]. <small>The truth of God's word is so far from being bettered by man's wisdom, that it is darkened thereby.</small>

The church of God must therefore be bound to none other authority than unto the voice of the gospel and unto the ministry thereof, as Esay saith, chap. viii. *Obsigna legem in discipulis meis*[9]. The prophet speaketh of such darkness, as should follow his time, concerning the coming of Messias, the true doctor of the church: therefore [he][10] prayed to preserve the true heirs[11] of the prophets, and that it would please him to confirm the doctrine of truth in their hearts, lest the word and true understanding of the word by the devil should be put out. And seeing the church is bound unto this infallible truth, the only word of God, it is a false and usurped authority that men attribute unto the clergy, and bind the word of God and Christ's church to the succession of bishops or any college of cardinals, schools, ministers, or cathedral churches.

[4 Ab apostolis usque ad nostri temporis fæcem, &c. Hieron. Op. Veronæ, 1735, Tom. II. col. 41.]

[5 Varronis Op. Amsterdam, 1623. De ling. Lat. Lib. IV. p. 6.]

6 Oldness corrupteth many things, and also taketh away many things. And the third age (quoth he) seeth not that man which they saw. R.

[7 Vid. Cic. de claris Oratoribus, cap. 18.]

8 In human things nothing is made perfect so soon as it is invented, but by use and exercise it is wrought out. So that some arts are by so much the more excellent as they have had continuance since the beginning, and since they were invented. R.

9 Seal my law in my disciples. R.

10 Supplied from R.

11 Hearers. R.

Paul would no man to give faith¹ to any person or minister in the church of God, but when he preacheth the word of God truly. Gal. i. Men may have the gift of God to understand and interpretate the scripture unto other, but never authority to interpretate it, otherwise than it interpretateth itself, which the godly mind of man by study, meditation, and conferring of one place thereof with the other², may find; howbeit some more, some less, as God giveth his grace. For the punishment of our sins God leaveth in all men a great imperfection; and such as were endued with excellent wit and learning saw not always the truth. As it is to be seen in Basilius, Ambrose, Epiphanius, Augustine, Bernard, and other, though they stayed themselves in the knowledge of Christ, and erred not in any principal article of the faith: yet they did inordinately and more than enough extol the doctrine and tradition of men, and after the death of the apostles every doctor's time was subject unto such ceremony and man's decrees, that was neither profitable nor necessary. Therefore diligently exhorted Paul the church of Christ principally to consider and regard the foundation of all verity; meaning that doctors of the church had their imperfection and faults. *Fundamentum (inquit) non potest poni aliud præter id quod positum est, quod est Jesus Christus*³. In these few words is stablished all our faith, and all false religion reprehended.

Upon this foundation some men build gold, to say, godly and necessary doctrine: as Polycarpus, that confuted the heresy of Marcion, *De essentia Dei*⁴, of the causes of sin; that the devil and man is the cause of sin, and not God, nor fatal destiny, nor the influence or respects of the planets. He maintained the true religion of God, and governed the church, as the scripture taught, which he learned of John Evangelist, and defended this⁵ truth with wonderful constancy and martyrdom.

Basilius and many other retained the articles of the faith;

Side notes: The ministers are not to be believed but as they preach the word of God truly. How the scripture may and ought to be interpreted. Imperfections are the punishments of sin in us. The greatest clerks of the church have erred in some points. Polycarpus confuted the heresy of Marcion. Polycarpus John's disciple.

¹ Faith or credit. R.
² Another. R.
³ Another foundation can no man lay than that which is already laid, which is Jesus Christ. R.
⁴ Of the essence of God. R.   ⁵ His. R.

but they instituted the life and rule of monks, and preferred that kind of life before the life of such as govern in the commonwealth the people of God, and persuaded men that such kind of life was a very divine and acceptable honouring of God.

<small>Basile allowed and maintained the life and rule of monks.</small>

After him followed such as augmented this ill, and said, it was not only acceptable unto God, but also that men might deserve therewith remission of sin.

Thus a little and a little the devil augmented superstition, and diminished the truth of God's glory: so that we see no where the church of Christ as it was in the apostles' time. Though many and godly verities hath been brought unto light in our time by men of diverse graces, yet is not the truth of necessary verities plainly shewed by them. Lest man should too much glory in himself, he permitted them to err in certain points: as Luther, of a blessed memory, which wrote and preached the gospel of justification, no man better; yet in the cause of the sacrament he erreth concerning the corporal presence of Christ's natural body, that there is no man can err more. I shall have occasion to write the truth concerning this matter hereafter. It is no reproach of the dead man, but mine opinion unto all the world, that the scripture solely and the apostles' church is to be followed, and no man's authority, be he Augustine, Tertullian, or other, cherubim or cherabim.

Unto the rules and canons of the scripture must man trust, and reform his errors thereby; or else he shall not reform himself, but rather deform his conscience. The church of the Romans, Corinthians, and other, the seven churches that John writeth of in the Apocalypse, were in all things reformed unto the rule and form prescribed by the everlasting God. The image of these churches I always print in my mind. And wheresoever I come, I look how near they resemble the afore rehearsed, and whether their preachers preach simply without dispensation of⁶ any part of God's most necessary word; and whether all the occasions of idolatry be taken away, as images, whom Gregory⁷ calleth the books of

<small>Reformation is to be made according to the canons of God's word.</small>

---

⁶ In. R.

[⁷ Quod legentibus scriptura, hoc idiotis præstat pictura cernentibus. S. Greg. Op. Paris. 1672, Tom. II. col. 938. Lib. IX. Indic. iv. Ep. ix.]

the laymen, though this title be against the second commandment, and never approved by the old testament nor the new, by word or example.

The occasion of idolatry is to be removed. God will not have his church pestered with any kind of idolatry.

Where as the occasion is not removed, the word of God must needs stand in hazard: for God will not (say the wisdom of man what it list) have his church pestered with any kind of idolatry; and to make God and the devil agree in one church, it is impossible. St John hath wonderful words in the Apocalypse, Chap. iii. unto the church of the Laodiceans: *Scio opera tua, quia neque frigidus neque fervidus. Utinam frigidus esses aut fervidus! itaque quoniam tepidus es, et nec frigidus nec fervidus, incipiam te evomere de ore meo*[1]. These words are very necessary to be borne in mind.

We must be fervent in advancing the truth, and not indifferent.

For he that is neither hot nor cold, but indifferent to use the knowledge of God's word and Christ's church with the word and gloss of man; that teacheth the use of images in the church, before he can prove by the authority of God's word that they may be suffered in the church, doth not well. They have been the occasion of great hurt and idolatry.

Neither the church of the old nor new testament did ever teach the people by images.

The church of the old testament nor the new never taught the people with images. Therefore it shall be the office of every man that loveth God and his word, to follow the scripture only, and to bewail the ignorancy of such as hath before our time, or now in our time, by words or writing defended the same; and with all humility and humbleness submit himself

The word of God is the judge of the doctors' writings.

to the judgment and censure of the judge of all judges, the word of God, that he may wisely and godly discern what is to be believed and accepted of any doctor's writings, and what is not to be accepted; what is to be pardoned, and what is not to be pardoned; and by the perils and dangers of other learn to be wise, that we commit not the same fault.

A fair gloss doth not good to an evil thing.

A fine gloss and fair[2] interpretation cannot make good an ill thing. If I should say, an image provoketh devotion;—holy water teacheth that the blood of Christ was sprinkled for my sins;—the holy bread teacheth that Christ's body

---

[1] I know thy works, that thou art neither cold nor hot: [I would thou wert cold or hot.] Therefore because thou art lukewarm, and neither cold nor hot, it will come to pass that I shall spew thee out of my mouth. R.

[2] Fere, 1547: farre, R.

was torn for my sins; what shall these glosses excuse the fact? Nay, nay, Christ, that died for our sakes, would not his death to be preached this way, but out of the scripture by the tongue of man, and not out of the decrees of bishops by a drop of water or painted post. He that took the pains to die and suffer his passion for the redemption of the world solely and only, solely and only hath taken the pains to teach the world how and which way they should keep this passion in mind, and left it unto the world in writing by the hands of his holy apostles: unto the which writing only he hath bound and obligated his church, and not to the writings of men.

Christ will have his death preached out of the scripture by the tongue of man, and not out of the decrees of bishops.

In this passage I admonish the christian reader, that I speak not of the laws of magistrates or princes, that daily ordain new laws for the preservation of their commonwealth, as they see the necessity of their realms or cities require; but of such laws as men hath ordained for the church of Christ, which should be now and for ever governed by the word of God. In this cause, look[3], as Eve offended, obeying the persuasion of the devil contrary unto the commandment of God; so doth every man offend, obeying any laws or decrees that commandeth any thing contrary unto the word of God. This law must prevail, *Oportet Deo magis obedire quam hominibus*[4]. The example hereof we have in Daniel, of the three children, that chose rather to burn in the fiery furnace, than to worship the image that Nabucadneser had made. So did the apostles, Acts v.

Though the church be tied always to the law of Christ, yet this letteth not, but magistrates may make new laws for the preservation of their commonwealth, as need requireth, so that they make no law against the law of Christ. God must be obeyed before all others.

Let all the world consider, whether these laws of the bishops,—the mass, which is a profanation of Christ's supper; to bind men's consciences to pray unto dead saints; to say, images be to be suffered in the temples; and constrain the ministers of the church to live sole, contrary unto their vocation,—are to be obeyed or not. They do no less offend God in obeying these laws, than Eve did in obeying the voice of the serpent. The wisdom of all the wits in the world cannot comprehend the greatness of this ill. Make what laws they will for the body, so they leave the conscience free, with patience it is to be suffered; only I lament the bondage

Men's consciences are not to be brought into bondage.

[3] Loke, 1547: looke, R.
[4] We must obey God, rather than men. R.

32   A DECLARATION OF   [CH.

Pighius, one of the pope's flatterers, preferreth adultery before holy wedlock.

of the conscience. Cursed be these[1] that make such laws, and cursed be those that with sophistry defend them. That parasitus and bondman of the bishop of Rome, Pighius[2], in his writings shameth not to say, It is less sin for a priest to keep another man's wife, than to have a wife of his own.

In what respect we may without sin use the indifferent things of man's ordinance, and in what respect we sin in them.

Concerning acts indifferent, which of themselves are neither good neither ill, as to refrain from eating of flesh the Friday, observing of the feasts kept holy in the remembrance of such holy martyrs as died for the faith of Christ, or in keeping holy Easter and Whitsunday; there are[3] two respects most diligently to be observed; the one good and to be suffered, the other ill and to be eschewed. Such as abstain from flesh, and think they do better service to God, and would likewise obtain remission of their sins by those works, do declare both themselves and their works to be ill. But such as abstain because the spirit may be more ardent, and the mind more given to study and prayer, doth well, and as they be bound to do; and to come unto the temple to pray for themselves and the church of Christ, and to hear the word of God, doth well. For as God commandeth his word to be preached and heard, so he hath appointed a certain time, as the sabbath, when people should hear it. And not only this order to be observed in the church, but also in every family and household. Of what degree soever he be, he should cause his family and children to read some part of the Bible for their erudition, to know God. Likewise he should

Parents ought to teach their children the knowledge of God.

[1] Those. R.

[[2] Such is the *tenor* of Pighius's argument, as will appear from the following sentences, with which he sums it up:

His, inquam, an saltem minus malum minusque damnabile erit nubere quam uri? Tu vide, quis pejor servus est? An qui gravatus servitio, et fortassis negligentius aut incautius agens, cadit sub onere, an qui jugum in totum projicit? Quis pejor discipulus? An qui ex præscripto ediscit, non quidem universum (quod forte potuisset, nisi crapulæ et somno indulsisset securius) tamen partem; an qui scholam prorsus deserit? Tentationi proinde quibus diximus remediis resistendum est. In quibus si quando remissiores ex infirmitate carnis ceciderimus, tolerabilius hoc peccatum est, quam si jugum in totum excutiamus, imo voto adversum votum Deo præstitum nos astringamus, tentationem non solum non sustineamus, non expectemus, sed præoccupemus etiam, &c. Pighii Controvers. præcip. Expositio. Controv. xv. De cælib. aut conjug. Sacerd. Coloniæ, 1542. Ff. 3, 2.]

[3] Is, 1547: are, R.

constrain them to pray unto God for the promotion of his holy word, and for the preservation of the governors of the commonwealth, so that no day should pass without prayer and augmentation of knowledge in the religion of Christ.

But our new evangelists hath another opinion; they dream of faith that justifieth, the which neither repentance precedeth, neither honesty of life followeth; which shall be to their double damnation, if they amend not. He that will conform his knowledge unto the word of God, let him likewise convert his life withal, as the word requireth, and as all the examples of Christ and his gospel teacheth; or else what will he do with the doctrine of Christ, which only teacheth, and sufficiently teacheth, all verity and virtuous life? Let him tarry still in the doctrine of man, and live as manly and as carnally as he list, and not profess to know God, neither his truth, rather than so to slander them both. This sufficeth to prove the only word of God to be sufficient to teach the truth; all other men's laws to be neither necessary neither profitable; and certain we be, that the church of the apostles did want these decrees that papistry of late days faithed[4] the church withal.

Repentance and honesty of life accompany a justifying faith.

CAPUT V.

[THE FIFTH CHAPTER.]

THE second office of Christ is to pray and to make intercession for his people. This office John writeth of in his first epistle: "If any man sin, we have an advocate with the Father, Jesus Christ," that maketh intercession for us. And as Paul saith, *Christus qui mortuus est, imo qui et suscitatus, qui etiam est ad dextram Dei, qui et intercedit pro nobis*[5]. In his name, and in the belief and confidence of his merits, we may obtain the mercies of God and life everlasting, as Paul saith: *Accedamus cum fiducia ad thronum gratiæ, ut consequamur misericordiam et gratiam inveniamus ad opportunum*

The second part of Christ's office, to make intercession for his people.

[4] Faythyd, 1547. Faced. R.

[5] Christ, which died, yea, which rose again, which sitteth also on the right hand of God; and which maketh intercession for us. R.

auxilium[1]. Heb. iv. This intercession of Christ only sufficeth. No man should seek any other mediator of intercession[2] or expiation of sin, as Paul saith, declaring the sufficiency and ability of Christ's death and intercession: *Christus manet in æternum, perpetuum habens sacerdotium. Unde et salvos facere ad plenum potest qui per ipsum adeunt Deum; semper-vivus ad hoc, ut interpellet pro illis*[3].

Unto this intercession and prayer in Christ's name he bound his church by express commandment: *Petite et accipietis*[4]. "Ask, and it shall be given you." And in the same place he sheweth the cause wherefore it shall be given[5]: *Quicquid petieritis Patrem in nomine meo, dabit vobis*[6]. "Whatsoever ye ask in the belief and confidence of my merits, it shall be given unto you." Saint Paul calleth Christ, sitting at the right hand of God, the minister and servant of the saints; to say[7], of such as be here living in this troubled and persecuted church, to solicitate and do all their affairs, as a faithful ambassador with the Father of heaven, until the consummation of the world.

This doctrine of Christ's intercession must be always diligently preached unto the people; and likewise, that in all necessities, calamities, and trouble, the afflicted person to seek none other means to offer his prayers unto God, but Christ only, according as the scripture teacheth, and as we have example of holy saints in the same. Not only in the New Testament, where as he commandeth us to pray in his name; and Stephen in his martyrdom, Acts vii., commended his spirit unto this only mediator, saying, *Domine Jesu, accipe spiritum meum*[8]; but also in the Old Testament thus prayed the patriarchs and prophets: Jacob, Gen. xlviii.,

---

[1] Let us come with boldness unto the throne of grace, that we may obtain mercy, and find favour to help in time of need. R.

[2] Need seek any other mediator for the intercession. R.

[3] Christ abideth for ever, having a perpetual priesthood: whereby he is able perfectly to save those which come to God through him; he liveth always to make intercession for them. R.

[4] Ask, and ye shall receive. R.

[5] Given you. R.

[6] Whatsoever you shall ask my Father in my name, he will give it you. R.   [7] That is to say. R.

[8] Lord Jesus, receive my spirit. R.

Benedicat pueris istis Deus et angelus qui eripuit me de cunctis malis[9]; and David, Psa. lxxi., *Et adorabunt ipsum semper*[10]. Forasmuch as Christ is daily in heaven, and prayeth for his church, the church of Christ must pray, as Christ hath taught it; as the patriarchs, prophets, and the apostles hath given us example, which never prayed unto dead saints; yea, as Christ hath given us example, hanging on the cross, saying, *Pater, in manus tuas commendo spiritum meum*[11]. *The patriarchs, prophets, and apostles, never prayed to dead saints.*

What intolerable ill, blasphemy of God, and ethnical idolatry is this, to admit and teach the invocation of saints departed out of this world! It taketh from God his true honour: it maketh him a fool, that only hath ordained only Christ[12] to be Mediator between man and him. It diminisheth the merits of Christ; taketh from the law of God her perfection and majesty; whereas God hath opened his will and pleasure unto the world in all things. It condemneth the old church of the patriarchs and prophets, likewise the church of the apostles and martyrs, that never taught the invocation of saints. It accuseth the scripture of God to be false, which saith, Thou shalt neither add, neither diminish any thing: it maketh Christ a liar, that said, *Spiritum quem ego mittam a Patre, docebit vos omnem veritatem*[13]. If the men that teach, *Sancta Maria, ora pro nobis*[14], be more holy than all the patriarchs[15], prophets and apostles, let the conscience of the christian reader judge. *Invocation of saints is a derogation of God's honour.* *Note here what evils follow the doctrine of invocation of saints.*

This distinction of mediators, to be one of expiation for sin—Christ, and another of intercession—the saints departed, is naught: it repugneth the manifest text of the scripture. It is the office only of Christ to be the mediator for sin, and likewise to offer the prayers of the church to his Father. John i. *Ecce Agnus Dei, qui tollit peccata mundi*[16]. *The vain distinction of mediators.*

---

[9] God bless these children, and the angel which hath delivered me from all evil. R.

[10] And they shall worship him for ever. R.

[11] Father, into thy hands I commend my spirit. R.

[12] That hath ordained Christ only. R.

[13] The Spirit which I will send from the Father shall teach you all truth. R.

[14] Saint Mary, pray for us. R.   [[15] (of) occurs in Ed. 1547.]

[16] Behold the Lamb of God, that taketh away the sins of the world. R.

As concerning intercession, he commandeth us only to ask in his name, and prescribed the manner how to ask, and what to ask. Luke xi.

Objection. Such as say, If the saints that we pray unto hear us not, nor profit a deal, yet[1] it hindereth not; we lost but our *Answer.* labour: this[2] much it hindereth; it declareth him that prayeth to be an infidel, to pray unto[3] that god or goddess, that is not able to help him, nor hear his prayer, and no better than he that prayed unto the image of Jupiter in Creta, that *God promiseth not only to hear our prayers, but also to grant our requests.* had neither ears nor eyes. It declareth him to contemn both God and his word, who assureth every man, in every time, and in every distress, not only to hear him, but also to give aid. Matt. xi. So now, this worshipper of saints departeth from the known and almighty God to an unknown *The worshipping of saints preferreth the doctrine of man before God and the truth of his word.* god, and preferreth the doctrine of man and the devil before the scripture of truth and the living God. I hope this detestable error is come to light, and all men taught to pray as the scripture canonical teacheth.

But there is another ill as great as this, to be reprehended of all such as know how to pray aright—the being *Against the having of images in churches.* of images in the temple, which the world saith may be suffered in the churches, and say they be good to put the people of God in remembrance of such godly saints as died for *When Satan cannot prevail openly; then he seeketh for subtle shifts.* Christ's sake. But this is always the subtilty of the devil, when a manifest ill cannot be borne withal, to seek a gloss and interpretation, that whereas he cannot walk in the church openly like a devil, and have candles sticked before a post, and the images kissed, yet to desire some man to put a fair coat upon his back, that he may have a place in the church to lurk in, until such time as occasion be ministered to shew himself again as he is. The authority of God's word re- *As invocation of saints is to be banished out of the hearts of men, so images out of their eyes in the church.* quireth me to pronounce this true judgment in the cause of images, that be not worshipped in the church, that their presence in the church is against God's word, as well as to say, *Sancta Maria, ora pro nobis*[4]. And as the one is to be eschewed and banished out of the heart, so is the other out of the eye in the temple, where as God's word is preached unto

---

[1] Ner profet adee, lyet. 1547. Profit us not. R.   [2] Thus. R.
[3] That man that so prayeth unto, &c. R.
[4] Saint Mary, pray for us. R.

the people, and the sacraments ministered. Thus I prove by
the authority of both Testaments, the Old and the New. The
Old saith, "Thou shalt make no image." Exod. xx. Deut. vi.
In the New there is no mention made of any image, but that
Christ concerning the law and precepts of the commandments
said: *Non veni solvere legem, sed adimplere*[5]. Matt. v. Forasmuch as Christ left the commandments of the old law unto
the church, in the which he saith, Thou shalt not make any
image; from whence hath these men authority, that say, if
images be not honoured, they may be suffered in the church?
It is but their opinion, contrary and beside the law of God.
And this commandment, *Non facies, non coles*[6], forbiddeth as
well the making of the image, as the honouring of it. Concerning the having of them in the place of public prayer and
use of his sacraments, such as would this occasion of idolatry
to remain in the church, by division of the commandments
would pass over this[7] second commandment, which saith, *Non
facies tibi sculptile, non adorabis ea*[8], and make of the tenth
commandment two commandments. But the text will not
suffer it. For as the Lord there forbiddeth the inward lust
and concupiscence of his neighbour's house, so doth he forbid
the lust and concupiscence of his neighbour's wife, servant,
or daughter, and all is but one commandment, Exod. xx.:
read the text in the Hebrew, and then it shall be more plain.
The second commandment which the defenders of images
neglect, forbiddeth not only the outward reverence and honour,
but also by the same express commandment forbiddeth to
make any image. They do injuries to the manifest text,
and their gloss is to be abhorred, and the plain text to be
followed.

The king's majesty, that dead is, willed not only all his *A simili-*
true subjects to have no familiarity with Cardinal Poule[9], but *tude.*

[5] I came not to break the law, but to fulfil it. R.
[6] Thou shalt not make—thou shalt not worship. R.
[7] The. R.
[8] Thou shalt not make to thyself any graven image, nor worship
them. R.
[[9] Thus the breach between him (Henry VIII.) and the pope was
past reconciling, and at Rome it was declared equally meritorious to
fight against him as against the Turk. But Cardinal Pole made it more
meritorious in his book. Yet the thunders of the Vatican had now lost

also to refrain his company, and not to have to do with him in any case, and not without good and necessary consideration. He that would, notwithstanding this command[1] of the king's majesty, have haunted Poule's company, and at the time of his accusation have said he was not with Poule for friendship nor familiarity to do him any honour, but haunted his company with such other persons as meant no ill to the king's majesty or his realm, doubtless this law should of right and equity condemn him: neither for friendship, neither other cause no man[2] should use his company. Doubtless, as the king's majesty and every other prince knoweth it to be dangerous daily to suffer his subjects in the company of his traitorous enemies; so God knew right well what danger it was to suffer man, his creature, to have company[3] with those idols, and therefore said, Thou shalt neither worship them nor make them. All the princes of the earth hath not had so many subjects betrayed and made traitors by their enemies, as God hath lost souls by the means of images: I make all the world judge that knoweth the truth.

God hath lost more souls by images than princes have lost subjects by the company of traitors.

It is so childish an opinion to say that images may be suffered in the church, so they be not honoured, that it needeth no probation at all. The gentiles, that Paul speaketh of, Rom. i., knew right well that the idol was not God. And all the idolaters that used images, that the New Testament speaketh of[4], 1 Cor. v. and x. 1 Pet. iv. 1 John v., knew right well that these images of gold or silver was not the devil that they worshipped. The apostles condemned not only their false religion, but also their images. John by express words calleth the image idolatry, and biddeth them beware of images, saying, *Cavete a simulacris*[5]. David, Psal. cxiv., saith, *Idola gentium argentum et aurum*[6]. He condemneth

their force, so that these had no other effect but to enrage the king more against all such as were suspected to favour their interests, or to hold any correspondence with Cardinal Pole.—Burnet's Hist. Reform. Part I. Book III. See also Turner's History of Henry VIII. Vol. II. ch. xxviii.]

[1] Commandment. R.   [2] Ought any man. R.
[3] Any company. R.
[4] Of whom the New Testament speaketh. R.
[5] Take heed of images. R.
[6] The idols of the gentiles are silver and gold. R. [Ps. cxv.]

not only their false religion, but also the images made by the hand of man, which were of gold and silver. Their false god was neither gold neither silver, but a wicked spirit, who had entered[7] for lack of faith into their spirits.

It is to be lamented, that God for our sins thus suffereth the world to be illuded by the devil. Of late years the images were in the temple, and honoured with *Pater noster*, heart and mind, with leg and knee. This use of images is taken away in many places, but now they be applied to another use, *scilicet*, to teach the people, and to be the[8] laymen's books; as Damascene[9] and many other saith. Oh! blasphemous and devilish doctrine, to appoint the most noble creature of God, man endued with wit and reason, resembling the image of the everlasting God, to be instructed and taught of a mute, dumb, blind, and dead idol! The brute beast that goeth by the way, and the ass that serveth for the mill, is not taught by the rod of the carter, but by the prudence of him that useth the rod; and should those painted blocks be the books of reasonable man? Full well can the devil transform himself into an angel of light, and to deceive the people under the pretence of true[10] religion. I had rather trust to the shadow of the church that the scripture teacheth, than to all the men's writings sith the death of Polycarpus. Christ saith not, Go preach unto the people by images; but said, *Ite in universum mundum, et prædicate evangelium*[11]. Matt. xxviii. They say, that images adorn and seemly deck the temple of God, whither[12] as people resort to hear the word of God, the more images, the more dishonoured is the temple. First, let them teach by the manifest word of God, that the temple should be decked with such idols that cannot teach nor speak. Some man's tongue must declare the history of the idol, or else they know not what the idol is; peradventure, take Saint Barbara

As one abuse is removed, Satan suborneth another.

Man is put to school to a dead idol.

The temple of God not honoured, but dishonoured by images.

---

[7] Who entered. R. [8] The, omitted in R.

[[9] Καὶ ὅπερ τοῖς γράμμασι μεμνημένοις ἡ βίβλος, τοῦτο τοῖς ἀγραμμάτοις ἡ εἰκών, καὶ ὅπερ τῇ ἀκοῇ ὁ λόγος, τοῦτο τῇ ὁράσει ἡ εἰκών. Damasc. Op. Basil. 1575. De Imagin. Orat. I. p. 708.]

[10] New. R.

[11] Go into all the world, and preach the gospel. R.

[12] Whither the. R.

for Saint Katherine, and Saint Concumbre for the rood of Paul's; Balaam and his ass, that for lucre attempted to curse the church of God, for Christ and his ass that came to bless and sanctify his church with his precious blood. It is the abuse and profanation of the temple to suffer them, and a great occasion for people to return to their accustomed ill. I would all men should indifferently ponder these reasons, and judge whether they be to be suffered or not.

<small>A recapitulation of the reasons why images are not to be suffered in temples.</small>

First, the most perfect churches[1] of the prophets, Christ, and his apostles, used no such mean to instruct the people. We ought to follow them and the word of God wroten by the prophets and apostles. Also the Greek church never consented willingly to admit the use of images in the temples. The ill that hath happened unto the people by the means of images is too plain and well known; God by idolatry robbed of his glory, and the idolater disherited of God's mercy, except he repented[2] in this life.

<small>An image brought into the church liveth a long time.</small>

An image once brought into the church liveth a long time. Grant, that at the beginning there was a good preacher[3] of the church: the preacher dieth, the idol the longer it liveth the younger it waxeth, as ye may see by the idol of Walsingham, Cantorbury, and Hayles[4]. They flourished most a little before their desolation

---

[1] Church. R.   [2] Repent. R.

[[3] agodd preachet, in the original.]

[[4] The image of "Our Lady" at Walsingham in Norfolk was so celebrated, that persons from foreign countries resorted thither upon pilgrimage. Erasmus has graphically described the gross idolatries and licentiousness connected with these pilgrimages. See his Colloq. Peregrin. religionis ergo. Dugdale's Monasticon, Vol. vi. p. 71, contains a long list of sovereigns who were pilgrims to this shrine. The last of these, Henry VIII., walked to it bare-footed from Barsham. In his reign the image was taken to Chelsea and burned. In "A Short Instruction," &c. set forth by Archbp. Cranmer, 1548, (Oxford, 1829, p. 23,) the following passage occurs: "The whiche abuses, good children, your owne fathers, yf you aske theym, can well declare vnto you. For they themselfes wer greatly reduced by certayne famouse and notoriouse ymages, as by our lady of Walsingham, oure ladye of Ippeswiche, saynt Thomas of Canterbury, sainct Anne of Buckestone, the roode of grace and suche lyke, whom many of your parentes visitide yerely, leaving their owne houses and familyes. To them they made vowes and pilgrimages, thinkyng that God would heare their prayers in that place rather than in another place. They kissed their feete devouteley, &c."—The cathedral of Canterbury was "full of idols," but the shrine of

in the reign of the king's majesty that dead is, Henry the VIII. of a blessed memory. At their setting up I suppose the preachers were more diligent and zealous of God's glory than afterward. But was not the original damnable, against the word of God, to give the people such a book to learn by, that should school them to the devil?

The words of Gregory *ad Serenum episcopum Massiliensium, parte X. Epistol iv.*[5] should move no man, though he say, *Quod legentibus scriptura, hoc idiotis pictura præstat cernentibus*[6]; and doth reprehend Serenus for the breaking of images, saying, that the like was not seen done[7] by any other minister[8]. This is but Saint Gregory's opinion. Epiphanius writing[9] in a certain epistle *ad Johannem Hierosolimitanum episcopum, interprete D. Hieronymo*[10], hath this sentence: *Audivi quosdam murmurare contra me, qui quando simul pergebamus ad sanctum locum, qui vocatur Bethel [* * * *] et venissem ad villam quæ vocatur [dicitur] Anablatha, vidissemque præteriens ardentem lucernam, et interrogassem quis locus esset, didicissemque esse ecclesiam, et intrassem ut orarem, inveni ibi velum pendens in foribus ejusdem ecclesiæ tinctum atque de-*

[Side note: Gregory the Great saith images are the books of the unlearned.]

Thomas à Becket stood pre-eminent, eclipsing there even the popular worship of the Virgin. See Erasmus above quoted, Burnet, and others.—At Hales Abbey, in Gloucestershire, the blood of our Saviour was pretended to be shewn. Collier has described the manner in which this fraud was practised. Latimer also in his seventh sermon before king Edward VI. has exposed the "great abomination of the blood of Hales;" of which he says, "What ado was it to bring this out of the king's (Henry VIII.) head." In his letter to M. Morice (see Foxe) he speaks of the people "coming by flocks out of the west country" to the blood of Hales.]

[5] To Serenus, bishop of Massile, in the X. part, Epist. iv. R.

[6] That an image performeth that unto the simple beholder which the scripture doth to the reader. R.   [7] Was not done. R.

[[8] Perlatum siquidem ad nos fuerat, quod inconsiderato zelo succensus sanctorum imagines sub hac quasi excusatione, ne adorari debuissent, confregeris. Et quidem quia eas adorari vetuisses, omnino laudavimus; fregisse vero reprehendimus. Dic, frater, a quo factum sacerdote aliquando auditum est, quod fecisti? Nam quod legentibus scriptura, hoc idiotis præstat pictura cernentibus. S. Greg. Op. Par. 1672. Tom. II. col. 938. Lib. IX. Indic. iv. Epist. ix.]

[9] Writeth, 1547. Writing. R.

[10] Unto John, the bishop of Hierusalem, according to the interpretation of Saint Hierome. R.

pictum, [et] habens imaginem quasi Christi vel Sancti cujusdam: non enim satis memini cujus imago fuerit. Cum autem [ergo] hoc vidissem in ecclesia Christi contra auctoritatem scripturarum hominis pendere imaginem, scidi illud[1], &c. whereas he willeth the occasion of ill to be taken out of the church, as Paul commandeth, 1 Thess. v. This doctor, as all men knoweth, was of singular learning and virtue.

Athanasius the Great denieth images to be the books of the lay people. Again, against the authority of Gregory the Great I set the authority of Athanasius the Great, who denieth by express words the images to be the books of the lay people[2]: *Adversus gentes sic scribit. Philosophi gentium et qui apud eos eruditi dicuntur, cum urgeri a nobis cœperint, non negant hominum et mutorum animalium formas atque effigies esse qui apud eos videntur Dii: verum hanc afferunt rationem, idcirco se illas imagines fingere, ut per eas sibi Deus respondeat et reveletur; non posse enim invisibiliter aliter nosse, quam per hujusmodi signa atque taletas. Alii his sapientiora se dicere arbitrantes eas esse veluti literas hominibus, quæ relegentes possint, per eam quæ ex illis insinuatur cœlestium spirituum revelationem, et Dei intelligentiam consequi. Ita quidem illi perquam fa-*

---

[1] I have heard certain murmur against me, who when we went together unto the holy place which is called Bethel, and I came to a certain village which is called Hnablatha, and saw as I passed by a candle burning, and had demanded what place it was, and had learned that it was a church, and had entered into it to pray, I found there a vail hanging on the doors of the same church dyed and painted, having as it were the image of Christ or some holy man. For I do not well remember whose image it was. But when I saw in the church of Christ the image of a man, contrary to the authority of the scriptures, to hang up, I tore it, &c. R. [Hieron. Op. Basil. 1565. Tom. II. p. 161.]

[2] He writeth thus against the gentiles. The philosophers of the gentiles, and those [who] were counted learned amongst them, when they are urged of us, do not deny but those are the forms and shapes of men and dumb creatures, which are reckoned for gods amongst them: but they render this reason, that they therefore make those images, that God by them may give answer, and be revealed unto them; for they think the invisible God cannot otherwise be known than by such signs and figures. Others, thinking they answer more wisely than these, say they are instead of books unto men, whereby the readers may through that revelation of celestial spirits which is insinuated by them, attain to the knowledge of God. Thus they speak very ridiculously, neither have they any more reason. R.

*bulose, neque enim rationabiliter dicunt*³. With great gravity and godly reasons this great clerk confuteth this fond opinion,—Images to be the books of the laymen.

The great and excellent clerk⁴ Lactantius Firmianus crieth so out against images, that he saith there can be no true religion where they be. Tertullian⁵, *De Corona Militis*⁶, judgeth the same. The law of God doth not only condemn the use of them in the church, and these holy doctors; but also the name of an image declareth it to be abomination.

_{Lactantius inveigheth against images.}
_{Tertullian condemneth images.}

Read all the scripture, and in every place where as thou findest this word, *ezeb*⁷, idol or image, it signifieth either affliction, rebellion, sorrow, tristes⁸, travail or pain, or else the wicked muck and mammon of the world, or the thing that always provoketh the ire of God, as Rabbi David Kimhy well expoundeth Psalm cxv. This Jew saith, that the idols bring men into hatred of God, expounding these words of David, *Quibus similes evadant qui ea faciunt et quicunque fidit eis*⁹; saith, the text must be understood by the manner of prayer¹⁰, as though David prayed Almighty God to make these gravers and carvers of images as dumb, as blind, as mute, and as insensible, as the idol that can nor speak¹¹ nor hear. Our Lord amend it!

Rabbi D. K. saith that idols bring men into hatred with God.

What should move men to defend in the church of Christ so necessary an ill and pestilent treasure, that hath

[³ Athan. Ora. contra Gentes. Par. Ben. Ed. 1698. Tom. I. cap. xix. p. 19.]

[⁴ Non est dubium quin religio nulla sit, ubicumque simulacrum est. Lact. Op. Lutet. Par. 1748. Tom. I. p. 185. Lib. II. de Orig. Erroris. cap. xix.]

[⁵ Longum enim divortium mandat ab idolatria, in nullo proxime agendum. Draco enim terrenus de longinquo non minus absorbet alites. Johannes, Filioli, inquit, custodite vos ab idolis: non jam ab idolatria quasi in officio, sed ab idolis, *id est ab ipsa effigie eorum*. Indignum enim est ut imago Dei vivi, &c. Tertul. Op. Paris. 1580. de Cor. Mil. p. 348. C.]

⁶ Of the crown of the soldier. R.

⁷ [עֶצֶב See Gen. iii. 17, &c.]   ⁸ Trouble. R.

⁹ To whom they are like that make them, and whoso trusteth in them. R.

[¹⁰ Similes illis fiant. Hoc imprecative dictum est. Kimchi in Psalmos. Paris. 1665. p. 525.]

¹¹ As is the idol that cannot speak. R.

seduced both our fathers and great-grandfathers[1]; where the church of the patriarchs, prophets, and apostles, never used them, but in all their writings abhorred [them][2]? Loved we God, we would be content with scripture. Every scholar of Aristotle taketh this for a sufficient verity, *Magister dicit*[3]: he will be contented as soon as he heareth his master's name. Cicero, lib. iii. *De Oratore*, was thus persuaded of those that were excellent orators[4]: *Sic estimat suavitatem Isocratis, subtilitatem Lysiæ, acumen Hyperidis, sonitum Æschinis, vim Demosthenis ac orationem Catuli, ut quicquid (inquit) aut addideris aut mutaveris aut detraxeris, vitiosius aut deterius futurum*[5]. And should not the patriarchs, prophets, Christ, and the apostles, as well suffice the church of God?

What, although many learned men hath approved images, should their wisdom[6] maintain any contrary unto the word of God? No: a christian man must not care who speaketh, but what is spoken; the truth [is][2] to be accepted, whosoever speaketh it. Balaam was as wise, learned, and replenished with God's gift[7], as [a][2] man could be; notwithstanding, his ass telling the truth must be believed better than he. The law of God teacheth no use of images, but saith: *Non facies, non coles*[8]. Exod. xx. Believe it. Yet the art of graving and painting is the gift of God. To have the picture or image of any martyr or other, so it be not put in the temple of God, nor otherwise abused, it may be suffered. Christ by the picture of Cæsar taught his audience obedience unto the

---

[1] Great graunt fathers, 1547. Grandfathers. R.

[2] Supplied from R.   [3] The master saith. R.

[4] And he so esteemed the sweetness of Isocrates, the subtlety of Lysias, the dexterity of Hyperides, the sound of Æschines, the power of Demosthenes, and oration of Catulus; that whatsoever thou shalt (quoth he) either add, or change, or take away, it will become the more corrupted and the worse. R.

[5] Suavitatem Isocrates, subtilitatem Lysias, acumen Hyperides, sonitum Æschines, vim Demosthenes habuit.—Quid jucundius auribus nostris umquam accidit hujus oratione Catuli? * * * quidquid aut addideris aut mutaveris, aut detraxeris, vitiosius et deterius futurum.—Cic. de Oratore, Lib. III. 7, 8.]

[6 -approuid imaginisshuld there wysdom, in the original.]

[7] Yeste, 1547. Giftes. R.

[8 Thou shalt not make, thou shalt not worship.]

civil prince, saying, *Cujus est hæc imago? Cæsaris, inquiunt. Ergo reddite quæ sunt Cæsaris Cæsari*[9].

But if man will learn to know God by his creatures, let him not say "Good morrow, master," to an old moth-eaten post, but behold the heavens which declareth the might [and][10] power of God. Psalm [xix.] Consider the earth, how it bringeth forth the fruits thereof, the water with fishes, the air with the birds. Consider the disposition, order, and amity, that is between the members of man's body, the one always ready to help the other, to save the other; the hand the head, the head the foot, the stomach to disperse the meat and drink into the exterial parts of the body. Yea, let man consider the hawk and the hound, that obey in their vocation, and so every other creature of the earth; and with true heart and unfeigned penitence come to the knowledge of himself, and say, All the creatures that ever the living God made, obeyeth in their vocation, saving the devil, and I, most wretched man.

The glory, majesty, and power of God appeareth in his creatures.

Those things were made to be testimonies unto us of God's mighty power, and to draw men unto virtue; not these idols, which the devil caused to be set in the temple to bring men from God. Thus did Christ teach the people his most blessed death and passion, and the fruit of his passion, by the grain of corn cast into the earth; and said, *Nisi granum frumenti cadens in terra mortuum fuerit, ipsum solum manet; si autem mortuum fuerit, multum fructum affert*[11]. He hanged not the picture of his body upon the cross, to teach them his death, as our late[12] learned men hath done.

Christ hath taught by similitudes taken from his creatures, and not by images.

The ploughman, be he never so unlearned, shall better be instructed of Christ's death and passion by the corn that he soweth in the field, and likewise of Christ's resurrection, than by all the dead posts that hang in the church, or [are][10] pulled out of the sepulchre with *Christus resurgens*[13]. What resemblance hath the taking of the cross out of the sepulchre, and going a procession with it, with the resurrection of Christ?

The ploughman may be instructed of Christ's death and resurrection better by the corn he soweth than by a rotten post.

---

[9] Whose image is this? And they said, Cæsar's. Then give unto Cæsar that is Cæsar's. R.   [10] Supplied from R.

[11] Except the corn fall into the earth and die, it abideth alone, but if it die it bringeth forth much fruit. R.   [12] (Late,) omitted in R.

[13] Christ rising again. R.

None at all: the dead post is as dead, when they sing, *Jam non moritur*[1], as it was when they buried it with, *In pace factus est locus ejus*[2]. If any preacher would manifest the resurrection of Christ unto the senses, why doth not he teach them by the grain of the field that is risen out of the earth, and cometh of the dead corn that he sowed in the winter? Why doth not the preacher preach the death and resurrection of Christ by such figures and metaphors as the scripture teacheth? Paul wonderfully, 1 Cor. xv., proveth[3] with arguments the death and resurrection of Christ, and ours[4] likewise, that nothing may be more plainly taught.

A dead post carried [in] a procession as much resembleth the resurrection of Christ, as very death resembleth life. People should not be taught nor by image nor by reliques, as Erasmus Rotterodam[5] in his third book of Ecclesiastes well declareth. Lactantius Firmianus[6] useth a wonder[ful] divine, eloquent, and plain manner in the declaring of this resurrection, which is sung yearly in the church, *De resurrectionis Dominicæ die*[7], with many godly and divine verses. The same Lactantius saith[8], that there can be no true religion where these images be. August. ad Marcellum repre-

Augustine against images.

---

[1] Now he dieth not. R.

[2] His place is made in peace. R. [Allusion is here made to the absurd ceremonies which were practised in the churches at Easter.]

[3] Paul thus doth wonderfully (1 Cor. xv.) prove. R.   [4] Us, R.

[[5] Huic affine est, quod quidam per imagines movent affectus, aut per ostensas sanctorum reliquias, quorum neutrum convenit gravitati loci, in quo consistit Ecclesiastes; neque enim legimus unquam tale quidquam factum vel a Christo vel ab apostolis. Alibi plurimum utilitatis habent imagines, vel ad memoriam vel ad rerum intelligentiam, &c........ Verum ea dignitas est concionis, ut ejusmodi adminicula gravatim admittat. Idem sentiendum arbitror de reliquiis sanctorum. Utrobique cavendum est a superstitione, quia par utrobique periculum. Erasmi Op. Tom. v. col. 987. D. Lugd. Batav. 1703—6.

For the more full expression of Erasmus' views on this subject, see also col. 501 of same Vol. De Amabili Ecclesiæ Concordia.]

[[6] Carmen de resurrectione Domini:
        Salve, festa dies, toto venerabilis ævo,
        Qua Deus infernum vicit et astra petit, &c. &c.
                Lactantii Opera Basil. 1582. fo. 113.]

[7] Upon the day of the Lord's resurrection. R.

[[8] See before, note 3, p. 42.]

hendeth them wonderfully in these words of David, *Os habent, et non loquuntur*[9]*;* saith[10] men may be soon deceived by images[11]. Likewise in the first book [12]*De Consensu Evangelistarum*[13].

Such as defend them have nothing but sophistical arguments to blind the people with. The scripture nor apostles' church used none: as for Gregory the Great and Theodosius[14], with other that defend them, all the histories declare, that men of greater learning than they by the scripture condemned them; as Leo III., the emperor Constantinus V. who assembled all the learned men of Asia and Grecia, and condemned the use of images, that Gregory and Martin the First had stablished[15]. But it forceth not, had all Asia, Africa, and Europa, and Gabriel the archangel descended from heaven, approved the use of images; forasmuch as the apostles neither taught nor wrote of them, their authority should have no place. The word of God solely and only is to be preferred, Galat. i., which forbiddeth images.

[9] They have a mouth, and speak not. R. [10] Sich. R.

[[11] Quis autem adorat vel orat intuens simulacrum, qui non sic afficitur ut ab eo se exaudiri putet, ac ab eo, &c. Contra hunc affectum, quo humana et carnalis infirmitas facile capi potest, cantat scriptura Dei, &c. Aug. Op. Basil. 1542. Tom. viii. in Ps. cxiii. (cxv.) col. 1307.]

[12] Of the consent of the Evangelists. R.

[[13] Nec discipulos ejus a sui magistri doctrina deviasse, cum deos gentium coli prohibuerint, ne vel insensatis simulacris supplicaremus, vel societatem cum dæmoniis haberemus, vel creaturæ potius quam Creatori religionis obsequio serviremus. Aug. Op. Basil. 1542. Tom. iv. De Consensu Evangelistarum, Lib. i. cap. xxxiv. col. 394.]

[[14] Theodosius. Possibly a misprint for Theodorus I. who zealously promoted the worship of images and relics, and was the immediate predecessor of Martin I. afterwards mentioned.]

[[15] See Platina.—Car. Mag. de Impio Imag. Cultu. Lib. iv.—Chemnit. Exam. Concil. Trident.—Tribbechovii. de Doctor. Scholast. Cor. &c.—Bellarmin. de Imag. Sanct.—Mosheim,—&c.]

CAPUT VI.

[THE SIXTH CHAPTER.]

The third Office of Christ is concerning his priesthood, to offer sacrifice unto God, and by the same to purge the world from sin.

<small>The third part of Christ's office.</small>

PAUL, Philip. ii., saith, that Christ humbled himself unto the death of the cross. Heb. ii. He was made partaker of man's mortal nature, that by death he might destroy him that had the imperie[1] and dominion of death, to say, the devil. John calleth him the Lamb that doth take away the sin of the world, John i. All the sacrifices of the old law were figures and types of this only sacrifice, which was appointed by God to die and to suffer the ire[2] and displeasure of God for the sin of man, as though he himself were a sinner, and had merited this[3] displeasure. The greatness of this ire, sorrow, confusion, ignominy, and contempt, neither angel nor man can express: his pains were so intolerable, and his passion so dolorous, his death[4] so obedient with the Father's will, that it was not only a sacrifice, but also a just recompense to satisfy for all the world solely and only, as Christ taught Nicodemus, John iii., as Paul, Heb. vii. viii. ix. x., Esa. liii., and so all the prophets and patriarchs; and such a sacrifice as once for all sufficeth, Heb. vii.

<small>Christ suffered for the sin of man, as though he himself had been a sinner.</small>

<small>Christ hath made satisfaction by his death.</small>

<small>Christ's sacrifice once offered sufficeth.</small>

These two offices of Christ should never be out of remembrance. They declare the infinite mercy of God, and likewise his indifferent and equal justice unto all creatures without respect of persons. The token of his mercy may be known in this, that he would not that all mankind should be lost, though in Adam all deserved eternal death. He opened his mercy unto Adam not only by word, but also by the fire that descended upon his sacrifices and his son's: so to Abraham, then to the world by the incarnation and death of his only Son, the promise of grace and the promise of everlasting life unto such as repent and believe in him.

<small>God opened his mercy to Adam not only in word, but also by fire that descended upon his sacrifices.</small>

---

[1] Empire. R.   [2] Wrath. R.
[3] His. R.   [4] [Deite, in original.] Death. R.

The signs of his ire and displeasure unto man is this, that he would not accept man again into his favour for no penance[5], no sorrow, no trouble, no adversity, no weeping, no wailing, no, nor for the death of any person, until his own Son, most dear beloved, by death appeased his displeasure, and became surety to satisfy the justice of God and the right that the devil had unto all mankind. This if [a][6] man remembered as deeply and as earnestly as the matter requireth, it should make his heart full sorry, and bring him unto an honest and virtuous trade of life; to consider this example of God's justice and equity in the appeasing of his own just conceived ire, and likewise that he would do no wrong unto his mortal enemy, the devil. Except the Son of God had been an equal and just redemption, a price correspondent to contrepece[7] and satisfy the culpe[8] and guilt of man's sin, God would not have taken one soul from the right and justice of the devil.

God declared his wrath against sin, in that he could not otherwise be appeased than by the death of his Son.

Now [out][6] of this infallible truth, that Christ hath sacrificed only for sin, and his death accompted only sufficient for the salvation of man, the church of Christ is aright instructed of two most necessary articles; first, of justification, and then of the right use of the sacrament of his holy body. Concerning justification thus the word of God teacheth.

CAPUT VII.
[THE SEVENTH CHAPTER.]

SAINT Paul, when he saith that we be justified by faith, Rom. iii. iv. v., he meaneth that we have remission of sin, reconciliation, and acceptation into the favour of God. So doth this word *justify* signify, Deut. xxv., *hisdich*[9], where as God commandeth the judge to justify, quit, and absolve the innocent, and to condemn and punish the person culpable.

Of justification, and what is the meaning when it is said that we are justified by faith.

Paul saith, We are justified[10] by faith, and not by works. To be justified by faith in Christ is as much to say as, we

---

[5] For any repentance, sorrow, &c. R.
[6] Supplied from R.   [7] Counterpeise. R. [counterpoise].
[8] Satisfy for the, &c. R. [Culpe, fault.]
[9] וְהִצְדִיקוּ Deut. xxv. 1. See Gesenius.]
[10] Weor iustied, in the original.]

[HOOPER.]

obtain remission of sin, and are accepted into the favour of God, by the merits of Christ. To be justified by works is as much to say as, to deserve remission of sin by works.

Paul declareth, that for the death and merits of Christ we be saved, and not by our own virtues. So that faith doth not only shew us Christ that died, and now sitteth at the right hand of God; but also applieth the merits of this[1] death unto us, and maketh Christ ours: faith laying nothing to gage unto the justice of God but the death of Christ, and thereupon claimeth mercy and God's promise, the remission of sin, and desireth God to justify and deliver the soul from the accusation of the law and right of the devil, which he is bound to do for his promise sake. Ezech. xxxiii. Matt. xvii. And although with this remission of sin he giveth likewise the Holy Ghost to work the will of God, to love both God and his neighbour, [yet][2] notwithstanding the conscience, burdened and charged with sin, first seeketh remission thereof. For this thing the conscience laboureth and contendeth in all fears and terrors of sorrow and contrition. It disputeth not, what virtues it bringeth, wretched soul[3], to acclaim this promise of mercy; but forsaking her own justice, offereth Christ, dead upon the cross[4], and sitting at God's right hand. Nothing maketh it the cause[5] wherefore this mercy should be given, saving only the death of Christ, which is *ton litron*, the only sufficient price and gage for sin.

And although it be necessary and requisite, that in the justification of a sinner contrition to be present, and that necessarily charity and [a][2] virtuous life must follow; yet doth the scripture attribute the only remission of sin unto the mercy of God, which is given[6] only for the merits of Christ, and received solely by faith. Paul doth not exclude those virtues to be present, but he excludeth the merits of those virtues, and deriveth the cause of our acceptation into the grace of God only for Christ.

And mark this manner of speech: *Fide justificamur;*

---

[1] His. R.   [2] Supplied from R.

[3] Wretched soul, omitted in R.

[4 For sakyng here awne iustice ofrithe Christ, ded upon the crosse, in the original.]   [5] There is no cause. R.

[6 Wliche is yeuyne, in the original.]

hoc est, fiducia misericordiæ sumus justi[7]. This word *faith* doth comprehend as well a persuasion and confidence, that the promise of God appertaineth unto him for Christ's sake, as the knowledge of God. For faith, though it desire the company of contrition and sorrow for sin, yet contendeth it not in judgment upon the merits of no works, but only for the merits of Christ's death. In case it did, it availeth nothing; for if a man desire to be delivered from the law, the law must be satisfied which saith, *Diliges Dominum Deum tuum ex tota mente, toto corde, et ex omnibus viribus*[8]. Deut. vi. Now there [neither][9] is, nor never was, any man born of the stock of Adam in original sin, that feared God as much as the law requireth, nor never had such constant faith as is required, nor such ardent love as it requireth: seeing those virtues that the law required be infirm and debile[10], for their merits we can obtain nothing of God. We must therefore only trust to the merits of Christ, which satisfied the extreme jot and uttermost point of the law for us. And this his justice and perfection he imputeth and communicateth with us by faith. *Our works imperfect.*

Such as say, that only faith justifieth not, because other virtues be present, they cannot tell what they say. Every man that will have his conscience appeased, must mark those two things: How remission of sin is obtained, and wherefore it is obtained. Faith is the mean whereby it is obtained, and the cause wherefore it is received is the merits of Christ. Although faith be the means whereby it is received, yet hath neither faith, nor charity, nor contrition, nor the word of God, nor all those knit together, sufficient merits wherefore we should obtain this remission of sin: but the only cause wherefore sin is forgiven, is the death of Christ. *Two things to be observed in our justification. The mean wherein we are justified, and that is Christ. The mean whereby we apprehend righteousness in Christ, and that is faith.*

Now mark the words of Paul: "Freely," saith he, "we are justified by his grace." Let the man burst his heart with contrition, believe that God is good a thousand times, burn in charity; yet shall not all these satisfy the law, nor deliver man from the ire of God, until such time as faith

---

[7] We are justified by faith; that is, through the confidence of his mercy we are just. R.

[8] Thou shalt love the Lord thy God with all thy mind, with all thy heart, and with all thy soul. R.   [9] Supplied from R.   [10] Weak. R.

letteth fall all hope and confidence in the merits of such virtues as be in man, and say, " Lord, behold thy unfruitful servant; only for the merits of Christ's blood give me remission of sins; for I know no man can be justified otherwise before thee, as David saith: *Non justificabitur in conspectu tuo omnis vivens*[1], Psal. cxliii. Again, *Beatus vir cui Dominus non imputat peccatum*[2], Psal. xxxii.

An opening of the communication between Christ and Nicodemus. He that would mark Christ's communication with that noble man and great clerk Nicodemus, John iii., should be satisfied how and wherefore man is justified so plainly, that no adversary of the truth should hurt this infallible verity, " sole faith to justify." Nicodemus, having a good opinion, although not a sufficient knowledge, of Christ, came unto him by night, and confessed him to be sent from God, and that because of such works and miracles as he had wrought. Christ made answer, " Truly, Nicodemus, I say unto thee, no man can see the kingdom of God, except he be born from above." Nicodemus, not understanding what Christ meant, asked him how an old man could be born again, and whether he could enter his mother's belly, and then be born again. Christ bringeth him yet near[er][3] unto the light, that he might know the means, and saith, " I tell thee truly, Nicodemus, that no man can enter the kingdom of God, except he be born of the water and the Holy Ghost, &c."

Nicodemus confessed yet again his ignorancy, and desired to be further instructed, saying, " How may these things be?" Christ answered, " Thou art the great master and rabbi in Israel, and yet ignorant of these things:" meaning, that great and horrible must the ignorancy of the people be, when their doctors know not the truth. Nicodemus confessing his ignorancy, and receiving reproach at Christ's hand, because he took upon him to teach other, and yet a fool himself in the religion of God, might for shame have left Christ and his gospel-yoke[4], because he now is made a scholar, that before was for his prudence and learning the chief of the Jews, a Pharisee of most notable estimation. Christ straightway comforteth him [and][3] all other,

---

[1] No man living shall be justified in thy sight. R.
[2] Blessed is the man unto whom the Lord imputeth no sin. Ps. xxxii. R.
[3] Supplied from R.   [4] yke, 1547. Omitted in R.

learned and unlearned, and saith, "No man ascendeth into heaven, except he that descended from heaven, the Son of man, which is in heaven." As though Christ had said thus: "Discomfort not thyself, Nicodemus, that although thou be a great learned man, and yet ignorant of the ways unto everlasting life. For I promise thee, there is no man, learned nor unlearned, that can of his own wit and learning ascend unto the knowledge of life everlasting, but only he that descended from heaven, the Son of man, which is in heaven."

Now Nicodemus, being destitute of all worldly and human prudence, and finding himself full unable by wit or learning to follow the effect of Christ's preaching concerning the means of salvation, dependeth only of[5] the mouth of Christ, and disputeth no more the matter. Then Christ sheweth him the way, and maketh a ladder for Nicodemus, wherewith he may ascend into heaven, and saith: "This way thou mayest understand the thing I speak of. *Sicut Moses exaltavit serpentem in deserto, ita exaltari oportet filium hominis.* As Moses lift up the serpent in the desert, so must the Son of man be lift up." This history of the serpent was not unknown unto this learned man, albeit he considered not the mystery and sacrament that it figured. Now Christ teacheth him in this place to understand the law; and because this oration of Christ wroten by St John is obscure, and lacketh a declaration somewhat of the purpose that Christ would prove, *omittit, Hebræorum more, alteram similitudinis partem*[6]. I will annex the type and figure with the effect and mystery of the figure, and make the text plain. *Sicut Moses exaltavit serpentem in deserto, sic exaltari oportet filium hominis*[7]. Moses was commanded to lift up this serpent in the wilderness for this cause, that whosoever was stung or venomed with the poison of the serpents, if he looked upon the serpent of brass, might be healed. Here is the cause and the effect declared, why the serpent was lift up. Now to the words of Christ: *Ita exaltari oportet Filium ho-*

[5] Upon. R.

[6] He omitteth, according to the manner of the Hebrews, the one part of the similitude. R.

[7] As Moses lift up the serpent in the wilderness, so must the Son of man be lift up. R.

minis, ut omnis qui credit in illum non pereat, sed habeat vitam æternam[1]. "So must Christ be lift up, that as many as believe in him shall have everlasting life." Here is Nicodemus taught the way unto everlasting life: and because he was a doctor of Moses' law, Christ by the law made open the matter unto him, and brought him from the shadow unto the true body, and from the letter unto the understanding of the letter, saying: As those that by faith beheld the serpent were healed of the stings of the serpent, so such as behold me in faith hanging upon the cross, shall be healed from their sickness and sin, that the devil by the serpent infected mankind withal.

<small>Christ teacheth Nicodemus out of the law.</small>

Now let us repeat the text of Moses again, that we may truly understand our Saviour's words: *Fac tibi serpentem urentem, et pone eum impalum in sublime sublatum, fietque, si serpens aliquem momorderit, intueatur eum, et incolumis erit*[2].

<small>The cause why the serpent was erected.</small>

In these words is declared three things:

First, why the serpent was set up: the cause, the people were stung with serpents.

<small>The fruit and effect of it.
The use of the serpent.</small>

Second, the effect, the health of the people.

Third, the use, that they should look upon him.

So John declareth why Christ was made man, the use and the effect of his humanity, in these words: *Sic Deus dilexit mundum, ut filium suum unigenitum daret, ut omnis qui credit in eum non pereat, sed habeat vitam æternam*[3]. The cause of his coming was the sin and sickness of man, bitten by the serpent in paradise. The effect of his coming was the health of this sickness. The use of his coming was to believe that his death upon the cross was and is sufficient for the remission of sin, and to obtain eternal life.

<small>The cause of Christ's incarnation.
The effect of it, and the use thereof.</small>

Here is the justification of man lively expressed, and how many things concur as necessary unto the remission of

---

[1] So must the Son of man be lift up, that whosoever believeth in him should not perish, but have everlasting life. R.

[2] Make unto thee a (fiery) serpent, and set it on high upon a pole; and it shall come to pass, that if a serpent sting any and he look upon that, he shall be safe. R. [Numb. xxi. 9.]

[3] God so loved the world, that he gave his only-begotten Son, to the end that whosoever believeth in him should not perish, but have eternal life. R.

sin; and yet man only justified by faith:—the word of God, the preacher of the word, Christ himself, the contrition of Nicodemus, the Holy Ghost that moved Nicodemus to come by night unto Christ, the consenting will of Nicodemus unto the words of Christ; yet only was he delivered from sin by the faith that he had in the death of Christ, as Christ saith: *Sic oportet exaltari Filium hominis, ut omnis qui credit in illum non pereat, sed habeat vitam æternam*[4]. This must be diligently marked. For as the fathers of the old church used the serpent, so must those of our church use the precious body of Christ. They looked upon him only with the eyes of faith, they kissed him not, they cast no water upon him, and so washed their eyes therewithal; they touched him not with their hands, they ate him not, nor corporally, nor really, nor substantially: yet by their belief they obtained health. So Christ himself teacheth us the use of his precious body: to believe and look upon the merits of his passion suffered upon the cross, and so to use his precious body against the sting of original and actual sin: not to eat his body transformed into the form of bread, or in the bread, with the bread, under the bread, behind the bread, or before the bread, corporally or bodily, substantially or really, invisible, or any such ways, as many men, to the great injury of Christ's body, doth teach.

But as the children of Israel only by faith ate the body spiritually, not yet born, so by faith doth the Christians eat him now, being ascended into heaven, and none otherwise, as Christ saith unto Nicodemus: *Omnis qui credit in eum non pereat*[5]. Grant that we could as well eat his carnal body as we eat other meat, yet the eating thereof nothing availed. And if the apostles had corporally eaten him in his last supper, it had profited nothing; for he took not his body of the holy Virgin to that use, to be eaten for the remission [of][6] sin, or to sanctify him that eat[eth][6] him, but to die for sin, and that ways to sanctify his church. As he saith himself, that only by death the fruit of his incarnation should be-

---

[4] So must the Son of man be lift up, that whosoever believeth in him should not perish, but have eternal life. R.

[5] That every one which believeth in him should not perish. R.

[6] Supplied from R.

dispersed into the world: *Nisi granum frumenti dejectum in terram mortuum fuerit, ipsum solum manet. Mortua prodest caro, non comesa*[1]. But of this I will speak farther in the chapter that followeth.

This example of Nicodemus declareth, that neither the works that go before justification, neither those that follow justification, deserve remission of sin. Though sole faith exclude not other virtues to be present at the conversion of every sinner, yet doth sole faith, and only, exclude the merits of other virtues, and obtaineth solely remission of sin for Christ's sake, herself alone: as Paul saith, Ephes. ii. *Gratia salvati estis per fidem, idque non ex vobis, Dei donum est; non ex operibus, ne quis glorietur*[2]. Where as plainly he excludeth the dignity of works, and affirmeth us to be reconciled by faith. So doth John, chap. i. attribute those two singular gifts unto Christ, grace and verity, saying: *Lex per Mosen data est, gratia et veritas per Jesum Christum facta est*[3]. Here grace signifieth free remission of sin for the merits of Christ: verity is the true knowledge of God, and the gifts of the Holy Ghost that followeth the remission of sin.

What evil followeth to deny men to be justified by faith only in the mercy of God. Therefore such as say they be not justified only by faith in the mercy of God through Christ, extenuate sin and God's ire against sin too much, and likewise spoil Christ of his honour, who is the only sacrifice that taketh away the sin of the world.

They that will justify themselves any other ways than by faith, doth doubt always whether their sins be forgiven or not; and by reason of this doubt they can never pray unto God aright. For he that doubteth whether God be his friend or not, prayeth not, but as an ethnick saith his *Paternoster*, without faith and godly motion of the heart. He that is persuaded by the gospel, though his own unworthiness fear[4] him from God, yet beholdeth he the Son of God,

---

[1] Except the corn being cast into the earth do die, it remaineth alone. The flesh profiteth in that it died for us, not in that it is to be eaten really of us. R.

[2] Through grace ye are saved, by faith, and that not of yourselves; it is the gift of God; not of works, lest any should boast themselves. R.

[3] The law was given by Moses, but grace and truth came by Jesus Christ. R.   [4 Fear, frighten.]

and believeth that both he and his prayers be accepted in Christ; and thus accepted into grace, will follow the life of a justified man, as Paul commandeth (Rom. viii. Coloss. iii.), and as all the scripture giveth example. For it is no profit to say sole faith justifieth, except godliness of life follow, as Paul saith: *Si secundum carnem vixeritis, moriemini*[5]. He that hath obtained the remission of sin must diligently pray for the preservation of God's favour, as David giveth example unto the whole church, saying: *Cor mundum crea in me, Deus, et spiritum rectum innova in visceribus meis. Ne projicias me a facie tua, et Spiritum sanctum tuum ne auferas a me. Redde mihi lætitiam salutaris tui, et spiritu principali suffulci me*[6]. Psalm l.

<small>Justification by faith bringeth forth sanctimony and holiness of life.</small>

This prayer containeth a wonderful doctrine, and necessary to be daily repeated with great attention and heed. First, he desireth to have a heart pure and neat, judging aright of God, to fear his justice against sin, and to believe steadfastly his promised mercy unto the penitent; and that this light and knowledge be not taken from him by the devil or vanity of the world, as daily we see such as hath the knowledge of God's word to live more worldly than he that knoweth not what God is. Then [he][7] prayeth to have the help of God to govern all his counsels, and all the motions of his heart, that they may be agreeable unto the law of God, full of faith, fear, and charity; that for sin he be no more cast out from the face and favour of God; prayeth to have strength in adversity, and to rejoice under the cross of affliction; not to murmur nor grudge at any trouble, but to obey willingly the pleasure of God; not to leave him nor mistrust his mercy for any punishment, but to suffer what God pleaseth, as much as God pleaseth, and when God pleaseth.

<small>The tenor of David's prayer.</small>

These virtues must man practise and use, after he is justified, as well as to obtain remission of his sin, or else he is not justified at all: he is but a speaker of justification, and hath no justice within him. As he maketh Christ only

<small>Being justified by faith after the example of Abraham, we must follow the example of Abraham's life.</small>

---

[5] If ye live according to the flesh, ye shall die. R.

[6] Create a clean heart, [and renew a right spirit] within me. Cast me not away from thy face, and take not thy holy Spirit from me. Restore unto me the joy of thy saving health, and stablish me with thy free spirit. Psal. l. R. [Psal. li.]   [7] Supplied from R.

his Saviour, so must he follow such as were of Christ's family; the patriarchs, prophets, and the apostles, in the life prescribed by Christ, as they did; or else they shall be no disciples of the prophets, that were the doers as well as the speakers of virtue, but rather the disciples of the poets, that only commended virtue and followed it not, as Ovid saith[1]:

> Est Deus in nobis: agitante calescimus illo;
> Sedibus æthereis spiritus ille venit[2].

These holy words availed nothing.

Such as cannot understand the Epistle of Paul to the Romans concerning justification, and what life is required of him that is justified, let him read diligently the first Epistle of John, and then he shall right well perceive another life to be required of the justified man than the gospellers lead now-a-day, that hath words without facts, which slandereth the gospel, and promoteth it not; as it is to be seen, the more pity! in such men and such countries, as the truth hath been preached a long time. For the receiving of it unworthily the Lord will doubtless take from them his word, and leave them unto their own lusts. For this is certain and too true: let the whole gospel be preached unto the world, as it ought to be; penance[3] and a virtuous life with faith, as God preached the gospel unto Adam in Paradise, Noe, Abraham, Moses, Esay, saying: *Væ! genti peccatrici*[4]; John the Baptist: *Pœnitentiam agite, appropinquat regnum cœlorum*[5]; as Christ did: *Resipiscite et credite evangelium*[6], Mark i.; and then of an hundred that cometh to the gospel there would not come one. When they hear sole faith and the mercy of God to justify, and that they may eat all meats at all times with thanksgiving, they embrace that gospel with all joy and willing heart. And what is he that would not receive this gospel? The flesh itself, were there no immortal soul in it,

---

[1 Ovid's words are:
> Est Deus in nobis, et sunt commercia cœli:
> Sedibus ætheriis spiritus ille venit.]

[2] God is in us, through his motion it is we are warm: this same spirit cometh from celestial places. R.

[3] Repentance. R.   [4] Woe be to the sinful generation. R.

[5] Repent, for the kingdom of heaven is at hand. R.

[6] Repent, and believe the gospel. R.

would receive this gospel, because it promiseth aid, help, and consolation, without works; and when it heareth that it may as well eat a pasty of venison upon the Friday as a herring, what is he that would not be such a gospeller? But now speak of the other part of the gospel, as Paul teacheth to the Romans, chap. viii.: *Si secundum carnem vixeritis, moriemini*[7]; and as he prescribeth the life of a justified man in the same epistle, xii. xiii. xiv. xv. xvi. chap.; Christ, Matt. x.; Peter, 2 Pet. i. He that is justified, let him study those canons to live by.

Saint Paul writeth to a justified church of the Corinthians, and to such as had received the knowledge of the gospel, and saith, *Si quis, cum frater appelletur, fuerit scortator, aut avarus, aut simulacrorum cultor, aut conviciator, aut ebriosus, aut rapax, cum ejusmodi ne simul capiatis*[8], 1 Cor. v. This part of the gospel is not so pleasant as the other; therefore men take the first liberty, and neglect the fruits that should follow the gospel, and think themselves to be rich in the gospel, as the church of the Laodiceans judged of themselves, Apocalyp. iii., when they be indeed miserable, and wretched, poor, and naked of all godliness. Paul declareth, Rom. viii., what it is to be justified, and to be in Christ, to walk after the Spirit: he saith, *Nulla condemnatio est lex his qui sunt in Christo Jesu, qui secundum Spiritum ambulant*[9].

For a conclusion, justification is a free remission of sin, and acceptation into the favour of God, for Christ's merits: the which[10] remission of sin must follow necessarily amendment of life, or else we receive the grace of God in vain. 2 Cor. vi. Rom. viii. 2 Peter i.

[7] If ye live according to the flesh, ye shall die. R.

[8] If any that is called a brother, be a fornicator or covetous, or an idolator, [or a reviler, or a drunkard, or an extortioner,] with such eat not. 1 Cor. v. R.

[9] There is no condemnation to those [that] are in Christ Jesus, which walk after the Spirit. R.

[10] After which. R.

CAPUT VIII.

[THE EIGHTH CHAPTER.]

<small>The doctrine which teacheth the true use of the Lord's supper ariseth out of the doctrine of justification.</small>

OF this infallible verity, "Only the death of Christ to be the sacrifice for the expiation of sin," may be necessarily taught the right and true use of the Lord's supper, which men call the mass.

First, it is manifest, that it is not a sacrifice for sin, as men teach, contrary unto the word of God, that saith, "Christ by one sacrifice made perfect all things," Heb. vii. viii. ix. x.; and as John saith, *Sanguis Jesu Christi emundat nos a peccatis*[1]: and there remaineth no more after it, as Paul saith, *Ubi peccatorum remissio, ibi non amplius hostia pro peccato*[2]; and, to take away all doubt that remission of sin cannot be obtained for the merits of the mass, Paul saith plainly, that without blood-shedding no sacrifice can merit remission of sin.

<small>A lively declaration of Christ's pain for our sins.</small>

Although Christ now sit at the right hand of God, and pray for his church, and likewise doth offer the prayers and complaint of us that believe, yet it is only for the merits of his death that we obtain the mercy of God's promise; in the which he sustained such pain, that the remembrance thereof, and the greatness of God's ire against sin, put his precious body and soul in such an agony and fear, that his passion of sorrow surmounted the passions of all men, that ever travailed or were burdened with the weight and peace of God's importable ire against man for sin; insomuch that he wept not only tears of blood, but so abundantly pain forced them to descend, that they trickled upon the ground. Sore troubled and overcome with sorrow was David, Psalm vi., when he washed his bed with tears for sin; but it was joy and mirth, if his pains be conferred to[3] these dolours of Christ; they wanted no augmentation. This sacrifice was killed a little and a little; from one place of judgment sent unto the other; and always from the flames into the ardent coals. His death upon the cross so differed, that although he was

---

[1] The blood of Jesus Christ doth cleanse us from all sin. R.

[2] Where remission of sins is, there is no more sacrifice for sin. R.

[[3] Conferred to: compared with.]

very God, and the dear beloved Son of the Father, his abjection was so contemptible and vile, that he cried out as a man most destitute of God's favour and love, and said, *Deus meus! Deus meus! quare dereliquisti me*[4]*?* And until such time as he offered his most holy soul unto the Father, and his blessed side pierced with the spear, his pains and sorrows increased. Lo! thus was the manner to offer Christ for sin! After this sort and cruel handling of Christ was the ire of God appeased.

If they sacrifice Christ in the mass, let them hang him [like][5] tyrants again upon the cross, and thrust a spear to his blessed heart, that he may shed his blood; for "without shedding of blood is no remission." The scripture damneth this abuse of the Lord's supper, and is the conculcation[6] of his precious blood.

As concerning the use of this sacrament and all other the rites and ceremonies that be godly, they should be so kept and used in the church, as they were delivered unto us of the high bishop Christ, the author of all sacraments. For this is true, that he most godly, most religiously, and most perfectly instituted and celebrated the supper, and none otherways than the evangelist doth record. The best manner and most godly way to celebrate this supper is to preach the death of Christ unto the church, and the redemption of man, as Christ did at his supper, and there to have common prayers, as Christ prayed with his disciples; then to repeat the last words of the supper, and with the same to break the bread and distribute the wine to the whole church; then, giving thanks to God, depart in peace.

The sincere use of the Lord's supper.

These ceremonies that God instituted not, but repugneth God's institution, be not necessary, but rather in any case to be left, because they abrogate the institution of Christ. It seemeth sufficient unto me, if the church do as Christ hath commanded it to do. St Paul to the Corinthians, after the ascension of Christ at least eighteen years, wrote his epistle, and said he would deliver them nothing but that he had received of the Lord, and wrote concerning the use of the supper, as Matthew, Mark, and Luke writeth.

[1 Cor. xi.]

[4] My God! my God! wherefore hast thou forsaken me? R.
[5] Supplied from R. [6] As the conculcation or treading under foot. R.

This is therefore an ungodly disputation that the papists contend about, the change and alteration of the bread; and also a false and pernicious doctrine, that teacheth the corporal presence of Christ, both God and man, in the bread. For although Christ said of the bread, "This [is]¹ my body," it is well known that he purposed to institute a sacrament; therefore he spake of a sacrament sacramentally. To speak sacramentally is to give the name of the thing to the sign; so yet notwithstanding, that the nature and substance of the sign remaineth, and is not turned into the thing that it signifieth. Further, the verity of the scripture, and the verity of a christian faith, will not suffer to judge and believe Christ's body, invisible or visible, to be upon the earth. Acts i., Luke ult., Mark ult., Acts iii.

How Christ spake when he said of the bread, "This is my body."

If we likewise consider the other places of the scripture, John vi. xvi. xvii., we shall find that Christ would not, nor meant not, to institute any corporal presence of his body, but a memory of the body slain, resuscitated, ascended into heavens, and from thence to come unto judgment. True it is, that the body is eaten, and the blood drunken, but not corporally. In faith and spirit it is eaten, and by that sacrament the promise of God sealed and confirmed in us, the corporal body remaining in heaven.

How we eat the flesh of Christ, and drink his blood.

In the twenty-fourth chapter of Matthew, Christ, giving his church warning of this heresy, to come by the preaching of false prophets, said: "They will say, 'Lo! here is Christ, lo! there is Christ!' believe them not; for as the lightning cometh from the east into the west, so shall the coming of the Son of man be;" meaning by these words, that his body is not a fantastical body nor invisible, as these teach that say his corporal body is corporally given in the bread, with the bread, and under the bread invisible. Against this error I will set the word of God, and declare the truth thereby, that they have but an imagination or idea² of Christ's body, and not the natural and corporal body.

And the first reason is this: Christ bid his disciples they should not believe him that should say, Lo! here is Christ! or, there is Christ! He spake of his body doubtless and human nature: for he commandeth us to believe that his

Reasons against the real presence in the sacrament.

---

¹ Supplied from R.   ² ydeam, 1547. ydea. R.

Godhead is every where, as David saith; and as he saith, "My Father and I am one." Likewise he told them by plain words, Matt. the last chapter, that he would be with them unto the end of the world. Christ having but two natures, one divine and the other human, by these express words now he declareth [himself]³ to be present with the one and absent with the other. These things marked, I put this matter in comprise, to be judged of every humble and charitable spirited man, who judgeth aright of the body of Christ; those that say bodily he is not in the sacrament, or these that say he is bodily and corporally there. If he be there corporally and bodily, as they say, why shall I not believe these words, *Ecce hic! ecce illic*⁴! and say, Christ lieth that said, Believe them not that say, Lo! here is my body, or, there is my body? Christ, having good experience of the devil's subtlety, that he would intoxicate the wit of man with more subtle reasons than the simple heart could eschew, prepared of his mercy a means to preserve the faith of the simple; and against the sophistical and crafty reason of the devil, God calleth man to the judgment of his senses, and saith, "Reason what they will of my body, and say it is here or there substantially, bodily, corporally, believe them not: trust to thine eye; for as the lightning sensible cometh from the east into the west, so shall the coming of the Son of man be." How so? Turned into fire? No, so visible and sensible. God wist right well, when he called man from reason to the judgment of his senses, what doctors and doctrine should follow of his sensible body: one to change a cake into his body, and another to teach, though the cake be not his body, yet is his body present corporally, substantially, really, bodily; the same body that hanged upon the cross, and is given by hand, with the bread, under the bread, and in the bread, and yet insensible.

Christ will have our senses to judge of the verity of his body.

Grant all their glosses and interpretations to be true, as they be most false; and say, as they would have it, that the very true humanity, and Christ in the true shape and form of a man, (as he is with all qualities and quantities, except sin and immortality,) to be in the bread, under the bread, or with the bread, after the bread, or before the

---

³ Supplied from R.   ⁴ Behold here! behold there! R.

bread; and say, "There is present, in the priest's hand, as great a body, and as natural a man, as the priest or minister is himself, the word of God made man," (so they would have it;) they shall never deceive a godly Christian with their glosses: for he will trust unto the simplicity of God's word that saith, *Nolite credere*, Believe them not, till they shew my body unto the senses; "for as the lightning," [&c.]

The defenders of this doctrine, because they be not able to answer unto such as writeth and preacheth the truth, they challenge and attribute unto themselves the only knowledge of truth, and say, their contraries[1] be not learned, nor cannot understand them. Grant there were none learned that defendeth this truth, as there be, hath, and ever, till the world's end, shall be; yet will the truth defend itself: and because no man should in this matter leave the truth, though better learned than he judge fantastically of a true body, Christ would his simple disciple to judge sensibly of his natural body, and let this sophistication pass, and saith his body shall be as sensible as the lightning in the air, and not invisible with a piece of bread; though that most religious sacrament ought to be most godly used for the mystery that it containeth, and likewise the promise of grace that it confirmeth.

They say, this place maketh not against the presence of Christ's body in the sacrament, but against such as should preach, in the latter days, false doctrine against Christ's doctrine, and make another Christ. True it is, he speaketh of such as should preach false doctrine: but what should be that false doctrine that could be overcome with these words, *Nolite credere; sicut fulgetrum coruscans venit ab oriente in occidente, ita erit adventus Filii hominis*[2]? What heresy readeth any man in the histories, to be vanquished by these words? Not of Samosatenus[3], that was condemned in the council of Nice; not of Nestor, that denied two natures to be united in Christ; nor of Eutyches, that said one nature was converted into the other: none of the heresies

[1] Adversaries. R.

[2] Believe them not; for as the lightning cometh out of the east and shineth into the west, so shall also the coming of the Son of man be. R.

[3] Paul of Samosata, bishop of Antioch, who lived in the 3rd century, and held heretical opinions on the Trinity. See Euseb. Hist. Eccles. Lib. VII. cap. 30.]

that the devil moved against the essence and divine majesty of God, as Marcion and the Manichees, that said there were two Gods and both eternal, the one good and the other ill, always the one repugnant to the other: neither yet the heresy of Valentiniane[4], that said there were innumerable gods: but this false doctrine Christ spake by such as would, after his ascension into heaven corporally, yet preach in the latter days[5] unto the people, that his body should be in the earth; and therefore gave them these words, "Believe them not; for as the lightning cometh from the east to the west, so shall the coming of the Son of man be."

Christ spake of those that should deceive the people in the time between his ascension and coming to judgment. For in the end of the world it shall be no need to bid us beware; for all false preachers shall be damned when his glorious body shall appear. He that believeth before[6] that the natural body of Christ can be here any way corporally, neglecteth the commandment of Christ, *Nolite credere*[7], Matt. xxiv.; and likewise forgetteth his creed, *Sedet ad dextram Patris, inde venturus est, &c.*[8] And Luke saith plainly, that as visibly as he ascended, so shall he descend at the latter day, and not before, as he saith Acto. iii. Because they defend their opinion by the wrong interpretation of the words in the articles of our faith, I will answer to one or two objections that they make.

First, they say that this word "Heaven" in the article of our faith, *Ascendit ad cœlos*[9], signifieth no certain and determinate place, but generally all the world, heaven, earth, and hell, wheresoever God's power be manifested; and so saith, that the right hand of God betokeneth no place, but the whole power of God: as when I say, *Sedet ad dextram Dei*[10], it is as much to say as, he is in his humanity every where, as his Deity is.

---

[4] [Nestorius held that Christ had two persons as well as two natures; Eutyches, that he had only one nature in one person; Marcion and Manes, that there were in the Godhead two opposing principles; and Valentine, thirty or more principles or æons.]

[5] In the latter days, omitted in R.

[6] Therefore. R.   [7] Believe them not. R.

[8] He sitteth on the right hand of the Father, from thence he shall come, &c. R.   [9] He ascended into heaven. R.

[10] He sitteth on the right hand of God. R.

[HOOPER.]

Answers to certain objections of the adversaries.

Unto the first this I answer, that heaven in no place of the scripture is so taken, though it signify sometime all the celestial bodies above, heavens eternal, and then it signifieth the air, as Psalm cxlix. *Aquæ quæ supra cœlos sunt laudent nomen Domini*[1]; and sometime it signifieth only the superior place of creatures, as in the same Psalm, *Laudate eum cœli supremi*[2]. Into these superior heavens Christ ascended, as the manner of his ascension declareth, Luc. ultimo, Acto. i. He took his disciples with him into the mount of Olivet, and bid them there farewell. He departed bodily from them, as their eyes bare them record; and a cloud received this[3] body, that it could no more be seen: yet what became of this[3] body after that it passed their sight? That no question afterward should be, where this body was become, Luke saith, *Ferebatur in cœlum, capit. ultimo*[4]. This mutation of place, to ascend from the earth, only his human nature suffereth: concerning his Godhead, it is every where, and can neither ascend nor descend.

Such as say that heaven and the right hand of God is in the articles of our faith taken for God's power and might, which is every where, they do wrong to the scripture, and unto the articles of our faith. They make a confusion of the scripture, and leave nothing certain. They darken the simple and plain verity thereof with intolerable sophisms. They make heaven hell, and hell heaven, turn upside down and pervert the order of God. If the heaven and God's right hand, whither our Saviour's body is ascended, be every where, and noteth no certain place, as these uncertain men teach; I will believe no ascension. What needeth it?— seeing Christ's body is every where with his Godhead. I will interpretate this article of my creed thus: *Christus ascendit ad dextram Patris. Patris dextra est ubique: ergo Christus ascendit ad ubique*[5]. See what erroneous doctrine followeth their imaginations!

God's right hand sometime betokeneth his power.

As concerning the right hand of God, it is taken some-

[1] The waters be above the firmament, praise the name of the Lord. R.
[2] Praise him ye heavens above. R. [Ps. cxlviii. 4.]   [3] His. R.
[4] He was carried up into heaven; in the last chapter. R.
[5] Christ ascended unto the right hand of the Father: but the right hand of the Father is every where: therefore Christ ascended to every where. R.

time for God himself and his omnipotent power. Psa. cxvii. *Dextra Domini fecit virtutem, Dextra Domini exaltavit me*[6]. Thus his right hand, taken for his power, it is every where. But it is not so taken, when we say Christ sitteth at the right hand of God, as Mark saith, capit. ultimo[7], and as Stephen said[7], Acts vii.: *Video Jesum stantem a dextris Dei*[8]. But it signifieth a certain place of joy, where as the souls of the blessed saints rest. Thither hath God translated the body of Christ to be in as much joy, as it was in contempt here in the earth, as Paul[7] saith, Phil. ii. Sitting thus at the right hand of God, his body is as true man as it was upon the earth; and in length, breadth, and weight, as physical, mathematical, and natural a body, as it was hanging upon the cross.

What the word heaven signifieth in our creed.

In the changing of mortal qualities the humanity of Christ is neither destroyed nor changed into his Deity; but as truly as his Godhead, concerning his essence, cannot be seen, so is his body, wheresoever it be, subject unto the judgment of the senses. And as he that maketh a house first conceiveth a true form in his imagination, and yet the imagination nor conceit of the mind is not materially the house; so [the conceit of][9] such as dream and imagine a certain fantasy, and reduce the form and figure of a true body into their imagination, is not a true body, but a conceit or imagination of a body, as those men have, that say Christ is in the bread[10] and with the bread, yet occupieth it no place, nor is not sensible. This is a wonderful doctrine, to make that glorious body of Christ to be a true body, and yet lacketh all the qualities and quantities of a body. If Christ could have such a dreaming body, as they speak of, yet may I not believe it is in the sacrament corporally, because Christ saith, *Nolite credere*[11].

And where they would better the matter with these words, that Christ in the time of his being upon the earth did many things above the nature of a body, and car-

[6] The right hand of the Lord hath done great things. The right hand of the Lord hath exalted me. Ps. cxviii. R.

[7] Saint Mark saith the last chapter—Saint Stephen saith—Saint Paul. R.   [8] I see Jesus standing on the right hand of God. R.

[9] Supplied from R.   [10] Christ's body is in the bread. R.

[11] Believe them not. R.

ried his body sometime invisible, and entered the house of the disciples, the gates being shut; they prove nothing, only they trouble the simple conscience, and stablish such as be more addict unto the writing of man, than unto the writing of God, in their error. Peter walked upon the water, yet was very man nothing the less: so it pleased God to use his creatures to his glory. Christ's body was nothing changed, although sometimes, for fear of the stones, he conveyed himself out of the way. Though his disciples knew not how he entered, the doors being shut, it is possible enough, that he opened the doors, and yet they perceived it not: men's eyes be obedient unto the Creator, that they may see one thing, and yet not another. The scripture so teacheth. Those ill men, that would have done villainy unto the angels in Loth's house, Gen. xix., were made so blind, they could not find the next door to them; yet bided Loth's house still in one place. The same may ye read, 4 Reg. vi., how God made blind the Assyrians' host, so that Elizeus led the whole army into the city of Samarie. Balaam saw to beat his ass, and yet could not see the angel, that the ass saw, till he was reprehended by the angel, Num. xxii. Here may ye see, that those reasons proveth nothing that they would, Christ's body to be[1] in the sacrament, because sometimes he would not be seen of his enemies.

marginalia: An answer to that objection which is gathered from the entering in of Christ to his disciples, the doors being shut.

marginalia: [2 Kings vi.]

This is our belief, that Christ is very man, and like unto his brothers, Heb. ii. Therefore, wheresoever his body be, it must have the qualities and quantities of a true man. If his body be corporally in the sacrament, and yet without all properties of a true body, this text is false, *Habitu inventus ut homo*[2]; likewise this, *Similis est fratribus per omnia*[3]. They grant that only the spirit of man eateth the body of Christ in the sacrament: then either the spirit of man is turned into a corporal substance, or else the body of Christ loseth his corporal substance, and is become a spirit. For it is not possible for the spirit of man to eat corporally a corporal body, no more than he that studieth the scripture, and commendeth the contents of the bible to his memory, eateth corporally the book: but by the help of God's

---

[1] Invisibly. R.   [2] In shape he was found as a man. Phil. 2. R.
[3] In all things he became like unto his brethren. Heb. ii. R.

Spirit and his own diligence he eateth the effect, marrow, and doctrine of the bible. And in case it were corporally and substantially with paper and ink in the bottom of the sea, yet the learned man may comfort himself, and teach the mariners in the ship with the contents thereof, though the corporal bible be drowned. So in the sacrament the christian heart, that is instructed in the law of God, and knoweth the right use of the sacraments by the Holy Ghost, and a firm faith that he hath in the merits of Christ's body and soul, which is ascended corporally into heaven, may in spirit receive the effect, marrow, sweetness[4], and commodity of Christ's precious body, though it never descend corporally. Thus doth faith and the scripture compel the church to believe.

When they say, it is in the sacrament, and yet moveth not from the right hand of God, I believe not their saying, but require a probation thereof. Christ hath not so great a body, to fill heaven and earth corporally; *Similis est fratribus, perfectus Deus et perfectus homo*[5]. They make him there, and yet occupy no place: then it is no body; for a true body, physical and mathematical, as Christ's body is, cannot be, except it occupy place. They say, I must believe, and say with the Virgin, *Ecce ancilla Domini*[6]; I may not seek to know the means how. Well, let them do as much to me in this matter, as was done unto the virgin Mary, and I am content. She could not comprehend how Christ was made man in her belly: yet the effect and corporal nativity of Christ ascertained both her reason and senses, that she had borne a true body. It shall suffice me if they make demonstration unto my senses, and warrant my reason, that they have present a corporal body: how it cometh, and by what means, I leave that unto God. But until such time as they shew me that glorious and perfect man's body of Christ, as it was shewed unto the blessed Virgin, their saying, "Believe, believe," shall not come into my belief; for Christ saith, *Nolite credere*[7].

[4] [heuen, man in sprit receaue theffect, Marrye, swetnys, in the original.]

[5] Corporally, omitted in R. He is like unto his brethren; [he is perfect God and] a perfect man. R.

[6] Behold the handmaid of the Lord. R.   [7] Believe them not. R.

Of Christ's words Marci xiii., *De die illo nemo scit*, "The moment of the last time no man knoweth, neither the Son of God," inasmuch as he is man, I gather this argument *a majori*[1]. If it be denied Christ concerning his manhood to know the last day, much more to be every where, or to be in divers places at one time, is denied his humanity: for it is more impossible and wonderful to be every where, than to know many things. I know the geographus[2] conceiveth and comprehendeth all the world in his head; but to be in all places, where as his thoughts and spirit is occupied, it is impossible.

Further, Christ's body hath not lost his corporal qualities; but wheresoever he be corporally, there is he with all qualities of a body, and not without qualities, as these dreamers imagine. I will not judge my Saviour, that died for the sin of the world, to have a body in heaven, sensible with all qualities of true man, and in the sacrament, without all qualities and quantities of a true body; but abhor and detest with the scripture this opinion as an heresy, so little differing from Marcion, that I can scarce put diversity.

As corporally is the corporal and substantial body of all England in the head of him that describeth by map or chart the whole realm in Italy or otherwhere; so corporally is the body of Christ in the heart of the Christian. The conceit, imagination, or form conceived of England is not the body, matter, nor substance itself of England: no more is the spiritual conceit of Christ's body the corporal body itself. Though Avicen and Averrois[3] would prove such a conclusion, yet the faith of our religion will not suffer it[4], a fantastical imagination to be a true substance.

To say that Christ's very[5] natural body is in the earth, and yet invisible, it is to destroy the body, and not to honour the body. Aristotle, Lib. v., *Metaphysicorum*, cap. 22, defineth what *invisible* is: *Invisibile (inquit) est quod non habet omni-*

---

[1] From the greater. R.   [2] Describer of the earth. R.

[[3] Avicenna and Averroes, two Arabian philosophers of the 10th and 12th centuries. The latter translated Aristotle into Arabic, and from his commentaries thereupon was called the Commentator. For the principles held by his disciples, reference may be made to the last council of Lateran, at which they were condemned.]

[4] It, omitted in R.   [5] Very—true. R.

*no colorem*⁶. Take this from Christ's body, that it is truly in the sacrament⁷ corporally, and yet invisible, is to say, Christ hath lost all the colour, shape, and form of his humanity. But what shall Aristotle do in this our faith? The scripture teacheth what we should believe: *Ascendit ad cœlos, sedet ad dextram Dei Patris Omnipotentis; inde venturus est judicare vivos et mortuos*⁸, Act. i. Mar. ultimo, Luc. ultimo, and hath left us a sacrament of his blessed body, the which we are bound to use religiously and many times, to exercise and stablish our faith; and he, being absent corporally, doth communicate by faith in spirit that most precious body, and the merits of the same: and would to God people would use it with more reverence and more awe⁹, as the scripture teacheth, with true amendment of life, and firm faith!

I put out a book in September last past, dedicated to my lord of Winchester¹⁰, wherein I have declared all my faith concerning this blessed and holy sacrament: therefore I will pass to the other office of Christ's priesthood.

CAPUT IX.
[THE NINTH CHAPTER.]

THE fourth office of Christ is to consecrate and sanctify these that believe in him. He is not only holy himself, but maketh holy others also; as he saith, John xvii., *Pro eis sanctifico meipsum, ut sint et ipsi sanctificati per veritatem*¹¹. {The fourth part of Christ's office.}

This sanctification is none other but a true knowledge of God in Christ by the gospel, that teacheth us how unclean we are by the sin of Adam, and how that we are cleansed by Christ; for whose sake the Father of heaven doth not only remit the sins wrought willingly against the word of God, {How we are sanctified.}

---

⁶ That is invisible, (quoth he,) which hath no colour at all. R.

⁷ To say Christ's body is truly in the sacrament, &c., it is to say. R.

⁸ He hath ascended into heaven, he sitteth on the right hand of God the Father Almighty, from thence he shall come to judge the quick and the dead. R.   ⁹ awght, 1547. fear. R.

¹⁰ [An Answer unto my Lord of Winchester's book entitled "A detection," &c. printed at Zurich, 1547. See the next work in this volume.]

¹¹ For their sake sanctify I myself, that they also may be sanctified through the truth. R.

but also the imperfection and natural concupiscence which remaineth in every man, as long as the nature of man is mortal. How the Father doth sanctify his people, the prayer of Christ sheweth, John xvii. *Sanctifica eos per veritatem tuam*[1], "sanctify them by thy word;" purge the[ir] heart, teach them, hallow them, make them apt for thy kingdom. Wherewith? With thy word, which is everlasting verity.

We are sanctified only by the blood of Christ. The means to sanctify is the word of God, the Holy Ghost, and faith that receiveth the word of our redemption. So doth Peter say, Acto. xv., *Fide purgari corda nostra*[2]. Here is the cause expressed, whereby we accept our sanctification; by faith, saith Saint Peter. Saint Paul, 1 Cor. vi., sheweth for whose sake, and wherefore we are sanctified: *Abluti estis, sanctificati estis, justificati estis, per nomen Domini Jesu, per Spiritum Dei nostri*[3], for the merits of Jesus Christ, by the operation of the Holy Ghost. This is to be always marked, that when Christ had prayed his Father to sanctify his church by his word, and by his holy Spirit, and desired him to preserve them from ill for his mercy's sake, he added the price, the merits, and just deserving of God's graces, and said, "I sanctify myself for them, because they may be sanctified by the truth." He sanctified himself for the church, when he died for the detestable uncleanness and filthiness thereof, more stinking and filthy than ever was the abhorred and leprous body of Lazarus. As though he had said, "Forasmuch as I offer and submit myself unto the bitter and cruel pain of the cross for the church, thou must, most holy Father, sanctify them, and accept them as sanctified, nourish them, love them, and defend them, for the price and satisfaction of my death."

Christ prayed not only for his apostles, but also for the whole church. What a consolation is this for every troubled conscience to understand! Although it be unworthy of remission of sin for the greatness thereof, yet for the prayer of Christ he shall not be a cast-away, so that he believe: as Christ said, he prayed not only for his apostles, but also for as many as should believe his word till the world's end. As many as will be gospellers, as they love the gospel and their own salvation, let

---

[1] Sanctify them by thy truth. R.

[2] Our hearts are purged by faith. R.

[3] You are washed, you are sanctified, you are justified by the name of Jesus Christ, and the Spirit of our God. R.

them not dally and play with it, as though God were a babe, to be pleased with a fig for sin: let him think upon the most vile and tyrannous death of him, that only was able to cleanse us from sin, and from hence beware of sin. It sufficeth, as Paul saith, that, "before we knew the truth, to live[4] wantonly." 1 Cor. vi.

Let all Christians beware of sin.

CAPUT X.

[THE TENTH CHAPTER.]

OF[5] this verity and truth, that the gospel teacheth us only to be sanctified in the blood of Christ, is confuted the blasphemous pride of the bishop of Rome, that nameth himself the most holy father, and taketh upon him to sanctify all other men of the earth, as God's vicar and lieutenant, to absolve *a pœna et a culpa*[6], to pull out of hell and send to heaven with his pardons, masses, and other abominations; whereas Christ only and solely doth sanctify, as it appeareth, John xvii. Likewise[7] by the title that Pilate gave him, hanging upon the cross, with these words, *Jesus Nazarenus Rex Judæorum*[8]. This title declareth him to be both Messiah, Saviour, and *Noser*[9], the protector and sanctifier of his church, as Matth. saith, chap. ii., *Nazaræus vocabitur*[10].

This office of Christ doth abrogate all other things that man's constitutions attribute any holiness unto, as bewitched water, candles, boughs, or any such ethnick superstition[11]: for only Christ sanctifieth, and all holiness we must attribute unto him, as John said, *Ecce agnus Dei, qui tollit peccata mundi*[12]. John i. Behold the Lamb of God, to say, destined and appointed by God to take away the sin of the world, and to sanctify his church.

[4] We lived. R.   [5] Out of. R.
[6] Both from the punishment and the fault. R.
[7 Soly dooth sanctifi ce as it apperyd Joan. 17. lik wice, in the original.]   [8] Jesus of Nazareth, King of the Jews. R.
[9 *Noser*, נזיר. See Numb. vi. 2, and Judges xiii. 5., &c.]
[10] He shall be called a Nazarite. R.
[11 —ony holynis unto as be wychyd water Candellis bowes or ony souch Ethnick supersticion, in the original.] ony—onely. R.
[12] Behold the Lamb of God, that taketh away the sins of the world. R.

Although baptism be a sacrament to be received and honourably used of all men, yet it sanctifieth no man. And such as attribute the remission of sin unto the external sign, doth offend. John, Matth. iii., preached penitence[1] in the desert, and remission of sin in Christ. Such as confessed their faults, he marked and declared them to be of Christ's church. So that external baptism was but an inauguration or external consecration of these, that first believed and were cleansed of their sin, as he declareth himself in the same place: *Ego (inquit) baptizo aqua:* I christen[2] with water. As though he said, My baptism maketh no man the better: inwardly, it changeth no man: but I call and preach to the outward ear, I exhort unto penance[1]; and such as say they do repent, and would change the[3] old sinful life, I wash with water. He that inwardly cleanseth, is stronger than I. His grace it is only, that purifieth the soul. I baptize in penance, to say[4], into a new life.

This new life cometh not, until such time as Christ be known and received. Now, to put on Christ is to live a new life. Such as be baptized must remember, that penance[1] and faith preceded[5] this external sign, and in Christ the purgation was inwardly obtained, before the external sign was given. So that there is two kinds of baptism, and both necessary: the one interior, which is the cleansing of the heart, the drawing of the Father, the operation of the Holy Ghost: and this baptism is in man, when he believeth and trusteth that Christ is the only author of his salvation. Thus be the infants examined concerning repentance and faith, before they be baptized with water; at the contemplation of the which faith, God purgeth the soul[6]. Then is the exterior sign added, not to purge the heart, but to confirm, manifest, and open unto the world that this child is God's.

And likewise baptism, with the repetition of the words, is a very sacrament and sign, that the baptized creature should die from sin all his life, as Paul writeth, Rom. vi. Likewise no man should condemn nor neglect this exterior sign, for the commandment's sake: though it have no power to purge from sin,

---

[1] Repentance. R. [2] Baptize. R.
[3] Their. R. [4] To repentance, that is to say. R.
[5] Went before. R. [[6] God purchith tha soule, in the original.]

yet it confirmeth the purgation of sin, and the act of itself pleaseth God, for because the receivers thereof obey the will of his commandment.

Like as the king's majesty, that now is, immediately after the death of his father, was the true and legitimate[7] king of England, right heir unto the crown, and received his coronation, not to make himself thereby king, but to manifest that the kingdom appertained unto him before. He taketh the crown to confirm his right and title. Had all England said nay, and by force, contrary unto God's laws and man's laws, with an exterior ceremony and pomp, crowned any other man, he should have been an adulterous and wrong king, with all his solemnities and coronation. Though this ceremony confirm and manifest a king in his kingdom, yet it maketh not a king, but the laws of God and of the land, that giveth by succession the right of the kingdom to the old king's first heir male in England and other realms. And the babe in the cradle hath as good right and claim, and is as true a king in his cradle uncrowned[8], as his father was, though he reigned a crowned king forty years. And this right of the babe should be defended and manifested, not only by the ceremony of coronation, but with all obedience and true subjection.

An apt similitude.

So is it in the church of Christ: man is made the brother of Christ, and heir of eternal life by God's only mercy received by faith, before he receive any ceremony to confirm and manifest openly his right and title. He saith, he believeth in the Father, the Son, and the Holy Ghost, and believeth (he saith) the remission of sin; doth not only deny the devil, the world, and sin, but saith he will forsake him for ever, and serve his master, the Lord of virtue, King of heaven and earth. Thus assured of God, and cleansed from sin in Christ, he hath the livery of God given unto him, baptism, the which no Christian should neglect; and yet not attribute his sanctification unto the external sign. As the king's majesty may not attribute his right unto the crown, but unto God and unto his father, who hath not only given him grace to be born into the world, but also to govern as a king in the world; whose right and title the crown confirmeth, and sheweth the same unto all the world. Where as this right by God and natural succession precedeth[9]

---

[7] Lawful. R.   [8] Crowned. R.   [9] Goeth not before. R.

not the coronation, the ceremony availeth nothing. A traitor may receive the crown, and yet [a]¹ true king nothing the rather. So an hypocrite and [an]¹ infidel may receive the external sign of baptism, and yet no christian man nothing the rather; as Simon Magus and other.

<small>Sacraments are to be used holily, and yet not to have the office of Christ given unto them.</small>

Sacraments must be used holily, and yet not to have the office of Christ added unto them. Solely it is his office to sanctify and purge from sin. I take nothing from the sacraments, but honour them and extol them in all things, as they be worthy; howbeit not too much. I call a sacrament a ceremony instituted in the law of God to this end, that it should be a testimony of God's promise unto all such as believe, and signs of God's good will and favour towards us. As Paul saith, that Abraham received a testimony, by the which God testified that he was received into grace, Rom. iv. And as the promise of God, the remission of sin, is received by faith; so must these sacraments, that be signs, tokens, and testimonies of the promise, be received in faith². Thus by Christ we are sanctified only; and as Peter saith, "A³ people chosen, a princely priesthood, a holy people, and peculiar nation, to declare the power of him that hath called us from the darkness of error and sin into his wonderful light." These words declare the manner how we are sanctified, and what our office is after we be sanctified; to preach the power of him that hath called us from the darkness of sin: as it is wroten, Esa. xliii., *Populum istum formavi mihi, ut laudem meam annunciet*⁴; and likewise chap. lxvi. The prophets and apostles doth use many times this word, "*annunciare*," pro "*laudare*," et "*gratias agere*⁵." So doth Paul, 1 Cor. xi., *Mortem Domini annunciabitis, donec veniat;* "ye shall shew the death of the Lord until he come:" *id est*, ye shall celebrate the death of Christ with all praises and giving of thanks.

<small>What our office is, when we are sanctified in Christ.</small>

Such as be sanctified by Christ, must live an honest and holy life, or else his sanctification availeth not. As God forsook the children of Israel for sin, so will he do us. They were elected to be his people with this condition, *Si*

---

¹ Supplied from R.
² Of his promise, be received by faith. R.   ³ The, 1547.—(A). R.
⁴ This people have I formed for myself, they shall shew forth my praise. R.   ⁵ "To tell forth" for "to praise and give thanks." R.

audiendo audieris vocem meam, et custodieris pactum meum, eritis mihi in peculium de cunctis populis[6], Exod. xix. He that favoured not the Israelites, but took cruel vengeance upon them, because they walked not in their vocation, will do, and doth daily the same unto us, Rom. xi. Therefore, one of these two we must needs do, that say we be justified and sanctified in Christ: either from the bottom of our hearts amend, or else be eternally lost with all our ghostly knowledge. For the axe is put to the root of the tree. So far is the malice of man proceeded, that the ire of God can be no longer deferred. A great time hath the gospel been known of many men, yet the life of the gospel as[7] new to seek, as though it were but now begun.

Therefore see we, how God beginneth again to permit the darkness of error to overwhelm the world. Such blindness ever followeth the contempt of God's word and the unthankful receiving thereof. Therefore, as we be sanctified by Christ, so let us bear him and sanctify him in our breasts, or else we perish, Rom. vi. For faith intendeth and always maketh haste unto this port, as Paul saith, Tit. ii., *Ut sancte, juste, ac pie vivamus*[8]. *(Mark this thing diligently.)*

Men knoweth not what the gospel is. They read it as they read Beuis of Hampton[9], or the gestes of Robin Hode[10]. If they may know what the scripture saith, they judge it sufficient; whereas it is clean contrary. Men should not only read the scripture to be wiser, but to be better. We bear the name of Christ, and confess him. We must therefore be those persons in whose life the steps of Christ must appear[11], or else we blaspheme our Master, whose name we bear, Rom. vi. xiii. Because after baptism we should live a modest and temperate life, Christ departed into the desert, and fasted, making this answer unto the devil, *Non in solo pane vivit homo*[12]. Man is not created to the fond pleasures of the world, but to regard what the will of God requireth. *(We must not only read the scripture to be the wiser, but also to be the better.)*

[6] If in hearing ye will hear my voice and keep my covenant, ye shall be unto me a peculiar people. R.   [7] is. R.

[8] That we may live holily, justly, and godly. R.

[[9] Sir Bevis of Southampton.
   Sir Bevis of renown,
   The right heir of South-Hamptoun.
See Ellis's Specimens of early English Metrical Romances, Vol. ii.]

[[10] Gestes, 1547. Jestes. R. The deeds of Robin Hood, *gesta*.]

[[11] Persones in whois lieff the stappes of Christ must appere, in the original.]   [12] Man liveth not by bread only. R.

They deceive themselves, that trust to faith, where as honesty of life followeth not. Faith is mistress[1] in the soul of the Christian, and entertaineth no such servants as be adulterers, thieves, slanderers, drunkards, covetous persons, swearers, ill and unoccupied raveners of the meat of the poor: but charity, peace, temperancy, prayer, liberality, and flying the occasion of ill. 2 Pet. i. James ii. 1 Cor. xii.

CAPUT XI.

[THE ELEVENTH CHAPTER.]

As the scripture teacheth Christ to be the very true Priest and Bishop [of][2] the church, [which][2] prayeth for the church, satisfieth the ire of God for the sin of the church, and only sanctifieth the church: so doth it prove Christ to be the King, Emperor, and Protector of the church, and that by the office and property of a king, that defendeth his subjects, not only by his godly laws, but also by force and civil resistance, as the enemies of his commonwealth shall minister occasion. By those two means every commonwealth is preserved, as the scripture teacheth; princes christened and ethnicks[3]—Aristotle in his politics,—Justinian in the Prœme of his Institutions,—the scripture everywhere.

Christ is not only our priest, but also our king.

Christ defendeth his church both by power and also by his laws.

Pharaoh, that would this church of God and commonwealth of the Israelites to be destroyed, was lost and all his army in the sea. The idolaters, that would make the commonwealth of Christ's church one with the commonwealth of Egypt, were destroyed.

Such as rebelled, Koreh and [the][2] Rubenites, against the governors of God's church, Moses and Aaron, were destroyed with the artillery of God's ire. All the princes and nations that possessed the land of Chanaan, God destroyed, to set his commonwealth in an order.

In the latter days, when the King of this commonwealth should be born, the angel declared unto the blessed Virgin, of what puissance and power this kingdom of Christ should be: *Regnabit, inquit, in domo Jacob in æternum, et regni ejus*

---

[1] Faith is matres, 1547. A matron. R.   [2] Supplied from R.
[3] Princes christian and heathen. R.

*non erit finis*⁴. Luke i. Although now the commonwealth of the church hath no certain place appointed where it shall remain, as it was appointed in the old law; yet certain we be, that this kingdom of Christ remaineth upon the earth, and shall do, till the earth be burned. Matt. xvi. xxviii. 1 Cor. xv. How-beit, as Christ won and obtained this kingdom in the latter days without shield or spear; so doth he preserve it with his holy Spirit, and not with carnal weapons. As Christ said unto Pilate, John xviii.: *Regnum meum non est de hoc mundo*⁵; meaning, that he would not reign in this world, as a prince of this world, with pomp and pride; but defend his people with his holy Spirit, that the devil, neither the world should not break their patience, though many afflictions and sorrows should fight against them for the truth's sake. Christ doth not deny to be the King of the world before Pilate, but that he meant not to reign worldly, to the hindrance and defacing of the emperor's⁶ dignity and title, as the Jews falsely accused him. As Cyrillus⁷, Lib. xii. cap. 10, in Johannem, saith: and so is the mind of Saint Augustine⁸ in the same place.

Christ ruleth not in his church with carnal weapons.

This kingdom is spiritual. Christ sitting at the right hand of God the Father prayeth for us, giveth us remission of sin, and the Holy Ghost, to fight and overcome the world; hath⁹ left here in the church his gospel, the only weapon to fight withal for the time of this mortal life, John xvii., where he defineth life everlasting to be the knowledge of God. So doth Paul, Rom. viii., prove this kingdom to be spiritual; and that¹⁰ concerning the body it appeareth, that Christ de-

Christ's kingdom is spiritual.

---

⁴ He shall reign (quoth he) in the house of Jacob for ever, and of his kingdom there shall be no end. R.

⁵ My kingdom is not of this world. R.

⁶ Temperours, 1547. Temporal. R.

[⁷ Liberavit a formidine Pilatum . . . . . . Christus autem Pilato respondens regem se esse non negat: mentiri enim non poterat. Sed regno Cæsaris non esse hostem ostendit; quia principatus suus mundanus non est, sed cœli, terræ, ceterarumque rerum omnium, &c. Cyrilli Op. Par. 1573, Co. 1002.]

[⁸ Dixit itaque ei Pilatus, Ergo rex es tu? Respondit Jesus, Tu dicis quia rex sum ego. Non quia regem se timuit confiteri; sed "Tu dicis" ita libratum est, ut neque se regem neget, (rex est enim cujus regnum non est de hoc mundo,) neque regem talem se esse fateatur cujus regnum patitur esse de hoc mundo, &c. Aug. Op. Basil. 1542. Tom. ix. Co. 540. Tract. cxv. De Evan. Joan. cap. 19.]   ⁹ He hath. R.

¹⁰ Though as. R.

fendeth not his people, because they live in such disdain and adversity, but hereafter it shall appear, as Paul saith, Col. iii., and John, 1 John iii.: *Nunc filii Dei sumus, sed nondum manifestum est quales erimus*[1].

<small>The estate of the church in this world.</small>

This kingdom shall be ever persecuted till the world's end. Psal. ii. cxv. lxxi. Esay the prophet described the church of this present life[2], saying: *Dabit vobis Dominus panem arctum, et aquam exiguam, et non auferet a te ultra doctorem tuum*[3], cap. xxx. Thus the church shall remain, but always in affliction. I know such as favoureth not the truth, will interpretate my words, that I condemn all princes and kings, as enemies of the gospel, because they peaceably enjoy their kingdoms. So I wish them always to do[4], with hearty prayer to the glory [of][5] God. But of this one thing I will assure every prince of the world: the more sincere he is in the cause of God, the more shall be his cross.

I report me unto the king's majesty, that dead is, which at the first brunt, as soon as he took God's cause in hand, that leopard and dragon of Rome did not only solicitate the whole foreign world against him; but also he suffered such an ungodly and detestable insurrection of his popish subjects, and other more crosses, that never should have been moved, had he not unquieted the beast of her rest, that sat above his majesty, and God also, in his own realm.

<small>To be a magistrate in the church of Christ is a great charge.</small>

They be flatterers of princes, that say every thing may be ruled with ease: they consider not what an enemy of God's order the devil is, that would not only the gospel of truth to be oppressed, but also every prince that studieth the preferment and setting forth of God's word. The devil never ceaseth to molest and unquiet every godly politic and commonwealth. Were there no scripture divine to detect the art[6] of the devil, Aristotle in the fifth book of his Politics were sufficient to manifest the devil's enmity against all commonwealths.

Further, the nature of man is infirm, and far unable to

---

[1] Now we be the sons of God, yet it appeareth not what we shall be. R.

[2] The state of the church in this present life. R.

[3] The Lord shall give you the bread of adversity, and the water of affliction; and he will no more take from thee thy instruction. R.

[4] Always so to do. R. [5] Supplied from R.

[6] No holy scripture to detect the heart. R.

sustain the office of any vocation, be it political, ecclesiastical, or domestical, without a singular aid of God. We see by Saul, that noble man, who in the beginning of his reign did many noble acts, yet the devil got the victory in the end. His successor David was likewise so entangled in the snares of the devil, that with much pain he could quit[7] himself from the witched coup[8] that the devil had once brought him good luck of[9]. Howbeit, God defended both him and his kingdom, so that not only the preachers, but also he himself, taught the word of God unto the people, as he had promised. Psal. vi. 1.

God preserveth above human reason his ministers, as he did Jacob from the hands of Esau, David from Saul, Daniel from the lions, and Paul[10] in the ship, where as no human hope of salvation was at all, but only the protection of God. Those examples declare, that he doth defend his people against all the world by his mighty power.

Likewise he governeth this church with his only laws, and would his subjects to know him, to honour him, and to obey him, as he hath commanded in his law. Paul expresseth this law, Rom. i.: *Evangelium virtus Dei est in salutem omni credenti. Marci ultimo: Prædicate evangelium omni creaturæ*[11]. The only law whereunto this congregation is bound, is the gospel, as Christ saith, John xiv. *Spiritus Sanctus docebit vos omnia, et rediget vobis in memoriam omnia quæ ego dixi vobis*[12]. Here Christ bindeth the apostles and all the church unto the things that he had taught them.

This commonwealth of the true church is known by these two marks; the pure preaching of the gospel, and the right use of the sacraments. Thus proveth Paul, Eph. ii., that the church is bound unto the word of God: *Super fundamentum apostolorum et prophetarum extructi estis*[13]. Likewise,

Two special marks to know the true church by.

---

[7] Could scarcely quit. R.   [8] Witched snare. R.

[9] Onsbrowght hym god Luk of. 1547. Brought him into. R.

[10] Saint Paul. R. [N.B. Rosdell frequently prefixes the word Saint where it does not occur in ed. 1547.]

[11] The gospel is the power of God unto salvation to every one that believeth. Mark, the last: Preach you the gospel to every creature. R.

[12] The Holy Spirit shall teach you all things, and bring all things to your remembrance which I have said unto you.

[13] You are builded upon the foundation of the apostles and prophets. R.

[HOOPER.]   6

Esa. lix.: *Spiritus meus qui est in te, et verba mea quæ posui in ore tuo, non recedent ab ore tuo, nec ab ore seminis tui in æternum*[1].

Of the right use of sacraments it is taught, 1 Cor. xi. Mar. ult. Luc. ult. and Matt. ult. Such as teacheth[2] people to know the church by these signs, [namely][3] the traditions of men, and the succession of bishops, teach wrong. Those two false opinions hath given unto the succession of bishops power to interpretate the scripture, and power to make such laws in the church as it pleased them. There is no man hath power to interpretate the scripture. God, for the preservation of his church, doth give unto certain persons the gift and knowledge to open the scripture; but that gift is no power bound[4] to any order, succession of bishops, or title of dignity. The princes of the earth doth give always such power of civil justice by succession: as one is chief justice for the time of his office, to do every thing appertaining unto the same, so hath always his successor the like.

Traditions of men and succession of bishops are but fallible tokens to know the true church by.

God hath given the civil magistrates power and authority to make such laws for the commonwealth, as shall be agreeable with reason and not against God's law; and likewise power to interpretate the same laws. But this is not to be admitted in the church, unto whom God hath given the gospel, and interpretated the same by his only Son; taught the meaning and contents thereof himself.

The tenor and contents of the law and word of God.

To know God and his ire against sin, the greatness of sin, the justice[5] given in Christ, the fear of God, the faith in his promises, the persecution of his members, the aid and help of God in adversity, the resurrection of the dead; where and what the true church is; of everlasting life; of the two natures in Christ; of the Father, the Son, and the Holy Ghost: these be [the][3] contents of the law whereunto God hath bound his church, and commanded her to hear his Son concerning the interpretation of these points. And at the commandment of Christ the apostles were sent to preach these verities in the Spirit of God. It is therefore necessary to

---

[1] My spirit which is in thee, and my words which I have put in thy mouth, shall not depart from thy mouth, nor from the mouth of thy seed for ever. R.   [2] Teach the. R.
[3] Supplied from R.   [4] Is not bound. R.   [5] Righteousness. R.

retain in the church the doctrine given unto us by the apostles, and to be the disciples of their doctrine, and not to feign interpretations of our own heads contrary unto their doctrine.

Such as will be the members of this church, must be a disciple of the gospel, and learn, in fear and humbleness of spirit, the articles of our religion, as they be taught there, and not stand unto the judgment of any man, whatsoever he be, though he say truth. For his truth is nothing, except the authority of God's word contain the said truth.

It is a great confirmation of our faith, when we see such as were godly persons before us interpretate the scripture, and use the sacraments, as we do. As when the heresy of Samosatenus[6] troubled the christian brothers, that said, this word, *Verbum*, in John, *In principio erat verbum*[7], did not signify any person nor substance divine; they were confirmed by the testimony of Ireneus, that heard Polycarpus[8], John the Evangelist's disciple, interpretate *Verbum*, [the word][3] in the gospel, for the Son of God, second Person in Trinity. Though we be bound to hear the church, to say, the true and faithful preachers of God's word, as was in this case Polycarpus and Ireneus; notwithstanding our faith is not grounded upon the authority of the church, but in and upon the voice of the gospel. We pray and invocate the Son of God, second Person in Trinity, because the scripture proveth him to be God: *Deus erat verbum*[9] [John i.][3]; also, *Pater meus usque modo operatur, et ego operor. Sine me nihil potestis facere.* Item, *Domine Jesu, accipe Spiritum meum*[10].

The adversaries of the truth defend many a false error under the name of the holy church: therefore these treasons and secret conspiracies must be taken heed of; and when the church is named, diligently to consider, when the articles they would defend were accepted of the church, by whom, and who was the author of them. Leave not, till the matter be brought unto the first, original, and most perfect church

The title and name of the church abused by the adversaries.

---

[6] Euseb. Eccles. Hist. Lib. v. cap. xxviii.]
[7] In the beginning was the word. R.
[8] See Euseb. Eccles. Hist. Lib. v. cap. xx.]
[9] The word was God. R.
[10] My Father worketh still, and I work. Without me ye can do nothing. Also, O Lord Jesus, receive my spirit. R.

of the apostles. If thou find by their writings, that their church used the thing that the preacher would prove, then accept it; or else, not. Be not amazed, though they speak of never [so]¹ many years, nor name never so many doctors. Christ and his apostles be grandfathers in age to the doctors and masters in learning. Repose thyself only [upon]¹ the church that² they have taught thee by the scripture. Fear neither of³ the ordinary power or succession of bishops, nor of³ the greater part. For if either the authority of bishops, or the greater part, should have power to interpretate the scripture, the sentence of the Pharisees should have been preferred before the sentence of Zachary, Simeon, Elizabeth, or the blessed Virgin. Consider, that many time⁴ the true church is but a small congregation, as Esay saith, *Nisi Deus reliquisset nobis semen, sicut Sodoma essemus*⁵. Therefore is not the interpretation of the scripture obligated unto an⁶ ordinary power, nor [to]¹ the most part; as Noe, Abraam, Moses, Samuel, David, and Christ's time testifieth.

Beware of deceit, when thou hearest the name of the church. The verity is then assaulted; they call the church of the devil the holy church many times. As Korah and the rest of the people said unto Moses many times, Why have ye deceived the people of God, and brought them out of Egypt? They were the church of God nothing the rather, though it was⁷ painted with this holy title; but the church of the devil, and a congregation of rebellious and seditious persons, as God declared⁸ both by word and fact. Moses called not them the church of God, but the church of Korah; not the people of God, but rebellious and God's enemies, as God declared⁸ them to be by his cruel revenging of them. So, many times, had the most part⁹ been preferred, then the truth had been confounded, and Moses and Aaron put to death.

The multitude is not always to be followed.

Remember, christian reader, that the gift of interpretation¹⁰ of the scripture is the light of the Holy Ghost given unto the humble and penitent person that seeketh it only to honour

---

¹ Supplied from R. ² That church which. R.
³ For. R. ⁴ Considering that many a time. R.
⁵ Except the Lord had left us a remnant, we had been as Sodom. R.
⁶ Bound unto the. R. ⁷ They were. R. ⁸ Declareth. R.
⁹ If the most part had. R. ¹⁰ Interpreting. R.

God; and not unto those persons that acclaim it by title or place, because he is a bishop, or followed by succession Peter or Paul. Examine their laws by the scripture, and then shalt thou perceive they be the enemies of Christ's church, and the very church of Korah. Remember, therefore, to examine all kind of doctrine by the word of God; for such as preach it aright, hath their infirmities and ignorancy[11]. They may depart from the truth, or else build some superstition and false doctrine upon the gospel of Christ. Superstition is to be avoided, false doctrine to be abhorred, whosoever be the author thereof[12], prince, magistrate, or bishop: as the apostles made answer, *Acto.* v., *Oportet magis obedire Deo quam hominibus*[13].

The superior power hath authority, and may make what laws they list for the wealth and preservation of their subjects, so it repugn not[14] the law of nature, nor the law of God. But as touching the church of Christ, which governeth the soul of man, only the law of God must be obeyed: the ceremonies ordained for a good order to be observed in the church, should not be neglected, as the assemblance of people in the sabbath-day, and other feasts, wherein the word of God is preached, and the sacraments rightly ministered. But these ceremonies, that partly superstition, partly avarice, partly tyranny, hath brought into the church, are to be eschewed; as the saying of private masses, blessing of water, bough, bread, bell or candle, with such like. As for the praying unto dead saints, or to have their images in the church, it is not a ceremony matter, but very plain and manifest idolatry, contrary unto the express word of God, who forbiddeth to make any image. And he that prayeth unto God in the name of any dead saint, is an ethnick, and knoweth not God; for he followeth his imagination, and not the word of God, who teacheth and commandeth that we should both know and pray unto him in his Son's name, John xiv. The neglecting of this commandment deserveth eternal pains.

Such as hath a knowledge[15] of Christ, from henceforth let them give him his right honour, and leave this idolatry and superstition; considering, that with great pain he won the

---

[11] Ignorancies. R. [12] Thereof, omitted in R.
[13] We must rather obey God than men. R.
[14] Repugnat, 1547. dooe not repugne. R.
[15] Such as have knowledge. R.

church out of the hands of the devil, defendeth it with his holy Spirit, and governeth it with the laws of his only word. And consider whether these injuries, blasphemies, trouble, unquietness, and destruction of God's people by the law of the bishops be to be permitted, though they cry till they be hoarse again, The holy church! (The holy church¹)! Were the like trouble in any realm among the king's subjects by the occasion and abuse of the king's majesty's laws, doubtless could they not shew under the king's seal their law to be of authority, they should, as right is, soon be put to silence, and their adulterous laws and sophistical glosses removed out of the way. Thus I know, that Christ knew best all the histories of the old law, was² the present teacher himself of all verity, and most wise to provide for the church such laws as should preserve it in his absence.

[THE TWELFTH CHAPTER.]

Of the knowledge of man, and of his office towards Christ.

³Now that we know what Christ and his office is in the church of God, it is likewise necessary for every man that is a member of this church to know, what man is, and his office towards Christ. For as God hath bound himself by his promise to be our God and helper for Christ; so hath he bound man by his commandment to be his servant, and in his word to follow Christ, and in Christ God, for the commandment's sake, until such time as the end wherefore man was made be obtained, which is eternal felicity, and man restored and made like unto the image of God, as he was at the beginning; full of justice, obedience, and love towards his Creator and Maker.

I will not, studying brevity and to be short, write particularly of every member and office thereof⁴, (wherewithal the whole mass and substance of man is framed)¹. That I refer unto the learned physicians, that writeth⁵ diligently of the parts of man, and unto Lactantius, *De Opificio Dei*⁶. Neither what

¹ Omitted in R.   ² He was. R.
[³ The xii. chapter commences here in R.]
⁴ Because I desire to be short, write particularly of every member of man's body, and what is the office thereof. R.   ⁵ Which write. R.
⁶ Writing of the workmanship of God. R. [Liber de Opificio Dei eruditus et lectu utilissimus est, hoc fine ab auctore conscriptus, ut Providentiam Dei ex miranda hominis structura comprobaret. Vide Lact. Op. Oxon. 1684. p. 774.]

man was at his beginning[7], before he sinned; full of godly knowledge, always lauding the goodness of his Creator, always obedient unto his will, always following the order of reason, without all ill and contrary concupiscence, or other[8] carnal resistance. To be short[9], man's nature had been in all things like unto the law and as perfect as the law of the decalogue, or ten commandments, had not he sinned: but what man is now after his transgression, thus the christian reader shall be advertised [by that which followeth][10].

Man, fallen from his first dignity and original perfection, is now the creature that fighteth with the law of God: full of darkness, ignorancy, and of the contempt of God; without obedience, fear, and love of God; oppressed and subject unto all calamities and wilful concupiscence, both of body and soul. What man is after his fall and transgression.

CAPUT XII.

THE enemy of God, Rom. viii. the image of the devil, the library of lies, the friend of the devil, right heir of eternal death, and the child of damnation, Eph. ii. murderers by the means of sin, not only of ourselves, but also of the Son of God, that never sinned. And yet, not understanding this our woeful case and condition, we neglect both God and his law, and feel not our infirmities and sickness: the more is our health to be despaired of.

He that laboureth with a dangerous disease, and yet feeleth not the grief thereof, shall never find remedy, neither have the ill removed. We see this to be true by natural reason. Of all diseases, frenzy is the most dangerous; yet the patient feeleth it not, nor cannot shew where nor how this woeful and miserable disease molesteth him. Therefore very seldom or never be such persons cured and made whole. It is a most dangerous thing not to have the feeling of sin.

---

[7] Neither will I write what man was at the beginning. R.
[8] Or rather. R.   [9] To conclude, how. R.   [10] Supplied from R.

Seeing the next way unto health is the knowledge of the disease, and man is in himself sick and infected with more diseases a thousand fold than I have rehearsed, it is not without cause that I say, to know what man is, to be necessary[1], although it seem not so unto such as be drunk with the pleasures of the world, and never think from the bottom of their heart to return unto penance[2]. If the scripture of God and writings of learned men cannot persuade them what the ire of God is against sin, my labours shall little avail, I know well. Yet is every disciple of Christ bound to search[3] the glory of God and salvation of his neighbour, and commit the success unto God.

How we may come to the knowledge of ourselves.

It is very difficile and hard for man to know himself. The only way thereunto is to examine and open himself before God by the light of the scripture. And he that will behold himself well in that mirror and glass, shall find such a deformity[4] and disgraced physiognomy, that he will abhor his own proportion so horribly disfigured. Let man seek no further than the first commandment, Exod. xx. Deut. vi., *Diliges Dominum Deum tuum*, &c., "Thou shalt love thy Lord God with all thy heart, with all thy mind, with all thy power, and thy neighbour as thyself:" then shall man perceive his wretchedness; how that he loveth nothing less many times than God or his neighbour; and perceive that he is the friend of the devil and of the world, and a contemner of God.

This ways Saint James teacheth man to know himself, *cap.* 1. *Qui perspexerit in legem, quæ est libertatis*, &c.[5] St James useth this word "law," in the Hebrew phrase[6], *thorah*, which signifieth a doctrine that teacheth, instructeth, and leadeth a man as well unto the knowledge of himself as of God[7].

So St Paul *admirandis enallagis et prosopopœis in Epi. Rom. vii. disputat*[8]. By the law cometh the knowledge of sin: he calleth the law the power and force of sin, 1 Cor. xv.

---

[1] I said it is very necessary to know what man is. R.
[2] Amendment of life. R.   [3] Seek. R.   [4] Deformed. R.
[5] Whoso looketh in the perfect law of liberty, &c. R.
[6] Feace, 1547. phrase. R. [*Thorah*, תורה from ירה.]
[7] A man's will unto the knowledge of himself and of God. R.
[8] With wonderful enallages and figures disputeth in his Epistle to the Romans, chapter vii. R.

Only the law declareth how great an ill[9] sin is; and the man that beholdeth the will of God in the law, shall find himself, and all his life, guilty of eternal death. Read the seventh chapter to the Romans with judgment, and then know what man is, how miserable, spoiled of virtue and[10] oppressed with sin. So Paul learned to know himself, and knew not what sin was till the law had made him afraid, and shewed him that he was with all his holiness, being a Pharisee, damned. *Peccatum occasione accepta per præceptum decipit me, et per illud occidit*[11], Rom. vii. And in the same chapter he sheweth plainly what he saw in the glass and contemplation of the law, that sin was manifested thereby, and the greatness thereof known, *Ut appareret peccatum, per id quod erat bonum mihi gignere mortem, ut fieret majorem in modum peccans peccatum per præceptum*[12]. Mark the travice[13] and play between the law of God and the conscience of Paul, and see how he giveth thanks unto his master the law, and proclaimeth it to be a spiritual and holy thing, as a light or torch to shew man his filthy and stinking nature; saying, *Lex spiritualis est, at ego carnalis sum, venditus sub peccatum*[14], a bondman of sin and traitor of God.

Here thou seest, good reader, what a miserable wretch man is; and how man may know his misery by the law. Howbeit, though we read it many times, we be neither the wiser, neither the better. We be not taught a deal by this mistress the law: she cannot make us good scholars. We dally and play so with the world; we live in such security and ease, that, say she what she list, we turn the deaf ear and will not hear.

Therefore, to make man to know himself, God sendeth another mistress to school man, *scilicet*, adversity. Then we begin to understand the law of God, that dissuadeth from

Because man will not be taught by the law of God to know himself, the Lord sendeth adversity to teach him.

---

[9] An ill, omitted in R. [10] verte, wand, 1547. wonderfully. R.

[11] Sin took an occasion by the commandment, and deceived me, and thereby slew me. R.

[12] Sin, that it might appear sin, wrought death in me by that which is good; that sin might be out of measure sinful by the commandment. R.

[13] [Travice: traverse, a term in fencing.]

[14] The law is spiritual; but I am carnal, sold under sin. R.

sin, and we then know our misery: as David crieth, that he is not able to bear the burden of sin, if the Lord execute justice, as the greatness thereof meriteth: *Si iniquitates observaveris, Domine, quis sustinebit*[1]*?* Psal. cxxx. David, when he felt the pains of his adultery, the death of his child, the conspiracy of Absalom, the vitiating of his wives, exile and banishment, and such other calamities; in this school of misery he learned this verse, Who can sustain the ire of God? Now, though these temporal pains be more than man can support, they be but sport and dalliance in respect of the pains eternal. Howbeit, man may learn by them how much God is displeased with sin, and know himself to be, as he is, a vile piece of earth, with all his pride and pomp, and a rebellion[2] unto his Maker, as no creature else is, saving the devil and he.

This inward and secret ill, rebellion of the heart, blindness of the intendment[3], and frowardness of will, is daily augmented by the malice of the devil and our own negligence, that regardeth not what the law teacheth [and][4] God requireth of man. Because the gospel teacheth, [that][4] we are only saved by the mercy of God for the merits of Christ, our gospellers hath set all at liberty[5], and careth not at all of such life[6] as should and ought to follow every justified man and disciple of Christ. [And][4] it is no marvel; for there is no discipline and punishment for sin: and wheresoever the gospel be preached, and this[7] correction not used, as well against the highest as the lowest, there shall be never a godly church.

Sin must needs flourish where there is no discipline and correction for sin.

As a king's army, though the[ir][4] hearts be never so good, cannot resist the force of his enemies without weapon and artillery necessary for men of war; no more can the king's majesty, the magistrates, and preachers, preserve the church against the devil and sin without the excommunication of such as openly offend the divine majesty of God and his word. For by this means the sinner is taught by the

---

[1] If thou dost mark what is done amiss, Lord, who shall abide it? R.

[2] Rebel. R.
[3] Understanding. R.
[4] Supplied from R.
[5] Have set up liberty. R.
[6] For such a life. R.
[7] This, omitted in R.

scripture to know himself. 1 Cor. v. *Congregatis vobis, et meo Spiritu, una cum potestate Domini nostri Jesu Christi, ut is, qui hoc patravit, tradatur Satanæ ad interitum carnis, ut spiritus salvus sit in die Domini nostri Jesu Christi*[8]. God would not only the *fideles*[9], but also the *infideles*, to be kept in an order by the discipline of the law, as Paul saith, *Lex est injustis posita*[10]; likewise, Deut. xix., *Auferes malum, ut audientes reliqui timorem habeant; non miserearis ejus*[11].

This political and civil use of the law teacheth man to know his faults; and this discipline of the law exterior and civil is necessary for man, [and that][4] for divers causes: first, to declare our obedience unto God; then, to avoid the punishment that always God, or else the magistrate, revengeth the transgression [by][4]; thirdly, because of a[12] public peace in every commonwealth, that the[12] one should not do injuries to the[13] other, neither in body nor in goods.

_{*margin:*} Divers causes why discipline is necessary and commodious in the church.

There is yet another cause, why this discipline of the law is necessary, which few men regard. Paul saith, that it is a schoolmistress, *pedagogia*[12], unto Christ, because such as leaveth not to sin, and to do the thing contrary unto the express word of God, to those Christ is not profitable. This use teacheth Paul, 1 Cor. vi., *Fornicatores, idolatri, adulteri, &c. regnum Dei non possidebunt*[14]. And so saith John, *Omnis qui peccat ex diabolo est*[15]. He that knoweth himself, must refrain from doing of ill, hear the gospel, and learn the gospel, that the Spirit of God may be efficacious[16] in him; which cannot be, as long as he hath a purpose to continue in doing of ill. Ezechiel speaketh of this use civil and politic

---

[8] When ye are gathered together, and my Spirit, in the name of our Lord Jesus Christ, that such one, I say, by the power of our Lord Jesus Christ be delivered unto Satan for the destruction of the flesh, that the spirit may be saved in the day of the Lord Jesus. R.

[9] Faithful. R.   [10] The law is ordained for the unjust. R.

[11] Thou shalt take away the evil from among you, that the residue which hear it may fear; and thou shalt not take pity on him. R.

[12] Omitted in R.   [13] An. R.

[14] This Saint Paule teacheth, 1 Cor. vi. saying. R. Fornicators, idolaters, adulterers, &c. R. [shall not inherit the kingdom of God.]

[15] Saint John. Every one that sinneth is of the devil. R.

[16] Effectual. R.

of the law, and likewise of the second use thereof, which is, as I said before, to shew man his sin, to accuse man before God, to fear him, and to damn man plainly¹: chap. xxxiii., *Vivo ego; nolo mortem peccatoris, sed ut vivat et convertatur*². These words declare, that as God would not the death of a sinner, so he requireth the sinner to cease from doing of ill, and to be converted unto virtue.

<small>The law delivereth not from sin.</small>

As for the second use of the law, which is to declare what sin is, I shewed before that it manifesteth the greatness and vileness thereof, as Paul writeth: it damneth sin, and³ delivereth not from sin: *Per legem, inquit, cognitio peccati. Lex iram efficit; per legem peccatum fit excellenter reum*. Rom. vii. *Aculeus mortis peccatum, virtus autem peccati lex est*⁴. 1 Cor. xv. In men that be addict unto the pleasure of this world, the law hath not this use, say the preacher what he list. Let the word of God threaten death eternal for sin; it availeth not. He thinketh that God is asleep, and will at last be pleased with a fig for sin. [But]⁵ we shall find the contrary to our great pain, as other hath before our time, that would not believe the word, till they felt the vengeance and punishment of God; as Caim, the drowned world⁶ with the flood, the burning of Sodoma, with other. It is a great and horrible offence to hide or extenuate the judgment of God against sin, and the voice of the law, that condemneth the same. God willeth his pleasure to be known openly: Hier. i. *Ecce, dedi verba mea in ore tuo, ecce, constitui te super gentes, ut evellas et destruas*⁷.

<small>It is a great offence to hide or extenuate the judgment of God against sin, and the voice of the law that condemneth the same.</small>

This use and office of the law none feeleth neither perceiveth so well as such as be God's friends, Adam, Abraam, Jacob, David, Ezechias, &c. David said that the fear of

¹ Condemn him. R.

² I live, saith the Lord, I will not the death of a sinner, but rather that he might be converted and live. R.

³ It condemneth, and. R.

⁴ By the law cometh the knowledge of sin. The law causeth wrath: by the law sin is made exceeding guilty. The strength of death is sin; and the strength of sin is the law. R.

⁵ Supplied from R.

⁶ The old world that was drowned. R.

⁷ Behold, I have put my words into thy mouth: I have set thee over nations, that thou mayest pluck up and destroy. R.

God's displeasure and ire was no less pain unto him, than though the fierce lion had rent and dismembered his body in pieces: *Sicut leo contrivit omnia ossa mea*[8], Psal. xxii. So saith Paul: *O infelix ego homo! quis me eripiet ab hoc corpore morti obnoxio*[9]*?* He that before said, *Ego aliquando vivebam sine lege, id est, fui securus, non sentiens iram Dei*[10]; now converted from a Pharisee to be an apostle, and brought to a knowledge of himself, he confesseth his imbecility and faults, and saith, *Novi quod non habitat in me, hoc est in carne mea, bonum*[11]. Yet Paul confesseth, that the law maketh us not afraid to be damned[12] because we cannot satisfy it, but that we should come to Christ, with these comfortable words: *Conclusit omnes sub peccato, ut omnium misereatur*[13]. A great consolation for every troubled conscience!

Thus man may know himself to be, as he is, a very wretched and damnable creature, were not the virtue of Christ's death.

CAPUT XIII.
[THE THIRTEENTH CHAPTER.]

WHAT the office of a justified man is, Paul declareth, Tit. ii.: *Apparuit enim gratia salutifera omnibus hominibus, erudiens nos, ut abnega[ta] impietate, et mundanis concupiscentiis, sobrie, pie, ac juste vivamus in hoc sæculo*[14]. By these words Paul forbiddeth all impiety and dishonest life, and sheweth

What is the office of every true Christian.

---

[8] As a lion hath he broken my bones in sunder. R.

[9] O wretched man that I am! who shall deliver me from the body of this death? R.

[10] I lived sometimes without law, that is to say, I was secure, not feeling the wrath of God. R.

[11] I know that in me, that is to say, in my flesh, there dwelleth no good thing. R.

[12] Afeard to condemnation. R.

[13] He hath shut all under sin, that he might have mercy on all. R.

[14] The grace of God that bringeth salvation to all men, hath appeared, and teacheth us, that we should deny ungodliness and worldly lusts, and that we should live soberly and righteously, and godly in this present world; looking for the blessed hope, and appearing of the glory of the mighty God, and of our Saviour Jesus Christ, who gave himself for us, that he might redeem us from all iniquity, &c. R.

man that is justified, what he should do: not to live after the concupiscence of the flesh, but soberly; not unjustly and doing wrongs unto other, but rather to profit[1] and do well unto all men. It sufficeth not man justly to keep his goods, but he is bound justly to dispense his goods with other[2], whether they be of[3] the body or of the mind; religiously, and not superstitiously. A notable word! *pie, inquit*[4]; as the word of God teacheth, and not as man's laws contrary unto God's law teacheth. *Expectantes beatam spem*, &c.[5] He provoketh men to live well, and taketh his reason of[6] the profit and commodity that followeth a godly life, which is immortal life at the coming of Christ to judgment.

Likewise with another argument, *a liberatione Christi petitum, et ab honesto: Dedit semetipsum pro nobis*, &c.[7] The Son of God gave neither gold nor silver for our purgation, but his own body and precious blood. It is therefore an unworthy thing, and not becoming a christian man, that by faith hath received this purgation, to live a vicious and ungodly life: but we should be an holy people, and followers of good works. There is a great virtue in this word, "Zeloten[8]." It is not sufficient to work well, except the justified man with a godly zeal and ardent desire follow this good work begun. Therefore Paul saith: *zeloten calon ergon, et non operatorem bonorum operum*[9]. Whereby we know, that although we be delivered from the malediction, curse, and damnation of the law, so that we retain a true faith, and with confidence in Christ repugn sin, and overcome the terrors thereof; yet are we bound to the obedience of the law, which is God's will to keep us from living ill[10]. And the more the justified man beholdeth the law, the more increaseth the knowledge of sin;

We are delivered from the curse of the law by Christ, not from the obedience of the law.

---

[1] Benefit. R.   [2] Unto others. R.   [3] Goods of. R.
[4] Godly (quoth he.) R.
[5] — teach, Looking for a blessed hope, &c. R.
[6] Occasion from. R.
[7] Being taken from the deliverance wrought by Christ, and from that which is honest. He gave himself for us, &c. R.
[8] Ζηλωτήν.] Zealous. R.
[9] Ζηλωτὴν καλῶν ἔργων. Zealous of good works, and not simply a doer of good works. R.
[10] In sin. R.

the more he beholdeth the mercy of God in Christ, the more his faith increaseth.

The law is also necessary for the justified man, to teach him with what works he should exercise his faith withal[11] and obedience unto God. We may not choose works of our own wisdom to serve him withal; but would us[12] to be governed by his word, as David saith: *Lucerna pedibus meis verbum tuum.* Also, *Frustra me colunt mandatis hominum*[13]. The wisdom of man, not governed by the word of God, doth soon err. It is carried for the most part with affections, and chooseth the works that be contrary to the law of God. Therefore this is true, that the ordinance of God still remaineth in the justified man immutable, that he must obey the law, and serve in his vocation according to the scripture; that the exterior facts[14] may bear testimony of the inward reconciliation. *The law teacheth the justified man what work he should do.*

The scripture is more diligent and more ample in teaching the christian, justified man the obedience unto God and virtuous life, than it is to shew us our salvation in Christ; and that is[15] for this purpose only, that we should not by our licentious liberty receive the grace of God in vain. It is more hard for man to know the gospel, than to follow the life of the gospel. Another man may preach Christ, but the auditor must follow Christ. The science of the scripture is practive, and not speculative; it requireth a doer and not a speaker only.

There be many that dissembleth faith, and hath a certain shew of religion, when indeed in the inward man is no faith at all. Let every man therefore search his own conscience, with what faith he is endued, and remember
    that Christ said, "It is a strait way and narrow
      that leadeth to life, Matt. vii., and but a few
        that walketh therein." Therefore our
          only remedy is to pray for grace
            and amend.

---

[11] Withal, omitted in R.

[12] Who will have us. R.

[13] Thy word is a lantern unto my feet. Also, In vain do they worship me by the precepts of men. R.

[14] Outward deeds. R.   [15] And that is, omitted in R.

PRYNTYD

IN ZVRYCH BY AV-

gustyne Fries. Anno M.

D. XLVII.

ANSWER

TO THE

BISHOP OF WINCHESTER'S BOOK.

[HOOPER.]

An Answer unto my

lord of wynchesters booke intytlyd a detection of the debyls Sophistrye wherwith he robbith the unlernyd people of the trew byleef in the moost blessyd sacrament of the aulter made by Johann Hoper.

Psalm. 119,

Vestigia mea dirige in verbo tuo domine, &
& non dominabitur mei ulla iniquitas,

Prynted in Zurych by Augustyne Fries.
Anno M.D.XLVII.

A DETEC
TION OF THE

Deuils Sophistrie, wher=

with he robbeth the un=

learned people, of the

true byleef, in the

most blessed Sa=

crament of the

aulter.

Timeo ne sicut serpens euam seduxit astutia sua: ita corrumpantur sensus uestri, et excidant a simplicitate. 2 Cor. xi.

1546.

[The colophon at the end is as follows:]

Prynted at London in Aldersgate
strete, by Jhon Herforde, at the
costes & charges of Roberte
Toye, dwellynge in
Paules churche
yarde, at the
sygne of
the Bell.

1546.

[Several answers were published to Bishop Gardiner's book. The first of these was by A. G. (Anthony Gilby) anno 1547, the 24 of January. Hooper's answer was dated Zurich, September, 1547. But the most elaborate and most important work in the controversy with Gardiner, upon the Sacrament of the Altar, was Archbishop Cranmer's, in folio, 1551.

The following is the dedicatory Epistle of the "Detection, &c."

Steven, Bishoppe of Winchester, to the reader.

Consyder gentle reader, how ful of iniquite this tyme is, in whiche, the hyghe mysterie of our religion is so openly assaulted. Byleue not euery spirite and mystruste thyne owne judgement, aboue the reache of thy capacite. If thou beest hungry for knowledge, take hede thou fallest not on every careyn[1]. Be desyrouse of the very truth, and seke it as thou art ordered by the direction of Christes Churche, and not as deceytful teachers, wold leade the, by theyr secrete waies. Follow God and his mynisters, whom he ordereth to rule, and rather conforme knowledge to agre with obedience, where Goddes truthe repugnethe not unto it, then with violation of obedience, which is a displeasaunt fault to enterprise the subuersion of Goddes honour and glory. Finally reade when thou readest, with favour, to that truth, whiche the consent of Christes church hath from the beginnynge commended unto us, and reuerentlye at theyr handes receyue the true understandinge of scriptures, whose true testimonie hath certified us of the selfesame scriptures.

And have alwaies in remembraunce the wordes of saint James, howe God resisteth the presumptuouse and arrogant, and giveth grace to suche as be in spirite, meke and lowly, whiche gyfte, God graunte the, and well to feare.]

[1 Carrion.]

＃ [DEDICATION].[1]

JOHAN HOPER wyshythe grace and the yefftes[2] of the Holy Gooste unto my lord of wynchester.

Your book, my Lord, entitled "A detection of the devil's sophistrie, &c." was delivered unto me in Zurych the 30th of April last past; the which I have with leisure and diligence perused, marked your intention, and how ye fence a wrong opinion with many fair[3] words and divers reasons sufficient to confirm the ignorant in his ignorancy, to stablish his error, and likewise it may put in danger the good and simple conscience unlearned, that is persuaded and seeth[4] the truth, yet for lack of knowledge cannot, nor is not able to defend the same, when arguments subtle and crafty shall assault his simple and plain faith, above the reach and capacity of his intendment.

Therefore, because I desire such as know the truth to persevere in the same, and such as yet be ignorant thereof to come unto the truth, that in Christ they might with the church of truth find eternal salvation, I have made this answer unto your book, to succour and warrant the conscience of the reader, from the snares and sophistications wherewithal

[[1] It appears that the only edition of this work of Hooper's was that printed at Zurich, which is, if possible, still more "pestered with gross and palpable faults, by passing through the press of an unskilful printer," than "the Declaration of Christ." The original text has been strictly adhered to, except where corrections were necessary in order to make sense of the passage; and in every such instance a literal reprint of the text has been added in the notes. The texts quoted have been placed in the margin for the convenience of the reader: they were not so printed in the book.]   [[2] Yefftes: gifts.]
[[3] Ffere, in the original.]
[[4] Seythe, in the original.]

you or any other should trouble and unquiet the peace and tranquillity of him that resteth only under the shadow and protection of God's holy word; being delivered from the darkness of Egypt, the detestable doctrine of man.

I have likewise dedicated the same unto your Lordship, to declare that it is against your cause and opinion that I write, and not against you, to whom I wish the same grace and favour of God that I would unto myself, and the love that Paul wished unto his countrymen the Jews, of whose salvation he was most desirous, though their obstinacy and blindness so merited the punishment and severity of God's ire, that he was compelled to write the indictment and condemnation of their infidelity, as it appeareth by his most loving and affectionate heart, Rom. ix., before his entry into that lamentable and severe disputation of their departure and rejection from the promise of God, taking God and his conscience to record that he wrote of no malice nor pretenced ill will, but constrained thereunto to serve the glory of God and the truth of his word, which must be preferred before all other loves of the world. Therefore wrote he, as I do, in the defence of the verity to gain such as he wrote unto unto God, and to defend them that knew the truth from the subtlety and craft of such as pretended the subversion of the truth by crafty and subtle argumentation.

It is not ignorant[1] unto you what may be done by the virtue of a fair and well ordered oration[2]; how much it availeth, whether it persuade a truth or a falsity. No need to seek examples thereof in Demosthenes, Cicero, or any other profane writer. The scripture is plain, that it hath such vehemency and effect in itself with the help of the devil, that it persuadeth the falsest lie of the world to be true; maketh man to believe not only that good is ill, the truth falsehood, but that God, his word, and all that speaketh his

[1 Ignorant: unknown.]
[2 The vetteue of afere and well orderyd oracion, in the original.]

word be false; as we may see, Num. xiii. by the oration of those ten that were sent by the church of the Israelites, with Jehosua and Caleb, to inquire and search the condition and nature of the land of Canaan: at their return, as traitors of the commonwealth, and not as faithful inquisitors, as it was commanded them in their embassage and commission, made this oration and advertisement of their expedition: *Venimus ad terram ad quam nos misisti, et utique fluit lacte et melle, et hic est fructus ejus. Nisi quod populus est fortis, qui habitat in terra, et civitates munitæ et grandes valde. Quin et filios Anac vidimus ibi. Amalec autem habitat in terra meridionali*, &c.³ This brief⁴ oration so prevailed among the Israelites, that it brought the whole multitude and congregation of the church into desperation, into a contempt of God and their lawfully appointed emperor Moses, and high priest Aaron. Num. xiii.

Confer the effect of this oration which ye may see in the beginning of the 14th chapter of Numbers, with God and all the miracles that ever he wrought for them: and yet more availed this false oration to persuade a false effect than God, his word, Moses, or Aaron. God, among all the people of the world, chose this people to be peculiar unto himself, and bid Moses say unto Pharao that he should dismiss his people to do sacrifice unto him, Exod. viii. This singular favour and privilege availed nothing: they would return into Egypt, Num. xiv. again, and serve Pharao, their mortal enemy, and leave the living God:—he that divided the Red Sea, killed all the first-begotten of Egypt, Exod. xii. fed them with meat from heaven, wonderfully preserved both their fathers and them, of his merciful favour promised them not

[³ We came unto the land whither thou sentest us, and surely it floweth with milk and honey; and this is the fruit of it. Nevertheless the people be strong that dwell in the land, and the cities are walled and very great: and moreover we saw the children of Anac there. The Amalekites dwell in the land of the south, &c. Num. xiii. 27—29.]

[⁴ Bryve, in the original.]

only life eternal, but also a pleasant, rich, and most commodious realm and kingdom in this world.

Now hath this false oration of the ten traitors wrought such an opinion in their heads, that they defy God, and hath no more trust nor confidence in him, nor will not hear him spoken of, insomuch that all the whole congregation agreed to stone Jehosua and Caleb to death, because they contraried their wicked pretence; yet was it not the fear of stones, fire, neither sword that could fear these two godly men from preaching the truth of God. They had words against words, and an oration against an oration, and said, "If it please the Lord, he can bring us into this land; and truly because he hath promised it unto us, he will give it. Be not ye rebellious against him, neither fear ye not the people of the land; they shall be our bread, we shall devour them; for *Zilam*[1], their protection, is departed from them, and the Lord is with us."

Little availed this godly oration; it persuaded nothing at all. Yet did these two their duties to shew the truth, which is an example that we should do the same; always confess the truth, and defend the word of God, though there be little hope or none that it shall take effect. Yet it is our duties, whether we be learned or unlearned, every man to confess his faith. For he that saith, "In thy heart thou shalt have no more gods but one," the same God saith, "Thou shalt not take my name in vain." Exod. xx. And in forbidding the negative he commandeth the affirmative. It is not sufficient to refrain the tongue from swearing and speaking of ill, but that it must confess the truth of God and speak well, as David saith: *Declina a malo et fac bonum*[2]. It is not sufficient to leave ill undone, but that we must do the good commanded by God and his law. As David saith, Psalm i. "Blessed is he that walketh not in the counsel

Exod. xx.

Psal. i.

[[1] צלם, *umbra illorum*.]
[[2] Depart from evil and do good. Psalm xxxiv. 14.]

of the ill, &c. but hath his meditations in the law of God day and night."

Wist I that my labour should never do good, nor help the conscience of one man, yet for the commandment's sake would I have written, to set one oration against the other, because I see the name of God blasphemed by the opinion that ye defend. But I have hope that it shall somewhat avail to confound the falsehood and bring the truth sooner to light. I know it is the condition of God to permit unto every oration his nature and condition; as we see sometimes by preaching of the true word of God people are converted unto faith; sometime by preaching the doctrine of men people are seduced and carried from the faith. It is not the nature of God to make the false orator dumb, when he would persuade a false opinion, neither to make his auditors deaf; but, as I say, he suffereth the oration to work his virtue, and leaveth free election unto the audience to embrace which part they list; by grace and a consenting will, the good; by the devil and their own malice, the ill. Now, the orator of God must persuade with none other arguments or words than the master of the school, Christ, hath taught, the prophets and apostles written. It is no orator of Christ's that, contrary unto his canons, rules, and precepts, would persuade in the church any thing more than is prescribed in the scripture; the which is most perfect and sufficient to persuade in causes of religion all things.

That law must needs be most perfect, that can have nothing added unto it, nor nothing taken from it. Of this condition is the scripture, as ye know by the words of Moses and the Revelation of John. Luke in his latter book saith: *Superiore volumine diximus, Theophile, de omnibus quæ cœpit Jesus facere et docere*[3]. The which words

[3 The former treatise have I made, O Theophilus, of all that Jesus began both to do and to teach. Acts i. 1.]

John Chrysostom thus interpreteth: [1]*De omnibus et non omnia; de omnibus ad salutem necessariis*[2].

Concerning doctrine, and how to lead our life, it is sufficiently taught in the scripture. Those that will stablish the mass, as ye do, my Lord, and defend idolatry, must prove the thing ye speak by the scripture, and plainly satisfy the places of the scripture brought against you: ye must not darken the places with glosses of your imagination[3]; but dissolve the places, and content both the scripture, which is your mortal enemy in this matter, and likewise satisfy the reason of man, which ye neglect in this cause of the sacrament, otherwise than ye should do; and for a good reason ye bring an invisible miracle. God, that can resuscitate the children of Abraham out of the hard stones, send you of his mercy full grace to take away the veil of blindness and give you his light! Amen. Tiguri, 9 Septembris, M.D.XL.VII.

JOHANNES HOPERUS,

Anglus voluntate ac legibus[4].

[[1] Not all, but *of* all; i.e. of all things necessary to salvation.]

[[2] Ἀλλ' οὐκ εἶπε, πάντα, ἀλλὰ περὶ πάντων, ὡς ἂν εἴποι τις, ἁδρομερῶς καὶ ταχυμερῶς· ἢ περὶ πάντων λέγει, τῶν συνεχόντων καὶ κατεπειγόντων. Chryst. Op. Tom. ix. p. 6. Ben. Ed. Par. 1837.]

[[3] Ymagyon, in the original.]

[[4] John Hooper, an Englishman in heart and by right.]

[ANSWER

TO THE

BISHOP OF WINCHESTER'S BOOK.]

It is daily prayed in the church of God, good christian reader, of as many as knoweth and feeleth in themselves their weakness, how soon man is carried away, either with affections, either by force of temptation, which the nature of man corrupted in no wise can resist, unto all kind of abomination; that God of his mercy would defend those dangerous assaults of the devil, the world, the flesh, and sin, and saith, *Ne inducas nos in tentationem:* "Suffer not us to be overcome with temptation," nor carried away by the force of the devil into the danger of sin and iniquity, but deliver us from ill; govern us with the light of thine eternal truth; that neither by ignorance of knowledge of thy most holy word, neither by the imbecillity and weakness of our infirm nature, we fall not away from thee[5].

Great and wonderful was the prudence of David; yet was he divers times carried away into many great sins, and so for the time made servant unto the devil and his own lusts, that with great difficulty and unspeakable penitence scarce could he in long time after moderate those wilful and rash affections: so dangerous a thing is it to be servant unto the devil, who would have all men, created unto the similitude of God, and redeemed with the most precious blood of his only Son, to be the eternal vessels of God's ire and vengeance, as he is himself. And to bring this wicked purpose to pass, he useth not one simple and plain way, but a thousand crafty and false subtleties, as he seeth occasion prompting to every man's nature and

[5 — gouerne us with the ligth of thyne eternal trnythe. that nether by ignoraynce of knolege of thy moost holy worde. nether by thymbecillite ant weakenys of our infirme nature, we fall not awaye from the, in the original.]

inclination, the sin that he is most prone and disposed unto, and leaveth not the man that he assaulteth until such time as he obtain the victory; except the wretched man keep himself with dread and fear under the protection of God's mercy, and desire him with ardent, vehement, and daily prayer, that in Christ he may resist the force of his mortal enemy, whose final pretence is none other than to bereave the soul of man of the joys eternal, and to have him his companion for ever, to curse the living God, and to blaspheme his holy name without end. But these temptations in Christ we may overcome. "He came into the world to destroy the works of the devil." 1 John iii. And no man may better overcome the devil, than he that is well persuaded of his malicious and insatiable ire towards God and man, knoweth and feeleth in himself that he is mortal enemy both unto God and unto all his most perfect works, ready always to pervert God's order in all things, as we may to our pain perceive in ourselves.

<small>1 John iii.</small>

The soul that was created unto the similitude of God, replenished with all virtue and grace, full of knowledge, prudence, and understanding in all things appertaining unto God, a heart most gentle, humble, and always obedient unto God and godliness, a will most ready and prompt to embrace, choose, and elect the things godly, and eschew, refuse, and avoid whatsoever God and reason judged to be ill; but now it is contrary: for knowledge, ignorancy; for light, darkness; for obedience, contumacy and rebellion of heart, both against God and his word; and for a will that would be inclined and choose nothing but virtue, and such things as might most appertain unto the glory of God, a will that now chooseth nothing less than to serve God, and rather to blaspheme God, than to refuse the ill offered by the devil contrary unto God.

Thus is man spoiled of all his original riches, daily wounded more and more with wounds, fresh and new; now pierced with this sin, now with that sin, and yet like unto men of no senses, we feel neither perceive how neither when we are wounded, neither care to seek a remedy of this ill; though right well we know that every sin that man committeth, of justice deserveth eternal damnation. But these things moveth nothing at all the man that is ignorant what the devil, the world, and sin is: he feeleth neither what his disease is, neither knoweth the craft, malice, and deceit of his enemy; and by those means departeth not only from God, but also from all honesty, and falleth, he knoweth not how, into such detestable crimes and ignorancy of God, that both God, the world, and their own conscience beareth testimony of their iniquity against them.

These our infirmities and great offences we must learn to know, and once known, diligently study to amend them, and to remove the causes of these ills; then the effect is soon destroyed. The way to remedy all this ill, and to lead an upright and honest life, is to know God by his true and holy word, who leadeth a man unto virtue only and solely, as David teacheth, Psalm cxix. *Quo pacto* *adolescens vitam inculpatam aget? Nempe si eam custodiat ut dictat verbum tuum. Quum autem te quæram in toto corde meo, ne sinas me errare a mandatis tuis*[1]. Whosoever conform his life unto the word of God, shall be out of the danger of his enemy the devil. Though he be subject unto the infirmities of the flesh, and must suffer the temptations thereof, yet shall he not be overcome, but in Christ able to resist, yea, and to be delivered from death, sin, and the devil; as all godly men before our time hath done, and likewise left behind them in writing how we may do the same. St Paul, that knew both the thoughts of the devil, 2 Cor. ii., and also his apert and open malice against those churches that he had preached the gospel of Christ unto; among other, he teacheth the church of the Galatians, that the principal remedy against sin is to believe stedfastly the gospel of Christ, that he preached unto them, and not to admit any false doctrine, or other learning, though an angel from heaven should preach the contrary, Gal. i.; not to admit any false addition or dream of man, but be contented to use the same as he left it: rebuked wonderfully such audacious persons, as took upon them to set any gloss or interpretation other than he had preached unto them. Thus taught Moses the children of

Psalm cxix.

2 Cor. ii.

Gal. i.

[1 Wherewithal shall a young man cleanse his way? By taking heed thereto according to thy word. With my whole heart have I sought thee: O let me not wander from thy commandments. Psal. cxix. 9, 10.]

Israel, and bid them observe the law as it was given from God, and threatened the transgressors and those that added unto the law the displeasure of God's ire, which should cause all men to tremble and quake for fear as many times as they thinketh, readeth, or heareth readen[1] any part of the holy scripture, because they receive it not with more reverence and honour, with hearty prayer that God will preserve them from all false, sinister, and perverse interpretations thereof, and with all study and diligence to follow and practise whatsoever be commanded them to do by God's word, in godly and virtuous living.

For the law was not given to be written in parchment or paper, but in the heart of man; not to babble and prate of it, but to live as it biddeth; not to bear it in the bosom, but to shew it unto the world in godly conversation and virtuous life; to mark all things therein contained, and to think verily that all together is spoken to thee, and that God requireth that honesty and godliness of life in thee that there is expressed, and would thee to beware how thou transgress his law, and to avoid his importable[2] displeasure, by the example of other. For as God letted not to punish the transgression of our forefathers, he is the same God still, and will do the like unto thee, if thou commit like offence. Remember that the original of man's misery, condemnation, and death, was first wrought by the false interpretation of the scripture; as thou mayest see by the horrible and most fearful example of Adam's wicked and detestable transgression, which made all his posterity and succession prisoners eternally unto death, hell, and sin, and compelled by the same means the Son of the eternal God to sustain the incarnation of mortal flesh, to appease the ire of God for man's transgression, that by the means and death of his most innocent body he might derive into himself the whole displeasure and vengeance of man's transgression.

Were there no more scripture but that that describeth the fall of man and the means how he was lost, it were sufficient to teach all the world to beware how to take the word of God in a wrong sense. If Adam had been contented to have used the word of God as it was given unto him, those miseries had never been known, neither

[1 Readen : read.]   [2 Importable : insufferable.]

by him, neither by his posterity: but he, wretched man, forgot God and godliness, yea, eke his own wealth, left the text and believed the gloss, as the devil had taught Eve, which wrought his woe and pain. And whereas he would not for the love of God believe the text of God's mouth, the pains that followed his transgression taught him to know that the gloss was diabolical.

Thus being instructed, let us beware of glosses and false interpretations, and in all matters of controversy and causes of religion, believe no man except he speak the word of God truly and in the same sense that God meant it. For, as Paul saith, "We are founded upon the foundation of the prophets and the apostles, the chief corner-stone being Christ." Eph. ii. And let us not doubt but only the scripture is sufficient to teach us all verity and truth concerning religion, and to govern our life in all godly and honest conversation. And by the scripture we may come alone unto all perfection, confute all heresies and false doctrine, though there had never doctor written, ne never decree made by any general council, as Paul teacheth, 2 Tim. iii. 2 Pet. i. [marginal: Ephes. ii. 2 Tim. iii. 2 Pet. i.]

Therefore, christian reader, as thou hopest to be saved, hearken diligently unto the words of our heavenly Father, and hear them not only, but understand them, believe them, and do them. His words be these, Matt. xvii. *Hic est filius meus dilectus, in quo mihi complacitum est; ipsum audite*[3]. A few words, but a great matter contained in them: the only salvation of all our health, sufficient authority to overthrow all false doctrine and all idolatry of the world. He that teacheth anything that Christ taught not, is not to be heard. Such as only hath their redemption in the only death of Christ, will believe nothing but that Christ commandeth, nor do any work that cannot be approved by the scripture. He holdeth always this text before his eyes, that the Father shewed unto the world, saying, "This is my Son, in whom I delight;" and doth also with reverence and honour embrace and receive his commandment, which is, *Ipsum audite*, "Hear him." [marginal: Matt. xvii.]

Now let us, with the help of his holy Spirit, see whether

[3 This is my beloved Son, in whom I am well pleased; hear ye him. Matt. xvii. 5.]

Christ ever taught this doctrine, that in the sacrament of his holy supper he meant any alteration, or transubstantiation of the bread into his very natural body, and the wine into his very natural blood, (as my lord of Winchester teacheth in his book,) or not; or whether, sith his glorious body was ascended into heavens, heaven, earth, man, and angel bearing record thereof with outcries and admiration, *Viri Galilæi, quid admiramini, aspicientes in cœlum? Hic Jesus, qui assumptus est a vobis in cœlum,* &c.[1] Acts i. (mark the manner of his visible and corporal ascension, and believe the scripture, the angels, and holy apostles' eyes, that saw him bodily ascend, and these words, *Sic veniet,* &c., better than these new massers;) whether it be possible that the seed of Abraam, the fruit and issue of the belly of that glorious virgin Mary,—being in all things, except sin, as consubstantial, equal, and like unto the nature of his mother, and nothing differing from the son of Adam, concerning his humanity, Heb. ii., as in his Godhead is equal and like in all things unto the Father eternal, that hath neither beginning nor ending,—can be or may be, against the nature of a true body, present bodily at the commandment of every priest, when he speaketh these words, *Hoc est corpus meum*[2]; which thing is as possible to be done by a word, as to make an end of the world when he would. For whensoever his glorious body shall descend from above, the end is come. Acts i., Matth. xxiv.

Until that day, christian reader, look not for him, but believe thy creed; and whatsoever thou hearest spoken by those ill persons of the new learning, that it should be present corporally in the mass, which is but a yesterday's bird, trust thou to the old learning of God's word, *Sedet ad dextram Dei Patris, inde venturus est judicare vivos et mortuos*[3], Acts i. 7., 1 John ii. Believe Christ's body to be really and corporally in the sacrament, when thou seest him there with thy corporal eyes, and not before; for Christ hath no body invisible nor insensible, as men dream,

[1 Ye men of Galilee, why stand ye gazing up into heaven? This same Jesus which is taken up from you into heaven, &c. Acts i. 11.]

[2 This is my body.]

[3 He sitteth on the right hand of God the Father; from thence he shall come to judge the quick and the dead.]

but a very true and natural man's body, like unto mortal man, except sin; and now likewise a glorified body immortal, as ours shall be in time to come.

And as many places of the New Testament proveth Christ's humanity, as proveth his deity, and more; and as the word attributeth unto the one nature divine all qualities, conditions, and properties appertaining unto the Godhead, so of the other part, it more manifesteth, openeth, and declareth his humanity to be a nature of other contrary qualities and conditions. Forasmuch as God differeth from man, so far doth the one nature in Christ differ from the other. And as I must believe that these words be true in all things concerning the Godhead of Christ, *Deus erat verbum*[4], like unto God, and very God; so must I believe this, *Verbum caro factum est*[5], John i., Christ to be in all things like unto man, and very true man in all things, except sin. And as the scripture proveth these two natures to be unite and knit in one person, and that God and man is but one Christ; so proveth it likewise the qualities of the one nature to be contrary unto the qualities of the other nature: the one mortal, the other immortal; the one to be buried in the sepulchre, the other to resuscitate the insensible and dead body, xxvii. xxix.,[6] Mark xv., Luke xxiii., John xix.; the one nature visible to be taken after forty days of his resurrection from the earth into heavens, Mark xvi., Acts [i.], the other nature invisible, to continue with his elects in the church until the world's end, Matth. xxviii. John i.

[Matt. xxvii. xxviii.]
Mark xv. xvi.
Luke xxiii. xxiv.
John xix. xx.
Mark xvi.
Acts i.
Matt. xxviii.

He that knoweth thus by the scripture, that the one nature of Christ, very man, is taken out of the world, and shall not be in the world till the great day of judgment, Acts iii., cannot be persuaded, contrary unto the word of God, that the same body may be naturally and corporally under the form of bread; but will diligently, in case the scripture seem by words to prove the same, search how that place may be agreed with the other, that manifestly repugneth the presence of Christ's body; and so agree them, that no contrariety may be admitted in the scripture: for if one place be false, there is none true, which were a blasphemy to say. The prophet David thus commendeth the scripture, Psalm xix., Acts iii.

Psal. xix.

[4 The word was God.] [5 The word was made flesh.]
[6 So printed in the original.]

[HOOPER.]

Lex Domini perfecta, convertens animas; testimonium Domini verum, imperitis sapientiam suppeditans. Decreta Domini recta sunt, cor exhilarantia; præceptum Domini repurgatum, illuminans oculos[1]. Therefore there must be as good heed given unto the meaning of the words as unto the words; or else they illuminate not the conscience, but rather darken the conscience, and lead it into all false doctrine and detestable heresies; as we may see here in those words of the Lord's supper, *Hoc est corpus meum*, Matth. xxvi.: leaving Christ's meaning plain, and constraining the letter, forcing it to serve a wicked purpose, men would make the people believe that these words consecrated the bread into the natural body of Christ, and telleth the people, that though it repugn never so much unto reason, yet it repugneth not unto faith, which believeth every thing against reason. Christ, saith they, spake these words, and made his body of the bread, and bid us do the same. Lo, these be they wherewith all this alteration of bread is made, the substance thereof turned into the substance of Christ's body, *Hoc est corpus meum*. Dispute not how, believe the words, and leave reason. Say with the blessed Virgin, *Ecce ancilla Domini*[2], Luke i. She held herself contented, when she knew by the word of God, that by divine operation of the Holy Ghost she should be the mother of God's only Son. She stayed herself by faith in the promise, and committed the means and doing thereof unto God. So, say they, ye must hold captive all your reason, and think that God is able to do it: believe, and it sufficeth. God is able to do all things, as indeed he can; and all these words be true that they persuade the people withal, if they were placed aright, and applied to prove a true conclusion, as they be alleged to stablish a false and detestable heresy. God could have given man wings to fly, as he gave unto the birds of the air, if he would; but he would not, therefore he could not: *Quia omnia quæcunque voluit, fecit in cœlo et in terra*[3].

[[1] The law of the Lord is perfect, converting the soul: the testimony of the Lord is sure, making wise the simple. The statutes of the Lord are right, rejoicing the heart: the commandment of the Lord is pure, enlightening the eyes. Psal. xix. 7, 8.]

[[2] Behold the handmaid of the Lord. Luke i. 38.]

[[3] For whatsoever the Lord pleased, that did he in heaven and in earth. Psal. cxxxv. 6.]

And as for the literal senses of these words, *Hoc est corpus meum*, which they say must be understand without any trope or figure, proveth nothing. Christ called himself a door, John x.; a vine, John xv.; and yet was neither door nor vine, except ye understand by a door the only gate into heaven, and by the vine the liquor of grace, that comforteth every troubled conscience, and quencheth the ire and displeasure of God the Father against us for our sins. So likewise in these words, *Hoc est corpus meum*, there is none other thing to be understand by them, but that bread represented unto his apostles, not only his precious body, but also the manner how and wherefore it should be torn and rent upon the cross: and as they themselves brake the bread between them, so were they the cause that Christ's body was broken and slain upon the cross; and that by the means and use of this sacrament, there might be always in the church of Christ a token of God's mercy towards us, and a remembrance of that glorious body that sustained most vile death for the sin of the world. Howbeit, the bread was no more the body, nor the wine his blood, than Christ was a lamb, as John called him, *Ecce agnus Dei, qui tollit peccata mundi*[4], John i. So, though he said the wine was his blood, and the bread his body, he meant none otherwise but that it represented his body; and he that corporally, with true repentance, did eat of that corporal bread and corporal wine in faith, did eat spiritually Christ's body and blood. John x.
John xv.

John i.

And if thou confer Matthew and Mark with Luke and Paul, thou shalt find that these words cannot be so grossly taken, as men say, without trope or figure. Whereas Matthew saith, xxvi., and Mark xiv., *Et accepto poculo, gratiis actis, dedit illis dicens, Bibite ex eo omnes, hic est enim sanguis meus, qui est novi testamenti, qui pro multis effunditur in remissionem peccatorum*[5]; Luke and Paul saith, xxii., 1 Cor. xi., *Hoc poculum novum testamentum est in meo san-* Matt. xxvi.
Mark xiv.

1 Cor. xi.

[4 Behold the Lamb of God, which taketh away the sin of the world. John i. 29.]

[5 And he took the cup, and gave thanks, and gave it to them, saying, Drink ye all of it, for this is my blood of the new testament, which is shed for many for the remission of sins. Matt.]

guine[1]. Here Luke and Paul saith plainly that the cup was the new testament, and attributeth the same to the cup that Matthew and Mark attributeth unto the wine, and saith that the cup, and not the wine contained in the cup, is the new testament in the blood of Christ, which was to be shed for the sins of the world.

These words of Luke and Paul they will understand by a figure, and let the letter pass. What authority have they to use the help and aid of a trope in these words of Luke and Paul? Whereas they say plainly, *Hoc poculum est testamentum novum in meo sanguine*[1], and expound *est* in this place *per metonymiam*, and that Christ meant not that the cup was the new testament, but the wine contained in the cup. Of equity and right, if they can take such licence to expound those texts that maketh against them, they must be contented that other men use them likewise, as many times as necessity requireth by contrariety of texts, or when without the aid of a trope we cannot save our faith inviolated. But it may fortune, they will say, that Luke and Paul must be understood by Matthew and Mark. Wherefore not rather Matthew and Mark by the words of Luke and Paul? Forasmuch as they do more manifestly declare the supper of the Lord than Matthew and Mark; and likewise these words better agreeth with the nature and propriety of a sacrament, *et rerum natura quæ in sacramento repræsentatur*[2], than the words of Matthew and Mark. Mark the word of Luke and Paul, and thou shalt perceive plainly that this pronoun (*hoc*) cannot be referred unto the cup only, but unto all the action of the whole[3] supper, wherein the Lord instituted a perpetual memory and sacrament of his glorious passion and death. But in case this pronoun (*hoc*) could be referred unto the bread and wine, as it cannot, yet can no man expound these words of the supper without a trope; for there is more difficulty in this verb (*est*) than in the pronoun (*hoc*). For in case, when Christ said unto his disciples, "This is my body," delivering them the bread,

[1 This cup is the new testament in my blood.]
[2 And the nature of things which is represented in a sacrament.]
[3 Whole: hole, in the original.]

it was indeed, as Christ said, his body, before he called it so; (for everything is called by his proper name, after that it hath his being, and not before: the light was not called the day, neither the darkness night, until such time as God had made the sun and the moon, and appointed each of them their proper office, Gen. i.; and the Son of God was not called the Son of Man, until such time as he received the nature of man in the belly of the blessed virgin: wherefore) if this verb (*est*), in these words of the Lord's Supper, must needs be simply and plainly referred unto the bread and wine of the sacrament, the bread and the wine was the body and blood of Christ, before Christ called it so, his body and blood, and before he spake these words that they call words of consecration, *Hoc est corpus meum*.

Gen. i.

When then began these external signs of bread and wine, that he gave unto his disciples, to be his body and blood? And what were the words that altered the substance of bread and wine into the substance of his most precious body and blood? It was not this word (*est*) that did it; for if it had not been his body before he called it so, Christ would never have named it so; for he cannot lie, he useth not to misname any thing. He leaveth fraud and false invented terms unto the devil, and such as mean no good faith by their words. Now if it were his body, very flesh, blood, and bones indeed, what words of the scripture, or what words used Christ to make this alteration? Peradventure he whistled[4] some other words, and put a piece of bread in his sleeve[5], and there secretly consecrated his precious body, and then said, "Take ye, eat ye, for this is my body." And so saith some of these new papish church, where before transubstantiation of bread was never spoken of.

The mother of this idolatry was Rome, and the father unknown. A bastard is this transubstantiation doubtless. Lanfrancus[6], that enemy of truth and true religion, that wrote

[[4] Whisselyd.—[5] Slyffe, in the original.]

[[6] *Lanfrancus*, Prior of St Bec, afterwards abbot of St Stephen's, at Caen, and in 1020 made Abp. of Canterbury. He opposed Berenger's opinions on the Lord's Supper in the council of Rome (1059,) and in some other councils, and died in 1089. See Labbe's councils.]

against Berengarius[1], Paschasius[2], Guymundus[3], Guydo Aretinus[4], Algerus Monachus Corbeiensis[5], Adelmannus Episcopus[6], Hugo[7], *et his recentiores*[8] Lombertus[9], Comestor[10], *et* Papa Innocentius[11], with other, begat this wicked woman, transubstantiation. Whereas Christ, neither his apostles, no, neither long after unto the council of Vercellense[12] in the time of Leo IX. about the year of our Lord 1052, and 300 years after the death of Bede[13]. A wondrous matter and an horrible practice of the devil, that contrary unto the scripture and unto the old fathers this mystery is happened unto the sacrament, that these masters of the latter days fight so sore to defend, an accident without a sub-

[[1] *Berengarius*, Archdeacon of Angers. He denied the corporal presence in the eucharist, for which he was condemned in several councils, and on more than one occasion retracted, and again relapsed; died 1088.]

[[2] *Paschasius*, (Radbert,) a Benedictine, who became abbot of Corbey. He wrote a treatise on the eucharist, in which he asserted that Christ was present in the sacrament in the same body which he took of the virgin Mary, and in which he ascended into heaven. At the desire of Charles the Bald, Bertram wrote against his views, as did also John Scotus, and others. He was said to be the first who asserted the real presence; but others deny this. Died about 865.]

[[3] *Guymundus*, (or Guitmundus,) a Benedictine monk, afterwards bishop of Aversa, who wrote on the reality of the body and blood of Christ in the sacrament, against Berenger.]

[[4] *Aretinus*, (Guydo,) a celebrated Benedictine, better known as the inventor of musical notes than for his theological writings; about 1028.]

[[5] *Algerus*, a monk of Clugny, who wrote on the eucharist against Berenger; he died about 1131.]

[[6] *Adelmannus*, bishop of Bresse, who also wrote on the eucharist against Berenger; died 1062.]

[[7] *Hugo*, perhaps Hugh de St Victor, who wrote on the sacraments; but Lombertus speaks of him as being in error. He was said to hold the opinions of St Augustine.]

[[8] And more recently.]

[[9] *Lombertus*, the well known Peter Lombard, Master of the Sentences.]

[[10] *Comestor*, Peter the Eater, born at Troyes, died a canon of St Victor, at Paris, 1198, author of historical and other works.]

[[11] *Innocentius*, (the IIIrd) Pope, who wrote on the sacrifice of the mass, &c. in the 13th century.]

[[12] Council of Vercelli held under Leo 9th, in which, as well as in those of Rome and of Paris, Berenger's doctrines were condemned.]

[[13] *Bede* the Venerable died 735. His works were published in eight vols. folio, at Basle and Cologne, 1612. See his Ecclesiastical History, published at Cambridge, 1644.]

ject, and hath taken from the supper the thing that we see, we touch, we taste, we eat, we drink, and we swallow through the throat, to say, bread and wine, as the apostles did, and yet say it is no bread nor wine. If it be altered, some were best, that best can maintain a lie, to shew how and by what words it is changed. By these words, *hoc est*, it is not done. For no man can do more by the virtue of those words than Christ himself. Now Christ by these words declared that it was his body, and not made his body. Then must ye shew the other words that wrought this marvellous transubstantiation; or else we should make Christ a liar, who is the fountain of all verity and truth.

But such as defend this alteration of bread, rather than they would say that by the words of Christ, *Hoc est corpus meum*, were not made the very body of Christ, they will expound this verb (*est*) per (*fit*,) and say thus: that by the power of God and virtue of his word spoken by the minister, the substance of the bread is altered into the substance of Christ's body; so is Christ's body made present by this word (*est*.) But this interpretation the letter without a trope will not admit, neither that *est* should be expounded by (*fit*,) neither that the bread should be made the body of Christ, but that it is already the body of Christ before these words be spoken, *Hoc est corpus meum*. If it be not before he call it the body, why doth he lie then, and call it otherwise than it is? If it be the body, as he saith it is, by what words of the scripture hath he made the bread the body, and the wine the blood? By these words, *Hoc est corpus meum*, there is neither bread neither wine altered. But the text saith, that the bread is the body and the wine the blood; which this new doctrine will not admit, that bread should be both bread and also the glorious body of Christ, for then *Duo corpora essent simul in eodem loco*[14]: which indeed reason will not grant[15]; no more than it is possible that a true body may be, and yet occupy no place.

Such as would defend a wicked and most damnable purpose, good reader, clean contrary to the nature of this verb (*est*), expounded *per* (*fit*), yet would they blind the people,

[14 Two bodies would be together in the same place.]
[15] Per naturam duo corpora non possunt simul esse in eodem loco. Jo. Duns Scoti, Lib. IV. Dist. X. Qu. II. folio 50, Paris, 1513. R.

and say they use plainly without trope Christ's words, and with open mouth cry out upon such as both reverently, godly, and learnedly, both write, use, and speak of the sacraments, and say they be heretics, people departed from God and all virtue, when they themselves use such a trope, as the scripture, from the beginning to the latter end, never useth. See their trope, in these words, *Hoc est corpus meum*. Christ said, Take ye, eat of this, this is my body: the Pope's doctrine saith, Under the form of bread is Christ's body. Thou seest that Christ said not so, but said, that the bread was his body; as no doubt it was, if Christ's meaning be taken, as well as his words, as it must be of every christian man: and where Christ said *est*, they understand *fit*, and teach Christ to speak, as though he could not for lack of words convenient express his mind in this matter.

But these words of the supper diligently considered, and one evangelist conferred with the other with judgment, it may easily be seen that these words, *Hoc est corpus meum*, make no more for the transubstantiation of the bread and the wine, than *In nova fert animus mutatas dicere formas corpora*[1], proveth *Verbum caro factum est, et habitavit in nobis*[2]. For if the bread and the wine be not really and substantially the corporal and natural body of Christ, this word *est* proveth nothing at all; and when they interpretate these words, *Hoc est corpus meum*, and say that under the term of bread is the body of Christ, I will not admit that interpretation, forasmuch as it hath no good ground neither in the scripture, neither in the ancient doctors, as I shall declare hereafter. But because they accuse other men for the use of a trope, I would not that they offend in the same: I require them to bide still in the letter, and to leave these glosses, under the form of bread, with the bread, in the bread, or under the bread. Christ used none of these terms, nor yet the holy fathers, but plainly said, "This is my body, that is broken for you." And whereas Christ says, "this is," they say, "under this form." Here is a very plain trope and figurative locution. Men saith that they admit *metonymian*, and say, under the form of bread is

[1] My mind leads me to speak of bodies transformed into new shapes.—Ovid. Metam.]

[2] The word was made flesh and dwelt among us. John i. 14.]

the true body of Christ, though it be as false as God is true that they say. A dumb thing without senses is no harbour nor dwelling-place for Christ's precious body, nor for the Spirit of God; but the penitent and sorrowful heart of the Christian by faith lodgeth this ghostly and spiritual guest. The soul of man, created unto the similitude of God, by faith is made the temple of God, to live in all virtue and godly conversation, following the steps of Christ, and to exalt the truth of his afflicted and persecuted church, till he come. Let these that defend this alteration of bread, do that themselves which they require of other, and interpretate the words of Christ without any trope; and then they may the better accuse other men that use a trope, in case they suppose their trope and manner of speech under the form of bread may better be made good[3] by the manner and phrase[4] of the scripture, than this trope that we use to call a sacrament by the name of the thing that is signified by the sacrament; the supper of the Lord, the Lord's body, present at the contemplation of faith, in spirit, spiritually and not corporally.

Forasmuch as I trust I have sufficiently declared that the papists doth use a trope, I would they should name their trope, and prove it to be true by the scripture that may warrant their trope to be good: they may not confirm their sayings with an old wife's tale, and say that the holy fathers believed so; for the contrary will be proved, that the ancient fathers believed as Christ taught: for both they and every man must be judged by the scripture.

Now likewise to the other part of the sacrament. If they will refer this pronoun *hoc* only unto the sign *et ad rem symbolicam*[5], behold Luke and Paul, and thou shalt see plainly that neither Christ called the wine that the apostles drank his blood, neither the priest, if he believe Luke and Paul, should not say that under the form of wine is Christ's blood, but under the form of the cup or chalice is the blood of Christ; for Christ's words be these: *Hoc poculum est novum testamentum in meo sanguine*[6]. Why doth the priest

[3 Good: in the original, godd.]
[4 Phrase: in the original, fraunse.]
[5 And to the symbolical thing.]
[6 This cup is the new testament in my blood. 1 Cor. xi. 25.]

speak of the form of wine, when Christ spake of the cup, and not of the wine? If there be no trope to be admitted in the words of the supper, (I will not admit this figure *continens pro contento*[1],) let them prove the golden chalice to be transubstantiated into the blood, and say there remaineth nor gold nor silver; the substance of the gold is changed into the substance of the blood of Christ; and then let them drink the chalice as well as the wine, and doubt no more of God's power in the cup than in the bread. For he that said by the bread, "This is my body," said likewise at the same time, that the cup was the new testament, and bid them drink of it,—them all. And if *Hoc est corpus meum* can alter the substance of the bread, then can *Hic calix est novum testamentum* alter the substance of the chalice; and thus, as they eat the bread, they should drink also the chalice; for these words of the cup were spoken by Christ, both God and man. The same word spoken by the same apostle is in one spirit, at one time, for one purpose, to one and to the same end. And he that can change the bread with *Hoc est corpus meum*, can change the chalice with *Hic est calix novum testamentum*, I trow; or Christ peradventure and his words availed not as much in the gold, as in the bread. And that were wonder; for the Psalmist saith: *Dixit, et facta sunt*[2], Psal. cxlviii. He made all the world with a word, and of nothing: and now should his mighty power be abridged? No, good christian reader! He can do now as he hath done beforetime, make the thing that he purposeth to make. But to make of bread his natural, physical, and corporal body, he never meant it: if he had done, he would have so made it, that thou shouldst have seen it, as thou seest heaven and earth. He would not be ashamed, and hide his body, now glorified, more than he was ashamed to betray himself, and open his own person unto the wicked company sent from the high priests and Pharisees, John xviii. It is not, therefore, as they say. For the scripture doth not testify, that our Saviour Christ Jesus ever took any other nature, than the nature of man in the belly of the blessed virgin Mary; and until such time as thou

Psal. cxlviii.

John xviii.

[[1] That which containeth, for the contents.]
[[2] He commanded, and they were created.]

seest the chalice eaten as well as the bread, believe it not³, that the bread is altered more than the chalice. For as of the substance of an old chalice sometime, though mass hath been often said withal, is made new groats; so of a new singing loaf, that hath been consecrated with *Hoc est corpus meum*, sometime hath creeping worms been engendered, yea, and sometime cast into the fire and burned, as Benno Cardinalis writeth of Gregorie VII., otherwise called Hil[de]brandus⁴. Good proof hath been taken, that bread remaineth after the consecration; for by the sacrament poisoned there was an emperor, and a bishop of Rome poisoned⁵. In what subject should this poison remain? In some subject, doubtless; for Aristotle's school will admit⁶ no accident to be without his subject, neither admit any accident to perish without his substance. And when these men say⁷, the mould and rot of the bread is nothing, every man that hath his senses knoweth it is a manifest lie: for so long it may be kept, that it will run round about the altar: yea, if man had no senses at all, and knew the scripture, it were sufficient to prove that bread remained still after the consecration. 1 Cor. xi. And there is no 1 Cor. xi. papist among them all, but will grant this most foolish and fond contradiction, something⁸ to be nothing. Force them to answer what it is that corrupteth, what it is that is moulded: then will they say it is nothing, though ye see the vermin engendered of the bread creep before your face. If this proposition of Aristotle should be disputed, *An generatio*

[³ Believe it not: in the original, belyued not.]
[⁴ Johannes Portuensis Episcopus, qui intimus fuerat a secretis Hildebrandi, ascendit in ambonem beati Petri, et inter multa, audiente clero et populo, ait: Tale quid fecit Hildebrandus et nos, unde deberemus vivi incendi: significans de sacramento corporis Domini, quod Hildebrandus, responsa divina quærens contra Imperatorem, fertur injecisse igni, contradicentibus Cardinalibus qui assistebant ei. See Vita et Gesta Hildebrandi, authore Benone Cardinali, in Brown's Fasciculus Rerum, Vol. I. p. 79, Londini, 1690. See also Innoc. III. Op. Col. 1575, Tom. I. p. 380.]
[⁵ Henry the VIth. Emperor, and Pope Victor the IIIrd.]
[⁶ Admitted, in original.]
[⁷ That say, in original.]
[⁸ Something: in original, some thynk.]

unius sit corruptio alterius[1], and they would say that the generation of worms in the sacrament were engendered of the corruption of nothing, he would not be able in Aristotle's school to answer unto one argument.

Further, it is such a blasphemy against God, that every christian man ought to abhor it, to say that any creature can have his being of nothing. This is properly the *Epitheton*[2] of God to be of nothing, but of himself; and if they say God hath made these corruptions in the sacrament of nothing, it repugneth the faith that we have in the scripture.

Gen. ii. Genesis ii. *Igitur perfecti sunt cœli et terra et omnis ornatus eorum*[3]. So that after those six days, wherein God made the matter of all things, sith that time never thing in this world was made of nothing: therefore we must, for the reverence and honour of our faith, seek a father[4] for these putrefactions in the sacrament. It shall be the bread, say what they will, both by the judgment of the scripture, and also by reason.

As for their terms that they cry, "Fie upon such manner[5] of speech, and fie upon them heretics that believe it is but bread and no sacrament, as long as it is kept in the pyx," it forceth not. God forgive them! they know not what they say: the devil hath closed their eyes; they have neither judgment of senses, nor reason. But this false doctrine Lanfrancus brought devilishly into the church, after that he had obtained of Leo IXth., that the good and godly man Berengarius should be condemned for an heretic[6], an excellent clerk of great learning and notable virtues, as [7]Platina maketh mention *in vita* Joan. XV., who taught and wrote that the corporal presence of Christ's body could not be in the sacrament.

These men hath conceived in themselves a certain persua-

[1 Whether the generation of one thing become the corruption of another. See Aristotelis Op. Tom. I. De generat. et corrupt. Lib. II. cap. 4.]

[2 Ἐπίθετον, epithet.]

[3 Thus the heavens and the earth were finished, and all the host of them.]

[4 Sek a fathere, in the original.]   [5 Man of, in original.]

[6 Concil. Omn. Coloniæ Agrip. 1567, Tom. III. p. 577.]

[7 Odilum Abbatem Cluniacensem, et Berengarium Turonensem, viros sanctitate et doctrina insignes. Platinæ Pontific. Vitæ. Paris, 1530. folio 164.]

sion of new and late invented doctrine, and holdeth the same as a principle of infallible verity. And rather than they would depart one jot from this adulterous doctrine, they will grant an heresy, not only foolish, but also detestable, a worm or mould in the bread to be engendered of nothing: which is so far wide from the faith of a christian man, that it needeth no probation. God, (saith Athanasius,) the Father, *a nullo est factus, nec creatus, nec genitus*[8]. God, when he would destroy the world with water, by miracle gathered together two of every kind that lived into the ark of Noah, that they might in their kind replenish the world again, as we at this day see, and made not every thing again of nothing. No; he made after the six days at the beginning never a thing of nothing; but that the substance of one thing was made by and of the substance of other creatures, every thing in his kind; man, by God and man; beast, by God and beast; Christ, himself God and man, by God and the blessed virgin Mary. The mould and beasts that are engendered in the bread, if there be no matter whereof they should be engendered, they were no creatures.

But what learning is this to be preached and defended among the people, good christian reader, to prove something nothing? God of his infinite goodness restore again his holy word unto the people, and the right use of his sacraments, and give grace unto the people to understand the manner of speech used in the scripture, and to admit that trope and figure in this holy supper of the Lord, that best appertaineth unto the nature of a sacrament, most commonly used and familiar in all other sacraments, and to the use of our sacraments, by the scripture, conferring one place with other; and not to send to the high priest of Egypt, or unto the book of bishops' decrees, to know what our sacrament mean. Let us search the scripture, and make it the guide of our study, as David did, Psalm cxix. *Lucerna pedibus meis verbum tuum, et lumen semitis meis*[9]. This we know, that as the supper of the Lord is a sacrament unto us, so was *Pesah*[10]

Psal. cxix.

[8 The Father is made of none, neither created nor begotten. The Creed ascribed to Athanasius, and from him called the Athanasian Creed.]

[9 Thy word is a lamp unto my feet, and a light unto my paths.]

[10 *Pesah*, פסח, the Passover. Exod. xii. 11.]

unto the children of Israel; and for our baptism they had circumcision.

As well was the promise of eternal life made unto them as unto us; as well they believed to be saved by Christ as we: they were of Christ's church as well as we. As well was Christ delivered[1] unto them in the use of their sacraments, as unto us; but not so openly, because he was not then born, nor had not suffered the death that their sacraments represented, as ours do, declaring unto us what Christ hath done for us, that now sitteth at the right hand of God the Father: so that the sacraments of the Old Testament and the New in effect be one; and give a right censure and judgment of the one, and then are we instructed aright in both.

For as all the promises of God, from this unto Adam, *Semen mulieris conteret caput serpentis*[2], Gen. iii., unto the last and final promise unto the apostles, *Sedebitis vos super sedes judicantes* xii *tribus Israel*[3], were made unto the church in Christ, and for Christ, to save such as believed from the curse and malediction of Adam's sin, and to stablish the weak infirmities of those that received by faith the promise; God annexed unto the promise these external signs, which we call sacraments, that they might set before our eyes the benefits of God's mercy due unto our faith in Christ, and were as seals and confirmations of God's promises, where he warranted and assured his church openly that he would be her God, and she to be his spouse for ever, made her[4] a dower of life eternal, and gave her these external signs, wherein she might always exercise her[4] faith, and in spirit have the godly conversation of Christ when she would; as we may have daily in the use of the sacraments, though not bodily, yet in spirit. And as verily as we eat and drink Christ in the holy supper, so did the fathers eat Christ in their sacraments; no less Christ's body then to be born, than we now that he is born; then to come in the flesh into the world, and now in the flesh departed out of the

[1 Delivered: delyuid, in original.]

[2 The seed of the woman shall bruise the serpent's head.]

[3 Ye shall sit upon thrones judging the twelve tribes of Israel. Matt. xix. 28.]

[4 Her: here, in original.]

world; as St Paul saith, 1 Cor. x. *Omnes eandem escam* 1 Cor. x.
*spiritualem comedebant, et omnes eundem potum spiritualem
bibebant. Bibebant autem de spirituali quæ illos comitabatur
petra. Petra vero fuit Christus*[5]. He teacheth manifestly
that the Fathers ate in their sacraments Christ to come, as
well as we that be after his birth in this earth and vale of
misery. This was Christ, the stone, that conjoined the
church of the prophets' time with the church of the apostles'
times, and made both these churches one; two in external
signs and sacraments, one in effect, to be saved in Christ,
and one concerning the substance and effect of sacraments.
I would allege for my purpose Saint Augustine[6], who understandeth and expounded one way and by one figure
and trope these two texts, *Petra erat Christus*, and *Hoc
est corpus meum*; saving that our faith is not grounded
upon St Augustine or any other man, but upon the word
of God, the only scripture; and also because I mind hereafter to declare the judgment of Augustine, and other of
the holy fathers, concerning this matter, because they make
with the old truth against this new papistry.

But first, by the word of God we must know what
the nature and use of a sacrament is. The office of a
sacrament is this: to shew unto us outwardly that the
merits of Christ is made ours, for the promise sake which
God hath made unto those that believe; and these sacraments by faith doth applicate and apply outwardly unto him
that in faith receiveth them the same grace, the mercy,
the same benefits that is represented by the sacraments, but
not so by the ministration of the sacraments, as though they
that receive them were not before assured of the same graces
and benefits represented by the sacraments. That were a
manifest error: for in case the sacraments could give us very
Christ, the promise of God were in vain, the which always
appertain unto the people of God before they receive any sa-

[5] They did all eat the same spiritual meat, and did all drink the
same spiritual drink; for they drank of that spiritual Rock that followed
them, and that Rock was Christ.]

[6] Nec tamen ait, Petra significabat Christum, sed ait, Petra erat
Christus.—Non enim Dominus dubitavit dicere, Hoc est corpus meum,
cum signum daret corporis sui. Aug. Op. Contra Adimantum, Cap. 12.
Tom. VI. col. 189, 187, Basiliæ, 1543.]

crament; but they be the testimonies of promise, and declare unto us for an infallible verity, and unto the church of Christ, that we be the people that God hath chosen unto his mercy, and that by faith we possessed before Christ; and in faith, friendship, and amity with God we receive these sacraments, which are nothing else but a badge and open sign of God's favour unto us, and that we by this livery declare ourselves to live and die in his faith against the devil, the world, and sin. But he that supposeth to make Christ his, and all Christ's merits, by the receiving of the outward sign and sacrament, and bringeth not Christ in his heart to the sacrament, he may make himself assured rather of the devil and eternal death, as Judas and Cain did. Matthew xxvi. Genesis iv. For the sacrament maketh not the union, peace, and concord between God and us, but it ratifieth, stablisheth, and confirmeth the love and peace that is between God and us before for his promise sake.

<small>Matt. xxvi.
Gen. iv.</small>

What is the most principal signification, and to what end every sacrament was ordained, it may be learned best by the promise annexed unto the sacraments. *Qui crediderit, inquit Christus, et baptizatus fuerit, salvus erit*[1]. Mar. ult. Therefore baptism is called a sacrament, because it is annexed unto the promise of eternal joy, to testify that the promise of grace verily appertaineth unto him that is christened.

<small>Mark xvi.</small>

Yet, to declare the virtue of this more plainly, let us consider the words of baptism, the which containeth in themselves the whole and sum[2] of the testament, the benediction wherewith we are consecrated, dedicated, and offered unto God, and God's name invocated upon us after this sort: "I," saith the minister, "by the commandment of God, and in the place of Christ, do christen thee; to say, do testify by this external sign thy sins to be washed away, and that thou art reconciled unto the living God of our Mediator Jesus Christ." And this is the sign wherewithal God marketh all that be living in this world; and his friends by these means he sealeth in the assurance of remission of sin, which thou hast first in spirit received by faith, and for the promise made unto thy father and his posterity.

[[1] He that believeth and is baptized shall be saved.]
[[2] The whole and sum: in the original, thole and somne.]

For the promise of God, the remission of sin, appertaineth not only unto the father, but also unto the seed and succession of the father, as it was said unto Abraam, Gen. xvii.: *Ero Deus tuus, et seminis tui post te*[3].   Gen. xvii.

It is ill done to condemn the infants of the Christians that die without baptism, of whose salvation by the scripture we be assured: *Ero Deus tuus, et seminis tui post te*. I would likewise judge well of the infants of the infidels, who hath none other sin in them but original, the sin of Adam's transgression. And as by Adam sin and death entered into the world, so by Christ justice and life. *Ut quemadmodum regnaverat peccatum in morte, sic et gratia regnaret per justitiam ad vitam æternam per Jesum Christum*[4]. Rom. v. Whereas the infants doth Rom. v. not follow the iniquity of the father, but only culpable for the transgression of Adam, it shall not be against the faith of a christian man to say, that Christ's death and passion extendeth as far for the salvation of innocents, as Adam's fall made all his posterity culpable of damnation. *Quia quemadmodum per inobedientiam unius hominis peccatores constituti fuimus multi, ita per obedientiam unius justi constituentur multi*[5]. The scripture also preferreth the grace of God's promise to be more abundant than sin. *Ubi exuberavit peccatum, ibi magis exuberavit gratia*[6]. Rom. v. Rom. v. It is not the part of a Christian to say, this man is damned, or this is saved, except he see the cause of damnation manifest. As touching the promises of God's election, *sunt sine pœnitentia dona et vocatio Dei*[7].

These temerous judgments of men hath brought into the church of Christ a wrong opinion of God, to say that he can nor doth save none, but such as be received openly into the church by baptism: whereas this sacrament and all other be but the confirmation of Christ's promises, which be in the person that receiveth the sacra-

[3 I will......be a God unto thee, and to thy seed after thee.]

[4 That as sin hath reigned unto death, even so might grace reign through righteousness unto eternal life by Jesus Christ our Lord.]

[5 For as by one man's disobedience many were made sinners, so by the obedience of one shall many be made righteous.]

[6 Where sin abounded, grace did much more abound.]

[7 The gifts and calling of God are without repentance. Rom. xi. 29.]

ments before, or else these external signs availeth nothing. This may be easily known by the use of baptism every where. The testimonies of the infant to be christened are examined in the behalf of the child; of faith, what they believe of God: *Credis in Deum Patrem, &c.? Credis et in Jesum Christum, Filium Dei, natum, et passum, &c.? Credis in Spiritum Sanctum? Credis sanctam Ecclesiam, remissionem peccatorum, resurrectionem carnis, et vitam æternam?*[1] The answer is, *Credo*[2]. Before yet or he be christened, he maketh this solemn vow, full little regarded of all the world in manner, that he will at the years of discretion practise and live godly after this faith. The minister saith unto him: "Thou shalt renounce the devil with all his works:" the answer is, "I do renounce him." This reason and account of faith given with a most earnest and pretensed vow, to live for ever virtuously, he is demanded whether he will be christened. "I" [will,] saith the testimonies[3]. Then is he christened in the name of God, the Father, the Son, and the Holy Ghost. The which fact doth openly confirm the remission of sin, received before by faith. For at the contemplation of God's promises in Christ, he is saved as soon as the conscience of man repenteth and believeth, and his sins be forgiven. John iii. and vi.: *Qui credit Filio habet vitam æternam; qui non credit non videbit vitam, sed ira Dei manet super eum*[4]. There is neither faith, neither sacrament, unto this christened creature in vain. Faith receiveth first Christ for the promise sake; then is he bold to take this holy sacrament for a confirmation of God's benefits towards him, and then to manifest, open, and declare unto the whole church, represented by the minister and such as be present at the act, Christ, that already secretly dwelleth in his soul, that they may bear record of this love, amity,

John iii. & vi.

[[1] Dost thou believe in God the Father, &c.? And (dost thou believe) in Jesus Christ...the Son (of God)...born...(and) suffered, &c.? Dost thou believe in the Holy Ghost? (Dost thou believe in) the holy... Church...the remission of sins, the resurrection of the flesh, and everlasting life...? Baptismal Service.]

[[2] I do believe.]

[[3] I saith the testimonies, in the original. I will, say the sponsors.]

[[4] He that believeth on the Son hath everlasting life: and he that believeth not the Son shall not see life; but the wrath of God abideth on him.]

peace, and concord, that is between God and him by Christ. And forasmuch as all displeasure, ire, vengeance, and hatred between God and him, is agreed upon by the intercession of Christ, whom faith before baptism brought before the judgment-seat of God, to plead this charter of remission; it is the office of the church, which hath an open and manifest declaration thereof, to give God thanks for the preservation of his church, and for the acceptation of this christened person into the commonwealth of his saved people; remembering, that only those be appertaining unto God, that be thus called openly into the visible church and congregation, except death prevent the act. And such as contemn this sacrament be not of God, as Paul saith: *Quos prædefinierat,* Rom. viii. *eosdem et vocavit*[5]. Rom. viii. When they may be received, as they were instituted, and ministered by such as the law of God appointed in the ministry of the church, no Christian should omit for any occasion the doing of them. But whereas such take upon them as be not lawfully called unto the ministration of sacraments, (as where the *sage femme*, or midwife, for danger of the child's soul will christen it,) it is a profanation[6] of the sacrament and not to be suffered. The child shall rejoice eternally in heaven with Abraam, Isaac, and Jacob for Christ's sake, whose merits appertaineth unto the infant for his father's faith.

This ungodly opinion, that attributeth the salvation of man unto the receiving of an external sacrament, doth derogate the mercy of God, as though his holy Spirit could not be carried by faith into the penitent and sorrowful conscience, except it rid always in a chariot[7] and external sacrament. This error hath ignorance brought into the church, because the ministers this many years knew not to what end a sacrament was instituted. They contend upon certain words of the scripture, John iii. Mar. ult. Howbeit, understood aright, John iii. and the circumstance of the text marked, it proveth nothing. Mark xvi. Nicodemus was a man of sufficient health and age, and no cause why he should not receive that holy ceremony of baptism. Mark's words appertain likewise chiefly unto such as were apt to hear the gospel, and such to be christened: notwith-

[5 Whom he did predestinate, them he also called.]
[6 Prophacion, in the original.]
[7 it ryd allwayes in a cherot, &c., in the original.]

standing they may likewise confirm thereby the baptism of infants by this reason, *Ero Deus tuus et seminis tui post te*[1]; deducing this argument of those words, to whomsoever the promise of God appertain, to the same the signs annexed unto the promise appertain. To the infants the promise appertaineth, *Ero Deus seminis tui*; likewise the signs of the promise. Whereas they say, that baptism appertaineth unto the salvation of all men that be of God's elects, I grant; but not unto every of God's elects. I except those that die before they be christened, the infants of the Christians, of whose salvation we may not doubt: of the infidels' infants I will temerously nor damn nor save. Saint Augustine[2] is of the contrary part against me: howbe[it], that holy doctor giveth me leave to leave his writings, and believe the scripture[3]. If it were my purpose to reason that matter, I would get great aid out of other his works to serve mine opinion: and as for the excuse of the midwives christening by the example of Zippora, Moses' wife, Exodus iv., that circumcised in the time of need, it may not prove the midwives' fact to be good; for of one private and singular fact no man may make a general law. Epiphanius[4], that great clerk, *libro iii. contra Hæreses, Tom* 2. *cap.* 79, proveth mine opinion with strong arguments: *Si mulieribus præceptum esset sacrificare Deo, aut regulariter quicquam agere in ecclesia, oportebat magis ipsam Mariam sacrificium perficere in novo testamento, etc.; at non placuit*[5]. Read the chapter. Moses

Exod. iv.

[1 I will be a God unto thee and to thy seed after thee. Gen. xvii. 7.]

[2 Si non baptizentur, inter eos qui non credunt erunt; ac per hoc nec vitam habebunt, sed ira Dei manet super eos. Sti Augustini Op. Basileæ, 1543, Tom. vii. contra Pelagianos ad Marcell. lib. 3. col. 720. c. See also col. 1034. a, and col. 1085. b. d. &c.]

[3 Quis nesciat scripturam canonicam veteris et novi testamenti certis suis terminis contineri, eamque omnibus posterioribus episcoporum literis esse præponendam, ut de illa omnino dubitari et disceptari non possit, utrum verum vel utrum rectum sit, quidquid in ea scriptum esse constiterit. Sti August. Op. Basileæ, 1543, de Baptismo contra Donatistas, Lib. ii. Cap. iii. Tom. vii. col. 392. B.]

[4 Εἰ ἱερατεύειν γυναῖκες Θεῷ προσετάσσοντο, ἢ κανονικόν τι ἐργάζεσθαι ἐν ἐκκλησίᾳ, ἔδει μᾶλλον αὐτὴν τὴν Μαρίαν ἱερατείαν ἐπιτελέσαι ἐν καινῇ διαθήκῃ. * * * ἀλλ' οὐκ εὐδόκησεν. Epiphan. Op. Coloniæ, 1682, Tom. i. Advers. Hæreses (Lib. iii. Tom. ii.) p. 1059.]

[5 If it had been commanded that women should sacrifice to God, or perform any thing ritually in the Church, it especially behoved Mary

was in danger of death, because he neglected the commandment of God, which was to circumcise the eighth day. Gen. xvii. As he supposed, after the judgment of the flesh, it should have hindered the child's health, because they had a long journey to travel: such good intentions, contrary unto the word of God, we see cruelly revenged divers times. The sacraments must be used as they be commanded, and to the same end that they be commanded. The ministry of Christ's church chiefly dependeth in the preaching of the gospel and the ministration of the sacraments; and as the preaching of the word is not the office of a woman, no more is the ministration of the sacraments.

To what end, and to whom the sacraments must be given, St Paul teacheth, Romans iv.; where he calleth circumcision *Sphragida ejus justitiæ acceptationis in gratiam Dei, quæ per fidem apprehenditur:* " It is the mark and seal of acceptation into God's grace, received before by faith." And this external sacrament was as the conclusion and sealing up of all that God had promised unto Abraam before: to say, *In te benedicentur omnes gentes terræ*[6], with many other promises, as is expressed in the book of Genesis from the 12th chapter unto the 17th, where as circumcision was given; for this word *sphragizo* signifieth *sigillo notare, insignire, et concludere*[7]. By the which word and text of Paul it is manifest, that by the sacraments God's promises be not first given unto man, but that by the sacraments the promise received is confirmed: for Paul *discernit applicationem gratiæ ab ipsa circumcisione*[8], as in the same 4th chapter he sheweth more plainly, where he declareth the condition of Abraam, what he was before he received this sacrament, proveth him first to be the friend of God: *Credidit Abraam Deo, et imputatum est ei ad justitiam*[9]. As a man first assured of God he received this sacrament, and sought not first to find him in an external sign. So doth all men at this day, if herself, under the new dispensation, to offer sacrifices, &c.; but it was not seen fit.]

[6 In thee shall all families of the earth be blessed. Gen. xii. 3.]

[7 Σφραγίζω, to seal, to sign, and to conclude.]

[8 Distinguishes the impartation of grace from circumcision itself.]

[9 Abraham believed God, and it was counted unto him for righteousness.]

they marked what is required of them before they receive any sacrament. There is not so much as the speechless infant, but by his parents is bound to give account of his faith before he be christened. And, as John saith, chap. i., *Dedit eis ut liceret filios Dei fieri, videlicet his, qui credidissent in nomine ipsius*[1]*:* so that none is admitted unto the sacraments, but such as be God's friends first by faith. *Abraam credidit:* "Abraam believed." The infant believeth. Cornelius believed, Acts x. and as one came unto the sacrament, our father Abraam, as the friend of God, so cometh all the world that follow his faith, and confirmeth God's promise with an external sign; as I shall declare more plainly from the first sacrament unto the last. Adam offered sacrifice unto God, so did Abel, Gen. iv. They had certain manifest and open sacraments given unto them by God, that their oblations were acceptable, because they sprang out of the fountain and life of all good works, from faith and the fear of God. Abel's lamb was by miracle burned with celestial fire, and Caine's sacrifice nothing accepted. Two brothers, having one father and one mother, what should be the cause that one received an open and external testimony of God's love, and not the other? Paul declareth the cause, Rom. xiv. Heb. xi.: *Sine fide impossibile est placere Deo ; accedentem ad Deum oportet credere*[2]. Abel, because before the sacrifice he was accepted by faith into God's favour, the religion of his heart was declared openly unto all the world. Caine, that thought God would be pleased with an external ceremony without an internal reconciliation, was openly declared to be an hypocrite, without faith or any godly motion. The rainbow given unto Noe was a sacrament of God's[3], and confirmed these words: *Non adjiciam ut amplius maledicam humo propter hominem*[4]. *Et, hoc signum fœderis quod ego do inter me et te, et inter omnem*

[1 To them gave he power to become the sons of God, even to them that believe on his name.]

[2 Without faith it is impossible to please God: for he that cometh to God must believe, &c.]

[3 The word "promise" appears to be wanting here to complete the sense.]

[4 I will not again curse the ground any more for man's sake. Gen. viii. 21.]

animam viventem, quæ est vobiscum in generationes perpetuas. Arcum meum posui in nube, &c.[5] Gen. ix. Had not Noe first believed the promise of God, and been accepted into the favour of God, this ark in the clouds had as much edified him, as all the miracles that [were] wrought by Moses in Egypt before Pharao, Exod. vii. viii. ix. x. xi. *Pesah,* Exod. xii. nothing availed; no, nor was not used without the due circumstances there prescribed, that such as ate of it were first instructed what it meant, and put in remembrance of God's benefits and mercies unto them, and then as people of godliness and godly religion they ate it with thanks.

What is there more to be said? As the promise of God is received by faith, so must the sacraments be also. And where as faith is not, no sacrament availeth. Read the eighth chapter of the Acts of the Apostles, and confer Simon Magus with the queen of Candes'[6] servant; and mark what difference is between him that looketh to find Christ in an external sacrament, and him that cometh with penitence and assurance that God is his through Christ. The one, Simon, would have had the power to have given the Holy Ghost to whom he list, not for his belief sake, but for money. Peter said: *Non est tibi pars neque sors in parte hac*[7]. The queen's servant, converted from the bottom of his heart, believing the preaching of Philip, would be a Christian also outwardly, said unto the servant of God: *Ecce aqua, quid vetat quominus baptizer? Dixit Philippus, Si credis ex toto corde, licet*[8]. "If thou believe with all thy heart, it is lawful." The godly man said: *Credo Filium Dei esse Jesum Christum.* "I believe the Son of God to be Jesus Christ." Thus first assured of Christ, took openly Christ's livery. The same diversity may be seen, Matt. xxvi., Mark xiv. and Luke xxii., by Judas and the rest of the apostles,

[5 This is the token of the covenant which I make between me and you, and every living creature that is with you for perpetual generations. I do set my bow in the cloud, &c.]

[6 Candes: Candace.]

[7 Thou hast neither part nor lot in this matter. Acts viii. 21.]

[8 See, here is water. What doth hinder me to be baptized? And Philip said, If thou believest with all thine heart, thou mayest....I believe that Jesus Christ is the Son of God. Acts viii. 36, 37.]

concerning the receiving of Christ's supper. So that I prove hereby, that all sacraments appertaineth unto none but unto such as first receive the promise of God, to say, remission of his sin in Christ's blood: of the which promise these sacraments be testimonies, witnesses; as the seal annexed unto the writing is a stablishment and making good of all things contained and specified within the writing. This is used in all bargains, exchanges, purchases, and contracts.

When the matter entreated between two parties is fully concluded upon, it is confirmed with obligations sealed interchangeably, that for ever those seals may be a witness of such covenants, as hath been agreed upon between the both parties. And these writings and seals maketh not the bargain, but confirmeth the bargain that is made. No man useth to give his obligation of debtor, before there is some contract agreed upon between him and his creditor. No man useth to mark his neighbour's ox or horse in his mark, before he be at a full price for the ox; or else were it felony and theft to rob his neighbour. Every man useth to mark his own goods, and not another man's: so God, in the commonwealth of his church, doth not mark any man in his mark, until such time as the person that he marketh be his. There must first be had a communication between God and the man, to know how he can make any contract of friendship with his enemy, the living God. He confesseth his default, and desireth mercy; useth no purgation nor translation of his sin, but only beseecheth mercy, and layeth Christ to gage[1], and saith, Forasmuch as thou hast given thy only Son for the sin of the world, merciful Lord, hast thou not likewise given all things, unto sinners that repent, with him? Then likewise, Lord, forgive me, and be my God, both in faith, and also in thy sacraments: and as truly shall I serve thee during my life, as these words pass my mouth, I renounce the devil, the world, and sin. Upon this faith and promise made to God, we be marked in God's mark, and none otherwise. For the church ever teacheth amendment of life, before he promise grace. So God preached to Adam, Gen. iii., Esa. i., Matt. iii., Mark i.: *Resipiscite, et credite evangelio*[2]. Men may not come like

Gen. iii.
Isai. i.
Matt. iii.
Mark i.

[[1] Layeth to gage, accepteth the challenge.]
[[2] Repent ye, and believe the gospel. Mark i. 15.]

swine unto the sacraments, with cry, God [have] mercy, good ghostly Father, and you³! But he must repent from the bottom of his heart, and leave the things that erst hath been committed against God; the idolater his idolatry, the swearer his oaths, the adulterer his adultery, the drunkard his drunkenness, men that tradeth in the world all false and unjust contracts, the slanderer his devilish tongue; or else never come to sermon, nor receive sacrament. But alas! with such faith as they receive the sacraments, in the same faith they liveth; not as people created unto the similitude of God, to obey justice and honesty, but to serve all uncleanliness and abomination; as it is daily to be seen, as well among them that yet live in superstition, as among them that professeth to know Christ's gospel, their living as much like unto a christian man's as antichrist unto Christ, and God unto the devil. If they that know, at leastway they say they know the gospel, will no better follow the gospel, let them cast the testament into the fire; for they know to their damnation, that will not follow their knowledge. To be a Christian, it is not so light as men make it: of all the crafts in the world it is the hardest; not to prattle and prate of it, but to practise it in life. For it is a science practive, and not speculative. *Consistit in actione, et non in lingua*⁴. God give grace, these holy sacraments may be more often and more reverently used! The neglecting of them is to be condemned, much more the contempt of them. But every man must be aright instructed, why and to what end he useth them, as well as to receive them. He that is ignorant of the causes can never judge aright of the effect. He that knoweth not the cause why God made man, shall live always like a beast, and apply his life to another end than God made it for, to serve him in justice and virtuous life. He applieth it more like a dog and brute beast, contrary unto the order of God, and maketh the image of God the image of Cacodemon, obeying ever lust, that repugneth unto the will of God. So far hath the devil and sin prevailed, that in manner there is neither the one sect of people called papists, neither the other called gospellers, that careth⁵ for the life of the

[³ god mercy godd gostely father and youe, in the original.]
[⁴ It consisteth in deed, and not in tongue.]   [⁵ Original, *caryd*.]

gospel. Such custom of ill hath made so weak our corrupt nature, that it flieth all honesty and honest laws that should keep it in order. And of a spiritual liberty given unto us by Christ in the gospel, we take a carnal licence and wantonness of life, so that we make very little or no resistance at all. *Assensus est infirmus, et cor habet contrarios impetus pugnantes cum lumine divinitus*[1] *insito mentibus*[2]. True are the words of Medea: *Video meliora proboque, deteriora sequor*[3]: ac, *Fertur equis auriga, nec audit currus habenas*[4]. Of every thing the principal cause must be known, to say, the cause final, the which is first to be considered: as in a commonwealth, the final cause of all laws and the commonwealth likewise is to live well; the final cause of physic to cure the sick well; the final cause of rhetoric to persuade well. And the principal and chief cause of all the sacraments that be now in the church of Christ, or ever were in the church of Christ, is, that they be and ever hath been the signs of God's will and pleasure towards us; testimonies and seals annexed unto the promise of grace. They be not the thing that they represent, but signs and remembrances thereof. Weigh the scripture diligently, christian reader, and search for the truth there.

God hath bound his church, and all men that be of the church, to be obedient unto the word of God. It is bound unto no title or name of men, nor unto any ordinary succession of bishops or priests: longer than they teach the doctrine contained in the scripture, no man should give hearing unto them, but follow the rule of Paul: *Si quis aliud evangelium docet, anathema sit*[5]. "He that teacheth any other gospel than Christ's, it must be accursed." God hath preserved in all captivities and persecution of the church miraculously one book, the holy Bible; delivered the same unto the church, and bound the church unto this book; as Christ saith, John

---

[1 dtuitus, in the original.]

[2 The assent is weak, and the heart has contrary impulses, contending with the light divinely implanted in the mind.]

[3 I see and approve the better, but pursue the worse. Ovid.]

[4 The charioteer is borne along by the horses, neither doth the chariot answer to the reins. Ovid. Metam.]

[5 If any man preach any other Gospel unto you than that ye have received, let him be accursed. Gal. i. 9.]

xiv.: *Paracletus autem ille, qui est Spiritus Sanctus, quem Spi-* John xiv.
ritum mittet Pater nomine meo, ille vos docebit omnia, et suggeret
*vobis omnia, quæcunque dixi vobis*⁶. He saith that his holy
Spirit shall teach none other doctrine than he himself taught,
and the same that he taught. Therefore withdraw thy heart
from this opinion, that they would deceive thy soul withal,
under the pretence of holy church. They only be the church,
that embrace this holy book, the bible, heareth it, learneth
it, and followeth the judgment of it. He is a christian
man, that leaveth the word of man, and keepeth the word
of God. *Si quis diligit me, sermonem meum servabit; et qui*
*habet præcepta mea, et servat ea, ille est qui me diligit*⁷. John John xiv.
xiv. Paul commanded Timothe to be studious in the scrip-
ture, and not to study in Talmud, nor Darash, or other
decrees of the Pharisees, 1 Tim. iv.: *Intende lectioni*⁸. Also, 1 Tim. iv.
Colos. iii.: *Verbum Christi abundet inter vos*⁹. To that pur- Col. iii.
pose the Holy Ghost would the scripture to be wroten, to
detect all falsehood, that God's name might be aright called
upon in Christ only, and not with invocation of dead saints;
and his holy supper to be used as a communion unto all
men under both kinds, and not to be made a mass of, that
blasphemeth God; for such as honour the bread there for
God, doth no less idolatry than they that made the sun
their God, or stars. David saith, Psalm ci.: *Scribentur* Psal. cii.
hæc in generatione altera, et populus qui creabitur laudabit
*Dominum*¹⁰. To what purpose hath Christ given us his sacraments, and wroten openly, manifestly, and sufficiently the
true use, how they should be used, in the scripture, when
no man, or few men, will observe the commandment of the
scripture, but rather the dreams and detestable decrees of
heretical and pharisaical bishops, and maintain their laws
in the church, be they never so devilish? It were as good
burn the bible, as to serve to no purpose. For the holy-

[⁶ But the Comforter, which is the Holy Ghost, whom the Father
will send in my name, he shall teach you all things, and bring all things
to your remembrance whatsoever I have said unto you. John xiv. 26.]

[⁷ If a man love me, he will keep my words, ver. 23. And he that
hath my commandments and keepeth them, he it is that loveth me,
ver. 21.]

[⁸ Give attendance to reading. 1 Tim. iv. 13.]

[⁹ Let the word of Christ dwell in you richly. Col. iii. 16.]

[¹⁰ This shall be written for the generation to come, and the people
which shall be created shall praise the Lord. Psal. cii. 18.]

water bucket sitteth in the church at the right hand of the bible, and not so hardy [as] once to melle[1] there, till the water-conjurer call him; and then must the holy bible serve, like a handmaid, a wicked purpose, to colour a stinking ceremony, that *asperges me, Domine,* may prove holy water to be a good and godly ceremony[2]: and *hoc est corpus meum,* after the invocation of dead saints, is called to make good the wicked mass; wherein is not as much as one thing good, saving the scripture, which they abuse to another purpose than it was wroten for.

Doubtless the princes of the earth, unto whom God committeth the civil governance of the people, shall sustain the ire of God for their negligent endeavour in this behalf, because they suffer such preachers and bishops to rule over the conscience of their subjects, where only the law of God should have place. These things should move all christian princes to a reformation of these wrongs, that God sustaineth by taking away his word from the people. The miserable blindness that the people be in, with danger of eternal damnation, because of idolatry, should cause princes to rue upon their woeful state and condition. Yea, their own estate and princely dignity, given unto them by God, should move them to remove this ill out of their realms; or else other men will usurp falsely their authority, and pervert the order of God in the commonwealth. Therefore in the most noble and famous commonwealth that ever was, the commonwealth of the Israelites, was this order appointed, Num. ix.: first God, then his word, the celestial signs, the pillar of fire and the cloud, which were as guides in their journey, to shew them when and where they should camp, and likewise when and which way they should march forward in the journey; in

Num. ix.

[[1] Melle, *idem quod* meddle. Lye in Junius.]
[[2] There is much obscurity in this passage in the original, where it is printed as follows:—

And meyntayne there lawes in the churche, be the neuer so deuillishe. It wer as god burn the Bible, as to serue, to no purpose, for the holy water boket, sittith in the church at te right hand of the Bible, and not so hardy ons to melle there till the water coniuryd call hym, and then moost the holi bible serue lik à hand maide awyckid purpose, to coloure à stinking ceremonie that aspringes my dominie. May proue holy water to be a good and godly ceremony.

For the ceremonies referred to in *asperges,* &c. see Durand. Ration. Divin. Officiorum, Lib. IV. cap. 4.]

the fourth place of this commonwealth was Moses appointed, as supreme head and prince next unto God; in the fifth[3] place was appointed the priests; then the princes inferior and captains; then the people; then all things necessary to maintain this commonwealth, whether it were in time of peace or time of war.

Now, he that considereth the face of this commonwealth may see many notable things, and specially for my purpose one, which shall prove that princes sustain wrong by such bishops as be within their realms. Though that Aaron and his sons, with the rest of the priests, had the ministry of the church committed unto them; yet were they never so bold to make any law for the people concerning conscience, or to bring any ceremony into the church, without the judgment and knowledge of God's word, and Moses the prince; as it may be well seen by such as could not celebrate Pesah in the time appointed, because of certain impediments rehearsed, Num. ix. This cause of religion was not brought unto the bishop and priests to be defined, but unto Moses, who counselled[4] the Lord, and thereupon advised[5] his subjects what was to be done in such a case. Read the place. This declareth that no general council, no provincial assembly, no bishops of any realm or province, may charge the subjects thereof with any law or ceremony, otherwise than the prince of the land by the word of God can give account to be good and godly. For the people are committed unto the prince to sustain the right of them all, and not only to defend their bodies, but also their souls, as it may be seen by the complaint of Moses unto God, Num. xi.: *Cur afflixisti servum tuum? Et quare non inveni gratiam in oculis tuis, ut poneres onus universi populi hujus super me, &c.*[6]*?* He was so careful that no law was among them, but that he was able to assure every of his subjects that God was the author thereof. Now, if we consider the commonwealth of Christ's church in our days, is there any prince that can warrant all the laws of the church to be good, and that God is the author thereof?

_{Num. ix.}

_{Num. xi.}

[3 Fifth: fight, in the original.]
[4 counselled: asked counsel of.] [5 advised: wysid, in the original.]
[6 Wherefore hast thou afflicted thy servant? and wherefore have I not found favour in thy sight, that thou layest the burden of all this people upon me? Numb. xi. 11.]

No: God knoweth they cannot do it; and right well I am assured such as make the princes believe they are good, cannot bring forth and make good the author, except they say the devil, author of all ill, is the author.

Now, to remove this pitiful and miserable ruin of the church, let all princes, for the love of God and for the restoring of their own princely honour, take Moses and the prophets, the evangelists and the apostles, to judge whether the yoke of their subjects be tolerable, or not: if it be not, of gracious pity to remove it, and, like a prince, warrant them from all other men's subjection and laws. And let not a bishop be check-mate and "hail fellow, well met:" if the prince rule the body, the bishop to sit in the quire and rule the soul; as indeed there is more bishops' decrees, laws, and statutes in the church for the soul, than civil laws in any realm for the body. Whereas every commonwealth ought to have but two governors, God and the prince, the one to make a law for the soul, the other for the body: all the king's officers to be ministers of the law made to the conservation of the commonwealth, and the bishops to be ministers in the church, of the law that is prescribed by God: as all justices, mayors, sheriffs, constables, and bailiffs, be ministers of the law made unto them, to govern the commonwealth; so must the bishops, priests, and all other preachers, be ministers of Christ, and govern the people in their vocation according unto the law prescribed by God. As Paul willed the people to judge of him and of his companions, 1 Cor. iv.: *Sic nos æstimet homo ut ministros Christi, et dispensatores mysteriorum Dei; quod superest autem, illud requiritur in dispensatoribus, ut fidus aliquis reperiatur*[1]. There is no more required of the bishop, but that he be diligent and faithful in the execution of God's word. It is not required that he should make any law for the people, but to preach God's law with all diligence and study, as they do most negligently.

The year last past, upon certain occasions, at my being in England, for lack of expedition of mine affairs, I was compelled to remain in a town longer than I

[1 Let a man so account of us as of the ministers of Christ and stewards of the mysteries of God. Moreover, it is required in stewards that a man be found faithful. 1 Cor. iv. 1, 2.]

would, having communication with certain of the citizens of many matters, sought of my part only to have occasion to help their poor conscience from the snare of ignorancy. When I perceived I had obtained their willing audience, I demanded of them when their bishop (for of the town the bishop hath his name) preached among them, and the contents of his sermons. They told me that he never preached sermon in the town. I asked, what deputies he had in the town, appointed to preach. They said, none; and I believe it the better, for as long as I was in that town there was never sermon. I lamented the people; for I found a great many apt and ready, by inspiration of God's Spirit, to hear the truth, if they had a preacher; for, at one talk and communication, as much as they could comprehend they believed; the rest they stood in doubt of. Then I willed them diligently to learn the gospel, to avance it in word, and to set it forth with the example of all honest life; and told them that there were two general rules to learn and know God by: the first, by his Word, whereby our fathers before thousands of years knew him; the second was, to know God by his dear Son, opened and declared in Hierusalem unto the world, and that God can nor will be known none other ways than by his Word, and by his Son Christ Jesus. John x. *John x.*

Here in this town the bishop of the diocese, from the time that he was appointed by the king's majesty unto that most painful office, he preached neither God, neither the devil, but let his flock wander as sheep without a shepherd. They say yet all, that their dioceses be well instructed and governed, and they do according unto their offices. Forsooth, as much their diligence is correspondent, and their facts agreeing with their name, (for they are called *diœcesani*, of *diœceo*, that signifieth to govern and to defend,) as Absolom's facts agreed with his name. His name signifieth the peace and tranquillity of his father; but his facts was the affliction of his father, and banished him out of his realm. 2 Sam. xvii. So doth *2 Sam. xvii.* the bishops govern the churches committed unto their charges, and defend them from false doctrine. They be instructed in the Pater-noster, the creed, and the commandments, and hath the sacraments ministered unto them, (would to God, aright!) What, all this? It is not enough. They may have all these things, and yet nothing the better. Hierome writeth of an heremite *in vitas patrum*, that said, *Nullum opus difficilius quam dicere preces Deo*[1]. "No work more difficile than to pray unto God." Howbeit many men think nothing to be more facile and easy.

_{John iv.} When Christ saith, John iv., *Veri adoratores adorabunt Patrem in spiritu et veritate*, "The true worshippers shall worship God in spirit and verity;" the difficulty is soon perceived: let invocation be in spirit, to say, in the godly motion of the heart, not with the tongue alone, nor with hypocrisy. It must be in truth, to say, in a true knowledge of God; directed unto God only by Christ, and by no dead saint. So that in prayer these two are necessary, a true knowledge of God, and the spiritual motion of the heart; or else prayer is but *inanis battologia et inutile murmur*[2]. The creed must weekly and daily, and also the commandments, be opened unto the people; thereby they may know God aright, fear his justice against sin, and take solace and comfort in his merciful promises for Christ. Only the commandments of God contain such a copious and profound doctrine, that it can never be known sufficiently, nor never with sufficient diligence declared unto the people. It is the abridgment and epitome of the whole bible, compendiously containing the whole law and the gospel. Not one proposition in the scripture but hath his common place in the ten commandments: and he that understandeth them well is a good christian man, if he follow them. He that understandeth not them can be no christian man. There is every man's office and duty described, what is to be done, whether it be towards God or man: and whether he be minister in the church, or in the civil-wealth, of what condition soever he be, there may he learn how to follow his vocation.

It is not sufficient for a christian man to believe one part

[Oratio maximum et difficillimum opus.]

[1] Interrogaverunt fratres Abbatem Agathonem dicentes, Pater, quæ virtutum in conversatione plus habet laboris? Et dicit eis, Ignoscite mihi, quia puto non esse alium laborem talem, quam orare Deum. Vitæ Patrum, (per Georgium Majorem, cum præfatione D. Doctoris Martini Lutheri). Wittembergæ, 1544. fo. 269.]

[2] An empty chattering and useless sound.]

of the scripture; but faith is a right persuasion and willing consent unto the whole word of God. For he that saith, *Credis in Deum Patrem, Filium, et Spiritum Sanctum*³? the same God saith, *Ambula coram me, et esto integer*⁴. What availeth the brag of faith, where as is no virtuous life? He that said, *Justificati igitur ex fide, pacem habemus erga Deum, per Dominum nostrum Jesum Christum*⁵, Romans v. Rom. v. et, *Nulla condemnatio est lex his, qui insiti sunt Christo Jesu*⁶, saith likewise, *Quod si quis Spiritum Christi non* Rom. viii. *habet, hic non est ejus*⁷; *et, Si secundum carnem vixeritis, moriemini*⁸, Romans viii. And as we believe that Christ died for our sins, so must we believe, that he died likewise to give us an example to die from sin and the concupiscence of the world. Paul saith, *Quod mortuus* Rom. vi. *fuit peccato, mortuus fuit semel*⁹, Romans vi. Peter saith, *Cum igitur Christus passus sit pro nobis carne, vos quoque* 1 Pet. iv. *juxta eandem cogitationem armemini; quod qui patiebatur in carne destitit a peccato in hoc, ut jam non concupiscentiis hominum, sed voluntati Dei, quod superest in carne vivat*¹⁰, 1 Peter iv. He that said unto Peter, *Pasce oves meas*¹¹, John xxi. John xxi., and to the rest of all the apostles, Matt. x. Matt. x. Acto. i., that they should be ministers of the church, taught Acts i. then likewise how they might please God in their vocation; said not, Go, bless a bucket of water, hallow bough, candle, bell, chalice, font, or any such beggary¹², Matt. xxix.; but bid Matt. [xxviii.] them teach that he had said unto them, and repeated the same,

[³ Dost thou believe in God the Father, the Son, and the Holy Ghost? John ix. 35.]

[⁴ Walk before me, and be thou perfect. Gen. xvii. 1.]

[⁵ Therefore being justified by faith, we have peace with God through our Lord Jesus Christ.]

[⁶ And, There is therefore now no condemnation (by the law) to them which are in Christ Jesus.]

[⁷ If any man have not the spirit of Christ, he is none of his.]

[⁸ And, If ye live after the flesh ye shall die.]

[⁹ In that he died, he died unto sin once.]

[¹⁰ Forasmuch then as Christ hath suffered for us in the flesh, arm yourselves likewise with the same mind; for he that hath suffered in the flesh hath ceased from sin, that he no longer should live the rest of his time in the flesh to the lusts of men, but to the will of God.]

[¹¹ Feed my sheep.]

[¹² —in there vocacion. Sayd not goblisse abucket of water. Holow, bowe. Candell, bell, chalice, fount, or ony soueh begery, in the original.]

[HOOPER.]

> Mar. ulti. *Ite in universum mundum, et prædicate evangelium omni creaturæ*[1]. "Preach the gospel unto the world."

Mark xvi.

This was the manner of Christ's ministry in the church, before this superstition and idolatry was heard of. So taught Paul, Acto. xx., 1 Tim. vi.; Peter, 1 Pet. v. Thus said God to Hieremye, Hier. i. *Fili hominis, dedi verba mea in ore tuo*[2]. He that speaketh in the church, must speak the word of God. He that will please God, must please him as it is prescribed in the scripture; or else all that ever he doth is naught. If the bishop or priest will please God, or any other man, let him apply only his vocation appointed by the scripture, and as the scripture teacheth him: if he be a judge, to keep justice without respect of persons; if a lawyer, to defend nothing but the right; if a physician, diligently to cure his patient, and not to take so many cures for avarice in his hand, as the one part may happen to die, whiles he cureth the other; if a bishop, not to have so many parishes in his diocese, as ten diligent, learned men cannot, once in a year, know the faith of such souls as hath the charge of Christ's flock, neither how the poor simple people believeth. Examine such as are bound to use the sacraments of Christ's church and among a thousand there is not one that knoweth what a sacrament is, more than an ass; and to such the sacraments be not profitable, but damnable, as ye may see, Esay i. Yea, when they be not used according to their institution, God so abhorreth them as things repugnant unto the law: as we read, Hiere. vii. *Non præcepi patribus vestris de holocaustis. Et* Psal. l. *Holocaustis non delectaberis*[3]. The prophets by these words declared, that no ceremonies are required of any man without the knowledge and confidence of the promise confirmed by the ceremony, or without true repentance and faith: for the sacraments in the church of Christ neither maketh the love nor reconciliation between God and man, nor retaineth it not; it must be received and kept by one means, to say, by lively

Acts xx.
1 Tim. vi.
1 Pet. v.
Jer. i.

Isai. i.

Jer. vii.
Psal. l.

[1 Go ye into all the world, and preach the gospel to every creature.]

[2 Son of man, (behold,) I have put my words in thy mouth.]

[3 I spake not unto your fathers, nor commanded them......concerning burnt-offerings. And, Thou delightest not in burnt-offering. Psal. li. 16.]

faith, Romans v. Judas by the sacrament received not the promise, nor by the sacrament was preserved from desperation, Matt. xxvi. *Rom. v.* *Matt. xxvi.*

But he that will be the friend of God, and godly use his sacraments, must use them after the form prescribed by him only, and know what a sacrament is by him; to say, an holy ceremony, a work of the third commandment, who saith, *Memento ut diem sabbati sanctifices*[4], Exod. xx.; and before the works of the third commandment, wherein all ceremonies are contained, must always precede the works of the first commandment and of the second, an inward faith and certain knowledge of God, and an outward profession of his holy name, to ascertain[5] the church that he is God's friend and reconciled in Christ; or else it were a preposterous order, to set the cart before the horse: like as if the king's majesty's officers should give his livery unto him that the king never meant to take into his service, so to wear his livery without profit. *Exod. xx.*

This I desired to admonish the good christian reader of, before I entered the disputation of this most holy cause, concerning the blessed sacrament of Christ's holy passion and death; that he should know, that God giveth his graces and promise of remission of sin, only for Christ's sake, which we receive by invisible faith, and stablish the same by the use and exercise of sensible sacraments; the which, in place and time, are never to be spoken against with tongue, nor wroten against by pen.

Now, that these words can make no alteration of the bread and wine, nor make the natural, corporal, nor physical presence of Christ's body; the first reason is, that the words, *Hoc est corpus meum*[6], proveth that the bread is already the body, before the words be spoken, or else they misname the thing, and call bread flesh. The second reason: if the words, and the thing meant by the words, be one, then is the cup, and not the wine in the cup, the testament in Christ's blood, Luke xxii., 1 Cor. xi. Thirdly, if it were the very body of Christ corporally present, Christ's words were not true; for he bid them do it in the remembrance of him. Now, the remembrance of a thing is not the same *Luke xxii.* *1 Cor. xi.*

[4 Remember the sabbath-day to keep it holy.]
[5 Ascertain: assure.] [6 This is my body.]

self thing that is remembered; as many men use to remember a weighty matter by a little ring upon their finger. If Christ's most honourable body were present corporally in the sacrament, it were no need remembrance at all; for the thing present presenteth itself without the help of memory.

Turn they which ways they list, these words, *Hoc est corpus meum*, will not serve for their purpose, except they add their interpretation. The best gloss they have is this, that these words, *Hoc est corpus meum*, bringeth with them the body of Christ. But this is their interpretation of the text, and not the meaning of the text. Ponder every word, and first this pronoun, *hoc*; which demonstrative they refer unto the bread and wine only, howbeit we may with Saint Paul refer *hoc* unto the whole action and ceremony of the supper, as well as unto the bread and wine. Paul saith not, *Hic panis est communio corporis Christi*[1], as though we should think that he spake of the bread only; but with plain words saith, *Panis quem frangimus*[2], to declare that the bread is not the sacrament of Christ's body, till it be broken unto the church, according to the institution of Christ; a spiritual meat, as Paul calleth it; so that the bread lift up over the priest's head, nor kept in the box, is not the sacrament, but the bread rightly distributed. And in the same place, he calleth the bread broken the table of the Lord, by the which is understood the whole institution of Christ's supper. And where men contend so much of this word, *corpus*, repeating the whole, *Hoc corpus meum*; St Paul, the true interpreter of Christ's words, resolveth them thus: *Nonne panis quem frangimus communio corporis Christi est*[3]? Where Christ said, "This is my body," Paul saith, "Is not the bread that we break a communion of the body of Christ?"

Now, what difference is between the communion of a body, and the body itself, and what Paul meant by this word *cœnonia*, communion, it will be best known by the process of the text, when we perceive what Paul's purpose

[[1] This bread is the communion of the body of Christ.]
[[2] The bread which we break. 1 Cor. x. 16.]
[[3] The bread which we break, is it not the communion of the body of Christ? 1 Cor. x. 16.]

was to prove in the same place. Paul meant, in that place, to withdraw such as had received the faith of Christ at Corinth, from feasting of such as used to eat of the meats dedicated unto idols. *Logismos talis est*[4]. His consideration and intention was, to declare that it was idolatry to eat of idols' meat with idolaters; and proveth his proposition, deducing his argument *a comparatis*[5]. If the Israelites, in eating the sacrifices dedicated unto God, were participant of the thing that the sacrifices were offered for, then such as ate of meats dedicated unto idols, were partakers of the same religion wherefore these meats unto idols were offered.

The first part of the reason is true, by the words that he allegeth out of Moses, *Videte Israelem juxta carnem, &c.*[6] They were sure to be partakers of the temple, that ate the meat dedicated unto the temple; so were they sure that ate of the meats dedicated unto idols, partakers of idolatry. Therefore Paul concludeth thus: *Non potestis poculum Domini bibere, et poculum dæmoniorum. Non potestis mensæ Domini participes esse, et mensæ dæmoniorum*[7]. They that communicated with the *fideles* were participant of their religion: they that communicated with idolaters were likewise participant of the idolatry.

Now, the same ways that the *infideles* were participant of the devils that they worshipped, the same ways the *fideles* were participant of Christ's body. In false faith were they knit and unite unto the devil; in true faith the *fideles* unite unto Christ. And as the idolaters did not by hand, with the meat dedicated unto idols, exhibit and deliver the devil to him that ate of the devil's sacrament; so those that ate of the bread broken by the minister, as Christ commanded, had not the body of Christ delivered by hand unto them, but were in communion and society with Christ, and therefore did eat of one bread, dedicated to be the mystery of his glorious death. So doth Paul's argument proceed, that because we are by faith one body mystically with Christ, we eat of one mystical bread, to testify the same. *Quoniam, inquit, unus panis et unum*

[4 Such is his reasoning.] [5 By comparison.]
[6 Behold Israel after the flesh, &c. 1 Cor. x. 18.]
[7 Ye cannot drink the cup of the Lord and the cup of devils: ye cannot be partakers of the Lord's table and of the table of devils. 1 Cor. x. 21.]

corpus multi sumus: nam omnes ex eodem pane participamus[1], 1 Corin. x. Paul in this place put two churches, one of Christ, and the other of the devil. All those at Corinth that were of Christ's church came unto Christ's sacrament, participated and communicated with the company and society of Christ's body. Such as were *infideles*, or such as were neither hot nor cold, associated themselves with like unto themselves, and so declared manifestly that they were of the devil, as the other were of God. Not that the devil was given, I say, by hand, (peradventure he had other business at Ephesus, or otherwhere;) but it sufficed him that his members assembled together, and, by participation of the meat dedicated unto his idols, in spirit communicated with his spirit.

Repeat again the proposition of Paul, 1 Corin. x., *Panis quem frangimus nonne communicatio corporis est*[2]? In this word, *communio*, dependeth all the weight of Paul's argumentation. I have shewed what communion is, and which ways it is made by a sacrament, concerning God or the devil, in this place of Paul, where he calleth *epulas immolaticiorum esse dæmoniorum cœnoniam, et illarum convivas dæmoniorum cœnonous*[3]. As *communio* in one place is taken in this purpose of Paul, so must it be taken in the other; or else Paul could prove no conclusion at all, by reason of equivocation of the word. And though the word *communio* be indifferent, and may be taken both actively and passively, *ut apud Latinos communicare dicimur, sive aliis impartiamus aliquid, sive ipsi cum aliis in participationem veniamus*[4]; but in this place of Paul it cannot be taken actively, as men say, that the minister doth exhibit and give by hand the corporal body of our most blessed Saviour Jesus Christ. For in case Paul had meant any exhibition, distribution, or deliverance of Christ's body, he would have declared his mind after another sort; and have said, We are one body, and that

[1 For we being many (he says) are one bread and one body; for we are all partakers of that one bread, ver. 17.]

[2 The bread which we break, is it not the communion of the body? ver. 16.]

[3 The feasts of them that immolate to be the communion of devils, and the guests at these feasts the communicants (*fellows*, in Wiclif's and the Rhemish translations) of devils.]

[4 As in Latin we are said to communicate, whether we impart any thing to others, or whether we ourselves participate with others.]

for the distribution and deliverance of Christ's body; and not have said, We are one body, and that by the participation of one bread.

These words sheweth plainly, that Paul meant nothing of giving or distributing of Christ's body, but taught the Corinthians that such as did eat of this holy sacrament, according to the institution of Christ, were partakers of the spiritual graces and communion of Christ's body and blood, represented by the bread. And as Christ was not really nor corporally present in those sacraments and sacrifices of the Israelites, that signified Christ to come, but by faith in effect they received the thing meant and represented by the sacrifices; so likewise we, though that glorious body of Christ be in heaven, that this holy and most honourable sacrament representeth, yet, when with true penitence we receive the external sacrament, faith receiveth the effect of that precious body represented by the sacrament. This is Paul's doctrine: he meant of no deliverance nor exhibition of that body ascended into heavens.

There is no place of the scripture sheweth the nature of Christ's supper better than this place of Paul, whose purpose was only to destroy this error among the Corinthians, that was repugnant to true religion. Such as had professed one God, thought yet they might eat and drink with infidels, of such meats as was offered unto idols. Paul denieth it, and saith, No man can be the member of two contrary churches. I would such as God hath given knowledge unto, what is true and what is false, would likewise remember these words better, and refrain from the doing of such things as their own conscience is persuaded to be ill. They be too favourable unto themselves a great deal, and extenuate God's ire and displeasure against idolatry too much. They will not be able to make good their act at the coming of the great Judge to judgment, to save a little muck and inconstant treasure of this world, and to offend the majesty of the living God, that hath power to lose both body and soul in eternal fire. Better it were to follow the commandment of Paul, *Carissimi, fugite idolatriam: vobis prudentibus loquor*[5]. God hath given unto many men this prudence, to know that the

[[5] Dearly beloved, flee from idolatry. I speak as to wise men. 1 Cor. x. 14, 15.]

mass is ill; yet as ill as it is, they let neither to say it nor to hear it, which is very idolatry, and shall be cruelly revenged[1] without they amend.

The nature of man, by the infection of original sin, is so corrupted, and the heart so oppressed with contrary motions and violent resistance unto virtue, that men never consent so willingly and stedfastly unto the knowledge of virtue, as they should do. Rom. i., *Sed veritatem Dei in injustitia detinent*[2]. This knowledge that men hath of God is detained with injustice, as prisoner captive: it can bear no rule in the soul for the impetie[3] of injustice, which repugneth this true knowledge. The man is drawn with his own lusts and love of the world unto the contempt of God, and consenteth not unto his true knowledge, neither unto the law that forbiddeth all dishonesty and idolatry. This aversion and malicious obstinacy of the will must be daily mortified; or else it will work thine eternal displeasure, and make thee the everlasting enemy of God. Lament abuse of knowledge, and that thou consentest not as well and as soon to the judgment of reason, and follow it in the principles practive, as speculative.

No man doubteth of this principle, "two and two to be four," "four and four eight," with all other geometrical and physical principles. Men doth not only acknowledge them to be true, but consenteth unto the same knowledge. The other should be likewise as manifest, and as soon consented unto as these; to say, the whole natural diversity of all things, honest and dishonest. And this light in man's reason the philosophers call, *Notitiam principiorum*[4]. And man should consent unto these principles and knowledge of them: *scilicet, Deo obediendum esse, adulterium est vitandum, honesta pacta sunt servanda; quod tibi non vis fieri, alteri ne facias*[5]. These, I say, should be as soon consented unto, as to consent, *quod bis quatuor sunt octo*[6].

[1 Cruelly revenged: severely punished.]
[2 But hold the truth in unrighteousness.]
[3 Impetie: probably impetus, or impetuosity.]
[4 A knowledge of first principles.]
[5 Namely, that God is to be obeyed, adultery is to be avoided, honest engagements are to be observed; that which you would not another should do to you, do not to another.]
[6 That twice four are eight.]

The knowledge remaineth of these things, but the assent is infirm, by reason of contumacy and rebellion of the heart; of all enemies an enemy most to be feared, whom Paul describeth with these words: *Sensus carnis inimicitia est contra Deum*[7]: an horrible description of man's natures, that it is the perpetual enemy of God, and will not be subject unto the law of God. This infirmity maketh that men be nor hot nor cold; cannot tell which part to take; in their chamber to profess God, where as none can bear record but a mouse, nor none [be] edified by his knowledge; abroad in the world, where as God should be spoken of, they know him not; but as wise and discreet men, will do then as the most part of people doth, and would all were well, though not long of them; for they will keep silence for ever, rather than to speak as they know, yea, and with their example stablish the thing that they know is naught. If God be God, why are people for fear so ashamed to confess? If he be not God, let him go. God abhorreth such as be nor hot nor cold. If Christ's body be in heaven, wherefore is any man so hardy to resort unto the place, where as the priests of Baal make a piece of bread both God and man, and teacheth people to honour it? Why doth they not consent unto their knowledge, and follow it? He that is partaker of the sacrifice in the altar, is partaker of the religion meant by the sacrifice; and those that be partakers of like signs and sacraments, be declared thereby to be the members of one church. We are unite and knit together, made one by one spirit of truth: why should we break this knot by external ceremonies? We are not made [one] by eating of Christ's body corporally, neither the scripture teacheth of no such union between him and his church, but by the Spirit of God received by faith; as thou mayest well perceive how God the Father and his Son our Saviour hath given this office and defence unto the Holy Spirit, like God with them. Remember thy creed, *Credo in Spiritum Sanctum, sanctam ecclesiam catholicam, sanctorum communionem*[8]; and think, that it is by the giving of God's Spirit into our hearts, for the most merciful death

[7 The carnal mind is enmity against God. Rom. viii. 7.]

[8 I believe in the Holy Ghost; the holy Catholick Church; the Communion of Saints.]

of Christ, that maketh this communion of saints, which is the church of Christ: and thus, already conjoined with God, we receive the holy meat of his blessed body in spirit by faith; not to make the union between God and us, but confirm the union in ourselves, and to shew the league of amity unto the church.

And to understand the better what this word, *cœnonia, communio*[1], is, read the fifth chapter of the first epistle of John, where as this word *communio* is four times rehearsed. There shalt thou see the communion between Christ's body and us, how it is made, and by what means. And then shalt thou see that Paul, 1 Cor. x. and John so well agreeth to mine interpretation, that the christian reader will be satisfied, I trust, in the Lord.

1 Cor. x.

For as all the true subjects, sworn to the king, by their faith and allegiance are prest[2] and ready; wheresoever they see the king's banner spleyde[3], resort thereunto and say, "Whatsoever the king hath to do, or with whomsoever he hath enmity withal, I will associate myself to be of this part, tide what betide, mayhap weal or woe; unto this prince I unite my life and death: the cause, he is my lord; the making good and reason of the cause, I am his sworn subject, faith given, and my conscience bound: therefore to manifest mine obedience and love, by this banner I proclaim life and death against his contraries": so those that be Christ's, when they see the banner of Christ, the holy supper and sacrament of the death that won the victory of death and the devil, they will there live and die, with this banner to declare their obedience.

They that be not of Christ, they care not under whose banner they be: so the avarice[4] mind and detestable love of the world be satisfied, it is good enough to them, with yea forsooth, and nay forsooth, as inconstant as the wind: like unto the bishops' laws in England, that ten times hath been changed, sithens[5] I knew the right hand from the left; and yet were they proclaimed as most certain and infallible

[1 Κοινωνία: communion.]
[2 Prest: not dilatory. Johnson.]
[3 Spleyde: displayed.]
[4 Avarice: avaricious.]
[5 Sithens: since.]

verities, with great penalty, as much as life was[6] worth. But what man will be so made[7] to lead his conscience by such inconstant persons, that hath laws to damn one year and to save another; that that is good and catholic this year, shall be heresy the next year? They be more inconstant than the wind. Our Lord of his mercy amend them, and give them grace to know their offences, and to promote the only word of God, and teach the people thereby to know God and his sacraments!

They would stablish the carnal presence of Christ's body in the sacrament by the words of Christ, John vi.: *Panis quem ego dabo caro mea est, quam ego dabo pro mundi vita.* "The bread that I will give is my flesh, which I will give for the life of the world." They say, that the first part of Christ's words is a promise unto the church, to eat his precious body in the sacrament, *Panis quem ego dabo caro mea est*[8]; and that Christ performed this promise in his last supper, when he made the bread his body: and the rest of the words, *quam ego dabo pro mundi vita*[9], is a promise that his body should be slain for the redemption of the world. Thus they interpretate the words of Christ, because *dabo* is twice repeated. "By the first *dabo* he promised his real and corporal body in the sacrament: by the second *dabo* he promised the death of his body." So that they would these words, *Hoc est corpus meum*, should be the fulfilling and deliverance of Christ's promise, John vi.: *Panis quem ego dabo caro mea est*[8]. Read the whole sermon of Christ, John vi., and then thou shalt perceive that this interpretation cannot be admitted.

Christ meant to bring his audience unto the knowledge of faith, that they might be partakers of God's promises through him only; and shewed them that he was the bread of consolation and solace, to satisfy the conscience of every hungry and afflicted person. *Ego sum panis qui de cœlo descendi: siquis ederit de hoc pane, vivet in æternum. Et panis quem ego dabo, caro mea est, quam ego*

[6] Iieue wz. So in the original.]
[7] Made: i. e. forced; unless it should be *mad*.]
[8] The bread that I will give is my flesh.]
[9] Which I will give for the life of the world.]

*dabo pro mundi vita*¹. Now mark the words: "The bread that I shall give is my flesh." He promised to give the bread, by these first words, that was his flesh: but how to give it? to be eaten, or to be beaten? to be invisible in the mouth of the apostles, or visible with all opprobrie and contempt before his judges? to be lift up over the priest's head, and there sacrificed, or else upon the cross to sacrifice himself? Christ, that always promiseth, with the thing promised, how the thing promised may be received and used, prescribeth the manner how, and after what sort, he would give his flesh unto the world: *Quam dabo pro mundi vita,* "I will give it for the life of the world." His body, rent and torn upon the cross, was the form and manner how he would give it for the life of the world: not to be in the sacrament, but to die upon the cross, as this relative *quam* declareth, *quam ego dabo pro mundi vita.* The same flesh that he spake of in the first part of the sentence, *Panis, quem ego dabo, caro mea,* of the same he speaketh in the second part, *quam dabo pro mundi vita.* And as the one part of the sentence speaketh of his body to be slain, and not eaten, so doth the other. This may be proved by Christ's words in the same place; for he speaketh of his body that should give life unto the world², which only is by the body slain, and not eaten, as Paul saith, Rom. vi., Heb. ix. and x.

Rom. vi.
Heb. ix. & x.

John vi.

As for the sacramental eating, where as Christ's institution is truly observed, there is nothing but a memory of this death, whereof Christ altogether spake in the sixth of John, and intepretateth many times in that place this word "eat" for "believe": *Qui confidit, inquit, mihi, habet vitam æternam*³. Neither the repetition of this word, *dabo,* is none other thing than accustomed repetition of one and the same thing by more express words. It is no marvel that people, for lack of knowledge and the Holy Spirit of God, so obstinately defend the carnal and bodily eating of

[¹ I am the living bread which came down from heaven: if any man eat of this bread he shall live for ever: and the bread that I will give is my flesh, which I will give for the life of the world. John vi. 51.]

[² Shuld yeue lyue un to the worold, in the original.]

[³ He that believeth (saith he) on me hath eternal life. John vi. 47.]

the body; for Christ, with all his words, could not bring his carnal audience to a spiritual understanding, as he meant.

These words, *Hoc est corpus meum, et, Panis quem frangimus, nonne communicatio corporis Christi est? et, Panis quem ego dabo pro mundi vita*[4], must be taken as Christ meant them, and as they may best agree with the other places of the scripture. Wonderful detriment should our faith take, if these words should not be taken with convenient tropes and figures. Without a trope, lo! what should follow? Christ's body to be *pantotopon*[5]. Christ must have so great a body as might fill heaven and earth, if it be corporally present both in heaven and in earth. Also, it were in vain to look for him at the day of judgment, or to complain that the spouse is taken away from us. For, as they say, they have him sure enough in the pix, and will have till the world's end. If it be true, I will say no more, *Inde venturus judicare vivos et mortuos*[6]. It needeth not to believe that he shall come from heaven to judge the quick and dead, but to believe that he shall come out of the pix that hangeth at every altar, now here invisible, and then shall be sensible. But how can this learning agree with the scripture, that saith, *Videte et palpate, quia spiritus carnem et ossa non habet, quæ me videtis habere*[7]? Luke xxiv.   Luke xxiv.

How doth this learning that saith Christ's body to be every where, agree with the words of the angels, *Surrexit, non est hic, venite et videte locum*[8], &c.? Matth. xxviii. Matt. xxviii. *Pauperes habebitis vobiscum, me non habebitis*[9]. Understand the words, *Hoc est corpus meum*, without a trope, and there shall follow such contradiction in the scripture as may not be admitted. Better it is to understand one place by many, than many should be made false by the mistaking of one. They would agree these places with *invisibi-*

[4 This is my body. And, The bread which we break, is it not the communion of the body of Christ? And, The bread which I will give for the life of the world.]

[5 Παντότοπον: in every place.]

[6 From thence he shall come to judge the quick and the dead.]

[7 Handle me and see: for a spirit hath not flesh and bones as ye see me have.]

[8 He is not here; for he is risen......come see the place, &c.]

[9 Ye shall have the poor with you, but me ye shall not have. Matt. xxvi. 11.]

liter[1] and *modo cœlesti*[2], to say that Christ's very natural body is here, but insensible, and doth occupy no place, although it be as very natural and true a body as man's body is, except sin and immortality. *Sed hoc dicere facilius est quam docere:* "It is not sufficient to say, but to prove that they say." This argument cannot be denied in Aristotle's school: *Corpus est finitum, ergo est in loco*[3]. If Christ have a true body, it must occupy place. In the sacrament it occupieth no place: then it followeth, it is not there.

Other probation have they none, but only the sound of these words, *Hoc est corpus meum.* The meaning of the words be against them. A man may not take the letter without the sense, in a matter of weight. Cicero, the ethnic, so willeth: *Semper autem in fide quid senseris, non quid dixeris cogitandum*[4], 1 Lib. Offic. Because we should never be troubled with these glosses, "invisible," "insensible," and "miraculousment," he caused his immortal and glorified flesh to be sensible, touched and tried by the fingers of Thomas, John xx. As for the words of Paul, *ad* Ephes. iv., Philip. ii., that seem to shew Christ's body now glorified to occupy no place, I refer it to the judgment and faith of the christian reader, whether[5] Paul meant any such doctrine or not: *Qui descendit, idem ille est qui etiam ascendit supra omnes cœlos, ut impleret omnia*[6]. The authors of this doctrine doth allege the text in a wrong sense: for the scripture in many other places doth confess Christ to be ascended into heavens; therefore, it is very like that Paul would not set him out of heaven. But rather by these words, "he ascended above all heavens", he would amplify the unspeakable joy of those glories that his most precious body possesseth; the which in the earth was debased and abjected unto most vile ignominy and contempt. So Paul declareth these two contraries, most vile in the earth, mortal, most glorious in heaven, immortal. *Illud ascendit, quid est, nisi etiam quod descendat prius in infimas partes terræ? Et addit,*

[[1] Invisibly.]   [[2] After a celestial manner.]

[[3] A body is finite, therefore it occupies space. See Aristotelis Physicorum, Lib. iv. cap. i.]

[[4] But in keeping faith, the meaning and not the words are ever to be regarded. Cic. de Offic. Lib. i. cap. xiii.]

[[5] Where, in the original.]

[[6] He that descended is the same also that ascended up far above all heavens, that he might fill all things.]

Qui descendit idem ille est qui ascendit supra omnes cœlos[7]. Paul doth weigh these two propositions, and setteth one against the other, *In infimas partes terræ descendere, et supra omnes cœlos ascendere*[8]. And he that will gather by these words of Paul such an argument, "Christ ascended above all heavens, therefore he is in no place, for out of heaven is no place," then may likewise gather of the other words this argument, *Christus in infimas partes terræ descendit; ergo nullum locum habuit in terra*[9].

But Paul, christian reader, meant no such subtleties in this place. His holy intention was to declare both his unspeakable contempt, that he had in this world, and also his most glorious joy and honour, that now the body hath in heaven; and doth interpretate himself, *ad* Philip. ii., *Quapropter et Deus illum in summam extulit sublimitatem*, &c.[10] My faith is, that his blessed body is in heaven, and doth abide still in heaven, and not out of heaven. Christ said, *Ubi ego sum, ibi erit et minister meus. Erimus autem in cœlis, non extra cœlos, aut supra cœlos, extra omnem scilicet locum*, i. [e.] *nullibi*[11]. Paul saith, *Nostra conversatio in cœlis est, ex quo exspectamus et Salvatorem*[12]: and doth likewise the same, 2 Cor. v. This is a true faith which I believe.

Phil. ii.

2 Cor. v.

And whereas they call Christ's body a thing celestial and divine; true, it is immortal, and delivered from all mortal qualities, according to Paul's words, Rom. vi., *Vivit Deo, et ultra non morietur*[13]. What can be inferred hereof? The fruit of the blessed Virgin hath not lost his humanity,

Rom. vi.

[7 Now that he ascended, what is it but that he also descended first into the lower parts of the earth? And he addeth, He that descended is the same also, &c. Eph. iv. 9, 10.]

[8 To descend into the lower parts of the earth, and to ascend above all heavens.]

[9 Christ descended into the lower parts of the earth; therefore had he no place in the earth.]

[10 Wherefore God also hath highly exalted him, &c.]

[11 Where I am there shall also my servant be. (John xii. 26.) But we shall be in heaven, not out of heaven, or above heaven, that is to say, out of all space, that is, no where.]

[12 Our conversation is in heaven, from whence also we look for the Saviour. Phil. iii. 20.]

[13 He liveth unto God, and shall not die any more.]

but in heaven his body is as very true flesh and blood, as it was hanging upon the cross; immortal, and yet very man; and so in this manhood sitteth at the right hand of God.

Seleuciani[1] did deny that Christ in his flesh did sit at the right hand of God; but the Christians believe the scripture. It is the nature of a contentious, arrogant, and proud heart to take out of the scripture some such propositions as sound for their purpose, to defend a wrong opinion, though the meaning make nothing at all of their part. And then they have none other word in their mouth, but the holy word of God, the plain and manifest text. "The Holy Ghost is the best orator of all, no man can speak more plain than he: he has the most apt and convenient words to express his mind withal." And when his wrong-conceived opinion must be defended, he setteth the words of the scripture in the forefront against his contrary; he cleaveth fast unto the letter, will admit no interpretation but as he pleaseth, no collation of places; he careth not whether it agree with other places, so the word sound for his purpose: which hath been the destruction of many famous and excellent clerks, as I shall repeat the names of a few, to school the christian reader in the fear of God; for it is not learning nor wit, that preserveth the faith of a christian man, but God's singular graces, which must be daily prayed for, that by affection he embrace none opinion, what men soever he is fantasied[2] unto, but say with David, *Turris fortitudinis nomen Dei*[3].

Anthropomorphitæ[4] said that God, that made man, was like unto mortal man; and took occasion to err by these words, Gen. i., *Faciamus hominem in imagine nostra, secundum similitudinem nostram*[5]. And doubtless the words, without a trope, sound even so; but the excellent divines, that knoweth

Gen. i.

[1 Seleuciani: the Seleucian Hermianists, who (after Hermias) adopted the errors of Hermogenes, applying stoicism to Christianity. See Tertullian and Origen.]

[2 Fantasied: inclined.]

[3 The name of the Lord is a strong tower. Prov. xviii. 10.]

[4 Anthropomorphitæ. Called by Epiphanius Audiani, from Audius, a heretic of the 4th century, and by St Augustine, Vadiani. Rutherius, Bishop of Verona, in the 10th century, wrote powerfully against this revived heresy. See D'Acheri's Spicilegium.]

[5 Let us make man in our image after our likeness.]

by the scripture what God is and what man is, will straightway perceive that there is a *tropote*⁶, and by the whole understand the part, to say, the soul of man.

Confer not the words of Moses, Deut. xxxi., with the other places of the scripture, *Pono ante te bonum et vitam, benedictionem et maledictionem: elige vitam, ut vivas,* &c.⁷, and then were the Pelagians' doctrine true. Deut. xxxi.

*Chiliastæ*⁸, by these words of Christ, "I will not drink of this wine from henceforth, till I drink it new in my Father's kingdom," said that we should eat and drink after this life in heaven.

*Sabelliani*⁹ said that God the Father suffered in the flesh as well as Christ, and took occasion by these words and like, *Ego et Pater unum sumus. Ego in Patre et Pater in me*¹⁰.

*Hebionitæ*¹¹ said Christ was only man, and not God, as the Jews at this present doth, by these words, *Deus meus, Deus meus, ut quid dereliquisti me?*¹²

*Helvidius*¹³, by the words of the scripture ill taken, conceived a wrong opinion of the blessed virgin Mary, and said she was mother of more children than one.

St Augustine¹⁴, *lib.* 21, *De Civitate Dei, cap.* xxv., writeth of a sort of heretics, that said, whosoever once received the sacrament of Christ's supper, could never be damned; and defended their opinion with these words, *Ego sum panis vivus qui de cœlo descendi: si quis comederit ex hoc pane, vivet in æternum*¹⁵.

[⁶ Tropote: trope, a figure of speech.]

[⁷ I have set before thee life and good, blessing and cursing: choose life, that thou mayest live, &c.]

[⁸ Chiliastæ: Millenarians. See Eusebius, Eccles. Hist. Lib. vii. cap. xxiv. p. 271. 1672. See also L'Eucharistie de l'ancienne Eglise, par Edm. Aubertin, Genevæ, 1633. p. 338.]

[⁹ Sabellius. See Wormii Hist. Sabell.]

[¹⁰ I and my Father are one. John x. 30. I in the Father, and the Father in me. John xiv. 11.]

[¹¹ Ebionites. See Epiphanius, Hæres. xxx. and Eusebius, Eccles. Hist. Lib. iii. cap. xxvii.]

[¹² My God, my God, why hast thou forsaken me? Matt. xxvii. 46.]

[¹³ Helvidius, an Arian of the 4th century, a disciple of Auxentius. Jerome wrote against him.]

[¹⁴ August. Op. Basiliæ, 1543, Tom. v. col. 1310, &c.]

[¹⁵ I am the living bread which came down from heaven: if any man eat of this bread, he shall live for ever. John vi. 51.]

Arius and Marcion, with many great learned men, defended most detestable heresies by the mistaking of the scripture: therefore no faith ought to be given unto the interpreter, that rather intendeth to stablish an error and false opinion, than to confer place with place, that no contradiction be found in the scripture, nor any violation of our catholic faith.

St Augustine[1], Lib. III. *De Doctrina Christiana*, teacheth a godly way to understand the scripture: he that will follow his counsel, shall not lightly err in expounding the scripture. He sheweth there, when the words may be taken, and when they may not be taken, without a trope. But, the more to be lamented, such is now the condition of all men deceived in religion, for the most part, they will rather run still the wrong race they have begun, than godly to return unto the truth: they will not repent, lest they should seem to have erred; such is the state and condition of our miserable nature. Where as there lacketh probation of the thing that should be proved, they tarry in the letter ill understood, and turneth themselves *ad petitionem principii*[2]. Ask how they prove, and why they make an alteration of the bread, and what place of the scripture proveth their proposition? They flee unto the text, *Hoc est corpus meum*. And for the probation of the proposition, they allege the proposition itself. *Hoc est corpus meum*, is the proposition whereupon all this disputation and contention dependeth.

They must prove by other places of the scripture, that those words alter the substance of the bread; what union is between the body of Christ and the bread; and how this union is made, and where the scripture proveth the Son of God to come into the world to be bread, and how he cometh, and what

[1 Nam in principio cavendum est, ne figuratam locutionem ad literam accipias............

Si præceptiva locutio est, aut flagitium aut facinus vetans, aut utilitatem aut beneficentiam jubens, non est figurata. Si autem flagitium aut facinus videtur jubere, aut utilitatem aut beneficentiam vetare, figurata est. Nisi manducaveritis, inquit, carnem Filii hominis, et sanguinem biberitis, non habebitis vitam in vobis; facinus vel flagitium videtur jubere. Figura est ergo, præcipiens passioni Domini esse communicandum, et suaviter atque utiliter recondendum in memoria, quod pro nobis caro ejus crucifixa et vulnerata sit. Aug. Op. Basiliæ, 1542, Tom. III. De doctr. Christiana, Lib. III. col. 43 and 53.]

[2 Begging the question.]

profit his body, made of bread, bringeth into the world; and whether any of the prophets ever prophesied of such a coming of God's Son into the world. Shew the scripture that proveth this proposition, *Hoc est corpus meum*, to have such a sense as ye say, that the conscience of those that ye would have believe this your doctrine, may repose herself in truth and verity of God's word; or else, no man will believe your doctrine. If Paul had no better fenced this general proposition to the Romans, *Arbitramur igitur hominem justificari per fidem absque operibus legis*[3], than still to have repeated the proposition, there would neither Jew, neither Gentile, believed his word: but he confirmeth the proposition, and disputeth the matter so *pro* and *contra*, that he confuteth all the arguments that seem to repugn his purpose.

These men that would have the bread to be turned into God and man, hath none other word, but still, like the cock, cry, *Hoc est corpus meum*, and will hear none other lay but, "This is my body." So may a man, after the same sort, prove our Lady to be John the evangelist' mother, and say always, whatsoever text of the scripture be brought against him, as Christ said, John xix., *Ecce* John xix. *mater tua!*[4] "Say what ye list, these words be true. Christ spake them; they be plain; they need no interpretation." If any man ask a reason and confirmation of the proposition, he may say still, *Ecce mater tua*[4]. "Ye must make no reason how it may be: it sufficeth to have the word of God, the manifest text; reason shall not melle[5] with the matter; it is a matter of faith." And after this sort a man may likewise prove John the baptist to be the person of Elias. Is not this a marvellous manner of reasoning?

When they be asked to prove the proposition, they repeat the proposition that is disputable, and so false as they take it, that the extreme contrary is true, as the scripture proveth, and calleth the signs of the most divine and sacrate supper of the Lord bread and wine, 1 Corin. 1 Cor. x. xi. x. and xi. "Whosoever eateth of this bread unworthily, shall be culpable of the body of Christ." These words be

[3 Therefore, we conclude that a man is justified by faith without the deeds of the law. Rom. iii. 28.]

[4 Behold thy mother!]   [5 Melle: meddle.]

more plain to prove the bread to remain after the words, as they call them, of the consecration, than *Hoc est corpus meum* are to make a metamorphosis of the bread. Now, if it be "the devil's sophistry," as my lord calleth it, to believe, with the authority of the scripture, with the judgment of reason, and by the consent and agreement of the senses, that bread is bread, and that God changeth not the just, true, and very body of his immaculate and glorious Son in so little a room as two inches of bread, then is the scripture the devil's sophistry, which teacheth to believe that Christ's body is in heaven, and bread in the sacrament: Acts i. iii. Matt. xvi. 1 Cor. x. xi. This doctrine only hurteth not[1] the faith of man, but also dishonoureth the dignity of man's creation; whereas it was given him to be lord of all the other creatures that God made, Gen. ii., and more to avail in reason. Now, by the malice of man, this order of God is perverted; and that that the birds of the air, beasts of the earth, and fishes of the water, know to be a creature, man maketh it his god, and proveth himself thereby to be inferior unto all other creatures, which is no small offence; the image of God in man not to know as much in a sensible piece of bread, as the beasts, unto whom God gave only the judgment of senses unto.

Then hath they another defence for this wrong opinion of the sacrament. They say it is done by miracle, that the body of Christ is present. Doubtless, if I saw the body present, and the thing done indeed, I would confess the same, and that it were a great miracle, to call Christ's most blessed body from heaven with a word. But now herein consisteth this whole matter: miracles of God be open, and the effect of the miracle so maketh manifest the miracle, that reason is contented[2] that God should do his pleasure, whatsoever reason would attempt to the contrary. As for an example: the blessed Virgin, when she heard the message of God by the angel, that she should bear a child in her virginity, it passed the capacity of her intendment; and though reason knew not how it might be, yet sought reason to know the means how it should be, and said,

[¹ Only hurteth not: not only hurteth.]
[² that reason is contendyth, in the original.]

Quomodo fiat istud?[3] When she was assured that it should be by no man, but by the Holy Ghost, she let fall reason, and believed the words of God. And as she in faith conceived by the Holy Ghost the Son of God, wonderfully above the reach of reason; so the Son of God, made man in the belly of that blessed virgin, naturally there increased for the space of certain months, and declared unto reason the fact that was done against reason; so that reason could not deny but that the blessed Virgin was with child, and had testimony thereof by the mother of John Baptist. *Unde hoc mihi, ut veniat mater Domini mei ad me?*[4] Luke i. With such a godly greeting as is comfortable for every Christian, this miracle was shewed afterward unto all the world by the acts that Christ did, which proved himself to be the Son of God. Luke i.

Now, mark, although man cannot comprehend which ways a miracle is done by reason, yet must the miracle be perceived and known by reason. Though the leper, Matt. viii., could not know by reason how he was healed suddenly of his disease, yet perceived he right well the effect of this miracle. The apostles of Christ, that knew not how so great a number of people, five thousand, beside women and children, should be fed with five loaves and two fishes, Matt. xiv., Mar. vi., Luc. ix., John vi. the miracle that passed their reason was shewed, not only to their reason, but also unto their senses. So all the world, that was made of nothing, against reason, by miracle, is declared manifest unto reason and senses, as we see at this day. Now, if they would prove Christ's body by miracle to be present, very God and man in the sacrament, though reason cannot comprehend how it may be, yet let them shew unto reason and unto the senses, that it is so; then men will believe it, and not before. Let them shew me any miracle that God did upon the earth, like unto their invisible miracle. All the world seeth the bread remain, and no body of Christ present; yet, say they, it is there. Is God so much the enemy of man, to give him his senses to his destruction? No. He hath of his abundant mercy given them to discern white from black, sour from sweet, chalk Matt. viii. Matt. xiv. Mar. vi. Luke ix. John vi.

[3 How shall this be? Luke i. 24.]
[4 Whence is this to me, that the mother of my Lord should come to me?]

from cheese¹, the glorious body of Christ from the sign of a sacrament, which is bread. Their miracle in the transubstacion² of bread is as much a miracle as the miracle of him that saith, he will make whole a man's blind eye, and yet the blind man seeth nothing the better. God useth no such blind miracles, but made every thing for man marvellously, because man should honour him in his works, according to our faith³: *Credo in Deum Patrem Omnipotentem, Creatorem cœli et terræ*⁴. It agreeth as well to make the body of Christ present in the sacrament, without his corporal qualities, as to make a great fire without heat.

Another gloss is there, which Eckius useth, to defend the alteration of bread withal, and saith, though Paul call the body of Christ bread, yet it is no bread indeed, but the very body of Christ⁵; and attempteth to prove his saying, by the rod that Moses used in Egypt before Pharao. When the rod was turned into a serpent, yet was the serpent called still a rod. This simile proveth nothing; for when the text saith, *Sed devoravit virga Aharon virgas illorum*⁶, Exod. vii., there remained nor form nor figure of a rod, but of a very horrible and fearful serpent. If this place serve to prove the alteration of bread into the natural body of Christ, let them shew me the form of bread changed into as natural a man, as the rod was changed into a natural serpent; and then I am content. I will not dispute of the name so greatly, though

[Marginal note: Exod. vii.]

[¹ yeuen them to decern, whit from blak, so warefrom swet chalke from chese, in the original.]

[² transubstacion: transubstantiation.]

[³ Our faith: our creed.]

[⁴ I believe in God the Father Almighty, Maker of heaven and earth.]

[⁵ Quæras autem, si non manet in sacramento substantia panis, cur tandem evangelistæ panem appellant? * * * * Quod autem Paulus et Lucas adhuc panem nominant, faciunt id sane more sacrarum literarum, quæ rem aliquam non semper appellant id quod jam est, sed quod ante fuit. Sic conversa jam virga Moysi in serpentem, similiter et virgis maleficorum mutatis in dracones, virga Aaron devoravit virgas maleficorum, ubi scriptura serpentem virgam vocat, eo quod antea serpens fuerat. Paulus etiam sacramentum hoc propter speciem vocavit panem, quoniam adhuc post consecrationem speciem habet et omnia accidentia panis. Eckii Op. Parisiis. 1549. Tom. IV. Hom. 31. De Transubstanti. folio 93.]

[⁶ But Aaron's rod swallowed up their rods.]

they called flesh and blood bread; but they must make demonstration of Christ's body unto the external senses, as Moses made of the serpent unto the Egyptians. When God called our first father Adam, because he was created of the earth, and Adam said by his wife, "Behold, a bone of mine bones," Gen. ii., there was neither Adam that had the form of earth, nor Eve the form of a bone. The one was a man, and the other a woman: howbeit, they kept still the name of the thing they were created of. Change the form of bread in the sacrament, and make thereof the form of a man: then these places will suffer the manner of speech right well, that a man may be called bread, if he be made of bread, as well as a serpent called a rod, because he was made of a rod. But forasmuch as there is no form of the bread changed in the sacrament; believe, with the evangelists and apostles, that it is in matter and substance very bread, how it [is] appointed to an holy use, to be ministered unto the church of God, in the remembrance of Christ's death, with these words, "Christ took bread and gave it to his disciples." Matt. xxvi. Luke xxii. 1 Cor. x. xi. These men agree with themselves in the Spirit of God, and teacheth a certain doctrine. Those that defend these masses and transubstantiation agreeth not with themselves, and hath nothing certain[7]. The one saith the thing that corrupted is nothing but accidents, the other saith that it is the very substance of bread. Read the book of Innocent III., *De Officio Missæ*[8], where as be these words: *Quod sicut miraculose substantia panis vertitur in corpus Christi, remanentibus accidentibus panis, ita miraculose redire substantia prioris panis possit, de qua generetur vel vermis vel quid aliud tale*[9]. Into what substance the water mingled in the cha-

Gen. ii.

Matt. xxvi.
Luke xxii.
1 Cor. x. xi.

[7 See Magister Sentent. Lib. IV. Distin. xi. and xii. Duns Scotus Lib. IV. Distin. xi. Quæst. 2.]

[8 The following passage appears to be that referred to: Si vero quæratur quid a mure comeditur cum sacramentum corroditur, vel quid incineratur cum sacramentum crematur; respondetur, quod sicut miraculose substantia panis convertitur in corpus dominicum, cum incipit esse sub sacramento, sic quodammodo miraculose revertitur cum ipsum ibi desinit esse, &c. Innoc. III. Coloniæ. 1575. Tom. I. p. 480. Myst. Missæ. Lib. IV. cap. xi. See also cap. ix.]

[9 For as by miracle the substance of bread is changed into the body of Christ, the accidents of bread remaining; so by miracle the substance of the former bread may return, from which are generated worms or the like.]

lice with the wine is turned, see the mind of Clement in the third book of the Decretals. It is turned, say he, into phlegm[1]. God of his mercy deliver his church from such doctrine!

Yet have they another reason wherewith they deceive themselves withal and other. "The power of God, that can do all things." And of these most holy words they frame many a false conclusion. Because God can do all things, therefore I must believe that the bread in the sacrament is turned into the body of Christ. I would believe it, were it not against his word. Now against his word he will do nothing, as full christianly saith Tertullian against Marcion: *Posse Deum, nihil aliud est quam velle; et e contrario non posse, idem esse in Deo quod nolle*[2].

It is the office of a Christian to know what God can do by the word of God, and not to be curious to search what his absolute power is. He could save the damned souls in hell, but he will not: it were against his word: *Non remittetur in hoc sæculo, neque in futuro*[3]. He could have saved Adam and all his posterity, otherwise than by the death of his only Son: for Augustine saith, Lib. IV. *De Trinitate, Mors Christi non fuit necessitatis, sed suæ voluntatis et potestatis*[4]: but he would not. By the cruelty of his death he would have us to know how horrible a thing sin is before the face of God, and thereby teach us to beware how we fall into his displeasure. But we be trunks, and in manner insensible: nothing moveth us to virtue. He is more curious than wise, to search to know the thing that apperteineth not unto him to know. It is the next

[1] Innocent III. condemned this opinion and said: Illud fuisse nefarium opinari...in sacramento videlicet Eucharistiæ aquam in phlegma converti. Corp. Jur. Can. Decretal. Greg. IX. Lib. III. Tit. 41. c. 8.]

[2] That God *can*, is nothing else than that he *will;* and on the contrary, that he *cannot*, is the same with God as that he *will not.* Tertullian's words are: Dei enim posse, velle est; et non posse, nolle. Tertul. Op. adv. Praxeam. p. 320. A. Par. 1530. See also Lombardus, Lib. I. Distinc. 42 and 43.]

[3] It shall not be forgiven him, neither in this world, neither in the world to come. Matt. xii. 32.]

[4] The death of Christ was not of necessity, but of his own will and power. These do not appear to be Augustine's words, but they convey his sentiments as expressed in his 13th chapter. August. Op. Basiliæ, 1543. Vol. III. De Trin. Lib. IV. co. 503.]

way, not only to bring a man out of the favour of God, but also out of his wit; for he that searcheth to know above the reach of a mortal man, shall be confounded with [the] immortal glory of God. Let no christian heart therefore trouble itself with this question, What God can do; but like a diligent scholar learn his lesson in the scripture, What he is bound to do. For the scripture was wroten to lead us unto God, and unto repentance of ill. It was wroten to teach us God and all godliness, and not to move such questions as engendereth nor faith nor virtue, but contention and discord, and words without end. It was wroten to be judge of all men's doctrine, and to save those that Christ redeemed with his precious blood from all heresies and false opinions. Therein is contained all truth and verity. And better was it with the church of God, when it was only taught and instructed by it, than after that any man's decrees were brought into the church. Man's wisdom giveth as much light unto the word of God, as a little candle giveth unto the bright sun in the mid-day.

Yet condemn I not the holy fathers, that hath wrote so much in the defence of Christ's religion; but give God thanks, that he hath such organs upon the earth, that would rather die, than to see the name of God and his holy word to be contemned of the world. And a notable thing is it to mark the godly fathers in their works, where as in the defence of the truth they allege not only the scripture, but also the testimony and example of the primitive church; not to stablish their faith, because it was so used of antiquity, but because they saw their elders use the word of God in the same senses that they did: as Epiphanius[5] writeth of one Peter, bishop of Alexandria, whom the tyrant Maximinus put to death. In this Peter's time there was one Meletius[6] that sowed a false doctrine, and said that every sin committed was irremissible, as the Novatians[7] and Catharenes say: this doctrine so prevailed, that the greater part of the people in Egypt and Syria believed it.

[[5] Epiphanii Opera, Coloniæ, 1682. Lib. II. Tom. II. cap. 68. p. 719.]
[[6] Meletius or Melitius, bishop of Lycopolis, in Egypt, in the 4th century. Hooper adopts Epiphanius' account (see above), which differs greatly from that of Athanasius, and Socrates, and Theodoret.]
[[7] Euseb. Eccles. Hist. Lib. VI. cap. 43, p. 241, &c.]

Peter resisted, not only by the scripture, but also, that the disciples of the apostles condemned this doctrine for an heresy. The like may ye read in the history of John the Apostle, *apud Euseb.* Lib. III. p. 60[1].

As Christ is true, and his word true, so hath there been always in the church such as hath followed the truth; and in that they have wroten truly we are greatly edified, to see that they and we agree in one faith, and understand the scripture alike, and use the sacraments as they did according to [the] institution of Christ. If any error be in their writings, we may leave it by the authority of the scripture, and offend nothing at all. They wrote, not to be judges of the scripture, but to be judged by the scripture.

Were it not to satisfy the weak conscience of those that yet be ignorant of the truth, I would not, in this matter of the sacrament, rehearse the mind of one doctor, because we may so fully and plainly know by the only scripture, what the supper is, and how it should be used; and think that such as hath wroten of late days to be the first authors of this doctrine, that the holy supper of the Lord should be a communion, and no private mass, or receiving of the sacrament by one man; no, though danger of death seem to require the same. If such as be sick will needs receive the sacrament, let them receive it as Christ hath instituted it, with such other as shall be present at the declaration of his faith; but alone no man may receive it, though his faith be never so good, and the minister never so godly. Howbeit, both the scripture and likewise the law civil doth rather improve[2] the act, than allow the doing of it. In this supper we should follow Christ and the apostles: their doings was absolute and perfect[3]. No man for a good intention, beside the word of God, should add any thing to the doing of this supper, or take any thing from it. We read not that they celebrated the supper in any private house for any sick person. The words of James

[1] Euseb. Eccles. Hist. Moguntiæ, 1672, Lib. III. cap. 23. Narratio de Joanne Apost. p. 91. This reference is to the well known history of St John pursuing and reclaiming a young Christian, who had fallen into gross sin, and become leader of a band of robbers.]
[2] Improve: disapprove of.]
[3] Perfeyth, in the original.]

seem to defend this religion, chap. v. *Infirmatur aliquis* James v. *inter vos? accersat presbyteros ecclesiæ, et orent super eum*[4], &c. Unto these sick people that he speaketh of, he would likewise have commanded the bread of the holy supper to have been brought, had it been the manner in the apostle's time. St Paul with many words declareth that this supper, whensoever it be celebrated, should be done with solemnity in the church: *Cum convenitis in ecclesia, inquit, audio dissidia esse*[5], &c. Again: *Igitur, cum convenitis in eundem locum, non licet Dominicam cœnam edere*[6]. 3. *Num sane domos habetis ad edendum et bibendum*[7]? 4. *Itaque fratres, cum convenitis ad edendum, alius aliud expectet; quod si qui esurit, domi edat*[8].

It shall not be prejudicial, nor nothing derogate the honour of the blessed sacrament, though it never be celebrated in a private house; nor he that abstaineth from the receiving of it out of the congregation, nothing the worse christian man. In time past it was sufficient for the people to celebrate openly this holy supper, and was not used to be brought unto the sick. Justinianus Imperator, *Constitu.* 57[9]. unto the archbishop of Constantinople, Meme[10], hath these words: Etiam [*Et*] *priscis sancitum est* legitur [*legibus*] *nulli penitus esse licentiam domi quæ sacratissima sunt agere, sed publice*[11], &c. And in the same place: *Omnibus* [*enim*] *interdicimus magnæ hujus civitatis habitatoribus, magis autem totius nostræ ditionis, in domibus suis habere quasdam quasi orationum domus, et in his sacra celebrare mysteria, et hinc*

[4 Is any sick among you? Let him call for the elders of the church; and let them pray over him, &c.]

[5 When ye come together in the church (saith he), I hear that there be divisions, &c. 1 Cor. xi. 18.]

[6 When ye come together, therefore, into one place, ye cannot eat the Lord's supper. 1 Cor. xi. 20. Marginal reading.]

[7 Have ye not houses to eat and to drink in? 1 Cor. xi. 22.]

[8 Wherefore, my brethren, when ye come together to eat, tarry one for another; and if any man hunger, let him eat at home. 1 Cor. xi. 33, 34.]

[9 Novellarum Constit. Justin. Paris. 1562, folio 114. (2).]

[10 Menna.]

[11 It was also ordained by ancient laws that no one should be at liberty to perform the most sacred rites in their own houses, but publicly, &c.]

fieri quædam extranea, catholicæ et apostolicæ traditioni contraria. Sed siquidem domos [*ita*] *simpliciter aliqui habere putant oportere, in sacris suis, orationis solius videlicet gratia, et nullo celebrando penitus horum quæ sacri sunt mysterii, id eis permittimus*[1]. This godly emperor reigned anno Domini 500, whereby it appeareth it was not the manner of those days to celebrate the supper nowhere but in the congregation openly, as the pesah[2] was commanded to be done: never part of the lamb brought unto the sick man, but eaten in their congregations, as ye read, Exod. xii. Num. ix. Whereas, Eusebius, Lib. vi. cap. 34, Eccles. Hist.[3] writeth of one or two to whom the bread was ministered in their private houses, it was done upon a singular consideration. The persons that received this sacrament in their private houses were before excommunicated by the authority of God's word, and before their reconciliation fell into this danger of death by sickness. The deacon was commanded to minister the bread unto them, that in the receiving thereof they might declare their true penitence unto the church, and die in the promises of God, that desireth not the death of sinners. In the time of Cyprian, it was used to give the bread of the supper unto children[4]. If

Exod. xii.
Numb. ix.

[[1] For we forbid all the inhabitants of this great city, or rather of our whole empire, to have in their own houses certain kinds of oratories, in which to celebrate sacred mysteries which might hence become foreign, and opposed to the catholic and apostolic tradition. But if, indeed, some think that their houses ought to have these among their holy things, solely for the purpose of prayer, and never therein to celebrate any of those things which belong to the sacred mysteries—that we allow to them.]

[[2] Pesah: The Passover.]

[[3] Old edition, Ecclesiastes. But the reference appears to be wrong. The case referred to is probably that of Serapion, mentioned by Eusebius, Lib. vi. cap. 44. Eccles. Hist. Moguntiæ, 1672, p. 246.]

[[4] Amiserunt parvuli, quod in primo statim nativitatis exordio fuerant consequuti. Nonne illi cum judicii dies venerit, dicent, Nos nihil fecimus, nec derelicto cibo et poculo Dei ad profana contagia sponte properavimus; perdidit nos aliena perfidia, parentes sensimus parricidas? Cypriani Op. Lugd. 1550. Tom. i. De Lapsis, p. 389.

Ubi vero solennibus adimpletis calicem diaconus offerre præsentibus cœpit, et accipientibus ceteris locus ejus advenit, faciem suam parvula instinctu divinæ majestatis avertere, os labiis obturantibus premere, calicem recusare. Perstitit tamen diaconus, et reluctanti licet de sacra-

it were given them as a sacrament, it was ill; but I cannot believe it. Grant it were, I will not follow Cyprian, but the institution of Christ. I know that he was but a man, and had his faults, as ye may see by his opinion, where he would such as were christened of heretics to be rebaptized[5].

We should not yet by this authority leave the example of the apostles, except it be in such places where as the common ministry of the church is corrupted, and the sacrament used contrary unto the institution of Christ: there every man may in his private chamber, with his christian and faithful brothers, communicate according unto the order of the scripture, as we see, Acts ii. xx., how the apostles did when the Pharisees and priests of the temple contemned Christ and his ministry, as well of the sacraments as of the preaching of the gospel. Where as the faithful may receive openly the sacrament, it sufficeth them; it is not need to have it brought unto the sick man's bed: for the doing thereof hath done hurt in the church of God, caused many times the poor sick man to put his hope and confidence in the external fact and receiving of the sacrament, and thought himself never sufficiently prepared to death, but when he had received this external sign. And thus was the abuse of the blessed sacrament. *Acts ii. xx.*

Men say it is neither commanded neither forbidden by the scripture, that the sick should use the sacrament in their private houses. The words of Paul, *Ego accepi a Domino*[6], &c., with the texts afore rehearsed, sheweth not only how the supper should be celebrated, but also where it should be celebrated. *Sufficiat nobis traditio apostolica*[7]. Let us conform ourselves unto them, as near as we may. Would to the Lord that there were no more ceremonies

mento calicis infudit. Tunc sequitur singultus et vomitus, &c. &c. Hoc circa infantem, quæ ad eloquendum alienum circa se crimen necdum habuit ætatem. Idem, p. 400. See also Aug. Op. Basiliæ, 1542, Tom. II. Ep. ad Bonifac. 23, col. 90, where in the margin we find, Etiam infantibus dabatur Eucharistia.]

[5 Cypriani Op. Ep. 6. ad Magnum, (in qua ostendit nisi quis in ecclesia et ab ecclesia catholica ordinatus fuerit, jus vitalis aquæ habere non posse.) Tom. I. p. 73, &c.]

[6 I have received of the Lord, &c. 1 Cor. xi. 23.]

[7 Let apostolical tradition suffice us.]

in the doing of this sacrament, or any other in the church, than the scripture maketh mention of. Then, blessed and fortunate were the poor ignorant people, that now bite and gnaw the bitter bark, and never taste the sweetness contained within these external signs: and no marvel. Their curates be as wise as they. The blind leadeth the blind into ignorancy. Such godly preachers hath their mother, the holy church, appointed to have the charge of those souls that Christ redeemed with his precious blood. Parson and vicar, patron and bishop, shall bewail, doubtless, this horrible sin, to deceive the people of God of his most holy word.

Were the givers of benefices so good unto their tenants, or poor people of the parishes, as they be unto their dogs and horses, it were well: for no man giveth his dog to keep, but unto him that hath skill how to diet him, and to keep him in breath, to maintain his course, to save him. He wax not mange his horse unto him that best can skill to handle him[1], as well in the stable as in the field. Every thing in the world is better provided for than the soul of man. Good mariners for the ship, politic men for the commonwealth, an expert physician for the body, a pleasant cook for the mouth, a well-practised captain for the war. None in any affairs concerning the body shall be admitted unto any office, but apt and convenient persons, the best that may be got. In the church of Christ it is no matter passed of who bear office, though he know no more what appertaineth to the charge that is committed unto him, than the least of his parish. They take great pain to visit the sick, and to minister the sacraments: it were better they never came anear the sick with the sacrament, except they knew better what a sacrament meant, and could shew them God's promises, which are not only sealed, but also openly declared unto the church by the sacraments.

And to make more open that the mass is no ceremony, nor the bread there used no sacrament, of God's, I will declare it unto the christian reader by the scripture, that teacheth us what the sacrament is, and how it must be

[1 To saue hym he wax not mange his horse unto hym that best can skyle to hand ill him, in the original.]

used; that the christian reader, by reason of the abuse, contemn not the thing itself. Though the abuse of sacraments is condemned, yet must we not contemn the sacrament. Though the abuse of prayer be naught, yet prayer as God commandeth is good. Though wine maketh men drunk, yet no man saith wine is naught. Remove, then, the abuse of every thing that is good, and let the thing remain still.

This is the definition of the Lord's supper. It is a ceremony instituted by Christ, to confirm and manifest our society and communion in his body and blood, until he come to judgment. Every word in this definition is in the scripture. That it is a ceremony instituted by Christ, Matthew, Mark, Luke, and Paul testifieth: that it confirmeth the conjunction and society of Christ and his church, these words of Paul proveth: *Quoniam unus panis, unum corpus multi sumus. Nam omnes ex eodem pane participamus*[2]. 1 Cor. x. And that it shall be done till the end of the world, Paul proveth, 1 Cor. xi. *Mortem Domini annunciabitis donec venerit*[3]. 1 Cor. x. 1 Cor. xi.

Now, the manner how it was instituted, and how it must be used in the church, it is wroten by Matthew, Mark, Luke, and Paul, in the places afore rehearsed. And Paul, by name, saith, *Convenientibus vobis*, &c[4]. would the supper of the Lord to be a ceremony of a public and common assemblance, and would in this assemblance the gospel to be preached, God to be called upon in the remembrance and faith of Jesus Christ, with giving God thanks that he would save us by the death of his Son. Therefore it is said, *Hoc facite ad recordationem mei:* "Do it in the remembrance of me." What the supper is, and how it was instituted, we see by the scripture.

Now, of the other part, behold the mass, and bring it to the gospel; then shall thou perceive it is no common ceremony instituted by Christ and his apostles; neither nothing done therein according to the scripture, but every thing contrary unto the scripture. Whereas Paul calleth it a com-

[2 For we being many are one bread and one body, for we are all partakers of that one bread.]

[3 Ye do shew forth the Lord's death till he come.]

[4 When ye come together, &c. 1 Cor. xi. 18.]

munion, and would all the church to receive it under both kinds; they say it is best to be a private mass, and eaten by one priest. Paul willeth the gospel of Christ to be preached unto the congregation: they mumble and dream a sort of collects, and other beggary unto dead saints, as neither profiteth themselves nor other, but blasphemeth God's holy name. Yet, say they, it is a godly thing; whereas God, neither the scripture, never meant such idolatry. It is a ceremony instituted by more bishops than twenty, to the great injury of God's word, and the authors thereof damned eternally, except they repented before they departed out of this world. For they no less deceived the people of God, than the devil in paradise: he was not content to suffer God's commandment as it was given, without a false gloss. Nor these members of the devil would not Christ's church to use Christ's holy supper, as it was given by Christ, without their devilish and detestable additions. Yet, wicked members of antichrist, they must be called the holy church, though all that ever they intend is the pest and destruction of the church, and their religion as contrary to Christ as darkness is to light, and say, if there were not such ceremonies added unto the Lord's supper, as they have in the mass, people should be provoked to no devotion, nor could not religiously honour that most holy sacrament; therefore, say they, is all these ceremonies added. A profound reason, doubtless, as meet for the matter as can be, and as far-fet[1] as he that never wist what a ceremony of Christ's testament is, but as one that never sucked other milk than of a cow that hath calved full many a thousand bulls of lead.

Therefore I will set before the eyes of the christian reader the ceremonies of this holy supper, contained in the scripture, and the signification of the ceremony, not feigned of my brain, but by the express words of the scripture; and so teach the Christian to love the ceremonies there expressed, and to detest the blind ceremonies of men. Christ, the same night that he was betrayed unto the Jews, sat at supper with his twelve apostles, and, among other godly talk, in his sermon unto them he said, that one of them should betray him: Matth. xxvi. Mark xiv. Christ, that knew the hearts of all men, saw the treason that

Matt. xxvi.
Mark xiv.

[1 Far-fet: far-fetched.]

Judas had wrought against him, and knew that he was at a full point with the Jews to deliver him unto them; the matter was fully concluded upon, and money received. This wicked man was not yet so far past, but there remained place of indulgence and forgiveness; or else Christ would never have admonished him so many times. Because God hateth sin, he admonished Judas in time to repent. But, as a wicked person, he contemned all admonitions, desired to finish his traitorous purpose, and after that he had eaten of that holy supper, he departed out of Christ's company, and with all diligence sought how to have his admonitor slain. John, xiii. xiv, declareth more at large Christ's words and facts at this supper. But these words of Matthew and Mark shall admonish the christian reader, what ceremony ought to be used in the church before the use of the sacrament, what the minister should do, and what the rest of the people should do. John xiii. xiv.

The minister's office is to make a solemn sermon, to admonish every man of his duty and office towards God, and to exhort all men unto godly and unfeigned repentance. The people's duty is every one to prove and examine his conscience and faith, and so to eat of the bread and to drink of the wine, as Paul teacheth, 1 Cor. xi.: and so to mark the word of God preached against sin, as though God himself spake it; and remember that when Christ said unto the apostles, that one of them should betray him, all were amazed at the words, and with sorrowful countenance the one beheld the other, with great fear who it should be. They heard a wonderful sin named: every one examined his own conscience, whether it were capable of any such sin or not, and with fear demanded who it should be. 1 Cor. xi.

This act of the apostles declares what every man's office is that cometh to the sermon, where by the word of God sin is accused, to examine his own conscience, and see that no such sin be in him that God condemneth by his word: if he be culpable, to repent from the bottom of his heart, and desire forgiveness. But now-a-days, when sin is rebuked, few men entereth into their own conscience, but rather into other men's; supposeth that the word of God rebuketh the sin of others, and not his; or else he judgeth himself to be no sinner, whereas every man hath abundance and too many, if he knew himself well, and such horrible faults as deserve eternal death. A good conscience will be soon pricked at the name of sin, and be ashamed that he hath offended so mighty a Lord, and afraid also of his judgments, and diligently amend his life. The conscience destitute of God's fear passeth not a deal of the word, is moved neither with fear nor with love, but contemneth both God and his word, as we may see by Judas, not only this sin of obstinacy and contempt of God's admonitions unto penitence, but also very hypocrisy, as reigneth now-a-days all over the world. Men associate themselves into the company of such as fear God, come unto the sermons to hear God's words, and be nothing the better; they amend their life nothing at all. They say it was a good sermon; the man spake well; but what availeth it that he spake well, and the hearer to live ill? What am [I] the better, that God and his word be holy, or another man virtuous, except I transform mine ill life unto the commandment of God, and live honestly? Nothing at all. The joys of Abraam, Isaac, and Jacob in heaven appertaineth not to such as know only the faith of them, but unto such as obey the commandment of God, as they did. Man must give place to the word of God, when it is told him, and refrain from all things repugnant unto the word, to promote the word, that God's kingdom may reign upon the earth. Whosoever preacheth it, heareth it preached, or permitteth it to be preached, except he follow it, nothing availeth him. Those the scripture declareth to be blessed that work the word, and have their meditations in the law of God. The sermon must not be heard only for to know God, but also to follow God in his commandments: *Beati immaculati in via, qui ambulant in lege Domini*[1], Psalm cxix. *Beatus, qui in lege ejus meditatur die ac nocte*[2], Psalm i.

Psal. cxix.
Psal. i.

Thus with an holy sermon Christ prepared the hearts of his disciples unto the holy supper, and not with saying of mass. He exhorted them to patience, and to contemn the world; the one to love the other, and the one to bear charitably the infirmities of the other. Read[3] the comfortable sermon of

[[1] Blessed are the undefiled in the way, who walk in the law of the Lord.]
[[2] Blessed is the man that...in his law doth meditate day and night.]
[[3] — thone to bare cheritable thinfirmites of thoter, rede, &c., in the original.]

Christ, from the thirteenth of John to the seventeenth; and then I make thy conscience, good christian reader, judge, which is the best ways to prepare the wretched and sinful man unto the supper of the Lord, and which of both is to be preferred, a sermon, as Christ used and his apostles, or those vile ceremonies that the bishops hath brought into the church. Every man beareth another in hand that he loveth Christ, and doth acknowledge him to be wiser than man. It appeareth not; for if they believed as they say, they would not leave his holy testament, sealed with his precious blood, and follow the superstition and idolatry that the testament condemneth. This holy sermon should prepare the hearts of such as purposed to communicate with the precious body and blood of Christ, lest they received this holy sacrament unworthily, to say, without penitence and the fear of God. For although sin of his own nature be detestable and condemned by God, they that without repentance receiveth this sacrament aggravate and double their sin, because without condign honour and reverence [they] contemptuously receive the body of Christ.

After this preparation unto the sacrament, consider the ceremony itself, without all men's additions, only prescribed in the word of God; and thou shalt perceive the action and doing of the supper preach unto thy senses faith and penitence. Christ took bread, gave thanks unto God, brake it, and gave it to his disciples, saying, "Take ye, eat ye, this is my body that is given for you." Matt. xxvi., Luke xxii., Mark xiv., 1 Cor. xi. The ears of the Christian heareth that the body of Christ was given, and his blood shed, for his sins. These words, and the breaking of the bread between him and his christian brother, doth certify him that the ire of God was great against sin, that would not otherwise be satisfied than by the death of Christ, his only Son. No godly heart can judge sin to be light ill, that was purchased with so marvellous a death and inestimable price. The calamities of man be great and his miseries wonderful, as we daily see: sickness, poverty, exile, banishment, war, not only in the field with our enemies, but also at home with all virtue and honesty, discord, debate, contention and strife, between them that should be in most peace and concord; yea, daily war in

Matt. xxvi.
Luke xxii.
Mark xiv.
1 Cor. xi.

every man's conscience between vice and virtue, loss of goods and loss of friends, the greatest loss of all losses, to be robbed of the true word of God. All these be sacraments and signs of God's displeasure and ire against sin; and we are troubled and afflicted with these miseries to admonish us of God's judgment and anger for sin.

But the testimony of all testimonies of this great and unspeakable ire is the Son of God sweating tears of blood, contending with the justice of God, and fighting against the devil and sin, only got the victory by death. He that is not moved nor feared with these thoughts of God's ire and the death of Christ, in eating and receiving the sacrament, understandeth not what the sacrament meaneth. Now, except Christ should come down from heaven and die again before our faces, his death cannot be more lively expressed than it is in the scripture. He knew what ways it might best be kept in remembrance, that suffered the death in his own body, and shewed the manner of this ceremony himself, and bid them do the same in the memory of him. Christ preached a sermon, brake the bread, and delivered the cup unto the whole congregation, Matt. xxvi. Mark xiv. Luke xxii.; so did Paul, 1 Cor. xi., and then gave thanks unto God and aided the poor, 1 Cor. xvi. And this was the memory of Christ's death; and unto this whole action and ceremony of the supper must these words be referred, *Hæc quotiescunque feceritis, in mei memoriam facietis;*[1] and not to the lifting up of the chalice over the priest's head, as it is used in the mass. Christ commanded this ceremony, to break the bread among the whole congregation, that by the doing thereof they might return unto true repentance, and think, when they break the bread and drink of that holy drink, that as they break the bread and drink of the cup, so it was their sin and their fathers' that caused Christ to die.

This ceremony is godly, and thus doth the scripture permit to interpretate the doing of the supper, and not to break the bread secretly, with *Per eundem Dominum nostrum Christum Filium tuum*[2], &c. as they do in the mass. What need hath the priest to break his cake

Matt. xxvi.
Mark xiv.
Luke xxii.
1 Cor. xi.
1 Cor. xvi.

[1 This do ye, as oft as ye do it, in remembrance of me.]
[2 Through the same thy Son our Lord Jesus Christ, &c.]

at all, if he mind not to depart[3] of it to his neighbour? He might eat it whole as well. It is but an apish counterfeiting of Christ to make good the thing that is naught, because Christ and Paul divided the bread unto the whole church as a communion. They will divide it in their private masses. Though it be ill done, yet hath it a certain shew unto the unlearned of virtue. Is not Christ well followed, good christian reader, of these men? Yes, hardly! Their mass and breaking of bread as like unto the blessed communion of Christ's body and precious blood, as vice is unto virtue, and false superstition unto true religion. The mass is no ceremony of Christ's supper, but a very profanation of Christ's supper; for this is a true and certain rule always to be had in remembrance. No ceremony hath the nature and strength of a sacrament, when it is not used as the word of God teacheth, but contrary unto the word of God, and to another end than the word of God assigneth it. The Jews and the Turks doth use at this day circumcision, yet is it no sacrament. This ceremony pleaseth not God, but it is a wicked superstition, damned by God, and done contrary unto the word of God.

Likewise the mass, where as one receiveth the bread and wine, the bearing about of the host in procession, keeping of it in the box, doubtless it is not a sacrament of Christ's most holy body, but a profanation of his holy supper. For of Christ's ceremony it was said, *Accipite et manducate:* "take ye, and eat ye." It agreeth nothing with a sacrament, that they do. They have not as much as one place of the scripture that speaketh of a private mass, bearing it about in procession, or keeping it in the box.

Beside that, they apply it to another end than it was instituted for, and make it of no less value than the death of Christ, who once for all sacrificed himself for sin upon the cross. Heb. ix. x. They cannot tell what this word "offer" Heb. x. ix. meaneth, when they say they offer the Son of God. It is a great matter to offer him. It is to acknowledge the ire of God against the sin of the world, and to submit himself unto this ire, and to be a Mediator between God and mankind: and likewise he must enter the Holy of Holies[4] unto God.

[3 Depart: part, impart.]   [4 Holy of holynis, in the original.]

Heb. ix.   Therefore it is said, Heb. ix. *Per proprium sanguinem intravit semel in sancta sanctorum, æternam redemptionem inveniens*[1]. Also, *Qui Spiritu æterno seipsum obtulit inculpatum Deo*[2]. It is an horrible heresy to say that Christ is offered in the mass for sin. Christ once offered himself. It is our office to confess and acknowledge that only oblation once offered, and to believe that by the virtue of it God is pleased only, and all our life give thanks to God for it.

Let the godly people consider these things, and conform themselves unto the example of the primitive church, and let the new massings go. I know that many men gathereth out of the scripture many places to defend this heresy of the mass; but it shall be the office of every godly man diligently to discern and judge *notha ac adulterina testimonia a veris*[3].

The manner of the apostles concerning this holy supper is best to be observed. First, in the church there should be rehearsed some godly lesson out of the scripture in a tongue known; the people instructed with an holy sermon, not out of the *festival* nor *legenda aurea*[4], but out of the holy bible. Then should there be common prayer, first for remission of sin, and the mitigation of the pain condign for the sin; for although these two concur together, remission of sin and deliverance from eternal pain, yet doth God many times punish the transgressors with wonderful afflictions in this life, as it may be seen by David and Manasses, with other. And to be short, what

[1 By his own blood he entered in once into the holy place, having obtained eternal redemption for us.]

[2 Who through the eternal Spirit offered himself without spot to God.]

[3 Spurious and false testimonies from true.]

[4 The Legend was a book used in the ancient church, containing the lessons to be read in the services. From this the *Legenda Aurea* took its name; chapters out of that book, containing absurd histories and lives of saints and martyrs, being read in the Romish church at matins, and at the refertories of religious houses. The *Festival* was a compilation from the *Legenda Aurea*, also used in the churches by the Romish priests. Strype, in his Mem. Vol. I, chap. 18, folio 138, gives "a taste after what manner the curates used to entertain their audience with the contents of this book." The use of the Festival was not altogether discontinued till the reign of Edward the VIth.]

trouble or adversity soever we see in this world, they be sacraments and signs that God is displeased with our sins.

Howbeit, the priest or minister hath no power to bind man to do this or that, to say this prayer or that prayer. His office is only to shew by the word of God God's justice against sin, and God's mercy in Christ to such as repent, and commit the rest to God, who sometime punisheth in this world, and sometime punisheth not. It is yet the custom of the old church to excommunicate such as were common adulterers, covetous persons, 1 Cor. v., idolaters, blasphemers, 1 Cor. v. slanderers, drunkards, and extortioners, and such as for fear denied the gospel of Christ; except they did open penitence, which was a commendable use and godly act, done to give other men fear, lest they should commit like offence. Also it was a good exploration of the transgressor's conscience, whether his penitence were true or feigned.

But ye must understand, that this act and discipline of the church is but an act politic and civil to such as hath professed to live in the commonwealth of Christ's church, in an order, lest that the vicious life of the person should be a slander unto the word of God. This open penance appertaineth not unto the conscience or remission of sin before God, which is done only for the penance of Christ: therefore the church must be diligently instructed of the doctrine concerning remission of sin before God. It must know the difference between the remission of the default, and the remission of temporal pain, in the which God would many times his displeasure should be known against sin; as in the pain of David and Manasses. There is no church can be governed without this discipline; for where as it is not, there see we no godliness at all, but carnal liberty and vicious life: as in the commonwealth, where a thief is as much esteemed as a true man, a brawler and breaker of the peace as an honest citizen; for a conclusion, where as virtue is not commended and vice punished, the commonwealth shall soon come to confusion. The ill-doers were always punished and banished the company of the good, not only among christian princes, and in the law of God, 1 Cor. v.; but also among the Greeks 1 Cor. v. and ethnicks such as committed murder and incest were excommunicated, and lost not only their offices in the commonwealth, but were put out of the company of all honest men, and marked with a sign in the upper vestment, that all men might know him to be, as he was, a man to be avoided, and none to eat nor drink with him as long as he bore that sign; as it is to be seen by Orestes, Peleus, Antilochus, and Adrastus, that came unto Crœsus with the sign of his transgression. They had also their execrations and curses against these malefactors and transgressors of honesty, as Phœnix declareth *in Homero: Propter stupratam conjugem patris contra se diras recitatas esse*[1].

These things were used of antiquity, that men should the more deeply think upon the greatness of God's displeasure and ire against those that had offended, and by that means the more to abhor from such abomination. The gentiles, that never knew God, keep the religion of their idols, and revenged the transgression and violation thereof better than the Christians. Would to God it were more diligently looked upon, vice more punished, and virtue more extolled!

After this prayer for reconciliation unto God, followeth prayer to obtain the protection and defence of the Holy Ghost against the devil, the world, and sin; and that it shall please God to govern every man in his vocation to do the will of God, and not their own wills: then to pray for the governors of the commonwealth, that they may govern and extol the word of God, and defend justice; then for the afflicted church of Christ, that God would deliver his people from the ravening wolves of antichrist, and give them true pastors and preachers, that would study to gather together the flock of Christ, so miserably dissipated and separated; then for those that be ignorant of the truth, that God would grant them grace to be saved in Christ with his church. More availeth this prayer unto God, than many thousands of men of war to defend the church and commonwealth of realms, as it may be seen by Moses: when he prayed, the church of Israel prevailed; when he ceased, it was put to the worst by her enemies.

There is not the poorest in any realm, nor most weak person, but may profit the commonwealth where he dwelleth very much, and help to bring it to the end and perfection that

[1] On account of his father's wife dishonoured, the furies were invoked against him. Homeri Ilias ix. 453.]

the commonwealth was and is ordained for. Though he be not able to fight in the field against man, he may fight at home by prayer against the devil, that moveth war and sedition to destroy the commonwealth. Though his vocation be not to bear rule in the commonwealth, yet may he pray that God give grace to such as rule to rule well. As the commonwealth is common for all men, so may all men profit this commonwealth, if they have the knowledge and fear of God. Thus meant Paul, 1 Tim. ii., where he exhorted unto prayer and intercession, with giving of thanks. Read the place, and mark to what end they should pray; to obtain the end of the commonwealth, and that by express words, *Ut placidam ac tranquillam vitam degamus cum omni pietate* *et honestate*[2], &c. But how negligent men be in this behalf, all the world seeth. I impute a great part of this fault unto ignorancy, that people knoweth not how great and difficile a matter it is for a prince and governor to rule godly in his vocation; neither how great a sin it is to be unmindful of such governors in the common prayers of the church.

1 Tim. ii.

Then after these prayers and invocations, there should thanks be given unto God for all his mercies: then the words of the supper rehearsed, and the sacrament distributed to as many in the church as would receive it, and demand to receive it. So with thanksgiving, and distribution of such goods as God hath given unto every man for the poor, to depart with joy and tranquillity of conscience.

This is the ceremony that is a sacrament of Christ's holy body and blood, expressed in the scripture, and the author hereof is Christ himself. A more godly and religious thing cannot be devised, as ye may see by the author of it, and by the diligent writing thereof by the evangelists and apostles. What should cause the people to leave this holy thing, whereof we be assured that it is good and godly, and to use a mass, that hath no certain author? Grant it were not ill, (as it is of all great ills the worst;) yet who would forsake a thing certain and most religious, for a thing uncertain, and superstitious invention of man? Use the sacrament with the same ceremonies and no more than be expressed in the new

[² That we may lead a quiet and peaceable life in all godliness and honesty, &c.]

testament, as Christ did, and it shall pass all the masses that are, or be to be said in the world. The external use thereof, where as faith is, may succour an inward and secret desperation of a troubled conscience, so that the mind be not destitute of knowledge: those that too much fear and tremble at God's severe and rigorous judgment, knowing that sin meriteth eternal death, the poor conscience thus afflicted by the means of the devil, and horror of sin, taketh not as great hope in the mercy of God, as fear of his justice; is borne in hand that mercy nothing availeth, but by justice to be eternally damned.

Against such imaginations and perilous temptations availeth greatly the ceremony and use of Christ's supper. For as man is by his senses drawn to accomplish the act of all inward and secret conceived mischief and sin, where as the senses find external matter and sensible occasion to satisfy the will that willeth nothing but sin; so where as a good opinion is conceived of God in the heart, the judgment of man persuaded aright that God is a merciful God, and will pardon every sin, though it be never so heinous, in Christ, the will that with great difficulty consenteth unto this assured promise of God in Christ, is the more constrained to obey the knowledge of faith, because the mind is not only inspired by divine operation of God's Spirit, that his sins be forgiven, but also by the object represented unto the external senses, to say, the doing and celebrating of this holy supper; where as the very woful and cruel tragedy of Christ's death is set before the senses with breaking of the bread and drinking of the cup, declareth that verily all hope of salvation were past, remediless, were it not for the pains, travails, death and blood-shedding of Christ, wherewithal he satisfied the ire of God, brake the prison of eternal death, and set man at liberty.

And lest this thing once done by Christ should fall into oblivion and out of remembrance, most diligently he himself shewed the manner and form, how he would his church might best be kept in mind of this inestimable benefit; gave and instituted this holy sacrament, to be used for the consolation of the *fideles*[1] till the world's end. And why should any man take upon him to change the tes-

[1 Fideles : faithful.]

tament of him that was so merciful to die for us, and of such wisdom, that heaven, and earth, and all other creatures were created and preserved by him? Truly, as he would no man should take upon him to change the order of any thing that he hath made, not to appoint the sun for the night, nor the moon for the day; the earth to bring forth the fishes of the water, and water the fruit of the earth; but every thing to remain in the order and state as he appointed unto them in their first creation; so no man ought to melle[2] in the blessed sacraments, to pervert any order instituted by God, or say, this is good to be added, and this to be taken away; for their imagination to deck a priest with so many vestments, and such other detestable pomps and Judaical apparels as is in the mass, and say, it is to the glory of God.

Take the holy communion from the people, and let the priest make a private mass thereof; is it not as much to say as Christ was a fool, and knew not how to celebrate the ceremony that represented his own death with condign honour and reverence? Doubtless it blasphemeth God. For, as he said these words, and would no man should add nor diminish any thing unto them, *Germinet terra herbam virentem, reptificent aquæ reptile animæ viventis*[3], Genesis i.; and as he said unto Abraam of circumcision, Genesis xvii., unto Moses of Pesah[4], Exodus xii., gave the sacraments, and how they should be used for ever, as he had prescribed; Abraam nor Moses, who were of marvellous and singular holiness, never added one jot unto the form prescribed of God. They knew they could use a sacrament with no more religion than when they observed [the] institution of the giver. All the prophets that were after Moses' time were as doctors and interpreters of Moses' law; yet never among them all none that added or diminished any thing unto the sacraments. We have a greater teacher in our church than Moses was, Christ himself, which gave us his sacraments, and the manner how they should be used. The apostles and evangelists that be the interpreters of Christ's

Gen. i.
Gen. xvii.
Exod. xii.

[2 Melle: meddle.]

[3 Let the earth bring forth grass. Let the waters bring forth (abundantly) the moving creature that hath life.]

[4 Pesah: the Passover.]

mind and pleasure, neither in the gospel, ne in the epistles, never changeth one jot of the sacraments, but used them as Christ commanded.

Such now-a-day, as turn and change the sacraments from the order given by Christ, maketh Christ inferior unto Moses, the gospel unto the law, and the church of Christ unto the church of Moses, and declareth themselves to be more contumelious against the gospel than the Jews against the law. Every Jew knew right well, that these sacraments were sufficiently prescribed and taught unto them by the express word of the scripture. These massers say that they can amend the form that Christ gave, and celebrate the supper with more religion than the scripture teacheth; and of a communion they make a private mass, and defend the same as a thing of all things most holy.

Doubtless, if their saying be true, and their mass of such holiness as they make it of, we are little beholding unto Christ, that he would not his church should have the use of the sacraments plainly known by his testament, as the use of the sacraments unto our fathers were known by the law. Fortunate, then, were these that were of the old church, before Christ was born; for they were certain of their ceremonies and sacraments, by the express word of God, which cannot lie; but we, in the time of the gospel, as they say, must believe the doctrine and tradition of man, and obligate both body and soul unto the same, as unto a truth infallible, and prefer it before the word of God: for where the word saith one thing, they say another. The scripture that affirmeth the supper to be a communion, they say it must be a private mass. Christ said, *Bibite ex eo omnes*[1]; and so said Paul, 1 Cor. xi.: they say, the one kind is sufficient for the people. Had any doctor among the Jews used such a blasphemy against the law of Moses, the people would not have brought the doctor unto the schools to have disputed the matter, but before the judge, to have had sentence of death against him, that they might have slain the blasphemer with stones. Unto us that be Christians, against Christ's law, they may say what they list, and have good thank for their labour.

1 Cor. xi.

[¹ Drink ye all of it. Matt. xxvi. 27.]

Better ear is given unto the word of man than unto the word of God: a tale of an old tub better heard than a godly sermon of the new testament. People could never have been brought unto this contempt of God's truth, had not the devil and the devilish laws of bishops taken the word of God from them, wherein only is declared the will of God unto us, what is good and what is ill, what to be chosen, and what to be refused. A thousand times more ignorant are the Christians of the gospel, and of the whole[2] scripture, than the Jews. Never met I with one Jew, but he could reason familiarly in any book of the old testament, as a great learned man among the Christians in any place of the new testament: yea, and likewise, some in the new testament also; and by the new testament, with many strong arguments, can prove the mass, and other ceremonies, to be against the new testament, to the great shame of christian men, that the enemies of Christ know better what is contained in the new testament, than those that hath professed Christ. And no marvel; for every Jew is able to instruct his own family in the bible, and beginneth to teach his child the xxth chapter of Exodus as soon as he can speak *Aleph.* God of his mercy turn them to his faith! and then I doubt not they will more advance God's gospel than we, and better keep the word of God in honour, without false glosses, than we.

I desire those that defend these masses and other robbery of God's glory in the church, to make some book of every thing that they defend; shew who was the author of their doctrine, and first brought it into the church; in whose days and what year it was done; and prove their book to be good by the word of God only, or else no man will believe it; and that their use of the sacraments is prescribed unto the church by the word of God, and tell us what difference is between a sacrament and the thing signified by the sacrament, or whether the sacrament and the thing meant by the sacrament be one thing; and what I should judge of the signs, and what of the thing signified by the signs. The scripture teacheth otherwise than the popish church teacheth of sacraments. God said

[² hole, in the original.]

unto Noah, that the rainbow was a sign of the covenant between God and him, Gen. ix.: *sic Abrahamo de circumcisione: Et erit* leooth *fœderis inter me et inter vos*[1], Gen. xvii.: *de pesah*, Exod. xii., *Et erit hœdum vobis in signum; et erit vobis dies ille in memoriam, et celebrabitis eum pro festo Domini in generationes vestras*[2].

Gen. ix.

Gen. xvii.
Exod. xii.

Now let the christian reader mark our sacraments, and the words that Christ used when he instituted them, and see how that Christ alluded unto the sacraments of the old church. He said that *pesah* should be celebrated, and the day of that solemnity kept holy as a memory of God's mercy done in Egypt, when he killed by his angel all the first-begotten in Egypt, and saved the Israelites. So saith he in the evangelists by his holy supper, "Do it in the memory of me:" and Paul saith, "As many times as ye do it, ye shall declare the death of the Lord till he come."

They of the old time kept in memory the fact of the angel in Egypt, and carried not with them always the angel in the sacrament of *pesah*; but the angel, when he had done his office appointed by God, returned again into heavens unto God. Such as be of Christ's church keep in memory the fact of Christ done upon the earth for the salvation of the world by the death of his innocent body, and doth not carry about in the sacrament the body of Christ itself; for that after forty days ascended into heavens, after that it had done the office that God appointed it unto, to say, to be slain upon the earth, and then to rise again and be exalted into the unspeakable joys of heaven: as Paul saith, *Ascendit ut adimpleret omnia*, Ephes. iv. "He ascended to fulfil all things," not with his corporal presence, as some men say, but to fulfil all things that was wroten of him in the law, the prophets, and psalms, and to leave us a sacrament of his blessed sacrifice in the church, to be a memory of that glorious death until the world's end. Which sacrament is not a bare sign and token of his death only, as many men imagine, as the picture of

Ephes. iv.

[[1] Thus to Abraham concerning circumcision: "And it shall be (לְאוֹת) *a token* of the covenant betwixt me and you." Gen. xvii. 11.]

[[2] Of the Passover: And the (*blood*) kid shall be to you for a token. And this day shall be unto you for a memorial, and ye shall keep it a feast to the Lord throughout your generations. Exod. xii. 13, 14.]

Hercles is Hercles, or the image of Jupiter to be Jupiter: but I put as much difference between the sacraments of Christ, and all other signs and tokens not appointed for sacraments, as I do between the seal of a prince, that is annexed unto the writing or charter that containeth all the prince's right and title that he hath unto his realm, and the king's arms painted in a glass window. Such seals, annexed unto so weighty writings, be no less esteemed than the whole right, title, or claim that is confirmed by the seal, though the matter of the seal be nothing but wax, not for the value of the matter, (for twopence will buy ten times as much wax,) but for the use that the matter is appointed unto. And he that would take upon him to deny the king's seal in such a purpose, and say, it is but a piece of wax, it were no less than treason, and a very contempt of the king himself; because the king hath appointed that seal to be honourably received and reverently used of all men. And as the writings sealed doth confirm and declare the right of the owner unto all the world; so doth the sacraments confirm the assurance of everlasting life unto the faithfuls, and declareth the same to all the world. And as the matter, substance, and land itself is not corporally nor really contained in the writing, nor annexed to the writing, neither brought (when any matter of controversy is for the land) before the judge with the writing; no more is the corporal body of Christ brought before the church, *neque cum pane, neque in pane, neque sub pane, neque per panem, neque ante panem, neque post panem*[3]. But when the minister delivereth unto me the thing that is in his power to deliver, to say, the bread and wine, rehearsing the words of Christ's institution, the Holy Ghost delivereth unto my faith, which is mounted and ascended into heaven, the precious body and blood of my Saviour Jesus Christ spiritually, and not corporally. So doth the merits of this precious body in heaven feed my poor wretched soul upon the earth; and no contradiction or impossibility for Christ's body so to do. It may be in heaven, and yet extend his virtue by the operation of the Holy Ghost into my soul, by the means of faith, which at the time of the receiving of this sacrament is in my soul, and out of my soul;

[3 Neither with the bread, nor in the bread, nor under the bread, nor by the bread, nor before the bread, nor after the bread.]

as the Spirit of God is in every godly heart, and out of the heart in heaven with God: so was God, at the creation of man unto his own likeness, in man and out of man.

Yet, to make it more plain, as the sun in heaven doth extend down his beams and lighten the earth, so doth Christ's body by faith, in spirit, expulse all darkness and sin out of the heart; moveth not bodily, but is every where, where faith is, spiritually, and at one time. As a man remaining in one place may address his thoughts into heaven or into hell, as many times as he listeth to meditate either the one place or the other; so Paul exhorteth the christian man, Heb. iv., *Accedamus ad thronum gratiæ, ut misericordiam et gratiam et auxilium opportunum inveniamus*[1], calling the throne of grace our sole mediator, to say, the peace-maker between God and man.

This body of Christ is only in heaven, and no where else, as St John saith, 1 Epist. ii. So doth Augustine[2] write, Tract. in John. 30. *Sursum est Dominus. Et iterum, Corpus enim Domini resurrexit, in uno loco oportet esse*[3]. So doth the Master of the Sentence allege his words, and not *in uno loco esse potest*[4], as the later edition readeth. How fond doctrine the schoolmen teacheth, it is plain: Lombertus[5] in the Sentence, Innocentius[6] in the Decretals, *de summa*

Heb. iv.

1 John ii.

[1 Let us...come...to the throne of grace, that we may obtain mercy and find grace to help in time of need. Heb. iv. 16.]

[2 Sursum est Dominus: sed etiam hic est veritas Dominus. Corpus enim Domini in quo resurrexit uno loco esse potest: veritas ejus ubique diffusa est. Aug. Op. Tract. xxx. Tom. ix. co. 24. Basilii (Frobenius) 1543.]

[3 The Lord is above: and again, For the body of the Lord is risen, it ought to be in one place. Lombardus quotes Augustine nearly as in the text: but in the Benedictine edition, as well as that of 1543, it is "as the later edition readeth." Pet. Lomb. Lugdun, 1570. Lib. iv. distinct. 10. p. 310.]

[4 Can be in one place.]

[5 Lombertus. See above, note 3, Pet. Lomb.]

[6 Una vero est fidelium universalis ecclesia, extra quam nullus omnino salvatur. In qua idem ipse sacerdos est sacrificium Jesus Christus: cujus corpus et sanguis in sacramento altaris sub speciebus panis et vini veraciter continentur, transubstantiatis pane in corpus et vino in sanguinem potestate divina: ut, ad perficiendum mysterium unitatis, accipiamus ipsi de suo quod accepit ipse de nostro. Et hoc utique sacramentum nemo potest conficere nisi sacerdos, qui rite fuerit ordinatus

Trinitate et fide cath. ca. Firmiter, and Nicolaus Papa[7] *de Consec. dist.* 2, *ca.* Ego Berengarius. This doctrine subverteth itself, if men mark it well. For as soon as they have confessed the bread to be the essential and substantial body of Christ, and the wine his natural blood, they add, *sed invisibiliter et ineffabiliter, et non ut in loco, non qualitative aut quantitative*[8]. So doth Thomas Aquinas, *part* III. *Quæst.* 76[9], and Lombertus *lib. sentent.* IV. *Distinct.* 10[10], sophistically dispute the matter. Is it not a wonder that men will not mark what contradiction is in their words? First they say, Christ's very natural, corporal, physical, substantial and real body is in the sacrament; the body that died upon the cross, was buried, that rose the third day, that was taken into heavens; and yet they make it without quality and quantity. Notice this: a marvellous doctrine, to say Christ now hath a body that is neither great neither small. Truly if he have now such a body as is invisible, without all qualities and quantities, then had he never upon the earth a true body, but a fantastical body, as they make him to have in the sacrament.

But I confirm my faith by the scripture, that teacheth of his incarnation and very manhood, Matthew i. Luke i. Romans i. Hebrews i. ii. ix. x. Matthew xxvi. xxvii. Mark xiv. 1, and by all the scripture; and let this false imagination of Christ's body pass, that they speak of to be in the sacrament; and would the christian reader not to be moved with this doctrine at all, but to set Saint Augustine against the Master of the Sentence and all other school doctors, be they realists or formalists. He declareth plainly

Matt. i.
Luke i.
Rom. i.
Heb. i. ii. ix. x.
Matt. xxvi. xxvii.
Mark xiv.

secundum claves ecclesiæ, quas ipse concessit Apostolis eorumque successoribus Jesus Christus. Corpus Juris Canon. Greg. XIII. Parisiis, 1687, Tom. II. p. 1.]

[[7] Ore, et corde profiteor .... panem et vinum, quæ in altari ponuntur, post consecrationem non solum sacramentum, sed etiam verum corpus et sanguinem Domini nostri Jesu Christi esse, et sensualiter, non solum sacramento, sed in veritate manibus sacerdotum tractari, frangi, et fidelium dentibus atteri. Nicolaus, ibid., Tom. I. p. 458.]

[[8] But invisibly and ineffably, and not as in any place, or quality, or quantity.]

[[9] Sum. Tot. Theol. tertiæ partis vol. secundi, Coloniæ Agrip. 1639, Quæst. LVII. Tom. VIII. p. 218, &c.]

[[10] See above, Pet. Lomb.]

that no body can be except it occupy place[1], *Epist. ad Dardanum* 57. *Spatia, inquit, locorum tolle corporibus, nusquam erunt; et quia nusquam erunt, nec erunt. Tolle ipsa corpora qualitatibus corporum, non erit ubi sint; et ideo necesse est, ut non sint.* Though Christ be absent bodily from his church, yet with his aid, help and consolation, he is present in spirit, which sufficeth until the end of the world, where as we shall see his glorious body indeed really and corporally, that now have but a sign and sacrament thereof, which sufficeth to keep that holy sacrifice in memory, and is profitable, so that the christian man be well instructed what difference is between the sign and the thing represented by the sign, and taketh not the one for the other, as Saint Augustine teacheth[2], *lib.* III. *de Doctrina Christiana, cap.* 5, 8, and as Paul teacheth Rom. iv. interpretating the words of Moses, Gen. xvii. *Hoc est pactum meum*[3]; and saith that Abraham received *sphragida justitiæ quæ per fidem apprehenditur*[4], and saith plainly that circumcision was not the alliance between God and Abraam, but the confirmation of the promise granted and given before. And so be all other sacraments, whether they be of the old church or of the new, called *sphragides*, signs and confirmations, *quia sunt vocalia, visibilia quædam, et palpabilia testimonia, ac veluti consignationes promissionis Dei acceptæ per fidem in Christo*[5]. Therefore it shall be necessary for the christian reader to learn by heart what a sign is, and to know the nature and office thereof.

A sign is a thing subject unto the senses, whereby is remembered the thing signified by the sign. This thing known, men must take heed they attribute no more nor no less

Rom. iv.
Gen. xvii.

[1 Aug. Op. Basiliæ, 1582, Tom. II. Ep. 57. *Ad Dardanum*, col. 275. Take away (saith he) the spaces occupied by bodies, and they shall be nowhere; and because nowhere, not in existence. Take away the bodies from the qualities of bodies, and they shall not be in any place; and therefore it is of necessity that they do not exist.]

[2 Nam in principio cavendum est, ne figuratam locutionem ad literam accipias, &c. Aug. Op. Basiliæ, 1582, Tom. III. col. 48, &c.]

[3 This is my covenant. Gen. xvii. 10.]

[4 A seal of the righteousness which is apprehended by faith. Rom. iv. 11.]

[5 Because they are certain vocal, visible, and palpable testimonies, and (as it were) sealings of the promise of God received through faith in Christ.]

unto the signs than is to be attributed of right. And whatsoever virtue be represented by the sign, yet must we judge of the sign according unto the nature of the sign. As in the time of war, if the captain either by a word, either by holding up of his hand, would signify unto the rest of the host when they should march forth, or retire back, it is neither the word, neither the beck of the hand, that is the marching forth or retiring back: but these signs declareth unto the soldiers when they should go back or forth.

By the examples of the scriptures I will make it more plain, that every man shall be able to judge aright of a sign. Read the tenth chapter of Numbers, where as the children of Israel departed from the desert of Sinai into the desert of Pharan in warlike order, every man appointed unto his captain, and under what banner he should be: every man that was of the tribe of Juda to be under Nahson, the general captain of that tribe, and under his banner; such as were of the tribe of Issachar, to be under Nethanael, and his banner; they of the tribe of Zebulon, under Eliab, and his banner; and so forth, as it is wroten in that chapter.

Now note what a sign is in this place. A mark, or open token, whereby every man in the host knew unto what captain and company he should resort; and when every man was in his proper place, the one knew by these signs and banners, of what lineage and progeny the other was. Here seest thou, christian reader, what a sign is, a declaration of the person unto what captain and tribe he appertained. The signs made no man of the tribe of Juda, but declared him that was in that ward to be of the tribe of Juda. Here is the sign, and the thing signified by the sign, well declared. Now were it ill done, to call the banner and sign the tribe of Juda, and say the sign were the thing represented by the sign. The sign therefore of every thing must be judged after his nature; if it be cloth, to say it is cloth. If a man should have made a garment of the banner of Juda, a sail-cloth, or any covering for such things as were in the tabernacle, they would have judged aright as the thing was, and called it a coat of cloth, according to the matter whereof it was made.

When the keys of any city or town be offered unto the emperor or prince, as unto the supreme governor thereof, it is a sign and sacrament of the citizens' obedience unto the prince to whom they be delivered: but if any man would ask what the sign of this obedience were, every man would answer, it is a key or keys, and not the subjects' obedience under the form of a key; or else say, that the city and citizens be turned into the keys, or the keys into the city or citizens, or any such like phrase[1]. But they know that obedience is in the heart, and a sign of the obedience is the keys. For in case the prince had no better assurance and warrant of the citizens' obedience, than is contained really and substantially in the keys, they might by fraud allure him with false hope unto the gates of the city, and then bolt the gates withinside against him, and not only keep him out of the city, but also by treason put him out of his life: then received he nothing in the keys. Likewise, if any man should feign himself to be the prince of the city, and the citizens, unawares thereof, should deliver the keys, and after the deliverance know that he is not their true prince; well, he may keep the sacrament and external sign of their obedience, but he shall not enter the city any thing the rather. Now, with this sign this counterfeited prince receiveth not at all the thing meant by the sign, no more than he that was of the tribe of Dan could make himself of the tribe of Juda with standing under the banner or sign of Juda. They say that the sign is not only a sign of the thing that it signifieth; but also there is contained in the sign, and with the sign, the thing that it signifieth. That is not so. No sign, insomuch as it is a sign, can be the sign and the thing meant by the sign. God commanded the children of Israel to blow the silver trumpets, when they entered battle against their enemies, that thereby they might remember that God had not forgotten them; yet was not the mercy of God and their victory inclosed in the trumpets. So these signs in the sacraments, because of God's promise and contract made with his church, are tokens that God will give the thing signified by the sacraments. No man therefore, upon pain of God's displeasure, should contemn these holy sacraments; nor no man of the other part should judge of them more than of right may be admitted. A hard thing

[1 Knays into the Cyte or Citicince or ony souch like frace, in the original.]

is it to keep the mean: or else we extol the signs overmuch, or else too much condemn them. Such as make the signs of the sacrament, which is bread and wine, God, commit idolatry, and knoweth not what a sign is. The people are not only abused in this sacrament, but also in every other thing used in the church, for lack of knowledge.

The ringing of the bells was instituted to convocate and call together the congregation of the church at a certain hour, to hear the word of God, and to use the holy sacraments; or else to shew when there should be any consultation and assemblance for matters touching the commonwealth. The thing is now come to that point, that people think God to be highly honoured by the sound of the bells. Some think that the sound hath power in the soul of man. They ring so diligently for the dead, that they break the ropes, to pull the souls out of purgatory. They say that the sound can drive away the devil, and cease all tempests. Other say, that the sound moveth and stirreth unto devotion. Doubtless they judge amiss: if devotion come while the bell ringeth, it cometh not thereby, but by God's Spirit; for it is not the nature of the sound to give it. It may be a sign of devotion, as the comet or blazing star may be called a sign of God's ire or anger, though the star of his nature is not to be feared. But there is another thing that feareth[2] the man, the fear of God's punishment. So the crowing of the cock is a sign of the drawing near of the sun unto our horizon. It may be also the occasion that man riseth early in the morning: howbeit the crowing of the cock causeth it not, but the business and affairs that he hath to do, the love that he hath to serve God in his vocation; or else he would not rise at the calling of the cock, but sleep as a slothful man, until he could sleep no more.

Howbeit it may fortune, men will object and say, that these signs that I have spoken of, and the signs of the sacraments ordained in the church be not like all one concerning the nature of signs. The diversity is by the word annexed unto the sign, and the use whereunto the sign is appointed. There are two kinds and diverse sorts of sacraments, and God is the author of them both. The

[2 feareth: alarmeth.]

one kind appointed unto the ministry of the church, always to be used in the congregation of God, and hath the word of God and promise of God's mercy annexed unto it; so that whosoever contemned the use of those sacraments were excluded from the promise of God, and also from eternal life. Of these sort of sacraments were two in the church of the Israelites, circumcision, and *pesah*; Genesis xvii., Exodus xii. Of the other sort of sacraments was the ark in the clouds, the which God called the ark of his alliance between him, of the one party, man and beast, of the other party, Genesis ix.; and likewise the celestial fire that consumed the sacrifice of our fathers in the beginning of the world, Genesis iv. There was none of these two appointed by God to be used in the ministry of the church, as circumcision and *pesah* was. But God at his pleasure, when he listed, shewed by such signs his love and favour unto the eyes of such as loved him. Notwithstanding, there was no promise annexed unto these sacraments, of life eternal. Now in both these sacraments, as well those that were appointed to the ministry of the church as those that were not, were none other than testimonies of the promise that God had made with them that used the signs, before they received the signs; and the cause why God would annex these signs unto his promise, though there be many, yet is this the principal, to admonish him that received them of God's pleasure and good will towards him, to excitate and confirm the faith he hath in the promises, to declare his obedience unto God, and by the use of these sacraments to manifest the living God unto the world, and give occasion to other for to do the same. Then are these sacraments as very chains and sinews, to conjunge and bind together all the members of Christ in one body, whereof he is the head; by the which exercise and use of sacraments the church of God declareth itself to be divided from all other nations that use not the same sacraments. But beware, christian reader, when thou speakest of the end wherefore the sacraments were instituted[1], that thou confound not the ends, and take one for the other. For if thou do, thou hast

Marginal references: Gen. xvii. Exod. xii. / Gen. ix. / Gen. iv.

[1 Thow speakist of then wherfore the sacramentes wkere institutid, in the original.]

ascended the next [de]gree to neglect the sacraments. Some say they are but signs of our profession, that discern us from other people; as in time past the Romans were known from all other nations by their apparel. But we must understand that the first, chief, and principal cause why the sacraments were instituted, to be testimonies of God's pleasure towards us, as Paul saith by circumcision, Romans iv. Behold the scripture, and then thou shalt see always that signs of God's favour were given unto the Rom. iv. faithful, and ceremonies annexed unto the promise of grace, from the fall of Adam unto this present day. And as the promise was renewed, so God gave new signs and testimonies of the promise: after the fire[2] unto Adam and Abel, circumcision unto Abraam, because the promise of salvation was renewed and made more open unto Abraam than unto Adam. *Inimicitias ponam inter te et mulierem, et semen tuum et semen illius,*[3] &c. Genesis iii. Now by Gen. iii. express words unto Abraam, *In semine tuo benedicentur omnes tribus terræ*[4], shewed that in his seed all the world should be blessed. And when this promise of God unto Abraam, by reason of the long captivity of Abraam's seed in Egypt, was like to have been forgotten, and the truth of God's word little regarded among the posterity of Abraam, God sent again new preachers of his truth, Moses and Aaron, to call this gospel unto remembrance, *In semine tuo benedicentur omnes tribus terræ*[4]. And with the restoring of this light again unto the church he gave likewise new signs, many a one, as the four latter books of Moses testifieth; namely, the killing of the lamb, which was a sacrament of Christ's death to come.

What occasions is there given to mortal man to render thanks unto God for the preservation of his church, that when the light of truth seemed to be clean put out, he kindled it again! After Noe, the preacher of the promise was Abraam; after Moses, Samuel, David and other: in

[2 Ffyer, in the original. Probably an allusion to the manner in which God testified his acceptance of their sacrifices.]

[3 I will put enmity between thee and the woman, and between thy seed and her seed, &c. Gen. iii. 15.]

[4 In thy seed shall all the nations of the earth be blessed. Gen. xxii. 18.]

the time of the Pharisees and Sadducees, Simeon, Zacharias, Anna, and Maria. When the light of the gospel was brought into the church, there was also new ceremonies and sacraments given to be signs of God's promise; baptism, and the supper of the Lord. The which two sacraments we have for circumcision and *pesah*, and are the same in effect with the sacraments of the old law, saving they signified Christ to come, and ours declare and signify Christ to be passed bodily out of the world; and that the elements and matter of our sacraments is changed from theirs. For the lamb that signified Christ to die, we have bread and wine that signifieth Christ to have died; and as Christ's body was not corporally in the lamb, no more is it in the bread and wine: for they be sacraments of one and the same-self thing, instituted by God to one and the same purpose; the one to prophesy the death of Christ to come, the other to preach and manifest the death to be past: the one commanded, to be a memory of the thing done in Egypt, Exod. xii.; the other, to be a memory of the thing done in the mount of Calvary, 1 Cor. xi. The memory of the one was not the thing that was remembered by the memory; no more is the other. For of things like must be like judgment given. In the one remained very flesh, the lamb; in the other, very bread and wine. In the one the judgment of senses was not reprehended; no more ought it to be in the other. The effect of the one sacrament, *scilicet pesah*, was only received by faith, and not by hand delivered into the mouth of the receiver; so is the other. The one had his promises, and proper ceremonies, how it should be used, by the word of God, and no man to change the use thereof; so ought the other. For the gospel is as sufficient to teach us all things, as the law was unto the Jews: and a better and more holy minister is Christ of our church, than Moses of the Jews' church.

The false interpretation of the Jews corrupted the judgment of our fathers, as ye may see by the scripture and vehement preachings of the prophets: so hath the decrees of bishops corrupted the judgment of the world in our time, as ye may see, when ye confer their doctrine unto the doctrine of the apostles. The malice of man could not utterly destroy the truth in our fathers' time;

no more shall it do in our time. Christ hath prayed for his church, and his prayer is heard. John xvii. It shall be upon the earth till he come to judgment, Matt. ult., though always afflicted and persecuted by such as contemn both God and his word. But it shall suffice the servant to be as his Master was: we read how he entered with many afflictions; so must every man that will be saved. Heb. xi., Rom. viii. The church of Christ may well be compared unto Daniel sitting among the lions, destitute of all human aid and defence. Deliver it out of the cave, yet shall it wander upon the earth as a contemptible thing, of no estimation, not knowing where to rest her head. Patience must suffer this opprobry and abjection; and when she cannot be received, as she is worthy, into the palace of the rich, she must be content to lodge in the stable with Christ among the brute beasts. Yet God many times doth resuscitate of his great mercy divers princes and godly-minded kings, for the defence of the church, as he did Cyrus and Constantinus, with many other. And in my days it pleased God to move the heart of the most noble and victorious prince Henry VIII., of a blessed memory, to deliver his subjects from the tyranny of the wicked antichrist, the bishop of Rome, with many other godly and divine acts, which brought the light of God's word into many hearts; beseeching the eternal and living God, that this our most gracious and virtuous sovereign lord, king Edward, his successor, may godly perform the thing that is yet to be desired, and leave no more doctrine in the church of England, nor other book to instruct his subjects withal, than the most godly young prince Josijahu[1] left in the land of Juda and Hierusalem. His most noble acts be wroten 4 Reg. xxiii. He removed all false doctrine and idolatry out of the church, and restored the book of the law into the temple, bound himself and all his subjects to honour and obey God only, as that book taught.

 Manasses, for the time of many years, conspired nothing but the abolition and destruction of God's word, killed the prophets of God, and many other godly persons. In that time of persecution some good man hid in the temple an exemplar of God's law, which by divine operation was found

[1 Josijahu: Josiah. So p. 204, Hilkijahu: Hilkiah.]

in the reign of Josijahu. A good act of him that hid the book, and a godly act of the king to bind his subjects unto that book. He that had sought all the churches in England before sixteen years, should not have found one bible, but in every church such abomination and idolatry as the like was not sith the time of Josijahu; every where idols, with all abomination. And as I perceive by a friend's letter of mine of late, in a certain church in England was an inquisition made for the bible by the king's majesty's officers, that instead of the bible found the left arm of one of those Charterhouse monks, that died in the defence of the bishop of Rome[1], reverently hid in the high altar of the church, with a writing containing the day and cause of his death: doubtless a very sacrament and open sign that they be hypocrites and dissemblers, and not persuaded of the truth in their hearts. And I trust to hear that the king's majesty never put his officers to great pain to bring them to Tyburn, but put them to death in the church, upon the same altar wherein this relic was hid, and burnt there the bones of the traitorous idolaters, with the relic, as Josijahu did all the false priests, 4 Reg. xxiii. And the doing thereof should not have suspended the church at all, but have been a better blessing thereof, than all the blessings of the bishops of the world: for God loveth those that be zealous for his glory.

<small>2 Kings xxiii.</small>

But what the cause should be now, that the little idols be cast out of the church, though the mother of them all be there yet, and yet people be idolaters, it is easy to be perceived,—the want of the word of God diligently preached. Read the 33rd chapter of the second book of Paralip., where as the good king Manasses, after his captivity in Babylon, was returned from his wicked life, and restored unto his kingdom, with great diligence he destroyed such idolatry as before he stablished in his kingdom, overthrew all the altars of idols with great diligence. Howbeit, in the fifty-fifth year of his reign, he departed out of his mortal life,

<small>2 Chron. xxxiii.</small>

[1] This appears to refer to the Carthusians, who were put to death for denying the King's supremacy. In Hall's Chronicle (27th year of Henry VIII.) it is recorded, "The 19th day of June, 1538, was three monks of the Charter-house hanged, drawn and quartered at Tyborne, and their quarters set up about London for denying the King to be supreme head of the church."

before he could conveniently restore the book of the law and the true word of God unto the people. So that, notwithstanding the king's godly pretence and destroying all idols, *Populus immolabat in excelso Domino Deo suo*[2], 2 Paralip. xxxiii. A manifest argument that it sufficeth not to remove the occasion of ill, but there must be given occasion of good. When idols be cast out of the church, the word of God solely and only must be brought into the church, and so preached unto the people, that their false-conceived opinion may be taken out of their hearts, and taught to abhor idolatry by knowledge; or else will they return again to their superstition, as many times as they have occasion. Give them the true word, and such as can preach it truly unto them; then will they swear in their conscience never to serve other than the living God of heaven, as ye may see, 4 Reg. xxiii., by king Josijahu and his subjects: *Stans rex juxta columnam percussit fœdus coram Domino, quod ambularent post Dominum, et observarent præcepta ejus, et testimonia ejus atque statuta ejus toto corde atque tota anima, et exequerentur verba fœderis hujus quæ scripta erant in libro illo. Stabatque cunctus populus consentiens fœderi illi*[3]. When they were persuaded by the word of God that idolatry was naught, it was no need to bid them beware of idolatry. In the time of Manasses, grandfather unto this virtuous king Josijahu, it was no marvel though the people left not their idolatry, because the king, being prevented by death, could not, with the taking away of the vice, plant virtue, as he would have done doubtless. But the merciful Lord vouchsafed to perform this old king's godly intention by the young, virtuous, and holy servant of God that was crowned king in the eighth year of his age; whose example I doubt not but that our most gracious king will follow, having so godly a governor and virtuous councillors, whose eyes cannot be dared[4] with these

2 Chron. xxxiii.

2 Kings xxiii.

[2 The people did sacrifice still in the high places, yet unto the Lord their God only. 2 Chron. xxxiii. 17.]

[3 And the king stood by a pillar, and made a covenant before the Lord to walk after the Lord, and to keep his commandments, and his testimonies, and his statutes, with all their heart, and all their soul, to perform the words of this covenant that were written in this book: and all the people stood to the covenant. 2 Kings xxiii. 3.]

[4 dared: dazzled.]

manifest and open abominations, to have a god of bread, or the holy and most blessed supper of the Lord's death thus abused. There is one notable thing to be marked in this young king Josijahu, when that Hilkijahu the high priest delivered unto the king's secretary, Saphan, the book of the law, that he had found in the temple, and Saphan read the contents of the book before the king; moved with a wonderful sorrow and heaviness of heart, for woe rent his clothes, and said unto those that were present, "Go, pray ye to the Lord for me, for the people, and for Juda; for great is the fury and anger of the Lord against us, because our fathers heard not the words of this book, and lived not thereafter;" declaring by these words that all the captivities, misery, and trouble that his predecessors sustained, was for the contempt and neglecting of God's word, the observation whereof is the preservation of all public and common wealths, the violation of it to be the subversion and destruction of the common wealth, as it may be seen by those two kings, Achas and Ezechias. 4 Reg. xvi. xviii. Ezechias was fortunate in his reign, because he was aided by God; Achas unfortunate, because he wanted the aid of God. To avoid God's displeasure, to instruct his subjects in the word of the living God, and for the preservation of his realm, [he] called assemblance of all the wisest of Juda and Hierusalem, came into the temple, and being present all the citizens of Hierusalem, the priests, prophets, with all other great and small, read himself unto the people the contents of the book that was found in the temple; which declareth that he would assure his subjects himself of God's true word, that no false preacher should afterward seduce their conscience with any false doctrine. So, I doubt not, but our most virtuous and noble king will deliver unto his subjects the only bible, to be preached in the congregation, and suffer none other man's writings to be preached there, to seduce his faithful subjects, and say with this noble king Josijahu unto all the bishops and priests of his most noble realm, *Auferte de templo Domini cuncta vasa quæ facta fuerant pro Baal, pro lucis, et pro universa militia cœli*[1]. Cast out all vessels, vestments,

2 Kings xvi. xviii.

[1 Bring forth out of the temple of the Lord all the vessels that were made for Baal, and for the grove, and for all the host of heaven.]

holy-water bucket, with *placebo* and *dilexi*[2] for the dead, with praying to dead saint, all other such trinkets as hath blasphemed the name of thy God; and use the testament and such sacraments there prescribed, and as they be there prescribed by the word. O how great shall the king's majesty and the council's reward be for their thus doing! They shall triumph for ever with God in such joys as never can be expressed with tongue or pen, without end in heaven, with David, Ezechias, and Josijahu.

The true preaching of God's word hath been so long out of use, that it shall be very difficult to restore it again, except men know the manner of speech used in the scripture. What hath brought this blindness and idolatry into the church but ignorancy? When the bible and true preachers thereof be restored into the church, God shall restore likewise such light as shall discern every thing aright; what God is, what a sacrament is, what saint is, and what honour is to be given unto them: where now is such confusion as the one thing confoundeth the other, praying unto saints as well as to God; attributing unto the sacraments and external signs that, that only should be attributed unto the promise of God ratified by the signs. Though the sacraments godly used be holy and godly things, yet be they neither God, nor God's promises; which thing men should use as confirmations of God's promises, and give only the honour unto God for the graces that they confirm, as they do that inherit their father's right and possession, useth to keep well their evidence and writings left unto them for the confirmation of their land; yet doth they neither honour the wax printed, annexed with the writings, as though it were their natural fathers, nor attribute the gift and donation of the land unto the writing and seal, but unto the giver of the land, that confirmed the donation or purchase of the land with the seal. The preaching of God's word is of all things in this world most necessary for the people, and Paul calleth the gospel "the virtue of God to the salvation of all that believe," Rom. i. Yet is the word of God of Rom. i. no such efficacy. For the words can do nothing but signify and confirm the conscience of him that believed. And when I say, the word of God "is the power of God unto

[[2] See Rituale Romanum, Officium defunctorum.]

the salvation" of those that believe, true it is, when it is preached, understood and followed. *Hoc est mens et medulla verbi*[1]*!* This is taught daily in our *Pater-noster*, when we say, *Sanctificetur nomen tuum*[2]. Give grace, that the knowledge of thy name may be preached in the whole world. Then followeth the second petition, *Adveniat regnum tuum*[3]; the which speaketh of nothing but of the effect of the first petition. Lord, when thou hast dispersed the voice of thy gospel into the world, so govern us with thy holy Spirit, that we may believe and receive the gospel. Here see we, *Quod Spiritus sanctus operatur salutem mediante verbo, quod est ipsa mens, sententia, et voluntas Dei; quam sententiam divinæ voluntatis tunc capit humanum pectus, quando trahitur a Patre*[4]. As ye may read, Acts xiii. xvi. John vi. Though it please God to send his holy Spirit into our hearts by this means, yet is not the word the grace given, nor the Holy Ghost that giveth it. Let us reverently use the means, and honour the giver of the grace only. Learn, good reader, to know God from his sacraments, that thou make not of honey gall, and of a profitable medicine, ordained for thy health, a necessary poison to thy destruction.

Acts xiii. xvi. John vi.

Remember the words of Epiphanius, Lib. III. *contra Hæres*. Tom. II. There were two sorts of people; the one, as he writeth, contemned the blessed virgin too much, the other extolled her too much. *Æquale est enim in utrisque his sectis detrimentum, quum illi quidem vilipendant sanctam virginem, hi vero rursus ultra decorum glorificent*[5]. *Revera sanctum erat corpus Mariæ, non tamen Deus*[6]. Mark well how he taketh

[[1] This is the mind and marrow of the word.]
[[2] Hallowed be thy name.]   [[3] Thy kingdom come.]
[[4] That the Holy Ghost worketh salvation by the instrumentality of the word, which is the very mind, purpose, and will of God; which purpose of the Divine will the heart of man then receiveth, when it is drawn by the Father.]
[[5] For the evil is the same in each of these sects, when the one despise the holy virgin, and the other on the contrary too highly honour her. Ἴση γὰρ ἐπ' ἀμφοτέραις ταύταις ταῖς αἱρέσεσιν ἡ βλαβή· τῶν μὲν κατευτελιζόντων τὴν ἁγίαν παρθένον, τῶν δὲ πάλιν ὑπὲρ τὸ δέον δοξαζόντων. Epiphanii Opera, Coloniæ, 1682, Tom. I. Adv. Hær. Lib. III. Tom. II. p. 1058.]
[[6] Truly the body of Mary was holy, but she was not God. Ναὶ μὴν ἅγιον ἦν τὸ σῶμα τῆς Μαρίας· οὐ μὴν Θεός. Epiphanii Opera, Tom. I. Adv. Hær. Lib. III. Tom. II. p. 1061.]

away from the blessed virgin such honour as she should not have, and yet giveth her due reverence. *Revera, inquit, virgo erat et honorata, sed non ad adorationem nobis data; sed ipsa adorans eum, qui ex ipsa carne genitus est, de cœlis vero ex sinibus Patris accessit*[7]. Again: *Sit in honore Maria. Pater, Filius, et Spiritus Sanctus adoretur. Mariam nemo adoret, non dico mulierem, imo neque virum. Deo debetur hoc mysterium*[8]. The saints are to be remembered, to follow their humility and patience, to preach the word of God as they did, to die from doing of ill as they did, to contemn the world as they did. They are not to be prayed unto, nor to be as God. The memory of saints is good, if it be well used. The right honour of saints is, to follow God by their example, as few men doth. God amend it! The thing they should do they leave undone, and that they do is forbidden them by the scripture. When they hear of the cruel martyrdom of any saint, they be moved with so great pity, they put the finger in the eye and weep, because the saint suffered so cruel pains for the defence of Christ's religion, and would please this blessed martyr with *Pater-noster* and *Ave-Maria*, that he should pray with him, and for him, as the Bishops' book in England teacheth, unto God. And doubtless the saint prayeth for him, (if at least way he know in heaven what is done upon the earth,) and his prayer is this: *Usquequo, Domine, qui es sanctus et verax, non judicas et vindicas sanguinem nostrum de his qui habitant in terra?* Apocal. vi. "Most holy and true God, when wilt thou revenge our blood upon

Rev. vi.

[7 Truly (saith he) the virgin also was had in honour, but not given to us to be adored, but herself adoring him who was born of her after the flesh, but came down out of heaven from the bosom of his Father. Ναὶ δὴ παρθένος ἦν ἡ Παρθένος, καὶ τετιμημένη, ἀλλ' οὐκ εἰς προσκύνησιν ἡμῖν δοθεῖσα, ἀλλὰ προσκυνοῦσα τὸν ἐξ αὐτῆς σαρκὶ γεγενημένον, ἀπὸ οὐρανῶν δὲ ἐκ κόλπων πατρῴων παραγενόμενον. Epiphanii Opera, Tom. I. Adv. Hær. Lib. III. Tom. II. p. 1061.]

[8 Let Mary be honoured; let the Father, Son, and Holy Ghost be adored. Let no one adore Mary. I say not, [let him adore] no woman merely, but no man also. To God alone this sacred service is due. Ἐν τιμῇ ἔστω Μαρία, ὁ δὲ Πατὴρ, καὶ Υἱὸς, καὶ Ἅγιον Πνεῦμα προσκυνείσθω. τὴν Μαρίαν μηδεὶς προσκυνείτω, οὐ λέγω γυναικὶ, ἀλλ' οὐδὲ ἀνδρί. Θεῷ προστέτακται τὸ μυστήριον. Epiphanii Opera, Tom. I. Adv. Hær. Lib. III. Tom. II. p. 1065.]

them that be in the earth?" Who shed their blood, but such idolaters as he that saith God's prayer unto saints? This martyr helpeth his client well to God, and saith, 'Lord, when wilt thou kill, and destroy all these idolaters that blaspheme thy name?' Leave praying unto them, and pray to God, to follow them in godly and honest life. Apply the words of Epiphanius unto every thing used in the church, and know what honour thou mayest give unto it. Though the sacraments be holy things, yet not to be honoured for God, nor for the thing they represent, though the scripture use to call the sacrament and sign the thing represented by the sign. As circumcision was an undersign and cutting away of the fore-flesh; the alliance signified by the sign was the knot and chain wherewithal God and Abraam was coupled together as friends; the one to be as master, the other as servant. The which conjunction and knot of friendship only the mercy of God and the consenting will of Abraam knit, and concluded that Abraam should be heir of eternal life, before any flesh was circumcised. And thus is it with all sacraments, for they do nothing but signify and confirm the thing that they represent; baptism, the absolution of sin, Matt. iii.; the sacrament of Christ's body, Christ's body. Though they be good, necessary, and commendable to be used of every Christian, yet not to be honoured for the thing that they represent, as these men teach that would alter bread into the body, and wine into the blood of Christ.

Matt. iii.

Every thing is good when it is well used. The apple that Eve saw in paradise, Gen. iii. was good; howbeit not to be eaten. She sought here wealth, and found here woe; as we most woeful wretches right well perceive. Black soap is good, but not to be laid unto a man's eye. The holy sacrament of Christ's body is good, but not to be honoured for Christ; it is good to be received of the congregation, and not to be massed withal. We must use every thing to the same end that God made it for; or else the thing is not used, but abused. Christ saw before, that false preachers would bring this idolatry into the church, to honour a sacrament for God; and therefore, to prevent the ill, he said, *Hoc facite ad memoriam mei*, "Do it in the memory of me." A gracious caveat and notable caution, were it not contemned! "Do it in the memory of me." He saw that people

Gen. iii.

would offer it as a sacrifice for the dead and the live, and make it equal with his death; therefore gave us his word, that sheweth us it is but a memory of his death. Repeat the words, and mark them: *Hoc facite ad memoriam mei*, "Do it in the memory of me." Two things in this word *memoria* is to be marked; the one present, and the other absent. The thing present is all the promises of God, the which the death of Christ hath merited; to say, the fruit of his blessed passion received by faith into the soul that is aright instructed what Christ hath done for us. For there is no faith where as is no knowledge. Joan. xvii. *Hæc est vita æterna, te nosse, et eum quem misisti Jesum Christum*[1]. To obtain the thing present in this holy supper, is to have Christ and all his merits delivered unto the soul by the Spirit of God through faith, which eateth neither flesh neither blood corporally, but feedeth upon the causes why and wherefore the body of Christ should die, and his blood to be shed, until such time as the Spirit of God warranteth and assureth the conscience where faith is; that as Christ died for sin, so because faith believeth and prayeth for remission of sin, the conscience shall not be condemned for sin. In this commemoration and remembrance of Christ's death by faith is apprehended not only a true knowledge and understanding of the mystery of Christ's death, but also the promise of life, remission of sin, and the gifts of the Holy Ghost, which necessarily followeth the remission of sin. Of these two things, the one is the light to judge all things aright, the other giveth strength to do all things aright; so that this faith delivereth from desperation and all other ill: *Adversus omnia nos erigat, et doceat mundum vincere: itaque ut memoratæ rei memoriam fides sequitur, sic ejus rei notitia memoriam præcedit*[2]. The thing present in this sacrament is Christ himself, spiritually; the thing absent is Christ's body, corporally. Knowledge of the scripture assureth me of the fact and death of Christ past, and

John xvii.

[1 This is life eternal that they might know thee......and Jesus Christ whom thou hast sent. John xvii. 3.]

[2 It lifteth us up against all things, and teacheth us to overcome the world. Therefore as faith followeth the memory of the thing commemorated, so the knowledge of that thing precedeth the memory thereof.]

no more present, but now is in heaven with the Father omnipotent. The Spirit of God by faith maketh present the fact past, and contendeth in judgment with God's ire upon the merits of Christ. And as always in man's nature is sin present, so is there always a remedy against sin present, the which we apply unto ourselves by faith, and desire mercy for Christ's sake. The punishment that man hath deserved, the Son of God, being made man, hath suffered for; and this sacrament is a memory thereof, and not the thing itself; though it be the manner of the Holy Ghost, in the scripture, to call the signs by the name of the thing signified by the sign. If we will needs add any words to make the matter more plain, let us not abhor from the old terms, *Panis est corpus Christi symbolice, vel sacramentaliter*[1]; and then by God's grace we shall be out of danger of all idolatry, and likewise keep the sacraments in their due honour and reverence. As for these new terms, transubstantiation, and then *essentialiter, substantialiter, naturaliter, corporaliter, mirabiliter, invisibiliter, ineffabiliter, in pane, cum pane, sub speciebus panis et vini*[2], these be terms that the old church knew not of. They have brought into the church of Christ great darkness, and too much caused the signs of the sacraments to be esteemed. They shall not be contemned nothing the rather, though their right use and nature be known: God forbid that any christian man should speak against them! But it is the office of every man to know the manner of speech in the scripture, and to judge according unto the meaning of the words, and not as they sound only; for then should we make divers Gods, where as is[3] but one. David, Psalm xxiv., calleth the ark the Lord of glory, which was but a sacrament of God's presence: *Tollite, O portæ, capita vestra; attollimini, fores sempiternæ, et ingredietur rex ille gloriosus. Qui est ille rex, ille gloriosus? Dominus fortis, et heros; Dominus virtute bellica insignis*[4]. Likewise, Psalm

Psal. xxiv.

[1 The bread is the body of Christ symbolically or sacramentally.]

[2 Essentially, substantially, naturally, corporeally, miraculously, invisibly, ineffably, in the bread, with the bread, under the forms of bread and wine. In allusion to the terms used by the Schoolmen.]

[3 Old edition, *it.*]

[4 Lift up your heads, O ye gates: and be ye lift up ye everlasting doors; and the King of glory shall come in. Who is this King of glory? The Lord strong and mighty, the Lord mighty in battle.]

lxviii., Iakum Elohim⁵, *inquit, Simul atque exsurgit Deus,* Psal. lxviii.
*inimici ejus disperguntur, et fugiunt a conspectu ejus, qui
ipsum odio habent*⁶. The scripture is full of such manner of
speech; yet was not the ark God, nor turned into God, but
the substance remained always, and not doubted thereof.
Great marvel is that christian men knoweth not the manner
of speech concerning a sacrament, as well as the Jews; they
had sacraments as well as we, and yet never brawled about
them as we do. And though many superstitions happened
in those days, and men put their whole confidence in the
external sacraments; yet made they not their sacraments
their God, as the Christians do. They failed of the end,
howbeit not in the matter and signs.

And to declare the matter openly, what we be bound to
believe of God's testament, what it is, I would that the
Christian should understand, that it was neither circumcision
nor *pesah* in the old law, nor baptism nor the sacrament of
Christ's body in the new law; no, neither the death nor blood-
shedding of our Saviour Jesus Christ itself, that is the testament or legacy that God hath bequest unto the faithfuls,
whereof Hieremy speaketh, *capit.* xxxi. The legacy and testa- Jer. xxxi.
ment is remission of sin and life eternal, which is promised us
for the merits of Christ. And this legacy and bequest is
made sure, sealed and confirmed by the death of Christ, which
the Father of heaven accepteth as a sufficient price for the
purchase of eternal life. And all the sacrament[s] that be, or
in time past hath been, are none other thing than testimonies
of this good-will and favour of God towards us, appointed
in the church to lead our faith unto Christ, the only sacrifice
for sin, whose merits extendeth not only unto us after his
passion: from the time that he was promised unto man in
the beginning of the world, Gen. iii., as many as believed Gen. iii.
in him were saved, as well before as after his passion; for
he was the Mediator between God and man from the be-
ginning; *Jesus Christus, heri, et hodie, et in sæcula*⁷, Heb. Heb. xiii.
xiii. *Abraam vidit diem meum, et gavisus est*⁸, John viii. Joh. viii.

[⁵ יקום אלהים]
[⁶ Let God arise, let his enemies be scattered, let them also that
hate him flee before him. Psal. lxviii. 1.]
[⁷ Jesus Christ, the same yesterday, and to-day, and for ever.]
[⁸ Abraham...saw my day...and was glad.]

14—2

*Patres eundem cibum et eandem escam comederunt et biberunt*¹,
1 Cor. x. Abraam, Isaac, and Jacob were justified by the
faith they had in Christ's merits to come; and were signs
of this only sacrifice to come. Joan. Chrysost.² *Homilia* 55
in Joan. et Irenæus *contra Hæreses*³, Lib. IV. cap. 13, doth
interpretate these words, *diem meum,* John viii. for the death
of Christ. St Augustine⁴, *tract. in Joan.* 43, doth understand
by these words, *diem meum,* as well the day of Christ's nativity as the life eternal. *Ego, inquit, non dubito patrem
Abrahamum totum vidisse*⁵. And that is consonant with
the words of the scripture, Luke xvi., where as is declared
the condition of such as died in the faith of Christ before
he suffered, and that they were in joy, and did not, as the
world now for the most part doth, believe that their sacraments were of such virtue to save them. They kept them
with reverence, and lived in the hope of the promise that
they confirmed, to say, the death of Christ to come. And
we believe in hope of God's promise for the merits of him
that hath died and is passed out of the world, as it is
signified by our sacraments left unto us by Christ in the
scripture, sufficiently there taught how they should be used,
and to what end; wherewithal people that have a good
opinion of Christ should be contented, and think verily that
all the wisdom of the world cannot devise a better way
how to use the sacraments, than he hath there taught
us, and that no man ever loved his church as well as
he that shed his blood for the redemption thereof. And
to ascertain us of this love he gave the testament and

[¹ Our Fathers......did (all) eat the same (spiritual) meat, and did (all) drink the same spiritual drink.]

[² Τὴν δὲ ἡμέραν ἐνταῦθά μοι δοκεῖ λέγειν τὴν τοῦ σταυροῦ, ἣν ἐν τῇ τοῦ κριοῦ προσφορᾷ καὶ τῇ τοῦ Ἰσαὰκ προδιετύπωσε. Chrysost. Op. Tom. VIII. p. 323. Paris. 1728.]

[³ Videret in spiritu diem adventus Domini et passionis dispositionem per quem, &c. Irenæi, Op. Oxon. 1702, p. 283.]

[⁴ Totum hoc vidit Abraham. Nam quod ait 'diem meum,' incertum potest esse unde dixerit; utrum diem Domini temporalem, quo erat venturus in carne, an diem Domini qui nescit ortum, nescit occasum. Sed ego non dubito patrem Abraham totum vidisse. Aug. Op. Basiliæ, 1542. Tom. IX. In Evang. Johan. Tract. XLIII. co. 323.]

[⁵ I have no doubt, saith he, that the patriarch Abraham saw the whole.]

his sacraments, wherewithal we might keep and preserve his love, were we so gracious to follow this book and testament only, and not the dreams of men. For the law of God is without fault and all imperfection: man's laws hath faults, and is unperfect. What should move man to depart from truth unto lies, from perfection unto imperfection, from the Holy Ghost in the scripture unto the lying spirit of man? Nothing have they to fear the simple man more withal, than to say, " If this learning be true, our fathers be damned; they believed not so;" and then rehearse a great many of holy men's names, whose doctrine they repugn, for they judged aright of sacraments. Grant, they did not; their authority must give place to the scriptures: and let the christian reader rather condemn the fact of all men that abuse the sacraments, rather than to say, the order that Christ hath ordained is not sufficient. Hold not with the most part, but with the better, and acknowledge them to be of the better part that use the sacraments as the scripture teacheth; and when they preach so much of their doctors' holiness, demand whether Christ was holy or not. And when they say the holy church thus teacheth mass to be good, think whether Christ were of the church or not: and when they would excuse their additions unto the supper of the Lord with their good and holy intentions, that it hath been so ordained by all learned men that hath wroten, demand who is better learned than Christ, or who meant better to the church than he; and if they have more wit to use the ceremony of Christ's supper than he, or better writeth of it than the evangelists, who writeth as clean against their use as light is to darkness, read the scripture well and see; and rather condemn all men of the world, than to grant that the scripture teacheth us not sufficiently the use of sacraments, and all other articles of our faith. Let the word of God be the lantern unto all thy life, and confirm thy knowledge thereby, and then art thou sure.

Now I will answer unto such arguments as my lord would stablish his opinion withal. He saith, "that it is the first and chief point of sophistry to make every man think of himself further than is indeed in him." These words may have diverse understanding, and be referred unto diverse ends. If any man unlearned, or meanly learned, would say he were as able to interpretate the scripture, to shew the art thereof, open the phrase thereof, declare the writer's intent and purpose, and refer all the sentences and arguments to the same purpose that the author meant them; and say he can defend and fence the proposition that[1] the prophet and evangelist with such other places of the scripture as may serve to the purpose, to confute all the arguments of his contrary; and say he is able by disputation to warrant both himself and the matter he taketh in hand, whatsoever his contrary may object, as well as a learned man exercised of long time in the scripture; it were not only the first point of sophistry, but the first and chief point of folly. I have heard but of few men that laboureth with that vice; but the unlearned glad to learn of him that is learned. If my lord meant a redress of such an ill, and tell the unlearned that it is not possible to be as good a divine as Augustine, as good an orator as Demosthenes, or as well know how to govern the commonwealth as Cicero, my lord's words were true. Howbeit, they mean another thing; to say, he that is unlearned cannot know nor comprehend the true use of the sacraments in Christ's church, and what they be, as well as the learned man, and say it shall be sufficient for them to trust unto other men's judgments.

This opinion of my lord's is not true. As the common laws of every city must be known of every man that will be a good citizen, so must the common laws of Christ's church be known of every one that will be a good Christian. It is not sufficient for a commonwealth, though he that pleadeth at the bar in Westminster Hall know there is nor ought to be in any monarchy more than one king, and all other to be subjects, but that the most unlearned of the realm must know the same, or else he should be judged for a traitor, to give such honour as is due only to the king unto another person that is not king. And is not God in the church as well to be known from a saint or sacrament of every christian man, as a king in his realm? Yes, doubtless; and as he that would make a subject the king, and so with tooth and nail proclaim him to be king, against the king's honour and against all

[[1] So the old edition. Qu. *of?*]

the laws of his realm, ignorancy could not excuse this transgressor from treason doubtless; no more shall these that proclaim and fight so sore for the god of bread, which is a creature and no god, be excused from idolatry. The king, of equity, is bound to kill the body of this traitor; and God can do no less of his justice than kill both body and soul of this idolater, if he repent not. And as no man is permitted to buy or sell, or to make any other contracts in any realm for his commodity, except in the doing thereof he observe the law of the land; no more can no man use to bargain or contract with God for his commodity in the church of Christ, except he observe the laws prescribed by God. As in a commonwealth all men cannot be princes and governors, nor all men learned; yet, forasmuch as the commonwealth is the society and conjunction of the prince with all his subjects, be they of noble parentage or of base lineage, learned or unlearned, it is necessary that as well the lowest as the highest, the unlearned as the learned, know how to live like a true subject, and not to run always unto a man of law to ask whether it be lawful to give the same honour unto the king's subject that is due only unto the king: so the church of Christ is not the assemblance of princes, bishops, and learned men only, but of all kind and degrees of people in the world; and the most inferior person of the church, he that lacketh his senses, is bound to know what God and his sacraments be, and the difference between the one and the other, as well as the best bishop of the church. For as the common proclamations of princes concerning faith, subjection, and obedience, is not given to one sort of his subjects, but unto all and singular persons of his realm; so is the gospel of Christ, concerning the articles of our faith and the use of sacraments, proclaimed unto all the members of Christ as well as unto one. God said not unto Moses and Aaron alone, *Ego Dominus Deus, qui duxi te de terra Ægypti, et non erunt tibi Dii alieni coram facie mea*[2]. Exod. xx. He would not Moses and Aaron alone to beware of idolatry, but all the church; not that they alone

Exod. xx.

[[2] I am the Lord thy God, which have brought thee out of the land of Egypt, and thou shalt have no other Gods before me.]

should know the word of God, but to make all the church to know the word.

Concerning the sacraments, every man was bound to know the use of them as well as Moses, and to teach their children to know what a sacrament was and how to use it, Exod. xii., Gen. xvii. What! was the commandment of Christ unto his apostles, to teach the learned to come to heaven only? No! He said: *Facite mihi discipulos omnes gentes*[1]. Mark xvi. "He that believeth and is baptized shall be saved: he that believeth not shall be damned." How can he believe well, that knoweth not God from a sacrament, a true body of Christ from the sacrament of his body? Mark all the sermons of the prophets and the apostles; and they appertained unto all the church, and not unto one learned man of the church. What learning is this, to say it is the devil's sophistry that a simple and unlearned man should not and is not bound to be as certain and sure to know God from an idol, and Christ's body from a sacrament of his body, as the best bishop of the world? Was not Joseph and the blessed virgin as well learned, trow ye, in the articles of their faith as Anna[2] and Caiaphas? They had been well assured, in case they had led their faith after the judgment of the holy church of the Pharisees, and not known God and his sacraments themselves by the scripture.

But I will put the Christian in mind of the first word of his creed, which is, *Credo*. I say, "I believe in God;" which is as much to say as, it profiteth nothing me that Abraam, Isaac, and Jacob, or that the apostles with other holy and learned men believe, but I must believe the promises of God, and I must live godly thereafter. Now, poor wretched man and comfortless person, how canst thou believe the thing thou knowest not? Thy conscience is a jakes for every devilish bishop's decrees; and as they change their law, now for avarice, now for fear, and now for *placebo*, so thy faith changeth as inconstant as the wind; and yet beareth thee in hand that the mother and nest of abomination, their universal church, cannot lie; when all histo-

Marginal notes: Exod. xii. Gen. xvii. Mark xvi.

[1 Make disciples or Christians of all nations. Matt. xxviii. 19. marginal reading.]

[2 Anna: i. e. Annas.]

ries declareth that the one bishop never stablished the other's decrees. Read Platina, and let those few bishops that I repeat, give thee occasion to learn thy faith out the law of God, and let their holy church go.

In the year of our Lord 900, Stephen VI. was bishop of Rome, and for a private hatred he had unto his predecessor and benefactor, Formosus, abrogated all the laws and statutes that he made in the time of his being bishop; plucked the dead body out of his sepulchre, cut off two fingers of his right hand, and cast them into the flood Tiber[3]. After the death of Stephen succeeded Romanus Primus[4], and after him two other, Theodorus Secundus[5], and Joannes Decimus[6]. These three disannulled all the decrees of Stephen, and restored the acts and statutes of Formosus, Stephanus' enemy. A little after was Leo the Fifth made bishop, and within forty days of his inauguration his very friend Christopher cast him into prison[7]; and he occupied the see and chair in Rome for the space of seven months, and then glad to flee unto a monastery as a banished man[8], as Platina saith. Then came Sergius

[3] Stephanus VI. pontifex creatus tanto odio persecutus est Formosi nomen, ut statim ejus decreta abrogaverit; res gestas resciderit. ....Refert Martinus scriptor, Stephanum tanta rabie desævisse, ut habito concilio, corpus Formosi e tumulo tractum, pontificali habitu spoliatum, indutumque seculari, sepulturæ laicorum mandaverit: abscissis tamen dexteræ ejus duobus digitis, illis potissimum quibus in consecratione sacerdotes utuntur, in Tiberimque projectis, &c. Platinæ Pontificum Vitæ. Paris. 1530. folio 151.]

[4] Romanus: ubi pontificatum iniit, Stephani pontificis decreta et acta statim improbat abrogatque. Ibid.]

[5] Theodorus II.: pontifex creatus, vestigia seditiosorum sequitur. Nam et Formosi acta restituit, et ejus sectatores in pretio habuit. Ibid.]

[6] Joannes Decimus: pontifex creatus, Formosi causam in integrum statim restituit. Ibid. folio 152.]

[7] Leo Quintus: pontificatum adeptus, a Christophoro, ejus familiari, dominandi cupido, capitur, et in vincula conjicitur......Christophorus itaque sedem occupat XL. Leonis in pontificatum die. Ibid. folio 153.]

[8] Christophorus: pontificatum malis artibus adeptus, male amisit. Septimo enim mense dignitate, ac merito quidem, ejectus, monasticam vitam, unicum calamitosorum refugium, obire cogitur. Ibid.]

Tertius, who so abrogated the laws made by Formosus, that such as were made priests in the time of Formosus were compelled to receive orders again, and took the dead body of Formosus out of his sepulchre, and caused it to be cast into Tiber[1]. I leave John the Eleventh[2] and John the Thirteenth. A more wicked person never occupied that Rome[3]. It were a whole book matter to name them all and their detestable acts. By these men we may see how little authority their decrees should have in conscience of a christian man, and cause every person to seek the truth only in the scripture, and not at the hand of any bishop or bishop's laws: for doubtless they have deceived themselves and other these many years. God give them grace to amend!

Account it not a point of sophistry, good christian reader, to know what a sacrament is by the scripture[4]: it

[[1] Sergius Tertius: pontificatum iniens......Formosi acta ita improbavit, ut denuo ad sacros ordines eos admittere necesse fuerit, quos Formosus antea sacerdotali ordine dignos censuerat. Neque hanc quidem ignominiam mortuo intulisse contentus, ejus cadaver e sepulchro tractum capitali supplicio ac si viveret afficit, corpusque ipsum in Tiberim projicit, tanquam sepultura et honore humano indignum. Platinæ Pontificum Vitæ. Paris. 1530. folio 154.]

[[2] Joannes undecimus: spiritus militares magis quam religioni deditos gessit. Ibid.]

[[3] Joannes XIII.: homo sane ab adolescentia omnibus probris ac turpitudine contaminatus: vir omnium qui unquam ante se in pontificatu fuere perniciosior et sceleratior. Ibid. folio 160.]

[[4] This seems to be in reference to what the bishop of Winchester said in the commencement of his book (see p. 99). "The first chief and principal point of deceit and sophistry is, to make every man think of himself further than is indeed in him, by this persuasion, that God granteth true understanding and wisdom to every man that would have it, hath need of it, and asketh it in his name; which hath such an evident truth in it, as no man can directly deny it and gainsay it: for so God doth indeed, and yet not so as the unlearned do take it, and thinketh it to be understood. This false persuasion of learning, wherewith the devil inveigleth the simple, and engendereth in them a pride of cunning and understanding which they have not, is the foundation and root, whereupon is builded and groweth false doctrine in the high mysteries of our religion, and specially in the most blessed sacrament of the altar, wherein divers have of late most perversely reasoned and unlearnedly spoken with such presumptuous pride and

is thy bounden duty; for if thou err[5] with thy preacher in the use of sacraments, thou shalt be an idolater with thy preacher, and God's enemy. Thy preacher was commanded to preach nothing unto thee but the word of God, as Christ taught: *Docete eos servare quæcunque præcepi vobis*[6], Matt. xxviii. And whether thou be learned or unlearned, as Matt. xxviii. thou lovest thy salvation, see thou be able to satisfy thyself in a true knowledge of the sacraments. Likewise be able to declare the same openly, apertly, and truly unto thy family and household. Remember the commandment of God unto all and singular of the Israelites: *Erit quoque, cum dixerint ad vos filii vestri, Quis est hic cultus vester? dicetis, Est oblatio pesah Domini, qui transcendit domus filiorum Israel in Ægypto, cum percuteret Ægyptios, et domus nostras liberavit*[7]. The fathers knew not only themselves what the lamb meant, but were bound to teach their infants the knowledge thereof, as they did by the word of God. Would to[8] our Lord christian men would study to do the same! first, to know themselves, and then to teach their family by the testament; and not to say unto their children, See thy God, kneel down serea[9], and hold up thy hands. The scriptures reproveth that idolatry. Teach the Lord's supper by the scriptures, and suffer not thy family to blaspheme God before they know what God is. And believe not this persuasion, that it is not a christian man's office to know what a sacrament is as well as the priest; for if thou do, thou makest thyself guilty of God's ire and displeasure, and declarest thyself to be none of

intolerable arrogancy, as declare plainly the same to proceed of the spirit of the devil, full of errors and lies, blindness and ignorance, by reason whereof they stumble in the plain way, and cannot see in the mid-day." A Detection of the Devil's Sophistry, &c. folio 5.]

[5 —bound on dewty for if thow ar, in the original.]

[6 Teach(ing) them to observe all things whatsoever I have commanded you.]

[7 And it shall come to pass, when your children shall say unto you, What mean ye by this service? that ye shall say, It is the sacrifice of the Lord's passover, who passed over the houses of the children of Israel in Egypt, when he smote the Egyptians, and delivered our houses. Exod. xii. 26, 37.]

[8 To, tho, in the original.]

[9 Serea, probably sirrah.]

Christ's. Read the tenth chapter of John, and he that will minister the sacrament unto thee, let him say as Paul said to the Corinthians, *Ego accepi a Domino quod tradidi vobis*[1], and know by the scripture that he saith truth. Trust not his word. If thou canst not read, desire some other to read unto thee [the] institution of Christ, and know whether he saith truth or not.

Every man is bound to know the commandments of God and the works thereof. Now the sacraments be all contained in this commandment, *Memento ut diem sabbati sanctifices*[2]. How canst thou honour the living God, and if thou be ignorant of his law? Was this precept given unto the priests alone, that they should only keep holy the sabbath? No! but as they by the word of God are bound to preach the gospel, and minister the sacraments with knowledge and reverence, so is every christian man bound to use them with knowledge; and in case he knoweth not what a sacrament is, and why it is used, refrain from the use of them; for God's promise and God's sacraments must be received one way, with knowledge and faith. This reason of my lord's is not godly; for doubtless he that goeth to plough all the week is bound to know truly what a sacrament is, and how, and why, and to what end it should be used, as well as my lord; and my lord with all the bishops and priests in England shall lament full sore their ignorancy, and their blood required at their hands, and yet the poor ignorant persons excused from the ire of God nothing the rather.

The second reason to stablish the alteration of bread he taketh of the nature of faith, who believeth things contrary unto reason and the judgment of carnal senses[3]. It

[1 I received of the Lord that which also I delivered unto you. 1 Cor. xi. 23.]

[2 Remember the sabbath day to keep it holy. Exod. xx. 8.]

[3 "To the carnal man the devil bringeth carnal reasons; and for the confirmation and proof of them, calleth to witness the carnal senses, both of the body and soul. And straight thine eye saith, there is but bread and wine; thy taste saith the same; thy feeling and smelling agree fully with them, &c."..."Wherefore, all such as ground their error against this most blessed sacrament upon the testimony of their sight, their taste, feeling, or smell, or otherwise upon their carnal understanding, because they cannot by their carnal reason com-

is true that faith so doth, as it believeth the world to be made of nothing, the Son of God to be made man in the belly of the virgin: this we believe because the scripture commandeth us to believe it; but my lord cannot infer thereby, that faith believeth every Canterbury tale. Faith is not a light opinion grounded upon man, but a firm persuasion and constant assurance stablished in the scripture, Heb. xi. It signifieth not only knowledge, but also firm confidence in the thing known: as the Hebrew phrase useth many times the word *believe* for *trust*. *Asre col hose bo*[4], Psalm ii. "Blessed are all that trust in him." Paul citeth a place out of Esay, 28th chap. *Hammaemin lo iahish*[5]: *Qui credit non festinet*[6]. Likewise Dan. vi.[7], and Psalm lxxviii. *Duo synonyma conjunguntur*[7]: *Quia non crediderunt Deo, et non confisi sunt in salutare suo*[8]. The examples of the Testament likewise declareth that faith signifieth confidence in the promise of God. *O mulier, magna est fides tua. Item, fides tua te salvam fecit*[9]. Thus doth *emeneh*[10] in the Hebrew, and *pistis*[10] in the Greek signify. Therefore Laurentius Val. and Budæus[11] in *Pandect. Juris Civilis*, calleth *pistis, persuasionem*, as Quintilian doth.

Heb. xi.

Psal. ii.

Isai. xxviii.

Dan. vi.

Psal. lxxviii.

prehend it, all such be beastly and blind, and far from the knowledge of the mysteries of our religion, as wherein our senses and reason be by faith condemned and reproved; finally, declare themselves to be such men as seem to require teaching in the principles and beginnings of our religion, wherein their gross carnal reasons, if they were truly mortified, they should not so stubbornly and arrogantly meddle in the discussion of the inscrutable mystery in the most blessed sacrament of the altar. For, if their senses were by true faith overthrown and put to confusion, &c." A Detection, &c. folio 6.]

[4 אשרי כל־חוסי בו Psal. ii. 12.]

[5 המאמין לא יחיש Isai. xxviii. 16.]

[6 He that believeth shall not make haste.]

[7 Because he believed in his God. Dan. vi. 23.]

[8 Two synonyms are joined together: Because they believed not in God, and trusted not in his salvation. Ps. lxxviii. 22.]

[9 O woman, great is thy faith. Matt. xv. 28. Also, Thy faith hath made thee whole. Mark v. 34.]

[10 אמונה, πίστις.]

[11 Quare fides non minus significat quam persuasio. Budæi Comment. Ling. Græc. Basil. 1556. Col. 152. 44. where Laurent. Val. and Quintil. are quoted.]

Now, if we be persuaded that the scripture is true, and that faith must be grounded thereupon, we must believe no alteration of the bread, but believe that the bread remaineth after the words of consecration, as Paul saith, 1 Cor. xi. The scripture saith it is a memory of Christ's body, and not the body. The scripture saith of Christ's body, *Ascendit ad cœlos, sedet ad dextram Dei, Patris omnipotentis, inde venturus judicare vivos et mortuos*[1]. *Expedit ut ego vadam*[2]. *Pauperes semper habebitis vobiscum, me non semper habebitis*[3]. Christ's body is above, and no where else. This saith faith, grounded upon the scripture.

1 Cor. xi.

And as for that my lord compareth such as trusteth unto their senses, and saith there still remaineth bread, unto the folly of the Epicures, that would believe the sun to be but two foot broad, because it seemed no greater unto the eye[4]; verily, if my lord would have studied a whole year, he could not have found a more apt and proper similitude to condemn the wrong opinion that he defendeth, neither better have accused his own ignorancy. The Epicures, by reason of the great distance between the Zodiac and the earth, could not judge the sun as big as it is indeed, but followed their senses, and said it was as big as they knew. These men that believe alteration of bread, be not so far off the altar, but they may judge what it is and how big it is. They may take the bread in their hand and weigh it, if they list; take and prove all experience, and warrant both reason and senses that it is a little piece of bread, and no man. Had the Epicures been as near the sun as the apostles

[[1] He ascended into heaven, sitteth on the right hand of God the Father Almighty; from thence he shall come to judge the quick and the dead. Apostles' Creed.]

[[2] It is expedient for you that I go away. John xvi. 7.]

[[3] The poor always ye have with you, but me ye have not always. John xii. 8.]

[[4] "Hereunto is added the carnal man's understanding, which because it taketh the beginning of the senses, proceedeth in reasoning unusually; and, as the Epicures did, concludeth that the senses together cannot be deceived. Whereupon also the Epicurians said the sun was but two feet broad, because their eye judged it to be no bigger. And from this they would not be brought, but remained as firm in that folly as some heretics do in this mischievous devilish misbelief against the most blessed sacrament of the altar." A Detection, &c. fol. 6.]

were unto the body of Christ at his departure out of this world, they would have judged of the sun otherwise; but forasmuch as they judged after their senses, they be more to be commended than those men that neither believeth the word of God, neither reason, nor their senses, but plainly deny the thing they see, and say a piece of bread is God and man, where as is not at all one inch of a man, nor of man's proportion. These men are worthy to be persuaded, as he that seeth the snow white, and yet will not believe it, *verberibus*[5], as the schools teacheth, *et non ratione*[5].

Then hath my lord another comparison, and would make God the thing that he purposeth, and saith: "Why be men more offended to believe the body of Christ to be in the sacrament, more than when that God, being *immensus*, could be wholly included in the Virgin's belly[6]?" The wherefore is, that the scripture commandeth us to believe the one, and not the other. *Conceptus est de Spiritu Sancto, natus ex Maria virgine*[7], Matt. i. ii. Luke i. ii. Men saw him in the world, Matt. i. ii. Luke i. ii. and when he departed out of the world. Now, my lord knoweth right well that in Christ be two natures, one divine and the other human; and each of them hath his proper qualities. God was wholly in the belly, and wholly out of the belly. Man was wholly in the belly, and not out of the belly till the time of his birth; then wholly out of the belly, and not within the belly. So saith Augustine[8]: *Fuit*

[[5] By stripes, and not by reason.]
[[6] "If in the mystery of the incarnation of our Saviour Christ the rebellion of man's senses were thoroughly trode under feet, and brought in due subjection to give place to faith, whereby we believe that the Son of God (which we confess truly to be *immensus*) was yet contained in the holy Virgin's womb, and a creature to contain the Creator, and as the church rejoicing doth daily acknowledge in worshipping the blessed Virgin Mary,

'*Quem totus non capit orbis,
In tua se clausit viscera, factus homo;*'

which to a man's reason implieth an insoluble contradiction, to say, that in her womb should be shut in that all the world could not contain." A Detection, &c. fol. 7.]
[[7] He was conceived by the Holy Ghost, born of the Virgin Mary.]
[[8] Non dimisit Patrem cum venit ad Virginem, ubique totus, ubique perfectus, quia nec divisionem incorporei simplicitas recipit, et Patris

totus in ventre, totus in cruce, totus in inferno, et totus in sepulchro[1]. But this is the property of his Godhead, and not of his manhood. That is in one place, and never without place; the other in all places, and yet in no place. *Deus est totus in toto, et totus in qualibet ejus parte*[2], as the soul of man is[3]. And as for the authority of John Chrysostom, he proveth not my lord's purpose, but disproveth; for he saith, *Oculis intellectus perspiciamus*[4]. There is no man but saith the body of Christ is present to the faith of man, howbeit not carnally, neither bodily received of him that receiveth the sacrament. *De modo præsentiæ est totum dissidium*[5]. Chrysostom[6] declareth how he is present in spirit unto faith, and not in the body unto the mouth: and godly spoken of this doctor. So said Irenæus[7] before him, that there is two things in the sacrament, one to the senses and the other to the spirit; for if there were nothing represented unto the faith by the sacraments, then were they no sacraments, but bare signs; which no man saith.

Then accuseth my lord those that say it is the bread that mouldeth; and saith the devil hath taught men to say

nomen plenitudo non novit. Erat ergo uno atque eodem tempore ipse totus etiam in inferno, totus in cœlo, &c. Aug. Op. Basiliæ. 1542, Tom. vi. contra Felic. Arr. Col. 788.]

[1 He was wholly in the womb, wholly on the cross, wholly in hell, and wholly in the sepulchre.

[2 God is wholly in the whole, and wholly in every part thereof. See Magist. Sent. Lib. iii. Distinct 22, c. fol. 257.]

[3 The Bishop of Winchester had quoted "the philosophers that said *Anima* was *tota in toto,* and *tota in qualibet parte.*" A Detection, &c. fol. 68.]

[4 Let us behold it with the eyes of the mind.]

[5 The whole difference is concerning the manner of his presence.]

[6 Ἐπεὶ οὖν ὁ λόγος φησὶ, τοῦτ' ἐστι τὸ σῶμά μου, καὶ πειθώμεθα καὶ πιστεύωμεν, καὶ νοητοῖς αὐτὸ βλέπωμεν ὀφθαλμοῖς. Οὐδὲν γὰρ αἰσθητὸν παρέδωκεν ἡμῖν ὁ Χριστός· ἀλλ' αἰσθητοῖς μὲν πράγμασι, πάντα δὲ νοητά. (The former part of this passage is quoted in the Bishop of Winchester's book, but not the latter.) Chrysost. Op. Ben. Ed. Par. 1836, in Matt. Hom. πβ. Tom. vii. p. 889.]

[7 Οὐκέτι κοινὸς ἄρτος ἐστὶν, ἀλλ' εὐχαριστία, ἐκ δύο πραγμάτων συνεστηκυῖα, ἐπιγείου τε καὶ οὐρανίου, &c. Irenæi Op. Paris. 1710, Lib. iv. cap. 18. Contra Hæres. p. 257.]

somewhat[8]. If it be not bread, let some man tell us what it is that mouldeth. It cannot be nothing. He would make men believe that nothing corrupteth by miracle. This is a wonderful miracle that is wrought in nothing. Here is three things: putrefaction, nothing, and a miracle by the power of God; and yet all three nothing, after my lord's mind. I deny any miracle at all to be in the sacrament; but every thing wrought by God accustomedly: by faith, remission of sin and augmentation of God's gifts, and the signs to remain in their proper nature. So doth Augustine deny any miracle to be in the sacrament[9], Lib. de Trin. III., cap. 10. It is Innocentius III. that would prove this wrong opinion of transubstantiation by miracle in his book, *De Officio Missæ*[10].

Then doth my lord name 1500 years that the church hath believed it[11]. If it be true, why doth not he name the authors that maketh good his saying? All the scripture and old doctors be against him. The breaking of the bread hath been used in the church this 1500 years and odd; but not in a private mass, as it is at this day, but

[[8] "Do we not see (saith the devil) the sacrament of the altar, that they call God their idol, (O blasphemous tongue!) sometime eaten of a mouse, sometime wax green mould, red mould, and blue mould? And here the devil refresheth his younglings with many abominable tales, such as a scoffing jesting wit could devise to have been done. Doth it not enter (saith the devil) into the body? and so forth; and speaketh that liketh him more than honest ears can endure, &c. &c." A Detection, &c. fol. 9.]

[[9] — sicut panis ad hoc factus in accipiendo sacramento consumitur. Sed quia hæc hominibus nota sunt, quia per homines fiunt, honorem tanquam religiosa possunt habere, stuporem tanquam mira non possunt. Aug. Op. Basiliæ, 1543. Tom. III. De Trin. Lib. III. cap. 10, fol. 289.]

[[10] Si vero quæratur quid a mure comeditur, cum sacramentum corroditur, vel quid incineratur, cum sacramentum crematur; respondetur, quod sicut miraculose substantia panis convertitur, cum corpus dominicum incipit esse sub sacramento, sic quodammodo miraculose revertitur cum ipsum ibi desinit esse, &c. Innocentii Papæ III. de sacro altaris mysterii libri sex, &c. Antuerpiæ 1545. Lib. IV. cap. 6. fol. 172. See also fol. 166, &c.]

[[11] "Doth not the priest daily in the mass, and hath done always, break the host consecrate in the sight of the people, without offence or slander, of such as have these fifteen hundred years, and do at this day, believe the presence of the natural body of Christ?" A Detection, &c. fol. 14.]

[HOOPER.]

unto all the church. Gregory's time was overcharged with superstition: yet was the communion of both kinds used then among the people[1]. And this man died not for 1500 years sithe[2]! He was created bishop of Rome 157 years after the death of Augustine[3], and died anno 604, in the reign of Phocas the emperor, that first decreed the church of Rome to be the head of Greeks and Latins, though the church of Constantinople never consented thereunto[4]. The name of the mass began then first to be known among the people. Howbeit, it was a communion and no private mass.

Such as make James the apostle, and Basilius, the authors of this wicked and devilish private mass, must prove that they say by good authority: except they mean by the name of the mass the communion of the Lord's supper. It should seem by the canon of the mass that is at this day read in, which was wroten in Gregory's time, that the mass was a communion. For the priest offered the gifts of the people, the bread and wine, unto God with thanks by these words, *Per Christum Dominum nostrum, per quem hæc omnia, Domine, semper bona creas, sanctificas, vivificas, benedicas*, &c[5]. So calleth Ireneus[6] and

[[1] —vobis adhuc parvulis incarnationis ejus tantummodo lambendum sanguinem trado. Sancti Gregorii Op. Paris. 1672, Tom. I. co. 935.]

[[2] And this manne died not for 1500 hundrithe yers sithe, in the original.]

[[3] Augustine died August 28, 430. Gregory was elected pope, September 3, 590.]

[[4] See Platina's lives of Gregory I. and Boniface III.]

[[5] Through Jesus Christ our Lord: through whom thou, O Lord, dost create, sanctify, quicken, bless, &c., all these things to be ever good. Missale Romanum, Parisiis, 1579. Canon Missæ, fol. 131.]

[[6] Ἐπειδὴ μέλη αὐτοῦ ἐσμεν, καὶ διὰ τῆς κτίσεως τρεφόμεθα, τὴν δὲ κτίσιν ἡμῖν αὐτὸς παρέχει, τὸν ἥλιον αὐτοῦ ἀνατέλλων, καὶ βρέχων, καθὼς βούλεται, τὸ ἀπὸ τῆς κτίσεως ποτήριον αἷμα ἴδιον ὡμολόγησεν, ἐξ οὗ τὸ ἡμέτερον δεύει αἷμα, καὶ τὸν ἀπὸ τῆς κτίσεως ἄρτον ἴδιον σῶμα διεβεβαιώσατο, ἀφ' οὗ τὰ ἡμέτερα αὔξει σώματα. Irenæi Op. Venetiis, 1734, Lib. v. cap. 2, § 2, Tom. I. p. 294.

Sed et suis discipulis dans consilium primitias Deo offerre ex suis creaturis, non quasi indigenti, sed ut ipsi nec infructuosi nec ingrati sint, eum qui ex creatura panis est accepit, et gratias egit, dicens: Hoc est meum corpus. Et calicem similiter, qui est ex ea creatura,

Tertullian[7] the bread of thanksgiving the creature of God, whereby is noted the difference between common bread, and the bread dedicated unto an holy use and memory of Christ's death: yet notwithstanding they call the bread and the wine creatures, and not the accidents of creatures, as our men of late days doth. Were there no more books but the mass-book, wherein is contained all this profanation and abuses of Christ's supper, it is easy to be proved by the prayers therein contained and used in Gregory's time, that the mass was a communion. Thus the priest and the people prayed, *Corporis sacri et pretiosi sanguinis repleti libamine, quæsumus, Domine Deus noster*[8], &c. Again, *Satiasti, Domine, familiam tuam muneribus sacris*[9].

Beda, that was ninety years after the death of Gregory, in the time of Sergius primus, knew not of transubstantiation, nor of private masses. No. In the time of Carolus the Great, two hundred years after [the] death of Gregory, there was no such massing as my lord speaketh of. But masses then began to come into estimation, when the order of Benedict enlarged their cloisters in France[10]. Other orders were not then begotten. These monks said private masses, and applied the merits thereof for the sins of other.

quæ est secundum nos, suum sanguinem confessus est, et novi testamenti novam docuit oblationem; quam ecclesia ab Apostolis accipiens, in universo mundo offert Deo, ei qui alimenta nobis præstat, primitias suorum munerum in novo testamento, de quo in duodecim prophetis Malachias sic præsignificavit. Non est mihi voluntas, etc. Ibid. Contra hæreses, Lib. IV. cap. 17, § 5, Tom. I. p. 249.]

[[7] Sed ille quidem usque nunc nec aquam reprobavit Creatoris qua suos abluit, nec oleum quo suos ungit, nec mellis et lactis societatem qua suos infantat, nec panem quo ipsum corpus suum representat, etiam in sacramentis propriis egens mendicitatibus Creatoris. Tertul. Op. Paris. 1664. contr. Marc. Lib. I. cap. 14, p. 372.]

[[8] We, replenished with the offering of thy sacred body and precious blood, beseech thee, O Lord our God, &c. Missale Romanum, in festo Visitationis beatæ Mariæ Virginis. Post-communio. Pro com. Sm. Martyr. Processi et Martiniani, fol. 222.]

[[9] Thou hast satisfied, O Lord, thy family with holy gifts. Ibid. In fest. invent. S. Crucis. Post-communio, fol. 209.]

[[10] Under the superintendence of Benedict (abbot of Aniane in Languedoc), who restored the rule of St Benedict, and required all the monasteries in France to conform thereto. He died 821.]

After the death of Carolus, reigned his son Ludovicus, anno 815, in whose days private masses came into such estimation, that people neglected the communion, and thought it sufficient if the priest said mass, and received the bread for them. Whereupon the prince made a law, that the people should communicate with the church three times in the year; as Ansegisus writeth, canon xxxviii., Lib. II[1]. Yet people esteemed the mass more holy and better than the institution of Christ, and passed neither of God, neither of the law of the prince. Then was there another law made, that all men should once in the year communicate and use the Lord's supper, as the canon "*Omnes utriusque sexus*[2]" testifieth.

This private breaking of bread is not of such antiquity as my lord speaketh of, as we may see by the decrees of Clement III., *De pœnitentia et remissione*[3], who lived in anno 1200. Lombartus[4] doth allege in the sentence no elder author than Sergius II., *Os porci cognominatum*, who reigned anno 842, thirty years after the death of Carolus Magnus.

The causes of this fraction doth Bonaventura[5] shew, *Distinct.* xii., Lib. IV:

[1 De corporis Domini et sanguinis communicatione laicorum.—Ut si non frequentius, vel ter laici homines in anno communicent, nisi forte quis majoribus quibuslibet criminibus impediatur. Capit. Caroli Magni et Ludovici Pii, Lib. VII. collecti ab Ansegiso, &c., Lib. II. cap. 45. Capitularia Regum Francorum, Stephani Baluzii, Paris. 1677, Tom. I. p. 750.]

[2 Omnis utriusque sexus Fidelis, postquam ad annos discretionis pervenerit, omnia sua solus peccata saltem semel in anno fideliter confiteatur proprio sacerdoti, et injunctam sibi pœnitentiam propriis viribus studeat adimplere, suscipiens reverenter, ad minus in Pascha, eucharistiæ sacramentum.—Decretal. Gregor. IX. Lib. v. Tit. 38, Can. XII. Corp. Juris Canon. Tom. II. p. 266, Paris. 1687.]

[3 See Jur. Can. Tom. II. p. 268, b.]

[4 Quid autem partes illæ significant, Sergius Papa tradit, inquiens, Triforme est corpus Christi. Pars oblata, in calicem missa, corpus Christi, quod jam surrexit, monstrat; pars comesta ambulantem adhuc super terram; pars in altari usque ad finem missæ remanens, corpus jacens in sepulchro significat, quia usque in finem seculi corpora sanctorum in sepulchris erunt. Mag. Sentent. Lib. IV. Lugduni, 1570, Lib. IV. Distinct. 12, F. fol. 315. See also Tho. Aquinat. Colon. 1639, 3 Par. Vol. II. Quæst. 83, Art. 5, p. 354.]

[5 Bonaventuræ Op. Moguntiæ, 1609. Tom. VI. fol. 92, col. 2.]

> *Hostia dividitur in partes tincta: beatos*
> *Plane*[6] *sicca notat vivos, servata sepultos*[7].

He that listeth to read more of this ill, let him read the fourth book of Lombert.

Their keeping of it in the box, and kneeling down at the time of sacring, is but the commandment of Honorius, third bishop of Rome, as it appeareth by his words, Lib. III. *Decretalium, titulo De celebratione missarum*[8]. And this Honorius died anno 1226.

As concerning the both kinds of the sacraments, it was not forbidden in the time of the Master of the Sentence[9], who lived anno 1182, *Frederico Suevo Imperatore Augusto*, nor in the time of Thomas Aquinas. For in a certain hymn[10] he speaketh thus of the distribution of the sacrament unto the whole church:

> *Sic sacrificium istud instituit,*
> *Cujus officium committi voluit*
> *Solis presbyteris, quibus sic congruit,*
> *Ut sumant et dent ceteris*[11].

If the priest gave unto the people that he received himself,

[6 Plene, according to Bonaventura.]

[7 The wafer dipped [in the wine] is divided into portions: clearly the dry denotes the blessed that are alive, that which is reserved, the buried.]

[8 Districte præcipiendo mandamus, quatenus a sacerdotibus eucharistiæ in loco singulari mundo et signato semper honorifice collocatæ devote ac fideliter conservetur. Sacerdos vero frequenter doceat plebem suam, ut cum in celebratione missarum elevatur hostia salutaris, se reverenter inclinet, idem faciens cum eam defert presbyter ad infirmos. Corp. Jur. Canon. Tom. II. Paris. 1687. Decretal. Greg. IX. Lib. III. Tit. 41. De celebra. Miss. cap. x. p. 193.]

[9 Sed quare sub duplici specie sumitur, cum sub alterutra totus sit Christus? Ut ostenderetur totam humanam naturam assumpsisse, ut totum redimeret. Panis enim ad carnem refertur, vinum ad animam: quia vinum operatur sanguinem, in quo sedes animæ a physicis esse dicitur. Ideo, ergo in duabus speciebus celebratur, ut animæ et carnis susceptio in Christo et utriusque liberatio in nobis significetur, etc. Magister Sent. Lib. IV. Distinct. xi. F. fol. 313.]

[10 Hymni qui in vesperis, matutinis, atque aliis horis canonicis in ecclesia Dei per totum annum leguntur. Parisiis, apud Johannem Ruellium, 1540. See Rituale Romanum. De Processionibus Hymnus. Sacris solemniis, &c.]

[11 Thus did he institute that sacrifice, the administration of which he willed to be committed to priests alone, whom thus it beseemeth that they should take and give it to others.]

there was no part of the sacrament taken from them, as it is at this day. Yet shame they not, ill men! to say their mass is 1500 years old. No, no! This ill came into the church after the condemnation of the great clerk, Berengarius, as is said before.

When my lord would stablish his doctrine by the authority of the doctors, because they say the wine and the bread is changed, they make not for my lord's purpose; for they speak of one alteration, and my lord speaketh of another. They say not that the substance and matter of the bread and wine is changed, but that the use of it is changed; for where before it was common bread and common wine, now it is with great religion taken for the presentation and confirmation of all God's promises unto his church, for the death of his Son. The doctors doth well to call the bread the body, and the wine the blood; for Christ so called it; as it hath been used, from the beginning of the church until this day, to call a sacrament by the name of the thing signified by the sacrament. Use thyself unto the scripture, christian reader, and then thou shalt perceive all the doctors, for the space of nine hundred years, to stand of thy part, and never minded this transubstantiation of the bread and wine. Read Augustine, *de sermonibus*[1] *fidelium. Quia Christus (inquit) passus est pro nobis, commendavit nobis in isto sacramento corpus et sanguinem suum, quem etiam fecit et nos ipsos. Nam et nos ipsius corpus facti sumus, per misericordiam ipsius, quod accipimus et nos sumus*[2]. And in the same sermon he saith, *In nomine Christi tanquam ad calicem venistis, ibi vos estis in mensa, et ibi vos estis in calice*[3]. As our bodies naturally are not the body of Christ, nor corporally our bodies be not in the chalice, but by faith we are his members, and spiritually conjoined with him in the chalice; so spiritually he giveth us his body.

[1 A mistake for *de Sacramentis fidelium*, as the Fragment is entitled in some editions. It will be found in Tom. v. p. 976. Serm. 229. Paris. 1670.]

[2 Inasmuch as Christ (saith he) suffered for us, he commended to us in that sacrament his body and his blood; the which also he hath made us. For we, through his mercy, are made his body, which we receive and [which] we are.]

[3 In the name of Christ, even as you have come to the cup, there you are on the table, and there you are in the cup.]

If Christ corporally be given unto us in the sacrament, then corporally are those that receive the sacrament in the chalice; which were an absurdity to grant. So likewise he interpretateth this spiritual receiving of Christ's body, *in Sermone ad infantes*[4], expounding these words of Paul, *Unum panis et unum corpus multi sumus*[5]. Tertullian, Lib. IV. *contra Marcionem*[6], doth expound these words, *Hoc est corpus meum*, and proveth thereby that the bread is not the body naturally of Christ, but proveth by these words that Christ had a true body, and was very man, saying: *Phantasma non capit figuram, sed veritas; aliud enim a pane corpus Jesus habet, nec pro nobis panis traditus, sed ipsum Christi verum corpus, traditum in crucem, quod panis figura in cœna exhibitum est*[7]. He calleth this sacrament the sign of his body, and yet never condemned for an heretic. And this should the better content the mind of man, that whereas Augustine, *in lib. heresibus*, doth note certain errors of Tertullian, yet concerning this matter of the sacrament he speaketh not one word against him: for Augustine himself believeth as Tertullian did, as he testifieth *contra Adimantum*[8]: *Non dubitavit Dominus dicere, Hoc est corpus meum, cum signum daret corporis sui*[9]. Why is not Augustine condemned for an heretic, and his books burned, because he saith that the

[4 Panis ille quem videtis in altari, sanctificatus per verbum Dei, corpus est Christi. Calix ille, imo quod habet calix, sanctificatum per verbum Dei, sanguis Christi est. Per ista voluit Dominus commendare corpus et sanguinem suum, quem pro vobis fudit in remissionem peccatorum, si bene accipitis: Apostolus enim dicit, *Unus panis, unum corpus multi sumus*. Serm. 83, de Diversis, entitled by others Ad Infantes.]

[5 We being many are one bread and one body.]

[6 Tertullian's words are: Figura autem non fuisset, nisi veritatis esset corpus. Ceterum vacua res, quod est phantasma, figuram capere non posset. Aut si propterea panem corpus sibi finxit, quia corporis carebat veritate, ergo panem debuit tradere pro nobis. Tertul. adv. Marc. Lib. IV. c. 40, Paris. 1580, p. 233.]

[7 It is not a phantasm which taketh form, but truth, for Jesus hath a body other than the bread: nor was the bread delivered for us, but the very body of Christ, which was delivered unto the cross, which [body] is shewn forth in the supper by the figure of bread.]

[8 Aug. Op. Basiliæ, 1542, Tom. VI. col. 187.]

[9 The Lord did not hesitate to say, "This is my body," when he gave a sign of his body.]

Lord doubted not to say, "This is my body," when he gave the sign of his body? Tertullian[1] denieth plainly the bread to be his body, Lib. IV. *contra Marcion.* speaking of the bread, *Acceptum (inquit) et distributum discipulis, corpus suum illum fecit,* &c. *Quomodo corpus suum fecit, si panis non est corpus, sed figura corporis ejus? panem fecit corpus, id est, sui corporis repræsentationem consecravit*[2]. So doth Cyprian[3], *Epistola ad Cecilium,* say of the chalice: *Non potest videri sanguis ejus, quo redempti et vivificati sumus, esse in calice, quando vinum desit calici, quo Christi sanguis ostenditur*[4]. The wine is put into the chalice to represent the blood of Christ. So in his sermon, *De oratione Dominica*[5], [he] saith that this supper is a mystical and sacramental eating and drinking of Christ's body by faith, and not carnally, as this opinion of transubstantiation would have it. *Mentis, non*

[1] Tertul. Adv. Marc. Lib. IV. c. 40, Paris. 1580, p. 233.]

[2] Having received (he said) and distributed the bread to his disciples, he made it his body, &c. How did he make it his body, if bread be not his body, but a figure of his body? he made the bread his body, that is, he consecrated it to be a representation of his body.]

[3] Cypriani Op. Lugd. 1550, Ep. 3. ad Cæcil. p. 117.]

[4] His blood, by which we were redeemed and quickened, cannot be seen to be in the cup, when wine is wanting from the cup, by which Christ's blood is represented.]

[5] No such expression has been found in the Sermo de *Orat.* Domin. Possibly allusion may be made to the comment on "Panem nostrum quotidianum da nobis hodie," commencing, Quod potest spiritualiter (et simpliciter) intelligi, quia et uterque intellectus utilitate divina proficit ad salutem. Nam panis vitæ Christus est, et panis hic omnium non est, sed noster est; et quomodo dicimus 'Pater noster,' quia intelligentium et credentium pater est, sic et panem nostrum vocamus, quia Christus noster, qui corpus ejus contingimus, panis est. Hunc autem panem dari nobis quotidie postulamus, ne qui in Christo sumus et eucharistiam quotidie ad cibum salutis accipimus, intercedente aliquo graviori delicto, dum abstenti et non communicantes a cœlesti pane prohibemur, a Christi corpore prohibeamur. p. 418. But more probably the reference is to the Sermo de *Cœna* Domini, where the following sentences occur: Sed in cogitationibus hujusmodi caro et sanguis non prodest quicquam, quia, sicut ipse Magister exposuit, verba hæc spiritus et vita sunt; nec carnalis sensus ad intellectum tantæ profunditatis penetrat, nisi fides accedat.—p. 316. Nisi manducaremus, &c. spirituali nos instruens documento et aperiens ad rem adeo abditam intellectum, &c.—p. 319.]

dentis, sacramenta sunt pabula, inquit Augustin[6]. St Hierome[7], *in Epist. ad Rusticum: Nihil ditius Exuperio Tolosæ Episcopo, ait, ut qui, vasis ecclesiæ pretiosis in pauperum alimonium distractis, corpus Christi in canistro vimineo et sanguinem portare in vitro*[8]. Also, Lib. II. *contra Jovinianum*[9], *et quæstione secunda ad Hedibiam*[10], he doth as Christ did, as the apostles did, as the scripture doth, call the sacrament of Christ's body the body itself. And so we read in St Ambrose[11], *Id quod panis erat ante consecrationem corpus esse*

[[6] Sacraments are food for the mind, not for the mouth, saith Augustine. *These words* have not been found in Augustine, but the same idea frequently occurs *in other words*. For example: Quid paras dentes et ventrem? Crede, et manducasti. In Evang. Joan. tr. 25. Noli parare fauces, sed cor—non ergo quod videtur sed quod creditur pascit. Sermo 112. De verbis Domini. Qui manducat intus, non foris—qui manducat in corde, non qui premit dente. Credere enim in eum, hoc est manducare panem vivum. Qui credit in eum manducat, invisibiliter saginatur, &c. In Evang. Joan. tr. 26. Flac. Illyr. quotes Aug. as saying, tr. 25: Non ventris, sed mentis est cibus. Catalog. test. Genev. 1608. p. 363.]

[[7] Sanctus Exuperius Tolosæ, viduæ Saraptensis imitator, esuriens pascit alios: et ore pallente jejuniis, fame torquetur aliena; omnemque substantiam Christi visceribus erogavit. Nihil illo ditius; qui corpus Domini canistro vimineo, sanguinem portat in vitro: qui avaritiam ejecit e templo, &c. Hieron. Op. Basil. 1516, Tom. I. Ep. ad Rusticum, fol. 23.]

[[8] Nothing (he saith) was more rich than Exuperius, bishop of Tolosa, who, when the costly vessels of the church had been sold for the maintenance of the poor, was wont to carry the body of Christ in a wicker basket, and his blood in a vessel of glass.]

[[9] Et nos Christi corpus æqualiter accipiamus, &c. Hieron. Op. Basil. 1516, Tom. III. Adversus Jovinianum, Lib. II. fol. 40.]

[[10] Nos autem audiamus panem, quem fregit Dominus, deditque discipulis suis, esse corpus Domini Salvatoris, ipso dicente ad eos, Accipite et comedite, hoc est corpus meum, &c. Si ergo panis qui de cœlo descendit corpus est Domini, &c. Hieron. Op. Tom. IV. Hedibiæ, Quæst. 2. fol. 63, D.]

[[11] Tu forte dicis, Meus panis est usitatus. Sed panis iste panis est ante verba sacramentorum; ubi acceperit consecratio, de pane fit caro Christi. Hoc igitur adstruamus. Quomodo potest qui panis est, corpus esse Christi? Consecratione.........non erat corpus Christi ante consecrationem, sed post consecrationem,—dico tibi quod jam corpus est Christi. Ambrosii Opera. Coloniæ 1616, Tom. IV. de Sacram. Lib. IV. cap. 4, p. 173, D and E. Antequam ergo consecretur, panis est: ubi autem verba Christi acceperint, corpus est Christi. Ibid. cap. V. p. 173, H.]

Christi post consecrationem[1], the bread was called the thing that the bread represented, because men should with the more reverence and often[2] use this holy sacrament. But what his censure and judgment was of the sign, it may be known in his Commentaries upon the First Epistle to the Corinthians, chap. xi.[3], where he saith that the supper is the sign of the thing, and not the thing itself. He calleth the cup the figure of the blood, and not the blood itself. The books "*De sacramentis*," that be named to be his, be not his, as those two reasons may well persuade. The doctrine of them agreeth not with the doctrine of his other works, neither with the writings of his scholar and disciple, St Augustine. Read his tenth book, *de humanitate Christi assumpta, in Lucam*[4]. *Ergo non supra terram, nec in terra, nec secundum carnem te quærere debemus, si volumus invenire. Nunc enim secundum carnem [jam] non novimus Christum. Denique Stephanus non supra terram quæsivit, qui stantem ad dextram Dei vidit. Maria autem quæ quærebat in terra tangere non potuit: Stephanus tetigit, quia quæsivit in cœlo*[5].

[1 That which was bread before consecration to be the body of Christ after consecration.]

[2 Often: owsten, in the original.]

[3 Ostendit illis mysterium eucharistiæ inter cœnandum celebratum non cœnam esse. Medicina enim spiritalis est, quæ cum reverentia degustata purificat sibi devotum. Memoria enim redemptionis nostræ est, &c. Quia enim morte Domini liberati sumus, hujus rei memores in edendo et potando carnem et sanguinem, quæ pro nobis oblata sunt, significamus, novum testamentum in his consecuti, &c. Nam et Moyses .... dicens, Hoc est testamentum. Hoc figura fuit testamenti quod Dominus novum appellavit per prophetas, ut illud vetus sit quod Moyses tradidit. Testamentum ergo sanguinis constitutum est, quia beneficii divini sanguis testis est. In cujus typum nos calicem mysticum sanguinis ad tuitionem corporis et animæ nostræ percipimus, &c. Si igitur apud veteres *imago* fuit veritatis, &c., quomodo hæreticis contrarium videtur vetus novo, cum ipsa tibi invicem testimonio sint? Ambrosii Opera Coloniæ 1616, Tom. III. In 1 Ep. ad Cor. cap. XI. pp. 183 and 184.]

[4 Ambrosii Opera. Tom. III. Lib. x. In Evang. Luc. p. 109, H.]

[5 Therefore we ought not to seek thee upon the earth, neither in the earth, nor according to the flesh; for now we know not Christ after the flesh. Finally, Stephen sought him not on earth, who saw him standing at the right hand of God. Mary who sought him on earth could not touch him; but Stephen touched him because he sought him in heaven.]

This doth Hilarius[6] godly declare in the cxxxvii. psalm. Wheresoever this later age could take occasion of any holy doctor's writing by the least word of the world, they wrested the word from the doctor's meaning to stablish their opinion of transubstantiation of bread. Every doctor of antiquity maketh against it, and yet they will not leave their miserable blindness.

I would repeat more places of the doctors, but it needeth not. Those that hath written against this falsehood before me, in Latin and in English, better learned than I, hath gathered so many places together, that it sufficeth every heart that is not wedded unto his opinion. Read Saint Augustine[7] in 6th chapter of John, and in the 98th Psalm: expounding these words, *Nisi manducaveritis carnem Filii hominis*[8], in the person of Christ [he] saith this: *Spiritualiter (inquit) intelligite quæ locutus sum. Non hoc corpus estis manducaturi quod videtis, et bibituri illum sanguinem quem fusuri sunt qui me crucifigent. Sacramentum aliquod vobis commendavi; spiritualiter intellectum* vivificat [*vivificabit vos*]. *Caro non prodest quicquam*[9], &c. Would to God the world could understand this kind of eating!

Such as would prove Christ's body to be here upon the earth, hath nothing but words of their own invention, without the scripture, wherewith they deceive the unlearned. It is soon done to make good a thing impossible, by words and a sweet oration, to such as be ignorant of the matter that is spoken of, as Cicero[10]: *Nihil tam incredibile quod non dicendo fiat probabile, nihil tam horridum quod non splendescat oratione*

---

[6] Deus (ut scriptum est) prope est his qui tribulato sunt corde. Non admiscetur autem arrogantibus, neque insolentibus prope est. Unicuique enim nostri pro fide diversitate aut proximus est aut remotus. Spirituali virtute ubi se dignum, &c. Hilarii Lucubrationes, Basiliæ, (Frobenius) In Psal. cxxxvii. (cxxxviii.), p. 692.]

[7 August. Op. Basiliæ, 1543, Tom. IX. Expos. in Joan. Evang. tract. 26, de cap. VI. col. 223, &c.]

[8 Unless ye eat the flesh of the Son of man, John vi. 53.]

[9 Understand spiritually (saith he) what I have spoken. You are not about to eat this body which you see, nor to drink that blood which they are about to shed who shall crucify me. I have committed unto you a certain sacrament: spiritually understood it shall quicken you. The flesh profiteth nothing, &c.]

[10 Paradoxa, ad Brutum.]

*et tanquam excolatur*¹; as it may well be seen in this matter of the sacrament, where as people by words are constrained to honour a piece of bread for God.

Then my lord would make good the wicked mass by diversity of terms, "institution and tradition²," and saith that Paul delivered unto the Corinthians by tradition the use of the Lord's supper, and would make the devilish mass to be the tradition of the apostles³ because Paul saith, *Cetera cum venero disponam*⁴. And of these words my lord would infer, that all this Romish rites and usages of massing were the tradition of the apostles: but the place serveth nothing to prove my lord's purpose. It is no need to go by conjectures, as my lord doth, to interpretate Paul's words. They mean nothing of the supper; for Paul saith concerning the use thereof, he delivered unto them the thing he received of the Lord. In the which words are two things to be noted. First, as concerning the use of sacraments in the church, it should be none otherwise taught nor ministered unto the people than God commandeth, and that only God is the author of every sacrament, and hath prescribed how they should be used. The second is, that

[¹ There is nothing so incredible that it may not be made probable by eloquence; nothing so rough that it may not shine out, and be, as it were, polished by the power of speech.]

[² Makgodd the wyckyd masse by diversice of termes instirucion and tradicion, in the original.]

[³ "And this word (institution) is often repeated, and yet the same word (institution) is not in scripture by those syllables; but St Paul speaketh of *tradition*, of the use of this sacrament, as he received it of our Lord, *Ego enim accepi a Domino, quod et tradidi vobis*, 'I have received of our Lord, which I have by tradition delivered unto you:' whereby and by that followeth, when he saith, *Cetera cum venero disponam*, 'I shall order the rest when I come,' it appeareth he had taught the Corinthians the sum of this high mystery, and the use of it, without writing before, and would add more when he came; which more he taught, and yet we have no writing of it; but the church hath not forgotten it, but hath taught it without writing, as she received it. And it appeareth in that epistle of St Paul, that, rehearsing such tradition as they had received of him, he blameth and reproveth them for the non-observation of it. And thus much for the word *institution* that pleaseth, which the scripture hath not, and the word *tradition* abhorred, that scripture hath; so as words go by favour, as this matter is handled." A Detection, &c. fol. 142.]

[⁴ The rest will I set in order when I come.]

the Corinthians were before in all things aright instructed according unto the institution of Christ in the use of the sacrament. But in other things Paul desired the church of Corinth to be reformed; therefore he said, *Cetera cum venero disponam*[4]. Theophylact is of my part[5]. But the use of the sacrament was plainly, absolutely, and most holily taught and used before in their church, as these words, full of emphasis and virtue, declareth: *Ego accepi a Domino quod tradidi vobis*[6]. I wonder what moveth my lord to say Paul meant these words of the supper, and would make Paul and the scripture author of such abomination as the mass is that now is used.

Those that readeth the histories and writings of our elders, knoweth what bishops of late days made this mass. The apostles and primitive church did celebrate the Lord's most holy supper without pomp and all this rabble of stinking ceremonies, most simply. My lord should not be offended with those that would the supper to be used simply. He should remember that the Lord himself and his apostles used it so, with the prayer of Christ, Pater-noster, as Hierome[7] and Gregory[8] testifieth; the one Lib. III. *contra Pelagianos*, the other Lib. *Epistolarum* VIII. *Epist*. 7.

The histories be plain, what the bishops of Rome hath done in this matter; how and by whom these ceremonies hath been augmented. The verb *paralambano*[9] [παραλαμβάνω] that Paul useth, signifieth, as Budæus saith, *in commentariis*

[5 *Ἡ περὶ ἑτέρων τινῶν ἁμαρτανομένων παρ' αὐτοῖς καὶ δεομένων διαταγῆς λέγει, ἢ περὶ αὐτοῦ τούτου φησὶν, ὅτι εἰκός ἐστί τινας ἀπολογίαις χρήσασθαι πρὸς ἃ εἶπον· ἀλλὰ τέως μὲν ἃ εἶπον φυλαττέσθωσαν. Εἰ δέ τις ἕτερόν τι ἔχει λέγειν, τῇ ἐμῇ παρουσίᾳ τοῦτο τηρείσθω. Ἐκφοβεῖ δὲ αὐτοὺς ὡς παρεσόμενος, ἵνα κατασταλῶσι καὶ διορθώσωνται, εἴ τι μὴ καλῶς ἔχοιεν. In Pauli Epistolas Comment. in loc.]

[6 I received of the Lord that which I delivered unto you.]

[7 Sic docuit apostolos suos, ut quotidie in corporis illius sacrificio credentes audeant loqui, Pater noster, &c.......statim in prima corporis communione Christi dicunt, et dimitte nobis debita, &c. Hieron. Op. Basil. 1526, Tom. III. Contra Pelagian. fol. 139, A.]

[8 Orationem vero Dominicam idcirco mox post precem dicimus; quia mos apostolorum fuit ut ad ipsam solummodo orationem oblationis hostiam consecrarent. S. Greg. Op. Par. 1672, Tom. II. col. 829, Lib. VII. Indic. 2, Epist. lxiv.]

[9 *prolambano*, in the original.]

linguæ Græcæ, Per manus traditum accipio, ut successor facit qui provinciam accipit. Significat et, A majoribus accipio et quasi per manus traditum accipio; et, A majoribus audiendo accipere[1]. Paul could not have delivered this supper of Christ unto the church, except he had first received it, nor Moses the law unto the Israelites. Is this a godly manner of speaking, to say, Moses gave the law unto the Jews? The apostles preached the gospel unto the Jews and gentiles. Paul preached and instituted the sacraments commanded by God. Therefore the law of God, the gospel of Christ, and his sacraments be the traditions of Moses and the apostles. They speak never of themselves, and gave nothing of their own brains unto the churches; but Moses and the prophets said this alway, *Sic dicit Dominus*[2]. So saith Paul, *Ego accepi a Domino quod tradidi vobis*. And God took from the prophets and apostles all authority clean, that they should speak nothing in the church but as they were taught: *Sic dices filiis Israel. Prædicate ea quæ ego dixi vobis*[3], Matt. xxviii. I will counsel the christian reader to leave the books of men, and learn the scripture, who only teacheth all truth and right use of the sacraments, and to follow the counsel of Cyprian[4]: *Si ad divinæ traditionis caput et originem revertamur, cessat error humanus, et sacramentorum cœlestium ratione perspecta, quicquid sub caligine ac nube tenebrarum obscurum latebat, luce veritatis aperitur.* * * * * * *Hoc ergo oportet facere Dei sacerdotes, præcepta divina servantes, ut in aliquo si nutaverit et vacillaverit veritas, ad originem dominicam, et evangelicam apostolicamque traditionem revertamur, et inde surgat actus nostri ratio, unde et ordo et origo surrexit*[5].

Matt. xxviii.

[[1] In his commentaries of the Greek language—I receive that which is handed over to me, as doth a successor [in a government] who receiveth a province. It signifieth also, "I receive from ancestors." And, to receive by hearing from ancestors.]

[[2] Thus saith the Lord.]

[[3] Thus shalt thou say unto the children of Israel. Teach them...... those things which I have commanded you.]

[[4] Cypriani Op. Lugd. 1550, ad Pompon. p. 126.]

[[5] If we return to the head and source of divine tradition, then human error ceaseth, and the meaning of these celestial sacraments being perceived, all that lay hid under the mist and cloud of darkness is laid open by the light of truth. This, therefore, ought the priests of God to do, keeping the divine precepts, that if, in any respect, truth hath faltered

The scripture and tradition of the apostles we must follow. The mass hath neither God, nor the scripture, nor honesty that defendeth it. For lack of authority they jangle an old wife's tale, that Gratianus[6] teacheth. Read of the foundation and founders of the mass more *apud Polydorum Urbinam*[7], *de rerum inventoribus.* Lib. v. cap. 9, 10. This is a woeful doctrine to preach unto the people that lacketh a father. My lord telleth a tale[8] of Ananias that was sent to Paul, Acts ix.; and of Moses, that led the children of Israel in the desert, yet were they believed of the people: but why? Ananias said, *Saule frater, Dominus misit me ad te*[9]. So said Moses. So said the prophets, whensoever they preached or taught any thing. We can prove by the scripture that they were sent from God.
^{Acts ix.}

Now these men that come to the people with transubstantiation, we know by the scripture they are against God and his truth. Therefore people must follow this commandment of Paul, *Omnia probate, quod bonum est tenete*[10]. For the scripture condemneth those that preacheth their own imaginations, and dishonoureth the truth. God forbid that any should condemn Moses or the prophets, or now him that preacheth the word of the living God! He commended Moses and other that preached truly, and condemneth such as preacheth falsely.

And where my lord saith[11], that in the 24th of Luke and Luke xxiv.

and wavered, we should return to our Lord's authority, and to evangelical and apostolical tradition, and that the rule of our action should be taken up from that point wherefrom the original law proceeded.]

[6 See below, Pol. Virg. cap. 12.]

[7 Pol. Virg. Urb. de inventoribus rerum, Lib. v. cap. 10—12.]

[8 "And all the outward teaching in this church hath been by men: all the apostles sent to teach the gospel were men. St Paul at his conversion from darkness to light, when it was said to him that it should be told him what he should do, then was Ananias by God ordered to go to Paul and declare what he should do. Moses, leader of the synagogue, the figure of our church, was a man; and the prophets were men." A Detection, &c. fol. 142.]

[9 Brother Saul, the Lord sent me unto thee.]

[10 Prove all things, hold fast that which is good, 1 Thess. v. 21.]

[11 "We read not in scripture that Christ did prescribe any such precise order of receiving or ministering: but as in his supper he indeed consecrated both kinds and ministered both kinds, whereby appeareth that all might receive both kinds, as all sometimes have done; so likewise when he ministered the sacrament to his disciples in Emmaus, and other

Acts ii. the 2nd of the Acts that the supper of the Lord was used under one kind, of bread, that is not so. Though only bread be named, yet was there wine ministered likewise; (for Christ is like unto himself always, and would not be a breaker of his own institution, under both kinds;) though there be but one made mention of in this place. My lord is not ignorant that bread is taken in the scripture for the whole feast and banquet, as we see Gen. xviii. In the Pater-noster we say, *Panem nostrum quotidianum da nobis hodie*[1], and by the bread understand all things necessary for the body. *Victum, pacem, defensionem, bonam valetudinem*[2], &c. This manner of speech was also used among the gentiles, as Erasmus[3] writeth in *Symbola Pythagoræ, Panem (inquit) ne frangito*[4]. The gentiles, at the making of peace and lowdes[5], eat together in one feast, which was as a confirmation of the peace. So doth christian men, when they be at peace with God through Christ. And as the Ethnicks were admonished to keep the peace reconciled by their sacraments, so be the Christians also. Why doth not my lord mark these words, Acts ii. *Erant perseverantes in doctrina apostolorum et communicatione et fractione panis et precationibus*[6]? Why doth they not study to restore the doctrine of the apostles into the church again, and let this adulterous tradition of men pass? That church was assured of Christ by his word; and this church that men defend hath cast out God's word, and the apostles' also.

Gen. xviii.

Acts ii.

Then my lord saith by the authority of Gregory Nazianzene[7], that it is not necessary to observe all things in the

among the apostles who understood Christ (Luke xxiv. Acts ii.) we read of the ministration of the one kind, whereby appeareth that the one kind under the form of bread may be ministered alone." A Detection, &c. fol. 146.]

[1 Give us this day our daily bread.]
[2 Sustenance, peace, protection, good health, &c.]
[3 Erasm. Rott. Op. Tom. v. p. 341, D.]
[4 The bread, saith he, do not break.]
[5 Lowdes, so in the original.]
[6 They continued stedfastly in the apostles' doctrine, and fellowship, and in breaking of bread, and in prayers, Acts ii. 42.]
[7 "And because the devil intendeth to subvert all, I shew also his sophistry in lower matters than is the sacrament of the altar......wherein he will have all observed as Christ ministered it, which Gregory Nazianzene saith is not necessary; but we should herein give credit to our

supper as Christ did. I grant the same, or else we should have our feet washed, as the apostles had. But let my lord prove that we should not use the supper as a communion distributed unto the whole church, under both kinds, and then hath my lord done somewhat.

Then by the authority of the prophet Malachi[9], chap. i., Mal. i. my lord would stablish the mass, and prove it to be a sacrifice: *Ab ortu solis usque ad occasum magnum est nomen meum in gentibus, et in omni loco incensum offertur nomini meo atque oblatio munda*[10]. The prophet's mind was, that all the ceremonies of the law should have an end when Messias came, and that all the Christians should offer "*mucktar*[11]" unto God, *thymiama vel incensam*. Now this word "*mucktar*" signifieth also prayer, Psalm cxli. *Adaptetur oratio mea velut incensum* Psal. cxli. *ante conspectum tuum*[12]. And the prayer of the Christians is this oblation spoken of by the prophet, and not the mass. Nor the word that followeth, "*minhah*[13]," helpeth the mass nothing at all, which signifieth *farinaceam oblationem sive molam*[14], and is taken, Psalm cxli., for the evening prayer. Psal. cxli. By this word *minhah* the prophet understood the vocation of the gentiles unto the faith of Christ. *Non est mihi in vobis beneplacitum, dicit Dominus, neque acceptum habeo munus*

mother, the church, the pillar of truth, and who truly teacheth us that is truth: who, forasmuch as with the observation of this feast, in receiving, eating, and drinking Christ's most precious body and blood, is also celebrate the perpetual only pure sacrifice prophesied by the prophet Malachi (Mal. i.) to be observed and kept continually in the church of Christ, which sacrifice is the body and blood of our Saviour Christ; the same church hath received one word of Hebrew to signify all together, and used in the Latin (missa), and in English (masse), wherein besides the glorious presence of the body and blood of Christ, the holy circumstances used, and ceremonies done, be also many godly and most devout prayers, &c. &c." A Detection, &c. fol. 138.]

[9 See above, note 2.]

[10 From the rising of the sun even unto the going down of the same my name shall be great among the Gentiles; and in every place incense shall be offered unto my name, and a pure offering: for my name shall be great among the heathen, saith the Lord of hosts. Mal. i. 11.]

[11 Mucktar, מקטר Mal. i. 11.]

[12 Let my prayer be set forth before thee as incense.]

[13 Minhah, מנחת Minhath, Psal. cxli. 2. Donum numini oblatum spec. sacrificium incruentum, opp. זבח sacrificio cruento. Gesenius.]

[14 A farinaceous offering, or meal cake.]

[HOOPER.]

ciborum, id est, oblationem de manu vestra, id est, a vobis oblatam. Etenim ab ortu solis ad occasum ejus usque, id est, erit tempus gratiæ, quo acceptabo munus gentium, quod offerunt mihi, in omni loco nomini meo incensum atque mola pura offertur, (erit) oblatum munus mundum: per cultum veteris legis intelligit cultum novæ, id est, optimæ preces et animæ fidelium[1]. Thus doth the great clerk, Vatablus[2], write in his annotations. *Divus* Theodoretus *Episcopus Cyrensis*[3] writeth in this manner: *Non est mihi voluntas in vobis, dicit Dominus omnipotens, &c. Funditus vos rejiciam, nam permultum detestor vestra facta; et victimas, quas offertis, execror, quarum loco universum orbem terrarum me summa religione colentem habeo. Nam omnium habitatores terrarum, quas sol exoriens et occidens suis radiis illustrat, cum ubique incensum offerent, tum etiam sacrum purumque mihi gratum conficient. Cognoscent enim nomen meum et voluntatem, et debitum honorem præstabunt, et accommodatum cultum adhibebunt. Sic* enim [*etiam*] *Dominus ad Samaritanam, Mulier, crede mihi, quia venit hora, quando nec in monte hoc neque* [*in*] *Hierosolymis adorabitis Patrem. Vos adoratis quod nescitis, nos adoramus quod scimus; quia salus ex Judæis est. Sed venit hora, et nunc est, quando veri adoratores adorabunt Patrem in spiritu et veritate. Paulus his edoctus, in omni loco jubet orare, levantes puras manus, sine ira et disceptatione. Et divinus Malachias plane nos ex his docet eam pietatem, quam nunc profitemur, in omni loco obitum iri; nam circumscriptio loci ad sacra obeunda deleta est. Omnis locus accommodatus ad Dei cultum est existimatus, et victimarum ratione carentium cædes immaculatus agnus, et tanquam signum virtutis odoratum incensum existit. Judæi autem juxta Malachiæ prædictionem*

[[1] I am not well pleased with you, saith the Lord, nor do I accept the gift of meats, that is, the oblation, at your hands, that is, as offered by you. For from the rising of the sun even unto the going down of the same [&c.], that is, there shall be a season of grace in which I will accept the offering of the gentiles which they offer unto me, in every place, [as] incense to my name and a pure cake is offered, there shall be offered a clean gift. By the worship of the old law he indicates the worship of the new, that is, the best prayers and aspirations of the faithful.]

[[2] Vatabli Com. in loco. Lutetiæ 1545, fol. 151.]

[[3] Theodoreti Op. Coloniæ, 1617, Tom. I. Interpret. in Malach. cap. I. p. 504.]

rejecti sunt : ideo [*quare eis dicit*] *nomen meum* (inquit) *magnum* inter gentes [*in gentibus.*][4] The prophet never meant, nor none other learned man that knoweth the tongues, to bring a Jewish ceremony into the church of the gentiles, and to inclose Christ in this mealy sacrifice of the altar. Read the twelfth chapter of Paul to the Romans, and see what sacrifice is required of the Christian.

My lord hath the sound of one word more of the Hebrew, "*Missah*[5]," and would that the sacrifice in the law called *missah* should be a figure and type of this popish mass. *Facies solemnitatem hebdomadarum Domino Deo tuo cum levatione voluntaria manus tuæ, quam dabis secundum quod benedixerit te Dominus Deus tuus*[6], Deut. xvi. God Deut. xvi. commanded in the end of harvest to celebrate this solemn feast, and to offer unto the Lord part of every grain that came of the earth; not only because they should give him

[4 I have no pleasure in you, saith the Lord of hosts, &c. Utterly will I reject you, for I greatly detest your deeds, and I abhor the victims which you offer; in the place whereof I have the whole circle of the earth worshipping me with deepest reverence. For the inhabitants of all the lands which the rising or the setting sun illuminates with his beams, wheresoever they shall offer incense, there also they shall render as holy and pure that which is grateful unto me. For they shall know my name and my will, and shall pay me due honour, and render befitting worship. Thus also the Lord to the woman of Samaria [said,] "Woman, believe me, the hour cometh when ye shall neither in this mountain, nor yet at Jerusalem, worship the Father. Ye worship ye know not what; we know what we worship: for salvation is of the Jews. But the hour cometh, and now is, when the true worshippers shall worship the Father in spirit and in truth." Paul, instructed by this, enjoins us to "pray every where, lifting up holy hands without wrath and doubting." And the divine Malachi clearly teacheth us in these [his words, Mal. i. 11] that that religion which we now profess, shall be exercised in every place; for the restriction of place in performing sacred rites is done away. Every place is accounted proper for the worship of God, and for the sacrifice of victims void of reason is the immaculate Lamb, and the odoriferous incense standeth for a sign of virtue. But the Jews according to the prophecy of Malachi were cast off; therefore my name, saith he, shall be great among the gentiles.]

[5 *Missah,* מסת, *missath,* tributum, Deut. xvi. 10.]

[6 Thou shalt keep the feast of weeks unto the Lord thy God, with the tribute of a free-will offering of thine hand, which thou shalt give unto the Lord thy God, according as the Lord thy God hath blessed thee, Deut. xvi. 10.]

thanks for the preservation of the people from hunger and famine, but also to acknowledge him to give all things only, and not to attribute the plenteous and abundant harvest unto fortune, as the Epicures doth; and likewise to confess that his grace and favour maketh rich, and his displeasure poor; and not to attribute the gifts they received unto the second causes, as the Stoics doth, that say God is bound to do as the second cause is disposed. It is not so: for he can make scarcity and need of corn where as is good fertile ground, and abundance in the barren fields. And now, if an oaten or barley sheaf that was offered for the purpose that I have shewed, figured the mass, let the christian reader judge.

I marvel my lord is so full of allegories, and speaketh nothing of the text; when an allegory proveth nothing, but is used to declare the thing that we would prove. Let him first prove his proposition by the scripture, and then I will admit the figurative locution, as truth shall force me.

My lord, in the end of his book, speaketh of "them that study to impugn this stablished verity (as he calleth it) of the church, the ministration of the sacrament under one kind;" and then saith: "They err not only in that high matter of the sacrament, but also in ceremonies; and namely, such as garnish Christ's religion, wherein he saith the devil useth a marvellous point of sophistry by division and examining parts alone, which parts so considered severally be nothing, and yet joined together be somewhat[1], &c." My lord "will open this point of sophistry," he saith, "which consisteth in division between the whole and the part," and putteth this example: "If one were asked whether a farthing would make a rich man, a simple man would say, Nay, &c." Then maketh he his simile: Likewise "in the discussion of ceremonies, seemliness, and orders, the devil frameth his questions by division, and asketh of each thing alone[2], as for example, whether a shaven crown maketh a priest? Then answer is made, Nay. Doth a long gown make a priest? Nay." And so forth, as my lord telleth his tale.

[1 A Detection, &c. fol. 148, &c.]

[2 Like wyssein the discussion of ceremonyes, semelynys, and oders, the devyll fframy the his quæstions by de vysyon and as kythe of eche thyng alone, in the original.]

My lord hath well opened a point of sophistry, doubtless, as he that meant nothing else but to set a witched candle before the eyes[3] of the simple, that they should not see the truth, and would carry them by sophistry whither he listeth. He that will argue of a similitude, must put always two things alike, that the one may open the other. Now, my lord maketh a comparison of two things unlike, as the qualities of gall should in sweetness be compared unto the qualities of honey. Every man knoweth that this is true, in twenty pound necessarily to be contained twenty nobles, twenty groats, twenty pence, twenty halfpence, and twenty farthings, and not possible to have the greater sum without the less. Is the like in the dignity of a bishop or priest, suppose ye, that whosoever was, or is a good priest, must have necessarily that shaven crown and long gown? I report me to the scripture. They be neither necessary nor commendable signs to know a priest by. As thou knowest the less number to be comprehended in the more, so be these virtues comprehended in a true bishop, and not a crown: *Maritus unius uxoris, vigilantia, sobrietas, modestia, temperantia, hospitalitas*[4], &c. 1 Tim. iii. Tit. i. What devil hath made a crown, a long gown, or a tippet, to be a thing necessary for a bishop? Restore it to Rome again, from whence it came, and divide the whole into his parts by the scripture.

1 Tim. iii.
Tit. i.

My lord speaketh of John Frith and others[5], and saith they made the sacraments acts indifferent, to be used and not to be used as it pleaseth man. I would to our Lord, my lord of Winchester spake, neither wrote, more ungodly of the sacraments than they! There was a sort of heretics called *Enthusiastæ*, that were of that ill opinion; but not Tyndall, Frith, nor none other that

[3 à whicche candell before the Iyes, in the original.]

[4 The husband of one wife, vigilance, sobriety, modesty, temperance, hospitality, &c.]

[5 The bishop of Winchester speaks of these men in no very measured terms: "Hath not Frith, in a detestable book......defamed Tertullian, &c.? And hath not Œcolampadius most maliciously and untruly, in falsely reporting those holy men, attempted the same? fol. 82—Joye, Bale, Turner, or such like, the devil's limbs—the blasphemy of some such wretches, as most villainously write, speak, and (as they dare) jest at this day, fol. 84.]

writeth or hath wroten in our days, except the ungodly anabaptists[1].

And as for that my lord saith Bucer, Luther, and many other, with the whole church of truth, be against such as would have no corporal presence of Christ's body in the sacrament; the church of truth is with them, and the word of God, as every man may see and read in their works: and that those great learned men be against them and the truth in this matter, it is an argument that faith is the sole gift of God, and cometh not into the soul of man because he is learned, but because his name is wroten in the book of life, and preserved by grace, that he honour not the beast that blasphemeth the living God. Apoc. xiii. God shall open both their eyes, and my lord's also, to see the truth, when it shall be his blessed pleasure; for the which every man is bound to pray that knoweth the truth in this matter, and not to boast nor brag his knowledge, but to remember he standeth only by the mercy of God and faith. Let him beware he fall not, according to the commandment of Paul, Rom. xi.

<small>Rev. xiii.</small>

<small>Rom. xi.</small>

He that is persuaded in his conscience by the word of God, that he knoweth God and his sacraments, I exhort him in Christ to follow and obey the word of God, and live thereafter, that the word be not slandered by his ungodly life; and beware he fall not from one ill into a worse ill, from a papist to be a libertine; but as he increaseth in knowledge, so to increase in godly and virtuous life, remembering that the kingdom of heaven consisteth not in words, but in the doing and practising of God's will and commandment. Eccles. xii. *Finis universæ rei auditus est: Deum ergo time, et præcepta ejus custodi, siquidem hoc omnis homo (facere debet)*[2]. Let every man fear

<small>Eccles. xii.</small>

[1 These "ungodly anabaptists" were a sect whom Mosheim characterises as "seditious and pestilential, furious and fanatical, whose tumultuous and desperate attempts were equally pernicious to the cause of religion and the civil interests of mankind." Their chief leaders were Munzer, Stubner and Storck. Menno subsequently reformed them, but their enthusiastic character remained unchanged.]

[2 Let us hear the conclusion of the whole matter: Fear God, and keep his commandments; for this ought every man to do. Eccles. xii. 13.]

of the sentence that followeth, wherewithal Solomon concludeth his book: *Nam omne opus adducet Deus in judicium una cum omni secreto, sive bonum sit sive malum*[3].

At that day it shall avail nothing the gospeller to say, Lord, I knew thy truth, and jollily prated of the same against the papist and such as defended idolatry and superstition; now give me the joys that the gospel promised. No! it shall be said unto him, Depart in the devil's name, thou wicked person, to eternal pain; for all thy religion was in the tongue: no man can possess the joys promised in the gospel, but such as study with all diligence to live after the gospel, as God give us all grace so to do! Amen.

Psalm cxix.
Bonum mihi, Domine, lex oris tui quam multa talenta nummorum aureorum et argenteorum.

[[3] For God shall bring every work into judgment, with every secret thing, whether it be good, or whether it be evil. Eccles. xii. 14.]

CORRIGENDA.

In page 118, note 7 was intended to have been printed thus:—

[7] Hugo, probably Hugo Lingonensis, or Hugh de Langres, who lived in the 11th century, and wrote against Berenger. Hugh de St Victor also wrote on the Sacraments, &c.

The treatise of Hugo Lingonensis is in the appendix to Lanfranc's works. See Lanfranci Op. Lutetiæ Parisiis. 1548. App. p. 68.

In p. 182, note 4, line 5, for *refertories* read *refectories*.

A DECLARATION

OF THE

TEN HOLY COMMANDMENTS

OF

ALMIGHTY GOD.

A Declaration

of the ten holy comaunde-

mentes of allmygthye God, wro-

ten Exo. 20. Deu. 5. Collectyd

out of the scripture Ca-

nonicall, by Joan-

ne Hopper.

Cum, and se: Joan. 1.

Anno M.D.XLVIII[1].

[Title page to the edition of 1548.]

[[1] The date on the title page is 1548, but the preface is dated Nov. 5, 1549.]

A Decla-
ration of the X.
holye commaunde-
ments of Almighty God
written Exo. xx. Deu. v.
Collected oute of the scripture Canonicall, by John
Houper, with certayne
new addicions made
by the same maister
Houper.
Cum, and se: John. i.
Anno. M.D.L.

[Title page to the edition of 1550[2].]

[[2] There appears to have been more than one impression of this date.]

A
Declaration of the X
holie commaundements
of Almightie God written

Exod. 20. Deut. 5.

COLLECTED
out of the scripture cano-

nicall, by John Houper, with

certaine new additions

made by the same Mai-

ster Houper.

Come and see: John, 1.

[Title page to the edition of 1588[1].]

[[1] This is said to be the date of it, but perhaps without sufficient authority. The book itself has no date.]

[In preparing the Declaration of the Ten Holy Commandments for the press, the foreign edition of 1548[2], that of (Richard Jugge) London, 1550, and the later edition " imprinted at London by Robert Walde-grave, for Thomas Woodcocke," (1588,) have been carefully collated. The second named of these three old editions seems to be in general an exact reprint of the edition of 1548; except that in the seventh commandment some additional matter is given, and at the close of the treatise a few sentences relating to the difficulty experienced in printing an English treatise at a foreign press, are omitted. The edition of 1588 appears to be nearly a reprint of the former editions, with the addition of marginal notes and references.

The text of the rare edition of 1550 has been followed in this reprint, as being that which received Hooper's own corrections and additions. Occasionally the readings in the foreign edition have been adopted, where they were evidently more correct, and the marginal notes and texts in the margin have been added from the edition of 1588. References will be made to the different editions by the letters A, B, C, in the order above given.]

[[2] "The date is a misprint, especially as the 'Epistle unto the Chrystiane Reader' is dated 5 Novembris Anno M.D.XLIX. in this as in (the) two other editions." Lowndes.]

THE TABLE.

CHAPTER		PAGE
	The Preface.	
I.	What the law is	271
II.	The use of the law	281
III.	A preparation unto the Ten Commandments	286
IV.	The First Commandment	293
V.	The Second Commandment	316
VI.	The Third Commandment	322
VII.	The Fourth Commandment	337
VIII.	The Second Table	351
IX.	The Sixth Commandment	367
X.	The Seventh Commandment	374
XI.	The Eighth Commandment	387
XII.	The Ninth Commandment	405
XIII.	The Tenth Commandment	409

CERTAIN OBJECTIONS THAT KEEPETH MAN FROM THE OBEDIENCE OF GOD'S LAWS SOLUTED.

XIV.	1. Of time and place	413
XV.	2. Exception of persons	414
XVI.	3. Presumption	415
XVII.	4. Curiosity	419
XVIII.	5. Desperation	422
XIX.	6. Ignorance	426

UNTO THE CHRISTIAN READER.

I COMMEND here unto thy charity and godly love, Christian reader, the Ten Commandments of Almighty God, written Exod. xx. and Deut. v., the which were given to this use and end, diligently to be learned and religiously observed. Deut. iv. Matt. vii. My mind and commentaries in them I beseech thee to read with judgment, and give sentence with knowledge; as I doubt nothing at all of thy charity or good willing heart towards me and all well-meaning persons. But forasmuch as there can be no contract, peace, alliance, or confederacy between two persons or more, except first the persons that will contract agree within themselves upon such things as shall be contracted, as thou right well knowest; also, seeing these ten commandments are nothing else but the tables or writings that contain the conditions of the peace between God and man, Gen. xix., and declareth at large how and to what the persons named in the writings are bound unto the other, Gen. xvii. xxii. Jer. vii., "I will be [your] God, and you shall be my people;" God and man are knit together and unite in one; it is necessary to know how God and man was made at one, that such conditions could be agreed upon and confirmed with such solemn and public evidences, as these tables be, written with the finger of God. The contents whereof bind God to aid and succour, keep and preserve, warrant and defend man from all ill, both of body and soul, and at the last to give him eternal bliss and everlasting felicity. Exodi xix. Deut. iv. Matt. xi. John iii. iv. v. vi.

Man is bound of the other part, to obey, serve, and keep God's commandments; to love him, honour him, and fear him above all things. Were there not love and amity between God and man first, the one would not bind himself to be master, neither the other to be servant in such a friendly and blessed society and fellowship as these tables contain. Before therefore they were given, God commanded Moses to go down from the mount Sinai to the people, to know of them whether they would confederate and enter alliance with him or not. Exod. xix., &c. Moses did the message, as God bade him, whereunto the people altogether consented. So that it was fully agreed upon, that God should be their God, and they his servants, with certain conditions, containing the office of them both: God to make them a peculiar people, to prefer them above all nations of the earth, to make them a princely priesthood and a holy people; their office to obey, and observe his holy will and pleasure. Deut. iv. Exod. xix.

[margin: Exod. xix. 3, &c.]

Here see we the alliance and confederacy made between God and man, and the writings given; likewise how it was made. But wherefore it was made, and for whose merits, yet by these texts we see not: why God should love man, that so neglected his commandments, favoured and loved, believed and trusted better the devil than God, Gen. iii.; so far offended the divine majesty of God, and degenerated from grace and godliness by custom of sin and contempt of God, that he bewailed and repented that ever he made man, Gen. vi., and decreed to destroy the creature man, that he created, as he did indeed: not only thus destroying man, but also protested openly, that better it had been Judas never to have been born. Matt. xxvi. And in the 25th chapter of the same gospel the displeasure of God is declared so great, that he appointeth man to another end than he was created for, saying, "Depart, ye doers of iniquity, from me unto eternal fire, prepared," not for man, but "for the devil and his angels."

[margin: For whom the law was made and given.]

[margin: Gen. iii.]

[margin: Gen. vi. 6.]

[margin: Matt. xxvi. 24.]

What is now more contrary one to the other, and farther at debate, than God and man, that now we see bound in league together as very friends? Moses, Deut. ix., sheweth that only mercy provoked God unto this alliance, to receive them into grace, deliver them out of Egypt, and to possess the plenteous land of Canaan: further, that God found just matter and occasion to expulse the inhabitants of that land, and found no merits in the Israelites to give it them; for they were a stiff-necked people, and intractable, as Moses layeth to their charge. Deut. ix. Howbeit God, having respect only unto his promises made unto Adam, Abraham, and his posterity, measured not his mercy according to the merits of man, who was nothing but sin, looked always upon the justice and deservings, innocency and perfection of the blessed Seed promised unto Adam, Gen. iii., and unto Abraham, Gen. xii. xv. xvii.

Deut. ix. 5. vii. 8.
Only mercy provoked God to the covenant.
Deut. ix. 6.
Gen. iii. 15. xii. 3. xv. 5. xvii. 4.

God put the death of Christ as a means and arbiter of this peace, Heb. ix. " For the testament availeth not, except it be confirmed by the death of him that maketh the testament." The which death in the judgment of God was accepted as a satisfaction for sin from the beginning of Adam's fall, as Paul saith, Christ's priesthood was and is like unto Melchizedec, that had neither beginning nor ending, bound neither to time neither to place, as the priesthood of Aaron. But as God accounted in Adam's sin all mankind, being in his loins, worthy death; so he accounted in Christ all to be saved from death, Apoc. xiii., as Adam declareth by the name of his wife, calling[1] her Heva, " the mother of the living," and not of the dead. Gen. iii.

The death of Christ the means. Heb. ix. 28.
Rev. xiii. 8.
Gen. iii. 20.

All these promises, and other that appertained unto the salvation of Adam and his posterity, were made in Christ and for Christ only, and appertained unto our fathers and us, as we appertained unto Christ. " He is the door, the way, and the life." John x. xiv. He only is the mediator

All the promises made in and for Christ.
John x. 9.
John xiv. 6.

[1 Calling, C. Called, A and B.]

between God and man, without whom no man can come to the Father celestial. John i. iii. vi. Because the promises of God appertained unto our fathers, forasmuch as they likewise unto Christ; hitherunto and for ever they were preserved from hell and the pains due unto Adam's sin in him, for whose sake the promise was made. The means of our peace and reconciliation with God is only in Christ, as Esay saith, cap. liii., " by whose passion we are made whole." Therefore Christ is called by John the Baptist, " The Lamb that taketh away the sin of the world." John i.

marginalia: John i. 12. John iii. 16. &c. John vi. 32. &c.
marginalia: Isai. liii. 4, 5.
marginalia: John i. 9.

And as the devil found nothing in Christ that he could condemn, John xiv., likewise now he hath nothing in us worthy damnation, because we be comprehended and fully inclosed in him; for we be his by faith. All these that be comprehended under the promise belong unto Christ. And as far extendeth the virtue and strength of God's promise to save man, as the rigour and justice of the law for sin to damn man. " For as by the offence and sin of one man death was extended and made common unto all men unto condemnation," as Paul saith Rom. v., " so by the justice[1] of one is derived life into all men to justification."

marginalia: John xiv. 30.
marginalia: Rom. v. 17, 18.

The words of the promise made unto Adam and Abraham confirmeth the same: they are these: " I will put enmity and hatred between thee and the woman, between thy seed and the woman's seed, and her seed shall break thy head." Gen. iii. For as we were in Adam before his fall, and should, if he had not sinned, been of the same innocency and perfection that he was created in; so were we in his loins, when he sinned, and participant of his sin. And as we were in him, and partakers of the ill; so were we in him when God made him a promise of grace, and partakers of the same grace, not as the children of Adam, but as the children of the promise. As[2] the sins of Adam with-

marginalia: Gen. iii. 15.

[1 Justice: righteousness.]   [2 As, C. And, A and B.]

out privilege or exception extended and appertained unto all Adam's and every of Adam's posterity; so did this promise of grace generally appertain as well to every and singular of Adam's posterity, as to Adam; as it is more plainly expressed, Gen. xv. xvii., where God promiseth to bless in the seed of Abraham all the people of the world; and Paul maketh no diversity in Christ of Jew nor Gentile. Gen. xv. 4, 5. and xvii. 1. Gal. iii. 28. Col. iii. 11.

Farther, it was never forbid, but that all sorts of people and of every progeny in the world to be made partakers of the Jews' religion and ceremonies. Farther, Saint Paul, Rom. v., doth by collation of Adam and Christ, sin and grace, thus interpretate God's promise, and maketh not Christ inferior to Adam, nor grace unto sin. If all then shall be saved, what is to be said of those that Saint Peter speaketh of, 2 Pet. ii., that shall perish for their false doctrine? And likewise Christ saith, that the gate is strait that leadeth to life, and few enter. Matt. vii. Rom. v. 15. 2 Pet. ii. 1—3.

Thus the scripture answereth, that the promise of grace appertaineth unto every sort of men in the world, and comprehendeth them all; howbeit within certain limits and bounds, the which if men neglect or pass over, they exclude themselves from the promise in Christ: as Cain was no more excluded, till he excluded himself, than Abel; Saul than David; Judas than Peter; Esau than Jacob; though[3] Mal. i., Rom. ix. it seemeth that the sentence of God was given to save the one and to damn the other, before the one loved God, or the other hated God. Howbeit these threatenings of God against Esau, if he had not of his wilful malice excluded himself from the promise of grace, should no more have hindered his salvation, than God's threatenings against Ninive, Jonah i.; which notwithstanding that God said should be destroyed within forty days, stood a great time after, and did penance. Mal. i. 2, 3. Rom. ix. 13. Jonah i. 2.

[3 Though, A. Through, B. By the scripture, C.]

Esau was circumcised, and presented unto the church of God by his father Isaac in all external ceremonies, as well as Jacob; and that his life and conversation was not as agreeable unto justice and equity as Jacob's, the sentence of God unto Rebecca, Gen. xxv. was not in the fault, but his own malice. For there is mentioned nothing at all in that place, Gen. xxv., that Esau was disinherited of eternal life, but that he should be inferior unto his brother Jacob in this world; which prophecy was fulfilled in their posterities, and not in the persons themselves.

<small>Gen. xxv. 23.</small>

Of this acceptation of the one and reprobation of the other, concerning the promises of the earth, speaketh Malachi the prophet, as the beginning of his book declareth, speaking in this wise: "I have loved you, saith the Lord: and ye say, Wherein hast thou loved us?" God answereth: "Was not Esau Jacob's brother? saith the Lord; notwithstanding I loved Jacob, and hated Esau." Wherein hated God Esau? The prophet sheweth: "I have made his possession, that was the mount Seir, desolate as a desert or wilderness of dragons." Malachi i. The which happened in the time of Nabuchodonosor. Wherein he loved Jacob, the text declareth. God transferred the right and title that appertained unto Esau, the elder brother, to Jacob the younger: likewise the land that was promised unto Abraham and Isaac, was by legacy and testament given unto Jacob and his posterities, Gen. xxv. xxvii.

<small>Mal. i. 23.</small>

<small>Gen. xxv. 23. and xxvii. 28, 29. Rom. ix. 11, &c.</small>

Saint Paul, Rom. ix., useth this example of Jacob and Esau for none other purpose, but to take away from the Jews the thing that they most put their trust in; to say, the vain hope they had in the carnal lineage and natural descent from the family and household of Abraham, and likewise their false confidence they had in the keeping of the law of Moses. Paul's whole purpose is, in that epistle, to bring man unto a knowledge of his sin, and to shew him how it may be remitted; and with many testimonies and examples of the scripture he proveth man to be saved only by mercy for the merits of Christ, which is apprehended and received by faith, as he at large sheweth, cap. iii. iv. v. of the same epistle. Rom. iii. iv. v.

In the understanding of the which three chapters aright is required a singular and exact diligence; for it seemeth by those places that Paul concludeth, and in manner includeth, the divine grace and promise of God within certain terms and limits; that only Christ should be efficacious and profitable in those that apprehend and receive this abundant grace by faith; and to such as hath not the use of faith, Christ neither God's grace to appertain.

Now seeing no man by reason of this natural incredulity, born and begotten with us, Rom. xi. Gal. iii., can believe and put such confidence in God as he requireth by his law, as experience of our own weakness declareth, though man have years and time to believe; the promise of God in Christ appertaineth unto no man. This sentence is plain, Mark, the last chapter: "He that believeth not shall be damned." Howbeit, we know by the scripture, that, notwithstanding this imperfection of faith, many shall be saved; and likewise notwithstanding that God's promise be general unto all people of the world, Matt. xi. Rom. xi. 1 Tim. ii. Gen. iii., yet many shall be damned. These two points therefore must be diligently discussed: first, how this faith, being unperfect, is accepted of God; then, how we be excluded from the promise of grace that extendeth to all men. Rom. xi. 32. Gal. iii. 22.
Mark xvi. 16.
Matt. xi. 28. Rom. xi. 32. 1 Tim. ii. 4.

I will not rehearse now the minds of other; but, as briefly and simply as I can, declare the mind of the scripture in this matter.

Saint Paul calleth this servitude of sin, naturally remaining in our nature corrupted, sometimes *apethian;* then *amartian;* at another time *asthenean*[1]. The first How faith being unperfect is accepted of God.

[1 Ἀπείθειαν—ἁμαρτίαν—ἀσθένειαν.]

word signifieth an impersuasibility, diffidence, incredulity, contumacy, or inobedience. The second signifieth error, sin, or deceit. The third betokeneth weakness, imbecility, or imperfection. So writeth Paul, 1 Cor. xv., man's body to be first born in imperfection or imbecility. Also that God concludeth all men under infidelity, Rom. xi. In the Epistle to the Galatians, cap. iii., he saith, that the scripture doth conclude all men under sin.

<small>1 Cor. xv.</small>
<small>Rom. xi. 32.</small>
<small>Gal. iii. 22.</small>

In those three places thou mayest see the three words that I rehearsed before, with the which Paul describeth the infirmities of man, which infirmities Esay liii. John i. doth testify that they are translated into Christ: not so that we should be clean delivered from them, as though they were dead in our nature, or our nature changed, or should not provoke us any more to ill; but that they should not damn us, because Christ satisfied for them in his own body. And Paul saith, Romans v. that "Christ died for sinners which were infirm," and calleth those sinners "the enemies" of God. Howbeit he calleth not them *theostygas*[1] in the scripture, that is to say, contemners of God. Every man is called in the scripture wicked, and the enemy of God, for the privation and lack of faith and love that he oweth unto God. *Et impii vocantur qui non omnino sunt pii;* that is to say, they are called wicked, that in all things honoureth not God, believeth not in God, and observeth [not][2] his commandments as they should do; which we cannot do by reason of this natural infirmity or hatred of the flesh, (as Paul calleth it, Rom. viii.,) against God. In this sense taketh Paul this word *wicked*, Rom. v., when he saith, that Christ died for the wicked. So must we interpretate Saint Paul, and take his words, or else no man should be damned.

<small>Isai. liii. 4, 5.</small>
<small>John i. 29.</small>
<small>Rom. v. 8. ἀσθενεῖς.</small>
<small>How we are called the enemies of God.</small>
<small>Rom. viii. 7.</small>
<small>Rom. v. 8.</small>

Now we know that Paul himself, Saint John, and Christ, damneth the contemners of God, or such as willingly con-

[[1] Θεοστυγής.]   [[2] not, supplied from C.]

tinue in sin, and will not repent. Matt. xii. Mark iii. Luke xii.; Paul, Rom. viii. 1 Cor. v. 2 Cor. vi. 2 Pet. i. Those the scripture excludeth from the general promise of grace. Thou seest by the places afore rehearsed, that though we cannot believe in God as undoubtedly as is required, by reason of this our natural sickness and disease; yet for Christ's sake, in the judgment of God, we are accounted as faithful, *fideles*, for whose sake this natural disease and sickness is pardoned, by what name soever St Paul calleth the[3] natural infirmity or original sin in man. And this imperfection or natural sickness taken of Adam excludeth not the person from the promise of God in Christ, except we transgress the limits and bounds of this original sin by our own folly and malice, and either of a contempt or hate of God's word we fall into sin, and transform ourselves into the image of the devil. Then we exclude by this means ourselves from the promises and merits of Christ, who only received our infirmities and original disease, and not the contempt of him and his law.

Matt. xii. Mark iii. Luke xii. Rom. viii. 1 Cor. v. 2 Cor. vi. 2 Pet. i.

How we are excluded from the promise of grace that is extended to all.

Christ received our infirmities, but not the contempt of the law and of God.

Further, the promises appertain to such as repent. Therefore Esay, chap. liii. said without exception, that the infirmities of all men were cast upon his blessed shoulders. It is our office therefore to see we exclude not ourselves from the general grace promised to all men. It is not a christian man's part to attribute his salvation to his own free will, with the Pelagian[4], and extenuate original sin; nor to make God the author of ill and our damnation, with the Manichee[4]; nor yet to say, God hath written fatal laws, as the Stoic[4], and with necessity of destiny violently pulleth one by the hair into heaven, and thrusteth the other headlong into hell. But ascertain thyself by the

[3 The, B and C. This, A.]
[4 For an account of the principles of the Stoics, and of the disciples of Manes and of Pelagius, see Mosheim, cent. 1. cap. 1. xxiii. cent. 3. cap. 5. and cent. 5. cap. 5.]

scripture, what be the causes of reprobation, and what of election.

The cause of damnation in man.
The cause of rejection or damnation is sin in man, which will not hear, neither receive the promise of the gospel; or else, after he hath received it, by accustomed doing of ill he fall either in a contempt of the gospel, will not study to live thereafter, or else hateth the gospel, because it condemneth his ungodly life, and would there were neither God nor gospel to punish him for doing of ill. This sentence is true, howsoever man judge of predestination: God is not the cause of sin, nor would not have man to sin.

Psal. v. 4.
Hos. xiii. 9.
Psalm v. *Non Deus volens iniquitatem tu es*, that is to say, "Thou art not the God that willeth sin." Osee xiii. it is said, "Thy perdition, O Israel, is of thyself, and thy succour only of me."

The cause of man's election. Rom. ix. 16.
The cause of our election is the mercy of God in Christ, Rom. ix. Howbeit, he that will be partaker of this election must receive the promise in Christ by faith. For therefore we be elected, because afterward we are made
Eph. i. 5. Rom. viii. 29.
the members of Christ. Eph. i. Rom. viii. Therefore, as in the justification or remission of sin there is a cause, though no dignity at all, in the receiver of his justification; even so we judge him by the scripture to be justified, and hath remission of his sin, because he received the grace promised in Christ: so we judge of election by the event or success that happeneth in the life of man, those only to be elected that by faith apprehend the mercy promised in Christ. Otherwise we should not judge of election. For
Rom. viii. 15, 16.
Paul saith plainly, Rom. viii. that "they that be led by the Spirit of God are the children of God;" and that "the Spirit of God doth testify with our spirits that we are the children of God." Being admonished by the scripture, we must leave sin, and do[1] the works commanded of God: or else it is a carnal opinion, that we have blinded

[[1] And to do, B.]

ourselves withal, of fatal destiny, and will not save us. *What declareth a lively faith.*
And in case there follow not in² our knowledge of Christ amendment of life, it is not lively faith that we have, but rather a vain knowledge and mere presumption.

John vi. saith, "No man cometh unto me, except my Father draw him." Many men understand these words in a wrong sense, as though God required in a reasonable man no more than in a dead post, and marketh not the words that follow: *Omnis qui audit a Patre et discit, venit ad me;* that is to say, "Every man that heareth and learneth of my Father cometh to me." God draweth with his word and the Holy Ghost; but man's duty is to hear and learn, that is to say, receive the grace offered, consent unto the promise, and not repugn the God that calleth. God doth promise the Holy Ghost unto them that ask him, and not to them that contemn him. *John vi. 44. How God draweth unto Christ.*

We have the scripture daily in our hands, read it, and hear it preached. God's mercy ever continue the same. Let us think verily that now God calleth, and convert our lives to it. Let us obey it, and beware we suffer not our foolish judgments to wander after the flesh; lest the devil wrap us in darkness, and teach us to seek the election of God out of the scripture. Although we be of ourselves bondmen unto sin, and can do no good, by reason our original and race is vicious; yet hath not the devil induced wholly his similitude into any of Adam's posterity, but only into those that contemn and of a set purpose and destined malice hate God, as Pharao and Saul. The one gathered all his men of war and would fight with God and his church, rather than obey his commandment. The other would, against God's express will and pleasure, kill David that God had ordained to be king. These sins Christ *Exod. xiv. 1 Sam. xviii. 11.*

[² In, omitted in A.]

<small>Matt. xii. 32.
Mark iii. 29.
Luke xii. 10.
1 John v. 10.
Heb. x. 26.</small> calleth "the sin against the Holy Ghost," Matt. xii. Mark iii. Luke xii.: Saint John, 1 John v. "sin unto death:" Saint Paul, Heb. x. "voluntary or willing sin."

We must therefore judge by the scripture, and believe all things there spoken. Know thereby the will of God, and search not to know the thing that appertaineth nothing to thine office. Remember how crafty a workman the devil is, and what practice he hath used with other. Chiefly and before all things he goeth about to take this persuasion, "that God's word is true," out of man's heart: as he did <small>Gen. iii. 4, 5.</small> with Adam, Gen. iii., that thought nothing less than to die, as God said. Then thought he wholly to have printed his own image in Adam for the image of God, and to bring him to an utter contempt and hatred of God for ever, as he had brought him to a diffidence and doubt of his word. Here let us all take heed of ourselves, that, daily with the word of God being admonished of ill, yet amend not.

We shall find at length God to be just in his word, and will punish with eternal fire our contumacy and inobedience; which fire shall be no less hot than his word speaketh of. So did he with Saul: persuaded the miserable wretch that God was so good, that though he offended, he would not punish him as he said, but be pleased with a <small>1 Sam. xv. 15.</small> fat sacrifice again. 1 Reg. xv. This doctrine is therefore necessary to be known of all men, that God is just and true, and requireth of us fear and obedience; as Saint <small>John viii. 26.</small> John saith, "He that sent me is true." David, Psalm cxlv., <small>Psal. cxlv. 17.</small> speaketh thus of his justice, "The Lord is just in all his <small>The justice of God intendeth itself to two divers ends.</small> ways." And understand, that his justice extendeth to two diverse ends: the one is, that he would all men to be saved, Gen. iii. xv. xvii. Matt. xi. Isai. liii. 1 Tim. ii. Rom. xi.; the other end, to give every man according to his acts.

To obtain the first end of his justice, as many as be

not utterly wicked, and may be holpen, partly with threatenings, partly with promises he allureth, and provoketh them unto amendment of life. The other part of his justice rewardeth the obedience of the good, and punisheth the inobedience and contempt of the ill. These two justice the elders call *correctivam* and *retributivam*. Jonas the prophet speaketh of the first, chap. ii. and Christ, Matt. xxv. of the second. God would all men to be saved, and therefore provoketh, now by fair means, now by foul, that the sinner should satisfy his just and righteous pleasure. Not that the promises of God pertain unto such as will not repent, or his threatenings to him that doth repent; but those means he useth to save his poor creature. 1 Cor. xi. This wise useth he to nurture us, until such time as his holy Spirit work such a perfection in us, that we will obey him, though there were no pain nor joy mentionated of at all. Jonah ii. Matt. xxv. 31, &c. 1 Cor. xi. 32.

Therefore look not only upon the promise of God, but also, what diligence and obedience he requireth of thee, lest thou exclude thyself from the promise. There was promised unto all those that departed out of Egypt with Moses the land of Canaan: howbeit, for disobedience of God's commandments, there was but one or two that entered. Of the other part thou seest, that the menaces and horrible threatenings of God, that Ninive, the great city, should be destroyed within forty days, nothing appertained unto the Ninivites, because they did penance and returned to God. In them seest thou, christian reader, the mercy of God, and general promise of salvation performed in Christ, for whose sake only God and man was set at one: so that they received the preaching of the prophet, and took God for their God; and God took them to be his people, and, for a certainty thereof, revoked his sentence that gave them but forty days of life. They likewise promised obedience unto his holy laws and com-

mandments, as God give us all grace to do! that though we be infirm and weak to all virtues, we exclude not ourselves by contempt or negligence from the grace promised to all men.
Thus farewell in Christ.

V. Novembris,
Anno 1549.

[Preface to the edition M.D.L.]

John Houper wysheth grace and
knowledge in Christ to
the christian
reader.

I JUDGED, christian reader, that in my former epistle I had sufficiently entreated thee to have read, and given charitable judgment of this well-meant and truly-written treatise upon the Ten Commandments. But both my labours and my request I see of many not only neglected, but also despised; and not despised only, but also condemned: yea, innocently, I dare well say, if men without affection read or hear read the thing which, of affection, temerously they condemn. And in case I had not prevented in time (before I wrote the work and printed it first) the same foolish judgment of foolish and ignorant people, that now speaketh slanderously of one unslanderous doctrine, I had written things, (and not contrary to God's laws nor man's laws,) which would have offended them more, as touching divorcement, whereof I soberly entreat in the seventh commandment, and truly, as I will answer to the same by God's grace. But I refrained, for two causes: the one is, that all things be not expedient, though they be lawful; the next, that I knew there lay under every stone a scorpion to bite and poison whatsoever I should write or say. But seeing no man's writings heretofore hath been clear and free from misconstruing and calumniation of such sycophants and serpentine tongues as hurt or[1] they warn, kill or they admonish, slander or they judge, proclaim victory or they fight; I must hold myself well contented to suffer obloquy

[1 Or: ere, before.]

and slander now, as they did then. And as they wished a better mind and prayed for their adversaries then, so do I now, that God in Christ may save and bring both them and me to the joys everlasting. Nothing desire I of thee but as I erst desired, that thou wilt read with judgment this little declaration upon the Ten Commandments; and in the seventh commandment thou shalt find added more than was before, for the confirmation of such divorcement as many of late have been offended withal: and then give sentence charitably, whether I give any liberty to sin, or elevate, diminish, extenuate, break or dissolve matrimony ungodly and without judgment, or no. Weigh the fifth and nineteenth of Saint Matthew with the tenth of Mark, and so shalt thou understand wherein standeth the state of the controversy, and so be able to give upright and true judgment; which God grant unto thee, that
thou mayest not only be able to maintain the
truth that thou knowest, but also search to
find out in all other doubtful questions
the truth that thou knowest not.
Thus the Spirit of peace,
love, and knowledge
be with thee now
and for ever!
Amen.

From London, 28th Julii, 1550.

A DECLARATION

OF

THE TEN COMMANDMENTS.

CAPUT I.

WHAT THE LAW IS.

SEEING that the least part of the scripture requireth in the writer both judgment and circumspection, that the interpretation of one place repugn not the text of God's word in another place; how much more diligence, circumspection, fear, and love requireth the two tables of the Ten Commandments, in the which is contained the effect and whole sum of all the scripture! And whatsoever is said or written by the prophets, Christ, or the apostles, it is none other thing but the interpretation and exposition of these ten words or ten commandments. So that it were no need at all to require the mind of any doctor or expositor, to know the will and pleasure of God manifested unto the world in his word, would they that hath leisure to read the scripture, study therein themselves; or such as be appointed to the ministry of the church in their sermons declared unto the unlearned, what and which commandment the evangelist, prophet, or history, that he preacheth, declareth. If this were done, then were it no need to bestow so many years in reading the gloss and interpretation of man. For let him write or say what he pleaseth, he that understandeth the text shall be always able to judge whether he write true or false, and so stablish his faith and knowledge upon the word of God, and not upon the interpretation of man; conform all his life to this rule and canon of the ten commandments, and not unto the decrees of man, as God commandeth. Deut. iv. *Diligence and circumspection in interpretation.*

Christ and the apostles expound the ten commandments.

The text of the scripture to be understood and interpreted best by scripture.

Deut. iv. 6.

These ten words hath been largely and at length written upon by many great and famous clerks; so notwithstanding, *Matter enough for every man to exercise himself in the exposition of the commandments.*

as they have yet left sufficient matter unto their successors, whereupon they may exercise both their learning and eloquence, as in a thing most inscrutable. There is no acuity[1] nor excellency of wit, no learning, no eloquence, that can comprehend or compass the doctrine and mystery of the learning that is contained in these commandments. They teach abundantly and sufficiently in few words, how to know God, to follow virtue, and to come to eternal life.

What the law teacheth.

Wherefore it behoveth every man of God to know as perfectly these commandments as he knoweth his own name; that all his works, words, and thoughts, may be governed according unto the mind and pleasure of this law: likewise, because we may by the knowledge hereof understand other men's writings and commandments, whether they be of God or of man, profitable or pernicious, leading to life eternal or to death everlasting. They teach what God requireth in the heart, and what in external conversation, both to God and man; what is to be done in the commonwealth, and what in every private cause; what is the superior's duty, and what the inferior's; what the husband's duty, and what the wife's; what the father's, and what the son's; what to be done to a citizen or landsman, and what to a stranger; what in the time of peace, and what in the time of war. So that in these ten precepts every man may see what his office is to do, without further travail or study in any other sort of other learning. I purpose therefore by God's grace, as well as I can, to open by other places of the scripture the true sense and meaning of these ten commandments simply and plainly, that the unlearned may take profit by the same. This order I will observe:

First, shew what this word, law or commandment, meaneth.

Then, how the law should be used.

Thirdly, prepare the reader's mind, that he may always read and hear these commandments with fruit and commodity.

Fourthly, interpretate every commandment severally, that the reader may perceive what God, the giver of the law, requireth of every man that professeth his name.

[1 Acuity: acuteness.]

Justinian, Lib. 1. Pandect. tit. i. saith, that "the law is a faculty or science of the thing that is good and right, as Celsus there defineth[2]". Or thus: "The law is a certain rule or canon to do well by, which ought to be known and kept of all men." Cicero de Legibus saith, that "the law is a certain rule proceeding from the mind of God, persuading right and forbidding wrong[3]." *Lib. i. Pandect. tit. i.*   *De Legibus.*

So that the law is a certain rule, a directory, shewing what is good, and what is ill; what is virtue, and what is vice; what profitable, and what disprofitable; what to be done, and what to be left undone. This declaration of the law general appertaineth unto all the kinds, members, and particular laws, made either for the body, either for the soul. So that whosoever be ignorant of the law and rules, that appertain unto the science or art that he professeth, can never come to the end or perfection that his profession requireth. As for example: the end of a christian man is eternal life; and his profession is, to know and learn the law and canons that most plainly and sincerely leadeth him unto this end of eternal felicity. As the law of God, which is a certain doctrine, shewing what we should be, what we should do, and what leave undone, requiring perfect obedience towards God, and advertising us that God is angry and displeased with sin, and will punish eternally such as perform not all things perfectly contained in this law, as ye may read, Matt. xxii. Exod. xx. Deut. vi. Those places shew that God requireth of us perfect obedience. What pain is due to the transgressor, ye may read in Deut. xxviii.: "Cursed be he that fulfilleth not the law;" and likewise, Matt. xxv.: "Depart from me, ye workers of iniquity, into eternal fire." *What the law is.* *By the law we come to the end of our profession.* *Matt. xxii. 34.* *Exod. xx. 1.* *Deut. vi. 5.* *Deut. xxviii. 15.* *Matt. xxv. 41.*

I declare now, good reader, what the law is, and not how it may be fulfilled. That I defer unto the end of the exposition of the law. Howbeit, I would thou shouldest most diligently mark this definition or declaration, "what God's law is;" that thou mayest know what difference is

---

[² Nam (ut eleganter Celsus definit) Jus est ars boni et æqui. Corpus Juris Civilis. Ant. 1726. Lib. I. tit. i. col. 1. Tom. I. p. 109.]

[³ Lex est ratio summa, insita in natura, quæ jubet ea quæ facienda sunt, prohibetque contraria. Cic. De Legibus.]

The difference of man's law and God's law.

between the law of God and the law of man. Man's laws only requireth external and civil obedience; God's laws, both external and internal.

Now he that is ignorant of the means, is ignorant of the end; being ignorant of the causes, must needs be ignorant of the effect. Only by the law of God the means is known; therefore only the law of God, if we will come to the end that God would us to do, is diligently to be learned: for like as the physician cannot communicate his health with the sick patient, or the living man his life with the dead body of another, (but every man enjoyeth his own health, and liveth with his own life;) so profiteth not him that is unlearned the knowledge of another man, but every man must know and learn himself the law of God, if he will be saved. John vi. Deut. iv. As he, that will be a physician, must learn the precepts that teacheth physic; a musician the rules of music; the orator the rules of rhetoric; the ploughman the rules of husbandry; and so every person the rules that belong unto his profession, or else he shall never profit in his science or art, nor be accounted a craftsman, that knoweth not the principles of his craft: no more before the majesty of God is he accounted a christian man, that perfectly knoweth not the commandments of God, though he be christened, and braggeth of the name never so much.

Deut. iv. 1. A notable similitude to prove that every man must learn the law of God.

No Christian is he that knoweth not the commandments of God.

Common excuse taken away.

And because that no man should excuse his ignorance, and say the bible is too long, and containeth so high mysteries and secrets, that the labouring man hath neither sufficient time neither convenient understanding to learn the law and commandments of God; it pleased his infinite goodness to collect and gather the contents and sum of the whole law into so short and compendious abridgment, that no science of the world hath his principles or general rules concluded with so few words.

Experience and proof declareth the same. The logician hath no less than ten general rules, called predicaments, wherein is contained the whole matter of his art[1]: the rhetorician, three manner and divers kinds of causes, demonstrative, judicial, and deliberative: the whole body of the law civil, these three principles, "Live honestly, hurt

[1 See Aristot. Topic. Lib. i. cap. 9.]

no man, and give every man his²," Justinianus, Lib. i. Institut.: the physician, as many principles as be kinds of diseases: the heavenly God eternal hath concluded all the doctrine celestial in ten words or commandments, Exod. xx. Deut. v. And yet, for a further help of our unapt memory to retain the will of God, he hath gathered the said ten commandments into two: Matt. xxii. Mark xii. "Love God with all thy heart, and thy neighbour as thyself," Deut. vi. & xxvi. Lev. xix. So that every dull and hard-witted man may sooner learn the principles and general rules of Christ's religion than of any other art or science, that he give his diligence any thing at all for the space of one month.

Justinianus, Lib. i. Institut.

Exod. xx. 1, &c. Deut. v. 6, &c. Matt. xxii. 38, 39, 40. Mark xii. 28.

There be many causes that should provoke man unto the study and knowledge of this law. First, the profit that cometh thereof, which is expressed, John xvii.: "This is life eternal, (saith Christ,) to know thee, O Father, and him that thou hast sent, Jesus Christ." David the prophet desired the knowledge of this law, and so copiously expresseth the commodity thereof in the most holy Psalm cxviii., that nothing of this world may be compared to it; for it leadeth to eternal life. What commodities it bringeth in this world, it is declared Deut. xxviii. and Psalm cxxviii.: "If thou hear the voice of thy Lord God, and observe it, thou shalt be blessed in the field and at home; blessed in all things that thou takest in hand to do." Read the chapter: "If thou wilt not learn the will of thy Lord, thou shalt be cursed in the field and at home, and unfortunate in all thy acts."

Many causes to provoke man to the study of the law of Christ. John xvii. 3.

Psal. cxix.

Further, without the knowledge and obedience of this law no person in the world can justly and conveniently serve in his vocation or condition of life, of what degree soever he be. Wherefore Moses commanded, Deut. iv. that no man should decline from this law, neither to the right hand neither to the left; meaning by these words, that no man should add or take anything from it, but simply to observe it, as it is given and written unto us. From this right line and true regle³ of God's word man erreth divers ways: sometime by ignorance, because he knoweth not or will not know, that only the express word of God sufficeth. He holdeth with the most part, and

Deut. iv. 32.

Man erreth many ways; 1. By ignorance.

[² Juris præcepta sunt hæc: *Honeste vivere, alterum non lædere, suum cuique tribuere.* Corp. Juris Civilis. Ant. 1726. Lib. I. tit. i. Instit. Tom. I. p. 9.]   [³ Regle: *regula*, rule.]

condemneth the better, as it is to be seen at this present day. This reason taketh place: "It is allowed of the most part, and stablished by so many holy and learned bishops, therefore it is true;" when they cannot by the scripture prove neither the learning, neither the life of their doctors to be good.

<small>2. The power of the world.</small>

The second way that leadeth from the word of God, is many times the power and authority of this world: as we see by the bishop of Rome and all his adherents, who giveth more credence and faith unto one charter and gift of Constantinus than to all the whole bible[1].

<small>3. Mistaking of the time.</small>

Another erreth by mistaking of the time, making his superstition far elder than it is, will not forsake falsehood for the truth, and saith, "Thus my father believed, and should I believe the contrary?" Thus rather will give credit to his father, being blind, than unto God, his great grandfather, that seeth; to the law of man more credit, than to the law of God. As the knowledge of man is thus withdrawn from the word of God by ignorance and ill-used customs; so is the life and conversation of man likewise not governed with the word of God, but with accustomed fraud and guile, every man in his vocation and condition of life: the spirituality with false received and ill deserved teaching, the temporality with false contracts and preposterous buying and selling. The princes and superior powers of the earth, for the most part, and all learned men, either in maintaining a wrong religion, or in not restoring the true, decline far from this simple and sincere verity contained in God's word. Some dispense with a less ill to avoid a greater harm. Some prescribe laws for the conscience of man for a time, until it may be farther deliberated upon or approved good by a general council. These men grievously offend[2] themselves, and causeth other to do the same. In case the law made for the time seem not good unto such as shall at a more leisure have the examination thereof, the law for the mean time shall be condemned as heretical and pernicious.

<small>Laws prescribed for a time.</small>

Then put the case[3], that many, or at the least some, of

[1 This probably is in allusion to the Edict of Constantine, A.D. 313, in favour of the Christians, or to that of March 3, 321, by which the Council of Nice was summoned. See Platina's Life of Silvester.]

[2 Offend: offended, A, B and C.] [3 Case, C, cause, B.]

those that led their conscience after the law made for the mean time die: how standeth then the case with these departed souls that were deceived whiles they lived by false doctrine? They doubtless are lost for ever and without time, if they died in any error of the catholic faith, as Christ saith, Luke vi. speaking of false interpreters of the word of God: "If the blind lead the blind (he saith) not only he that leadeth shall fall into the ditch, but both." Therefore it is not sufficient that people have a law for the mean time, but whatsoever the conscience beginneth withal, it must end in the same; that is to say, no law at all should be spoken of concerning the conscience, but the only word of God, which never altered nor cannot be altered. Matt. v.; Luke xvi.; Psal. xviii. David, Psal. cxix., proveth the immutability of God's word by two strong reasons: if heavens and earth, made by the word, cannot be altered, how much more the word itself! Read the two verses that begin with the letter *Lamed;* in English thus: "Thy word, Lord, abideth for ever, as the heavens testify." [Luke vi. 39. Matt. v. 18. Luke xvi. 17. Psal. xix. 7. Psal. cxix. 89.]

Unto the which law the conscience of man, in matters of faith, is bound only. For whensoever or whosoever prescribeth any law for the cause of religion, and giveth it this title, "for the mean time, until it may be judged by a general council, or otherwise decreed by the assemblance of learned men," the author of the law declareth himself not to know whether his law be true or false, leading to hell or to heaven, to save the conscience of man, or to damn it; but leaveth it in doubt, and maketh it as uncertain as these that shall have the censure and judgment thereof preferred unto their discretion and learning. I would wish therefore, and heartily pray unto Almighty God, to put into the hearts of all superior powers of the earth grace and knowledge to choose four indifferent judges to appease all controversies in religion.

If the clergy should judge, the world would and might say, they are too partial, and for many respects would too much favour their own commodity. If the temporalty should judge, the clergy would think something to be done of displeasure or malice, that always in manner hath remained between the parties. Further, if a Papist, Lutheran, or Zuinglian, should judge, they agree so ill one with the other, that the matter could not want suspicion. Therefore I would have once these four indifferent judges to break the strife, the Bible in Hebrew, the Bible in Greek, the Bible in Latin, and the Bible in English, or in any other vulgar tongue, according to the speech of the realm where this communication should be had. Then, doubtless, these judges that favoureth not more the one part than the other, no more one person than the other, would soon set men at peace, in case they loved not dissension. But as long as the authority of any general council or judgment of man is accounted equivalent and equal with the word of God, the truth cannot be sincerely known.

Such as can interpretate nothing well, but looketh to find occasion to calumniate the good meaning of the thing well spoken, will say, I have an ill opinion of God the Eternal in heaven, and likewise of the superior powers [1] in earth, because I damn the disciples of the false doctors with the doctors, and take from all powers[1] of the earth authority to prescribe unto their subjects any law touching religion of the soul.

As concerning the judgment of God against those that be seduced by false preachers or makers of false laws, Saint Luke vi. and Ezech. iii. and xiii. judgeth as I do. And as touching the question, what I should then say of our forefathers, that ever sith the time of Constantine the Emperor, and Sylvester the bishop of Rome, hath always in manner been seduced by the false doctrine of man, I can judge none other than the scripture teacheth. Both he that leadeth unto damnation, and he that is led, falleth into the pit. And in the same place Christ saith, that it sufficeth the disciple to be as his master is.

_{Luke vi. 39.
Ezek. iii. 17,
&c.}

_{Luke vi. 39.}

_{verse 40.}

St Paul describeth the nature of such as preach false doctrine thus, 2 Tim. ii.: They lead unto iniquity, and their communication " eateth as the disease of a canker:" meaning, that false doctrine hurteth not only him that is seduced, but likewise such as shall be his hearers. And as this disease, called a canker, if it be in any part of man's body, it infecteth always the next parts unto it; as Galenus writeth *De causis morborum*, likewise Leonardus Fuchsius *De compendio medicinæ*, and Ovidius, thus,

_{2 Tim. ii. 17.}

_{De Causis
Morborum.
De Compendio Medicinæ.}

"*Utque malum late solet immedicabile cancer
Serpere, et illæsas vitiatis addere partes,*"

[¹ Powers: power, B.]

which is the same description of the disease written afore: so doth false doctrine. And as every member of man may be in danger of this disease, yet chiefly the members that wanteth sinews and bones; *Ut fœminarum mammæ, quod raræ et laxæ sint, ac crassissimam atræ bilis materiam prompte excipiant:*[2] even so the preaching of false doctrine may deceive every man, but specially the simple and unlearned, as it is to be seen at this day (the more pity!) everywhere. Easier for a soul that can do nothing but bless a tub of water[3], to keep an hundred in superstition and the adulterous doctrine of man, than for him that is well learned in the law of God to win ten unto Christ. Notwithstanding, I believe that in the midst of darkness, when all the world (as far as man might judge) had sworn unto the bishop of Rome, that Christ had his elects, that never consented unto his false laws, neither walked not after strange gods, though unknown unto man; as it was in the time of Elie the prophet, 3 Reg. xix., where God said he had preserved seven thousand that never bowed their knees nor kissed Baal. _{1 Kings xix. 18.}

In every age so God preserveth some, that no false doctrine may corrupt them, though the nature thereof be, as St Paul saith, to infect as a canker. So God impeacheth many times and would not things to execute their natural operation: as we read, Exod. iii. where the bush burned, and yet consumed not; likewise of the three children in the fiery furnace, Dan. iii.; and as Christ saith, John x., that his sheep hearkened not unto the voice of the false preachers. As many therefore as died before us, seduced by false preachers, without penance, the scripture condemneth. _{Exod. iii. 2. Dan. iii. 25. John x. 5.}

As many as believed them not, but trusted to the scripture, or else deceived, yet called to grace before they died, live eternally in joy and solace, and are saved, as John saith, Apoc. xiii. in the blood of the Lamb. I judge therefore in this point God to be no more severe than the scripture teacheth, wherein he teacheth us what we should believe and judge of him. Thus I have spoken largely and[4] truly, to admonish my good reader to beware _{Rev. xii. 11.}

[2 This sentence is omitted in C.]

[3 An allusion to the method in the Romish church of consecrating water for what is termed holy water.]

[4 And, supplied from A and C.]

of man's laws in the cause of religion. As touching the superior powers of the earth, it is not unknown unto all them that hath readen and marked the scripture, that it appertaineth nothing unto their office to make any law to govern the conscience of their subjects in religion, but to reign over them in this case as the word of God commandeth. Deut. xvii. 1 Reg. xii. 2 Par. viii. Soph. vi.

<small>Deut. xvii. 16, &c. [1 Sam. xii. 2 Chron. viii. Wisdom vi.]</small>
Howbeit, in their realms, provinces, and jurisdictions, they may make what laws they will, and as many as they will; command them to be kept as long as it pleaseth them, and change them at their pleasure, as they shall see occasion for the wealth and commodity of their realms, as we see in all the notable commonwealths among the Greeks and Romans, with other. Unto the which superior powers we owe all obedience, both of body and goods, and likewise our daily prayer for them unto Almighty God to preserve their honours in grace and quietness. Rom. xiii. 1 Tim. ii. 1 Pet. ii. Matt. xxii. Mar. xii. Luk. xx. And as many divers commonwealths as there be, so many divers laws may there be. Howbeit all christened kings and kingdoms, with other magistrates, should reign by one law, and govern the churches of their realms solely by the word of God, which is never to be changed; as I declared afore in the definition of God's law, that it is a rule never to be changed by superior power or inferior. Psal. xviii. and cxviii. So doth the holy prophet David, that honoured God, reverenced the powers of the earth, loved the common sort of people, teach, Psalm xvii.: "Shew me, good Lord, thy way, and lead me in a right path, for fear of those that lay wait for me." So commandeth Job, chap. xxii., to learn the law at the mouth of God.

<small>Rom. xiii. 1. 1 Tim. ii. 2. 1 Pet. ii. 13. Matt. xxii. 21. All realms are to be governed by God's laws only.</small>

<small>Ps. xxv. 4.</small>

<small>Job xxii. 22.</small>

I follow therefore the commandment of God, persuading every man to learn his faith in his law, as Moses did, Deut. xxxi., commending the law unto the priests, the sons of Levi, not only that they should know it, but to shew it unto the whole multitude of the people, men, women, children, and strangers, that they might hear it, learn it, fear the Lord God, and observe his commandments. So Christ commanded his apostles to preach, and their audience to hear the thing he commanded, Matt. xxviii. Mark xvi. With what diligence, and how it should be preached, learn in the viiith and ixth chapter of Neemi.

<small>Deut. xxxi. 11, 12, &c.</small>

<small>Matt. xxviii. 19, 20. Mark xvi. 15.</small>

CAPUT II.

OF THE USE OF THE LAW.

It is well known by the places afore rehearsed, that the law of God requireth an inward and perfect obedience unto the will of God: the which this nature of man, corrupted by original sin, cannot perform, as St Paul proveth manifestly in the seventh and eighth chapter to the Romans. There remaineth in man, as long as he liveth, ignorance and blindness, that he knoweth not God nor his law, as he ought to do, but rebelleth by contumacy against God. For no man suffereth God's visitations [or]¹ punishments with such patience as is required. No man can abide to hear his defaults rebuked by the law, but hateth his admonitors, and would that there were neither God neither law, so that he might, unpunished, satisfy his pleasure. Likewise the will as froward and perverse, that it willeth nothing of God nor of his law, so that if it diminish any part of such goods or pleasure as the world requireth: as we may see by daily defection and departure from the knowledge of God's word in those that once were as ardent as fire, but now, as the Gadarenes did, Matt. viii. Luke viii. Mark v. &c., they desire Christ to depart out of their country, rather than they would lose their swine. Where is now the will that freely and frankly should forsake all the goods of the world, and also this mortal life, rather than to leave Jesus Christ, which, as John saith, only "hath the word of eternal life," chap. vi.?

<small>The obedience which the law requireth, man's corrupt nature cannot perform.</small>

<small>Matt. viii. 34.
Mark v. 1, 2.
Luke viii. 26.</small>

<small>John vi. 68.</small>

It is not need to prove this perverseness and wicked resistance against God and virtue by the example of other; but every man may find himself too much infected with this disease, would he look upon his own life, and be as equal a judge of himself, as he is temerous in judging of other. Then should he flee the same ill in himself, that he seeth in another, and every man damned before God, except such as believe in Jesus Christ, Rom. v., and study to live after his law. 1 Cor. v.; Luke i.; Tit. i.; Matt. vii.; Psal. vi.

<small>Rom. v. 1.</small>

Seeing the works of the law cannot deserve remission of sin, nor save man, and yet God requireth our diligence

[¹ Supplied from C.]

and obedience unto the law, it is necessary to know the use of the law, and why it is given us.

The first use of the law.

1 Tim. i. 9.

The first use is civil and external, forbidding and punishing the transgression of politic and civil ordinance, as Paul writeth, 1 Tim. i.: "The law is given to the unjust." Wherefore God commandeth the magistrates and superior powers of the earth to punish the transgressors of the law made for the preservation of every commonwealth, as we read, Deut. xix., "Thou shalt remove the ill done in the commonwealth, that other may fear to do the same: thou shalt have no pity" upon the transgressor; for such pity as is used of man against this commandment towards the transgressors is rather a maintenance of ill, than works of mercy.

Deut. xix. 19, 21.

The second use of the law.

The second use of the law is to inform and instruct man aright, what sin is, to accuse us, to fear us, and to damn us and our justice, because we perform not the law as it is required, Rom. i. and vii. Howbeit the law concludeth all men under sin, not to damn them, but to save them, if they come to Christ. Rom. xi. Gal. iii.

To whom these two uses appertain.

These two uses of the law appertain as well unto the *infideles*, as to the *fideles*;[1] to such as be not regenerated, as to those that be regenerated: for those that she cannot bring to Christ, she damneth.

The third use of the law.

The third use of the law is to shew unto the Christians what works God requireth of them. For he would not that we should feign works of our own brains to serve him withal, as the bishops' laws that teacheth another faith, and other works than the old testament or the new; but requireth us to do the works commanded by him, as it is written, Matt. xv., "They worship me in vain with the precepts of men." Therefore David saith, "Thy word, Lord God, is the light unto my feet." Psalm cxix. By the knowledge of this law we judge all other men's writings, Christians and ethnicks, whether they write well or ill: and without a right knowledge in this law no doctrine can be known, whether it be true or false.

Matt. xv. 9.

Psal. cxix. 105.

This law judgeth, who defended[c] the better part, Marcion or Tertullian; Augustine or Arius; Christ and his apostles,

[1 The infidels as well as them that believe, C.]
[2 Defended: defendeth, A.]

or Caiaphas and his college of scribes and Pharisees; the poor preachers, that with danger of life set forth the glory of God, or the pope with his college of cardinals, that with wicked laws study to deface the glory and majesty of Christ's church; where and what is the catholic church of the Christians, and where the synagogue of antichrist? No falsehood can be hid, if men seek the truth with this light.

If we examine our deeds or other men's by this law or canon, we shall soon perceive whether they please God or displease. If we be praised and have an honest estimation among people, bring both our conscience and praise of the world unto this rule of God's word; and then shall every man judge himself, whether he be inwardly the same man that people esteem him for outwardly. In case man sustain likewise dispraise and contempt of such as be in the world, if the law of God bear testimony with his conscience, that it is rather the malice of the world than his demerits that oppresseth thus his good fame with the burden of slander; he shall rather rejoice that God hath preserved him from the crimes that he is falsely accused of, than impatiently suffer the malicious world maliciously to judge God to be evil[3], as it is his accustomed manner.

This law judgeth, that Aristotle[4] in his morals teacheth better doctrine, when he condemneth the external fact, in case the mind and will concur not to the doing thereof, than the bishops in their decrees, that attribute the remission of sin neither to contrition, nor faith, neither to Christ, but unto the external sprinkling of a drop of water. For thus they say of the water and of the bread in the exorcism or conjuration of the water, *Fias aqua exorcizata ad effugandam omnem potestatem inimici, etc.*[5], " I conjure thee in the name of God," as it is at the beginning of

[3 good to be ill, A.]

[4 Ἔτι οὐδὲ ὅμοιόν ἐστιν ἐπί τε τῶν τεχνῶν καὶ τῶν ἀρετῶν· τὰ μὲν γὰρ ὑπὸ τῶν τεχνῶν κ. τ. λ. * * * * τὰ δὲ κατὰ τὰς ἀρετὰς γινόμενα οὐκ, ἐὰν αὐτά πως ἔχῃ, δικαίως ἢ σωφρόνως πράττεται, ἀλλὰ καὶ ἐὰν ὁ πράττων πως ἔχων πράττῃ· πρῶτον μὲν ἐὰν εἰδώς, ἔπειτ' ἐὰν προαιρούμενος, καὶ προαιρούμενος δι' αὐτά, τὸ δὲ τρίτον καὶ ἐὰν βεβαίως καὶ ἀμετακινήτως ἔχων πράττῃ. Arist. de Moribus, Lib. II. cap. iv. see also cap. vi.]

[5 Ordo ad faciendam aquam benedictam. Missale Romanum ex dec. i. i. Conc. Trident. rest. Pii. v. Pont. Max. jussu editum.]

the conjuration, "to be a water blessed to expel all the power of the devil." Of the bread thus: *Benedic, Domine, istam creaturam panis, ut omnes gustantes ex eo tam corporis quam animæ recipiant sanitatem;* that is to say, "Bless, Lord, this bread, that as many as taste thereof may receive health, both of body and soul[1]." By this law thou mayst judge who defendeth the better opinion; Numa Pompilius, that forbid images, or else the bishops' laws, that say, idols can teach the unlearned people, and be to be used. Bring the matter to judgment, and see which opinion God's law will defend. *Non facies, inquit Deus, sculptile aut ullam similitudinem,* "Thou shalt make no image," &c. Whose law is more consonant with God's laws; the decrees and precepts of Cato, that saith, *Parentes ama, magistratum metue;* that is to say, "Love thy father, and fear the magistrate;" or the bishops' laws, that park young children in cloisters, that never know their parents' need; and likewise exempt the clergy from all obedience of the higher powers?

Exod. xx. 12.
Rom. xiii. 1.

God's laws saith with Cato, *Honora parentes: Omnis anima potestatibus supereminentibus subdita sit,* Rom. xiii.; Exod. xx., that is to say, "Honour thy father, and every man be subject unto the superior powers." The Romans reprehended and deposed likewise the tyrant Nero for his cruelty, and killed the vicious prince Tarquinius Sextus for vitiating of the chaste matron Lucretia. The bishops' laws saith thus: *Si Papa suæ et fraternæ salutis negligens deprehenditur, inutilis, et remissus in suis operibus, et insuper a bono taciturnus, quod magis officit sibi et omnibus; nihilominus innumerabiles populos catervatim secum ducat, primo mancipio Gehennæ, cum ipso plagis multis in æternum vapulaturus; hujus culpas istic redarguere præsumit mortalium nullus: quia cunctos judicaturus, ipse a nemine judicandus*[2]: that is to say, "If the pope care neither for his own health, neither for his brother's; be found unprofitable and neg-

---

[[1] Benedic, Domine, creaturam istam, ut sit remedium salutare generi humano: et præsta per invocationem sancti nominis tui, ut quicunque ex ea sumpserint, corporis sanitatem et animæ tutelam accipiant. Benedictio panis. Missale Romanum.]

[[2] Corpus Juris Canon. Paris 1687. Tom. I. p. 53. Decreti. 1 Pars. Distinct. xl. col. 6.]

ligent in his works; further, a man apt to do no good, (so I English *taciturnus a bono, i. qui sua natura omni honestate probitateque facile tacet,*) that hurteth himself and other, leadeth with him people innumerable by legions unto the devil, to be punished with him in pains most dolorous for ever; being pope, no mortal man should presume to reprehend his faults; for he judgeth all men, and is to be judged of no man." What law was there ever written more pernicious or contrary unto God's laws than this?

Cyrillus against Julianus[3] allegeth the writings of the philosopher Pythagoras, who proveth to be one only God, who made, and preserveth only[4] the things made. So do Sophocles[5], Cicero, Lib. II. of the Nature of Gods, Lib. I. *Tuscul. quæst.* Lib. I. *de Legibus,* Seneca[6] unto Lucilius, Epist. Lib. xv. Bring these ethnicks' laws unto the word of God with the law of bishops, that teacheth the invocation and aid of saints departed out of this world; and then thou shalt see that the ethnicks' laws are approved by God's word, and the bishops' laws condemned. For God's laws saith, " I am the Lord thy God, and thou shalt have no more before my face." Exod. xx.; Deut. v. And if we pray for any thing, God's word commandeth to ask in Christ's name. John xiv. Seeing the knowledge and use of God's word is so necessary, and only telleth us what is good and what is ill, what true and what false, every man should give diligence to know it, setting all other business of the world apart.

Lib. ii. De natur. deor. [29, &c.]
Tusc. quæst. lib. i. [70.]
De legibus, lib. i. [7.]
Epist. lib. xv.

Exod. xx. 3. Deut. v. 7.

John xiv. 13.

[3 Itaque Pythagoras dicit: Deus quidem unus, et ipse non, ut quidam suspicantur, extra mundi gubernationem, sed in ipso totus in toto circulo, omnes generationes considerat, contemperatio existens omnium seculorum, et lux suarum virtutum et operum, principium omnium, lumen in cœlo, et pater omnium, mens et animatio omnium, circulorum omnium motio. Cyrilli, Op. Paris. 1573, Tom. II. col. 526, B. Contra Julianum, Lib. I.]

[4 Preserveth only: alone preserveth.]

[5 Quin et Sophocles sic dixit de Deo: Unus, verissime unus est Deus, qui cœlum ordinavit, et terram ingentem, pontique jucundam undam, et ventorum vim. Plerique autem mortales, &c. Ibid. col. 527, E. See Soph. Fragm. LI. Brunck. with the editor's note.]

[6 Hæc exemplaria rerum omnium Deus intra se habet, etc. Seneca Epist. ad Lucil. LXV. See the whole Epistle. The reference xv. appears to be a mistake.]

CAPUT III.

A PREPARATION UNTO THE TEN COMMANDMENTS.

Necessary rules as preparatives.

Moses, before he repeateth the ten commandments in the book of Deuteronomy, prescribeth certain necessary rules and instructions, which he useth as preparatives and means to dispose and make apt the hearts of the people to receive this holy and most blessed sermon of Almighty God, the ten commandments, with condign honour and reverence; and that this law and precepts might work their operation and virtue in man, which is, to purge and cleanse the soul and mind from all unwholesome and contagious disease and sickness of sin, and to preserve the body in health and all honesty of life.

As a purgation made for the body (which Galenus calleth *humorum qui sua qualitate molestant evacuationem,* that is to say, cleansing of such humours as be hurtful,) many times worketh not his operation by reason of the ill temperature of the body, or else of the region that too much by reason of heat draweth humours of man into the exterior parts of the body: so the word of God, poured into the ears and understanding of man, worketh not many times his operation in cleansing the soul from the humours and corruption of sin, by reason of the ill temperature and disposition of the persons that useth to read and hear the scripture. As the physician therefore giveth the patient first some preparative, to dispose and make apt the body to receive the purgation with fruit and commodity, so doth Moses prepare first to make his auditors apt to hear the commandments, that afterward they might receive them with fruit and profit. How to proceed in the science and practice of physic, learn of Galen and Hippocrates, or of such as professeth that art.

Seven rules or precepts serving as preparative to the law of God.

My purpose is to shew, how Moses proceedeth in the celestial science of divinity, to cure the soul of man. He prescribeth unto his audience seven rules, or precepts, wherewith he prepareth them unto the receiving of the ten commandments; and without them it availeth nothing to hear or read the commandments, or any other place of the scripture.

The first rule is, confidence and a right persuasion of God's word, that all his promises be true; and will doubtless give the good promised unto the good, and the ill promised unto the ill, though it seem never so impossible unto the flesh. This preparative is most necessary for all men, that will be the disciples and hearers of God's word. For when men think that God is not indeed as severe, and will punish sin according as it is written in his commandments, and likewise favour and preserve them that fear him; they never take profit, nor never shall do, in hearing or reading the scripture; for they have no more credence to it than to a vain and faithless tale. The first preparative.

This misbelief and incredulity towards God's word is the occasion and let, that the word heard or readen worketh not his operation, and the man no better at night than in the morning, in age than in youth. Moses therefore persuadeth them unto a certain right confidence, saying, *Ecce, dedi in conspectu vestro terram, venite et possidete terram quam juravit Dominus patribus vestris Abraham, Isaac, et Jacob, ut daret eis atque semini eorum post eos:* Deut. i., that is to say, "Behold, I have presented before your face the land which the Lord promised to give unto your fathers, Abraham, Isaac, and Jacob, and to their posterity: come and possess ye the land." Jacob and his posterity were in such bondage in Egypt, that it seemed impossible that ever they should possess the land of Canaan promised by God. Read the fourteen first chapters of Exodus, and see. Then, as thou canst not choose but believe him to be true in the one promise of his help towards the good; so believe him that he will likewise punish the ill. Though he suffer and dissemble for a time at our sin, to call us unto penance, Rom. i., yet at length we shall be assured he will keep promise as well in punishing the ill, as in doing good to those that repent. If thou read the scripture, thou shalt find examples of both, how he favoured and kept promise with the good and the bad: Noha saved and his family; the whole world damned with water: Lot saved, and the cities burned. Josua and Caleb entered the land promised; all the rest died for their sin in the desert. If thou canst not read Deut. i. 8. Rom. ii. 4.

to stablish thy faith in the word of God, yet canst thou lack no master to teach thee this confidence in God. Turn thine eye of which side thou list, up or down. Behold the birds of the air and the flowers of the field, Matt. vi. Luke xii., and acknowledge not only the power of God that made them, but also his providence in feeding and apparelling them; for they be seals and confirmations of God's promises, that will clothe thee, feed thee, and help thee in all necessities. They were not created only to be eaten and smelled[1] unto, but to teach thee to credit and believe God's promises. Matt. vi.; Luke xii.

Matt. vi. 26. Luke xii. 22.

Matt. vi. 30.

The second preparative.

The second rule or preparative is, that thou have a right opinion of the magistrates and superior powers of the earth, that thou give them no more, neither no less honour nor reverence, than the word of God commandeth. This he declareth by the twelve princes that were sent to explorate and search the privities and condition of the land of Canaan. Two of them persuaded the people to believe God's promise, and not to fear the people that dwelled in the land; unto these godly princes was no faith nor credit given of the people. The princes that persuaded the thing contrary unto God were believed of the people, and their counsel admitted. By this we learn, that such magistrates, as persuade the people by God's word, should be believed and obeyed, the other not. In the cause of conscience there must God only be heard, Acts v. Matt. x., or else people shall fail of a right faith. For he that knoweth not what his duty is to God and his laws, will believe rather a lie with his forefathers, than the truth with the word of God; and this man is no meet auditor nor disciple of the word of God.

Acts iv. 19. [v. 29.] Matt. x. 28.

For lack of this preparative, the world hath erred from the truth this many years, to the dishonour of God and danger of christian souls. Men doth not look what God's word saith, but extolleth the authority of man's laws, preferring the decree of a general or provincial council before the word of God: which hath brought this abomination and subversion of all godly doctrine into the church of Christ.

The third preparative.

The third preparative is obedience both unto God and

[1 Spellyd, A, spelled, B.]

man. It were as good never to read the scripture, nor to hear sermon, in case we mind not to obey unto the word of God spoken or readen. Therefore doth Moses upbraid[2] and reprehend them, Deut. i., when they knew the land to be good by the fruit that the twelve princes brought unto them, that[3] they would not proceed forth in their journey to possess the land, but murmured against God; wherefore they perished in the desert. _{Deut. i. 26.}

Therefore we must bring with us unto the reading of the word of God obedience, and be ready to do everything it commandeth, though it seem never so difficile: as Abraham did in leaving his country, Gen. xii. and offering his son Gen. xxii. and as Christ commandeth all that will be his disciples, Matt. x. Luke xiv. The thing that God commandeth must be obeyed, what danger soever happen; yea, if it be the loss of our life. Luke ix. xvii. Matt. xvi. Likewise the commandment of the superior powers, and no man should detract, neither deny his obedience, because he is a Christian, 1 Peter ii. Rom. xiii. Eph. vi. Col. iii. Tit. ii.; not only with eye-service, but from the heart; sustaining not only such charges as the necessities of the commonwealth shall require, but also with life to defend the same, not fearing how strong an enemy is against him, nor how many; but rather to consider how strong God is, that hath promised to preserve every man's right, and given commandment that no man shall do the other wrong. Deut. v. Exod. v. *Non facies furtum;* "Commit not theft." Again, *Honora parentes;* "Honour thy father:" the which commandment requireth obedience to all superior powers. Only obey the word of God, whatsoever shall happen unto man in his godly vocation, as Moses commanded, Deut. xx. "If thou see horsemen and chariots more than thou hast, fear not; God is with thee," as we have example in Abraham, Gedeon, Josaphat, and others.

The fourth preparative is, that they should observe the common laws used among all people, which is called *jus gentium;* that they should peaceably pass by the possessions of the children of Esau, the Mount Seir, and likewise by the Moabites; not to molest them, neither their goods, but buy such things as they wanted for money, till they passed

[² Abraide, A, abrayde, B.]   [³ That, supplied from C.]

their limits and bounds; the which law bound them not to spoil, rob, and burn wheresoever they came, as well their friends as their foes, as it is used in our time among Christians, that say, *Silent leges inter arma*; that is to say, "Laws be dispensed withal in the time of war." Contrary unto this devilish opinion, God required them to pass as true men, and not as thieves; as those that were obedient unto all honest and godly laws, and not as exempt and privileged persons from all virtues and godliness.

<small>The fifth preparative.</small>

The fifth preparative is, that they should esteem this doctrine of the commandments as it was worthy, and declared the estimation thereof with many reasons: the first, of the utility and profit that it bringeth. Whereof he speaketh in the fourth chapter of Deuteronomy: *Hæc est sapientia et intelligentia vestra coram populo*; that is to say, "This is your wisdom and prudence before the people;" this is the doctrine only and law that teacheth how to live well, and to avoid the displeasure both of God and man, and leadeth to eternal felicity. "What other people is there of the world," saith Moses, "that hath their gods as present as our Lord God, as many times as we invocate and call upon him?" This doctrine was given from heaven, and the author thereof is God: a doctrine always to be learned and observed, not in paper or parchment, but in the heart of man, and daily taught unto the world, as the manner of the giving of it declareth. Exod. xxix. Unto all the people it was preached, not in an obscure and dark place, but in the mount, clearly and openly, that no man should doubt of it, as though it came out of Trophonius' cave, Saint Patrick's purgatory, or the privy chamber of the bishop of Rome: both the law and the lawgiver known of all the people. Minos was familiar with Jupiter, as the poets feign. Numa had communication with Ægera the goddess, but no man was record thereof: he might therefore feign what he list, as many superstitious hypocrites hath done.

<small>The estimation of the law.
Deut iv. 6.

Deut. iv. 7.

Exod. xix. 17.</small>

There appeared unto Gregorie a child in the bread of the altar[1]; the which vision, if it were true, was devilish,

---

[[1] Nos sane credimus post benedictionem ecclesiasticam illa mysteria esse verum corpus et sanguinem Salvatoris, adducti et veteris ecclesiæ auctoritate et multis noviter ostensis miraculis. Quale fuit illud quod beatus Gregorius exhibuit Romæ; quale quod Paschasius narrat conti-

and wrought by the devil to deceive the people of God. Brygitta[3] saw likewise in her contemplations wonders. The bishops in their Decretals seeth likewise marvels and mysteries[4], that no man else can see, except he be sworn to renounce God's laws; for they teach one faith, and the gospel another; one kind of good works, and Christ another.

This law is of another sort and perfection, openly manifested by God, not unto one prince or learned man, not unto twelve or seventy heads and principals among the people, but unto all the whole congregation; and not suddenly, but with great deliberation and preparation of the people for the space of three days. Exod. xix. This law therefore Moses would the people to esteem as a thing of all things most to be esteemed; as they do nothing at all, that say the scripture containeth not all necessary doctrine for the health of man, but needeth man's decrees.

Exod. xix. 15.

The sixth preparative is, a true and right understanding of the law; not to constrain the letter against the mind of the text, but behold always the consent of the scripture, and to do no wrong unto the Author thereof.

The sixth preparative.

Some men call this a dispensation of the law, when the extremity thereof cannot with justice and equity be executed against the transgressor; as we see Deut. iv. where Moses appointeth certain cities to be as refuges or sanctuaries for them that by chance or against their will

Deut. iv. 41.

gisse Alemanniæ, presbyterum Plegildum visibiliter speciem pueri in altare contrectasse, et post libata oscula in panis similitudinem conversum, &c. Malms. de gestis reg. Angl. Lib. III.]

[3 Brygitta. Brigida, devotissima Christi mulier, Suetiæ princeps. Platina. Her revelations were printed in eight books, which John de Torquemada defended in the council of Basil. Sion House, in Middlesex, was once a monastery of the order of Saint Bridget.]

[4 In the "Vitæ Patrum," Par. I. cap. 162, is a story "of a Hebrew man that saw a child between the hands of Saint Basil, when he divided the body of our Lord." The child, as it seemed to him, was by this said Basil parted and divided, and the chalice seemed filled with blood.—Paschasius Radbertus, in his treatise on the body and blood of Christ, cap. xiv. relates a story of a priest, who prayed earnestly to *behold* the real presence. —Tum venerabilis presbyter pavidus, ab imo vultum erigens, vidit super aram Patris filium, puerum, &c. Hence, one of the questions among the schoolmen is, "Utrum quando in hoc sacramento miraculose apparet caro vel puer, sit ibi vere corpus Christi." Tho. Aquin. Vol. II. Par. 3. Quæst. 76. Art. 8.]

should happen to kill any man. The law is, that whosoever shed the blood of man, shall satisfy the law with his blood again. Gen. ix. Matt. xxvi. Apoc. xiii. This law extendeth not as far as the words sound, but as far as the mind of the letter permitteth; that is to say, unto such as of hatred, rash and wilful madness, or to satisfy an ill and undigested passion, that hateth his neighbour, killeth his neighbour, contemneth God in the superior powers, who should reverence and punish the ill-doer, and not he himself. Those and such-like should suffer death again, and not such as kill against their will. Thus doth the scripture of God interpretate itself, and sheweth how every law should be understood: the which is a very necessary rule and precept to be always observed everywhere, lest the figure[1] and force of the letter should do injuries unto any circumstance of the text.

Gen. ix. 6. Matt. xxvi. 52.

Therefore I would every man in the reading of the scripture should mark two things in every doubtful text: first, the consent of other places; then, the allegory of the letter. As for an example, this proposition Matt. xxvi.: "This is my body." First, look the other places of the scripture, what Christ's body is, and what qualities it hath; how it was conceived and born, and whither it is ascended. Then thou shalt by the consent of other places be constrained to understand these words according to the analogy or proportion of faith, and not after the letter. Then consider by the scripture, why Christ by an allegory called the bread his body, and the wine his blood. Then it shall be easy to understand, that they be rather confirmations of our faith, than the body itself: sacraments and memorials of the things past, and not the thing they represent and signify. Rom. iv.

Two things to be marked in every doubtful text: 1. The consent of other places. 2. The allegory of the letter.

Rom. iv. 11.

The seventh preparative is, to add nothing unto this law, neither to take any thing from it. Who can be a convenient disciple of God and his doctrine, that believeth not all things, and every thing necessary for the salvation of man, to be contained openly and plainly in the scripture canonical? Or how can he be a christian man, that believeth one commandment of God, and not the other? He that said, "Thou shalt have but one God," saith likewise, "Thou shalt neither

The seventh preparative.

Deut. iv. 2.

[[1] Rigure, A, figure, B, vigor, C.]

add nor take any thing from the scripture," Deut. iv., but shalt observe it as it is given. So said Christ, Matt. xxviii.; so saith Saint John, chap. xxi.: likewise in the Revelations of Jesus Christ our Redeemer, chap. xxii. What is more necessary for him, that will read the scripture or hear it preached, than this preparative? First to be persuaded, that all verity and necessary doctrine for our salvation is contained therein, and that the holy church of the patriarchs, prophets, and apostles, believed, preached, and died for the same, and in the same doctrine. If thy heart be not thus prepared, but judgest that God's law containeth one part of such doctrine as is necessary for man's salvation, and the bishops' laws another part; thou contemnest and dishonourest the whole law and giver thereof, and offendest the commandment given, Deuteronomy iv. xii., and Proverbs xxx. Read diligently those places. Further, remember that this opinion is so ungodly, that the whole scripture endeth with this sentence: "If any man add unto the word of God, God will put upon him all the maledictions contained in the book. And if any man diminish any thing of this prophecy, God will take from him such part as he hath in the book of life." Apocalypse xxii.

<small>Matt. xxviii. 20.
John xxi. 24.
Rev. xxii. 18.

Deut. iv. 2. & xii. 32.
Prov. xxx. 5, 6.

Rev. xxii. 18, 19.</small>

THE FIRST TABLE.

CAPUT IV.

I am the Lord thy God, that brought thee out of Egypt, from the house of servitude: thou shalt have no strange gods before me.

THIS precept or commandment hath two members: the first requireth that we accept, account, and take the God that made and preserveth all things, the God *Sadai*[1], omnipotent and sufficient, not only to be God, but also to be our God, that helpeth us, succoureth us, saveth us, and only defendeth us. The second part forbiddeth all false gods.

<small>The principal part of the first commandment.</small>

[1 El-Shaddai, אל שדי, Exod. vi. 3.]

This first part is the ground, original, and foundation of all virtue, godly laws, or christian works. And where as this precept and commandment is not first laid, and taken as the only well whereof springeth all other virtues; whatsoever be done, seem it never so glorious and holy unto the world, it is nothing but very superstition and hypocrisy, as Paul saith, Rom. xiv.; Heb. xi.

Rom. xiv. Heb. xi.

What putteth difference between the death of Socrates and Esaias, Diogenes and Hieremy, Sophocles and Zachary, Euripides and Stephen, Homer and Saint John Baptist, saving only the knowledge and confidence in this commandment, "I am the Lord thy God?" What difference were there between the church of the Pharisees, scribes, and hypocrites, and the church of God, were not the knowledge of this commandment that containeth two most necessary things, the true knowledge of God, and the true honour of God? Deut. iv. xii. Exod. xix. xx. Gen. xii. xvii. The which foundation and ground of our religion both the testaments every where teacheth: also the image of God in our soul. Though we be born in servitude of sin, and blind unto all godliness, such a sparkle and dim light notwithstanding remaineth in the soul, that our own conscience crieth out against us, when we utterly contemn the reverence and divine majesty of God. As it appeareth by the horrible and fearful death of such as thought it more easy to destroy their own living bodies, than to endure the conflict and dolours of their own conscience with the judgment and contempt of God's laws; as it is to be seen, (leaving profane examples apart,) in Saul, and Judas, with all other such in our time, that are the causers of their own death.

This first commandment containeth two notable things.

1 Sam. xxxi. 4. Matt. xxvii. 5.

The subtilty of the devil.

The subtilties of the devil must be taken heed of therefore, and known betime, lest he shew us God in another form than he sheweth himself in his word, and this commandment, where he saith that he is our God, to say, as well ready to punish us if we contemn him, as to help us if we love him. The devil goeth about another thing, and would all men, as long as they have a purpose and bent will to sin, think that God is a merciful God, a gentle, sweet, and figgy[1] God, that winketh and will not see the abomination and accustomed doing of ill. But when the

[1 Fyggie, A and B, loving, C.]

conscience feeleth the displeasure of God, and seeketh redress, he amplifieth and exaggerateth the greatness of sin, sheweth it as foul and as horrible as it is indeed, and more extenuateth the mercy of God; maketh him then a cruel and an unmerciful tyrant, as impossible to obtain mercy of, as to suck water out of the dry pumps[2] or burning coal.

Wherefore, seeing his majesty is invisible, and cannot be known of mortal man, as he is; and likewise because man giveth little credit, or none at all, unto his blessed word, he presenteth all his works, heaven and earth, unto man, to be testimonies and witness of his great power; that man, seeing those creatures and wonderful preservation of the same, might think upon[3] God, the maker of all things, and thank him with all the heart, that he would say these words unto him, a vile creature and worm's meat: "I am the Lord thy God." By his works he shewed himself thus unto Adam, Gen. ii., and unto the natural phi-[losopher,[4]] Rom. i.; also unto every reasonable man, Deut. xxx. Howbeit, so far hath the devil blinded many (would to God, only the infidels and not such as be accounted Christians!) that they take as much knowledge of God by the contemplation of his works, as Midas the king by the contemplation of his gold. Gen. ii. 15. Rom. i. 20. Deut. xxx. 19.

Wherefore, seeing we believe with such difficulty this word of God, "I am the Lord thy God," and the devil hath blindfolded and dared our sight, and so bewitched all our senses, that we hear nor see any thing to the glory of God and salvation of our souls; he addeth yet other testimonies to ascertain us that he is our God, and leaveth nothing undone, that might draw us unto a firm and constant belief in him; setting before our eyes the glorious and wonderful deliverance and defence of the people, when he brought them out of Egypt. Such testimonies added he unto his word to stablish our faith always: to Adam and Abel, when the fire from heaven burned their sacrifice, Gen. iv. ix. xvii. Exod. xii.: so unto us, unto whom he hath given the same word, Rom. i. [he] hath given for the confirmation thereof his dear Son Jesus Christ, born, dead, and resuscitated from death, to shew us himself, and to

[2 Pumpesse, A and B, pump, C.]
[3 Think of, A.]   [4 Supplied from C.]

teach us that he is our God to save us from the servitude of hell and sin, and to help us as many times as we call unto him in Christ's name. For only in him we come to that knowledge of God, that he will be our God.

Though the Jew and the Turk know there is but one God, and after their religion would honour him; yet doubt they whether he taketh cure of them, will hear their petitions, will be honoured of them, and how he will be honoured. For they have not the word of God, as Christ gave it, but as they falsely interpretate it, to the contumely and dishonour of Christ. But we know him to be our God, as this commandment saith, in Christ Jesu. John i. Matt. xi. John xvi. When we have a true knowledge of him by his word, we must give him the same honour that his commandment requireth, to say, obedience and fear, faith and love. Repeat the words again of the commandment, and mark them: "I am the Lord thy God." If he be Lord, then hath he power over body and soul; obey him therefore, lest he destroy them both. "Thy God:" if he be God, all things be in his power, and hath sufficient both for thee and all other, and will give it thee because he is thy God. He needeth for himself neither heaven, neither earth, nor any thing that is therein; and to put thee out of doubt thereof, he brought not only the people out of Egypt to warrant his promise, but also send his only Son to die for thy sake, that he might be thine, and thou his. Rom. vi. Esa. liii.

<small>John i. 18.</small>
<small>Matt. xi. 28. John xvi. 29.</small>
<small>Rom. vi. 3. Isai. liii. 4, 5.</small>
<small>The effect of this commandment.</small>

The effect now of this part of the commandment is to declare and bring man unto a knowledge of God, as ye see; and once known by his word, requireth also man's duty to honour him in true and perfect religion, the which consisteth in fear, faith, and love: the which three points Moses diligently and at large declareth in the 6th, 7th, 8th, 9th, 10th, 11th chapters of Deuteronomy, and doth nothing else in all them but expound this first commandment. I will shew thee partly how; and then read the places, and learn more by thyself.

In the beginning of the sixth chapter he sheweth wherefore thou shouldest fear him, and keep his commandments, saying, "It shall be to thy profit." This is the manner of all men that would have any thing done: first, to shew what profit followeth the doing of it, that the commodity might excitate the mind and study of him that should do it. Moses saith, "It shall be well with thee, God will multiply thy seed, and give thee a land flowing with milk and honey." Now, if thou fear the Lord God, this shall be thy reward, and the same self promise thou shalt find many times annexed with the fear of God, before thou come to the end of the 11th chapter. All health and joy followeth the fear of God. Mark those words well, and print them in thy heart; fear of no ill nor sickness, contagious air or disease, so thou have this medicine of God's fear in thy soul, which preserveth health, and expulseth all diseases.

Galenus hath written books, *De tuenda Sanitate*, that is to say, to preserve health: so hath Hippocrates, Cornelius Celsus, and other. They prescribe those six things to be observed of as many as would live in good health: [1.] The temperature and condition of the air. 2. Moderate use of meat and drink. 3. Motion and exercise of the body, and rest of the same. 4. Sleep and watch, as the complexion by nature shall in time convenient require. 5. Fulness and emptiness of the body. Gale. Lib. II. *Aph. commenta.* 17, et Lib. II. *de compos. medic.* 6. Perturbations and passions of the mind. For many hath died with such passions of the mind; with sudden sorrow, as P. Rutilius[2], Plinius Lib. VII. cap. 36., and M. Lepidus[3]; some with sudden joy, as the noble woman Policrata[4], as Arist. writeth. So died Diagoras, as Gellius[5] writeth; and other, as ye may read, Plin. Lib. II. cap. 53, Valer. Max. Lib. IX.

Galen. lib. ii. Aphor. com. 17. et lib. ii. de compos. medic. Plinius, lib. vii. cap. 36. Gell. lib. iii. cap. 15. Plin. lib. ii.[1] cap. 53. Val. Max. lib. ix. cap. xii. Plin. lib. [v]ii.[1] cap. 53.

[¹ Several of these references are evidently wrong.]

[² P. Rutilius morbo levi impeditus, nuntiata fratris repulsa in Consulatus petitione, illico expiravit. C. Plinii Secundi Hist. mundi, Lib. VII. cap. xxxvi. Basiliæ, 1545, p. 116.]

[³ Lepidus. Cum autem non multo M. Lepidus nobilissimæ stirpis, quem eventi anxietate diximus mortuum, &c. C. Plinii Sec. Hist. mundi, Lib. VII. cap. liii. p. 124.]

[⁴ Policreta.—See Plut. de claris mulier.]

[⁵ Gellius. Is Diagoras tres filios adolescentes habuit, &c. Eosque omnes vidit vincere, coronarique eodem Olympiæ die; et cum ibi eum tres adolescentes amplexi, coronis suis in caput patris positis suaviarentur, cumque populus gratulabundus flores undique in eum jaceret, ibi in studio inspectante populo, in oculis atque in manibus filiorum animum efflavit. Auli Gellii Noctes Atticæ, Coloniæ, 1541, pp. 151, 2.]

cap. 12. Some died for shame, as Diodorus[1], Plin. Lib. II. cap. 53; Homer, Valer.[2] Lib. IX. cap. 12. The physicians promiseth health, if these six rules be observed. But God saith, all those be in vain without the fear of him. Deut. xxvii. xxviii. xxx. There see the word of God. And look the second book of the Kings, chap. xxiv. how it was proved true, where as the pestilence infected the whole land of Canaan, from the city of Dan unto the city of Bersabee, in three days, so that there died seventy thousand men in that short space.

Plin. lib. ix. cap. 12.

[2 Sam.]

In the end of the sixth chapter of Deuteronomy Moses exhorteth the people to fear God, to avoid the punishment that followeth the contempt of God's commandment: and this is the most apt and best way to persuade people that careth for no virtue, nor will not be moved with any promise or reward that followeth well doing. "I am a jealous God, and the Lord thy God is in the middle of thee." Which words declareth, that when people will not obey his commandments, and receive his love and favour, he waxeth angry, and useth the extreme remedy, the scourge of adversity, that whosoever will not willingly by fair means bow[3], by force shall be constrained to break; for nothing can resist when he will punish.

Three points of religion.

The first point therefore of religion is the *fear* of God.

The second is *faith* and confidence in his word. Therefore saith Moses: *Audi, Israel, Dominus Deus noster unus est;* that is to say, "Hear, O Israel, the Lord our God is one God; that in this one God thou shalt put all thy trust, and believe."

Deut. vi. 4, 5.

To persuade this faith into their hearts, Moses put not only the deliverance out of Egypt before their faces, but also the seven most mighty princes of the world: Hytheum, Girgaseum, Nemorreum, Cananeum, Pherizeum, Hiveum and Jebuseum. Deut. vii. And in the same chapter he repeateth and inculcateth into the ear this religion and

Hittites, Girgashites, Amorites, Canaanites, Perizzites, Hivites, Jebusites. Deut. vii. 1. [9].

[1 De mortibus repentinis. Pudore Diodorus, sapientiæ dialecticæ professor, lusoria quæstione non protinus ad interrogationes Stilbonis dissoluta. C. Plinii Sec. Hist. mundi, Lib. VII. cap. liii. p. 124.]

[2 Homer. Non vulgaris etiam Homeri mortis causa fertur: qui in insula, quia quæstionem a piscatoribus propositam solvere non potuisset, dolore absumptus creditur. Val. Max. Lib. IX. cap. xii. 3.]

[3 Bow: boghe, A, bought, B and C.]

faith, saying, *Scias itaque quod Dominus Deus tuus ipse est Deus, Deus fidelis,* &c. that is to say, "Know thou that the Lord thy God, he is the only and true God," and so forth. Then read unto the end of the eleventh chapter, how busy and diligent Moses is, heaping argument upon argument to persuade the people to believe God and his word, and to stablish this commandment, and root it in their and our hearts. All the works of God, heaven and earth, all the miracles wrought in the Old Testament and in the New, were done to prove unto mortal man this precept to be true, "I am the Lord thy God," and by none other thing but interpretations of this commandment to stablish the verity of this[4] word. ver. 6.

The third is *love:* wherefore he saith, "Love the Lord thy God with all thy heart, all thy soul, and with all thy power." Deut. vi. Moses, in the end of the chapter, sheweth wherefore this our God should be loved. "He will give you," saith he, "the land that ye never deserved, freely for his promise sake." And in the seventh chapter he promiseth to destroy a people more strong than they be. In the eighth chapter he saith, that he fed them in the wilderness with meat from heaven, which they, neither their fathers, never knew. By these and other many reasons he provoked the people to this part of religion, the love of God. In case any benefactor, or he that doeth good to another, be to be loved[5], specially this our God is to be loved, saith Moses. We may likewise consider his benefits towards us, and so expulse this detestable and horrible unkindness towards him; as is the leaving unto us of the scripture, whereby we know his blessed will, for the grace of the Holy Ghost, that leadeth us to knowledge, defendeth us from ill, and preserveth us in virtue. The greatest argument of all, the birth and death of his only Son, given for our redemption. Deut. vi. 5.
ver. 1.
ver. 3.

Then doth Moses teach how we should love him, Deut. vi. "with all our heart, all our soul, and all our force." Of these parts consisteth man: for the heart is the original of all affects and desires. When the law requireth the love of God with all the heart, it requireth all men's[6] affections to be Deut. vi.

[4 His, A, this, B and C.]
[5 Be to be loved, A, to be beloved, B, is to be beloved, C.]
[6 Meenes, A, meanes, B, man's, C.]

sincere and pure, and wholly directed unto the love and obedience of God. For he is a jealous God; he is not content with the fourth part, or the half, but requireth the whole heart, mind, will, affections, and life of man. He is not content that we love him with one part, and the world with the other.

These words forbiddeth not, but that we may love our honest friends, parents, and other, as it is written, Exod. xx. Deut. v., so that their love be in God and for God, not equal nor above the love of God. If election happen, that in the loving of the one follow the hatred of the other, thou art bound to hate thy father, thy friends, and also thine own life, for the love of God. Matt. x. Last of all, thou must love him with all thy force; by the which word is understand all the powers, both of body and soul, the senses interior and exterior, whatsoever they be, and as the Holy Ghost hath given them; so that neither the inward man, neither the outward man, be defiled by sin, as Saint Paul saith, 1 Thessal. v.

These words must be thought upon, that man apply the gift of the Holy Ghost aright to the glory of God, and profit of his church, whereof we be all members. One hath the gift of prophecy, to judge of things to come: another, of knowledge, to open the mysteries hid in the scripture: another, the gift to comfort and give consolation to the afflicted: the other, the gift truly to dispense and distribute the goods of this world without fraud: the other, the gift to persuade by the word of God people to amendment of life with the tongue: another, with the pen: one, the gift to serve God in the ministry of the church: the other, to serve God in the ministry of the commonwealth: the one, apt and strong, wise and prudent in affairs of war: the other, to keep good rule and govern in peace: the one, apt to one thing, the other, to another. Every man therefore remember this commandment, "Love God with all thy force," and apply the gift that the Holy Ghost hath given thee, to the glory and service of God. It is an horrible sin before God, the abuse of his gifts, whether they be of the body or the soul. Matt. xxv.

Moses now, as thou seest, hath taught us to know God, and shewed us how to honour him in faith, fear, and love; and shewed many reasons, why we should give him this honour and obedience; so that the first part of the first commandment, "I am the Lord thy God," may be understood of every man that is willing to know God and his own salvation.

Before he expoundeth the second part of the commandment, "Thou shalt have no strange gods before me," he admonisheth the people of a very necessary doctrine, that is to say, how they should behave themselves in prosperity and wealth, and use the commodities of this world. We know by experience and daily proof, that nothing more withdraweth man from the honour, love, and fear of God, than those two, felicity and adversity; as Christ teacheth, our Saviour, Matt. xiii., Mark iv., Luke viii., by the similitude of him that sowed, and part fell by the way-side, part upon the stones, part among the thorns. By the seed in the stony ground Christ understandeth such as leave his word for the calamities and affliction of this world: by the seed among the thorns, such as hear the word of God, howbeit it bringeth forth no fruit by reason of the cares of this world and deceit of riches. Moses therefore sheweth, like a good prince and faithful preacher, what is to be done in both these states and conditions of life, in prosperity and adversity. So that, if this[1] counsel be followed, there is neither prosperity, neither adversity, can withdraw man from the will and pleasure of God.

A necessary doctrine how to behave ourselves in prosperity.

Matt. xiii. 1. Mark iv. 1. Luke viii. 5.

Moses' rule to be observed in time of prosperity.

The first doctrine, to keep man from the displeasure of God in prosperity, is written Deut. vi. *Erit cum introduxerit te Dominus Deus tuus in terram quam juravit patribus tuis Abraham, Isaac, [et Jacob], et dederit tibi civitates magnas atque bonas quas non ædificasti, domos quoque plenas omni bono quas tu non implevisti, et cisternas excisas quas tu non effodisti, vineas et olivas quas non plantasti; comederisque, et satiatus fueris; cavebis tibi ne forte obliviscaris Domini qui te eduxit de terra Ægypti, de domo servorum*: that is to say, "When the Lord thy God shall bring thee into the land which he promised to thy fathers Abraham, Isaac, and Jacob, and shall give thee great cities and good, which thou never buildedst, houses furnished with all necessaries, which thou replenishedst not, and water-pits that thou diggedst

Deut. vi. 10.

[¹ This: Is, A, this, B and C.]

not, vines and olives that thou plantedst not, and thou eat and be satisfied; beware thou forget not the Lord that brought thee out of Egypt, from the house of servants."

Here seest thou, what danger and peril is annexed with abundance and prosperous fortune in this world; and how common an ill it is, in manner taking effect in all men that possesseth the goods of the world, as Esay saith, "Let us eat and drink, to-morrow we shall die." As Moses saith, Deut. xxxii., "The people replenished themselves with the gifts of God and rebelled, using prosperity and good fortune, forsook God." ["He that should have been upright, when he waxed fat, spurned with his heel: thou art gross, thou art fat, thou art laden with fatness; therefore he forsook God that made him, and regarded not the strong God of his salvation."][1] And, Luke xii., the rich man said, "My soul, thou hast great riches, and shalt use them many years; take thine ease, eat, drink, and be merry."

Isai. xxii. 13.

[Deut. xxxii. 15.]

Luke xii. 19.

Two precepts in the rule of Moses.

By these examples thou seest, that Moses prescribed not without cause this regle, how to use ourselves in prosperity. The which rule containeth two precepts; the one, to use moderately the gifts of God, and not to abuse them; the other, to acknowledge them to come from God, and to put no trust in them. The riches of the world abused engendereth pride and forgetfulness of God: therefore Moses admonisheth chiefly man in his wealth to beware he forget not God. And in the eighth chapter he sheweth the cause, why we[2] should not glory nor trust in them, although they be most justly and right wisely[3] gotten: "God giveth them," saith he, and be not gotten with our labours and pain.

I know what men are wont to say, when they heard[4] any of these new gospellers, that a rich man acknowledged not God for God, and confess the same unto other: so much may every man, that is not out of his wit, confess. David saith not, "The fool saith with his tongue, there is not God;" but in his heart, Psal. xii. Verily, to acknowledge

Psal. xiv. 1.

[1 This sentence in brackets is found only in C, where it is substituted for that which here immediately precedes it.]
[2 Why we, A, whych, B, whie wee, C.]
[3 Wysly, A and B, easily, C.]   [4 When heard, A.]

only God to be God, only to trust unto him, and not unto the creatures of the world, it is a rare thing in prosperity.

Few think, by how small a thread all the certainty of riches hangeth, and that suddenly they may perish. Then should man most suspect the fortune of this world, when she smileth most, because she is brittle and inconstant, as the poet Horace teacheth: when prosperity promiseth security and rest in the goods of this world, it is a hard thing and rare, verily to think only God to be the giver thereof, and can suddenly take the things away that hath been gathered with great pains and travails. Therefore he maketh many times of a rich man a poor man; of one that ruled all, contemned of all; of Crœsus, Irus; and so punisheth, because men followeth not this precept and commandment of Moses: "Abuse not the gifts of God, and forget him not in the time of prosperity."

The other impediment, that leadeth us from this religion of God, fear, faith, and love, is adversity; whereof he speaketh, chap. viii. Deut. "God led thee forty years in the desert to punish thee and to tempt thee, to know what was in thy heart, whether thou wouldest keep his commandment or not; punished thee, and suffered thee to hunger, fed thee from heaven, which meat thou knewest not, neither thy fathers knew not, to declare unto thee that man only liveth not by bread, but by all things that proceed from the mouth of God liveth man." *Adversity another impediment that leadeth from God. Deut. viii. 2.*

When man is oppressed with adversities and trouble in this life, then cometh thoughts as thick as hail, whether God love him that is punished; disputeth why and what should be the cause of these troubles and adversity; then he revolveth, tosseth, and turneth both the nature of God and man in his cogitations, knoweth God to delight in doing well unto man, and that man of all creatures is the most excellent. He findeth God severe, and of all creatures man most miserable, and subject to adversities; and the more man applieth unto the commandments of God, the more miseries of this world are heaped upon his head. It is not therefore without cause that Moses prescribeth a remedy, lest man should depart (being in the thrall[5] *What thoughts follow adversity.*

[5 In thrall, B.]

and brake of adversity) from this religion, "fear God, believe in God, and love God."

<small>Moses sheweth why God doth punish so that he might give us a remedy against this temptation. Rom. v. 12. Job xiv. Isai. xl. 6. Psal. cvii. 39.</small>

Moses would keep man in his obedience and office towards the law, in declaring the causes why God punisheth; sheweth that it is for no hatred that he punisheth, but for love; and that he findeth always in man just matter worthy punishment. As Paul saith, Rom. v., that "death by reason of sin entered into the world;" so that the integrity and perfectness of man's nature by sin is lost, and made like unto the nature of the brute beasts, fruits, and herbs of the field, Job xiv. and Esay, cap. xxii. xl. Ecclus. xiv. Psal. cvii.; therefore God, for sin being angry, punisheth the miserable nature of man, being spoiled of his original and first perfection, with many calamities. As David saith,

<small>Ps. xc. 7.</small> Psalm lxxxix., *Defecimus in ira tua*: that is as much to say, "Thou being angry for sin, we are subject unto death." Read the whole psalm, if thou canst. It is Moses' prayer, wherein is declared how brief and miserable the life of man is for sin.

<small>Natural corruption and wilful malice joined in man.</small>

Unto this natural corruption is annexed our wilful malice and contempt of God, as we see in Cain and Esau; likewise in this people of Israel, which were diligently instructed and godly brought up by Adam, Isaac, and Moses; yea, in ourselves, that daily read and hear the word of God, yet nothing the better. Therefore Moses saith, that "God led them in the wilderness to punish their sin," which is the principal cause of all calamities. Then punisheth he, to prove such as be his, whether they will persevere with his commandment or not. Thus tempted he Abraham, and Jacob for the space of all his life; and layeth more adversities many times upon such as be of his true church, than upon other.

As these examples declare: Manasses the tyrant cut Esay the prophet asunder with a saw: Apries killed Hieremy; the bishops, Zachary; Herod, John Baptist, with other. When such adversities happen, let no man depart from the true word of God, but say with Micheas <small>Mic. vii. 9.</small> the prophet, chap. vii., "I will sustain the punishment of <small>Isai. lxiv. 5.</small> God, for I have offended him;" with Esa. lxiv. chap., "Behold, we have offended and long continued in sin, wherefore thou art angry." God, when he punisheth, worketh two good deeds at one time; correcteth the sin, and calleth the sinner to penance, as we have examples in David, Osias, and Manasse. And Saint Paul saith, 1 Cor. xi., "We are punished of the Lord, lest we should be damned with the world." If thou be a good man, and yet punished, rejoice: for the punishment is a testimony of the doctrine and religion that thou professest; and hast many fellows, the patriarchs, prophets, Christ, and the apostles, which would rather suffer death than deny the profession of the gospel. Matt. xvi. 2 Tim. iii. Psalm cxv.

<small>Two good things in punishment. 1 Cor. xi. 32. Matt. xvi. 21. 2 Tim. iii. 12. Psal. cxvi.</small>

There be many other causes why God punisheth, and why the punishments should be patiently taken; it were a book-matter to rehearse them. I will only speak of one cause more, that Moses writeth in the same eighth chapter, and pass over the rest. God "made them hungry, and fed them with meat from heaven, that they should know man lived not only by bread, but of all things that proceed from the mouth of God." Some men understand that Moses meaneth, that the body liveth with bread corporal, and the soul with the word of God; seeing that man consisteth of those two parts, the body and the soul. It is true, and a good interpretation: howbeit, if these words be referred only to the body in this place of Moses, it shall be consonant with the circumstance of the text, and declare his purpose the better. Though man put meat into his body, that of his own nature men judge to nourish, yet except the favour and grace of God digest and dispose it into every member of the body, it nourisheth not; as we see in many men that eateth much and many times in the day, yet is nothing the stronger. The physicians call this disease *apepsian, cruditatem*, when there is no digestion at all; sometime *dyspepsian, depravatam concoctionem*, when the meat is turned into a contrary quality; sometime *bra¹dy-pepsian, tardam concoctionem*, when the stomach digesteth with difficulty and long protract of time.

<small>Another cause why God punisheth man. Deut. viii. 3.</small>

This I speak only to this purpose, that neither meat, neither medicine, neither physician availeth, except God say, Amen. If thou wilt take profit of the thing thou eatest, follow the physic of Paul, 1 Tim. iv., speaking of the meat: *Sanctificatur per sermonem Dei ac precationem.* "It is sanc-

<small>1 Tim. iv. 5.</small>

[¹ Bra: *aura*, C.]

[HOOPER.]

tified by the word of God and prayer." It is not only lawful for thee to eat it, but also God will give thee nourishment. That the meat and drink feedeth not the body without the favour and blessing of God, it is declared, Levit. xxvi., Ose. iv., Miche. vi. "Ye shall eat, and yet not be satisfied." Thus doth Christ's answer unto the devil prove, Matt. iv., when he hungered in the body, and not in the soul; therefore his answer must be referred only to the body. God's punishment therefore taught the Israelites this doctrine, that God giveth not only meat, but also virtue thereunto to nourish him that eateth. Seeing now that the Israelites by adversity were brought unto the knowledge of their sin, and instructed with this further doctrine, that God giveth as well virtue unto the meat to nourish him that eateth, as the meat itself; there is no occasion that they should therefore leave God, but rather accept the punishment with thanks, as a good schoolmaster sent to teach them their health and the will of God. As David saith, Psal. cxviii.: *Utile mihi est quod in miseriam dejectus sum, ut discerem decreta tua;* that is to say, "It availeth me greatly that I am punished, to learn thy commandments."

The first part of the first commandment containeth, as thou seest by the interpretation of Moses, the fountain and original of all true religion; and is as the foundation and root, from whence springeth all the other commandments; and is comprehended in these four words; knowledge of God: fear of God: faith in God: and love of God.

Further, in the interpretation of the same he hath taught his people and us, how to use ourselves in prosperity and adversity. For each of them draweth man from the four afore rehearsed virtues, except the mind of man be fully persuaded by the word of God, how a means and godly moderation may be kept, when man hath abundance; and how, to whom, and when use liberality and dispensation of his goods: likewise, how man should with patience sustain the hand of God in adversity for the time of this present life, which Job describeth, chap. xiv. to be nothing but a vanity by these words: "Man born of a woman liveth but a few days, and is replenished with all[1] affliction; springeth and withereth all away as a flower;

[¹ All, omited in A.]

fleeth as shadow, and cannot long endure." So saith Esay xxii. xl. If thou read the book that wise Salomon wrote, *De contemptu mundi*, that is² to say, of the contempt or vanity of the world, called Ecclesiastes, thou shalt not only learn what the world and man is, but also take adversities in the better part, if thou follow his counsel. The book containeth but twelve chapters; read and mark every month one, then at the year's end thou shalt read it over. If thou put the riches thereof into thy head, think thou hast gained well that year, though by the punishment of God thou hast lost otherways all thy goods in the world, unto thy shirt.

Now followeth³ the second part of the first commandment:

Thou shalt have no strange gods before my face.

This part of the commandment removeth all false religion and superstition, wherewithal the glory and majesty of God might happen to be diminished or darkened in the soul of man: which chanceth⁴ as many times as man attributeth unto any creature the thing that is due only unto God; or when we would honour God, or do any thing acceptable unto him, as we feign of our own brains, and not as his word teacheth. This honour we owe only unto God, faith, love, fear, and prayer. Now to attribute any of these to any creature is idolatry, and to have false gods before his face. Only God should be our hope, faith, love, and fear: him only should we pray unto. Esay viii. Psal. xviii. xxviii.

Idolatry.

Isai. viii. 13.
Ps. xxix. 9.
& xxv. 1, 2.

To pray or trust in any dead saint departed out of this world is idolatry against⁵ this commandment: and those that do it hath neither commandment nor example in the scripture to approve their doings. Such as fear the menaces and threatenings of the devil or of devilish people, that mindeth the subversion of God's holy word, and persecution of such as follow it, and believeth not that God hath power to keep them under, and will do so for his

[² That is, omitted in A.]
[³ Followeth, A and C, follow, B.]
[⁴ Chanceth, A and C, changeth, B.]
[⁵ And against, A.]

word's sake, hath false gods before his face; for only he is to be feared. Matt. iv. x., Esa. li.

Matt. iv. 10. & x. 31.
Isai. li. 7.

Such as be given to astronomy, or other, that superstitiously observe the course and revolution of the heavens, [and]¹ think they can do good or harm, give good fortune or ill, as those think and judge that elevate the figure of heaven to judge what shall follow them, when they perceive by their nativities under what sign they were born, offend against this commandment. The which abomination hath not only been used before our time of superstitious persons, but also now-a-days of them that hath a right knowledge of God.

Such as give over-much faith unto medicines, or the nature of stones and herbs, as ye see, 2 Paralip. xvi., commit idolatry.

2 Chron. xvi. 12.

Such as give faith unto the conjuration or sorcery of superstitious persons; as to priests, that bless water, wax, bone, bread, ashes, candles; or other to witches or soothsayers, where they abuse the name of God to singe out the fire of him that hath burned his hand, to stanch blood, to heal man or beast; or to such as destinieth what shall happen unto man, and what plenty shall follow of grain and fruit in the earth, health, or sickness in the air, committeth idolatry. Levit. xx., Deut. xviii.

Lev. xx. 27.
Deut. xviii. 10, 11.

I speak not against the knowledge that man seeketh for, whether it be in the heavens or in the earth, so that they extend their study to this end, to glorify God in his works, and not to make the works God. Well we be assured by the scripture, Hie. x. and also by those that knew not the scripture, that no constellation of heaven, mistemperature of the air, water, or earth, can hurt him that feareth God; as the testimonies of the scripture declare. Only the disobedience of man towards God maketh man subject unto these diseases and sicknesses that man is troubled withal. Exod. v. ix. Lev. xxvi. Numb. xiv. Deut. xxviii. 2 Reg. xxiv. 3 Reg. viii. 1 Par. xxi. 2 Par. vi. Ezek. vi. vii. xiv. xxviii. xxxiii. xxxviii. Read the 91st psalm, that beginneth, "Whoso resteth in the secrets of the Highest, lodgeth in² the harbour of the Omnipotent. In Latin it beginneth after the old translation: *Qui habitat in adjutorio*

Jer. x. 2.

[¹ And, supplied from C.]   [² In, supplied from A.]

Altissimi, in protectione Dei cœli commorabitur. In the which psalm is shewed, how sure and free from all ill and diseases he is, that putteth his trust in God; and that heaven, neither earth, or any thing that is in them, shall molest him. Read and see.

Cicero[3], in the first book of Divination, mocketh these blind conjectures and foredestinies: *Quærit unde Jupiter cornicem a læva, et corvum a dextra canere jubet,* asketh in derision of those soothsayers, how happeneth it that Jupiter commandeth the crow to sing at the left hand, and the raven at the right hand. Lib. i. Divin.

Esa. cap. xxx. and xxxi. sheweth another kind of idolatry, which was used and punished in our fathers; and likewise daily we see the same with our eyes; confidence and trust in the power of the flesh, when such as be in league and confederacy together too much trust in their own strength and power. Read those two chapters, how the Israelites entered league with the Egyptians, and what was their end; and confer the same unto our time: what cities, what princes, and what strength, after the judgment of the world, was unite together; but because God was out of the league, see the end, how it availed nothing. To the same confusion shall at length come all kings and kingdoms, that trust more in their riches, munitions, and confederacy with men, than in God. Isai. xxx. 2. & xxxi. 1.

There is forbidden in this part of the commandment, that no man should give thanks for any thing received in this world to any other saving to God. Therefore Osee the prophet calleth the synagogue of the Jews a whore, because she attributed the gifts she received of God unto her false gods. The same teacheth Esa. lvii. This idolatry is at large written, Hiere. ii. Read the chapter, and confer it with our time, that parteth the thanks and praises, that only should be given unto God, with the saints departed out of this world. Every man, as his superstition leadeth him, he commendeth his riches to God and Saint Eras.[4]; his ox to God and Saint Luke; his horse Isai. lvii. 9.
Jer. ii.

[3 Quod faciebat etiam Panætius, requirens, Jupiterne cornicem læva, corvum a dextra canere jussisset. De div. Lib. i. 7.]

[4 Probably Saint Erasmus, bishop and martyr, who suffered in the reigns of Diocletian and Maximianus. See his Life, per Adonem Episc.

to God and Saint Loye[1]; for every disease he hath a diverse patron, and honoureth him with the prayer that only should be said unto God Almighty in the name of Christ. John xv. xvi.

<small>Whereby idolatry is to be examined.</small> This idolatry hath in manner infected all the Latin church. The nature of this secret and pernicious ill must be by the word of God well marked, lest under the cloak and shadow of true religion it deceive men of the truth. For this idolatry saith and beareth men in hand, that she doth not so desire help of saints, or thank them for the benefits received, as though she neglected or offended the high and only God; but granteth and confesseth God to be the chief giver of all things; howbeit not only for his mercies' sake and the merits of Christ his Son our Saviour, but also at the intercession and prayers of the dead saints. Thus craftily and under a pretence of true religion doth she sunder and divide the glory and the honour due only unto the Father, the Son, and the Holy Ghost, with the saints in heaven, that knoweth nothing of <small>Isai. lxiii. 16.</small> our condition and state in this world. Esay lxiii.

By this means our elders, both the Jews and the gentiles, mingled the rabble and multitude of gods with the only God and Maker of all thing: not that they thought the idols or images to be God; but thought that way God would be honoured. The which is very idolatry: for the

<small>Treverensem, in Aloysii Sanctorum Historia. Lovanii. 1565. Tom. II. p. 141. It is mentioned in Petr. de Natalibus, Lib. v. cap. 75, that when Saint Erasmus was imprisoned by Maximianus, the archangel Michael set him free, "*eidem ducatum præbens,*" which may perhaps account for the name of this saint being invoked in prayers for riches. Becon in his Reliques of Rome, Vol. III. folio edit. 361, p. 2, mentions "five special gifts and singular benefits granted to the fraternity of St Erasmus. The first of these is, that he shall have reasonable goods to his life's end." After reciting four other benefits, it is added:—"All these * * * * benefits shall all they have, that give any part or portion of their goods to the upholding and maintaining of the holy place of Saint Erasmus."]

[1 Saint Loye or Eloi, was Treasurer to Dagobert and Bishop of Noyon. He excelled in some of the mechanical arts, particularly in working in gold. He was also eminent for zeal and liberality in the discharge of his episcopal office. His having made for Dagobert a saddle of peculiar excellence may have led to his being regarded as the tutelar saint of equestrians. See his life by Saint Ouen, Paris, 1693. He died, 658.]</small>

law saith, "Thou shalt not do the thing that seemeth good in thy eye, but the thing I have commanded thee to do." Therefore, to avoid all false religion and superstition of the mind and inward man, God saith, "Thou shalt have no strange gods before me." The conscience therefore must be pure and nett from all privity and secret thoughts of idolatry, apostasy, or defection, if we would God should approve our religion to be true. Every thing that we do for the honour of God, not commanded by his word, is as strange, and not accepted of God: as all good intentions, feigned works by man, and all things commanded by general councils, not expressed in the word of God, by the patriarchs, prophets, Christ, and the apostles, which be and ever were before God the holy and catholic church, and sheweth us whosoever add any thing to their laws are the church of antichrist. Deut. iv. and xii., Apoc. xxii. So called God the fire of Aaron's sons, Nadab and Abihu, a strange fire, to say, such as he commanded not. God will have none other works of man, than he requireth in his express word. Deut. iv. 2. xii. 32. Rev. xxii. 18, 19.

He condemneth by this law the wicked sacrifice and idolatry committed in the private masses, where as people doth not only take from God and Christ their due honour, but also make another god of bread, which is no more the living God than the golden calf of the Israelites; as not only the scripture, but also the reason of man and the senses of all brute beasts of the field, ox and sheep, with all other the birds of the air and fishes of the water, doth bear record.

This unspeakable and most abominable ill is taken for the principal article and chief pillar of the true and apostolical church, of such as believe not the apostles' writings. But how can it be the apostolical church, when it repugneth and is clean contrary to the apostles' writings; Matt. xxvi. Mark xiv. Luke xxii. 1 Cor. x. xi.; likewise contrary to the testament, will, and institution of Christ Jesu, our only Saviour, the author and first giver of this blessed sacrament of his most honourable and precious blood in his church? If it be not lawful to change man's testament, nor to add or take any thing from it, but to execute and do every thing as it is there expressed, and none otherwise; much more no man should take upon him to change the testament of Christ.

Oh that people, for whom Christ hath shed his most innocent blood, would understand and perceive this sensible and manifest abomination, why they believe these seductors and deceivers of christian souls, that hath not as much as one iota or prick of the scripture to help themselves withal! Read, read, I beseech thee, christian reader, Matthew xxvi. Mark xiv. Luke xxii., and see how far their abominable mass is from the word of God: and think, who was the priest that ministered this sacrament, and what people received it. Then shalt thou find the Son of God, the Wisdom of the Father, the Light of the world, the Lamb that died for thy salvation, to be minister of this holy sacrament, and the church or people that received it to be the elect and chosen apostles, Christ's friends, that taught the gospel in all the world, and died for the same, as testimonies of the truth. Acts ii. Then doubt not but thou wilt soon perceive this idolatry; except (which God forbid!) thou doubt, whether Christ and the apostles be the true, old, and catholic church, or not.

They that defend this idolatry deceive thee with lies and false feigned laws out of their own heads, and not taken out of the scripture. Believe Christ and his word, which sheweth the truth only; and then thou canst not err no more than Christ himself erreth, neither be damned; except Christ, all the patriarchs, prophets, and apostles be damned with thee. These make thee believe that holy sacrament, used as a communion under both kinds, is a new and late invented doctrine by man. Thou shalt find the contrary in the word of God, Matt. xxvi. Mark xiv. Luke xxii., that it is a thousand five hundred and odd years old, and that Christ and his apostles so used it. Let those be thy fathers, and follow thou their faith, and let the rest go. Such as teach contrary doctrine be likewise the followers of the apostles and disciples, but not of Peter nor Stephen, but of Judas, as Saint Bernard saith of the pope, who hath been the chief doer in the defacing of God's holy word and in planting of this idolatry.

Such as trust in adversity to be holpen by any saint, and not only by God in Christ, make them strange gods, as they do that call upon the saint departed in the time of war; as in time past the Englishman upon Saint George[1], the Frenchman upon Saint Denys[2], the Scot

[1 The accounts of Saint George, the patron saint of England, are very contradictory. By some he has been confounded with the Arian Bishop of Alexandria (see Gibbon), by others, (Heylin, and Pettingale, &c.) he has been regarded as merely a symbolical device, perhaps derived from Grecian mythology or Egyptian hieroglyphics. One writer has attempted to prove that George is a corruption of Gregory. In Aloysii Lipomani Veron. Sanctorum Historia are copious details of the life and martyrdom "Sancti Georgii Magni." In these it is recorded that "patria ipsius fuit Cappadocum regio, altrix vero Palestina, Christianus inde usque a proavis, ætate juvenis, sapientia canus, corde rectus, et utraque re adversus impietatem exultans: qui in armorum certaminibus bene ab ipsa pueritia excelluerat, ac fortitudinem bellis gerendis convenientem ita exercuerat, ut militaris ordinis Tribunatus ejus fidei commissus fuerit. (p. 131.) Comes a Diocletiano constitutus est antequam Christianus esse cognosceretur. (p. 117.) Having avowed himself a Christian and denounced the worship of the gods in the presence of the Emperor, it is related—Tunc in eum intuens Diocletianus Imperator, velut sævus aliquis Draco, &c., after which follows an account of his martyrdom by the emperor's command, and of the miraculous manner in which, in the first instance, all efforts to destroy his life failed, until he had converted many around him to Christianity. Perhaps this may have been the origin of the emblematic device of St George encountering the Dragon, which has been considered as typifying the christian soldier conflicting with his spiritual foes. Some have imagined that this device was borrowed from the conflict between Michael and the great beast in the Apocalypse. It is found in Russia among the pictures used in the Greek church. The adoption of St George as the tutelary saint of England appears to be connected with the Crusades, as may be gathered from the legends concerning Robert of Normandy and Richard the First. Edward the Third identified him with England in the establishment of the Order of the Garter, and by invoking his aid as a saint in the preceding year (A. D. 1349), at the siege of Calais, at which time and subsequently his name was used by the English as a war cry. Some trace this as adopted from William, Duke of Aquitaine, grandfather to Henry the Second's Queen, who resigned his sovereignty and became a hermit in 1137. He had been celebrated as a warrior, and his war cry was "Saint George." The angels coined in the reign of Edward IV. have the device of St George and the Dragon. See Sti Georgii Magni vita et martyrium per Simeonem Metaphrastem; also Martyrium, a Pasicrate ejus servo scriptum, and Encomium per eundem Sim. Metaph. in Aloysii Sanct. Hist. Lovanii. 1655. Tom. II. pp. 117. 124. 130.]

[2 Saint Denis, (Dionysius,) the patron saint of France, was the first bishop of Paris. He is said to have suffered martyrdom during the

upon Saint Andrew[1]; which is nothing else but a very gentility, and ethnick custom; as though their private gods and singular patrons could give the victory and upper hand in the field, or Saint George favour him that Saint Andrew hateth. What thing is this else but to set two souls at bate, as the gentiles did their gods Juno and Minerva with Venus? Virg. Æneid I. and II. Ovid. Met. XII. *Hector adest secumque deos in prœlia ducit;* that is to say, "Hector is come and hath brought his gods with him to the field." What is there between the Greeks that trusted in Juno and Neptunus, and the Englishman that trusteth in Saint George; or between the Trojans that trusted in Venus and her friends, and the Scots, that trust in Saint Andrew, if they hope by their help their wars shall prosper?

But, praised be the mercy of God! I hear say, and believe it, that Englishmen hath resigned Saint George's usurped title to the living God, the God of battle. No good man will take me as though I meant Juno, Pallas, or Venus, were as good as Andrew or the saints that be in glory for ever with God. But I say that these superstitious persons, that maketh their patrons or singular helpers, of the saints, differ nothing in this point from the heathen or gentile: for as the one honoureth he knoweth not what, so doth the other; both following their own imagination and superstition without testimony and commandment of the scripture. Read the commentaries of Thom. Valois and Nicol. Triveth, in the fourth book of Saint Augustine *De Civitate Dei,* cap. xxx. and they will

persecution under Valerian in 272. His remains are preserved as well as those of his companions in martyrdom (Rusticus and Eleutherius) in three silver shrines. The legend is that they suffered death upon Montmartre (Mons Martyrum) so called from that circumstance.]

[[1] Saint Andrew, who was adopted as the tutelary saint of Scotland, is said, in the Romish legends, to have visited the northern regions; and some assert that his relics were removed to Fifeshire by a Grecian monk, A.D. 368, and gave the name to St Andrew's in that county. Others attribute the adoption of this saint by the Scotch to Hungus, one of their princes, having had a dream, in which he saw Saint Andrew as about to assist him in an approaching conflict. In accordance with this dream it is related that a St Andrew's cross appeared in the heavens, and secured the victory on the side of Hungus.]

tell thee, if thou believe not the scripture, what superstition is; where as be these words: *Superstitio autem* Lib.iv.c.30.
*vocatur omnis cultus superfluvius, quocunque modo superfluus;
sive ex superfluitate eorum quæ coluntur, sive eorum quæ in
cultum assumuntur, sive ex modo assumendi. Hoc enim
istud intelligitur nomine superstitionis, undecumque nomen
originem habuerit:* that is to say, "Superstition is a superfluous religion, what ways soever it be superfluous;
whether it be of the superfluity of the things honoured,
or of the things used for religion, or of the manner in
religion. This doubtless is understood by the name of
superstition, from whence soever the name hath his beginning: whatsoever thou do to please the Almighty, if
it be not commanded in his word, it is superfluous superstition."

Remember therefore this part of the commandment,
"Thou shalt have no strange gods before my face;" and
honour God, save thy soul, avoid idolatry, as his only
word teacheth, and beware of man's laws.

CAPUT V.

THE SECOND COMMANDMENT.

Thou shalt make thee no image, or any similitude of things in heaven above, in earth beneath, or in the water under the earth. Thou shalt not worship nor honour them: for I am the Lord thy God, a jealous God, punishing the iniquity of the fathers in the children that hate me, in the third and fourth generation.

<small>The sum of the first commandment.</small> IN the first commandment we learned that God is the only and sole God, and that we should not think nor feign any other besides him. Further, that commandment expresseth, what this our one God is, and how affectionated or minded towards us, full of mercy, and ready always to succour and aid both soul and body in all affliction: sheweth us further, how we should honour and reverence this our almighty and merciful God: so that the end and whole sum of the first commandment is, that only God would be known of his people to be God and honoured as God. So doth God first instruct the mind and soul of man, before he require any outward work or external reverence; or else all together were hypocrisy, whatsoever shew or perfection it seemeth to have in the eye of the world. He layeth therefore the first commandment as a foundation of all true religion, as the original and spring of all virtue, and openeth the well and fountain of all mischief and abomination in these <small>The sum of the rest of the commandments of the first table.</small> words: "Thou shalt have no strange gods before my face." This second precept, and the two other that follow in the first table, teacheth us how to honour God in external religion or outward works, and to shew the fear, faith, and love, that we bear unto God in our hearts unto the world.

Two of these last commandments sheweth what we should do; and the third, which I now expound, what we <small>The end of this second commandment.</small> should not do. The purpose, end, and will of this second commandment is, that God's pleasure is unto us, that we should not profane or dishonour the true religion or honour of God with superstitious ceremonies or rites, not commanded by him. Wherefore, by this second commandment he calleth man from all gross and carnal opinions or judgments of God, the which the foolish and ignorant prudence and wit of man conceiveth, where as it judgeth without the scripture; and forbiddeth external idolatry, as in the first internal.

This commandment hath three parts. The first taketh from us all liberty and licence, that we in no case represent or manifest the God invisible and incomprehensible with any figure or image; or represent him unto our senses, that cannot be comprehended by the wit of man nor angel. *(The parts of the second commandment.)*

The second part forbiddeth to honour any image.

The third part sheweth us, that it is no need to represent God unto us by any image.

Moses, Deut. iv. giveth a reason of the first part, why no image should be made: "Remember," saith he to the people, "that the Lord spake to thee in the vale of Oreb. Thou heardest a voice, but sawest no manner similitude, but only a voice heardest thou." Esay, cap. 40, 41, 45, 46. diligently sheweth what an absurdity and undecent thing it is, to profane the majesty of God incomprehensible with a little block or stone; a spirit with an image. The same doth Paul, Acts xvii. The text therefore forbiddeth all manners of images, that are made to express or represent Almighty God. *(Deut. iv. 15. Isai. xl. 18. and xliv. 9. and xlvi. 5.)*

The second part forbiddeth to honour any image made.

The first word, "honour," signifieth to bow head, leg, knee, or any part of the body unto them, as all those do that say they may with good conscience be suffered in the church of Christ. To serve them is to do somewhat for their sakes, as to cense them with incense, to gild, to run on pilgrimage to them, to kneel or pray before them, to be more affectionate to one than to the other, to set lights[1] before them, with such-like superstition and idolatry. God be praised! I may be short or write nothing at all in this matter, because such as I *(What it is to honour images.)*

[1 Set high lights, C.]

write unto, my countrymen, be persuaded already aright in this commandment.

The second part sheweth us, how idolatry proceedeth and taketh place in men's conscience. The mind of man, when it is not illuminated with the Spirit of God, nor governed by the scripture, it imagineth and feigneth God to be like unto the imagination and conceit of his mind, and not as the scripture teacheth. When this vanity or fond imagination is conceived in the mind, there followeth a further success of the ill. He purposeth to express by some figure or image God in the same form and similitude that his imagination hath first printed in his mind; so that the mind conceiveth the idol, and afterward the hand worketh and representeth the same unto the senses.

Therefore God first forbiddeth this inward and spiritual idolatry of the mind, when he saith, "Thou shalt have no strange gods before my face." If the mind be corrupted, and not persuaded aright, then followeth the making of images, and after the honouring of them. The cause therefore of external idolatry is internal and inward ignorance of God and his word, as Lactantius[1] writeth in his book of the Original of Error. As it cannot be otherwise, but where as the air is corrupted, there must follow pestilence and infection of the blood, Galen. Lib. I. De diff. feb. cap. 5.; so where the mind is not purely persuaded of God, must follow this gross and sensible idolatry, that would honour God in an idol.

The original cause why they are made, is, that man thinketh God would not be present to help him, except he be presented someways unto their carnal eyes; as the example of the Israelites declareth, that required Aaron to make them gods that might lead them in their journey. They knew right well that there was but one God, whom

[1 Hæc fuit prima gens quæ Deum ignoravit; quoniam princeps ejus et conditor (Chanaan) cultum Dei a patre non accepit, maledictus ab eo, itaque ignorantiam divinitatis minoribus suis reliquit. * * * * * Ceteri autem, qui per terram dispersi fuerunt, admirantes elementa mundi, cœlum, solem, terram, mare, sine ullis imaginibus ac templis venerabantur, et his sacrificia in aperto celebrabant; donec processu temporum potentissimis regibus templa et simulacra fecerunt; eaque victimis et odoribus colere instituerunt: sic aberrantes a notitia Dei, gentes esse cœperunt, &c. Lact. De Orig. err. Lib. II. cap. 13. Oxon. 1684, p. 190, 191.]

they knew by the miracles that he wrought among them; but they thought he would not be present and at hand with them, except they might see him in some corporal figure and image, and that the image might be a testimony of his presence. So see we, that no man falleth into this gross idolatry, but such as be first infected with a false opinion of God and his word; then, say they, they worship not the image, but the thing represented by the image[2]. Against whom writeth Saint Augustine, in Psalm cxviii. and cxiii., in the 4th book of the City of God, cap. 5, that "images take away fear from men, and bring them into error. The ancient Romans more religiously," saith he, "honoured their gods without images[3]." Psal. cxix. and cxiv. and De civit. Dei. lib. v. cap. 5.

Seeing there is no commandment in any of the both testaments to have images, but, as ye see, the contrary; and likewise the universal catholic and holy church never used images, as the writings of the apostles and prophets testify: it is but an ethnick verity[4] and gentiles' idolatry to say God and his saints be honoured in them, when that all histories testify, that in manner for the space of five hundred years after Christ's ascension, when the doctrine of the gospel was most sincerely preached, was no image used. Would to God the church were now as purely and well instructed, as it was before these avaricious ministers

[[2] Videntur autem sibi purgatioris esse religionis qui dicunt, Nec simulacrum nec dæmonium colo, sed per effigiem corporalem ejus rei signum intueor, quam colere debeo. * * * * Itaque Apostoli una sententia pœnam istorum damnationemque testatur. Qui transmutaverunt, inquit, veritatem Dei in mendacium, et coluerunt et servierunt creaturæ potius quam Creatori, qui est benedictus Deus in sæcula. Nam priore parte hujus sententiæ simulacra damnavit, posteriori autem interpretationes simulacrorum. Aug. Op. Basil, 1542, Tom. VIII. co. 1306—7. In Psalm. 113.]

[[3] Dicit enim [Varro] antiquos Romanos plusquam annos centum et septuaginta Deos sine simulacro coluisse. Quod si adhuc, inquit, mansisset, castius Dii observarentur. Cujus sententiæ suæ testem adhibet inter cetera etiam gentem Judæam: nec dubitat eum locum ita concludere, ut dicat, Qui primi simulacra deorum populis posuerunt, eos civitatibus suis et metum dempsisse, et errorem addidisse: prudenter existimans deos facile posse in simulacrorum stoliditate contemni. Aug. Op. Basil, 1542, Tom. v. co. 272. De Civ. Dei, Lib. IV. cap. 31.]

[[4] Qu. *vanity* ?]

and dumb doctors of the lay people were made preachers in the church of God! Read Augustine, Epist. xlix.[1] et [Psal. cxiv.] Psal. cxiii. Therefore Saint John biddeth us not only beware of honouring of images, but of the images' selves.

Thou shalt find the original of images in no part of God's word, but in the writings of the gentiles and infidels, or in such that more followed their own opinion and superstitious imaginations than the authority of God's word[2].

i. Lib. 2. Herodotus[3] Lib. II. saith, that "the Egyptians were the first that made images to represent their gods." And as the gentiles fashioned their gods with what figures they listed, so doth the Christians. To declare God to be strong, they made him the form of a lion; to be vigilant and diligent, the form of a dog; and, as Herodotus[4] saith, Lib. II., Mendesii formed their god Pana with a goat's face and goat's legs, and thought they did their god great honour, because among them the herdmen of goats[5] were had in most estimation.

So doth those, that would be accounted Christians, paint God and his saints with such pictures as they imagine in their fantasies: God, like an old man with a hoary head, as though his youth were past, which hath neither beginning nor ending; Saint George, with a long spear upon a jolly hackney, that gave the dragon his death-wound, as the painters say, in the throat; Saint White, with as many round cheeses as may be painted about his tabernacle. No difference at all between a christian man and gentile in this idolatry, saving only the name. For they thought not their images to be God, but supposed that their gods would be honoured that ways, as the Christians doth.

[1 Quæst. 3ᵐ solvens docet, Latriam nec hominibus piis nec angelis bonis exhibendam: multo minus saxis et hominibus. Aug. Op. Basil, 1542. Tom. II. co. 197. Ep. 49.]

[2 See above, p. 318, note 1.]

[3 βωμούς τε καὶ ἀγάλματα καὶ νηοὺς θεοῖσι ἀπονεῖμαι σφέας πρώτους, καὶ ζῶα ἐν λίθοισι ἐγγλύψαι. Herodoti Hist. Lib. II. 4.]

[4 τὸν Πᾶνα τῶν ὀκτὼ θεῶν λογίζονται εἶναι οἱ Μενδήσιοι· τοὺς δὲ ὀκτώ, κ. τ. λ.—γράφουσί τε δὴ καὶ γλύφουσι οἱ ζωγράφοι καὶ οἱ ἀγαλματοποιοὶ τοῦ Πανὸς τὤγαλμα, κατάπερ Ἕλληνες, αἰγοπρόσωπον καὶ τραγοσκελέα, κ. τ. λ. Herodoti Hist. Lib. II. 47.]

[5 The herd men of gotes, A, they hearde men of gotes, B, the heard men of gotes, C.]

I write these things rather in a contempt and hatred of this abominable idolatry, than to learn any Englishman the truth. For my belief and hope is, that every man in England knoweth praying to saints and kneeling before images is idolatry, and instruments of the devil to lead men from the commandments of God; and that they are appointed in many places to be as doctors to teach the people: these doctors and doctrine the bishops and pastors shall bewail before the judgment-seat of God at the hour of death; and likewise the princes of the world, whose office is daily to read and learn the scripture, that they themselves might be able to judge the bishops' doctrine, and also see them apply the vocation they are called unto. It is not only a shame and an undecent thing for a prince to be ignorant, what curates his subjects hath through all his realm; but also a thing so contrary unto the word of God, that nothing provoketh more the ire of God against him and his realm, than such a contempt of God's commandment.

The third part declareth, that it is no need to shew God unto us by images, and proveth the same with three reasons. First, "I am the Lord thy God," that loveth thee, helpeth thee, defendeth thee, is present with thee: believe and love me, so shalt thou have no need to seek me and my favourable presence in any image. *That it is not needful to shew God unto us by images, three reasons.*

The second reason, "I am a jealous God," and cannot suffer thee to love any thing but in me and for me. When we two were married and knit together, for the love that I bore unto thee I gave thee certain rules and precepts, how in all things thou mayst keep my love and good-will towards thee; and thou promisedst me obedience unto my commandments. Exod. xix. So honour me and love me, as it standeth written in the writings and indentures written between us both. I cannot suffer to be otherwise honoured than I have taught in my tables and testament. *Exod. xix.*

The third reason is, that God revengeth the profanation of his divine majesty, if it be transcribed to any creature or image; and that not only in him that committeth the idolatry, but also in his posterity in the third and fourth generation, if they follow their father's idolatry; as I "give mercy into the thousandth generation," when the children follow their father's virtue. Then to avoid the ire of God, and to obtain his favour, we must use no images to honour him withal. This ye may read, Num. xii. Jer. xxxii. and Esa. xxxix., how king Hezekiah's sons lost their father's kingdom, and were carried into captivity for their father's sin. Read the xiii. xiv. and xvth chapters of Deuteronomy, and see how Moses interpretateth this second commandment more at large.

<small>Isai.xxxix.2.</small>

God's laws expulseth and putteth images out of the church, Exod. xx. Deut. v.: then no man's laws should bring them in. As for their doctrine they teach the unlearned, it is a weak reason to stablish them withal. A man may learn more of a live ape than of a dead image, if both should be brought into the school to teach.

CAPUT VI.

THE THIRD COMMANDMENT.

Thou shalt not use the Name of the Lord thy God in vain.

<small>The end of this law.</small>

THE end of this precept is, that we always use reverently the name of God; that is to say, the majesty and essence divine, that consisteth in one divine nature and essence, and in three[1] persons, the Father, Son, and the Holy Ghost.

<small>Three things to be taken heed of in naming God.</small>

This most honourable, fearful, and blessed name no man should unreverently profane or temerously without good advisement once think upon or speak of, but diligently take heed of these three things:

First, that whatsoever we think or speak be agreeable and consonant unto the excellency and holiness of his name, and extend to the setting forth of his glory. Second, that we abuse not his holy word, nor pervert the meaning and mysteries thereof to serve our avarice, ambition, or folly; but as he hath opened himself and his will in his word, so to know him, so to fear him, so to love him, so to serve, so to instruct ourselves in faith, and so to teach other. Thirdly, that we reverently speak and judge of

[1 There, A, their, B, three, C.]

all his works, without detraction or contumely, acknowledging his inscrutable prudence and justice in all things with laud and praise, as well in adversity as in prosperity. Psal. xxxiv.

They obey this commandment, and use the name of God aright, that preach Almighty God as he commandeth in his word; that pray unto him as it teacheth; to give him thanks for adversity and prosperity, as it teacheth; to confess him before the world, as it teacheth. These be the works of this third commandment, and be commended unto us in all the scripture, as well unto the princes and magistrates of the world and every private person, as unto such as be appointed unto the ministry and office of the church: that every private person is bound to teach such as be under him; the fathers their children, the elders the younger, as thou mayst read in these places of the scripture; Deut. iv. vi. xi. Ps. lxxvii. Job i.: that the princes should do the same unto their subjects, read Deut. xvii. 2 Reg. i. 3 Reg. x. Job iv. Ps. xxx. 1. As for the ministers' duty, there be as many places that commandeth them to do their office, as be names of books, and in manner chapters in the bible: as be for prayers unto God and thanksgiving, how and when it should be done, the book of Psalms, writings of the prophets and apostles; likewise the commandment of our Saviour Christ declareth. Matt. vi. John xiv. The confession of God and his word before the world is commanded in both Testaments, and confirmed with the example of all men that loved the truth from the beginning; as Abel, Seth, Noha, Esaias, Christ, and his apostles; yea, of the simple maid and prisoner in the house of Naaman Syrus, 4 Reg. v., that feared not to confess the living God in a strange country before them that were God's enemies. This maid shall damn in the last judgment all those that for fear, not only in a strange country, but also at home, dare not confess the truth.

The right use of this commandment.

[Deut. iv. 9. & vi. 7. Psal. lxxviii. 4, 6. Job i. 5. Deut. x. 18. [2 Sam. i. 1 Kings x.]

[2 Kings v.]

In these four works are contained all other that appertain to the setting forth of God's glory, as be these; to learn the word of God, teach it unto other, to promote it with example of honest and godly life, when the glory of God, the defence of the truth, the conservation of justice, and deliverance of innocency requireth to make open an unknown truth, and to confirm the same.

To swear or take an oath before a lawful judge is the work also of this commandment, and setteth forth God's glory. Deut. iv. For as Paul saith, all controversies are ended by the virtue of an oath; so have we examples in Paul, Rom. ix., in Abraham and Isaac with Abimelech, Jacob and Laban, Gen. xxxi., between Booz and Ruth, Ruth iii.: so of good Abdias[1], 3 Reg. xviii. The oath thus taken declareth him that received it to acknowledge and give unto God only this honour, that he alone knoweth what is in man's heart; and likewise bindeth God to revenge and punish him, if he swear false; unto the which pain the condition and tenor of the oath bindeth him, and maketh himself the vessel, wherein God may exercise his displeasure and justice. For God will not leave him unpunished, that taketh his name in vain; as it is written in the second part of this commandment. Exod. xx. Deut. v.

Rom. ix. 1. Gen. xxi. 23. Gen. xxxi. 53. Ruth iii. 13. 1 Kings xviii.

Of whom the works of this commandment may be done.

These be the works required of us in this third commandment; the which can be done of no man, but of such as first know God in Jesu Christ, and for his merits be reconciled, and hath his sins forgiven. Then they spring out of the fountain and original of all good works, faith, love, and fear of God, which be works of the first commandment. All other, whether it be prayer, preaching of God's word, confession of his name, or giving of thanks, with such as follow in the next commandment, and likewise in the second table, pleaseth God none otherwise than they proceed of faith in the mercy of God through Christ Jesu our Saviour.

Works repugnant to this commandment.

As these works agree with the commandment, so be there works contrary and repugnant unto this commandment that saith, "Thou shalt not take the name of the Lord thy God in vain;" the which is done divers ways, as it shall appear in the numbering of certain daily used vices, and horrible blasphemies daily used, not only unpunished, but also as a thing commendable, and worthy praise of the most part of people.

The most horrible abuse of this holy and most fearful name is among such as think there is no God to remunerate virtue nor to punish vice, as the Epicures say. Would to God the same blasphemy had corrupted none that bear the name of Christianity!

[[1] Abdias: Obadiah. Old editions, *God* Abdias.]

THE THIRD COMMANDMENT.

There were always in the church such, as it appeareth, Esay xxii. cap. and Luke xiii., and be at this day a great number, that say, not platly[2] and plainly, " there is no God ;" but by certain circumlocutions and paraphrases, as well by words as ill conversation of life, think there is no heaven nor hell, and believeth not as much the scripture of God, as the words of him that knoweth neither God nor godliness.

Isai. xxii. 13.
Luke xii. 16.

The second sort that abuse this holy name of God be those, that under the pretence and name of God, his word, and his holy church, seek their own glory and profit. As the pope, under the title and pretence of God's ministry, hath gotten himself not only a bishopric, but also the whole monarchy, in manner, of all Europe; a richer kingdom than any prince of the world; which never ceased from his beginning to move christian princes to most[3] cruel and bloody war, under the cloak and mantle of God's name. What means and craft hath he found to maintain this whorish and antichrist[ian][4] seat of abomination; idols, peregrinations, masses, dispensations, absolutions, defensions of all things abominable; tyrannies against virtue, stablishments of his own laws, abrogations of God's laws, emptying of heaven, and filling of hell, blessing of things exterior, oil, bell, bread, water, with other that be not cursed, and cursing of the souls that Christ redeemed with his precious blood; with a thousand more such abominations, under the name and pretence of God and his holy church, the which neither the patriarchs, neither the prophets, Christ, neither his apostles, never knew of, as both the Testaments doth bear record.

The same doth such as preach in the church of God their own imaginations, decrees of men; for be their doctrine never so false, it hath a fair title and name of God's word, when it is but a subtle quiddity of Duns, a vain sophism of Aristotle, a superstitious decree of the bishops' laws, a copy of vain glory and crafty connexion of words, to satisfy the most part of the audience, and to flatter the richest; wresting and writhing the simple verity of God's words into as many forms and divers sentences, as be vain

[2 Platly, A and B, flatly, C.]
[3 To most, A and C, to the most, B.]   [4 Supplied from C.]

and carnal affections wrought within his ungodly heart. So for the law of God they preach the law of man; for the gospel, judaical superstition; for Christ, themselves; which honour not God's name, as the law of the holy and catholic church of Christ teacheth, but dishonoureth and taketh it in vain, with the church of antichrist and the devil. For Christ bid his disciples preach none other than he himself commanded them, Matt. xxviii. cap.; yea, he shewed that the Holy Ghost, the Spirit of truth, should teach none other thing than by him was taught, John xv.

<small>Matt. xxviii. 20.</small>
<small>John xvi. 13.</small>

Therefore such as will occupy the office of a preacher, first must be well learned in the things that appertain unto the gospel, then free from all such affections as rather seeketh himself and the world, than the furtherance of the doctrine he preacheth. It is not enough that he preach the truth, but that only he have a respect unto the glory of Christ: then shall he boldly speak the truth without respect of persons, not tempering his oration with colours of flattery, but hardly call virtue virtue, and vice vice, as he seeth occasion, whosoever be his audience. Saint John, in his epistle, chap. iii., sheweth who is apt for this office, to preach the word of God. So doth Christ, Matt. x. So doth Paul, 1 Tim. iii., Titus i. So doth Moses and the prophets. Nothing more blasphemeth the name of God than false doctrine, and such as seeketh themselves, and can use the word of God[1] as they see their audience, and not as it is commanded them by the word of God. Such preachers hath brought the superior powers of the earth unto a contempt of God's word, hatred of the preacher, when he telleth truth, and the unlearned into blindness and ignorancy.

Those abuse the name of God that seek help of damned spirits, or of such souls as be departed out of this world, as Saul did, 1 Reg. xxviii.; or those that by necromancy, or such like enchantments, abuse the name of God to resuscitate dead bodies, or call spirits departed unto the body again; which is nothing else but an illusion and craft of the devil to make men believe lies. Those men in English be called conjurers, who useth arts forbidden by God's laws, and also by the laws of ethnicks, before Christ was

<small>1 Sam. xxviii. 7.</small>

[[1] Of God, omitted in C.]

born. Titus Livius[2], Lib. I. *de urbis origine,* writeth of Numa Pompilius, that was instructed *disciplina tetrica;* the which discipline St Augustine[3] calleth *hydromanciam* either *necromanciam.* Lib. De Civit. VII. cap. 35. The which arts were forbidden, as it appeareth by Apuleius,[4] which in his book *De Magia* defendeth himself against one that accused him of necromancy. The law of the twelve tables, that were in Rome long before the birth of Christ, forbiddeth those arts, as Cicero[5] writeth, *De Repub.* The more I wonder, that any such superstitious books should be printed under the privilege of any christian prince or magistrates, as be the books of John Tritemius[6] and Henry Cornelius Agrippa[7], specially his third book *De occulta philosophia,* that is to say, of secret philosophy; with many other that spared no labour in setting forth such ungodly works.

They brought first the abuse of God's name into christian men's hearts, and taught them the same superstition that once was, namely, among the Persians and Egyptians. Valerius, Lib. VIII. cap. 6[8]. For as among the gentiles there were some called *augures,* that by observation

Marginal notes: Lib. I. De Civit. Dei, lib. VII. cap. 35. Valerius, lib. VIII. cap. 6.

[2 Suopte igitur ingenio temperatum animum virtutibus fuisse opinor magis: instructumque non tam peregrinis artibus, quam disciplina tetrica ac tristi veterum Sabinorum, quo genere nullum quondam incorruptius fuit. Livy, Lib. I. cap. 18.]

[3 Nam et ipse Numa, ad quem nullus Dei propheta, nullus sanctus angelus mittebatur, hydromantiam facere compulsus est : * * * * Quæ sive hydromantia sive necromantia dicatur, id ipsum est, ubi videntur mortui divinare. Aug. Op. Basil. 1542. Tom. v. co. 423.]

[4 Aggredior enim jam ad ipsum crimen Magiæ, quæ ingenti tumultu, ad invidiam mei, accensum, frustrata expectatione omnium, per nescio quas anileis fabulas deflagravit, &c. Apulei. Op. Lugd. Bat. 1588, p. 324, Apologia. I.]

[5 This seems to refer to a fragment of Cicero, to be found quoted by Augustine, or some other of the Fathers.]

[6 John Trithemius, a man of profound learning, who was Abbot of Spanheim, &c. He died in 1516. His cabbalistical writings were republished, enlarged, and translated into French by Collange, in 1561.]

[7 Henry Cornelius Agrippa was an eminent scholar, and reputed to be a magician. He wrote upon the occult sciences, and died 1535. His works were printed in 2 vols. 8vo. apud Beringos fratres.]

[8 There is some error in this, as in many of the other references: it probably should be, Lib. VIII. cap. 2. 1.]

of the birds of the air in their flying, crying, and eating, made men believe they knew things to come; so among the Christians be some that think they can do the same: as if the pye chatter, they look for guests; if the crow cry, they say we shall have rain; if the owl howl, it is sign of death.

And as there were some that by the observation of the stars took upon them to speak of things to come by certain superstitious and devilish incantations, which the Persians call *Magos*; the Greeks, *Philosophos*; the Latins, *Sapientes*; Galli[1], *Druidas*; the Egyptians, *Sacerdotes*; the Indies, *Gymnosophistas*; the Assyrians, *Chaldeos*: so is there amongst the Christians the same sort of people, which be called soothsayers or prognosticators, that write and speak of things to come. As when Jupiter ruleth the constellations above, and is not impeached nor let by the conjunction of his contrary planet, we shall have a good year and a plentiful. If Saturn, and such as astronomers attribute contrary qualities unto, reign, we shall have scarcity and dearth of things.

Lib. xviii.

Pliny, lib. xviii. writeth of such, as by only words or with some other thing annexed with the words, worketh things above nature, as the devil hath done always, as histories record, Luca. lib. vi. Valer. lib. viii. cap. 1[2], writeth of one of the goddess Vesta's nuns, that was falsely accused of an unchaste life, desired the goddess to deliver her innocency in that crime by some miracle, as she did. The maid went to the river called Tyber with a sieve, and brought it full of water into the temple of the goddess. So among christian men be the same sort of people, that by the abuse of God's name, through the help of the devil, doth many times work the same in healing man; and lest, as not many years sith I was borne in hand of a poor man that erred by ignorance, that this medicine could heal all diseases, + *Jesus* + *Job* + *habuit* + *vermes* + *Job* + *patitur* + *vermes* + *in* + *nomine* + *Patris*

Valer. lib. viii. c. 1.

[1 Galli, A and B, the French, C.]

[2 Arrepto enim cribro, Vesta, inquit (Tuccia Virgo), si sacris tuis castas semper admovi manus, effice ut hoc hauriam e Tiberi aquam, et in ædem tuam perferam. Audaciter et temere jactis votis sacerdotis, rerum ipsa natura cessit. Valer. Max. Lib. viii. cap. i. 5.]

+ *et* + *Filii* + *et* + *Spiritus Sancti* + *Amen* + *lama zabacthani* +. God opened his heart afterwards to know the truth.

Such as be given to the arts practive, as geometry, music, astrology, and arithmetic, taketh upon them to judge of men's conditions by the sight of their faces[3]. Gell. lib. [I.] cap. 9, lib. XIV. cap. 1. So be there among people christened, that know neither art nor science, that take upon them to know the same by their countenance, the lines of their hands, or by their paces or going. Lucan[4] the poet writeth, that one resuscitated from death to life shewed unto Sextus Pompeius, what should be the success and end of the battle in the fields of Thessaly. So writeth Pliny, Lib. XXXVII. cap. 11, and Tully, Lib. I. *Tusc. Quæst.* So did the shadow of Samuel shew the death of Saul. 1 Reg. xxviii. The same doth the devil shew unto many, that by the abuse of God's name use superstitious conjurations and enchantments, when they seek the truth of the devil and dead bodies, and leave the word of the living God.

Augustus, the emperor, forbid this superstitious art, and Claudius, the emperor, clean abolished it. Cæsar, lib. VI. How the law of christian emperors hath forbidden and punisheth these ungodly arts, thou mayest read Cod. lib. IX. tit. 18. The law civil punisheth it with banishment, with the sword, and to be torn with beasts. *Culpa similis est tam prohibita discere quam docere:* that is to say, the fault is one, to learn and teach the things forbidden. Read the xviiith chap. of Deuteronomy, and there thou shalt find as many names of those that use forbidden arts, as be rehearsed by Constantine and Julian[5] the emperors, Cod. lib. IX. tit. 18,

Deut. xviii. 10.

[3 Qui sese ad discendum obtulerant ἐφυσιογνωμόνει. Id verbum significat mores naturasque hominum conjectatione quadam, de oris et vultus ingenio, deque totius corporis filo atque habitu sciscitari. Aul. Gell. Noct. Atticæ. Lib. I. cap. 9. p. 25. Coloniæ, 1541.—Adversus eos qui Chaldæi appellantur, et ex cœtu motibusque siderum et stellarum, fata se hominum dicturos pollicentur. Ibid. Title to Lib. XIV. cap. 1. p. 507.]

[4 Lucan. Lib. VI. ad finem.]

[5 Nemo aruspicem consulat, aut mathematicum, nemo auriolum augurum et vatum prava confessio conticescat. Chaldæi, ac magi, et ceteri, quos *maleficos* ob facinorum magnitudinem vulgus appellat, nec ad hanc

and likewise the same arts¹. And as Moses forbiddeth all the people those ungodly arts, so doth those emperors. Both Moses in God's laws, and these emperors in man's laws, punisheth with death the transgressors of this commandment.

<small>Deut. xiii. 5.</small> Moses, Deuteronomy xiii. prescribeth this pain, *Propheta ille aut somniator somniorum occidi debet, eo quod aversionem loquutus sit a Domino Deo vestro*: that is to say, "that prophet or dreamer of dreams must be slain, because he hath spoken a defection or apostasy from the Lord <small>Levit. xx. 6.</small> your God." More at large is this pain written, Levit. xx. <small>Isai. xlvii. 12.</small> and Esay, capit. xlvii. Read the places, the execution of <small>[1 Sam. xxviii. 2 Kings xxiii.]</small> the pain against the transgressors. Read 1 Reg. xxviii. <small>Cod. lib. ix. tit. 18.</small> 4 Reg. xxiii. In the law of man we read thus, *Sileat omnibus perpetuo divinandi curiositas, etenim supplicio capitis ferietur gladio ultore prostratus, quicunque nostris jussis obsequium denegaverit*, Cod. lib. ix. tit. 18.² that is to say, "The superstition of fore-destinying is forbidden always unto all men; and whosoever obey not our commandments is condemned unto the sword, and shall suffer the loss of his head."

Though I do by the authority of God's laws and man's laws damn this damnable art mathematical, I do not damn such other arts and sciences, as be associated and annexed with this unlawful astrology. As is geometry and arithmetic, those be necessary for every man: specially arithmetic, for she extendeth, as a necessary aid, not only unto all sciences, but also to every liberal art and condition of life. And among all arts mathematical arithmetic is accounted the first: music, geometry, and astronomy wanteth her aid, and she not theirs. Plin. Lib. xxxv. cap. 10. They be the gifts of God, and to be honoured, because they come from him only, that giveth all goodness. <small>Jac. i.</small> Jac. i.

<small>partem aliquid moliantur. Sileat omnibus perpetuo divinandi curiositas. Etenim supplicio capitis ferietur gladio ultore prostratus, quicunque jussis nostris obsequium denegaverit. Impp. Constantius A. et Julianus C. ad populum. Corpus Juris Civilis Cod. Lib. ix. tit. 18. cap. 5. (Antv. 1726. Tom. ii. p. 411.)]</small>

<small>[¹ Ars autem mathematica damnabilis est, et interdicta omnino. Ibid. cap. ii.]</small>

<small>[² See note 5, p. 329.]</small>

Further, the emperors of the world, Diocletian, Maximianus, Tiberius, Cod. lib. ix. tit. 18, doth permit these arts. *Artem geometriæ discere atque exercere publice interest; ars autem mathematica damnabilis interdicta est*[3]: that is to say, "It is expedient or profitable to learn and exercise the art of geometry, but the damnable art mathematical is forbidden." The law meaneth astrology and astronomy, which are used well but of a few men. The astrologer is he that knoweth the course and motions of the heavens, and teacheth the same; which is a virtue, if it pass not his bounds, and become of an astrologer an astronomer, who taketh upon him to give judgment and censure of these motions and course of the heavens; what they prognosticate and destiny unto the creatures of the earth, man, beast, and other; what shall be the temperature of the air, the condition of the earth, the state and success of such fruit as it bringeth forth.

By this knowledge they fore-speak of pestilence and other diseases, and seeth the death of great men to come, and such commotions and wars, as shall follow between the princes of the world. And thus they say, they know by the course of the heavens, where as they see the conjunctions of many planets of rigorous and fatal disposition and quality concur, by reason of whose influence into these inferior parts all those calamities must happen. Here they abuse not only the name of God and the natural discourse of reason, which hath comprehended the motions and course of heavens, but also heavens itself; and attribute unto the heavens the thing that only appertaineth to God: to say, the health of man and sickness of man, the plenty of the earth and scarcity of the same, the regiment of commonwealths, and the life and death of the governors thereof.

Their knowledge and practice in these things is nothing at all. For Almighty God hath not made the heavens to that end and purpose, that man should learn of them good fortune or ill: as it is plain, Gen. i. In the second day God made the firmament and the superior spheres, which the text calleth *rakiah*[4], to this end, that it should "separate the waters that be under the firmament,

[3 See note 1, p. 330.]   [4 Rakiah, רָקִיעַ Gen. i. 6.]

from those that be above the firmament; and God called the firmament heaven." In the fourth day God made the sun, the moon, and the stars, and sheweth to what purpose and end he made them; the one to have dominion in the day, the other in the night: and God put them in the firmament of heaven to give light unto the earth. Those rule in the day and night, and put diversity between light and darkness; to divide the year into his parts, the spring, summer, autumn, and winter. They are in signs likewise, saith the text, the which the husbandman, that tilleth and soweth the ground, observeth without superstition, to sow and reap his corn. He casteth it into the winter, and receiveth it again in the summer.

So doth the mariner mark the revolution of the moon, his decrease and increase, whereby he knoweth the tides, the ebb and flow of the sea.

And the later physicians, Avicenne and Averroys[1], hath likewise assigned their use in man's body. Therefore they appoint diversity of days in the practice of physic, one to be more apt for letting of blood than other, to purge and to balm than the other. If they may be observed without superstition, it may be suffered: so notwithstanding that such, as observe not these latter rules, may both minister and receive medicines; for the heavens were made to serve us, and not to master us; were created for man, and man not for them. Therefore it is a false superstition, to say good or bad, plenty or scarcity, sickness or health, war or peace, dependeth of the influence of the heavens: or he that is born under one sign to be more fortunate than he that is born under the other; as this Egyptiacal and ethnicks' foolishness beareth men in hand. The prognostication of these blind prophets is good to be borne in a man's bosom, to know the day of the month. The rest of their practice is not worth one haw, as Moses teacheth, Deut. xxviii. xxix. xxx. Levit. xvi. [Lam. ii.] Thre. ii. Mal. ii.; where as ye may see that all these ills, and many more than the astronomers speaketh of, cometh

[[1] Avicenne, or Avicanna, was a celebrated physician as well as philosopher; his works were translated into Latin, and printed at Venice, 1564. Averrois taught medicine, rather than practised it. See note 3, p. 70.]

unto us for sin and the transgression of God's commandment. It is neither sun, neither moon, Jupiter nor Mars, that is the occasion or matter of wealth or woe, plenty or scarcity, of war or peace. Neither is the cause of pestilence the putrefaction of the air, as Galenus writeth, Lib. I. *de diff. feb.* cap. 5: but the contempt of God's commandment is the cause, as thou mayest read in the chapters of the scripture a little afore rehearsed: the air, the water, and the earth hath no poison in themselves to hurt their lord and master, man. But first man poisoneth himself with sin, and then God useth these elements ordained for the life of man to be the occasion of his death.

Read the places and know, that good health is numbered among the blessings of God, and appertaineth unto those, that fear and keep God's commandments, and not to those that be destined to live long by the favour and respects of planets. And the ill, of what kind soever it be, is the malediction of God against sin. The physicians say, that the chiefest remedy against pestilence is to flee from the place where the air is corrupt: God's law saith, Flee whither thou wilt, *adhærere faciet tibi Dominus pestilentiam, donec consumat te desuper facie terræ,* Deut. xxviii.; that is to say, "The Lord shall make the pestilence cleave and associate thee, till it consume thee from the world." Again, in the same chapter, " The disease or sickness shall be faithful," that is to say, stick fast to thee, use what medicines thou wilt. Deut. xxviii. 21.

Galenus saith, Lib. I. *de diff. feb.* cap. 4, that the chief remedy to preserve from pestilence is to purge the body from superfluous humours, to have a free and liberal wind, and to avoid the abundance of meat and drink. God saith, nothing preserveth, but the observation of his commandments. If we offend, the best remedy is penance and amendment of life. It maketh no force, how corrupt the air be, so the conscience of man in Christ be clean from sin. Though there die a thousand of the one side of thee, and ten thousand on the other side, thou shalt be safe. Psal. xc. He will let thee live, to serve longer in the world to the glory of his name; and if thou die, it is because no malice of the world should corrupt thy life, and bring thee from God; further, to take away the miseries of Psal. xci. 7.

this world. If such as care not for God escape in the time of pestilence or war, it is to call them unto a better life, Rom. ii.: if they amend not, they are reserved to a greater pain. This is spoken, not as though I contemned the gifts of God, philosophy and physic; but to take from men all vain hope in the artificial medicines, and give only the glory unto the name of God.

Rom. ii. 4.

They abuse the name of God, that perform not the thing they promise in God's name by any oath or vow made according to the law of God; whether it be between man and God, as in the holy sacrament of baptism and the holy supper of the Lord, where as we swear and promise to live after his will and pleasure: or when man to man bindeth himself to any conditions or promises by the invocation of God's name, or testimony of his own conscience. If the one keep not touch and promise with the other, he that offendeth abuseth not only his own faith, which should be always simple and true, but also contemneth the majesty and omnipotency of God, in whose name the oath was taken.

And not only the law of God, but also the law of man punisheth this horrible perjury, as ye may read, Levit. xxiv., how he that took the name of God in vain was stoned to death. So saith David, Psal. v. So saith this commandment, "God will not leave him unpunished that nameth him in vain." Example we have in Ananias and his wife. Acts v. The children of Israel were slain for perjury. Esay x.

Psal. v. 6.

Acts v. 1.
Isai. x. 2.

The emperor Justinian, *Novellis constitut*[1]. 77, commandeth to put to death the blasphemers.

Novel. constit. 77.

Such as trust in their own strength or riches abuse and blaspheme this name of God: which never was nor never shall be unpunished in this world, in the world to come, or in both. Examples we have in Assur, Esa. x., Holofernes, Judith xiii. Ajax, that said he could overcome his enemies without God, at length was not overcome of his enemies, but killed himself.

Isai. x. 13.
Judith xiii. 8.

Those that swear by the name of God, and likewise by the name of saints, offend this commandment. As when the form of their oath is thus: "As HELP ME GOD and all

Deut. vi. 13.

[1 Ultimis subdere suppliciis. Corp. Juris Civilis, Tom. II. Auth. Collat. VI. Tit. VI. Novell. 77. cap. I.]

saints." For the oath must be only in the name of God: Deut. vi. x. Josu. xxiii. How this sin in swearing by any than God is punished, read Hiere. v., Soph. i. Read the seventh chapter of Josua, and learn the form of a true oath there, when he constrained Achan to confess the truth by the virtue of an oath. It is a manifest argument of impiety and false belief, when people swear by any creatures: such as give their books a holy and religious title, and the contents thereof is none other than the defence of superstition and inquiry of vain glory, or his own private commodity, abuse the name of God. *Jer. v. 7. Wisd. i. 5. [Zeph. i. 5.]*

They offend grievously this commandment, that swear without necessity: more grievously, when for every light trifle or matter of nothing; most grievously, when men swear to maintain a false cause, to obtain an ill purpose, to oppress the truth, or to justify the wrong. The oath therefore must be, as Hiere. saith, cap. iv., in verity, judgment, and justice. There the prophet exhorteth the Israelites to reverence the name and glory of God, and that they believe stedfastly the universal providence of God, that they abstain from false oaths and perjury. For God seeth not only the works of man, but also the words and thoughts of the heart. Therefore no man should swear, except he know perfectly the thing to be true that he sweareth. *Jer. iv. 2.*

That is the first thing that man should have in his conscience before he swear. The second, that he swear not temerously nor lightly, without reverence of God's majesty, but with judgment: that is to say, when necessity constraineth, for the glory of God or defence of virtue, at the commandment of a just and lawful appointed judge. Thirdly, that it be in justice, that the oath extend to nothing that is against God's laws. If the oath have not these three companions, it is perjury, whatsoever be sworn, and blasphemeth God's name: as all those that swear to please and flatter the superior powers, when they make ungodly laws; and those that swear in the laws of men under the pretence of holy church, and persecute Christ's true members.

As for those that be common swearers, and be suffered to blaspheme without punishment, it is so abominable, that the magistrates, they that swear, and all the commonwealth where as they dwell, shall at length smart for it. Regulus, the Roman, and the Saguntines, shameth christian men, that would not for any pain or punishment of the world violate or break their oath made by their false gods. Of whom writeth Saint Augustine[1], *libro De civitate Dei*, xxii. cap. 6, lib. i. cap. 15, Cicero[2], lib. iii. *De Officiis.* Valerius[3], lib. ix. The Saguntines burned themselves; Regulus returned from his native country and city of Rome to his most cruel enemies in Africa, and would rather suffer the extreme tyranny of his enemies than violate or break his oath that he had sworn.

[[1] Unde merito quæritur, utrum recte fecerint Saguntini, quando universam suam civitatem interire maluerunt, quam fidem frangere, qua cum ipsa Romana republica tenebantur: in quo suo facto laudantur ab omnibus terrenæ reipublicæ civibus. Aug. Op. Basil. 1542. Tom. v. col. 1337. De Civ. Dei, Lib. xxii. cap. 6. Habent tamen isti de captivitate religionis causa etiam sponte toleranda, et in præclaris viris nobilissimum exemplum. Marc. Attilius Regulus * * * * * Nec * * * * ad hostes redire compulsus est; sed quod juraverat, id sponte implevit. At illi eum excogitatis atque horrendis cruciatibus necaverunt. Aug. Op. Basil. 1542. Tom. v. col. 58. De Civ. Dei, Lib. i. cap. 15.]

[[2] Neque vero tum ignorabat se ad crudelissimum hostem et ad exquisita supplicia proficisci: sed jusjurandum conservandum putabat. Cic. de Off. Lib. iii. c. 27.]

[[3] Valer. Max. Lib. vi. De fide publica, Cap. vi. Externa 1.]

CAPUT VII.

THE FOURTH COMMANDMENT.

Remember to sanctify the sabbath day. Six days thou shalt labour, and do all thy works. The seventh day is rest unto God thy Lord, thou shalt do no work in it; neither thy son, neither thy daughter, thy servant, nor thy maid, neither thy beast, neither the stranger that is within thy doors. For in six days God made heaven and earth, the sea and all things that is therein, and the seventh day rested. Therefore blessed God the seventh day, and sanctified it.

THE cause and end why this commandment was instituted is divers. First, because man should upon this day call his intendment and thoughts from the lusts, pleasures, vanities, and concupiscence of the world, unto the meditations of God and his works, to the study of scripture, hearing of the word of God; to call upon God with ardent prayer, to use and exercise the sacraments of God, to confer and give, according to his ability, almose to the comforting of the poor. [sidenote: The end why this commandment was instituted.]

Then likewise God by this commandment provideth for the temporal and civil life of man, and likewise for all things that be necessary and expedient for man in this life. If man, and beast that is man's servant, should without repose and rest always labour, they might never endure the travail of the earth. God therefore, as he that intendeth the conservation and wealth of man and the thing created to man's use, commandeth this rest and repose from labour, that his creatures may endure and serve as well their own necessary affairs and business, as preserve the youth and offspring[4] of man and beast, till it come to a sufficient age and convenient force to supply the place and room of such, as death or disease shall private or disable from the execution and use of such travails as this careful life shall necessarily require. So saith Ovid, *Quod caret alterna requie, durabile non est;* that is to say, "The thing cannot endure that lacketh rest."

[4 Offspring, C, offrynge, A and B.]

That man and beast therefore might breathe and have repose, this sabbath was instituted, not only that the body should be restored unto strength, and made able to sustain the travails of the week to come; but also that the soul and spirit of man, whiles the body is at rest, might upon the sabbath learn and know so the blessed will of his Maker, that only it leave not from the labour and adversity of sin, but also by God's grace receive such strength and force in the contemplation of God's most merciful promise, that it may be able to sustain all the troubles of temptation in the week that followeth. For as the body, being always oppressed with labour, loseth his strength, and so perisheth; so doth the mind of man, oppressed with the cares and pleasures of this world, lose all her force, lust, and desire, that she had to the rest to come of eternal life, and so dieth not only the death of sin, but hasteth, what she can, to hate and abhor all virtue.

Almighty God therefore, not only in his commandments, but also at the first creation of the world, sanctified the seventh day, Gen. ii.: that is to say, appointed it to an holy use, or separated it from other days, wherein men travail in the business of this world. So is the meaning of this Hebrew phrase, or manner of speech: as ye may read, Joshua xx. chapter. *Sanctificaxerunt Kades in Galilea*, that is to say, "They sanctified Kades in Galilea." It is as much to say in English, they chose or appointed the city of Kades to be a refuge or sanctuary for murderers, to be safe there till the cause of the murderer might be known. Howbeit, ye may not think that God gave any more holiness to the sabbath than to the other days: for if ye consider Friday and Saturday, Saturday or Sunday, inasmuch as they be days and the work of God, the one is no more holy than the other, Cod. lib. iii. tit. 12. *de Feriis*. But that day is always most holy in the which we most apply and give ourselves unto holy works. To that end he sanctified the sabbath day: not that we should give ourselves to illness, or such ethnical pastime, as is now used among christian people[1]; but, being free that

[1 Omnes judices, urbanæque plebes, et cunctarum artium officia venerabili die Solis quiescant. Corp. Jur. civ. Cod. Lib. III. Tit. 12. cap. 3. De die Dominico. Dies festos, majestati altissimæ dedicatos, nullis volu-

day from the travails of this world, we might consider the works and benefits of God with thanksgiving; hear the word and law of God, honour him and fear him; then to learn who and where be the poor of Christ, our brothers in necessity, that wanteth our help. The observation therefore of the sabbath doth extend as well unto the faith we have in God, as unto the charity of our neighbour; and not only that, but also unto the beasts that travail in our business and be our necessary servants, the which we should in no wise abuse, not only for their labour's sake, but also for the love of him that hath commended them unto our service, Almighty God.

How far the observation of the sabbath extendeth.

Thirdly, the sabbath hitherunto from the beginning of the world was and is a type and figure of the eternal and everlasting rest that is to come; as St Paul diligently sheweth in the epistle to the Hebrews, cap. iv.: so doth Saint Augustine[2], Lib. xi. cap. 31. *De civit.* Such as believed the promise of God declared by Moses, were led by Josuah the prince into Palestina, and rested in Chanaan: such as hear the word of God and obeyeth it, shall be carried into the celestial heavens by Jesus Christ, and rest in[3] eternal joy. Read diligently that chapter, and thou shalt find a very necessary doctrine, what is the cause that the most part of men enter not into this eternal rest; the contempt of our captain's words, Jesu Christ, who would lead us thither, haled we not back, and left not his commandments.

Heb. iv. 8. De civit. Dei. lib. xi. cap. 31.

Consider the persons rehearsed in this commandment: " Thy son, thy daughter, thy man-servant, and thy woman-servant, thy beast, and the stranger within thy doors." Those thou must not without necessity constrain to any servile work upon the sabbath; but see that they exercise themselves upon the sabbath in hearing the word of God; and see they frequent the place of common prayers,

The persons rehearsed in this commandment.

mus voluptatibus occupari, nec ullis exactionum vexationibus profanari. Dominicum itaque Diem ita semper honorabilem decernimus, et venerandum ut, &c. Nec hujus tamen religiosi diei otia relaxantes, obscœnis quemquam patimur voluptatibus detineri. Ibid. cap. 11.]

[2 De die septimo, in quo plenitudo et requies commendatur. Aug. Op. Par. 1432, Tom. v. col. 656.]

[3 In, A, into, B and C.]

and use the sacraments, as God commandeth. For those God hath commanded unto thy charge, as long as they be with thee; not only that thou give them their wages that is due, but also see them aright instructed in the law of God, and live thereafter. For if they perish by thy negligence, their blood shall be required at thy hand.

The stranger likewise within thy port[1], though he be of another religion, thou shouldest assay to win him unto the knowledge and rites of thy religion, as thou seest here commanded unto the Israelites, and consequently unto us all. For we are bound no less, but rather more than they, to the love of God and our neighbour, and by express words commanded to do the same. Matt. xxii. Jac. v. Here let us all cry out and say, *peccavimus*, "We have offended," and study to amend: for there is here condemned the avarice of all men, that care not for God nor his law a deal, but useth ungodly and uncharitably their servants and beasts, as though they were made only of God to serve his avaricious appetites, and not rather to serve the necessaries of their masters, and likewise to glorify God, as his word commandeth.

<small>James v. 19.</small>
<small>What is condemned in this commandment.</small>

Likewise in this commandment is condemned our uncharitable behaviour towards our neighbour, and likewise the ungodly and carnal fear that we have to teach a stranger the knowledge of God. We give him the thing we owe him not, saving by the law of nature, and the thing that he may well lack, or else obtain of another, a supper or dinner for his money, or love; and never make mention of the thing we owe him, inasmuch as we be Christians. Thus can Aristotle entreat his guests, and Plato give his alms. Our office is to communicate the knowledge of God with him, so[2] to move a communication, that the one might know the other's faith. But this charity and hospitality is used but of few men. In case a man should make mention of any such almose, or entreat any place of the scripture at dinner or supper, it were a cloying of the stomach and taking away of the appetite; an ill-savoured mess, and the worst dish that can be brought to the table. Men say, that folk should be merry at the table, and let the preacher talk of scripture; as though the law of God

[1 Port: gate.]   [2 So, A, for, B and C.]

made men sorry, which containeth not only the solace and joy of man in this world, but also in time to come for ever. God take out of the hearts of men all fear and shame, that we freely confess him, as occasion shall be given, with Loth, Gen. xix. cap., that sat in the gates of Sodoma to invitate the strangers that came to the city into his own house, to keep them in virtue, and preserve them from vice. Read the chapter, and see wherein consisteth true hospitality. Gen. xix. 1.

Further, thou seest by this commandment, that the Israelites might constrain the strangers within their city to hear and see their religion upon the sabbath: as every well-ordered commonwealth now in the time of the gospel should do the same, and constrain all people to hear the word of God, and see the ministration of their sacraments. This day is appointed also for man to consider and expound the works of God, the which he made in six days. For the least creature that God made shall teach man a knowledge of the Creator, if it be considered accordingly. So that man should not only use them, but also give God thanks for them, to augment faith, to roborate[3] hope, and provoke love. Therefore God blessed the sabbath, to say, made it honourable, sanctified it, appointed it to an holy use, gave it certain privileges, and would men to be that day holy. Strangers to be constrained to religion.

For as he hath appointed six days for us to exercise ourselves in the business and travails of the world; so hath he appointed the seventh to exercise the ceremonies of the church, which are instituted for the preservation of the ministry of the church: as to use common prayer, hear the sermon, use the blessed supper of the Lord, and to give alms. 1 Cor. xi. xiv. and xvi. Although the ceremony of the sabbath be taken away, Col. ii. which appertained only unto the people and commonwealth of the Hebrews; yet one day of the week to preserve and use the word of God and his sacraments is not abrogated. 1 Cor. xi. 17. xiv. 23. and xvi. 2. Col. ii. 16.

Therefore in this commandment are two things to be observed, the one ceremonial, during for the time; the other moral and never to be abolished, as long as the church of Christ shall continue upon the earth. The patriarchs before the law, Gen. ii., the prophets in the Two things are in this commandment to be noted.
Gen. ii. 3.

[3 Roborate: corroborat, A, roborat, B, confirm, C.]

time of the law, Exod. xx. Deut. v., we being delivered from the damnation of the law, 1 Cor. xvi., have one day to rest from labour, and to apply ourselves to the works of the Spirit; which secretly in ourselves should be done every day, with our handy labour; upon the Sunday openly without the labour of our hands.

Exod. xx. 10.
1 Cor. xvi. 2.

Sunday not the precept of man.

This Sunday that we observe is not the commandment of man, as many say, that would, under the pretence of this one law, bind the church of Christ to all other laws that men hath ungodly prescribed unto the church; but it is by express words commanded, that we should observe this day (the Sunday) for our sabbath, as the words of Saint Paul declareth, 1 Cor. xvi., commanding every man to appoint his alms for the poor in the Sunday. The text saith, "in one of the sabbath." It is an Hebrew phrase, and is as much to say as, "in the Sunday;" as ye may read the same manner of speech, Luke xxiv. and John xx., of the women that came to the sepulchre to anoint the dead body of Christ. Luke saith, "In one of the sabbaths early they came to the sepulchre;" and so saith John by the same words: the which was the Sunday, as no man doubteth. For it is our faith that Christ rose the third day. So may ye read, Gen. i., where the text saith, "It was evening and it was morning one day;" that is to say, the first day, which we call the Sunday. And thus also saith those that were best learned in the tongues among christian writers: John Chrysostom[1], Lactantius[2], and Erasmus[3].

1 Cor. xvi. 2.

Luke xxiv. 1.
John xx. 1.

Gen. i. 5.

For the preservation of the true meaning of the word of God, and right use of his blessed sacraments, he hath given unto the church apostles, prophets, pastors, doctors, and other, Eph. iv., that should teach us the scripture and writings of the prophets and apostles, which was declared to be true with many signs and tokens: that we should not waver with every wind, and be carried into errors by

Eph. iv. 11.

[1] Μίαν σαββάτων τὴν κυριακὴν ἐκάλεσε. Chrysost. Op. Paris. 1835. Tom. III. p. 302.]

[2] See Lactantii Op. Basiliæ, 1532. De vera Sapientia, Lib. iv. cap. xix. fo. 60.]

[3] Cur igitur septimus dies versus est nobis in octavum? &c. Erasmi Opera, Lugduni Bat. 1704. Tom. v. co. 1190.]

the doctrine of man: that we should not feign new doctrine out of our own brains, but believe as the holy church of the patriarchs, prophets, Christ, and the apostles; which taught the people as they wrote, and wrote as they taught; that no man after their death should deceive the people, that Christ redeemed with his precious blood, with false and imposterous doctrine. Those ethnick and Jewish doctors of the pope, howsoever they brag of the name of holy church, be none other than the defenders of the synagogue of antichrist.

Sure we be that Christ, the patriarchs, prophets, and apostles, be saved, and believed no more, nor none otherwise, than they have left unto us by writings. Better it is to be certain of our doctrine and salvation with this holy church, than to associate ourselves with the rabble of liars, that boasteth and braggeth their abominable and ethnical ceremonies, which be condemned in the scripture, to be laws for the holy church. God give thee grace to read the holy bible, and to have a little understanding of it! Then shalt thou see, who and where is the holy church, that these dreamers attribute unto their father the devil and antichrist of Rome. And if they say unto thee, that thou must not take the text after thy own mind, but after the mind of the holy doctors, that hath written in the scripture; think with thyself, that God hath given thee the scripture to read therein to thy salvation, as well as unto the doctor.

Further, that thy doctor preach not a lie for the truth, God hath given thee the scripture to judge thy bishop, doctor, preacher, and curate, whether he preach gall or honey, his own laws or God's laws.

Further, say boldly and fear not, (for it is true,) that in matters and causes of weight the doctors agree not one with the other, no, many times not with themselves; as every man knoweth, that hath read them with judgment. And as good arguments shalt thou find in them to disprove, as to prove the things, that this late-found catholic church of the devil would stablish.

Again, think which was the most pure church and free from heresies: the church before the doctors wrote, that only was taught by the simple text and words of the apostles, or the church that hath been taught this many years by the blind doctrine of men? Then thou shalt see, that those doctors that they speak of hath put out God's laws and brought in their own, as the Pharisees and rabbins did in the old church. Be not afraid of their holy name, but trust to the holiness of scripture: then shalt thou not be deceived. They say, the holy church must be heard and obeyed. True it is: but our faith is not grounded upon those that be of the church, though they be the true ministers of God's word; but upon the word itself, as it appeareth, Matt. xvi. Therefore, when the authority or testimony of the church is alleged, man that loveth his salvation must search where and what the church is, what times and when the writers were most sincere; and not believe these yesterday's birds, that sing as the papegay[1], they know not what, as they be taught out of a shameless school, that began with murder, is maintained with sacrilege, and shall be destroyed with the clarity[2] and brightness of the Son of man coming to judgment.

Matt. xvi. 18.

It appertaineth unto no man, in what authority soever he be, to judge who preacheth false, or who true; but unto the word of God only, which interpretateth itself, when it is with judgment conferred. But of this is required a more prolix work, which God shall give in time.

Now the works of this precept be also these: godly to preach his word, and to use the sacraments as he teacheth in his word, to hear them reverently that truly preacheth, to honour the word of God, and help to the preferment thereof as much as may be, to succour the professors thereof, which be, hath been, and ever shall be (if they preach truly) in the most miserable condition of the world. Matt. x. Luke xxi. Mar. xiii. Joh. xv. xvi. To neglect the preaching of God's word, as these do that look for the fleece and care not for the sheep, [is a work against this commandment.][3]

Matt. x. 22.

To abolish the preaching of the word, as those do that hath brought into the church massing and mumbling of

[¹ Papegay, A and B, popingay, C. A parrot.]
[² Clertye, A and B, cleernesse, C.]
[³ Added from C.]

canonical hours (as they call them), which neither they that say them, neither those that hear them, understandeth not, [is a work also against this commandment.][4] They say, God understandeth them: what then? So he understandeth likewise the cuckoo and the lowing of the cow, which is as good and better praise unto God than the superstitious and unknown prayer that thou mumblest. For they use the gift that God hath given them, to sound an unknown voice: and thou abusest the gift of God, which gave thee a tongue, to edify thyself and thy neighbour, likewise to preach the Lord omnipotent; but thou makest thy tongue an instrument to speak thou wottest not what. When thou shouldest cry for mercy and say, *Sana animam meam quia peccavi tibi*, that is to say, "Lord heal my soul, for I have offended thee;" thou sayest, *Custodivi vias Domini, nec impie gessi a Deo meo*, that is to say, "I have kept the ways of the Lord, and have not departed by iniquity from my God." Thus the Psalms and books of the scripture thou readest without judgment, and knowest not what psalm is meet for thy necessity and state of the people that be present, no more than he that never saw the scripture. Yea, sometime thou readest a false history, and either thou attributest the honour due to God unto the saint thou worshippest, or honourest him in the earth, whose soul, peradventure, is in hell. For Augustine[5] so saith, that all be not glorified souls with God, whose relics men worship in the earth.

To teach false doctrine, is a work against this commandment. Likewise to depravate the use of the sacraments otherwise than they be taught in the scripture, is against this commandment; to use them to another end than they were instituted; to honour them, as they do that enchant the water of the font, and chafe it with many a suspire[6] and deep-fet breath; such as honour the bread

[[4] Added from C.]

[[5] The exact words have not been found in Augustine as here quoted. In the book De opere Monachorum, Cap. xxviii, this expression occurs: Alii membra martyrum, si tamen martyrum, venditant. Aug. Op. Basiliæ, 1542. Tom. III. col. 800.]

[[6] Suspire: *suspirium*, sigh, fetching breath. "Tunc *sufflet* ter in aquam versus tres partes, etc." Rituale Romanum, *De sacramento Baptismi*.]

and wine, which the scripture doth not only teach to remain in their substantial essence and nature without changing, but also the reason and all the wits of man. Further, the beasts of the earth, fowls of the air, and fishes of the water, knoweth there is no change of bread nor wine, and beareth record that the scripture is true; bread to remain bread, and wine wine. 1 Cor. x. xi.

Further, to augment the ceremonies of the church, and bring in a new Judaism and Aaronical rites, is against this commandment. As the bishops hath used the matter, there be more ceremonies in the church of Christ than were in the church of the Jews; as it shall easily appear to him that will confer our church with the books of Moses. Seneca[1], in his book *contra superstitiones*, reprehended the rites of the Jews, and chiefly the sanctifying of the sabbath. What would he say, if he saw our churches, that have not the ceremonies commanded by God, but by man to the dishonouring of God?

Contra superstitiones.

To neglect a charitable deed to our neighbour upon the sabbath day, is to break the sabbath, Matt. xii., Luke vi. xiii.: not to cease from doing of ill, but to abuse the rest and ease of the sabbath in sports, games, and pastimes, keeping of markets and fairs upon the sabbath, is

Matt. xii. 12.
Luke vi. 9.

[1 Quid de Judæis Seneca senserit. Cap. xi.

Hic inter alias civilis theologiæ superstitiones reprehendit etiam sacramenta Judæorum, et maxime Sabbata, inutiliter id eos facere affirmans, quod per illos singulos septem interpositos dies septimam fere partem ætatis suæ perdant vacando, et multa in tempore urgentia non agendo lædantur. August. Op. Tom. v. De Civ. Dei, Lib. vi. Cap. xi.

From the preceding chapter it appears that Augustine is quoting from "eo libro quem contra superstitiones condidit," and Hooper probably derived his knowledge of this opinion of Seneca's from Augustine; for, as Ludovicus Vives mentions, " Libri Senecæ nonnulli sunt amissi, ut *hi de superstitionibus, &c.*" The following passage occurs in another part of Seneca's writings. Accendere aliquem lucernas sabbatis prohibeamus, quoniam nec lumine Dii egent, et ne homines quidem delectantur fuligine. Vetemus salutationibus matutinis fungi, et foribus assidere templorum: humana ambitio istis officiis capitur; Deum colit qui novit. Vetemus lintea et strigiles Jovi ferri, et speculum teneræ Junoni. Non quærit ministros Deus. Quidni? Ipse humano generi ministrat. Ubique et omnibus præsto est. Sen. Op. Lib. xv. Epist. 96, p. 216. Basil. 1529.]

to abuse the sabbath. It is as much as to fery[2] unto God, and work to the devil; for specially all unlawful plays and sports be used upon that day.

It is against this commandment to keep or dedicate any feast to any saint, of what holiness soever he be. Therefore saith the law, "Ye shall celebrate the feast unto the Lord." Exod. xxiii. This honour should be given only unto God. In the old testament was no feast ever dedicated unto any saint, neither in the new. It happened after the death of the apostles, as it is written in Euseb[3]. Eccles. Hist. Lib. iv. cap. 15. And better authority have they not, that be the authors of these holy days, the which the council of Lugd. hath given us: they have not above two hundred and seventy-three years in age, and is the leaven of the pope. In Trip. Hist. Lib. ix., cap. 38, there is no mention of saints' holy days; few of St Hier.[1] i. 4, cap. ad Galat., and likewise of St Augustine[5], ad Janu. cxviii. Epi. The Sunday and the hours thereof appointed for a decent order, to preach the word of God, use the

marginal notes: Exod. xxiii. 11. Eccl. Hist. lib. iv. c. 15. Lib. ix. cap. 38. Jerome i. 4. ca. ad Galat. Aug. ad Janu. cxviii. Ep. i.

[2 Fery, A and B, ferrie, C. To keep a feast or holiday.]

[3 After relating the death of Polycarp by martyrdom, and the burning of his remains to ashes, Eusebius says, οὕτως τε ἡμεῖς ὕστερον ἀνελόμενοι τὰ τιμιώτερα λίθων πολυτελῶν καὶ δοκιμώτερα ὑπὲρ χρυσίον ὀστᾶ αὐτοῦ, ἀπεθέμεθα ὅπου καὶ ἀκόλουθον ἦν. ἔνθα ὡς δυνατὸν ἡμῖν συναγομένοις ἐν ἀγαλλιάσει καὶ χαρᾷ, παρέξει ὁ Κύριος ἐπιτελεῖν τὴν τοῦ μαρτυρίου αὐτοῦ ἡμέραν γενέθλιον, εἴς τε τῶν προηθληκότων μνήμην, καὶ τῶν μελλόντων ἄσκησίν τε καὶ ἑτοιμασίαν, &c. Euseb. Eccles. Hist. Moguntiæ, 1672. Lib. iv. Cap. xv. p. 135.]

[4 Dicat aliquis, Si dies observare non licet, et menses et tempora et annos, nos quoque simile crimen incurrimus quartam sabbati observantes, et parasceven, et diem dominicam, et jejunium quadragesimæ, et paschæ festivitatem, et pentecostes lætitiam, et pro varietate regionum diversa in honore martyrum tempora constituta. * * * * * Quotus enim quisque est, qui saltem *hæc pauca quæ statuta sunt,* vel orandi tempora vel jejunandi? Hieron. Op. Basiliæ, 1519. Tom. ix. fol. 90.]

[5 Illa autem quæ non scripta sed tradita custodimus, quæ quidem toto terrarum orbe observantur, dantur intelligi vel ab ipsis Apostolis vel plenariis conciliis, quorum est in ecclesia saluberrima auctoritas, commendata atque statuta retineri; sicuti quod Domini passio et resurrectio et ascensio in cœlum, et adventus de cœlo Spiritus Sancti, anniversaria solennitate celebrantur: et si quid aliud tale occurrerit, quod servatur ab universa quacunque se diffundit ecclesia. There is in a marginal note "festa paucissima." Aug. Op. Basiliæ, 1542. Tom. ii. col. 556. Epist. 118.]

sacraments, to have common prayers, to provide for the poor, is to be observed, that all things may be done in order. 1 Cor. xiv.

<small>1 Cor. xiv. 40.</small>

As for the other laws that they have made concerning fasting and satisfaction for sin, and would defend them under the pretence and title of mortification of the flesh; that gloss serveth not for their purpose. But their hypocrisy layeth wait to destroy the true doctrine of Christ, if it be not avoided. They teach neither what mortification is, neither how the flesh may be best kept under to obey the Spirit. Mortification signifieth either patience, which God requireth in the time of adversity; either temperance, commanded of God to refrain the lusts and concupiscence that fighteth against the Spirit. It signifieth not such voluntary fasts, celebrating of masses, or any such other doings of superstitious ceremonies, as man chooseth to do without the commandment of God. Of patience under the cross, and of adversity, Saint Paul speaketh, 2 Cor. iv.: "We always," saith he, "bear about with us the mortification of the Lord Jesu in the body, to that end that the life of Jesu may be manifested in the body." And in the same place: "Always we, that be living, for the love of Jesu are delivered to death, that the life of Jesu might appear in our mortal flesh." This calleth Saint Paul mortification, that is like unto the affliction of Christ, and speaketh of the same, Rom. xii., and David, Psal. l., Mic. vii.

<small>2 Cor. iv. 10.</small>

Of temperance and sobriety in meat, drink, and all other things, it is written, Luke xxii. "Beware your hearts be not oppressed with gluttony and drunkenness." Matt. xvii. "These kinds of spirits be not cast out, but with fasting and praying." Likewise, Ephes. vi. Whether we speak of patience in adversity, or temperancy in felicity, both these [be]¹ works commanded of God. And it is lawful for every man to choose for himself such exercises, as best be convenient to his own age and condition of his body; therefore Paul saith, 1 Cor. ix., "I chasten my body and bring it into servitude" to this end, that intemperancy letted not the Holy Ghost, withdrew not his mind from prayer, made him not unapt to study and to the vocation he

<small>Luke xxi. 34.</small>
<small>Matt. xvii. 21.</small>
<small>Ephes. vi. 11.</small>
<small>1 Cor. ix. 27.</small>

[¹ Supplied from A.]

was appointed unto. This is the end why we should do these works, not to merit our reconciliation for sin, but to labour against the devil, the world, sin, and the flesh with the Holy Ghost, to preserve ourselves in the favour of God.

Temperancy is in general commended unto all men and all times. Howbeit, not one manner of exercise in this virtue can be appointed for all men; but every man may choose for himself, what exercise he listeth, and is most convenient for his disease. Such as be passed in age, and with cares of this world hath lost the strength of their bodies, needeth not so great abstinence from meats and drinks as these that be young and in the midst of their strength. As we may see in one man, David, that needed more exercises before he was put into exile than after; when scarce could the bones bear about the weak body, that was far broken with the troubles and care of this world. Health is the great gift of God, Deut. xxviii., and fairest beauty of man or woman, Arist. Lib. Rhetori: therefore it must not be hurt, neither with overmuch abstinence, neither with dissolute living. Would to God people would follow the scripture in this mortification! then the world would amend doubtless: but there is now nothing but a carnal liberty of the gospel, which hindereth much the glory of God.

^{Temperancy.}
^{Health.}

The pain of such as violate this commandment, and doth any vile work without necessity, is written Numb. xv., that he should be stoned to death.

^{Num. xv. 32.}

Thus I have rudely opened the first table of the ten words, that containeth four commandments: the which division doth Josephus[2], Antiq. Lib. vi. cap. 3, Origen, Homil. in Exod. viii., Ambrose[3], in vi. cap. Epist. ad Ephes. Augustine[4], Lib. iii. ad Bonifac. approve. In his Quæst. in

^{Antiq. lib. vi. cap. 3. Hom. in Exod. viii. In cap. 6. Eph. lib. iii. ad Bonif.}

[2 Joseph. Antiq. Lib. iii. Cap. v. par. 5. Tom. i. p. 229. Amsterd. 1726. Josephus here enumerates the commandments in accordance with the method of the English church.]

[3 Sed quia prima quatuor mandata ad Deum pertinent, hæc in prima tabula contineri subintelliguntur, cetera ad hominem, &c. Ambros. Op. Tom. iii. p. 243. Col. Agrip. 1616.]

[4 Aug. Lib. iii. ad Bonif. (contra Duas Epistt. Pelagianorum) enumerates the ten commandments in accordance with the present method. Tom. vi. col. 899.]

In Exod. quæst. 7.	Exod. Quæst. 71[1], he numbereth but three in the first, and seven in the next table, by reason of a certain allegory. And
Lib. iii. Distinct. 40.	him doth the Master of the Sentence[2] follow. Lib. III. Distinct. 40. Howbeit the first division is true, as the text in Exod.
Exod. xx. 1.	xx. is plain, where as the tenth commandment, "Thou shalt not covet," is but one commandment; as I have diligently searched all the editions that we have in the Hebrew tongue. With one punct, period, and sentence he concludeth the whole tenth commandment, which many men divide into two: "Thou shalt not covet thy neighbour's house," that is one with them: "Thou shalt not covet thy neighbour's wife," is another. But the text declareth manifestly, that it is but one: for all is comprehended within one and under
Deut. v. 21.	one sentence. In Deuteronomy, cap. v., certain later editions maketh divisions of the text; but that is nothing to the purpose. There Moses repeateth the words unto them that knew before the division of the tables. Further, the printers therein followeth the mind of one Maimon[ides], an Hebrew, and not the original in Exodus, cap. xx. Further, in the oldest edition and print that I have seen (as far as I know, there is none elder; if there be, it is but one), the tenth commandment in Deuteronomy is not di-

[[1] Quæritur decem præcepta legis quemadmodum dividenda sint; utrum quatuor sint usque ad præceptum de sabbato, quæ ad ipsum Deum pertinent; sex autem reliqua, quorum primum, "Honora patrem et matrem," quæ ad hominem pertinent: an potius illa tria sint et ista septem, &c. &c.

Mihi tamen videntur congruentius accipi tria illa et ista septem, quoniam Trinitatem videntur illa quæ ad Deum pertinent insinuare diligentius intuentibus. Aug. Op. Basiliæ, 1541. Quæst. super Exod. cap. xx. 71. Tom. I. col. 147, 148.]

[[2] Habet enim Decalogus decem præcepta, quæ sunt decachordum psalterium. Quæ sic sunt distributa, ut tria quæ sunt in prima tabula pertineant ad Deum, scilicet, ad cognitionem et dilectionem Trinitatis; septem quæ sunt in secunda tabula ad dilectionem proximi.

Primum in prima tabula est, Non habebis Deos alienos. Non facies tibi sculptile, neque omnem similitudinem, &c. Hæc Origenes dicit esse duo mandata, sed Augustinus unum, &c. Pet. Lomb. Lib. III. Distinct. 37. Lugduni, 1570, fol. 281.

In Distinct. 40. the title is "De sexto et septimo præcepto secundæ tabulæ."

Sextum præceptum est: Non desiderabis uxorem proximi tui. Septimum est, Non concupisces domum proximi tui, &c.]

vided, the which edition Venice gave unto us, anno 1494. Further, Onkelos, the Chaldee interpreter, in Deut., maketh but one commandment of the tenth. I wonder that some, which be not ignorant of the tongues, follow not the truth of the text, but maketh the commandment that forbiddeth images a precept ceremonial. So I might say this were also ceremonial, "Thou shalt have no strange gods before my face." For all the commandments be of one virtue and strength. If the one may be in effect ceremonial, so may the other: but these opinions I pass over at this time.

THE SECOND TABLE.

CAPUT VIII.

Honour thy father and mother, that thou mayest have long life in the land that the Lord thy God shall give unto thee.

As in the first table are comprehended all the works that appertain unto such religion and honour as belongeth only unto God: as in the first precept, knowledge, fear, faith, and love of God; in the second is forbid all external idolatry; in the third, external profession of God's name, his word, and his works, as by prayer, thanksgiving, preaching, and confessing his truth before the world; in the fourth, how we should honour him with public sacraments and ceremonies in the church: so in this second table is comprehended all such works as appertain unto God and man. And in this table is prescribed how, and by what means, one man may live with another in peace and unity in this civil life, during the time of this mortal body upon the earth.

Many noble wits hath applied great diligence and study to prescribe such laws as might best and most commodiously govern and keep the people in a politic felicity, to live quietly, prosperously, and wealthily: as Lycurgus the Lacedæmonian, Solon, Plato, Aristotle, the Greeks: Numa

Pompilius, Cicero, and other, the Romans: amongst Christians, Constantine, Justinian, and other. Those men hath done somewhat to associate people in cities and realms by wisdom, to keep them in an honest order with virtuous laws, and to remove the occasion of vice and discord by justice.

Howbeit, none of them all, nor all they together, hath not prescribed so perfect and absolute a form of a politic wealth, as Almighty God hath done unto his people in this second table and six rules: neither so equally pondered the diversity of sin and transgression of justice, as this law doth; nor so indifferently prescribeth correction and punishment according to the gravity and greatness of the fault, but is too cruel in the less offence, and too merciful in the greater: as ye may see the injuries of theft punished, and blasphemy of God with adultery unpunished.

After that he had gathered together this people into one company and multitude, brought them out of Egypt, and appointed them a land and cities, where they should live, as members of one commonwealth, he prescribed unto them certain laws, without the which no commonwealth can long endure. For it is no less mastery to keep a royalme in wealth from the dangers to come, than to win it from adversity, when adversity is present.

The first law to preserve a commonwealth is, that the people thereof know how to reverence and honour God aright, who is the president and the defender of all cities and realms. If he be neglected, there followeth doubtless a ruin and change of the commonwealth. Thus saw all those that wrote laws for the preservation thereof: not only Moses and christian writers, but also the ethnicks, Aristotle[1], Lib. VII. Polit. cap. 8, where as he numbereth the works to be done in the city: *Quintum, inquit, ac primum circa aram divinam cultus, quod sacrificium vocant;* that is to say, "the fifth and principal work is religion at the altar of God, which men call sacrifice." They knew that no city nor realm could continue long in wealth, except they had the favour of God; though they could

[[1] Πέμπτον δὲ καὶ πρῶτον, τὴν περὶ τὸ θεῖον ἐπιμέλειαν, ἣν καλοῦσιν ἱερατείαν. Aristot. Pol. Lib. VII. cap. 8. Jenæ, 1660. p. 733.]

not tell how to honour him aright. We likewise know the same, the favour of God first and chiefly to preserve the commonwealth, Ps. cxxvii. Deut. xxxi.; and be assured by his word how we may honour him, to say, as it is taught us in the first table and four first precepts.

The second law necessary for every commonwealth is, that the people among themselves live in peace and concord, without discord and dissension. As Sallust[x] saith, "Little things by concord increaseth, and great things by discord decreaseth." That saw the poor shepherd Melibœus in Virgil, when he said: *En, quo discordia cives perduxit miseros*[3]*!* that is to say, "Lo! whither (or into what miseries) hath discord brought the wretched citizens!"

Not only Rome, and other most noble commonwealths, lost their liberties and themselves by discord, but also the commonwealth of the Israelites. As ye may read, 3 Reg. xii., 1 Kings xii. how of one kingdom was made two, for the discord that God suffered to be among themselves for the idolatry of king Salomon, 3 Reg. xi.; where as ye have an example, that no commonwealth can endure, where as the precepts of the first table be neglected.

Almighty God therefore, after that he hath taught the people what is to be done towards him in the first table, he sheweth in the second table what we should do, one to the other of us, that peace and concord might be among us; which cannot be, where as one knoweth not, what reverence and honour should be done to the other. For where as all men will be like, there is neither wealth nor virtue; but contention and hatred, which is the matter and ground of all calamities and mischief. The law of God therefore, in the first front of this second table, doth appoint and institute a certain impery and dominion to be had among his people, that one person might be known from the other; commandeth obedience unto the superior powers, saying, "Magnify or reverence thy father and mother." If this order be kept, there is a reward appointed for the observation thereof, as the text saith: "Thou shalt live long upon the earth." After that people

[2 Nam concordia res parvæ crescunt, discordia maximæ dilabuntur. Sallustii, Bellum Jugurthinum—Micipsæ oratio.]

[3 Virg. Bucol. Ecl. i. l. 72.]

[HOOPER.]

of a commonwealth know each of them their duties, it is necessary there follow a law to maintain them in peace and unity. Therefore followeth it in the table: "Thou shalt not kill," which precept is a munition and defence of the peace.

Howbeit, because there followeth alteration and change in every commonwealth by reason of death, and the persons present cannot live for ever, the law-maker for the commonwealth must provide how the places of those that die may be again furnished; that with the departure of one may follow the success of another. Wherefore God putteth the sixth[1] canon that defendeth marriage, whereby is preserved this commonwealth, and as godly continue, as it began; the which law is not only necessary for the preservation of the commonwealth to come, but also to preserve the state present in peace and tranquillity. For never was there greater occasion of discord and hate between commonwealth and commonwealth, prince and prince, private persons and private persons, than for the abuse and violating of marriage, and committing fornication, with such like vices: as it is to be seen by Dina, Gen. xxxiv.: by Thamar, 2 Reg. xiii.: by the priest's wife abused of the Benjamites, Judicum xix., xx. read the place. For the rape of Helena Troy perished: for the oppressing of Lucrece at Rome, and other. Then as there be laws to preserve the person's self of the commonwealth, so must there be laws to preserve such goods as appertain unto the members of the commonwealth, that one do no wrongs unto the other, but every man be content with his own condition and proper goods, and not to usurp authority over his neighbours. Therefore the eighth law is concerning the defence of proper and private goods, "Thou shalt do no theft."

Gen. xxxiv. 25.
2 Sam. xxviii.
Judges xix. xx. xxi.

Howbeit, seeing we are frail and so ill, that many times we transgress some or all these laws that preserveth the commonwealth, it is necessary to find and prepare some remedy to have the transgressor punished, and the person that is hurt and offended restored unto his right. Therefore is there this clause and rule in the law; "Thou

[[1] Sixth canon: the sixth commandment, as enumerated by the church of Rome and the Lutherans; the seventh in the arrangement usually followed by protestants.]

shalt give no false testimony against thy neighbour:" which is the ninth commandment, and bindeth as well the superior powers to see equity and justice without respect of persons, as the cause requireth, observed; as such shall be testimonies in a doubtful matter to say as they know truly: and likewise, that in buying and selling, and in all other contracts, men use no fraud to get their goods. These laws now I will open, in order as they stand, plainly and simply as I can, to the understanding of the text. As for them[2] I will speak of severally: these be the fountains and original of all politic laws.

The first law that stablisheth the authority of the superior powers, beginneth with the name of the father and mother. For after and next unto God we owe most reverence unto them, of whom we have received this natural life by the help of God: and they likewise hath sustained the pains of our education and bringing up. Then under the name of the parents is concluded all other persons to whom we owe our obedience and love; as the country where we were born, or where we have our living, that we be true and faithful unto it, garnish it what we may, and enrich it with all godly knowledge, arts, and other commodities; nor to hurt it, but to die for it, as justice shall require: then the prince or magistrate, that hath the defence of the country and the people of the same committed unto his charge: tutors appointed for youth, such as teacheth any craft or handy means to live by: the doctors and teachers in the ministry of the church, whom the scripture calleth the father of the people, 1 Cor. iv.: then such as be by nature and parentage our kinsfolk; also all that be our elders, unto whom we owe obedience. These be the persons, that be understanded by the father and the mother.

Fathers and mothers.

Our country.

The prince and magistrate.

Tutors and masters over youth.

Ministers.

1 Cor. iv. 15.

Kinsfolk.

The text saith, that I should honour them. The which word in the Hebrew hath a greater energy[3] and strength than one word in Latin or English can express. *Cabad*[4] signifieth, to set much by, to have in estimation, to prefer and extol; and requireth these affections in the heart,

Honour.

[2 As for the then the law, A. And of them, C.]
[3 Force, C.]   [4 Cabad, כָּבֵד. Exod. xx. 12.]

and not only external reverence, as be fair words, outward gestures, without the love of the heart; to obey them in all things honest, agreeing with the law of God, not contemn them, neglect them, hate them, or be unkind to them; to help them as we be able, if necessity require; to put our lives for them, and to pay them their due, Rom. xiii., and that without murmur and grudge. For all those that I have rehearsed be as our fathers, and as it were a second God appointed for us upon the earth.

Therefore, if thou wilt have a very true image to express God Omnipotent, thy sole God and Maker, unto thy reason and external senses, set those superior powers before thine eye, which hath or doth travail for thy wealth and commodity; thy father and mother, as is before said; the prince and king, how[1] to keep thee in thine own country in wealth and felicity, that thou be not made prisoner nor bondman unto a strange nation, thy contraries[2] and thy mortal enemies. The land itself bringeth thee fruit and all things necessary for thy life, the which thy fathers won with their blood, and maintained with their body and goods. Thy preacher telleth the will of God, and all his study is to bring thee to eternal felicity. Unto those thou owest of duty a filial reverence and honour; to thy father, Exod. xx., Deut. v., Prov. x., Eph. vi., Eccles. iii.; to thy prince and lawful magistrate, Josh. i., Rom. xiii.; Eph. vi., Tit. iii., Heb. xiii., 1 Pet. ii.; to thy elders, Levit. xix, 1 Tim. v.; the which was observed also among the gentiles, as Juvenal the poet saith, that thought it a fault worthy death if the younger honoured not the elder[3]. As for the defence of the country, it was and is [granted][4] of all natural men, that there needeth nor testimony nor example: Moses, Deut. xx.; the profane writers, as Horace, thus speaketh, [that][4] "*Dulce et decorum pro patria mori;* that is to say, "It is sweet and decent to die for the country." The Lacedemonians, that were slain in Termin[5], had this epitaph on their graves:

Hospes, dic Spartæ, nos te hic vidisse jacentes,
Dum patriæ sanctis legibus obsequimur.

[1 That travaileth how, C.]   [2 Adversaries, C.]
[3 Juv. Sat. xiii. 54.]   [4 Supplied from C.]
[5 Thermopylæ. See Cicero, Tusc. Quæst. i. 101.]

"Thou stranger, say, that thou sawest us here dead, whiles we obeyed the holy laws of our country." As for our honour and reverence to such as teach us the word of God, it is shewed, and also the examples of the Corinthians, and likewise of the Galatians, that were so prompt to obey Paul before they were seduced, that they would have plucked out their own eyes to have done Paul honour. Galat. [iv. 15.]

Valerius Maximus[6], libro II. capit. 1, [writeth][7] how in Rome the elders were always taken as fathers of the younger, and that no youth should sit at any feast till their elders had place; they should be the last that sat, and the first that rise from the table.

Every man should reverence and honour these superior powers, not for fear, but for love. And consider that God beginneth not this second table with the dominion and empire of the father in vain, or without cause; but meaneth, that we should none otherwise love the superior powers of the earth, and be affectionated unto them, than unto our natural parents, and obey them in all things that is consonant or not against the law of God.

Likewise the superior powers should be none otherwise affected with love towards their subjects, than the father is against[8] the son. Consider the work and ordinance of God in this superiority and dominion, that preserveth the good, punisheth the ill, advanceth virtue, and oppresseth vice, to the preservation and wealth of the republic[9].

Thine office is to consider, in what place the superior is set, and how the devil travaileth without ceasing to trouble the tranquillity, peace, and good order of every commonwealth by sedition, treason, war, and lascivious and dissolute manner of living. Further, he laboureth continually to subvert the prince and governor thereof, to

[6 Senectuti juventus ita cumulatum et circumspectum honorem reddebat, tanquam majores natu adolescentium communes patres essent. —Invitati ad coenam diligenter quærebant, quinam ei convivio essent interfuturi; ne senioris adventum discubitu præcurrerent: sublataque mensa priores consurgere et abire patiebantur. Valer. Max. Lib. II. cap. 1. 9.]

[7 Supplied from C.]   [8 Against, A and B. Towards, C.]
[9 Republic, A and B. Commonwealth, C.]

bring him from virtue to vice, that they may both with ungodly laws and ill example pervert the people and bring them from God. As thou mayest see by David and Saul, two virtuous and godly kings at the beginning of their reign. Saul he utterly lost[1] in this world, and in the world to come. He so intricated and wrapped David in the snares of sin, that scarce could he find[2] his colour, and return to grace. Mark how he did dare and blind Salomon, the wisest that ever reigned, and brought him to idolatry.

Remember that they that rule be men, and hath likewise their infirmities, and without a singular grace cannot govern well: as Salomon saith: *Ut oculus videat, et auris audiat, Deus facit utrumque;* that is to say, "That the eye see, and the ear hear, God giveth both." The meaning of which text is, that if the magistrate have good counsel, and see what is best for the commonwealth, and the people obey it, it be the works of God. No human sapience, diligence, and industry is sufficient for this vocation. Therefore Paul saith, 2 Cor. iii. "Our ability and sufficiency is of God."

2 Cor. iii. 5.

When we have considered the malice of the devil against such as rule in the world, and likewise the rulers' proper infirmities, then let us consider likewise our own sins and naughty life, for the punishment whereof God giveth many times cruel and ungodly governors, Job xxxv.; as he giveth good, wise, and loving princes to such as fear his name. 2 Par. ix. If they happen to fall from God and follow vice, it is not thy duty straightway to calumniate, speak, move sedition, cast off obedience, love, and fear, that thou owest unto them; but pray for them, study what thou canst to call them again to God; be prone to forget and remit the offence. Remember David and Saul, that fell and yet returned; dissemble at such faults as be curable, lest the public peace be troubled. Remember, though he be naught that ruleth, the place and office that he is in is the order and work of God. So if thou put difference between the office itself, which is good, and the officer, that is evil; it shall keep thee in a fear, that thou reverence a good and godly governance in an ill governor: as Paul loved

[2 Chron. ix.]

[1 Ruined. Old editions, *loost.*]
[2 Find: Fend, A. Fynde, B. Finde, C.]

the policy and laws of Rome, and never taught sedition, though he hated Caligula and Nero, the emperors, that occupied the empire and dominion.

Beware, therefore, of contumacy and disobedience against the superior powers; obey them in all things, where they command thee nothing against God's laws. So commandeth Paul, Eph. vi.; for they are appointed unto that place of governance to be God's vicars, to execute his law, his will, his pleasure, to bring men to God, and not to carry men from God. For in case they instigate their subjects to the transgression of God's laws, we must obey neither them, neither their laws: they be not then our fathers, but rather strangers, that would draw us from the obedience of God, which is our very Father. It is not decent, that their authority should be above, and God's authority under. For as man's authority dependeth of God's, so should it bring men, and lead men to God. Where as they command nothing against God's law, thou hast heard before what reverence thou owest unto them. *Eph. vi. 1.*

A thing more unnatural is there not, than to see the son dishonour the father, the subject his superior; as we learn not only by the scripture, but also by the examples of all other beasts of the earth and fowls of the air, except a few. Therefore, the book of Job sendeth us unto them to learn wisdom. Job xii. So doth Pliny[3], Lib. VIII. cap. 27, shew what wisdom the beasts of the earth hath taught man. Be not as the viper, that gnaweth out the belly of her dam, and seeketh her own life with her dam's death. Follow the nature of the cicone[4], that in her youth nourisheth the old days of her parents[5]. Plin. Lib. x. cap. 23, Nat. Hist. Thus thou art bound to do. Exod. xx., Deut. v., Deut. xvii., Exod. xxi., Prov. xv., Rom. xiii., Jer. xxxv. If thou do it, thou shalt have the reward; which is, to live long upon the earth. If thou do it not, be assured that God will punish it, though man do not. Read the *Job xii. 7. Nat. Hist. lib. vii. cap. xvii. Plin. Nat. Hist.lib. x. cap. xxiii. Exod. xx. 12.*

[[3]. C. Plin. Nat. Hist. Basiliæ, 1545. p. 137, &c.]

[[4] Cicone: *ciconia*, stork.]

[[5] Ciconiæ nidos eosdem repetunt, genetricum senectam invicem educant. C. Plin. Nat. Hist. p. 176. See also Aristotelis de Hist. Anim. Lib. ix. cap. 13, from which Pliny's account appears to be taken.]

five-and-thirtieth chapter of Hieremy the prophet, and mark how God punished the children of Israel for disobedience, and rewarded the Rechabites for obedience of their father's will.

The duty of superiors. Now, it is necessary to know the superior's duty. First, the father's to the son; then of others that bear rule in the world.

Of fathers. The fathers' office is, to teach and bring up their children in the knowledge and discipline of God, to know him aright, and keep them from wantonness and ungodly life, Eph. vi. Deut. vi. Exod. xxi.; not to provoke them to ire, but gently win them to virtue and love, without severity and rigour, if fair means can avail; if not, to use rod and the punishment, as he seeth the cause require; and not to be remiss and negligent in correcting his child's fault, neither to wink at his ill doings. Read the place: Prov. xiii. xxii. xix.; Eccles. xxx. But, alas! how can this be done, whereas the parents themselves can scarce repeat by heart the articles of the faith, the *Pater Noster*, and ten commandments? How can those miserable persons teach their children the meaning of their belief, the virtue of prayer, the danger of sin, or right use of the sacraments? This the world oweth unto the holy church, that is extolled into the higher heavens, that hath robbed people not only of the scripture in a known tongue, but also preferred unto the cure of souls such as sing *sol fa*, and can do nothing less than the thing that appertaineth unto their office.

Eph. vi. 4. Deut. vi. 7.

Prov. xiii. 24. & xxiii. 13. Ecclus. xxx. 1. &c.

Now, what the prince and magistrate should be, what their office is towards their subjects, what is their reward if they govern well, and what their pain if they do the contrary, it shall appear by the scripture.

Of Kings. Deut. xvii. 14. What the king should be, it is written Deut. xvii. and likewise, what things they should do, or not do. "If thou wilt," saith God unto the Israelites, "have a king, thou shalt take him that I choose in the midst of thy brothers (understand that now all kings, be they good or bad, are put in their authority by God); thou canst make no stranger king over thee." In these words is declared, that whosoever will govern a commonwealth aright, must love it and the members thereof, as the father his children: as Xenophon saith[1], "a good prince differeth nothing from a good father." Aristotle[2] Lib. Politicorum, v. cap. 9. sheweth many conditions, that are necessarily required in him that should be preferred to the governance of a commonwealth.

Lib. Politi. v. cap. ix.

The first is, that he love it and the state thereof. Thus required likewise Christ in Peter, when he commended the people unto his charge, saying, "Peter, lovest thou me?" "Yea, Lord," said he, "and that thou knowest." "Then, Peter, feed my sheep." John xxi. He shall not profit in the regiment of the civil wealth, nor ecclesiastical, without a singular love unto the preservation thereof.

John xxi. 17.

The king there is forbidden to multiply horses, and to carry the people again into Egypt: not that the king should have no horses, or permit none of his subjects, if occasion required, to travel into Egypt; but that he should not glory in his own strength, and cause the people to trust in the might and power of the flesh, as though by man their commonwealth might be preserved, or their enemies so overcome in time of war, as Pharao and the Egyptians did.

Farther, it is forbidden the king to have many wives; and the cause is, lest they should withdraw his heart from God. Neither should the king multiply for himself great abundance of gold and silver. But thus the king must do, when he reigneth in his kingdom: cause an exemplar of Deuteronomy be written out, and that book should be with him, and he to read therein all the days of his life, and learn to fear the Lord his God, and to observe all the precepts thereof, and laws, to do them.

Farther, his heart should not be lift up above his brothers, and should not decline from the precepts of the book, neither to the left hand, neither to the right; that he may prolong his days in his reign, he and his children, in the midst of Israel. Deut. xvii.

Deut. xvii.

[1 Ἀλλὰ πολλάκις μὲν δή, ὦ ἄνδρες, καὶ ἄλλοτε κατενόησα ὅτι ἄρχων ἀγαθὸς οὐδὲν διαφέρει πατρὸς ἀγαθοῦ. Xenoph. Cyrop. lib. Η΄.]

[2 Τρία δέ τινα χρὴ ἐχειν τοὺς μέλλοντας ἄρξειν τὰς κυρίας ἀρχάς. κ.τ.λ. Aristot. Polit. Lib. v. cap. 9. Jenæ, 1660. p. 552.]

The first cure and charge of the magistrate or prince must be, to see their subjects instructed in the first table and the precepts thereof; which cannot be, except they appoint learned and convenient ministers in the church, that teach none other doctrine than the holy bible containeth.

Psal. ci.

Concerning their office in civil governance, it is described Psalm c.; to live well himself, and to observe mercy and justice, to punish vice, and to extol virtue. Read that psalm: there shalt thou see a prince's office, his life and family described; how he should live after the word of God, govern his people thereby; what servants he should have in his court, and what persons should be banished out of the court; to use the industry of such as be good in public and private business, as it is in the sixth verse. It may happen, a prince to have ill servants, extortioners, pollers, pillers, oppressors of the poor, nor commodious for his majesty nor for the people of his realm. Such as live in illness, blaspheme God, and can do none other thing than devour the bread of the poor; those David saith, in the eighth[1] verse, he will banish out of the court.

In the ninth[2] and last verse he saith, he will not only rid his court of such ill persons, but also daily give diligence to purge and cleanse all his realm of such ill doers. The princes that hath this study to maintain the glory of God, and to preserve justice and equity, if by infirmities they fall sometimes, must be borne withal, and their faults either hid or healed; as it is to be seen in Salomon and David. If their offence be hurtful and slanderous to the word of God, and pernicious to the commonwealth, the preacher of God's word must not dissemble to correct it by the word of God plainly, without colour or circumlocution, as Nathan did David; Elias, Achab; John, Herod. For that that is spoken to all men, is as though it were spoken to no man. So doth Paul teach.

The princes are called *reges a regendo;* that is to say, they are called kings, which name cometh of a verb that signifieth to govern. They must lead the people and themselves by the law, and not against the law; to be ministers

[1 Eighth, A and B, seventh, C.]
[2 Ninth, A and B, eighth, C.]

of the law, and not masters over the law. Cato saith well therein, "Obey the law that thou madest thyself." It should not offend the magistrates to be reprehended by the preacher of the law of God, but rather take it in good part, and thank God that he hath one to admonish him of ill in time; remembering the words, Ecclesiasticus x. *Rex hodie, et cras morietur,* that is to say, "To-day a king, and to-morow shall die." *Eccles. x.*

All the estates of the world, in their honour, should remember the words written, Gen. ii. *Formavit Dominus hominem lutum de terra;* that is to say, "The Lord God made man clay of the earth." Which words should admonish all men of their condition and original. *Quid igitur superbis, cinis et lutum?* Ecclus. x.; that is to say, "Why then art thou proud, ashes and clay?" Thus should all other remember, that boast so their nobility, and think there be no men but they. In time past men were accounted noble for virtue and justice; such as had done some noble act, either in peace, in governing the commonwealth, or in war for the defence of his country, and the heads thereof. They were born no gentlemen, but made gentlemen for their noble and virtuous acts. The nobility now-a-days is degenerate. It applieth no study to follow the wisdom, learning, and virtues of their predecessors, but thinketh it enough to have the name, without effect. Their wisdom and learning once ruled other; now they contemn learning, and scarce can understand a learned man when he talketh of wisdom and learning. Trajanus the emperor said unto the captain of his horsemen, when he gave him a sword, "Use this sword for me, if I command the things that be right; if not, use it against me." There should no vice be excused, neither defended, under the pretence and cloke of God's works; neither for the dignity of any place, manifest injuries and wickedness permitted to reign. But the word of God should always, without respect of persons, stand in his full strength and power; whose office it is to teach the ignorant, rebuke the transgressors, chasten the intractable, and to institute man to all kind of virtue. 2 Tim. iii. *Gen. ii. 7. Ecclus. x. 12. 2 Tim. iii. 16.*

They should remember, that kingdoms be altered and changed because of sin, Job xxxv. and that God removed likewise princes from their dignities by reason of sin; as it is to be seen by Saul, the first king among christian people. 1 Reg. chap. xvi. All kings and commonwealths of Christianity were instituted, specially to preserve the ministry of the church, and the estimation of God's word, that people might know and live according to it, and as it teacheth; to decline all unjust wars and battles, to defend themselves, their realms, and all other that be persecuted for justice; as Abraham did his neighbours and Loth his nephew, Gen. xiv.; to promote peace and make concord, that they may be the children of God, Matt. v.

margin: 1 Sam. xvi. 1. Gen. xiv. 16. Matt. v. 9.

No christian man will take me here, as though I extenuated the princely honour of kings and other magistrates, commended to us by God: whom I honour, reverence, and love; and know by the scripture what I owe unto them, to say, both goods and life. Rom. xiii. Ephes. vi.

margin: Rom. xiii. 6. Eph. vi. 3. Cod. lib. xi. Tit. 74, 75.

Farther, what man's laws giveth, Cod. Lib. xi. Tit. 74. 75. I would all men should observe. The subjects of every civil wealth must bear the charges and burden that is necessary for the preservation thereof, and must not refuse to pay tribute unto the superior powers, under the pretence of a christian liberty; but pay it without grudge, whatsoever lawfully and of duty is demanded; remembering, the liberty that Christ hath given us is deliverance from sin, from death eternal, the horror of hell; and to restore us to everlasting life; and not to deliver us from the obedience of princes in such civil cases. Matt. xxii. Luke xx. Rom. xiii. "Give the thing to Cæsar that is due to Cæsar, and to God the thing due to God."

margin: Matt. xxii. 21.

Christ putteth difference between those two great lords, God and the civil magistrate, that people should beware they give not the thing that is due to the one unto the other. But this order is changed: for where God commandeth to give tribute and other exactions, helps, or subsidies unto Cæsar, the people are made so blind by the falsehood of antichrist's ministers, that they will rather give a gold crown to the building of an abbey, foundation of a chantry, or for a mass of requiem, than one silver penny for the defence of their commonwealth. And the thing that is due to God, they give unto Cæsar, or the civil magistrate; to say, their belief and knowledge of

God. This is only due unto God and his word, and not to king nor emperor, or any other magistrate. Thus is to change God's institution.

We see daily, how the princes of the world persecute the gospel and the gospel-like use of the sacraments. We pervert, therefore, God's law; which commandeth to give tribute to princes of the commonwealth for the preservation thereof, and in matters of religion to give ourselves, both body and soul, unto God; and learn not only by the scripture to love the superior powers, God's ordinance, but also consider other examples, where as he shall see obedience and love of the subjects to their prince to be the strength of their realm.

Scipio was demanded, when he came in warfare into Africa, how he durst to enter so strong and mighty a realm? He said, "the obedience of his soldiers." For they were so obedient, that if he bade any of them fall from the top of a steeple into the water, they would not have disobeyed him. See the order and concord among the beasts in the air, as long as their king liveth; among the cranes, Plinius[1] libro 10, capit. 23. Natur. Hist., and the little bees[2], Virgilius Georgicorum, lib. 4. Now, if they govern not the people well, which be their brothers, they may read their own damnation, Ecclesiastes ix. x. Ezechiel xix. Hieremy xxxix. xlii.; and likewise the ire of God, that they hearkened not to the voice of the preacher, Deut. xvii. [Plin. Nat. Hist. lib. x. cap. xxiii. Virgil. Georg. lib. iv. Eccles. x. 16. Ezek. xix. 1. Jer. xxxix. 7. Deut. xvii. 14.]

It is, therefore, the office of every magistrate to learn how to reign over the people by the law of God, and to desire wisdom of him, to know and follow the things that appertain to the ministration of the commonwealth. For of him alone cometh all wisdom. James i. Ps. cxxvii. Thus knew the godly rulers, and were fortunate in their governance. 2 Reg. vi. vii. 3 Reg. iii. If the magistrate would read every morning, before he entreat any matter for the commonwealth, the 101st Psalm, it should lead him to a singular wisdom and marvellous dexterity in judgment. [2 Sam. vi. vii. 1 Kings iii.]

[1 Quando proficiscantur consentiunt, volant ad prospiciendum alte, ducem quem sequantur eligunt, &c. C. Plin. Hist. p. 174.]

[2 ———Rege incolumi mens omnibus una est;
 Amisso, rupere fidem: constructaque mella
 Diripuere ipsæ, et crates solvere favorum. Virg. G. IV. 214.]

The people should daily pray for their magistrates; for of them dependeth the peace and tranquillity of the commonwealth. 1 Tim. ii. Psalm xx. xxi. It is a great iniquity for people to neglect their office herein. There be proper psalms written by the prophet David, that appertain unto this purpose: as the creation, coronation, or inauguration of the magistrate, Psalm cx., where people made supplication at the coronation of king Salomon, 1 Par. xxviii. xxix., for a prosperous governance of the commonwealth: when the magistrate shall take any battle or war in hand, Psalm xx.: when God giveth victory, xxi.: and so for all other necessaries, that they may defend the orphalings and poor widows with all other oppressed wrongfully. For the palace of a prince, or a magistrate, should be the refuge and sanctuary of the poor, where as they might offer boldly, as before God, their griefs and oppressions.

<small>1 Tim. ii. 2. Psal. xx. xxi.</small>

<small>[1 Chron. xxviii.xxix.]</small>

So it appeareth in the prayer of the people for king Salomon, Psalm ci., saying, *Da, Deus, regi judicia tua;* that is to say, "Give, O God, thy judgments unto the king." For no magistrate can govern without some form of judgment and certain laws. But because all judicials and decrees, statutes and laws made by man, doth many times fail, either for their own proper imperfection, either by the partial and corrupt ministration of the judge; the people desired God to give their king his judgments, which are written in his laws, and those the magistrate must observe, Deut. i. x. and xvi.; as Moses did, Exod. xviii. Levit. xxiv. Num. xv. Josua i. By the which words we know, that all godly laws should be asked and sought out of the scripture.

<small>Psal.lxxii.1.</small>

The sum and conclusion of this fifth precept, and all that I have spoken in it is: that such as the Lord hath appointed in the earth over us to rule, those we must reverence, honour, and obey, with all fear and love; and that we derogate nothing of their dignity with contempt, contumacy, or unkindness. For seeing God would his ordinance that he hath instituted to be inviolated, it is our office to observe the degrees and order of pre-eminence as he hath instituted.

CAPUT IX.

THE SIXTH COMMANDMENT.

Thou shalt not kill.

I SAID before, that concord and peace best preserved always the commonwealth, which dependeth of the love of God and our neighbours. Therefore doth God, immediately after the institution of the commonwealth and civil assemblance of his people, before set in order, and every man appointed to a certain place and vocation: the one to be the father, the other son; the one to be the master, the other servant; the one to be a disciple, and the other an instructor; the one to be the younger, and the other the elder. And each of these knoweth by the precept and commandment afore, what his office is, and how he should live in his vocation.

In this precept he removeth the occasion of discord and debate, that might happen between the members of this commonwealth by reason of murder and manslaughter. Therefore forbiddeth he all injuries, violence, force, and other uncharitable means, wherewithal we might hurt our neighbour's body; and likewise requireth, that in case we can do any thing for the help of our neighbour, we diligently apply our service to his use, and to procure the things that appertain unto his tranquillity, to save him from adversities, and to give him our helping hand, when his troubles shall require; seeing there is nothing more dear to man than his body and life, as the law of nature teacheth. God by this law defendeth it against the devil and devilish wilful hatred of man, that sometime is so carried away with affections of the flesh, that he honoureth not this precept; but contemneth the image of God in his neighbour, hateth his own flesh, and executeth a beastly rage and tyranny in his brother's body, more like a furious lion and mad dog than a reasonable creature; not only to the destruction of him that is killed, but to the loss and perdition of his own body and soul for ever, if he repent not.

<small>The purpose of God in this commandment.</small>

God in this commandment forbiddeth not only the murder done with the hand, but also the murder of the heart and of the tongue. Matt. v. 1 John iii. In the murder done of the hand is forbidden all private revenging between private persons, that will be judges in their own cause; which begin with blows, then followeth hurting of some members of the body, or clean destruction of it; at the last, murder of the whole body. Some kill with the sword, some with poison, some with enchantments; some dissemble, as though they played, and so in bourding[1] putteth him out of the way that he hateth. Some kill not themselves, nor will not be seen to break the peace; but shoot their bolts by other men, and wound and kill him that is an hundred mile from him. These the laws punish with death, Gen. ix. Matt. xxvi.; likewise the laws of men. Justin. Lib. iv. Tit. 18.

(margin: Matt. v. 21. 1 John iii. 15.)
(margin: Gen. ix. 6. Matt. xxvi. 52.)

Such as procure and search the death of man privily, the law punisheth more cruelly; not with the sword, neither fire, or any other solemn manner of death; but he should be inclosed in a trunk with a dog, a cock, a snake, and an ape, and so be cast into water, and die amongst these rigorous beasts[2].

(margin: Just. lib. iv. Tit. 18.)

Those yet less offend than such as conspire the death of any prince, or governor of the commonwealth, or by treason intend the destruction of the commonwealth, or any man that governeth therein. Those have their pain of death appointed *Lege Juliana*, Justin. Lib. iv. Tit. 18. *de publicis Judiciis*[3]. So hath the law respect of the persons, and will know who is killed, a private person, or governor;

(margin: Just. lib. iv. Tit. 18. de publicis judiciis.)

[1 Bourding: mocking, mock-fighting.]

[2 Alia deinde lex asperrimum crimen nova pœna persequitur, quæ Pompeia de parricidiis vocatur: qua cavetur, ut si quis parentis aut filii, aut omnino adfinitatis ejus quæ nuncupatione parentum continetur, fata præparaverit (sive clam, sive palam id ausus fuerit), necnon is cujus dolo malo id factum est, vel conscius criminis existit, licet extraneus sit, pœna parricidii puniatur, et neque gladio neque ignibus, neque ulli alii solenni pœnæ subjiciatur; sed insutus culleo cum cane et gallo gallinaceo, et vipera, et simia, et inter eas ferales angustias comprehensus, vel in vicinum mare vel in amnem projiciatur. Corp. Jur. Civ. Institut. Lib. iv. Tit. 18. §. 6.]

[3 Lex Julia majestatis, quæ in eos, qui contra Imperatorem vel Rempublicam aliquid moliti sunt, suum vigorem extendit. Ibid. §. 3.]

a man, or a woman; one of his own blood, or a stranger; that the pain may be according. In the ministration whereof the magistrate or prince should always observe justice, as well against one man as the other, without respect of persons; remembering that it appertaineth nothing unto their office to save or damn, to give one a charter of life, and put another that hath done the like offence to death.

The magistrate is but a minister of the law, and is bound for the law's sake to suffer him to live, that transgresseth not the law: so is he bound to put him to death, that hath offended the law. So God commandeth, Deut. xix., that the judge shall have no mercy upon the offender, and sheweth three causes why: the one, that he should take the ill out of the commonwealth; the other is a promise of God's grace for his so doing; the third is, that other might fear to do the same. We have examples thereof in the captains that were hanged against the sun, Num. xxv., and of Mary[4], the emperor Moses' sister, that, when she was a leper, was compelled to obey the law, as well as the poorest of the congregation. Num. xii.

Deut. xix. 13.

Numb. xxv. 4.

Numb. xii. 14.

It is ill done, therefore, of princes and magistrates, to give charters and privileges to such as by the law should die; and a shrewd example for other, that think, when need is, I shall have friends likewise to beg me my pardon. In case it cannot be obtained, he that laboureth in the cause will scarce be contented that his request can take none effect, the matter being of no greater weight, than before by other obtained grace. Thus, in dispensing of an ill fact, is both God and man offended; and the prince or magistrate that dispenseth with the fault of another, maketh himself culpable of the same crime, as is written, Prov. xvii. Sap. vi.

Prov. xvii. 15.
Wisd. vi. 1.

Of the other part, the judges, that condemn the right and deliver the wrong, commit the same horrible offence, and worthy by the law to suffer the pain that is due unto him that should for his offences die: likewise, should such, as by letters or otherwise defence[5] or procure the let

[4 Mary: Miriam.]

[5 Likewyce souche as be letters, or otherwyce defice, A. Likewyse shulde such as by letters or otherwyse defence, B. Like paine should such suffer, as by letters or other defence, C.]

[HOOPER.]

or delay of justice in saving or reprieving the offender, which is an horrible offence, and daily used, (the more pity!) in every assize and sessions. They pretend a work of charity and good deed to save a man, that is worthy of death; but the judge of all equity, mercy, and justice saith, they should not extend their mercy to such a person nor in such a case, but commandeth without mercy to put them to death that justice condemneth.

Men will be in an ill cause more merciful than the fountain self of mercy: but where as they should be merciful in remitting a private displeasure done unto them by a poor man, then will they execute not only justice, but also tyranny. So pervert they the law of God, and judge ill good and good ill, and likewise reprehend the ordinance of God. God gave certain privileges, that whosoever killed against his will might flee to a sanctuary to save his life; but he that killed of malice or of a pretended purpose, might be brought to the gallows, not only out of the sanctuary, but from the altar. Deut. xix. And this is not only the law of Moses, but also the law of Christ, that saith, Matt. xxvi. capit. "He that striketh with the sword, with the sword shall perish." When it pleaseth God such a transgressor to be taken, the judge that judgeth, and the person that is judged, should think this is the time that the commonwealth should be delivered from an ill person: and he that must suffer should think, This is the time that God will punish me for my sin, and call me to his mercy.

Deut. xix. 12.

Matt. xxvi. 52.

The prince should suffer the ordinance of God to take place. For, as Terence saith: *Male docet facilitas multa, Heautontim.* that is to say, "Over-much pity teacheth many things ill;" the which vice he teacheth men beware of in *Hecy. Etsi ego meis me omnibus scio etiam adprime observantem, sed non adeo ut facilitas mea illorum corrumpat animos*[1]. Therefore he that would purchase a charter, should rather come to the prison to comfort the afflicted man, and say: 'This trouble is the preacher sent from God to bring thee to acknowledge of thy sin, and to call thee to penance. Thou seest how the devil hath prevailed against

[[1] Though I know myself to be especially attentive to all my friends, yet not so as to let my easiness of temper corrupt their minds.]

thee. Following the blindness of thine affection, thou gavest place to the devil, who delighteth in the ill doings of men. Therefore thou must suffer the pain of the law, and from henceforth thou shalt give no place more unto him. Know Christ, and believe that in him thou shalt suffer no pain for thy transgression, but only the death of the body. He shall now carry thee from the gallows into eternal joy, as he did the thief on the cross. Obey therefore the commandment of God in this public ministration of justice. For now is thy[2] time to die, not that God hateth thee, but of a singular love that thou shouldest hurt no more thyself and other. Beg with me in Christ thy charter of God, and his mercy shall give thee eternal life, which thou mayest boldly by the law acclaim:'—and not to put him in a false hope of man's remission, that can give no pardon at all, if they do well.

In case a private person, a man that loveth peace, happen to be oppressed at any time of those breakers of peace, or robbers by the highway-side or otherways, cannot defend his life and body without using resistance; and the oppressor will not be content, neither with reason neither with fair words, neither the man oppressed may in no wise find place to avoid the fury of this oppressor in defending his own life; if he kill his adversaries, he no more offendeth God's laws neither man's laws, than though he killed a wolf or mad dog; as Moses killed the Egyptian, or as the godly magistrate killeth privately the thief, or openly defendeth himself by war, when he cannot maintain or recover the right of his commonwealth otherwise. Then to use the extreme remedy of battle he offendeth not. So is it to be judged of those that will oppress by violence other, that either offend not, either be ready to offer their causes to the vicars of God, the judges of the earth. If they find their own death, it is to be judged that it is none other thing than the just judgment of God, that the one should defend his life, and the other perish. A great ill is it, that those ill men that dare not bring their cause to be judged before the lawful magistrate, are permitted so licentiously to trouble the peaceable people of a realm without punishment; which is against God's laws

[[2] Thy, A, thys, B and C.]

and man's laws, and the occasion of great murder, which provoketh the ire of God against the magistrates for the sufferance of so great an evil.

I know how men that govern after Aristotle's politics, will excuse this evil. They will say, that laws must be made according to the nature of the people to whom they are prescribed. But God's laws saith, man must obey the law, and not the law man. If they be Christians, it shall not be a servitude to live after the laws of Christ, who should govern chiefly both the superior and the inferior. And so saith also Aristotle[1], Lib. v. Polit. cap. 9. *Non est servitus vivere ad formam reipublicæ, sed salus*[2]. I Englished this the second verse before. It should not be difficile[3] to remove this evil, if every man that shall see the peace broken in a city, had authority to sunder the persons and bind the peace-breakers to a peace by their words; and he that brake his faith and promise to him that required it, to lose his head, in the name of a pain, as it is used in some commonwealths.

<small>Polit. lib. v. cap. ix.</small>

Murder is committed likewise by hand by such as are every man's men for money; as these runagates and lance-knights are, that sell both body and soul to such as will hire them, they care not whether the cause be wrong or right. They should neither receive by the law of God, neither any christian man give them any thing, except the cause be good. If it be, every man is bound to defend it; if not, no man. This cannot be known of all men; but if the cause be naught, God excuseth no man; but esteemeth him a murderer of his own life, and the magistrate that hireth him, the occasion thereof.

<small>Murder of the heart.</small>

This precept is not understood only of external murder, but forbiddeth also the murder of the heart; which though it deserve no punishment in the world, yet God accounteth it worthy of death: as it is to be seen, Gen. iv., where as God accused Cain for the murder of his heart, before he laid hands on Abel to kill him. So doth Saint John,

<small>Gen. iv. 6.</small>

[[1] Οὐ γὰρ δεῖ οἴεσθαι δουλείαν εἶναι τὸ ζῆν πρὸς τὴν πολιτείαν, ἀλλὰ σωτηρίαν. Aristot. Politic. Lib. v. cap. 9. ad finem. Jenæ, 1660, p. 557.]

[[2] It is no servitude to live after the form of the commonwealth, but safety. These words are in the text in C.]

[[3] Difficile, A and B, hard, C.]

1 Epistle iii. say, "He that hateth his brother is a murderer." <small>1 John iii. [15.]</small>

Then is there the murder of the tongue worthy death before God, not only of the body, but also of the soul; the which is committed by a cursing, slandering, and a convicious tongue. Of a cursing tongue Christ speaketh, Matt. v.: "He that saith to his brother, Raah, is guilty of council;" the which word, *Raah*, in English signifieth ill or affliction. Christ meaneth there, that he only is not a murderer, that by hand killed his brother; but also he that curseth or desireth evil to his neighbour: as those do that bid the pestilence, the fever quartern, Saint Antone's evil, or such other execrations, and should be punished as heretics and blasphemers of God; as ye may read, Levit. xx., Gen. xxvii., Levit. xix., 1 Cor. v., 1 Pet. iv. Such evil sayers hath no part in the kingdom of God. He that calleth his brother "fool," that is to say, contemn him, mock him, or as men call it now-a-days, lowting of a man, committeth such murder as is worthy hell-fire and eternal damnation. The which vice is reprehended, Psal. lvi., and was so abhorred of the gentiles, that many would rather suffer death, than sustain the slanders of a pestilence tongue. <small>Murder of the tongue. Matt. v. 22. Levit. xx. 9. Gen. xxvii. 41.</small>

The derision of the simple, how great a sin it is, and equivalent with murder, we see by the punishment of Cham, who was so cursed of his father Noah, that his posterity suffered for his offence. *Maledictus Cham; servus servorum erit fratribus suis:* that is to say, "Cursed be Cham, who shall be unto his brothers the servant of servants." Gen. ix. <small>Gen. ix. 25.</small>

Samson was accounted of the Philistians for a fool, but he would rather die than suffer that opprobry unrevenged. Judic. xvi. David was lowted of Michol, Saul's daughter, but she was made therefore barren all her life. 2 Reg. vi. How David revenged the contumely of his ambassadors contemned of the Ammonites, read 3 Reg. capit. x., and then thou shalt perceive that mocking is none other but murder. In the fourth book of the Kings, capit. ii., see how the boys mocked the preacher of God's word, Elizeus the prophet, and how God punished the same with death more cruel than the magistrate punisheth the murderer. <small>Judg. xvi. 30. 2 Sam. vi. 23. 2 Sam. x. 7. 2 Kings ii. 23.</small>

Of these places we see what murder is, and how many ways it is committed. The occasion thereof is ire, envy, hatred, disdain, indignation, and such like. We see also the pain appointed by God's laws and man's laws. Lib. iv. Inst. Cod. Lib. ix. But of these places infer not, that it is not lawful for the magistrate to punish the evil doer by death; the father to correct his child; the master his servant; or the preachers the vice of the people. These laws appertain unto all private persons, and not unto such as God hath given jurisdiction over other. Of the magistrates we have Rom. xiii., which offend not in punishing the evil: of the fathers' correction, Eph. vi. Stephane called the Jews traitors and murderers, Acts vii., and Paul the Galatians fools, Gal. iii.: yet offended nothing against this law, "Thou shalt not kill;" but served the place of their vocations, as it was commanded them by God.

Anger is no sin, so that the original thereof and the end whither it extendeth be virtuous, and proceed with charity. Moses was angry, and brake the tables of God in his zealous and godly passion: he put the idolaters to death, but the end was to destroy vice, and to maintain virtue. So was David, so was Paul, so was Christ: but it sprang of a love towards God, and extended to a virtuous end, the[1] punishment of vice and commendation of virtue.

Marginalia: Just. lib. iv. Cod. lib. ix.; Rom. xiii. 4; Eph. vi. 4; Acts vii. 51; Gal. iii. 1.

CAPUT X.

THE SEVENTH COMMANDMENT.

Thou shalt commit none adultery.

The end of this law.

THAT there should never fail succession and posterity to preserve the commonwealth that God had ordained for man, as well before his fall in paradise, as after in this vale of misery; he ordained matrimony between man and woman, which is the institution and ordinance of God, approved by the law of nature, the law of Moses, and the law of man, and the law of the gospel: meaning and willing this ordinance to be reverently observed of all men, hath

[¹ The, A and C, to, B.]

given this precept, that no man should dishonour, defile, or contaminate himself with any undecent or intemperate kind of life.

This is the end and purpose why this law was given; to avoid a dissolute, common, and libidinous life, with other uncleanliness; to love and keep chastity and purity of life, which consisteth either in sincere virginity, or faithful matrimony, as Chrysostom writeth, Homil. de invent. cruc. *Primus gradus castitatis est sincera virginitas, secundus fidele matrimonium;* that is to say, "The first degree of chastity is pure virginity; the second, faithful matrimony[2]." The same division of chastity approveth the scripture, 1 Cor. vii., where as Paul defineth and sheweth, that virginity is a chastity of the body, conjoined with the purity of the mind, by these words: *Cœlebs cogitat, quæ Domini sunt, quomodo sancta sit corpore et spiritu;* that is to say, "She that is unmarried thinketh the things that be of God, how she may be holy both in body and in spirit." Of matrimony and the purity thereof it is written, Heb. xiii., *Honorabile est inter omnes matrimonium et cubile impollutum;* that is to say, "Matrimony is honourable among all (nations), and the bed impolluted."

<small>Wherein chastity consisteth.</small>
<small>Homilia de inventione crucis.</small>
<small>1 Cor. vii. 34.</small>
<small>Heb. xiii. 4.</small>

No man should continue in a sole life, but such as hath no need of matrimony, following the word of God and ordinance of man's nature, according to the examples of the patriarchs, prophets, and the apostles; which were not excluded from matrimony, although they were ministers of the church; nor never made law to exclude their successors, but reciteth the matrimony of the ministers among the virtues and necessary gifts that is required in the minister, 1 Tim. iii., Tit. i., and calleth the prohibition of matrimony the doctrine of the devil: the which the iniquity of our doctors, that defend with sword and fire the sole life of the ministers, would put from them unto the old heretics the Tatians[3], who forbid matrimony to all men.

<small>1 Tim. iii. 2. 1 Tim. iv. 1.</small>

[2 The passage will be found in the Opus Imperf. in Matth. Homil. xxxii.]

[3 Tatian was a disciple of Justin Martyr. His followers were ascetics of the severest caste. They condemned the use of wine and women, and were therefore called Encratites. For the opinions of Tatian, see Clemens Alexandrinus, Epiphanius, and Origen. Or the English reader may consult Mosheim, (by Soames,) Vol. I. p. 187.]

And they damn not it, but only forbid it to the order of ecclesiastical ministers; as though they damned not matrimony, because they forbid it not to all, but to some. It is like as if the physician should say to two men of one age, one disposition, and sick in one disease, that the medicine that healeth the one will kill the other. But the scripture is against them, and also the fathers for the most part. The council of Nice condescended to the mind and sentence of Paphnutius[1], that said, faithful marriage was chastity; and not unto superstitious persons, that always dream some novelties to be accounted glorious.

What the commandment forbiddeth. The temerity of these laws and law-makers hath been godly and learnedly all times confounded. It sufficeth us loyallement and with good faith to hear this commandment, "Commit no adultery;" which forbiddeth not only to abstain from another man's wife, the which both God's laws and man's laws, Christians' and gentiles', punisheth with death, Deut. xxii., Levit. xxvi.; Lib. Instit. iv. Tit. *De publicis Judiciis*[2]: also the desire and lust of the heart is forbidden, Exod. xx., Deut. v., Matt. v.

Deut. xxii. 22.
Levit. xxvi. 10.
Matt. v. 8.

Further, all other women are forbidden, whether it be virgin, widow, or other common woman[3]. The policy of Moses put to death only the man and woman [married][4], that committed adultery. Howbeit all kinds of adultery in this precept are forbidden, as Paul writeth, 1 Corinth. v., where he equalleth and maketh like fornication and rape with adultery, (read the place,) and biddeth to flee fornication. So doth he, Ephesians v., and saith, that the ire of God

1 Cor. v. 11.

Eph. v. 36.

[1 See Sozomen, Lib. i. cap. 23. and Socrates, Lib. i cap. 11. where Paphnutius is described as strenuously and successfully opposing at the Council of Nice the attempt to compel the married clergy to separate from their wives. Baronius (58. §. 21.) denies the truth of these statements by Sozomen and Socrates, and maintains that the discipline of the church was then otherwise, all the clergy being bound to continence. Father Lupus, however, acknowledged the history of Paphnutius' conduct herein at the Council of Nice to be true. (Lup. in Can. p. 114.) But Valesius in his notes upon Socrates expresses doubts upon the subject.]

[2 Lex Julia de adulteris coercendis, quæ non solum temeratores alienarum nuptiarum gladio punit, sed eos qui, &c. Corp. Juris Civ. Instit. Lib. iv. Tit. 18. (p. 51.)]

[3 "To transgress this commandment" is here added in C.]
[4 Supplied from C.]

accustometh to come for such sins. Likewise we see by the punishment of fornication, and oppression of virgins, which is not inferior to adultery: the city of Sichem and the inhabitants thereof were destroyed, for the oppression of Dina, Jacob's daughter, Gen. xxxiv. Judas commanded Thamar the widow to be put to death for dishonouring of widowhood, Gen. xxxviii. Phineas killed Simri, the Israelite, with his whore Casbi the Midianite, Numb. xxv. So that all kind of adultery is forbidden, and nothing in this case to be admitted, but the lawful conjunction between man and woman. Gen. xxxiv. 17. Gen. xxxviii. 24. Numb. xxv. 8.

But this is not all that this precept forbiddeth: for as it forbiddeth the act itself, so doth it the adultery of the heart and of the eye; likewise the adultery of the mouth, as unchaste and filthy communication; the adultery of the hands, that provoketh or moveth the person that is not his. Salomon saith, "He shall burn his coat that beareth fire in his bosom; and burn his feet that walketh upon the coals." Here is forbidden likewise the adultery of apparel; and so consequently all excess of meat and drink, and other occasions that are inductions to this ill, and cometh of the concupiscence of the heart, forbidden in the scripture.

Peter saith, 1 Pet. iii., "The habit and apparel of a woman shall not be in broided and splaid hair[5], neither in laying on of gold, or costly array." Ye see in our time, that many bear more upon their backs than they be worth: a woman pampered up with precious stones and gold, knotted behind and before with more pearls than her husband and she bestoweth in alms all days of their life. And other sort, that lacketh wherewithal to bestow these charges, are a-dilling and burling of their hair a longer time than a godly woman, that readeth the scripture to follow it, is in apparelling of three or four young infants. If this were only in the woman, it were the less harm; but it is also in men: for there is not as much as he that hath but forty shillings by the year, but is as long   1 Pet. iii. 3.

[5 In brodyd and splayde here, A. In broyded and splayde heere, B. Imbrodered and splaid heare, C. *Broided* is the word used in our Authorised version of 1 Tim. ii. 9, ed. 1611, now generally printed *broidered*.]

in the morning to set his beard in an order, as a godly craftsman would be in looming of a piece of kersey. And not only they, but also such as should give their servants an example of sobriety, as well in the clergy, as among the civil governors of the earth.

I speak not against a decent and seemly apparel of man nor woman, every person in his degree; but that each of them should avoid the excess and ill thereof, that is forbidden in God's laws, and rather study to commend himself by virtues, than to be esteemed by his apparel. Thus doth not God [only], but also ethnicks teach; as Cicero, 1. Offic. *Adhibenda est munditia, non odiosa nec exquisita nimis, tantum quæ fugiat agrestem et inhumanam negligentiam;* that is to say, "Such a means should be kept in apparel, that should be not too neat nor too filthy, but such as might avoid a rude and beastly negligence[1]."

Matt. v. 29.   In the v. Matt. and Luke vi. we see how Christ interpreteth this precept, not only to avoid the evil itself, but also the occasions of it; saying, "If thine eye or right hand offend thee, cast them off:" where as Christ sheweth, there is no occasion that can excuse adultery or fornication. As this sin hath degrees in itself, as ye see and may perceive by the pains rehearsed; so is it more offence in one person than in the other; more in age than in youth, more in the magistrate or prince than in a private person, more in the teacher of God's word than in the hearer.

And as the condition of the persons aggravate the offence, so should justice aggravate the punishment thereof; and not to punish the one, and let the other go. There is no man more privileged than the other. As justice is executed against the inferior, so should it be against the superior; for as the one is subject unto the law of God, so is the other.

There is another kind of adultery forbidden in this
Matt. v. 32. precept, which Christ speaketh of, Matthæi v. and xix. cap.
& xix. 9. which is unlawful divorcement of matrimony, where as the man putteth away the woman, or the woman the man for unlawful causes. The same authority hath the woman to put away

[[1] Cic. De Officiis, Lib. i. cap. 36.]

the man, that the man hath to put away the woman. Mark Mark x. 12. x., Christ saith, there is no lawful cause to dissolve matrimony, but adultery. For when the woman giveth the use of her body to another man, she is no more her first husband's wife; nor the husband no longer the husband of his wife, than he observe the faith of matrimony with her. Wheresoever this fault happen, and can be proved by certain signs and lawful testimonies, the persons may by the authority of God's word, and ministry of the magistrates, be separated[2] so one from the other, that it shall be lawful for the man to marry another wife, and the wife to marry another husband, as Christ saith, Matt. v. and xix. So that the man shall not need to keep at home with him a woman that is no more his than another man's; neither the woman such a husband, as is no more hers than another woman's, Mark x.

[3]Of these few words uncharitably construed, good christian reader, there is by ignorant and lascivious persons much controversy risen between many men: not by such as be able to judge and give sentence in the matter; but by those, that neither have seen my work, that they might with knowledge have condemned it, or with charity have sought with communication, or writing, to have solicitate me to a recantation and condemnation of my judgment in this behalf; and by such as use will for reason, and spite for charity.

Wherefore, seeing my work will eftsoons be imprinted, as my friend the printer advertiseth me; I thought good to strengthen and succour this my true doctrine, grounded upon God's word, with such helps as I may help and warrant the same by the word of God; most humbly praying mine adversaries in the blood and passion of Christ, not to condemn me nor my book of affection; but either to answer me and my book with disputation, where and before whom they will, so they be subjects to God's word, and to the censure and judgment of the holy and catholic church; whose judgment and learning hath and doth defend my learning and sentence in this behalf; either cha-

[2 Separated, A and C, departed, B.]
[3 The following passages to page 382 were added in the edition of 1550.]

ritably to write unto me, that of their writings I may learn (as God knoweth I most desire) wherefore to amend and revoke this my learning so uncharitably condemned.

And I do by this my last addition and maintenance of my first doctrine protest and declare unto all the world, that my first doctrine in this question is and shall be for evermore true. And I will stand to the defence thereof when and where it shall please the magistrates to appoint, with the danger of God's displeasure and theirs, to whom I bear obedience, love, and fear, according to my most bounden duty. Wherefore, my friend, of friendship be not too friendly to favour me too much; nor thou, mine enemy, of enmity condemn me not too soon. Hear now my defence, I beseech thee; and judge of knowledge, as thou wouldest be judged, how I fence the innocency of my cause, forced thereunto by thine occasion and uncharitable slanders, that wouldest defame thou knowest not what, or win the victory thou knowest not when.

This is now to help my first doctrine by the word of God upon the divorcement that I have written. But seeing the divorcement cannot be understand what it is, nor when it is lawful, except men know first what matrimony is; what is the dignity thereof, and how it should be contracted; I will passingly[1] by the way shew what matrimony is. And note it, I pray thee, that thou mayest answer for me, whether I judge contrary or beside the word of God of divorcement between man and woman.

The definition of matrimony. Matrimony is a lawful conjunction of man and woman to be one flesh, to bring forth children, either to avoid fornication.

Out of this definition may be gathered the dignity, and also the beginning of matrimony.

First, I say, matrimony is a lawful conjunction of one man and one woman. Matt. xix. And by this part of matrimony be excluded all whoredoms, adulteries, and unlawful conjunctions of man's and woman's bodies contrary to the law of God and the law of nature. And then, where he saith "in one flesh," that is to say, the husband shall keep his body for the wife only, and the wife her body for the husband only, is excluded that foolish and carnal

[1 Passingly, omitted in C.]

opinion that saith, a man may have two, three, or more wives, and the wife as many husbands.

Secondly[z] the ends of matrimony be two; the first for the procreation of children, that they might be the preservers of true and godly religion, by whom his word might be set forth when the parents be dead; as ye may see by the history of Tobie and Isaac. And here be damned as many as seek riches, honours, or any other like vain things of this world, before virtue; also such as care not of what religion their wives be, neither how their children be brought up. This negligence lost Salomon, and also the children of Israel: Esdras i. *The ends of matrimony.*

The other end of matrimony is to avoid fornication. Seeing the Lord made man to be a creature, prone and ready to associate another sex and kind like to himself; as God said, Gen. ii., "It is not good that man be alone;" lest there should be any unlawful connexion, God did institute and command matrimony, to all such as after the fall of Adam were in danger of fornication. 1 Cor. vii. By the which institution and commandment they be condemned, that for poverty, foolish vows, or for easiness of life avoid and refuse matrimony, yet tarry in the mean season in the present danger of fornication and concupiscence of the flesh. *Gen. ii. 18.* *Matrimony not to be avoided for poverty or any such cause.*

Wherefore the Lord approveth this to be christian matrimony, where as the man and woman consent lawfully in the fear of the Lord, to live in the justice and chastity, that may bring forth and bring up their children in the fear of the Lord. But this matrimony is contemned now-a-days, which provoketh the ire of God; for three manner of ways men offend in this behalf. First, men woo and covet matrimony for affection. Then be they well conjoined together of their own consent; their parents' and fathers' good will either neglected or avariciously blinded, rather with the respect of honour and riches, than well persuaded for estimation of virtue. *Christian and approved matrimony.* *Three ways offence in matrimony.*

Thirdly, being thus conjoined, there is brought forth the fruits of ungodly and unadvised matrimony; to say, discord and debate. Whereof springeth the accustomable and ungodly manner of divorcement, which might be avoided,

[[z] Printed *Thirdly* in B and C.]

if men would use this only remedy; if they would, as Isaac and Tobie did, first pray unto the Lord, then to have rather respect unto the man's and woman's virtues than to their riches; thirdly, when they be conjoined together, the one to bear godly with the other's conditions, and know their states, the man to be the head, and the woman glad to acknowledge the pre-eminence and superiority without disdain for the ordinances of God.

<small>Remedies against these offences.</small>

But seeing these circumstances be seldom and rarely observed, many divorces happeneth, more than should be, or can be lawful. Christ putteth only one cause of divorcement, fornication. Matt. v. xix., Mark x.

<small>Matt. v. 32. & xix. 9. Mark x. 12.</small>

Therefore, to speak of divorcement, as we have of matrimony, we will take it from his definition and nature, which is this.

<small>Divorcement, what it is.</small>

True divorcement is a separation and departing of man and wife from the bonds and law of matrimony, for the breaking of the faith and promise of matrimony, which made the man and the wife two in one flesh. I will not entreat of other causes of divorcements than fornication, because my book maketh no mention of any other.

But I will come to the state of all this controversy between my contraries and me, whether it be as lawful for a woman upon due and sufficient circumstances to put away her husband, an adulterer, as the man to put away his wife upon the same circumstances, being adulteress and harlot. Of this controversy mark, gentle reader, the resolution and answer, and mark without affection; so shalt thou please God, instruct thy conscience, and not offend me thy friend and brother in Christ.

First, it is known to all men, that it is lawful for the man to put away his wife for fornication: for such a fault breaketh the knot of matrimony. The same is also lawful for the wife, as it may be thus proved. First, that the man breaketh as well the bonds of matrimony by the giving the use of his body to an harlot, as the woman the use of her body to the adulterer: so that the law of reason admitteth the lawful union and conjunction of two to be one, and disalloweth the violation of the same as well in the man as in the woman.

<small>That a woman may put away her husband for fornication.</small>

Then Christ, in the cause of divorcement for fornication, equalleth and maketh like the man's and the woman's cause in the respect of adultery. Mark the x. Read the place, and note it. For there he giveth the same authority to the woman for fornication, that he giveth to the man. Thirdly, the civil law admitteth and licenseth the same[1], Cod. Lib. v. l. *consensu legitima*. Read Eusebius[2], Lib. IV., and tell me, whether thou have an example or not of a woman that put away her husband for fornication.

Mark x. 12.

Cod. lib. v. l. consensu legitima. Euseb. lib. iv.

But they object: and first out of the old law, that it was not lawful for a woman to put away her husband, but the man might put away his wife. I grant the same, but I am sure the poor woman was not compelled to live with her adulterous husband; for the law commanded such a villain to be slain, and so put the honest party to liberty: and so should it be now-a-days, and then the question of divorcement would be ended. And in the same cause of divorcement, and to marry another, Christ is plain, Mark x.; where as he giveth equal power, as well to the man as to the woman, and to the woman as well as to the man.

An objection.

The answer.

Mark x. 11.

Then say they again: Yea, but the man is the head of the woman. Hereof infer they some privilege and pre-eminence to appertain to the man, that is denied and taken from the woman. True it is, and no man denieth it, the man to be the head of the woman, as long as they be one flesh, and very matrimony remaineth between them both: or else the husband is the member of a harlot, and not the head of his wife; and the wife, the whore and adulteress of an adulterer, and not the true wife of her husband; after that the fault of adultery is known, proved, and condemned by the word of God and the judgment of the magistrate, as is aforesaid.

A second objection.

The answer.

[¹ Si qua igitur maritum suum adulterum aut, &c. * * * vel ad contemptum (sui) domusve suæ ipsa inspiciente cum impudicis mulieribus (quod maxime etiam castas exasperat) cœtum ineuntem,—probaverit, tunc repudii auxilio uti necessario ei permittimus libertatem, et causas dissidii legibus comprobare. Corp. Juris Civ. Cod. Lib. v. Tit. 17. cap. 8. Impp. Theodos. et Valent. (Tom. II. 237.)]

[² γυνή τις συνεβίου ἀνδρὶ ἀκολασταίνοντι—ὅπως μὴ κοινωνὸς τῶν ἀδικημάτων καὶ ἀσεβημάτων γένηται, μένουσα ἐν τῇ συζυγίᾳ καὶ ὁμοδίαιτος καὶ ὁμόκοιτος γινομένη, τὸ λεγόμενον παρ' ἡμῖν ῥεπούδιον δοῦσα, ἐχωρίσθη, &c. Euseb. Eccles. Hist. Moguntiæ, 1672, Lib. IV. cap. 17. p. 139.]

The third objection. Yet object they again, If it should be lawful for the woman to make a divorce with her husband, marriage could never be sure nor constant, for women would change *The answer.* still at their pleasures. I answer, that there is given no such liberty to man or woman by the word of God; nor no honest man or honest woman will seek any such liberty, but rather fear the Lord, and wish that neither they themselves, nor any other, should need this permission and liberty of God's word granted. Matt. v., xix. Mark x.

Further, I dispute not of the fact, but of the law itself; whether the fact being done, as I have spoken before, may be suffered and accounted lawful or not. Also I would not that divorcement should be lightly, or at the will of every man or woman, done, but to observe all these things.

First, I would that both the man for his part, and the woman likewise for her part, should not for any affection seek occasions, or false suspicions, neither yet credit every slanderous tongue.

Then, if it happen, either of them to find his companion culpable and guilty, to attempt all manner of means, secretly between them both, to amend the fault: if that avail not, to solicitate the same by honest arbiters and godly friends; and in the mean time, the innocent party to pray diligently unto God for the party that is in the lapse.

Thirdly, if none of these means profit, then to appeal unto the magistrates, who be bound to punish the adulterer or the adulteress, and so to set the man or the woman civilly in the world at liberty, as the crime and fault hath already sundered them before God. For as the congregation and magistrates be testimonies and judges of the matrimony, when two persons are coupled together lawfully; so be they testimonies and judges of the separation, which is granted for the unlawful violating of matrimony. Neither doth the magistrate dissolve that God hath bound, nor discouple that God coupled; but be judges of the adultery and unlawful fact, that hath of itself before dissolved that God conjoined. Thus seest thou, good reader, that I give no licence nor liberty to elevate or diminish the dignity of matrimony, nor never will, by God's grace[1].

St Paul, 1 Cor. vii., sheweth another cause of divorce- ment, when the one of the persons being married is an infidel, and of a contrary faith. If this person will not dwell with the other, that is his fellow in matrimony, and a Christian; it is lawful to break the faith of matrimony, and marry with another. So saith Saint Ambrose[2], writing in the same place of St Paul: *Non debetur reverentia conjugii ei qui horret Auctorem conjugii;* that is to say, "The reverency of matrimony is not due unto him that contemneth the Author of matrimony." And in the same place: *Contumelia enim Creatoris solvit jus matrimonii circa eum qui relinquitur, ne accusetur alii copulatus;* that is to say, "The contempt of God breaketh the right of matrimony concerning him that is forsaken, lest he should be accused, being married to another."

1 Cor. vii.

Thou seest, that the Lord, Matt. v. xix. giveth licence for adultery to divorce and marry again; and Paul for infidelity. The divorce that the bishops permit in their laws, is no divorce, but only the name of it: for they will not permit those persons thus divorced to marry again. They say, what God hath conjoined, man should not separate. Who denieth that? God speaketh of the woman that standeth by the law and ordinance of God, being lawfully married, and do the office of a wife.

If adultery or the case of infidelity chance, man dissolveth not the matrimony, but the person's self that offendeth; and the magistrate is but a testimony of his or her ill fact, that hath broken and dissolved that that God coupled, and protesteth to the world that they, thus dissolved, may marry again, notwithstanding the former marriage. Though man's laws admit it not, God's laws doth, whose words may not be wrested out of tune, but always applied to the end they were spoken.

The Pharisees, Matt. xix. capit. demanded of Christ, whether it were lawful for a man to divorce his wife for every

[1 Here close the additions referred to in the preliminary address to the christian reader prefixed to the edition 1550 of the Declaration, &c. See p. 377.]

[2 Ambrosii Op. Colon. Agrip. 1616, Tom. III. p. 174. G.]

cause, and to marry another, as all those did in the time of Moses. Deut. xxiv. Christ answered directly to the question, and said, it was not lawful for a man to put away his wife, and marry another, except she committed adultery. Then and for that cause it is lawful now in the time of the gospel, as it was in the time of Moses' law. But for the frowardness of conditions, or tediousness of manners, men should not separate their wives, neither from bed, neither from board; much less marry another. He or she that cannot with wisdom amend the displeasant and crooked manners of his or her mate, must patiently bear them; remembering, if Christ command us to be of such a tolerancy and patience to endure the obloquy and injuries of all men, though they be our enemies; how much more the morosity and injuries of a domestical companion! A hard cross! But patience must lighten it, till God send a redress.

Matt. xix. 5. Christ yet speaketh of another adultery, Matt. xix. which those commit, that marry at one time two wives, and say, if a man have an hundred, (as he may have as well as two,) yet all be but two, and one flesh in the Lord. Christ doth not so interpretate two, Matt. xix. capit., but referreth two to one man and one woman, as the text that he allegeth out of Gen. cap. i. ii. declareth, saying, "Have ye not readen, that he that made from the beginning, made them male and female; therefore shall man leave father and mother, and officiate his wife, and shall be two in one flesh?" This text admitteth no pluralities of wives, but destroyeth plain the sentence of those that defend the conjunction of many wives with one man.

For as the beginning of matrimony was but one man and one woman created and married together; no more should there be now in one matrimony; as Christ there teacheth, and expoundeth, "two in one flesh," and not three or four in one flesh. The word of God must be followed, and not the example of the fathers, in this case. It is also forbidden by man's laws, Codic. Lib. v. Tit. 5. *De incestis et inutilibus nuptiis, Neminem, qui sub ditione sit Romani nominis, binas uxores habere posse vulgo patet, &c.* "It is commonly known, that no man being

Marginal notes: Deut. xxiv.; Matt. xix. 5.; Gen. i. 27. & ii. 24.; Codic. lib. v. Tit. v. de incest. et inutilibus nuptiis, cap. ii.

under the jurisdiction of Rome can have two wives," saith the emperors Dioclesian and Maximianus[1].

Saint Paul, 1 Cor. vii. giveth a godly precept, if it were godly used: read the chapter at the beginning; the conclusion of the sentences is thus, speaking to the persons married: "Depart not the one from the other, except it be for consent for a time, to apply fasting and praying, and then come together again, lest the devil tempt you for your intemperancy." If Paul could do any thing with men that be married, they would not for their pleasures or private lucre make so many voyages out of their countries, or within their countries, leaving their wives, children, and households, as forsaken orphans.

1 Cor. vii. 3, &c.

How light soever this ungodly people make their gaddings or peregrinations, they shall be culpable and accountable for as many faults, as is done by his family through his absence and negligence, before God. How this sin of adultery is punished, read Gen. xii. xx. and xxxix. Job xxxi. *Legem Julia. Just.* Lib. iv. Tit. 18. *De pub. judiciis:*[2] and look not how man useth now to punish it, that rather accounteth it a virtue than a vice; but see what punishment God appointeth for it in the scripture.

Gen. xii. 17. & xix. 24.

CAPUT XI.

THE EIGHTH COMMANDMENT.

Thou shalt not steal.

THIS eighth law extendeth to this end, that we give unto every man that that is his. And in so doing, we resemble the Master of this law, God Almighty, that abhorreth all injustice, and loveth equity and right. As here is forbidden to steal the goods of other, so is there commanded and required to employ diligence in keeping the goods that be our own; remembering that every man

[1 Corpus Juris Civilis.]   [2 See note 2, p. 374.]

receiveth at God's hand his goods and parcels thereof, and not by fortune, or his own travail. Therefore to abuse them is not only a loss of the goods, but also injuries unto the dispensation of God, who willeth the rich to give gladly, and with thanks, unto the poor; the poor to receive religiously, as out of the spence[1] or cellar of the Lord, with thanksgiving; the rich to exercise his faith in giving, and to think that the way to be rich is not to muck up in the coffer, but to be liberal, and to put out much to the poor, for the commandment's sake, and think the promise of God will send it in again; the poor to exercise his faith in receiving, when he hath nothing at home, yet God hath opened the heart of one or other to give him his necessaries, and that always God is faithful in his promise, and will give bread to the hungry at all times opportune. Psal. cxlv. 4 Reg. iv. cap.

Psal. cxlv. 16.
2 Kings iv. 43.

This law principally forbiddeth all injuries that afflict or diminisheth the riches, faculties, glory, estimation, fame, and all other things expedient for body and soul; all actions and traverse of the law, that might be ended charitably without breach of love; and all other uncharitable expenses, all violent and forcible oppressions by night or day, as well of them as rob with the hand by the highway side, as of them that by counsel, affection, avarice, hatred, or by request of letters, invert and pervert justice.

Likewise all fraud and guile in buying or selling, and breaking of promise in all bargains and contracts; or when there is taken from the law that which is hers: that is to say, when she taketh execution and punishment of one ill doer, and not of another, not because their causes differ or be unlike, but that she is robbed by force of her justice by the unjust persons and judges, that judge not by the law, but against the law. As this robbery of justice is used commonly against God's laws and man's, so hath it obtained a common soothsaying among all people: *Dat veniam corvis, vexat censura columbas;*[2] that is to say, "He giveth pardon to the ravens, and oppresseth the doves with exaction." The sentence meaneth, that the great thieves and robbers are at liberty, and sometime occupy the seat of justice, when the little thieves are hanged. He is not only a

[[1] Spence: a buttery or store-room.] [[2] Juvenal, II. 63.]

thief, that by day robbeth, and breaketh men's houses by night; but also those that by any means let the thing to be paid that is due, whether it be to the law, or to those that be under the law. Two manner of ways all injuries and wrongs are done: the one in[3] withholding another's right, and the other in taking away another's right.

The things unjustly withholden are the goods of the body, or of the mind. Of the body are these: the husband, the wife, the children, the servants, the patrons, and the pupils; money, ware, and all such other things as is used in the life of man necessary for the body. If these things be truly gotten, the owner must godly use them to his glory, and to the profit of his neighbour. If they be gotten with fraud, guile, and deceit, keep them not, for they be none of thine; restore them to the right owner, or else it is theft, and no man can dispense with thee for them, though thou shrive thyself to the priest, and cause all the masses of the world to be said for thee, or, if thou be delivered from that superstition, boast of the gospel never so much.

Let them that trade the course of merchandise in their vocation, beware of this danger. Such as hath the cure of souls beware they hold not their stipends, and deserve them not. Such as be servants, that they eat not their masters' bread, and receive their wages for nought. As for those men that give their wages to such as live an evil and unoccupied life, as the most part of the nobility doth now-a-days; it is against God's laws to keep any such in their house, for they maintain illness[4], which is forbidden, 1 Thess. iv. 2 Thess. iii.; and the servant that receiveth it committeth theft, for he is commanded to labour with his hands to feed himself and other. Though it be used of princes, potentates, and all men of the world, yet that excuseth not the fault before God: for it was never readen in the law of God, nor in the law of any man that had knowledge in a commonwealth, that an ill man was accounted as any member thereof; as ye may read in Plato and Aristotle,[5] what persons be meet to

1 Thess. iv. 11.
2 Thess. iii. 7.

[³ In, A, omitted in B, by, C.]
[⁴ Ilenys, A, ylnes, B, ilnesse, C. Perhaps, *idleness.*]
[⁵ Arist. Polit. Lib. vii. cap. 7.]

dwell in a commonwealth. How unruly a sort of people the evil men be, thou mayest see by the writings of Cicero, when the empire of Rome fell out with itself by sedition, libro vi. *de republica*, and in an Epistle[1] *ad Varronem: Crudeliter enim otiosis minabantur; eratque iis et tua invisa voluntas, et mea oratio.* No man should retain the wages of his servant, but satisfy always his covenants.

Further, they offend against this law of God, that by force or violence, fraud, or any other way, unjustly withhold and keep any man's child or servants; as those do that by force or fraud marry any man's child against the will of his parents.

Such as hath great forests or parks of deer or conies, that pasture and feed upon their neighbours' ground, or columbaries, where as doves assemble and haunt, and those feed of the poor's corn; I refer it to the charity of every man, whether the keeping of such beasts be not against God's laws and man's laws, and whether it be not suffered rather for a few men's pleasure, than for many men's profit. If any man should kill any of those beasts, it were felony in many places: whereas the law civil[2] calleth those wild beasts the goods of the owner no longer than they bide at home, or have a purpose to return home, which will never be as long as they find good bait in the poor man's pasture or corn, except they be chased home: whether those beasts be not as well the poor man's, if he can take them in his pasture, as the owner's, read the law, Just. Lib. ii. Tit. 2. *De rerum divisione et acquirendo illarum dominio.* I cannot tell with what good conscience any man can fare well with the detriment of his neighbour: let every man judge with charity, whether it be well done or not.

<small>Inst. lib. ii. Tit. 2. de rer. divisio. &c.</small>

As it is sin to retain unjustly these goods of the body, whether they be ours or other men's, so it is to retain the goods of the mind; as good counsel, learning, wisdom,

[1 Epist. vi.]

[2 Feræ igitur bestiæ, et volucres, et pisces, et omnia animalia, quæ mari, cœlo et terra nascuntur; simul atque ab aliquo capta fuerint, jure gentium statim illius esse incipiunt: quod enim ante nullius est, id naturali ratione occupanti conceditur, nec interest, feras bestias et volucres utrum in suo fundo quis capiat an in alieno. Corp. Jur. Civ. Instit. Lib. ii. Tit. 1. 12.]

or any other thing else, that may aid our brother in things of religion and virtue: and as every man that seeth his brother want things necessary for the body, in case he help him not, hath no charity in him, as John saith, 1 John iii.; so he that seeth his brother want the knowledge of God and good counsel, in case he aid him not the best he can, is culpable of his brother's damnation. ^{right-margin:} 1 John iii. 17.

The other part that containeth the transgression against this law, is in taking away another man's right or goods, which goods likewise be of the body, or of the soul. Of the body, as I rehearsed before; which are taken away by force or violence, secretly or apertly; as by thieves, pirates, and other, that against God's laws and man's laws spoil and rob. Likewise such as war in the defence of any commonwealth, and under the pretence of warfare thinketh all spoils and rapes to be lawful; as those do, that under the name of justice commit unpunished all injustice. Such as by fraud and craft in buying or selling, making of bargains or other contracts, deceive any man, is condemned by this law of theft; as those that sell wares that be naught or corrupted for things lawful, the things that be good for more than they be worth; which useth not their craft to profit many, but for their own private commodity.

Of this avarice cometh usury, fraud, false contracts, breaking of faith and promises, contempt of all truth and honesty, forestallings and ingrossing of markets, compacts and agreements between the rich, that things may not be sold as they be worth, but as their avarice hath agreed upon. This maketh scarcity of all things, and robbeth the poor members of every commonwealth, and bringeth the greater part of such commodities as be in every realm into a few rich men's hands, so that they cannot be sold as common goods of the civil wealth, but as the goods of one private person; the which monopoly or selling of one man is forbidden, not only in the law of God, but also by the law of man, Cod. Lib. IV. 79, and that under a great pain, *Bonis propriis exspoliatus perpetuitate damnetur exilii;* that is to say, forfeiting his own goods, and to be damned to perpetual exile or banishment. Justinian saw well, when

Cod. lib. iv. cap. 79[3].

[3 Cod. Lib. IV. cap. 59.]

one solely bought because only he might sell again, [it] was not profitable, but hurtful, for the commonwealth.

As it is in buying and selling of things moveable forbidden to use fraud, so is it in the goods of the earth unmoveable; as lands, houses, and possessions, which now in manner are only the goods of the rich, and so hanced[1], that the poor cannot get as much as a cottage to put himself, his wife and his children in, which crieth vengeance in the ears of the God of battle. Esay v. Read the chapter, and see the curse of God against those insatiable raveners and eaters of the poor: yet when they have all together, and suffereth not the poor to have nor house nor rent, they will occupy yet all crafts and trade of buying and selling, that the poor man shall have neither goods nor handycraft[2] to help himself withal. How doth these men hear or read the word of God, that biddeth them give their own goods to the poor; which neither giveth their own, neither suffereth them not to buy at a reasonable price the thing that is not theirs?

Isai. v. 8.

Cod. lib. iv. Tit. 63. de commerc. et mercat.

The emperors Honorius and Theodosius, Cod. Lib. IV. Tit. 63, *de commerc. et mercat.* gave other laws for their commonwealths, writing in this manner: *Nobiliores natalibus et honorum luce conspicuos, et patrimonio ditiores, perniciosum urbibus mercemonium exercere prohibemus, ut inter plebeios et negotiatores facilius sit emendi vendendique commercium*[3]; that is to say, "Such as be of noble parentage, and bearing rule in the commonwealth, and rich by patrimony, we forbid to exercise buying and selling, which is hurtful to cities; that among the common sort of people and occupiers the[4] trade of buying and selling might be the more facile or common." This faculty and trade of merchandise, that now is used for avarice, was invented for a good purpose, to communicate such things as was necessary for the life of man, and not to the use that now it is applied. Plin. *in Pan. Diversasque gentes ita commercio commiscuit, ut quod* gentium [*genitum*] *esset usquam, id apud omnes gentes natum esse vide-*

[1] i.e. enhanced. Haunsid, A, haunsed, B, hansed, C.]

[2] Nor goddes not handie crauffte, A, nother goods nor handye crafte, B.]

[3] Corpus Juris Civ. Cod. Lib. IV. Tit. 63. c. 3.]

[4] Old editions, *in* the trade.]

retur[5]. Such as God hath given goods unto, or possessions of the world, should live upon the same; and he that hath one craft to live by, should not occupy two, for fear of doing wrong to his neighbour.

As for usury, and applying of money or any thing else to an unreasonable gain, it is none other than theft. I would men should rather refrain from giving of money to a gain altogether, than break the law of charity, that helpeth without looking for gain, Luke vi. Levit. xix., and also, Exod. xxii. Deut. xxiii. because usury is plain forbidden. The laws and constitutions of the magistrates civil admitteth certain gain and usury, as ye read, Cod. Lib. iv. Tit. 32.: though they be in many things scarce to be borne withal, yet I would they were well observed; but such is our time, that every man is in this case a law to himself, and taketh what he can. [margin: Cod. lib. iv. Tit. 32.]

Here is forbidden also all games for money, as dice, cards, cloyshe,[6] and other; which is very theft, and against charity, that would rather augment his neighbour's goods, than make them less: so[7] the diminution of any man's fame; as when for vain glory any man attribute unto himself the wit or learning that another brain hath brought forth, whereof many hath complained, as this of Virgil:

"Hos ego versiculos feci, tulit alter honores[8]."

They make a fair shew with another bird's feathers, as Æsop's crow did. This offence Mart. III. calleth *plagium: Imponens plagiario pudorem*, speaking of him that stole his books.

Such as are appointed to be common and public receivers, that twice ask the thing due of the people, once for themselves, and once for the Lord; or such as bear office, to see the treasure of a commonwealth preserved and augmented as it is need, with the revenues that belong to the same; as receivers, auditors, treasurers, paymasters, with other; commit more than theft, if they use any part of the goods belonging to a commonwealth to a private

[[5] C. Plinii. See Panegyricus, cap. 29.]

[[6] Cloyshe, B, cloysshe, A, omitted in C. Cloish or closh was a game something like ninepins, prohibited by statute in the reigns of Edward IV. and Henry VIII.]

[[7] So, A, for, B, also, C.]

[[8] I wrote these verses, another bore away the honour.]

use, Pandect. Lib. XLVIII. Lex Jul.[1], and causeth the superior magistrates to charge their subjects with new exaction; which should not need to be done, if all things paid by the people were truly brought home, and faithfully laid up to the use it was gathered for.

A greater theft yet is it to constrain any person that is free, to do any thing against his liberty, as many times the father doth his son; sell him as a bondman, and marry him where he list, and to whom he list.

Thus offend likewise those that persuade any man's child to forsake his parents, or any servants their master, and is punished in the law with death or exile. It is also theft to oppress any just cause, that is in controversy, by force, affection, or authority of any superior power, or request by letters, not only against God's laws, Deut. xxv. but also against man's law, Codic. libro II. Tit. 13., where as be[2] these words: *Divine admodum constituit D. Claudius consultissimus [princeps] parens noster, ut jactura causæ afficerentur ii, qui sibi patrocinium potentiorum advocassent: ut hoc proposito metu judiciariæ lites potius suo marte discurrerent quam potentiorum domorum opibus niterentur*[3]; that is to say, "The godly and most prudent prince, our father Claudius, very[4] godly decreed, that those should lose their suit, that obtained the help of noblemen; that by this fear all causes of controversies might be used indifferently, rather than to depend of the estimation of any superior power." If this theft were avoided, poor men's causes should find more grace, and rich men's conscience more virtue; especially the judges, that forget what place they be in, and serve the world more than God.

How devilish and great offence it is before God, thus to corrupt justice, they may learn of David, Psalm LXXXII. that beginneth in Latin, *Deus constitit in cœtu Dei*, that is to say, "God sitteth, or is present in the senate or place of judgment." This psalm all judges should learn by heart, and practise it; likewise mark the second verse of the psalm, that saith thus: "How long will ye judge perversely, and corrupt justice at the request of the ill?" In the end of

[1 Tit. 13.]   [2 Old editions, *by*.]
[3 Corp. Juris Civ. Cod. Lib. II. tit. 14. 1.]
[4 Very, A, were, B.]

this verse is a word in Hebrew, *Selah*, the which of the Hebricians is diversely interpretated; Psalm iv.: but to pass over other meanings, wheresoever thou read it, think there is in the same verse some special and notable thing to be marked. It is[5] in this verse. Selah here signifieth as much in English, as though David had said: "Oh, how great offence is it before God, to pervert at any man's request justice!" Or else David put this word Selah there, as though he had said: "It is a common fault and accustomed manner of judges to have respect of persons in judgment." The psalm containeth but eight verses: the judges may the sooner learn them, and the better bear them in mind.

The greatest thiefdom of all is sacrilege, in robbing of the goods appointed to an holy use; the goods appointed for the poor, for the maintenance of schools to bring up youth in, in such learning as shall be necessary for the ministry of the church, and governance of the commonwealth.

Or in taking from the ministers the condition and goods whereupon they live, who should by God's laws honestly be provided for by the heads of the commonwealth, 1 Thess. v.; it is an horrible offence to take these goods away from the godly use they be appointed to. So is it the like offence to enjoy them undeserved; as those do, that hath hospitals, spitals, and other such almose, appointed for the poor, and apply it to their own use, the which crieth vengeance before God.

Also those that are appointed in colleges or schools to learn or teach for the stipend they receive, if they do not their office, commit sacrilege.

Such as live of spiritual tithes, pensions, lands, or other goods appointed to teach the people the word of God, and minister his holy sacraments, in neglecting their office and duty offend in the same offence; or when one man, (and such a one which chanceth many times,) that doth not, or cannot do half a man's office for such a place, hath many men's livings. But of whatsoever gifts he be of, he should not have two men's livings, which the bishops' laws admit by pluralities and totquots. But this is, "Claw me, and I will claw thee." If the bishops permitted not their priests to

[5 As is in, A, it is in, B, in C.]

have two benefices, it may fortune the priest would likewise say, "The bishop should be bishop but of one city;" and indeed so it should be: and until the magistrates bring them to that point, it shall be as possible to hear a bishop wade godly and simply through the scripture in all cases of religion, as to drive a camel through the eye of a needle.

A great pity it is to see, how far that office of a bishop is degenerated from the original in the scripture: it was not so at the beginning, when bishops were at the best, as the Epistle of Paul to Titus testifieth, that willed him to ordain in every city of Crete a bishop. Titus i. cap. And in case there were such love in them now, as was then towards the people, they would say themselves, there were more to do for the best of them in one city than he could do. They know that the primitive church had no such bishops as be now-a-days, as examples testify, until the time of Silvester the First. A little and a little riches crept so into the church, that men sought more her than the wealth of the people; and so increased within few years, that bishops became princes, and princes were made servants: so that they have set them up with their almose and liberality in so high honour, that they cannot pluck them down again with all the force they have.

Tit. i. 5.

What blindness is there befall in the world, that cannot see this palpable ill, that our mother, the holy church, had at the beginning such bishops as did preach many godly sermons in less time than our bishops' horses be a-bridling; their household was the school or treasure-house of good ministers, to serve the word of God, and ministration of the sacraments. If it be so now, let every indifferent man judge. The magistrates, that suffer the abuse of these goods, be culpable of the fault. If the fourth part of the bishopric remained unto the bishop, it were sufficient; the third part to such as should teach the good learning; the second part to the poor of the dioceses; and the other to maintain men of war for the safeguard of the commonwealth; it were better bestowed a great deal; for it is now ill used, and bestowed for the greatest part upon those that hath no need of it, or else upon such ill men as should be maintained with no man's goods.

It were well done to provide for such as by ill bringing up cannot now otherwise live, and provide such means that hereafter no more offend in that kind of life. If any man be offended with me for my thus saying, he loveth not his own health, nor God's laws, nor man's, out of which I am always ready to prove the thing said to be true: further, I speak it of love, and of no hatred.

The Acts of the Apostles doth shew, that in the primitive church such as were converted unto Christ used a singular liberality towards the poor; and likewise other writers, namely, Saint Augustine[1], Lib. I. *De civitate Dei,* that many men were found rich in Rome when it was taken by the Gothes; and again within fourteen year after, by Geysericus, the king of Vandale: but they were rich for the poor, and not for themselves, or such as were rich: and maketh mention of one Paulinus, the bishop of Nole, a city in Campania, that was exceeding rich, but for the poor; as our bishops should be, that now apply the best part of their bishoprics to a prodigal use in their own houses, or in large fees and gifts, hospitality, and other benevolence upon the rich.

Let all men, yea, themselves (affection put apart, and the love or study of many) judge in this case, whether ever they read in the new testament, or have any one godly bishop in the primitive church for an example, that used the goods of the Holy Ghost, the riches of the poor, the possessions given for the preservation of godly doctrine and the ministry of the church, as they do: if it seem good unto the higher powers that this ill may be tolerable, and borne withal, for the honour of the realm, and doings of such expeditions as shall be expedient for them to do, when they be commanded; their honours knoweth right well, that nothing commendeth a realm more than where every man in his degree is as rich as the scripture of God permitteth;

Lib. i. De civitate Dei.

[¹ Unde Paulinus noster, Nolensis Episcopus, ex opulentissimo divite, voluntate pauperrimus, et copiosissime sanctus, quando et ipsam Nolam Barbari vastaverunt, cum ab eis teneretur, sic in corde suo, ut ab eo postea cognovimus, precabatur: Domine, non excrucier propter aurum et argentum: ubi enim sint omnia mea, tu scis. Ibi enim habebat omnia sua, ubi eum condere et thesaurizare ille monuerat, qui hæc mala mundo ventura prædixerat. Aug. Op. Basil, 1542. Tom. v. fo. 57. De Civ. Dei. Lib. I. cap. 10.]

and that bishop doth most honour unto the realm, that keepeth his household, and disposeth the same according to the form and rule of the word of God. 1 Tim. iii. Tit. i.

^{marginal:} 1 Tim. iii. 1. &c.

As for such expeditions in the civil wealth, as should be committed unto these ministers of the church, the common treasure-house should bear it: they should be reasonably provided for, and the rest and overplus taken from them, and put to some other godly use. Look upon the apostles chiefly, and upon all their successors for the space of four hundred years; and then thou shalt see good bishops, and such as diligently applied that painful office of a bishop to the glory of God, and honour of the realms they dwelt in. Though they had not so much upon their heads as our bishops hath; yet had they more within their heads, as the scriptures and histories testify. For they applied all the wit they had unto the vocation and ministry of the church, whereunto they were called: our bishops hath so much wit, they can rule and serve, as they say, in both states; of the church, and also in the civil policy: when one of them is more than any man is able to satisfy, let him do always his best diligence. If he be so necessary for the court, that in civil causes and giving of good counsel he cannot be spared, let him use that vocation, and leave the other: for it is not possible he should do both well. And a great oversight of the princes and higher powers of the earth, thus to charge them with two burdens, when none of them is able to bear the least of them both. They be the king's subjects, and meet for his majesty to choose the best for his court that be of the realm: but then they must be kept in their vocation to preach only the word of God, and not to put themselves, or be appointed by other, to do things that belongeth not to a bishop's vocation.

This is theft of such goods as appertain unto the body.

There is another kind, of the soul; as when the ministers give not unto such, as be committed unto their charge, the word of God simply and plainly, in a tongue known, and lead not the people towards the life everlasting, as the word of God teacheth, to know, that for Christ's sake only, without all respect of works, sin is forgiven, and that we are bound to do the works that God commandeth us to do, and be expressed in the scripture, which is the regle and rule to lead the church by. John xv. *John xv. 14.*

Such as preach man's laws, and works not commanded in the scripture, robbeth the scripture of her riches.

Likewise those that attribute more than is due, or less than is due, unto the holy sacraments instituted by Christ, committeth sacrilege.

They take from the sacraments too much, that say, they be but external signs to know the church of Christ by from such as be not of the church; as the Roman once was known from another citizen by his gown: or those that say they may be done and left undone, as it pleaseth man that useth them.

They add too much to the sacraments, that attribute as much unto them as unto the grace and promise that they confirm: as to the sacrament of baptism remission of sin, when it is but an external confirmation of it. Rom. iv.: and *Rom. iv. 11.* unto the holy supper of the Lord they attribute a distribution, deliverance, or exhibition of Christ's natural body; whereas it is but a confirmation of the grace and mercy, that he bought for us upon the cross with shedding his precious blood, and death of his innocent body: as the words sheweth plainly, Luke xxii., 1 Cor. xi., where Christ saith, he *Luke xxii. 19.* did not institute his last supper that men should bodily eat *1 Cor. xi. 24.* his body, but that they should do always the same in the remembrance of his death, and consider the grace that he obtained for us in his body and blood, and be thankful for the same.

Great pity it is that the devil hath so prevailed in many men, that obstinately without reason and authority of the scripture preach their fantasies unto the people of God, and would persuade that their imagination or dream of Christ's holy body were [a][1] true and substantial body: but such is the devil's malice, now that many men are persuaded that the substance of bread remaineth, and can no longer deceive them in sensible things, he carrieth them to as great an ill or worse than that, and would make them believe that a fantasy or dream of a body, that hath neither quantity

[[1] Supplied from A.]

nor quality, to be a true body. My good reader, without all affection consider the reasons and authority of God's word, that I shall rehearse here briefly against those thieves that rob the humanity of Christ of all human qualities and quantities.

First, they judge the body of Christ, that is in heaven, to have all properties and conditions of a true man; and of the same self body in the sacrament they take away all the conditions and qualities of a true man's body. They must shew by the scripture, that one and the same body, Jesus of Nazareth, the Seed of the holy Virgin, perfect God, perfect man, consisting of man's flesh and a reasonable soul, hath and hath not, at one and the same time, a body with all dimensions, qualities, and quantities of a true man in heaven, and without all dimensions, qualities, and quantities, at the same time in the sacrament.

This put as a pillar and foundation of thy faith, that as he is perfect God, with all the properties and conditions of a true God, wheresoever he be; so is he perfect man, with all the qualities of a true man, wheresoever he be, consisting of a reasonable soul and man's flesh. John i., Heb. i. They say, thou must not judge so carnally and grossly of Christ's body. Believe thou the scripture, and bid them shew thee the place in the scripture, that thou shouldest not judge so of a true physical and mathematical body, which Christ now hath, as the fingers of St Thomas beareth record, John xxi., the hands and eyes of all the apostles, 1 John i., and also his ascension beareth record. Acts i. Let them prove that they speak by the scripture, and shew where Christ was ever present in one place, visible; and in another place present at the same time, invisible.

<small>John xx. 27. 1 John i. 1. Acts i. 9.</small>

They say, we must speak as the scripture speaketh, that saith by the bread, Matt. xxvi., Mark xiv., Luke xxii., "This is my body;" and of these few words ill understanded, they dream wonderful mysteries, that the substantial body of Christ's humanity is present, by miracle and a way celestial, passing all men's capacities, with many other far-fet imaginations and new-found terms, which the scripture never knew of. Howbeit, if thou mark their conclusion, thou shalt find nothing but the name of a body, which they have

<small>Matt. xxvi. 26. Mark xiv. 18. Luke xxii. 14.</small>

given to this chimera and monster that their fantasy hath conceived. They speak of the letter, and none goeth further from it than they. Christ said, "This is my body that is betrayed for you;" the which was a visible and sensible body, as the eyes of those that saw him hang upon the cross testify. They say, it is an invisible body, that occupieth not place; but the scripture saith the contrary, as thou seest by the words of the supper. Luke xxii.

Hold them therefore by the scripture fast; and when they name the most holy humanity of Christ, and would have it with the bread, bid them shew thee the body. For the text saith, that he shall come as visible unto us, as he departed from us. Acts i. If they say, that place speaketh of his coming to judgment, and not of his presence in the sacrament, deny their saying; for the text saith, that he shall be in heaven, till that time of judgment. Acts iii. *Acts i. 11.* *Acts iii. 21.*

It is evil done of any man to speak as the scripture speaketh, and not to take the meaning of the scripture. God of his mercy give men grace to know the truth! Before Christ in his supper called the bread his body, see how he foresaw this after evil and fantastical dreams, that men would take his words contrary unto his mind. In the sixth of John he telleth his disciples, that to eat his body was to believe in him: that availed not; but straightway said, "The words that I speak be spirit and life," and calleth them from the letter. Yet again, the third time in the same place saith, "What if ye see the Son of man ascend where as he was first?" By these reasons he took away all bodily eating, and rigour of the letter. Likewise after the supper, lest they should dream yet of a bodily presence, because sacramentally he called the bread his body, he repeated again the same words; John xvi., "It is expedient that I depart." Again: "I go to my Father. I came from my Father into the world. I forsake the world again, and go to my Father." Why should not these places hold their authority, and teach us to understand these words, "This is my body;" seeing that both before and after the supper Christ told them by plain words, he would not be in the world? And so doth the institution of it declare, that this sacrament was and should be a memory of his blessed passion and pains suf- *John xvi. 7.*

[HOOPER.]

fered in the flesh, and not a distribution of the flesh itself. Luke xxii.; 2 Cor. xi. None of them that put this corporal presence in the bread, yet hitherunto never could interpretate the words of the supper aright. I would be glad to hear it once.

If they will not admit the alteration of the bread with the papists, they will, and can do none otherwise, but interpretate the words thus: "This is my body;" that is to say, very bread, and my body; and refer the verb "is" to two diverse substances, to the body of Christ, and to the bread; which is plain against the nature of a verb substantive, to be at once two diverse substances.

Rom. iv. 11.   Seeing Saint Paul doth interpretate and expound this word "is" in the sacrament of circumcision, (and all sacraments be of one nature,) by this word "signifieth," or "confirmeth," Rom. iv.; what should men mean, thus to trouble and vex the church of Christ with new doctrine? Also, it is a common manner of the scripture, to attribute unto the sign the thing meant by the sign. God knoweth what a weak reason this is, to say, people must speak as the scripture doth, and would prove thereby a real and bodily presence of our Saviour, that died for us, and ascended into heaven, sitteth at the right hand of God Almighty, and from thence shall come to judge the quick and the dead.

Did not Arius defend his heresy with as good an argument as this, when he spake as the scripture doth, and said, *Pater major me est*, "My Father is greater than I?" Or might not a man prove by the same reason that Elie, Esay, and all other prophets before Christ came, to be deceivers

John x. 8.   of the people, and false preachers? For Christ said, John x., "As many as came before me were thieves and murderers:" he that speaketh thus, speaketh as the scripture speaketh. There is not, nor never was, christian reader, heretic, but spake in the defence of his heresy as the scripture speaketh; but took not the meaning with the word, as we must do, except we intend to rob the holy scripture of her true sense, and ungodly force the letter from the true meaning thereof; as those do, that rather constrain the unlearned conscience with fear, than persuade them with good arguments out of the scripture.

They intricate the wits of men with sophistry and illusion,

that they know not what they hear, neither they themselves what they say, when the oration is ended. For a true body they shew a blank shadow, or rather fantasy of a body: and all their words hath brought forth nothing less than a body, that they promised to deliver unto him that they would persuade; as those that Horace speaketh of: *Parturiunt montes, nascetur ridiculus mus*[1].

They say, he that believeth not their words, that they have a true body, with *hoc est corpus meum*, was never well persuaded of the first article of his faith; *scilicet*, "I must believe that God is omnipotent." So we do. But with this reason they subvert themselves, because ye see in the sacrament God doth not make the thing they speak, and therefore it is not there: for if he would it should be, it must be a man's body with all the qualities thereof; for Christ hath none other body but that he took of the holy Virgin, and is always visible and subject unto the senses wheresoever it be, John xxi. 1 John i.

When they trouble thee with the words of the supper, "this is my body," return unto all the sacraments of the old testament, Gen. xvii. Exod. xii.; and thou shalt find that they were the confirmations of the things they were called, and not the thing itself. Romans iv. Then look upon other places of the scripture, John vi. Mark xvi. Luke xxiv. Acts i. iii. vii.: believe thy *Credo;* "he ascended into heavens, sitteth at the right hand of God the Father Almighty, from thence shall come to judge the quick[2] and the dead." Gen. xvii. 12. Exod. xii. 1. John vi. 63. Mark xvi. 18.

Wilt thou not believe all these places as well as the dream of them that choketh thee with one place of the scripture evil[3] understand? Let those untractable men judge what they list of the sacrament and holy supper of the Lord: believe thou with the scripture, that it is but a memory of Christ's death, a confirmation and mystery of our redemption, Luke xxii.; 1 Cor. xi. Luke saith, "Do it in the memory of me;" and lest any man should say, that memory is to receive the corporal body of Christ, Saint Paul, 1 Cor. xi., interpretateth it plainly, and saith; "The eating of the bread, and drinking of the wine, is done Luke xxii. 19. 1 Cor. xi.

[1 The mountains in labour bring forth an insignificant mouse.]
[2 Live, A.]   [3 Ill, A.]

to shew the death and passion of Christ's body, till he come."

We must therefore, in this kind of theft, and all other, study to make restitution, and to pay every man his; as it is written in the law and prophets. Exod. xxii. Esay iii. Amos iii. Luke x. Of the which restitution writeth Saint Augustine[1], ad Macedonium, Epist. 54; the which no man should prolong, nor commend the doing thereof unto his executors; but he that hath committed the fault must make the mends in this case unto him that he hath deceived.

_{Exod. xxii. 1.}

If thou canst not remember whom, neither how much thou hast defrauded, let that be thy daily study, to call to remembrance some way, as well to restore the goods ill gotten, as thou foundest means to obtain them: and be no more ashamed to return to grace, than thou were to lose[2] it. If thou find no persons to whom thou shouldest restore it, give it to the poor, and not to such as shall sing *requiem* for thee after thy death. And give no less than thou hast taken away.

The goods, that be truly thine, thou shalt use aright, if thou observe these two rules. First, if thou put no trust in them. Read the sixty-first Psalm. Matt. vi. 1 Tim. vi. Second, if thou use them to the honour of God, to the necessity of this present life without excess; moderately with thy friends for humanity, and abundantly with the poor for charity: so shalt thou have enough, and leave enough, as Abraham did to his son Isaac.

Psal. lxii. 10.
Matt. vi. 19.
1 Tim. vi. 17.

[[1] Si enim res aliena, propter quam peccatum est, cum reddi possit non redditur, non agitur pœnitentia, sed fingitur: si autem veraciter agitur, non remittetur peccatum, nisi restituatur ablatum: &c. &c. &c. Aug. Op. Basil, 1542. Tom. 2. co. 248. Epist. 54. Ad Maced.]

[[2] Old editions, *lost*.]

CAPUT XII.

THE NINTH COMMANDMENT.

Thou shalt be no false witness against thy neighbour.

In the eighth commandment ye see how God bound the hands of man from robbing of his neighbour's goods: the which is, as it were, a manacle or hand-shackle to keep them from doing of ill. So doth he in this ninth commandment bridle the tongue from hurting his neighbour: which is, if it be well used, the most precious member of man; if the contrary, most detestable, and pernicious, and ill, incorrigible, full of pestiferous poison. James iii. This precept commandeth a moderation of the tongue, and requireth the truth always to be said, as occasion requireth: that no man hurt his neighbour, which may happen, where this law is neglected, many ways; in the soul, in the body, in his name, or in his goods; and is committed either by word, writings, simulation, dissimulation, or by any other beck or sign, which are all there forbidden. *James iii. 5.*

Likewise, that no man, being called to bear testimony in any matter, should speak other than the truth, for he that is a false witness offendeth both against God and his neighbour.

Here is forbidden all kind of lies that be contrary to charity. There be three kinds of lies: the first men call *jocosum mendacium;* when in bourding[3] they merrily[4] speak of things untrue, that rather extend to exhilarate the company, than to any man's harm. This kind of bourding is not commendable among christian men, that should seek other means to occupy the time withal, and hath more vice and lightness than virtue and gravity. *Three kinds of lies.*

The second sort of lies is called *mendacium officiosum,* and is required, when otherwise ill or murder cannot be avoided. As ye read, Exod. i., where the midwives, being commanded of Pharao to kill all the males among the *Exod. i. 19.*

[3 Bording, A and B, boording, C, jesting. See p. 368.]
[4 Merelie, A, merely, B, merrily, C.]

Israelites at the time of their birth, said, the women of the Hebrews were delivered before they came to them. 1 Sam. xix. Michol, David's wife, by the same means saved David; so did Jonatha's, cap. xx.; David in the xxi. by this means obtained bread of Abimelech the high priest in Nobe, and avoided the hand of Achis the king of Gath.

<small>1 Sam. xix. 14.
1 Sam. xx. 28.
1 Sam. xxi. 2.</small>

The third kind is called *mendacium perniciosum*, a pernicious and hurtful kind of lying, that cometh of malice, hatred, envy, or disdain; and extendeth to the hurt of his neighbour. This kind is damnable, whether it be in civil causes, or matters of religion: specially to be abhorred in divines and preachers of the church, that cause men to err from the way of salvation taught us by the scripture, and to bring people from the old learning of the patriarchs, prophets, and apostles, to the new learning of men; from our mother the holy church, and the spouse of Christ, Ephes. v., from a church builded upon the doctrine and foundation of the prophets and apostles, Ephes. ii., unto the synagogue of the devil, builded upon the doctrine of antichrist. Here is forbidden all things that hurteth, and not the thing that can honestly and charitably profit the truth and a good cause.

<small>Eph. v. 23.
Eph. ii. 20.</small>

This law extendeth against those that by any false means contend in judgment to overcome a right cause, or molest an honest person with slanders and lies: or such as feign untrue accusation and crimes against any man; who is not only damned by this law of God, but also by the law of man. For when an ungodly and malicious person is suffered to lie, and speak what he listeth unpunished, there is nothing more pernicious in the world to make debate and to break charity. Therefore, not only God's laws requireth the slanderer to be punished with the same pain that is due for the offence that falsely he hath accused his brother of, Deut. xix. Matt. vii. Luke vi.; but also by the law of the twelve tables in Rome. August.[1] De Civit. Lib. xxi. capit. 11. Instit.

<small>Deut. xix. 16.
Matt. vii. 1, 2.
Instit. lib. iv. tit. 18.</small>

[[1] The title to this chapter in Augustine is, "An hoc ratio justitiæ habeat, ut non sint extensiora pœnarum tempora, quam fuerint peccatorum."]

Lib. iv. tit. 18.[2] libro Pandect. de iis qui infamiam irrogant. Slanderers be not unpunished.

Likewise those that secretly intend dissension or debate between persons, and bearers of tales that they themselves have feigned out of their own malicious interpreting of a thing done to a good purpose, or the words spoken to an honest end, contrary to the true meaning of them. Against such speaketh Saint Augustine, De Civit. Lib. xix. cap. 6: *Qui ponit in judicio debet pœnam similem sustinere, quamvis sint vera, quia occulta manifestanda non sunt;* that is to say, "He that propoundeth the thing he cannot prove, though it be true, he should suffer the like pain himself; for things secret should not be opened." Understand, that if the matter appertain unto God, charity, the governors of the commonwealth, or unto the commonwealth itself; then should the ill charitably be opened, if it cannot be secretly remedied. Deut. xiii. [Aug. De Civit. Lib. xix.]

Here is forbidden all flattery and currying of favour; an ill that destroyeth city and world, reigneth in Moses' chair, in the court of princes, and every private house; where as men careth not, so they may keep themselves in favour, or come into favour; what they praise, or what they dispraise: so it please their masters, these parasites and servile sort of men hold up "Yea," and "Nay," as the wind bloweth; which is of all servitudes the greatest. It is not without cause, that so many wise men hath given counsel to beware of this pestiferous kind of people. Cato, *Cum quis te laudat, judex tuus esse memento;* that is to say, "If any man praise thee, remember to be thine own judge:" Cic. De Offic. i. *Cavendum est ne assentatoribus pate-faciamus aures, ne adulari nos sinamus;* that is to say, "We must beware we open not our ears to such as praiseth us falsely, and not suffer ourselves to be flattered." None be so much in danger of these ill men, and dangerous sin, as the princes, nobles, and superior powers of the earth. Therefore Ovid saith, *Agmen adulantum media procedit in aula;* that is to say, "The cluster of flatterers walk in the [Lib. i. cap. 26.]

[[2] Lex Cornelia de falsis,—pœnam irrogat ei qui testamentum vel aliud instrumentum falsum scripserit, signaverit, recitaverit, subjecerit; vel signum adulterinum fecerit, sculpserit, expresserit, sciens dolo malo. Instit. Lib. iv. Tit. 18. 7.]

midst of the court." To this inhonest and filthy gain either poverty or avarice storeth them, as Cicero[1] writeth, ad Heren. Lib. IV.: *Duæ res sunt quæ possunt homines ad turpe compendium commovere, inopia atque avaritia.*

Further, there is here forbidden the judge to admit, or any man to offer in judgment, any partial, fore-wrought, or concluded cause. In case it be known, the person accused may appeal to a higher judge, and refuse the testimonies that speak of hatred, or being corrupted other ways, by love, or money, whether it be already paid or yet to be paid. Cod. Lib. IV. tit. 20.[2] When the law saith, "Thou shalt not answer as a false witness against thy neighbour;" it declareth, that it is lawful to shew the truth, when he is required: which condemneth the opinion of those that think it not lawful for a christian man to contend in any cause before the civil magistrates of the earth.

Remember those four things in giving of testimony; and then thou shalt not offend.

First, remember God and the truth, and do for them as much as thou mayest.

Second, put apart all affections, fear, love, and hatred. Consider what the cause is, and not whose the cause is. If any man speak good or ill, keep one ear stopped with thy finger, and hear him that speaketh with the other. So did Alexander the Great; and when he was demanded why he did so, he said, he kept the one ear close, to hear the other part. And that is the greatest testimony that any man can have to commend his wisdom: and so we be commanded, Exod. xxiii. Levit. xix. Read the chapter.

Exod. xxiii. 3, 6, &c.

Third, see thou feign nothing, nor add nothing to the cause, whether it be good or bad; as the Pharisees did against Christ, and his holy martyr, Saint Stephen.

Fourth, see thou hide nothing, nor dissemble, but speak plat[3], and plainly as much as thou knowest.

If thou observe not these four things, it is not only theft against charity, but also sacrilege against God, which

[[1] Item utrum igitur avaritiæ causa an egestatis accessit ad maleficium, &c. Cicero ad Heren. Lib. IV. sect. 38.]
[[2] De Testibus.]
[[3] Platle, A, plat, B, truth, C.]

he abhorreth, Prov. vi., read the chapter, and shall not be unpunished. Deut. xix., read the place. The end of this precept is, that we use in all things a simple verity towards all men without fraud, deceit, or guile in word and deed.

Prov. vi. 19.
Deut. xix. 16.

And all that is before spoken in many words, the sum and whole is, that we violate not nor hurt with slanderous words; calumniate not the thing well spoken or done, nor otherway our brother's name; but be glad in all things to promote him, both in goods and fame.

CAPUT XIII.

THE TENTH COMMANDMENT.

Thou shalt not covet thy neighbour's house, neither desire thy neighbour's wife, either his man-servant, either his woman-servant, either his ox, either his ass, either any thing that is thy neighbour's.

As much as is necessary for man to live an upright and godly life in this world, both towards God and man, is repeated in the nine commandments afore, if they be observed according to their institution, and mind of Almighty God, the giver of the same: as he desireth all the external acts of man to extend unto the glory of God, and utility of our neighbour; so doth he in this last precept require, that the mind and soul of man be replenished with all affections and desire of love and charity; that whatsoever we do, it be done without vain-glory and hypocrisy, from the heart, not shewing one thing outwardly, and have another secretly in the heart. And this commandment is referred to all the other, as Christ saith, Matt. v.; though the words of the commandment make mention only of the concupiscence of such things as be our neighbour's possession, as his house, his wife, with other such goods as be his.

The purpose of this commandment.

And in this precept is declared specially our infirmity and weakness, that we are all miserable sinners; Rom. vii. for never was there, or ever shall be, only Christ excepted, but offended in this precept, to what perfection or degree of holiness soever he came unto.

Rom. vii. 7.

No creature born into the world could satisfy this law; and all holy saints had sin remaining in them, as long as they lived. Psalm cxlii. 1 John i. Rom. vii. 1 Cor. iv. Psalm cxxix. xvi. xxxi. Job ix. Exod. xxxiv. Of the which places we may learn to call for the great and inestimable help of God, that we may be quit and saved from this imperfection in Christ Jesu, and accounted in him the children of God and satisfiers of the law. Rom. viii. For by this law is required such a charity and sincere love towards God and man, that the mind should not have as much as any contrary motion, or any resistance at all, to stain the glory and beauty of this love, which comprehendeth all those commandments afore rehearsed. As Christ saith, Matt. xxii. Mark xii., and likewise Matt. vii. "All things that ye would men should do to you, the same do ye to them; this is the law, and the prophets."

1 John i. 8.
Rom. vii. 14.
1 Cor. iv. 4.

Rom. viii. 16.

Matt. xxii. 35.
Mark xii. 28.
Matt. vii. 12.

So that by these words ye may know, what is the scope and end of the law: truly none other thing, than to bring men to justice and honesty of life, and to make him like unto the law, and so unto Almighty God, whose image the law expresseth; and the more man conformeth himself to live after the law, the more he resembleth the Almighty God, giver of the law. Moses, when he would briefly call unto remembrance the sum of God's laws, saith: *Et nunc, Israel, quid petit abs te Dominus Deus tuus, nisi ut timeas Dominum, et ambules in viis ejus; diligas eum ac servias ei in toto corde et tota anima; custodiasque mandata ejus?* Deut. xx., that is to say, "Therefore now, Israel, what doth the Lord thy God ask of thee, saving that thou shouldest fear the Lord, and walk in his commandments, love him, and serve him, with all thy heart and life, and to keep his commandments?"—and repeateth the same words again, 22nd chapter. The law would that our hearts should be replenished with the love of God, of the which love proceedeth the love towards our neighbour, as Paul writeth, 1 Tim. i.

Self-love.

The occasion of all hatred that we bear unto God, his holy word, and our neighbour, is the love of ourselves, and the vanity of this world. In this commandment is not only forbid the effect of ill, but also the affect[1] and desire towards ill: not only the affect[1], lust, concupiscence, proneness, inclination, desire, and appetite towards ill; but also, when man is most destitute of sin, and most full of virtue, most far[2] from the devil, and nearest to God, out of hell, and in heaven, Philippens. iii.; yet is his works so imperfect, that if it were not for the free, liberal, and merciful imputation of justice in Christ Jesu, man were damned, Rom. vii. viii. Psalm cxliii. He that considereth this precept well, shall the better perceive the greatness of God's infinite mercy, and understand the article and doctrine of free justification by faith. *Phil. iii. 20. Rom. vii. 25. Rom. viii. 1. Psal. cxliii. 2.*

For although grace prevent the doing of good, and follow it never so much; yet is the work unperfect, and satisfieth not the perfection of the law: only it is Christ's merits that we be saved by. The which article the devil most envieth, and goeth about to oppress as much as is possible. Confess thyself therefore in thy most perfection, and say: "Lord God, have pity and compassion upon me always and for ever, thy unprofitable servant," Luke xvii. *Our works cannot fulfil the law. Luke xvii. 10.*

And when thou speakest of grace, remember it is not only the free gift of God to prevent thee in doing well, and to follow thee in the same; but also free imputation of life eternal, which thou canst not merit, neither with grace, neither without grace. For, as I said before, to what perfection soever thou be come unto, this law accuseth thee: "Thou shalt not covet." But because thou trowest and believe in Christ Jesu, thou shalt be saved, John iii. iv. v. vi.: and whereas the law promiseth nothing but upon such condition as we perform it to the uttermost, Christ Jesu taketh from her the rigour and extremity of her justice in us, and layeth it upon himself; so that the bliss eternal, that the law promiseth for works, God giveth unto us by grace, for his sake that only satisfied the law, Christ Jesus. Rom. v. Ephes. i. Coloss. i. Galat. iv. *John iii. iv. v. vi. Christ hath performed the law for us. Rom. v. 1, 2. Eph. ii. 7. Col. i. 14. Gal. iv. 6.*

[¹ Old editions, *theffect*.]
[² Ferrist, A, farrest, B, far, C.]

And in this argument of free justification writeth Saint Paul in the eleven first chapters in the epistle to the Romans; where as in the fourth [chapter]¹ he putteth Abraham for an example, that is the father of all believers, in whom we may see how the friends of God are justified, or obtain the favour of God; and saith, that Abraham was justified by faith, Gen. xv., and before circumcision. Where as thou seest two things: one, that the uncircumcised was justified; the other, that no man was justified by the merits or benefits of the sacrament. Likewise, he was promised to be the heir of the world, because of him should be born Christ Jesu, the Lord of the world. *Id credidit, non per legem meruit:* "This he believed, and not by the law merited." Gal. iii.

Another reason Paul allegeth, that Abraham, and all other, are justified by faith. It is not possible, that the promise of God should be irritated or made vain; but if it dependeth of the justice of the law, it could not be certain: therefore addeth he, "Freely by faith." Which faith, in obtaining remission of sin, beholdeth only the mercy of God in Christ Jesu, and looketh upon none other merits.

Yet mark more: he saith that grace is the heritage of the believer, by the justice of faith. Romanorum iv. Then it is not merit. *Hæredes nascimur, non emimus:* "We are born heirs, and buy it not;" as those say that attribute remission of sin to works or sacraments; which doth testify or confirm the friends of God, and not make them God's friends. Rom. iv.

Thus thou seest, what the law is, how thou art bound studiously to obey it, and how it is fulfilled in Christ Jesu; whose justice is thine, if thou believe in him, as though thou hadst perfectly satisfied the law thyself.

[¹ Supplied from C.]

CERTAIN OBJECTIONS, THAT KEEPETH MAN FROM THE OBEDIENCE OF GOD'S LAWS, SOLUTED.

CAPUT XIV.

1. *Of Time and Place.*

As it is the manner of all orators, not only to stablish the matter they entreat of with such reasons, arguments, and probations, as best may confirm and stablish their purpose; but also add such reasons, as may incline the hearers to favour the thing spoken, and likewise leave in their minds such persuasions, as might in manner prick them forth, and by force constrain them to put in effect and practice the thing spoken of; and then to remove such impediments, and break the force of such contrary arguments, as may be objected, to let the thing they would obtain and prove: so doth Moses in the book of Deuteronomy, as thou heardest before, leave no argument nor reason unspoken of, that might excitate, stir up, provoke, and force us to the love, obedience, and execution of God's laws, as the 28th chapter of Deuteronomy sheweth. In the 29th and 30th he removeth all the objections, impediments, and lets, that withholdeth us from the obedience and doing of God's laws. *[The custom and manner of orators. Moses, his forcible persuasions to obey the law of God. Deut. xxviii. Deut. xxix. Deut. xxx.]*

The first sophism or carnal objection is, when men say, "It is no place nor time now to learn or obey the word of God: we be not in a monastery, in the school, or in the temple; we be in the broad world, and must do as other men do, and rather serve the place we be in, *et ululare cum lupis*, bark with the wolf, than speak of the scripture." So doth they reason of time likewise: "Now it is too dangerous a season to reason any matters; let it pass till the world be more quiet;" and such like. As the Israelites might have said to Moses, that commanded to observe this law when they came into the land of Canaan: We observed not these precepts in the wilderness; wherefore then more in Canaan? We kept them not for the *[The first objection. Proverb.]*

space of forty years, no more will we hereafter. This objection he breaketh, and proveth that the law should be always observed, and in every place; and sheweth how the observation of the law was rewarded, and the neglecting of it punished; and declareth the same by examples. God fed his friends in the desert by miracle from heaven, and preserved all their apparel, that it consumed not, nor perished in the wearing for the space of forty years. Then of Pharao, and the two great kings of Hesbon and Basan, Sehon and Og.

<small>Deut. xxix. 5 6, 7.</small>

CAPUT XV.

2. *Exception of Persons.*

<small>The second objection.</small>

THE second objection is, when men put from themselves the obedience of the law unto other, saying, "Let the priests and monks keep the law, and learn it; what should a prince, magistrate, or gentleman be bound to learn and keep all those holy rules?" Further, "Youth cannot be tied to so strait canons; it must not so be bridled. Such as be parked in with high walls, and separated from the world, must observe these commandments of God."

This wicked acceptation of persons Moses destroyeth, and most godly repeateth and numbereth the members of the church, the orders and degrees[1] of the same; repeateth the words of the alliance, saying: *Vos omnes hodie statis coram Domino Deo vestro, principes vestri, tribus vestræ, seniores vestri, præfecti vestri, atque omnes viri Israel, parvuli quoque vestri, uxores vestræ, et peregrinus tuus, &c.;* that is to say, "All ye this day stand before the Lord your God, your princes, your tribes, your elders, your officers, and all men of Israel, your children, your wives, and thy guest," and so forth. Read the place. And why they stood before the Lord, the text declareth, to enter alliance with him. No manner of person is excluded from the league: whereby we know, as God's mercy is common for all men, which

<small>Deut. xxix. 10, 11, 12.</small>

[¹ Old editions, *decrees.*]

is the first part of the condition expressed in the league; so alike is the obedience towards the law required of all men, specially of such as be the governors of the people in the ministry of the church, or else in the governance of the commonwealth. If the preacher be ignorant of God's word, and of a dissolute life, what godliness or virtue can there be in his hearers? If the king, prince, magistrate, or rulers of the commonwealth, nor know God's laws, nor follow justice, equity, temperancy, nor sobriety; what honesty or virtue can they look to have in their subjects? They must give example of all virtue. Let them beware betime, that use these objections: for if they think to have God for their God, let them observe his alliance; for he will punish the transgressors without respect of persons, whosoever it be.

Like obedience to the law required of all.

CAPUT XVI.

3. *Presumption.*

THE third objection or satanical sophism is presumption or security of God's will; when men knoweth what is to be done, yet against his knowledge, presuming of God's mercy, doth the thing that is ill. This horrible sin extendeth wondrous far. The one sitteth in judgment, and falsely judgeth; the other climbeth to honour and riches by flattery, usury, simony, extortion, fraud, and pilling of the poor; the other holdeth in the truth to be spoken, and letteth out the lies that should be kept in, with all such other like vices, as reign now-a-days in the world. They hear by the words of God, that those ills and abominations be cursed of God; yet hope they the contrary, and think yet to have God's favour, as the text saith, Deut. xxix. Read and mark it: *Cum audierit verba juramenti hujus, benedicat sibi in corde suo, dicens, Pax erit mihi, etiamsi incessero in imaginatione cordis mei, ut addat ebriam sitienti;* that is to say, "When he heareth the words of this oath (where God sweareth to punish the ill, Deut. xxviii.), he promiseth good to himself, saying in his

The third objection.

Deut. xxix. 15.

heart, Yea, if I walk in the imagination of my heart, and take my pleasure, there is no danger."

Presumption the occasion of continuance in sin. This diabolical presumption is the occasion that men not only fall into divers kinds of abomination, but also persevere in the same ill. Let every man judge his own conscience, and see. Against the word of God he taketh hope, as it seemeth him, of God's mercy; which is no hope at all, but the very withe and halter of the devil to strangle at length him that is thus persuaded in this ill and dangerous opinion. They think it is faith, whereas it is very arrogancy; a true knowledge of God, when it is but a devilish illusion, and false opinion of man, as it appeareth in the same place by Moses' words: *Non agnoscit Dominus, ut propitietur ei; sed fumabit tunc furor Domini, et zelus ejus in virum istum, et cubabit super eum omnis maledictio quæ scripta est in libro isto, delebitque Dominus nomen ejus sub cœlo.* Deut. xxix. *Deut. xxix. 20.* that is to say: "The Lord will not favour him, but then be angry, and kindle his ire against this man; so that every malediction written in this book shall rest upon him, and the Lord shall destroy his name under heaven." Read the place, and learn to avoid such security and sinister judgment of God and his nature.

The original cause of presumption. The original and fountain from whence this presumption springeth is ignorancy, and a trust in other men's virtues, for whose merits they think to be saved. Some say, they have angels and archangels, and many other holy saints in heaven, that commend their salvation to God. Another trusteth to such works as may be done upon the earth for him, and he do nothing himself, but live as he list, in a vain hope, to have solace in iniquity.

How presumption is nourished. This great offence is nourished divers ways: first, when men judge not aright of God's nature, that he is as angry with sin as the scripture saith.

The second, when men judge amiss of God's works: when they see he punished one for sin, he thinketh not that the same punishment appertaineth unto him. Moses teacheth, and setteth before the people the works of God, his wonders and marvels done in Egypt, in the cities of Sedom and Aemorra, Adma and Seboim, the which the Lord *Deut. xxix. 23.* subverted in his ire and fury; and said these works only punished not those that offended, but also should teach all other men to avoid God's displeasure; for to that end miracles of punishments be done, as Christ saith, Luke xiii. to forewarn men of the ill to come; and thus hath he always called men to penance.

Luke xiii. 3, 5.

If they would still be naught, at length he punished cruelly: as not only the holy histories of the bible testify, where as ye see kings and kingdoms changed and destroyed; but also in profane writers ye shall see by what miracles God called the magistrates and people of the commonwealth to repentance. Titus Livius, *libro tertio de secundo bello Punico*, writeth that an ox calved a horse[1]. In the seventh book a pig with a man's mouth[2], and a child born with an elephant's head[3]. Valerius[4] writeth, libro i. cap. iv. that a mare foaled a hare in the king of the Persians' camp, called Xerxes, who, as some writers record, brought against the Athenians 1,700,000 men of war, whom Themistocles, the captain of the Greeks, overcame in the sea. Herodotus writeth this history at large[5]. Had king Xerxes considered the work of God, he might have learned that there was a God that would turn the force and courage of his horsemen into the fear and timidity of the timorous and fearful hare. Livius[6] lib. III. *de urbis origine*, writeth how the heavens burned and divided itself in two; Lib. II. *de secundo bello Punico*, the sea-banks burned,[1] the sun was seen to fight with the moon[7], and likewise two moons to be seen in the day. Lib. III. he saith that the sea burned.

Strange miracles sent of God to call men to repentance.

Liv. lib. iii. & lib. vii.

Valer. Max. lib. i. c. iv.

Liv. lib. iii. De urb. origine.

[1 Mare arsit eo anno: ad Sinuessam bos equuleum peperit. Liv. Lib. XXIII. cap. 31.]

[2 Tarquiniis porcum cum ore humano genitum. Ibid. Lib. XXVII. cap. 4.]

[3 Cum elephanti capite puerum natum. Ibid. Lib. XXVII. cap. 11.]

[4 In exercitu Xerxis, quem adversus Græciam contraxerat, equæ partu leporem editum constat, eodem montem Athon vix tandem transgresso. Quo genere monstri tanti apparatus significatus est eventus, &c. Valer. Max. Lib. I. cap. 6. Externa. I.]

[5 Herodoti. Hist. Lib. VII.]

[6 Cœlum visum est ardere plurimo igni: portentaque alia, &c. Tit. Livii. Lib. III. cap. 5. Eo anno cœlum ardere visum, terra ingenti concussa motu est; bovem locutam cui rei priore anno fides non fuerat, creditum, &c. Ibid. cap. 10.]

[7 Arpis parmas in cœlo visas, pugnantemque cum luna solem: et Capenæ duas interdiu lunas ortas. Ibid. Lib. XXII. cap. 1.]

These supernatural works might have taught the people of those days amendment of life, had they not been blind, as we be; that never take profit by any work of God, otherwise than to eat the revenues of the earth, as the brute beasts of the same, nor no more knowledge of God by the motions of the heavens, than the ox or horse, that likewise see them, and yet neither the wiser, neither the better. If we marked the eighth and nineteenth psalms, we should know they were made to another end. The gentiles shame us all away, that learned by the revolution of the year, that nothing was durable in this mortal life:

Immortalia ne speres monet annus, et almum
Quæ rapit hora diem[1].   Horat. Carmin. Lib. IV.

[Marginal: Psal. viii. Psal. xix.]
[Marginal: [Od. vii.]]

The third reason is, that men judge amiss of God's promises, that saith he will punish doubtless for sin all manner of people, be they never so strong, as the prophets always testify. Hieremy in especial: he said, if the people converted not from their doing of ill, God would keep promise with them, and destroy their land: but they believed it not, but said, *Templum Domini, templum Domini, templum Domini*; "The temple of God, the temple of God, the temple of God." They judged then, as many do now-a-day; when they see their cities and country strong, they think it not possible to be overcome. So thought the Trojans, and deceived themselves, as the prophecy of Nereus forespake:

[Marginal: Jer. vii. 3, 4.]

Post certas hyemes uret Achaïcus
Ignis Iliacas domos[2].   Horat. Carm. Lib. I.

[Marginal: Hora. lib. i. Od. xv.]

Another so esteemeth the force of the people, and putteth their confidence in the same, saying: "Let this babbling preacher say what a' list; God is not so cruel as he speaketh of: it shall cost many a broken head before any enemy enter any parcel of our commonwealth." But trust to it, if sin be not banished, the ire of God will find a way in at last; and the deferring thereof is only to call us to a better life, and not that he is asleep, or approveth

[1 The revolving year, and the hour which hurries away the beautiful day, admonishes us not to hope for immortality.]

[2 After a certain number of winters the Grecian fire shall burn the houses of Troy.]

our ill life: Rom. ii. As thou seest example of the Israelites Rom. ii. 4. in the land of Canaan, which was passing strong, and the inhabitants thereof the only commonwealth of God, as they said, "The temple of God, the temple of God;" yet at the last Nabucadnezer, that they looked not for, was their destruction, Esay xxii. Mark the punishment and the Isai. xxii. cause thereof, which was sin; and learn to beware, taught by another man's ill.

CAPUT XVII.

4. *Curiosity.*

THE fourth let or impediment is curiosity, and overmuch searching the privities and secrets of God; when men of an ill and licentious life return not to penance, as the scripture biddeth, but mounteth straightway into God's providence and predestination; contemning the will of God that is made open to him in the scripture, that God would him now to repent, and to receive grace; searcheth to know the thing that never was made open to man or angel, the event and end of things to come; thus reasoneth with himself: "Who knoweth what his last hour shall be? Wherefore favoureth God the one, and not the other? Sometime the good maketh an ill end, and the ill a good." In this opinion and inscrutable mystery he weareth all his wits, and at the end of his cogitations findeth more abstruse and doubtful objections than at the beginning; so that he cometh from this school neither wiser neither better. *The fourth impediment.*

Moses, Deut. xxix., removeth this ungodly let and impediment, saying: *Secreta Domini Dei nostri revelata sunt nobis et filiis nostris usque in sæculum, ut faciamus omnia verba legis hujus;* that is to say, "The secrets of the Lord our God are made open unto us, and unto our children for ever, that we do all the precepts of this law." The which words plainly condemneth our foolish and audacious presumption, that seeketh to know what shall happen unto us Deut. xxix. 29.

in the hour of death, and will not know the thing that should be done in all our lives; to say, that God would have us know the thing that is opened unto us in the scripture, God's mercy promised in Christ Jesu, and follow him in all virtue: if we offend, to repent, and leave sin; then hath he promised mercy, and will give it; as[1] Moses saith, cap. xxx. Deut., "Do the thing that thou art bid to do, and follow the will of God made open unto thee in his word."

Deut. xxx. 8.

As for the[2] disputation of God's providence, is a curiosity and no religion, a presumption and no faith, a let of virtue and furtherance of vice. When thou hearest penance spoken of, learn that lesson out of hand, lest peradventure thou be never good scholar in theology[3] of God's laws. It fareth many times with us, that long go to school in divinity, and yet never good divines, as it fareth in the school of rhetoric: where as if at the beginning the scholar profit not, as Aristotle saith, shall never be good orator. Therefore Moses saith in the 29th chap. Deut., *Non dedit Dominus vobis cor ad intelligendum et oculos ad videndum atque aures ad audiendum usque in præsentem diem;* that is to say, "God gave you not a heart to understand, eyes to see, nor ears to hear until this present day." Here doth Moses speak *ironice*, and seemeth to deny the thing he would affirm. As Aristotle or Cicero might say, when they have applied all their labour, and done the best they can to make their scholars learned, yet profiteth nothing, then depart out of the school, and say unto their audience, "I never opened unto you the science that I taught you;"—not that the fault was in them[4], but in the auditors that neglected their diligence and doctrine: so doth Moses now speak of God; not that the fault was in him, that those unkind people understood not the doctrine he taught, but in themselves, as it appeareth in the text: for he useth now the rod of persecution, punisheth them, beateth them, yea, and killeth them, because they would not learn the thing he taught them: yea, farther, he sheweth that his pleasure was they should choose the good, and leave the ill, to be in wealth, and avoid the woe.

Deut. xxix. 4.

[[1] As, supplied from A.] [[2] Thy, A, the, B and C.]
[[3] Theology, A and B, divinity, C.]
[[4] Them, A, him, B and C.]

This argument he proveth of his own nature, which is amiable, loving, and holy, inclined to do well unto man, and to be at peace with him. But because man of his own malice contemneth the word and doctrine of God, he is not only rigorous and severe against man, but also he waxeth so angry for sin, as he that chafeth and moveth himself, that all men may perceive by his countenance he is offended: therefore saith the text, *Fumabit furor Domini*, Deut. xxix.; that is to say, "the fury of God shall smoke against the sinner." Deut. xxx. 19.
Deut. xxix. 27.

Our gospellers be better learned than the Holy Ghost. For they wickedly attribute the cause of punishment and adversity to God's providence, which is the cause of no ill, as he himself can do no ill; and of every mischief that is done they say, it was God's will. The Holy Ghost putteth another cause, as it is written here, Deut. xxix.; that is to say, sin in man, and the contempt of his holy word.

Further, the pain is not inflicted by predestination to lose[5] man; but both predestination and the affliction extendeth to call man from damnation. Ezech. xxxiii., 1 Cor. xi., Psal. cxviii., Apoc. iii., Esay xxvi., Heb. xii., Prov. iii., Matt. xi., Rom. xi., Esay lxi. The blind soothsayers that writ of things to come, are more to be esteemed than these curious and high-climbing wits; for they attribute the cause of ill unto the ill respects and sinister conjunctions of the planets. Ezek. xxxiii.
1 Cor. xi.
Psal. cxix.
Rev. iii.
Isai. xxvi.
Heb. xii.

Refuse not therefore the grace offered, nor, once received, banish it not with ill conversation. If we fall, let us hear Almighty God, that calleth us to repentance with his word, and return. Let us not continue in sin, nor heap one sin upon the other, lest at last we come to a contempt of God and his word; for remission is promised to as many as repent, as Moses sheweth in the 30th chapter of Deuteronomy, and likewise all the scripture, and examples thereof. Deut. xxx. 1, 2.

But remember what the text saith, that thou must convert unto God, [and] that by the means and mediation of Christ, and that with all thy heart; and then thou mayest find remedy. Convert not to superstition, and buy [not][6] a mass for thy sins, or look [for][6] help of any saint, but

[5] i. e. *ruin*, cause him to be lost. Lost, A, lose, B, loose, C.]
[6] Supplied from C.]

only of God, as his word teacheth, John xv.; for he that strake thee for sin, can heal thee again. Say not in adversity, as Cicero did, *Nisi quis Deus vel casus aliquis subvenerit, salvi esse nequeamus,* Lib. xvi. Epist. 148. ["Except God, or some good hap do save us, we cannot escape."][1] For there is nothing in heaven nor earth that saveth, but God alone.

John xv.
Cic. lib. Ep. xvi. [12, init.]

CAPUT XVIII.

5. *Desperation.*

The fifth impediment.

The fifth let or impediment is desperation, when as men think they cannot be saved, but are excluded from all mercy. And this is not a light and small let for men that hath offended; and is contrary unto presumption. For presumption hath some simile and shew of hope; for although man offend the will of God, yet doth he trust in the doing and perseverance of ill, that God will not punish: the which impiety and wickedness taketh from God his justice.

Desperation detracteth from God's mercy.

Of the contrary nature is desperation; it taketh from God his mercy: for when they offend and continue in sin, they think there is no mercy left for them; the which sin and blasphemy thus proceedeth in man. The desperate person hath now his eye in God's justice; readeth, heareth, and seeth, how cruelly and with rigour he revengeth the transgression of his law; beholdeth the examples in whom God executed the same rigour and punishment, that his conscience is oppressed withal; considereth his own strength which is prone unto nothing but unto ill; seeth how difficile and hard the things be that God commandeth, specially because of his accustom and long continuance in sin.

How men become desperate.

This discourse and progress in that knowledge of sin beareth him in hand, that it is impossible to return unto God: then doth they for the most part abridge and shorteneth their own days, or else choose another kind of life than God appointeth in the scripture. As Sardanapalus,

Sardanapalus.

[[1] Supplied from C.]

the last king of the Assyrians, prescribed at his death this rule to live by, and left the word of God; of whom Justinus writeth, Lib. I. [cap. 3.]

> *Ede, bibe, lude; post mortem nulla voluptas:*
> *Cum te mortalem noris, præsentibus exple*
> *Deliciis animum: post mortem nulla voluptas.*

That is to say, "Eat, drink, play, for after death there is no joy."—Juvenalis,

> *Et Venere et cœnis et plumis Sardanapali.*[2]

Moses, like a good physician, teacheth a remedy against this dangerous disease, and sheweth the way unto God; declareth that God is full of mercy, and ready to forgive; and beginneth his oration in this manner unto such as be afflicted and oppressed with sin: *Cum itaque venerint super te omnia verba ista;* that is to say, "When there cometh upon thee all those things," Deut. xxx. Read diligently the chapter, and mark it. Moses saith there, "When God hath afflicted thee for thy sins, and thou returnest unto him with all thy heart, he shall deliver thee from captivity, and receive thee to his mercy again[3]." Of the which text learn this doctrine, that God will always forgive, how many and how horrible soever the sins be. Rom. v., Ezech. xxxiii., Rom. xi., John iii., Matt. xi. And learn to fear of presumption, and to beware of desperation. *(marginal: Deut. xxx. 1, 2. Rom. v. Ezek. xxxiii. John iii. Matt. xi.)*

God desireth thy obedience towards the law, though thou canst not fulfil it. Likewise, he desireth to do well unto thee, and not to punish thee. Hieremy xx. Read the place, and also Esay, chap. xlix., Luke xv.; and see, what paternal and more than fatherly love God Almighty beareth unto all us miserable sinners in Christ Jesu his only Son, who is ours by faith; which faith solely and only leadeth us to eternal life, as Christ saith, John iii. "So the Father loved the world, that he would give his only Son for it, that all that believe in him cannot perish, but hath life everlasting;" and so, John vi. "He that believeth in me hath everlasting life." *(marginal: Jer. xx. 12. Isai. xlix. John iii. 16. John vi. 40.)*

[2 Juv. x. 362. The lust and feasting and downy beds of Sardanapalus.]

[3 These words are here added in C.]

But unto this way of life (to Christ by faith) all men be not brought after one sort: for as man's life is not maintained with one kind of meats, but the child with pap, the full age with stronger meats, the health with common meats, the sickness with such as be of lighter digestion; so is it in bringing man to faith in Christ Jesu, our Saviour. One doctrine and learning cannot do it, because there be divers sorts of people in the world: some hypocrites, that would justify themselves by their works; these know not the greatness of sin, neither their own imperfection, neither the damnation of God against sin. John xvi. This man should not have the free remission of sin in Christ Jesu preached unto him; but the law and ten commandments, that by it he learn first to know the horror of sin, and greatness of God's ire against it.

<small>John xvi.</small>

Another sort live without all fear and honesty a filthy life, as well of those that confess the gospel, as those that hateth it. Those, because they know not the abomination of their sin, and the severity of God's anger against it, be not meet to have the gospel of remission of sin preached unto them; but to be instructed in the law, and rather brought to a fear of God's punishment, that remaineth for all impenitent persons. They should be excommunicated and punished with the discipline of God's word, that first they might know their sin, and acknowledge their damnation.

Thus Christ taught the young man that trusted in his own works; Matt. xix., Mark x., Luke xviii.: because he was an hypocrite, he preached not unto him the gospel of free remission of sin, but send him to the law, and to the works thereof; not that he meant man could fulfil the law, or justify himself by the works thereof, or that Christ would not he should be partaker of his mercy; but that the hypocrite might come to a knowledge[1] of his sins, the ire of God, and damnation of himself by the law: the which thing known, he should be constrained of necessity to seek his salvation by faith in Christ Jesu, except he would perish in his sin.

<small>Matt. xix. 16.
Mark x. 17.
Luke xviii. 18.</small>

Saint Paul did not bid the Corinthians preach faith and remission of sin unto the adulterer that continued in sin; but bid them excommunicate him, and as many as did

[¹ Old editions, *acknowledge*.]

like offence, and that no man should eat or drink with him. 1 Corin. v. But unto such as know their sins, and be troubled with the heaviness thereof, (as David was, that said, Psalm xxxviii., "Thy darts, Lord, are shut[2] in me, and thy hands oppresseth me; no part of my body free from pain, because I have sinned; for I am drowned in sin, and the punishment thereof is more weighty than I can bear; the sores and wounds that thou hast stricken me withal for my sin stink, and speweth out filth and corruption for my transgression;" and so forth with a dolorous and lamentable oration. Read the psalm; it beginneth, "Lord, chasten me not in thy ire:" there shalt thou learn true penitence:) to him and such-like, as the law hath wrought her office in, appertaineth the preaching of the gospel of remission of sin, and deliverance from hell in Christ Jesu. *1 Cor. v. 1.* *Psa. xxxviii. 3.*

So Christ preached unto Mary Magdalene, Luke vii.; for as she had most grievously[3] offended, so knew she herself, and was afflicted with the dolours of hell. When she came to Christ to know the way to heaven, he send her not unto the law; for the law had first done her office in her, and made her afeard: therefore, poor wretch, she heard, "Thy sins be forgiven, and thy faith hath saved thee." *Luke vii. 48.*

There is another sort meet to hear the gospel, and not to be feared with the law; to say, such as hath through Christ remission of their sin, and walketh by faith in the vocation of God, yet during this mortal life beareth about with them the relics and remnant of sin in their bodies: to these men preacheth Saint Paul the gospel, Rom. viii. *Nulla condemnatio est iis qui insiti sunt Christo Jesu;* that is to say, "There is no condemnation unto them that are grafted in Christ Jesu;" lest this man should too much sustain the weight of the law, as Paul maketh exclamation for fear of the rigour of it in the seventh chapter [of] Romans. *Rom. viii. 1.* *Rom. vii. 24.*

Further, unto this man it is also necessary to mingle the law now and then, to this end, to keep him in his office, in the fear of God; that by the law the affections of the flesh may be kept under, and by the gospel may be preserved the spirit and order of faith.

[[2] Shut in, A and B, light on, C.] [[3] Grounslie, A.]

This is to preach in the church of God: not to fear the sorrowful conscience with the rigour of the law; neither to flatter those hypocrites, epicures, and lascivious gospellers with the promise of faith, until such time as they amend, and the law done his office in them. And in case preachers had used and applied the scripture to the use it was written, and as their auditors had need, there had never been such a sudden and horrible defection from the gospel in many places, as now we see.

CAPUT XIX.

6. *Ignorance.*

THE sixth let or impediment, wherewith men excuse themselves from the obedience of the law of God, is the pretence of ignorancy, the which they think shall excuse them. Thus they say: "The scripture hath so many mysteries in itself, and is too hard for our capacity. Sometime the letter, sometime the spirit, and sometime both must be understood." Further they say: "The doctors brawl and chide between themselves, and how should the unlearned understand it aright?" "Who can tell," saith another, "whether this be the true law or not? If it were the true law of God, then should it contain all verities, and have no need of man's laws."

Now, the greatest part of such as hath the name of Christianity, say, that God's laws saveth no man, instructeth no man aright; no, it is not wholesome for man, except it be holp and aided by the law of the bishops. Thus the world oweth to the bishops' decrees, that have called the authority of the holy testament that containeth all truth, (whose sufficiency and verity is sealed with the precious blood of Christ,) into doubt; and not into doubt only, but clean abrogated it, and preferred their own laws. Confer their preachings and ministration of the sacraments with the holy word and law of God, and see.

Other say, I have no wit to understand the word of God; and if I had, yet have I no leisure to learn it. Against this objection Moses answereth and saith, This law is sufficient, is simple, and plain, easy to be understood, a perfect doctrine, and required of all men. Thus he proveth it: *Præceptum istud, quod ego præcipio tibi hodie, non est mirabiliter supra te nec procul positum*, Deut. xxx.; that is to say, "The commandment that I prescribe unto thee to-day, is not far above thee, nor put far from thee." Read the last half of the chapter. By the which words it appeareth, that God hath made his will and pleasure simple and plainly open unto his people, with apt sentences and open words; and also put the same near unto us, that we should not seek it with great danger of our life, to sail into the Indies for it, or look it in heaven above, as those that receive all things by revelation or apparitions of angels, or other such means. But Moses saith, it is no need of any such ambassadors; and so saith Abraham, Luke xvi. For man may learn out of the scripture what is to be done, and what not to be done, what is the condition of the good and of the bad: no need to seek the knowledge thereof in Egypt, Athens, or Rome. *Sed valde propinquum est tibi verbum in ore tuo, et in corde tuo, ut facias illud;* that is to say, "The word is present, and at hand with thee, in thy mouth, and in thy heart, that thou shouldest do it." Deut. xxx. 11.

Luke xvi. 29.

By these words we see, that in the greatest sinner that is, is a certain rule and knowledge to live well by, if he did follow it. So confounded St Paul the gentiles, Romans i., of sin, because they knew the evil they did was condemned by the testimony of their own conscience. For the law of God to do well by, is written naturally in the heart of every man. He that will diligently search himself shall soon find the same; and in case man would behold his own image both in body and in soul, though there were no law written, nor heavens over our heads to testify the goodness and justice of God, and the equity of Rom. i. 21.

_{Rom. ii. 15.} an honest life, man's conscience would tell him, when he doth well, and when evil. Romano. capit. ii.

Farther, the judgment and discourse of reason desireth not only to live justly in this world, but also to live for ever in eternal felicity without end; and that cometh by the similitude of God, which yet remaineth in the soul after the sin of Adam. Whereby we see plainly, that those excuses of ignorancy be damnable, when man seeth he could do well if he followed the judgment of his own mind, and could not live an evil life; for when he doeth evil, he knoweth that he doeth against the judgment of his own conscience: so that we see that the law of God is either outwardly or inwardly, or both, opened unto man; and by God's grace might do the good, and leave the evil, if it were not of malice and accustomed doing of sin. The which excuseth the mercy and goodness of God, and maketh that no man shall be excused in the latter judgment, how subtilly soever they now excuse the matter, and put their evil doings from them, and lay it upon the predestination of God, and would excuse it by ignorancy; or say, he cannot be good, because he is otherwise destined.

[ι. i. 39, 40.] This stoical opinion reprehended Horat :—Epist. i.

Nemo adeo ferus est, ut non mitescere possit,
Si modo culturæ patientem commodet aurem :

that is to say, "No man is so cruel, but may wax meek, so that he give a willing ear to discipline."

Although thou canst not come to so far a knowledge in the scripture as other that be learned, by reason thou art unlearned, or else thy vocation will not suffer thee all days of thy life to be a student; yet mayest thou know, and upon pain of damnation art bound to know, the articles of thy faith; to know God in Christ, and the holy catholic church by the word of God written; the ten commandments, to know what works thou shouldest do, and what to leave undone; the *Paternoster*, Christ's prayer, which is a bridgment, epitome, or compendious collection of all the psalms and prayers written in the whole scripture; in the which thou prayest for the remission of sin, as well for thyself as for all other, desirest the grace of the Holy Ghost, to preserve thee in virtue and all other, givest thanks for the goodness of God towards thee and all other.

He that knoweth less than this cannot be saved; and he that knoweth no more than this, if he follow his knowledge, cannot be damned, John xvii. There be two common verses that all men in manner knoweth, and doubtless worthy, that telleth us to know Christ, though we know no more, is sufficient:

Hoc est nescire, sine Christo plurima scire:
Si Christum bene scis, satis est si cetera nescis:

that is to say, "To be ignorant, is to know many things without Christ. If thou know Christ well, it is sufficient, though thou be ignorant of all other things."

Thus I have said in the ten holy precepts of Almighty God according unto the scripture. Fare ye well in our only and sole joy and consolation, Christ Jesu.

[The following sentences are here added in the first edition, printed in 1548.]

(And where as thou shalt find in any word a letter too much or too little, or perchance one for another, or true orthography not observed, the sentences not well at all times, and aright pointed, or for lack of putting on of ink, or slack drawing of the press, the letters not plainly expressed,—remember, I pray thee, that it is not in manner possible to print in a known tongue a whole work without faults: how much more impossible, where as the setters of the print understandeth not one word of our speech, and wanteth also such as knoweth the art of true correcting! Where as such faults or other shall happen, thou shalt without all difficulty and labour, by the lesson and process of the matter, straightway understand my mind and meaning, and as need requireth, add or take away a letter from a word, or change the whole word, if one be put for another in an open and plain sentence; as in the letter H, at the number xciv. in the fifth verse thou shall find *penitence* for *pestilence.* Such faults charitably bear withal, I pray thee; for although it be not as well done as I would wish, and as every christian reader would desire, yet is it as well as I could have it done: take it therefore well at worth, and remember the saying of Horace, Lib. i. Epi. i. [v. 32.]

Est quoddam prodire tenus, si non datur ultra.

Farewell in our only and
sole joy and conso-
lation Christ
Jesu.)

FINIS.

⁋ Imprynted at London in
Paules churche yarde at
the sygne of the Byble by
Rycharde Jugge.

AN

OVERSIGHT AND DELIBERATION

UPON THE

HOLY PROPHET JONAS.

An oversighte and deliberacion uppon the holy prophet Jonas: made, and uttered before the kinges maiesty, and his most honorable councell, by Jhon Hoper in lent last past.

Comprehended in seuen Sermons.

Anno . M . D . L .

Except ye repent, ye shal
al pearish.
Lu. xiii.

An ouersight,

and deliberacion upon the holy Prophete Jonas: made and uttered before the kynges maiestie, and his moost honorable councell, by Jhon Hoper in lent last past, Comprehended in seben Sermons.

Anno. M.
D.L.

Excepte ye repente, ye shall al peryshe.
Luke xiii.

Cum priuilegio ad impri mendum solum.

[These sermons on Jonas were preached on the Wednesdays during Lent, in the year 1550, before the king and council; Ponet preaching on the Fridays.

Hooper, in one of his letters to Bullinger, preserved in the Archives at Zurich, dated June 29, 1550, says, that at Easter, after the sermons were ended, it pleased his majesty and the council to offer the bishoprick of Rochester to Ponet, and that of Gloucester to himself.

Three editions of these sermons appear to have been printed during the year in which they were preached; two by Day and Seres, and one by Tisdale. The former are page for page alike, except in the Epistle (dedicatory), and seem to be almost exact reprints, with variations only in the spelling. Tisdale's edition also very closely corresponds with those of Day and Seres; the variations being generally very trifling.

These three editions have been collated for the present work, and the differences noticed where the sense appeared to be affected by them. They are distinguished in the editorial notes by the letter T. for Tisdale's edition; D. 1. for that of Day, in which a page of corrections occurs at the end of the volume; and D. 2. for the other.]

THE EPISTLE.

To the most puissant prince and our most redoubted sovereign lord, Edward the Sixth, by the grace of God, king of England, France, and Ireland, defender of the faith, and in earth, next and immediately under God, of the churches of England and Ireland the supreme head: and also unto the most wise, godly, and most honourable lords of his highness' privy council; his most humble, loving, and obedient subject, John Hooper, elect and sworn bishop of Gloucester, wisheth all grace and peace from God, with long, and the same most godly and prosperous, reign over us, in all honour, health, and perpetual felicity.

Among all other most noble and famous deeds of kings and princes, none is more godly, commendable, nor profitable to the commonwealth, than to promote and set forth unto their subjects the pure and sincere religion of the eternal God, King of all kings, and Lord of all lords. Then shall justice, peace, and concord reign, the door of idololatry be shut up, by the which hath entered all evil, and kings and kingdoms fallen into jeopardy, as the writings of the prophets do testify. But the more this noble fact is glorious, godly and princely, the more difficile and hard it is; for the enemy of God and of all mankind, the devil, customably is wont to deceive the princes of the world; so that either they utterly neglect the religion of the true God, as a thing foolish and of no estimation, either provoke them cruelly to persecute it. If he can bring neither the one, neither the other of these to pass; he will do the best he can to preserve a mixed and mingled religion, that shall neither plainly be against, nor wholly with him; and so use the matter that partly God's truth shall take place, partly the superstitious invention of man. The which mingled and mixed religion is so much the more dangerous, as it is accompted for pure and good: therefore it is earnestly forbidden by God, as the examples of the scripture declareth. Jehu, the king of the Israelites, when he had removed all gross and sensible idololatry, and with the sword had taken away all the idololatrical priests, 3 Reg. x., is reproved of God nevertheless, because he walked not in the law of God with all his heart, and left not the ways of Jeroboam. And against these minglers and patchers of religion speaketh Elias the prophet, 3 Reg. xviii. "How long," saith he, "will ye halt on both sides? If the Lord be God, follow him; if Baal, go ye after him." Even so we may justly say: If the priesthood and ministry of Christ with his notes and marks be true, holy, and absolutely perfect, receive it; in case it be not, follow the pope. Christ cannot abide to have the leaven of the Pharisees mingled with his sweet flour. He would have us either hot or cold; the lukewarm he vomiteth up, and not without a cause.

For he accuseth God of ignorance and foolishness, that intendeth to adorn and beautify his doctrine and decrees with human cogitations. What king or prince of the world would suffer his statutes, laws, and testament to be cut off and set on, at every man's liberty and pleasure? Should not the same glory, majesty, and honour be given unto the laws and testament of Christ, that is sealed with his precious blood? The word of God, wherewith he governeth and ruleth his church, is a sceptre of iron, Psal. ii., and not a rod of willow, to be bowed with every man's finger, either a reed to be broken at man's will; no, neither a piece of leather to be stretched and reached out with any man's teeth.

These things be spoken of me, most gracious and virtuous king, to commend your majesty's and your most honourable council's doings, that seek the glory of God and the restitution of his holy and apostolical church. The which thing as your highness, and your most honourable and wise council, have graciously begun, God's mercy in the bowels of Christ Jesu grant you most graciously to perform! The people of England were oppressed with the violent and cruel tyranny of antichrist; darkness and ignorancy occupied the minds almost of all men, so that few knew the true way to eternal salvation. And yet many princes and wise men delight and tarry in this darkness, and cannot or will not bear nor suffer the radiant and shining beams of the gospel, more than the night-crow can the beams of the sun; but the merciful Father of heaven shall better their sight, when his good and merciful pleasure is. But, the Lord be praised! your majesty, your most honourable and wise council, have not cared what the greatest part, but what the better doth, that the law of the high and mighty God may be known to your highness's people; as did David, Josaphat, Ezechias, and Josias. And in your majesty's so doing, ye bind not only the true and living members of Christ to give God thanks in this behalf, but also declare yourself to be the very fautor[1], nurse, and helper of the word of God, according to the saying of Esaye, xlix. Persevere, gracious king, in this quarrel and dangerous enterprise. Your highness shall not need to fear either the strength or cautelles[2] of your enemies; for there is no wit, wisdom, nor counsel against the Lord, as Salomon saith, Prov. xxi. No, although they had silver as the gravel of the sea, and gold as common as the clay of the streets, Zach. ix. For albeit the horse is prepared for the day of battle, yet the victory cometh from the Lord, Prov. xxi. "I am he," saith the Lord, "that do comfort you: what art thou that fearest mortal man, either the son of man, that shall be made as hay? canst thou forget the Lord thy Maker, that stretcheth forth the heavens and layeth the foundation of the earth?" Esa. li. Let these diabolical sounds and speakings of evil men nothing trouble your highness, nor your wise and godly councillors, "As long as the king is in his tender age, his council should do nothing in matters of religion." For those men's foolishness, rather I should say malice, is condemned by the word of God, that teacheth how a king in his young age, with his wise and godly council, should abolish idololatry, and set forth the true and godly religion of the living God. Thus declareth the notable and godly fact of Josias, that followed the religion of his father, not Ammon the idolater, but of David, nor declining to the right hand, neither to the left hand; and destroyed not only the images of his father, but

[1 Fautor: favourer.]   [2 Cautelles: precautions, plots.]

2 Kings xxii. xxiii. also of Jeroboam and of Salomon. 4 Reg. xxii. xxiii. This fruit of Josias holp his godly councillors and virtuous priests. Even so Joas, being but a child, was holp by his councillors in the like proceedings and reformation of religion. In case the princes, bishops, and priests, had not known it to be the commandment of God to have obeyed these two young and godly kings, they would not have consented unto their[1] proceedings.

But we see how glad they were to do it. The princes and councillors moved no sedition; the bishop and the priests sought not for the defence of their proper doctrine, either to mingle theirs with God's, but were content with the sole and only law of God. Ye noble princes and councillors, praise be unto the living God for your great wisdom and godly assistance in this behalf! And the Lord be magnified in all the godly and learned bishops and others of this realm, that have and do put to their helps and studies to bring the church of Christ to her old and reverend perfection again; and all other that hinder your majesty's godly purpose, openly or secretly, God will doubtless revenge at length.

The godly and virtuous beginnings, most noble prince, of your father the king's majesty, Henry the eighth of a blessed memory, shall by your highness godly be ended in Him that can and will do all things for Christ his dear Son's sake. And a thousand times the rather shall your majesty restore again the true ministry of the church, in case ye remove and take away all the monuments, tokens, and leavings of papistry: for as long as any of them remain, there remaineth also occasion of relapse unto the abolished superstition of antichrist. Seeing I see in the writings of the prophets God to require the observation of his law only, concerning religion; and threateneth all princes, priests and prophets, with his displeasure, that neglect or contaminate it with their own cogitations; I can do no less, howsoever the world shall take my doings, but exhort and pray the magistrates to bring the church to her first perfection: for if I should study to please man herein, I were not the servant of God. And I am afraid lest the disease that infected the Pharisees, infecteth also many now-a-days, that

[[1] Their, T. and D. 2, his, D. 1.]

minister in the church, unto whom Christ spake, John v.,
"How can ye believe, that seek glory one of another, and the glory of God ye contemn?" God give grace, I may not say, *Hinc illæ lacrymæ²*! Help ye therefore, O ye bishops and priests, the king's majesty's and his noble council's proceedings, that all things may be brought to a perfect and apostolical reformation. It is not enough to lay the foundation of the temple, but there must be builded upon it gold, silver, and precious stone. But in any case we must take heed we lay no straw nor stubble upon the foundation; if we do, it will be burned. 1 Cor. iii. If we do not build up upon the foundation, then shall we be shent³ as the Israelites were, Aggeus i.

Let no man excuse himself upon the king's majesty's age; for the age cannot excuse the king's majesty itself. If his religion in his youth be according to God's word, he hath the favour and promises of God to bless, preserve, and keep his majesty and his realm, though the devil and his members would say nay. If in youth his majesty take a wrong religion, he shall be assured of God's displeasure, as it is to be seen 4 Regum xxi. Manasses, being of twelve years old, was crowned king, and in his youth revoked the idololatry that his father Ezechias had abolished, and in his so doing displeased heinously the majesty of God, and at length was sore afflicted and punished for his so doing. Behold the displeasure of God in a young king for a false religion. Jeoachim, crowned the eighth year of his age, for the evil he did in the sight of the Lord, he was taken prisoner by the king of Babylon, 2 Par. xxxvi., with all the goodly vessels of the Lord. This king reigned but three months and ten days, before the Lord revenged the false doctrine he maintained.

These examples, I doubt not, most godly king and virtuous councillors, moveth you to be careful of the true religion. The Lord hath strength and power enough: seek ye him, and give no place to the infirm persuasions of the flesh; for the Lord shall be with you.

Such as think peace and quietness shall come to the realm a better way than to have the true religion of God restored, they shall know the contrary in the prophet, Jer.

[² Hence these sorrows.]   [³ Shent: blamed, disgraced.]

<small>Jer. vi.</small> chapter vi., the which chapter if the king's majesty bear in mind and follow, it is worth a king's revenue: if a lord, the value of his land: if the bishop, the estimation of his bishoprick: if the merchant, the gains of his labour: if the husbandman[1], his oxen and plough. And the same com-
<small>Levit. xxv.</small> manded God, Levit. xxv. "Observe my statutes and my judgments, then shall ye dwell safely in the earth: and the earth shall bring forth her fruit; ye shall eat and be satisfied, and dwell in the earth without fear." It is a fond opinion, most gracious king, and unmeet for a christian man to bear the magistrates of God in hand, that in case the doctrine of Christ and his holy sacraments should not be decked and set forth with these plausible and well liking ceremonies, (that is, to speak plainly, with papistical superstition,) it were to be feared of sedition and tumults. Doubtless, if the pope's members would not deceive the people, but teach them God's word, the people would soon see the truth, and willingly leave as much as God and their king should command them, as the gests and facts of Josias and Joas declareth.

Most gracious king and noble councillors, as ye have taken away the mass from the people, so take from them her feathers[2] also, the altar, vestments, and such like as apparelled her; and let the holy communion be decked with the holy ceremonies that the high and wise priest, Christ, decked and apparelled her in[3] first of all. And from whence, mighty prince and sovereign lord, springeth war and sedition? Come they not from the only God being angry for the neglecting of his law? So we be taught
<small>Isai. l.
Jer. ix.</small> by Esa. l.; and Jeremy ix. saith, "Who is wise and understandeth this, and he unto whom the mouth of the Lord hath spoken and declareth, wherefore the earth perisheth, and is like unto the burned wilderness, that no man may pass by it? And the Lord said, Because they have forsaken my law which I put unto them, and heard not my ways, and walketh not therein; but followed the desire of their own[4] hearts, and after Baalim, as they were taught by their fathers." And because we mingle men's inven-

[1 Husband, old editions.]
[2 Feathers: fathers, T. and D. 2, fethers, D. 1.]
[3 In, omitted in D. 1.]   [4 Own, omitted in T. and D. 2.]

tions with his law; for he saith, "Men worship him in vain with the precepts of men." Matt. xv. And in the ninth of Jeremy the Lord declareth other manner of causes of war and sedition, the forsaking of his law, not to hearken unto his voice, nor to walk in his ways, to go after the pravity and evilness of our own hearts; the vitiating and abuse[5] of the Lord's Supper, 1 Cor. xi.; also the neglecting of widows and orphelens' causes, not to judge right judgment to the poor, Jerem. v. These causes must be avoided, or else truly the saying of Jeremy will take place, chapter vii.: "You trust in yourselves and in lies that nothing profiteth." The next way to return the hand of God's anger and great displeasure against us, is to follow Josaphat, the king, that appointed good judges and godly priests in every city; the judges to judge after the true laws of the realm, and the priests to do all things in the church according to the word of God, which teacheth such knowledge and fear of God, and of the magistrates, that all the wisdom, laws, and books that ever were made, be but counterfeit and foolish in respect of it. Nor ever had God in heaven, or king upon the earth, such a friend as is the holy Bible; for it teacheth the people and subjects of the realm the fear of God, obedience to the king's majesty and his magistrates, and all mutual and fraternal love. This example and counsel of Josaphat, if it be neglected, there can no godliness be among the people, as the text saith, "When prophesy wanteth, the people shall be dissipated and scattered abroad." Proverbs xxix. *Matt. xv. Jer. ix. 1 Cor. xi. Jer. v. Prov. xxix.*

To the doings of these godly offices should all men be exhorted, specially such as bear the name of bishops and priests. If they will not be desirous and glad to have and help the ministry of the church to the primitive and perfect state again, the Lord doth cry vengeance towards them, and will not only require the loss of themselves, but also of all the people at their hands. Ezech. iii. xxxiii. Let them remember the complaint of God himself, Jerem. l. "My people hath been a lost flock, my shepherds have deceived them, and have made them go astray upon the hills." If these threatenings will not amend them, gracious *Ezek. iii. xxxiii. Jer. l.*

[5 Abuse, T. and D. 2, just use, D. 1.]

king, and you, my honourable lords of his high council, must do with them as the mariners did with Jonas. What that is, seeing it pleased the king's majesty and you, my lords of his most honourable council, in the Lent, to hear by me, I have now, at the request of many godly persons, caused it to come abroad; and dedicated the same to your princely majesty and most prudent council, that your highness may be both judge and record of my doctrine unto your majesty's true and loving subjects. The which doctrine is catholic and godly in all things, nothing dissenting, but agreeable with the prophets and the apostles; as I am, according to my bounden duty, ready at all times to make answer, if anything shall be attempted to the contrary. In case there be now and then added a word more or less, or, peradventure, some sentence, yet I know well the matter is not changed nor altered, otherwise than I spake it before your majesty: for I have memorials wherein I wrote before the invention, order, and disposition of all the matters I would entreat upon; as I use, and ever will do, of all things I speak in God's behalf to the people, write myself, or cause another to write, the pith and disposition of all things I speak upon, that I may as well learn a farther knowledge myself thereby, as make answer to mine enemies, if any should accuse me of false doctrine. The God of all strength and consolation govern your majesty and your most honourable council with his holy Spirit, and give you the victory of all your enemies! Amen.

Anno MDL., Septembris vi. Since the angel of God slew, in the army of Sennacherib, God's enemy, a hundred fourscore and five thousand men, Anno MMCCLXXXVIII.[1]

[[1] The Reformers sometimes dated their letters and other publications from remarkable events and particular eras.]

THE
FIRST SERMON,

MADE THE 19th DAY OF FEBRUARY,[2] IN THE YEAR OF OUR LORD,
A. M.CCCCC.L., BEFORE THE KING'S MAJESTY AND HIS MOST
HONOURABLE COUNCIL, BY JOHN HOPER, PREACHER,
UPON THE HOLY PROPHET JONAS.

A PREFACE UNTO THE PROPHET.

IT is the office and duty of every good child, that studiously laboureth to obey and follow his father's commandment, before all things to know perfectly the nature and condition of his father's will. Whereof[3] if he be ignorant, many times in the same things he judgeth best of, he most offendeth; and the things most pleasant and acceptable, as things most displeasant and unacceptable unto his father, he flieth and refuseth. Even so we, that be subjects and the children of God the Father Almighty, can do nothing gratefully and acceptable unto his Majesty, except we first know his good-will and pleasure towards us: or else we shall there most offend him, where as we mind most to please him; and again, haply[4] to improve, as pernicious and heretical, that his wisdom approveth to be most godly and profitable. Wherefore, as the first point of a loving child is to know what pleaseth and what displeaseth, what contenteth and what discontenteth his father, lest he should by ignorance displease where as his son-like affection, by natural zeal, would please; so is it the second point of a good child, his father's will once truly known, diligently to observe and keep the same, lest he should, by negligence or contempt, be seen wilfully to contemn the thing he hath, with diligence and study, obediently submitted himself unto. And in case (as such cases be most common and daily) that infirmities, or other occasion, lead the son from the obedience of his father, the third point of his duty is, speedily to acknowledge his

[2 February, T. and D. 2, March, D. 1.]
[3 Whereof, D. 1, wherefore, T. and D. 2.]
[4 Haplye, T. and D. 2, happyly, D. 1.]

offence, and desire pardon and mercy for his transgression; as the prodigal and disobedient son did, Luke xv.; and David, 2 Samuel [xii.]; and so, after the remission and pardon obtained, to be more circumspect and wise how he fall and transgress again. Psal. li.

<small>Luke xv.
2 Sam. xii.
Psal. li.</small>

These propositions and sentences be so true that no reasonable man doubteth of them. But as the devil hath left in the world no truth nor verity, which by argument and question he hath not called into doubt; so troubleth he in this case the minds of men with two questions. The first is, How and from whence the will of God may be known? The second, What the will of God is? So hath he prevailed among men for sin, that the truth of these questions is unknown to the greatest part of the world, as it was in Moses' time, Christ's time, and now in our time, more ignorant and far from God than they. He persuaded in those days that the will of God was not known[1]; not from heaven, nor out of the scripture canonical, as the patriarchs, prophets, and the apostles taught; but that it was known by the writings, decrees, and statutes of men, that were in the earth, and that the will of God was to do that man commanded, and not that God commanded.

But as Almighty God left not his church then without some that should keep the truth of both these questions among the people, to preserve them from the danger that must needs follow where as truth is not known; so hath he done now at this present time: and by the same authority as the devil, author and father of all questions and lies, was confounded then, so is he now. Moses, instructing the people in the truth of the first question, whence the will of God should be known, commandeth them neither to look [for] it in Ægypt nor elsewhere, but in the word of God, Deut. xxx.; and Saint Paul doth the same, Roma. x. and St John i. saith, "No man hath seen the Father, but the Son, and he unto whom the Son hath opened the Father" unto. God, therefore, and his blessed will, is known unto us, because he hath spoken unto us by his dear beloved Son, Heb. i., as he spake beforetime unto the world by his prophets. From Christ, therefore, and

<small>Deut. xxx.
Rom. x.
John i.</small>

<small>Heb. i.</small>

[1 Was known, D. 1, was not known, T. and D. 2.]

his word cometh the knowledge of God's will; for the
Father bid us hear him. Matt. iii. xvii. John x. Matt. iii. xvii. John x.
Now, what his will is, the truth also appeareth out of the
book of God, and out of none other man's writings. Mark i. Mark i.
His will to the world is this, "Do penance, and believe the
gospel;" that is to say, let every man bewail and repent
him of his sins, and desire the remission and pardon thereof
for Christ's sake, for whom, the gospel sheweth, our sins shall
be forgiven. John i. iii. iv. v. vi. Matt. xi. Rom. v. Eph. i. John i. iii. iv. v. vi. Matt. xi. Rom. v. Eph. i.
This doctrine, from the fall of man, hath been always
taught in the catholic church of Christ unto all nations,
as the writings of the prophets and apostles doth testify;
in whom is fully and abundantly contained all truth and
verity, and left here for our doctrine and consolation.
Rom. xv. Among the which is also contained, as a most Rom. xv.
faithful witness of all truth and verity, this holy prophet
Jonas; who was sent by God to the city of Ninive, to
preach unto them God's pleasure and amendment of life,
or else within forty days both they and the city should
be destroyed.

This prophet have I taken to interpretate for two
causes. The one, to declare unto the king's majesty and
his most honourable council, that the doctrine we preach
unto his majesty's subjects is one and the same with the
prophets' and apostles', and as old as the doctrine of them
both, and not as new as these papists, and new learned
men of papistry, would bear the people in hand. The
second cause is, to declare which way the sinful world
may be reconciled unto God. And for the better understanding of the prophet, I will divide him into four parts.
The first containeth, into what danger Jonas fell by disobeying of God's commandment. The second part containeth, how Jonas used himself in the fish's belly. The
third part containeth the amendment and conversion of
the Ninivites at the preaching of Jonas. The fourth part
containeth an objurgation and rebuke of God, because Jonas
lamented the salvation of the people and city.

THE FIRST PART.

The first part is divided into three members: the one
containeth the embassage and legacy of Jonas unto Ninive:

the other containeth Jonas' disobedience: the third containeth the pain and punishment of Jonas' disobedience.

The embassage is described with these words:—

> The word of the Lord came unto Jonas, the son of Amithai, saying; Arise, and get thee to Ninive, that great city, and cry out against it; for their wickedness is come up before me.

It is not the least help that the reader or teacher of any prophet or other part of the scripture shall have, to know of what place, under what king, in what state of commonwealth, the prophet lived that he purposeth to interpretate: all these things, as touching our Jonas, is declared in the iv. book of the Kings, the xiv. chapter. He lived in Samaria, under an idololatrical king, Jeroboam, the son of Joas, a detestable idolater; and in Juda at that time reigned king Amasias: and this Jonas laboured in the ministry of God's word at one time with Amos, Oseas, and Joel, the true prophets of God. The state and condition of the commonwealth was troublous and very unquiet; for because the Israelites, by their idolatry in following the learning invented by man, and leaving the word of God, God punished them with many great and cruel wars; yet after his accustomed pity and compassion upon those that he punisheth, to remove the occasion that worketh God's ire and displeasure, he sent them divers times his holy prophets, that should call them from their idolatry and corrupt living, as Elias, Elizeus, and this our prophet Jonas; but all in vain. They would be naughty idolaters and vicious livers continually, maugre God's head, and would (as we now-a-days for the most part do) rather give faith unto the prophets of men and liars, than unto the prophets of God, that be true men. But their reward was, as ours shall be except we amend, utter destruction and loss, both of themselves and their commonwealth.

The commonwealth and state of Israel and Juda thus troublously being afflicted, the commandment of God came unto this our Jonas, that he should go to the great city of Ninive, as the text saith. In the which words note first,

Kings xiv.

that no man can or may teach truly the word of God, but he be called ordinarily, or extraordinarily: *ordinarily*, where as is no corruption of the ministry in the church, neither in doctrine, neither in the right ministration of the sacraments, which be as seals and conclusions of God's holy words. Where as this integrity, I say, remaineth in the church, no man ought, without the appointment of the higher powers, to intrude or appoint himself to preach or minister; as it was in Moses' time and the apostles'. *Extraordinarily* is, when immediately any man is called by God, where as the ministry of the church is corrupted, as it was in the time of the prophets and of Christ, that called to minister such as the common face and greatest multitude of the world would not admit, no, not the high bishop, and those that then were called the holy church; as is to be seen by Amos, Jonas, Hieremy, Moses, and Paul, with other. They are to be rebuked, therefore, that intrudeth and put themselves without lawful calling into the ministry of the church, either with money or prayer, and buy themselves into the church; which thing through all papistry is a common practice, and daily used thing. For in case they sought not of their bishoprick more riches and honour, than the necessary travails and labours that be annexed unto the vocation, they would not strive so sore who might leap up first to the bishop's and parson's vocation. There would not so many princes contend and labour for the seat of Rome, the nest of abomination, if there were not in it rather the patrimony of Judas and Simon Magus, than the labour of Christ and Peter; more ease than pain, more riches than burden.

The text saith, that this prophet, being called by God, was sent to Ninive. Of this city's original read the tenth of Genesis. It was the chief city of the Assyrians, unto the which Jonas was sent; and the consideration thereof, that in case the head city be well instructed of a realm, there is the better hope of all the rest. Therefore God hath used, from the beginning of commonwealths, to be merciful unto the greatest cities thereof, and hath sent the most preachers of the truth; as it is to be seen in these days what God hath shewed upon London. And as he offereth them first the tokens of his mercy, so first he revengeth their unkindness with his punishment, if they neglect and contemn the grace offered.

It is to be noted that this city of Ninive was idololatrical and gentilish; never under the discipline and doctrine of Moses. Yet unto it sendeth the Lord his prophet, to declare unto the Jews that the ceremonies and works of the law, whereof they most gloried and extolled themselves, were not necessary to salvation; but given for a time, to exercise their obedience in the commandment of God, and to trust in Christ, of whom their rites and sacrifices were figures and shadows of: further, the Lord declareth by this embassage unto Ninive, that the ignorant and superstitious gentiles be more ready to receive the living word of God than the hard-hearted Jews; as it is to be seen at this present day. More easy it is to convert unto God ten simple and ignorant souls, than one that hath been brought up, and is wedded to the ungodly doctrine and traditions of men. Moreover, the Lord, in seeking the wealth of these Assyrians, declareth that he is not only the God of the Jews, but also of the gentiles. Rom. iii. Acts x. The text declareth, to what end Jonas was sent to the city. What to do? to bring in the ceremonies of Moses' law? Nay, but to cry out against it. That is to say, plainly and openly to shew God's pleasure unto them: and not against one or two of the city, but generally against the whole city, without respect of persons; against the king, the princes, the lawyers, the priests, and the common people. And this was the duty and office of all the prophets. Esay lviii. "Cry out and cease not." Also Hier. ii. vii. The same commandment was given to all the apostles, Mark xvi. Matt. xxviii. The same commandeth St Paul, 2 Tim. iv., "Preach in time and out of time." This is the note and mark to know the bishops and ministers of God from the ministers of the devil, by the preaching tongue of the gospel, and not by shaving, clipping, vestments, and outward apparel.

The text maketh answer to an objection that might be demanded, wherefore God would send Jonas, a man of base sort, to rebuke so great a king with his council, and commonwealth.

Because their sins are come up before the face of the Lord.

Of this answer we learn three things. The *first*, that the Lord seeth, marketh, and is displeased with our sins, although we live in all security, and careless, as though our sins offended God nothing at all.

The *second*, as many times as God sendeth such preachers, as without fear sheweth unto the world God's word and punishment for sin, that their sin is full ripe, and that they must either amend at the preaching, or utterly to perish under the plague and scourge of God. Thus Noah was preacher before the flood, Jonas before the destruction of Ninive, Loth of Sodom, Christ and his apostles of Hierusalem. Seeing now that God hath sent his word, his king, his magistrates, and his preachers into England, it is (take heed of it) a very token that the sins of England is ascended up into his sight, and that out of hand we amend, or suddenly to look for the most severe and cruel punishment of God. All men confess that sin never so abounded; but none of us say, "It is I that provoke the ire of God, and I will amend." The nobility putteth all the fault in the people, the people in the nobility, in the bishops, merchants, priests, and other. But will ye be judged, at one word, by the testimony of a noble wise man? Noble Esay, the prophet, saith, "The ox knoweth his lord, Isai. i. and the ass his owner's stable: woe is me, ye sinful people, people laden with iniquity, a seed malicious, lost children! ye have forsaken the Lord, and the Holy One of Israel ye have provoked;" as Esay i. Let every man look upon himself, knowledge his sin, and study to amend it from the highest to the lowest; for the Lord is ready to smite.

The *third* doctrine out of this place is a description of God's nature, and long-sufferance towards kingdoms, realms, public and private persons: for whereas he might most justly punish and take vengeance upon us for sin, he is yet so merciful that he premonisheth and forewarneth of his scourge to come, by his prophets, apostles, and preachers, and willeth the world to amend. In case they so do, he will turn his ire from them; if they will not, no remedy but utter destruction; as ye may read Gen. vii. of the

[HOOPER.]

_{Gen. vii.
xix.
Exod. xiv.} flood, Gen. xix. of Sodom, Exod. xiv. of Pharao. But let us rather follow the example of the Ninivites, and amend, than the example of the Egyptians, and perish. Thus much is to be taken heed of in the legacy of Jonas, in the first part of the chapter.

Now followeth the second part, containing Jonas' disobedience, after this sort in the text:

> Whereupon Jonas rose to fly from the face of the Lord into Tharsis, and came to Japho, and found a ship pressed towards Tharsis: paying his passage, he went into her, to come with them unto Tharsis.

Jonas was commanded to cry and preach against the Ninivites; but being afeard, and suspecting the difficulty of the vocation, flieth another way. Here, first, are two things to be noted; whither he flieth, and from whence he flieth: the text saith he fled to Tharsis, which some men think is the sea called *Mare Mediterraneum;* but the more true opinion is, that Tharsis is the city called Tunes or Carthage. Japho is the city called Joppe, a haven town in Palestina. He flieth from the face of God; that is, to wit, from the benevolent and merciful God, that appointed him to the vocation of preaching.

Of this text we learn many godly doctrines. First, how hard and difficult a vocation it is to be a preacher, that in case he be not with a singular mercy of God comforted and strengthened, he cannot, nor is it possible he should, preach truly God's word; as it is to be seen by Moses, _{Exod. v. vi.
Isai. vi.
Jer. i. ii.
Matt. x.} Exod. v. vi. Esay vi. Hier. i. ii. Matt. x.; and in this ye may see the diversity between the ministry of God and of the devil, of Christ and of antichrist. Christ's ministry is full of labours, pains, slanders, and calamities: antichrist is full of ease[1], pleasures, commodities, and honours, as ye may see through all the kingdom of the pope; for there is not a bishoprick nor benefice can fall, but ten are ready to take it or it come to the ground; yea, and help away

[1 Ease: care, D. 1.]

the incumbent with an Italian fig before-time, as ye may read of Victor the Third².

The second doctrine is, that whosoever leaveth undone the office commanded unto him by God, flieth from the favour and good-will of God, as it is to be seen, 1 Reg. xv. Here be all bishops and priests admonished to beware how they leave their duties and cures. They fly from the face of God, as many as bear that name, and preach not the word of God, and instruct not the people after the mouth of God. Miserable and cursed is our time of God's own mouth, that there be such dumb bishops, unpreaching prelates, and such ass-headed ministers in the church of God. Christ instituted neither singers nor massers, but preachers and testimonies of his true doctrine. Mark xvi. Matt. xxviii. Luke xxiv. Acts i. He that leaveth this doctrine untaught in the church, or teacheth a contrary doctrine, flieth from the face of God, and do incur the danger and damnation that is written, Ezech. xxxiii. iii. "I will require their loss," saith God to the preacher, "at thy hand." Let no man, therefore, be offended, if the crier speak against the faults of all degrees without exception, seeing he is commanded so to do upon the pain eternal of his soul; and Paul saith, "Woe be unto me if I preach not!" 1 Cor. ix. Let all men take heed to do the thing that appertaineth to their office, least they depart from the face of the Lord; as kings do, if they make any laws contrary to the law of God and the law of nature, or suffer their subjects to be taught in any doctrine for the salvation of their souls beside and contrary to the express word of God. The justice departeth from the face of God, when that he for favour, preposterous pity, or for bribes, judgeth not justly. The gentlemen, when beside charity they help³ themselves with the hurt of their neighbours. The commons of every realm departeth from the favour of God, when seditiously and inobediently they make tumults and sedition, lifting up weapon against their king and rulers, which leadeth to eternal damnation. Rom. xiii. Num. xvi.

[² William of Malmsbury relates that Victor III. had poison administered to him in the cup at the sacrament. Platina says that he died "not without suspicion of being poisoned."]

[³ They help: seek, D. 1.]

But a man might say, Tush! it is not so great a matter if a man walk not in his vocation, neither yet is God so much offended with disobedience. But this fleshly and perverse opinion may soon be corrected, if men would consider the dangers that this poor man Jonas fell into for his disobedience. They be in number six. The first is, the perilous winds that troubleth the ship. The second, his sin and disobedience is detected and made open by lots. The third, he is examined what he is. The fourth, he is constrained to give sentence of death against himself. The fifth, the shipmen cannot save him. The sixth, he is cast into the sea.

The first danger hath two parts: the one sheweth the danger of the ship; the other sheweth how the mariners behaveth themselves in the time of their danger. Of the first thus saith the prophet:

> The Lord hurled a great wind into the sea, and there arose a mighty tempest in the sea, so that the ship was in jeopardy of going in pieces.

Well we may think to escape the danger of God, though we neglect our duty and vocation; but truly it cannot be so. "Whither," saith David, "should I go from thy Spirit, and whither should I flee from thy face?" Psal. cxxxix. There is no corner of the world wherein man may hide himself from the knowledge and punishment of God, if we neglect the works of our vocation. He hath all things in his hand, heaven, earth, the winds, and the waters, with the which he useth to punish the wickedness of transgressors withal at his pleasure, when he will; as it is to be seen, 1 Sam.

Ps. cxxxix.

1 Sam. vii.

Of this place of the text we learn, that whosoever, contrary to God's commandment, studieth to avoid one evil, falleth into many. The bishop or the preacher, that for the love or fear of the world letteth to speak the truth, falleth into the burning and damnation of his own conscience. The people that against God's law would defend the poverty of their bodies, lost body, soul, wife, children, and all together. The corrupt judge in searching to serve his own turn or his friend's in corrupting of justice, bringeth both himself and his friend into the danger of eternal damnation.

The text proceedeth, that sheweth how the mariners behaved themselves in this danger, which thing is diligently to be noted; for in them is expressed a very lively image of all men that lacketh faith, how they fear above measure in the time of trouble. Their doings is expressed four ways: first, their faith[1]; second, each of them calleth upon his own God; third, they exonerate the ship; fourth, they wake Jonas out of his sleep.

The fear declareth the greatness of the danger they were in, and their ignorance of God, who only comforteth in the days and hour of trouble.

That every man calleth upon his own God, it appeareth there were people of sundry and divers nations: and also, what is common to all men under the sun, that have not lost the use of reason; when we be left destitute of human help, we call upon God, not for love, but for fear; as it is said, *Metus primus in orbe Deos fecit*, that is to say, "Fear was the first that made gods in the world." These mariners are of some part to be followed, of some part not: that in the day of trouble they pray, we ought to follow them; that they pray not to the one and sole God, but every man to a sundry god, they may not be followed: for there is but one patron and helper for all men, and he is never, nor nowhere, known but by his word. Man's reason knoweth right well in the time of trouble, that there is a God; but who he is, reason cannot tell: therefore worshippeth reason an idol of his own head, under the name of God; and then followeth man either his own opinion, either the tradition of his elders. And this is the fountain of idololatry; when that every man thinketh him to be his god, that he himself, his elders, or custom hath taken to be God. From hence came such diversity of gods among the gentiles, and so many patrons among the superstitious sort of Christians. These gods altogether be forbid. Exod. xx. Deut. vi. xxxii. Exod. xx.
Deut. vi.
xxxii.

They lighten the ship. When they felt that prayers availed nothing, they turn to labour, which also eased

[[1] So the old editions. A mistake for *fear*.]

them nothing: whereby we learn, that all gods and goddesses be but vanity, saving our God, the Father of Jesus Christ; and no labour nor travail availeth without the favour of God. Luke ix. The woman had spent all she had on physicians, yet nothing the better: so doeth the papists in masses, and yet their conscience nothing more delivered from sin; and those that pray to saints attaineth nothing. If their request be sometime granted them, it is none other than a punishment of their idolatry, 2 Thes. ii.

<small>Luke [viii.]</small>

<small>2 Thess. ii.</small>

The fourth thing they do, they wake Jonas.

> But Jonas gat him under the hatches, where he laid him down and slumbered.

The text noteth two things: one, that Jonas slept; the other, how the mariners awoke him to call upon his God. Jonas' sleep signifieth two things. First, that when we think ourselves most at rest, then be we most in danger, as it is to be seen by Baltheser[1], in the prophet Daniel, and Matt. xxiv. 2 Thess. ii. Luke xii. The second is, to declare the nature of sin. Whiles it is a committing, the prick and danger thereof is not felt, but it delighteth rather man: so without fear ate Adam and Eve the apple; Peter denied Christ. And because God out of hand punisheth not our sin, the devil bewitcheth our minds and wits, and beareth us in hand that he will never punish, and that God seeth not our sin, nor is not so grievously offended with our sins. So yet sleepeth the sin at this day, of them that persecute God and his holy word; the sins of false or negligent bishops and priests, the sin of the corrupt judges, and seditious people: but it will awake one day, as ye may read, Gen. iv. and here by our Jonas. At the hour of our death sin will awake, and with our own sin the devil will kill us eternally, except we awake betime.

<small>Matt. xxiv.
2 Thess. ii.
Luke xii.</small>

That they desire Jonas to pray unto his God, it declareth that all idolatry and superstitious persons think one God to be stronger than the other: as it is to be seen in papistry at this present day, whereas it is disputed

[1 Baltheser: Belshazzar.]

which lady is best, our lady of Bullayne², or our lady of Rome; Saint James in Italy, or Saint James at Compostella³. Farther, this text declareth that idolaters always seek new gods, where as their old god deceiveth them. So is it among Christians; when the matter is plain desperate, they lot the matter between three or four idololatrical pilgrimages, which one of them shall be the patron of his health. Where as the word of God is known, there is no suit but unto one God by the mediation of Christ, beside whom there is no health⁴. This God I commend unto you; unto this God make your prayers; forsake that heretical doctrine that divideth your hearts in prayer, part to God, and part to saints departed; for God is sufficient to help, and will help alone. Esay lxiii. To him be all honour and glory now and for ever. Isai. lxiii.

The end of the First Sermon.

[² This shrine of the Virgin seems to have been in great repute. The English delivered up Bologne to the French, on Saint Mark's day, 1550. The French king entered in triumph fifteen days after, and "offered one great image of silver in the church there which was called 'Our Lady Church'; the which said image he had caused specially to be made in the honour of the said Lady, and caused the same to be set up in the place where the like image before did stand, the which before was taken away by the Englishmen at the winning of the town." Hollingshed Chronicles, Vol. II. p. 1062.]

[³ See Cave's lives of the Apostles; where a full account is given of the fabulous history of St James' body being transported into Spain after his martyrdom. Compostella, the name of the place where the Apostle's remains are said to have been deposited, is described as a corruption of Giacomo Postolo. (Ad Jacobum Apostolum.) The relics of this saint are reported to have wrought such incredible miracles, that Baronius calls Compostella "the great storehouse of miracles lying open to the whole world."]

[⁴ Salvation.]

THE SECOND SERMON UPON JONAS,

MADE BY JOHN HOPER, 26th OF FEBRUARY.

❡ THE PREFACE.

UNTO every man is appointed his vocation; to one this, to another that; one to a private, another to a public vocation; and each of them either is lawful or unlawful. That is unlawful that fighteth and repugneth with the word of God; as the vocation of bawds, idolaters, mass-mongers, common receivers, and maintainers of dicers and dice-houses, with such like. In these, or any like, whosoever continueth[1] still without repentance, is subject to eternal damnation.

The other vocation is lawful, and standeth with the word of God; of the which St Paul speaketh: "In what vocation any man is called, in the same let him abide." But this lawful vocation we transgress two manner of ways: either when we bear the title or name of the vocation, and do nothing appertaining thereunto, which is condemned by God, in that he commanded in Adam all men to avoid idleness, Gen. iii. "In the sweat of thy brows thou shalt eat thy bread;" and Paul, 1 Thess. 2 Thess.: either when we do in the vocation that we should not do; as, for example, a bishop to teach false doctrine for a true; a judge, that should judge truly, corrupteth judgment for favour or money; a merchant to wax richer by false contracts or corrupt wares. Into what danger each man falleth, that any way transgresseth his vocation, it is to be seen by this our Jonas, who in voiding of one danger falleth into six, as ye have heard before: of the which six we have spoken but of one; and in the one noted

Gen. iii.
1 Thess.
2 Thess.

[¹ Continually, D. 1.]

many and profitable doctrines, as well declaring man's infirmity, that cannot help itself out[2] from the dangers of the body; as of the power and good-will of God, that can and will save both from the dangers of body and soul. All men confess him to be the true God, that can and will help all diseases, the Jews, the Turks, the gentiles, the good, the bad. But therein standeth the danger, lest for the true God we call and invocate a false god, and under the name of god we honour and worship the devil, as these mariners did when each of them called to a sundry god; and as the gentiles doth that David speaketh of, Psal. cvi., that they sacrificed their children to the devil, and not to God. David saith, they offered to the devil that they thought was offered to God. And Paul, 1 Corinthians x., calleth the religion of the heathen the table of the devil.

_{Psal. cvi.}

_{1 Cor. x.}

So did the Jews before us; and so do they in these days now, that for every disease they have a sundry god and patron; for the pestilence, St Roch[3]; for the war, St Barbara[4]. In this danger of idololatry be all they that call upon God, and pray unto him, otherwise than he hath appointed by his word. And here we be admonished of two things. The first, that we offer none other obsequy and religion unto God than he himself by his word requireth: if we do, we offer an idol of our own head, and honour the devil under the person and name of God; as those doth that erect and build up images, and altars to say mass upon in the honour of God, which God never commanded. Exod. xxii. Deut. v. The next

_{Exod. xxii. Deut. v.}

[[2] Out: not, in the second edition.]

[[3] St Roch is said to have lived at the close of the thirteenth century. Being on a pilgrimage at Rome, he cured many persons of the plague, but afterwards was himself seized with that disorder at Placentia. Retiring into a forest, he was attended by a dog, who daily brought him a loaf of bread, and licked his sores till he recovered. He died in 1327, at Montpellier, his birth-place. See Maldura's life of St Roch.]

[[4] St Barbara was a celebrated martyr in the third century, whose father, it is related, beheaded her with his own hands, after she had suffered the most cruel tortures for her determined adherence to the christian faith. Simeon Metaphrastes gives a fearful account of her sufferings and death. See Aloysii, Lip. Veron. Sanctorum Historia. Tom. ii. p. 106. See also Asseman. in Calend. Univ. Vol. v. p. 108.]

we be here admonished of is, that we call upon God only in the name of Christ: for he is the door, the way, and the truth; John x. and he alone sheweth us the Father. John i. and vi. Here be condemned not only the Jews and gentiles, but also as many as would know and come to the Father by invocation of the saints departed, by bulls, pardons, peregrinations, mass, and other. Let this error be corrected, and let us leave calling every man to his own god, and call only upon the only God that can and will, in Christ, hear us, as he heard the patriarchs, prophets, and the apostles. And that this be done, it is the office of the king's majesty, his council, and all his magistrates, to see the true book of God, the holy Bible, to be taught and received of his majesty's subjects, after the example of Moses, Josua, David, Josaphat, Ezechias, and Josias, the noble princes of God's people. There was and is one doctrine more, in that the mariners did not only pray, but also lightened the ship. That they prayed and were not heard, ye learn what a vanity it is to pray after the opinion of man; nothing at all it availeth; it never cometh before God, nor easeth the conscience of him that prayeth. Further, that they do not only pray, but also labour, we see our duty; that as God freely giveth help, so we must travail, and do the best we can with prayer, not only to receive and obtain the free help of God, but also to keep it. Thus I thought good to speak before the second danger, which is this: Jonas' sin is detected by lots; so saith the text:

marginal: John x. John i. vi.

They said one to the other, Come, let us cast lots, that we may know for whose cause we are thus troubled: and so they cast lots, and the lot fell upon Jonas.

When they perceived the tempest ceased not with prayer and devotion every man unto his god, they understood that such desperate danger could not come but only from the ire and displeasure of God, for some notable and wonderful crime; and the more was the fear, because the crime was not known, nor no man would be seen culpable of it. They thought it good, therefore, to search the guilty offender by lots; and missed not of their purpose a deal, but found Jonas, the rebellion of God, to be the occasion of their trouble.

Of this text we be learned, that the cause of all trouble, in public and private persons, is sin, as we read, Deut. xxviii. Levit. xxvi. That understood the mariners; and in case be we wise, we will understand the same, and amend it, and not to attribute our adversities to sun or moon, star or planet, as fools do. [Deut. xxviii. Lev. xxvi.]

Of this text we learn again, howsoever sin be hid for the time, yet at length it will be known; some by one means, some by the other: by lots, as our Jonas and Ahab[1], Judicum and 1 Samuel xiv.; by their own confession, as David, 2 Samuel [xii.] Let no man, therefore, think to keep always his sin hid. [Josh. vii.] [1 Sam. xiv.] [2 Sam. [xii.]]

Farther, here we learn how every kingdom and commonwealth may be appeased when it is troubled. If the chief captains and principal occasions of the trouble be known and removed, then shall peace, joy, and quietness follow in the commonwealth; else never, except the scripture of God be false. Men of the best judgment in civil matters many times, under the name and similitude of a ship, understand the commonwealth. In case the ship, which is the commonwealth, be troubled, the master of the ship, that is the king with his council, inquireth[2] diligently of the authors of the trouble, or else the tempest of trouble shall never cease. At this day, gracious king, the ship of the commonwealth is sore moved with winds and tempests. Here your majesty and your most honourable council may not cease, if ye would the ship to come to rest, but take the pain to find out the authors of these troubles.

In case ye will, as indeed ye must, by some means find out the occasions of these troubles and unquietness within your majesty's realm, ye shall not find, as many report, the gospel to be the cause thereof; for it is the word of peace, and the disciples thereof be assured of all grace and God's favour, Deut. xxviii.; and Christ appeased with his presence the troublous waves of the sea, John vi. Upon whom then will the lot of unquietness and trouble [Deut. xxviii.] [John vi.]

[1 Ahab: Achan, Josh. vii.]
[2 Inquireth: inquire, D. 1.]

fall? Upon Jonas; that is to say, upon every man that neglecteth his vocation, and doeth not as he is bid: as when he that should steer the rudder[1] in a ship leaveth her to waves, he that should strike the sails, stretcheth them to more wind; and so, to conclude, none taketh heed of that he should. My gracious lord and king, and ye, my lords of his most honourable council, how many Jonases should there be found in England? Doubtless, too many in every condition and sort of people within this realm, among the nobles, lawyers, bishops, priests, and the common people. Examine all apart, and prove: the nobility make unprofitable expenses, more than their ability can or is able to sustain; they feed a sort of idle and never commended sort of people, neither by God's laws, neither by man's laws; they themselves live idle, and will not labour, neither with hand, neither with wit. What must follow but trouble of the ship, that is to say, oppression of the poor? Esay v.

Isai. v.

The lawyers in all causes hath more respect to lucre and vantage than to justice; insomuch they rejoice, and of other fools be rejoiced at, when they can overcome in a false cause, and so their thievery catcheth up the labours and sweat of the poor.

The bishops and priests unquiet the ship of this realm two manner ways; one by the neglecting of their true duty, the other by a defence of a false and damnable superstition. In the primitive and apostolical church, the office of a bishop and priest was to teach in the congregation of the faithfuls the doctrine of the prophets and apostles, according to the commandment of Christ. Matt. xxviii. Mark xvi. Eph. ii. Now is this integrity turned into false idololatry and devilish superstition—to sing and say mass in the congregation of God. Thus, like thieves and murderers, they do the abomination commanded by man, with massing, conjuring the holy-water bucket, and such like, and leave the preaching of God's word as God commandeth, and as the prophets and apostles hath left us example; and say, when godly kings and magistrates require and command a reformation of their evils, the ministry of the church is contemned with such false slanders,

Matt. xxviii.
Mark xvi.
Eph. ii.

[1 Steer the rudder. Stirre the rother. Old Editions.]

as the ignorant people will do more for the bishops and priests of Ball[2] than for God, God's word, or his anointed magistrate, as it appeared this last summer[3].

The people and commonalty of this realm trouble the ship of this commonwealth. For do the king and magistrate what he can, the people will never be content. Many of them live in idleness, and will not labour; and in case they cannot have that they would, they convert themselves to sedition and treason, and care no more to kill and oppress their lawful king and magistrates, than the devil cared to kill Adam in paradise. Gen. iii. They should call unto the Lord for redress of their things, and not to redress it themselves. Psal. l.

Gen. iii.

Psal. l.

How is it possible, where every sort offendeth in the commonwealth, but that the ire and vengeance of God should send unto our ship winds of adversity? I know that Jonas was never better known to be the occasion of this tempest in the sea, than I know these four sorts of people to be the trouble, and will be the destruction, of this commonwealth, if they be not found out by lot and wisdom betime. But a man might ask, what should the king's majesty do in such a case with all these four sorts of Jonases? Let his majesty learn of these mariners; then shall he do well; and as they did with Jonas, so the king's majesty must do with these four sorts of people. What they did, the prophet shall tell his own tale, and declare the third danger he fell into, which is the examination of Jonas in this form:

> They said unto him, Shew us, I pray thee, how this trouble happeneth unto us? What is thine occupation? Whence comest thou? What countryman art thou? Of what nation art thou?

[2 Ball : Baal.]

[3 This has reference to the insurrections in Devonshire &c. Cranmer speaks of "some seditious priests" who encouraged the people to rebel; and Burnet mentions "that the priests inflamed the enraged multitude with all the artifices they could imagine." Hist. Reform. Part II. Book 1, pp. 375, 376. London, 1841. See also Archbishop Cranmer's answers to the fifteen articles of the Rebels, 1549. Strype's Life of Cranmer, Vol. II.]

In these ethnical mariners we see a singular discretion, wit, and humanity. What, if our mariners, Christians, had suffered the like danger and detriment for any man's sake within their ship? Doubtless, they would have sworn, and out of hand, without examination, have cast him into the sea. But these men be wise, that they do not only search to know his fault by lots, but diligently seeketh to know all the circumstances, how he fell into this danger, lest Jonas should account himself unjustly condemned. Of this doing of the mariners we learn two things: one, humanity towards the afflicted persons; the other, that all kings and magistrates ought to condemn this law as a thing pestiferous and damned by God's laws, to execute sentence against any man, before his cause and matter be heard: for it is contrary to the law of God, the law of nature, and the law of man; yea, God commandeth that no man should be condemned with the testimony of one man. Deut. xvii.

Deut. xvii.

Here is for the king's majesty and his council one more doctrine to be learned of these mariners. I said, that four sorts of people were the occasion of the trouble of his majesty's ship, this realm of England; but I said not that every man of these four sorts was guilty of the tempest: therefore there must be lots, and examination of every degree, and of each person in his degree, that the innocent be not punished, neither the transgressor favoured. And these must be examined by the master and his shipmen; that is, to our purpose, of the king's majesty and his council; so that, in case the godly without respect of persons seek to know, and upon truth and knowledge punish as they know, the ship of this commonwealth shall rest in peace and quietness: if it be not searched for and amended, the ship of the commonwealth shall at last be burst in pieces, which the Lord defend! Amen.

THE THIRD SERMON UPON JONAS,

MADE BY JOHN HOPER, THE 5th OF MARCH.

☞ THE PREFACE.

WE never read in any writers, whether they be holy or profane, of any kingdom or commonwealth that continually endured without tumults, sedition, or war, either by foreign and outward enemies, either among itself by conspiracy, treason, and disobedience of subjects of the same realm: and the same evil not being in time taken heed of and redressed, brought always the kingdom or commonwealth from trouble and sedition unto utter ruin and confusion. We will omit and pass over to speak of the kingdom of the Assyrians, the Persians, Greeks, and Romans; although of their original, continuance, and destruction, the holy Bible maketh in Daniel the prophet, and other places of the scripture, much mention of. We will speak but of two kingdoms, of Juda and Israel. What troubles, contention, wars, sedition, and rebellion they suffered, and at last came clean to nought, the books of the Kings and Chronicles doth record, and the prophet Jeremy. What the causes of these troubles and destruction were, the godly readers of the scriptures be not ignorant; but the men of that time, the princes, the kings, neither the priests, would understand, but assigned false causes: the preaching of God's word, 3 Reg. xviii. For thus saith Ahab unto Elias the prophet: "Art not thou he that troubleth Israel?" And so saith the people, Hiere. xliv. "The word of God that thou hast spoken unto us in the name of the Lord, we will not receive it; but we will do whatsoever seem unto us good, that we may do sacrifice unto the queen of heaven, and offer our offerings unto her, as we have done and our fathers, our kings and our princes, in the cities of Juda, and in the streets of Jerusalem. Then had we abundance of all things, and well was it with us, and we felt no evil. As soon

1 Kings xviii.

Jer. xliv.

as we left offering to the queen of heaven, and sacrificed no more sacrifice unto her, we lacked all things, and be consumed with war and hunger." Hiere. xliv. But the true prophets of God shewed the true causes of these evils to be the contempt of God's word, as Elias said unto Ahab: "I trouble not Israel, but thou and thy father's house troubleth it. For ye have forsaken the commandment of the Lord, and thou goest after Baalim." But the princes and the people continually defended the false causes, and accounted the prophets of God, that would have corrected their error, to be seditious and traiterous persons, and even so persecuted and killed them for their true preaching; till at the last they perished, and their realm with them: as ye may read, 4 Reg. xvii., and in the last book of the Chronicles, in the last chapter. Unto the lesson of those two chapters I exhort the wise and godly hearer; for ye shall gather of those places, that the contempt of God's word was the occasion of the loss of these realms.

The same evil vexeth us at this present day. The ship of this commonwealth of England is tossed upside down, and the occasion thereof is imputed and laid unto Christ, and his holy word, though falsely; for Christ's nature is to appease and quiet all troubles and tempests with his presence, John vi. Therefore this false and preposterous cause of trouble must be taken heed of, if we wish the ship of this kingdom to come to rest. We shall never bring it to pass, until such time as we agree and confess that Jonas is the occasion why the realm is thus unquieted; that is to say, as many as be in this realm, that neglect or pervert their appointed vocation.

I said, O king, that Jonas might be found among four sorts of people within your majesty's realm; among the priests, noblemen, lawyers, and the common people. But lest any man should think I condemned every man within the ship of your commonwealth, we will follow the wisdom and commendable doings of these shipmen, which were not only content to have found out Jonas the cause of their trouble by lots, but also diligently they examine him. So the same thing, most gracious king, we must do. But before we take upon us their examination, we will pray unto Almighty God for his holy Spirit of wisdom, lest in this

necessary and profitable examination we err and be
deceived; and also that they upon whom the lots
do fall, and cannot justly excuse their faults,
may learn to amend them and turn
unto the Lord, and from henceforth may live in purity and
innocency of truth and
virtue, all the days
of their lives.
So be it.

The end of the Preface.

Ye have heard how Jonas for the contempt and disobeying of his vocation to have fallen into six great dangers. Of two we have spoken, and now we be come to the third, where as he and his facts be diligently examined, which doubtless was a great cross and trouble unto him; for there is nothing that displeaseth man more than to have his faults hidden to be brought unto light and knowledge. God, notwithstanding, suffereth that many times for our good and profit; that we being brought unto a knowledge of our sins, might hate the same and pray for the remission thereof: and so is it better, howsoever the blind flesh judgeth, to have our sins, if God will, opened for our salvation, than hid to our loss and damnation.

In this examination we see not only the danger of Jonas, but also the office of every good magistrate that meaneth to quiet and rest his commonwealth, being in trouble.

Those should be examined, that by any sign, or probable suspicion, seem to be the authors of tumults. And this using moderation in examining, the innocent and good shall be free from pain and punishment; and the culpable and guilty found worthy of correction. First, therefore, let us examine the bishops and priests, whether those that know the will of God by his holy word, diligently teach and preach the same unto other. Then, whether any man of that vocation teach false doctrine in the church of Christ. If the one do too little in the first, and the other too much in the second, or the one neglect the first, and the other too diligent in the second, both these be Jonas, and occasion that the ship is moved. Against the negligent sort speaketh Ezechiel, iii. xxxiii., and Agge i. with vehement words, and threateneth eternal damnation to such as preacheth not, nor buildeth up the temple of God's congregation: likewise St Paul, 1 Cor. ix. Against those that teach false doctrine, speaketh Christ, John x., and Paul, 1 Tim. iv. Hiere. xiv.

<small>Ezek. iii. xxxiii. Hag. i.</small>
<small>1 Cor. ix.</small>
<small>John x. 1 Tim. iv. Jer. xiv.</small>

Among the noblemen, Jonas that troubleth the commonwealth may be found among two sorts of them. The one of them hath enough given him from God, yet is not content therewithal; but for avarice and love of himself, and his insatiable covetousness, scrapeth and gathereth together, whether with the law, or against the law, it maketh no force, so he have it. So this Jonas and troubler of the ship with all injuries and wrongs rather would add somewhat where indeed is too much, than to depart[1] a little where as is nothing at all. And in vain glory and pride of the mammon of the world, they will condemn and disdain the very image of God in the poor. Against whom speaketh Salomon, Prov. xiv. "He that calumniateth the poor, abraideth his Creator." Take example hereof out of the ninth of John, how the general council of the Pharisees laid to the poor blind man his blindness. Their reproach of God's work was reprehended; and the insatiable and covetous hearts of them be condemned by Esay the prophet, chapter v.: "Cursed be ye that join house to house, and field to field." The experience of this curse had Ahab, that ungodly took from Naboth his vineyard. If these men that hath enough will not move the ship of your highness's commonwealth, let them leave their ravening, and give God thanks for that they have, and to their ability help, and not rob the poor. The other sort of noble or gentlemen, that make more expense than their revenues and condition is able to bear, and liveth by dice, cards, whoredom, fraud, guile, deceit, theft, and such like; indifferent examination, not only by God's laws, but also by man's laws, will prove them not only to be disobedient Jonas, but also stark thieves.

<small>Prov. xiv.</small>
<small>John ix.</small>
<small>Isai. v.</small>

The lawyers, if they be examined diligently, there will

[1 Depart: part with, give.]

be so many found among them to unquiet the ship of this commonwealth, that few or none will be found clear. And among the lawyers I put judges and justices: the one for gain careth not to defend the falsest cause and most unjust matter that can be brought unto him, and promiseth, like a thief, the cause to be good, till he have emptied his poor client's purse. Then washeth he his hands with as much foul honesty as he can, and referreth the doubtful cause, above his learning, to the ignorant men of the shire, to be judged at home, like a fool, where as his purse can no longer cause his prattler and ignorant lawyer to keep his cause aloof and out of the shire. And indeed such a subject as cannot find in his heart, after God's laws, to end his contention without strife by the arbitrement of those that be his neighbours, is worthy to find such a Jonas as will never leave blowing at his purse, till he have unladed it even to the bottom, and have caused him to spend as much in recovery of twenty shillings by lease, as he might have purchased twenty shillings in fee simple. I damn not the law, that is good; but these thieves that abuse the law: for their doings is nothing but guile and deceit, and a noble kind of thievery. Against the which speaketh Zachary in his fifth chapter; and God, Exod. xx. Deut. v.: "Thou shall commit no theft;" "Thou shalt give no false testimony against thy neighbour." These Jonases doth not only give false testimony, but also for lucre defendeth the same; and not for a day, but for a year, and years: the more shame it is to be suffered. The justices be also Jonas; for they receive rewards and bribes, which blindeth the eyes, Deut. xvi., and maketh them to corrupt justice, to their eternal damnation if they amend not. Against whom speaketh Salomon, Prov. xvii.: "He that quitteth the evil doer, and condemneth the innocent, be both execrable and damned before God." *Zech. v. Exod. xx. Deut. v. Deut. xvi. Prov. xvii.*

Among the common people ye shall also find many Jonases; but that we may the better espy them out, we will divide them into the rustics, or people of the country, and into the citizens. All and every country or husbandman that liveth not of his labour, and giveth himself to idleness, and so moveth sedition and treason against their lawful king and magistrate; or privily in their conventicles and assemblies speak evil, curse or provoke any thing against their magistrates, they can nor will learn neither to know God, neither to obey their prince; these be those among this sort of people that be Jonases, and troubleth the state of this realm. Among the citizens be a great number that trouble the ship also, as adulterous unpunished, the fraud and guile of the merchandise, idleness the mother of all mischief, theft, murder, blasphemous oaths, conspiracy, and treason, with open slander and rebuke of God's most holy word. These things and such like tosseth the poor ship, that hardly she can sail above the water; and so displeaseth the majesty of God, that he will never cease from sending of tempests, till those Jonases be amended, or cast into the sea.

But before I come to Jonas' answer upon his examination, because I know this saying to be true, *Obsequium amicos, veritas odium parit*, that is, "flattery obtaineth friendship, and the truth displeasure;" lest any man should for my truth and liberty be offended, I will briefly purge myself. Doubtless it were pleasure to me to speak nothing at all, in case the necessity of my vocation, the danger of these Jonases, and the salvation of this ship of our commonwealth forced me not thereunto. As touching myself, I am called unto this place to cry: in case I do not, I know all the blood of these Jonases shall be required at my hand; which God forbid! It were better I should call so hard as heaven and earth might sound again of my voice.

The salvation of these wicked Jonases moveth also to speak in this matter, and with the trump of God's word to wake them out of their sleep, lest they slumber and rest so long in their wickedness, that they go sleeping to eternal damnation. These therefore I call upon for the amendment of their knowledge and life.

Farther, the love I bear unto the king's majesty and to this commonwealth of England compelleth me to speak; seeing I see the angry hand of God already stretched forth to punish us, if we awake not out of sin. Last of all, be it known to all men, that I speak in the condemnation of the evil, and commendation of the good. And that all men may easily find out and know, among these four sorts of people, the Jonases and troublers of this ship and commonwealth of England, I give you one most true and general rule, which is this: whosoever, or of whatsoever degree he be, that is, or sheweth himself to be, offended with this my free and indifferent speaking of God's word, he or they, be they what they may[1], are the very Jonases and troublers of this commonwealth. And these men love more darkness than light, more to trouble the ship than to rest her. But now to the text wherein is contained Jonas' answer upon his examination.

He answered them: I am an Hebrew, and fear the Lord God of heaven, that made the sea and the dry land.

When as Jonas perceived he could no longer cloak and hide his offence, he doth not only confess his fault, but also maketh them privy and uttereth his faith and religion he hath in God unto them. In that he confesseth his fault, we learn that the first gree[2] and proceeding to mercy and remission, is the knowledge of the sin, which is a thing most difficile and hard to the flesh, to say, I have offended the Lord, and will amend; for either we deny our sin with Cain, or extenuate and excuse it with Saul. Would to God our Jonases would acknowledge their faults, and not excuse it nor extenuate it! It is but a mockery once in a year to acknowledge and murmur our faults in the priest's ear; but we should from the heart repent the neglecting of our bounden duties, and unfeignedly amend it, which is not only painful to the flesh, but also grateful unto God. I exhort all men therefore that knoweth themselves guilty—as indeed there is none of us of all parts innocent—we say with David: "We have offended the Lord." Yet is not this enough, to confess our faults; but therewithal we must make a confession of our faith: but not such a confession as most men use, but such as may most be like unto Jonas'. And let them embrace only Christ and his doctrine, and worship God in spirit and verity, as his word teacheth. This I mean: let the priests teach according to the word of God, the noblemen govern and rule thereby, the lawyers conform their law to

[[1] What they be may, in the old editions.] [[2] Gree: degree, step.]

God's law, and such laws as be contrary to God's laws abrogate and abolish. The people should hear the word of God, give faith unto it, and follow it. And so say every man of us with Jonas: "I am an Hebrew," that is to say, "I am a christian man, and will from henceforth forsake my sin, that disquieteth not only mine own conscience, but also the whole commonwealth." It followeth how the mariners took Jonas' answer.

> Then were the men exceedingly afraid, and said unto him, Why didst thou so? (for they knew that he was fled from the presence of the Lord, because he had told them), and said moreover unto him, What shall we do unto thee, that the sea may cease from troubling of us? For the sea wrought, and was troublous.

In these mariners we see three things; fear, rebuke of disobedience, and taking of counsel how to save the ship. This fear, it is most like, sprang of this: that the mariners had heard Jonas say, how he was commanded by God to preach unto the Ninivites their destruction, and the city's also, for their sin. The mariners, knowing themselves guilty of the same, themselves being both idolaters, infidels, and of corrupt condition and living, feared the like punishment. Who is it, that will not tremble at the angry countenance of God's displeasure? But now-a-days our stony and indurate hearts be past all fear, and turneth the threatenings of God to a laughter, saying in their hearts, There is no God.

That these gentilish mariners rebuke Jonas of disobedience, it declareth the fault to be so great when any man leaveth his vocation, and specially the vocation of preaching, that it meriteth and is worthy to be rebuked of all men. But such is now the proud minds of bishops and pastors, that it will suffer no rebuke or christian admonition; but will be lauded and praised, yea, in evil doing and omission of their vocation, as it is to be seen in that horrible and wicked decree: *Si papa*[1]. And not only

[1 *Si papa suæ et fraternæ salutis negligens, deprehenditur inutilis, et remissus in operibus suis, et insuper a bono taciturnus, quod magis*

the pope, but also every man that sleepeth and delighteth in his sin, refuseth all manner of admonitions. If Jonas took well at worth the reprehension of the heathen, it is more than a shame one Christian to forsake the admonition of another.

In that they ask counsel of Jonas how to save the ship, they declare a singular humanity towards a stranger; that although by the means of him they stood in danger both of life and goods, yet would they leave no means they could to save him, though it were with their great loss and danger.

Thus we be bound to do as occasion shall serve; not cruelly without discretion to revenge, but charitably with patience to bear with the weak, until such time as the law requireth execution of the evil. Now followeth the answer of Jonas wherewithal he condemneth himself, as it is plain in the text, and it[2] is the fourth danger he fell into.

Take me and cast me into the sea; so shall it let you be in rest: for I wot it is for my sake that this great tempest is come upon you.

In this answer we learn and know, what is the nature and condition of every penitent man, to judge himself worthy pain and punishment. And that is so true, in case we judge not so of ourselves, and say, "Heretofore I was accounted and took myself for a christian man, but indeed I was the contrary; wherefore I am worthy of punishment;" we be but hypocrites and dissemblers. Thus should the nobleman say, the lawyer, the priest, and the common sort of men, as David teacheth. 2 Sam. xxiv. When he saw 2 Sam. xxiv. the commonwealth punished, and in danger of destruction for his offence, he said unto the Lord, as Jonas did: "I have sinned, I have done evil; what hath these sheep of-

officit sibi et omnibus; nihilominus innumerabiles populos catervatim secum ducit, primo mancipio Gehennæ, cum ipso plagis multis in æternum vapulaturus; hujus culpas istic redarguere præsumit mortalium nullus: quia cunctos ipse judicaturus, a nemine est judicandus, nisi deprehendatur a fide devius: pro cujus perpetuo statu universitas fidelium tanto instantius orat, quanto suam salutem post Deum ex illius incolumitate animadvertit propensius pendere. Corpus Juris Can. Dec. 1. Par. Dist. xl. c. vi.]

[2 It, omitted in D. 1.]

fended? let thine ire and displeasure be against me and my father's house."

But, O my gracious lord and king, such penitent and sorrowful Jonases be far out of your realm; for none will confess their faults. They will rather say, Let the Bible in English, and the preacher of God's word, be cast into the sea, and so shall follow quietness, for it was never well sith preaching began. But these be, most gracious king and honourable councillors, Caiphas' fellows, that said, "Ye understand not." John xi. chapter. But what followed? It happened unto the wicked as he feared. They lost their commonwealth, as their fathers did before, and came into bondage both of body and soul.

<small>John xi.</small>

Now followeth the fifth danger that Jonas fell into. The mariners cannot save him, as the text saith.

> Nevertheless the men assayed with rowing to bring the ship to land: but it would not be; because the sea wrought so, and was so troublous against them.

In these mariners the Holy Ghost teacheth us two things: the one, how they would have saved the troubler of the ship; the other, that they could not save him. In the first is noted the nature and condition of every godly magistrate that would, if God would, and the law, all men to be saved: as Moses did pray for the people that rebelled, for Aaron and Mary¹, his brother and sister. Josua called disobedient Ahab² son. Here is the partial and corrupt judgment of kings, magistrates, judges, and such as bear office in the commonwealth, horribly condemned, that serve not the law, but master the law; and for lucre or affection damneth him the law quitteth, and saveth him the law condemneth, contrary to the doctrine of Salomon. Prov. xvii. Deut. xix. Luke xxii. Rom. xiii. James iv.

<small>Prov. xvii.
Deut. xix.
Luke xxii.
Rom. xiii.
James iv.</small>

That they could not save Jonas, we learn that no commonwealth can be quieted except the transgressors be punished. Josh. vii. God giveth no victory to the children of Israel, till Ahab² be punished. The plague ceased not from the Israelites, till Phinees had slain the adulterous. Num. xxv.

<small>Josh. vii.</small>

<small>Num. xxv.</small>

[¹ Mary: Miriam.]   [² Ahab: Achan.]

And the Lord saith, in Ezechiel xxxiii. "Ye lift up your Ezek. xxxiii. eyes to your idols, and shed blood; and think ye, ye shall possess this land? Ye pollute each another's wife, and should ye inhabit this land?" Hitherunto alludeth Saint Paul, Eph. v. "Let no man seduce you with profane words; for Eph. v. these things cometh the ire of God upon the children of distrust."

Generally, we learn that there is no more pestiferous hurt can come unto a commonwealth, than over much lenity and preposterous pity, to suffer the laws of a realm to be broken and neglected, without punishment of the transgressor: as it shall be more declared hereafter. Now to the text, which containeth the prayer of the shipmen in this wise.

Wherefore they cried unto the Lord, and said, O Lord, let us not perish for this man's death, neither lay thou innocent blood to our charge: for thou, O Lord, hast done even as thy pleasure was.

Of this oration, first, we learn that the mariners were converted unto God by the preaching of one Jonas. Before each man called upon a sundry God, now all call upon one God. They excuse not their old idololatry for their old custom's sake, nor yet for the authority of their forefathers; but simply they embrace the truth. The same should we follow, and for our doctrine it is written, as saith Saint Paul, in the fifteenth chapter of his epistle to the Romans: "Whatsoever things are written, are written for our learning; that we, through patience and comfort of the scriptures, should have hope." Casting away all idololatry and false honourings of God, we should, in Christ, embrace and receive the everlasting God and his infallible word; seeing we be not moved thereunto by one Jonas, but by many; by king, by council, and many other men of God.

The second thing we learn out of this prayer is, how they desire God not to impute unto them the death of Jonas, which had not hurt them, but himself in disobeying the Lord's commandment: wherein we may see how the gentiles and ethnicks abhorred murder and manslaughter, and accounted it horrible and a thing damned by the law of nature.

They were in the sea, and no man could have accused them of murder; yet perceived they well, that the eyes of God could mark them wheresoever they were, and would punish the fact. And wisely they judged: for so teacheth us all the scripture of God, as it shall now appear; for I will somewhat touch this horrible crime of murder more at large. Murder is commit two manner of ways, by chance and ignorantly, or of malice and wittingly. Ignorantly, when against his will, doing and meaning nothing less than murder, against his will killeth. Such a murderer by the law should not die; for God absolveth and quitteth him, and prepared in the commonwealth of the Israelites sanctuaries and refuges for them, whither as they might flee for their safeguard, Exod. xxi. Numb. xxxv. Josh. xx., lest their blood should be shed again. He that of malice and willingly killeth a man, should noways be saved; for unto such the Lord commandeth death again. Exod. xxi. Levit. xxiv.

Exod. xxi.
Num. xxxv.
Josh. xx.

Exod. xxi.
Lev. xxiv.

And also in the time of the law of nature this was the commandment of God for murder, Gen. ix. "He that sheddeth a man's blood, shall have his blood shed again:" and so saith Christ: Matt. xxvi. "He that striketh with the sword shall perish with the sword." This sin is so horrible, that no indulgence or pardon should pity the offence, nor pardon the fault; but the murderer, in case he fled to the high altar, he should be fet[1] forth: as ye may see the experience in Joab at the commandment of Salomon: 3 Regum ii. and read Num. xxxv. If the magistrate dispense, either for fear of him that should suffer execution, or for any profit or gain, and punish it not, what doth he other than provoke the ire of God against himself and the whole realm? for the Lord saith, he will not dwell in the earth till it be purged with the blood of him that shed the blood, Num. xxxv. Let all men therefore in the commonwealth know and fear this doctrine of Paul: Rom. xiii. "The magistrate beareth not a sword in vain." Let the magistrate take heed of two things: first, that under the pretext and cloak of the law, he serve not

Gen. ix.

Matt. xxvi.

1 Kings ii.
Num. xxxv.

Num. xxxv.

Rom. xiii.

[¹ Fet: fetched.]

his affection or gain, nor punish the innocent. In this offended the kings and magistrates of the Israelites, that for the maintenance of their superstition, false religion, and corrupt manners, killed and put to death the prophets and the apostles. So Jesabel caused Naboth to be slain. 1 Kings xxi. 3 Regu. xxi. The second, let the magistrate take heed he absolve not him that God condemneth, and commandeth to be punished, for gain, affection, good intention, or else for any foolish and preposterous pity: for so doing Saul lost his kingdom: 1 Sam. xv. read the place. And Ahab, 1 Sam. xv. the king of Israel, for dimissing of Bennaud, God said, "Thy soul shall be for his soul." 3 Regum, fourteen. 1 Kings xiv.

Even as here is occasion to admonish of justice towards evil-doers, so it is to speak of war, and how it may be used lawfully by magistrates. The magistrate offendeth when he beginneth or continueth any unjust battle, or of affection punisheth any innocent person: so Josias offended, although he was a good man, in making war with the Egyptians, where as honest conditions of peace was offered, and was slain for his labour. The magistrate, of the other part, may offend, if he, in case he see his subjects oppressed, and will not defend them, as Abraham did his nephew Loth, and other. Again, this battle he is daily bound unto,—to war against vice, and to punish sin; and in case he see any rebellion to resist the just execution of justice, not to fear; for God will help his proceedings. Deut. xiii. And it may be seen, that God will favour the Deut. xiii. magistrate that fighteth against his own brother, if it be to amend vice and to kill sin; for in manner the whole tribe of Benjamin was destroyed for the defence of adultery. Further, a magistrate fighteth justly, when he resisteth unjust force, whether it be of foreign enemies, or of his own rebellious subjects. Of such laws as should be kept in the time of war it is written, Deut. xx. xxiii. Luke iii., Deut. xx. xxiii. Our warriors have made of war a means and way to all robbery and spoil. The captain by his faith is bound to have as many as his allowance chargeth him withal: but like a thief, he deceiveth the king both of his number of men, and robbeth him of his goods; and, for lack of true payment to the half number that he is appointed unto, he wearieth the good will of the poor soldiers, that Luke iii.

extreme poverty, with sickness, for lack of payment of their wages, causeth them to pass neither of the king, neither of the commonwealth.

And as these unjust and already damned captains, (except they repent,) with receivers, paymasters, victuallers, and other, destroy not only the law and majesty of arms, but also deceive the king, by pilling and polling[1] the poor and needy soldiers; so decay and undo they the whole commonweal; for they come to serve the commonwealth of little or no value at all: in serving of the commonwealth they enrich themselves unjustly, to the utter impoverishing and beggaring both of the commonwealth and the heads thereof.

And well both magistrate and soldier meriteth the same: for the one trusteth he knoweth not whom, other than upon report; the other prepareth himself to the war for defence of his country with whoredom, theft, and all abomination; and by false and thievish means bringeth more to the war than is his own. No marvel then, though God set such a thief over him as will give him less than is his due. True men were wont to go to battle, and such as prepared themselves with the fear of God to live and die for their magistrate and country; now the verier thief and blasphemer of the God of battle, the better soldier. Well, God may give the victory to such blasphemers for a time; but doubtless it will not, nor cannot continue. Look upon all the wars that Moses writeth of in his five books, and then shall ye know the same. Wherefore I humbly require all magistrates, both in peace and war, to punish chiefly these two vices, adultery and blasphemy, in case they would have either victory in war, or quietness in peace.

As touching swearing and blasphemy, it is known unto all men of God, how the law condemneth it in the first table: Exod. xx. Deut. v. "Thou shalt not take the name of the Lord in vain; for God will not leave unpunished such as abuse his name." Of an oath, I think it therefore convenient to speak somewhat. There is two manner of oaths: the one of custom or of sport; the other serious and grave, required and taken before the magis-

Exod. xx.
Deut. v.

[1 Robbing and cheating.]

trate or judge. The first is devilish, damnable, and naught of every part, and forbidden by God to all christian men. The other, that is taken for the glory of God, the defence of the truth, or help of a man's neighbour, as necessity shall require, is lawful and godly. But in this lawful oath a man may offend two manner of ways: first, if his heart and mind be not according to his words, but that his mouth speaketh one thing, and the heart thinketh another thing; the second, if he that sweareth swear by any creatures. Both these be blasphemous before God.

And in case it be damnable in a naughty matter to swear by creatures, is it not the same, trow ye, daily and foolishly, of custom, to swear by a man's hand, his head, by the mass, and such like? The more vile the thing is we swear by, the more is the oath detestable before God. Wherefore, in things not necessary and required lawfully, to swear by any thing is sin. In weighty matters, to swear by any thing except by God is no less offence.

That may we see four manner of ways: by reason; the holy scripture; examples; and the canon law. By reason, thus: To swear is to protest and promise the thing we swear to be true before him that knoweth the thoughts and cogitations of the heart: that knoweth only and solely God: therefore is it blasphemy to swear or attribute the same to any creature, as they do that sweareth by creatures.

Again, every oath hath annexed with it an invocation and execration: an execration, that he by whom we swear may punish and curse us if we swear false; an invocation, that he by whom we swear would help us if we swear true. But only God can save and lose: reason would then him only to be sworn by.

The authority of the scripture. This also is double: the one teacheth by whom we should swear, the other by whom we should not swear: that is, by God and by no creatures. Deut. vi. x. "Thou shalt fear the Lord thy God and worship him, and also swear by his name." Esay xlv. "Unto me shall every knee bow, and every tongue swear." In the lxv. speaking of the calling of the gentiles, he sayeth, "He that will swear shall swear by the

<small>Jer. xii.</small> true God." And Jer. xii. "They shall swear, The Lord liveth."

That no man should swear by creatures, ye have Exod. xxiii. "Ye shall not think upon the name of strange gods; neither shall it be heard out of your mouths." <small>Josh. xxiii.</small> Josue xxiii., the people be admonished not to swear by the names of the gods that the people used, whither they <small>Jer. v.</small> were going. Hierem. v. it is said that the people offended, because they sweared by the gods that were not God. And the people think it is no sin to annex a creature with God: hear what Sophony[1] the prophet <small>Zeph. i.</small> saith, chap. i. "I will, saith the Lord, destroy them that worship and swear by Malchon," that is to say, by their patron. Where as the prophet meaneth, they that swear by God and creatures matcheth and setteth God and the devil in one chair and seat.

Examples, out of the scriptures: "Abraham sware by the most high God." "God sweareth by himself." Polycarpus would rather suffer the flames of fire, than to swear by Cæsar's fortune. Euseb. Libro iv. chap. xv.

The canon law[2]. Causa xxii. Q. i. *Clericum per creaturas*, and, *Et si quis per creaturas*, and, *Si aliqua causa*, also, *Movet te iterum*; thus the laws begin: and the gloss[3] upon the same places requireth us to swear only by God.

I have tarried the longer in this matter, because I

[1] Sophony: Zephaniah.]

[2] Clericum per creaturas jurantem acerrime esse objurgandum: si perstiterit in vitio, excommunicandum.

Si quis per capillum Dei vel caput juraverit, vel alio modo blasphemia contra Deum usus fuerit; si in ecclesiastico ordine, deponatur; si laicus, anathematizetur. Et si quis per creaturas juraverit acerrime castigetur, &c.

Si aliqua causa fuerit, modicum videtur facere, qui jurat per Deum. Qui autem jurat per evangelium, majus aliquid fecisse videtur. Quibus similiter dicendum est: stulti, scripturæ sanctæ propter Deum sunt, non Deus propter scripturas.

Movet te, utrum ejus fide utendum sit, qui ut eam servet, per dæmonia juraverit. Ubi te volo prius considerare, utrum si quispiam per Deos falsos juraverit se fidem servaturum, et eam non servaverit, non tibi videatur bis peccare. Si enim &c. Corp. Juris Can. Decret. 2 Pars, Caus. xxii. Q. i. can. 9. 10. 11. 16.]

[3] Hic patet quod non est licitum jurare per creaturas, &c.—Decretum Gratiani. Antverpii 1573. co. 1300.]

happened to see of late a certain book for the making of
deacons, priests, and bishops, wherein is required an oath
by saints; whereat I did not a little wonder[4]. And how
it is suffered, or who is the author of that book, I well
know not. I am led to think it to be the fault of the
corrector in the printing, for two causes: one is, because
in the oath for the bishop is no mention made of any
saints; the other cause is, that in the same book the
minister must confess, at the receiving of his vocation, that
the book of God, the holy scripture, to be perfect and
sufficient for the salvation of man. Yet do I much marvel
that in the same book it is appointed, that he that will
be admitted to the ministry of God's word or his sacraments, must come in white vestments; which seemeth to
repugn plainly with the former doctrine, that confessed the
only word of God to be sufficient. And sure I am, they
have not in the word of God, that thus a minister should
be apparelled, nor yet in the primitive and best church.
It is rather the habit and vesture of Aaron and the
gentiles, than of the ministers of Christ. Further, where,
and of whom, and when have they learned, that he that
is called to the ministry of God's word, should hold the
bread and chalice in one hand and the book in the
other hand? Why do they not as well give him in his
hand the fount and the water? for the one is a sacrament
as well as the other. If the fount be too great, take him
a basin with water, or such like vessel. But in this
matter and in other, as tolerable things be to be borne with
for the weak's sake awhile, so I think it not meet, before
the king's majesty and his most honourable council, to
halt in any part, but to say the truth; that they, knowing the same, may redress it as soon as may be, as my
part is, and all other private persons', to pray them to do
the same, and beseech God to restore us to the primitive
church, which never yet had nor shall have any match
or like. Before all things beware of an oath by any creatures, except ye will be glad to have God's displeasure.

[4 See the Form and Manner of making and consecrating of archbishops, bishops, priests, and deacons, Grafton, 1549. which is reprinted
in "Documents of the Reign of King Edward VI.," by the Parker
Society. See also the notes in Keeling's Liturgiæ Britannicæ, 1842.]

Now followeth the sixth danger of Jonas how he is cast into the sea.

So they took Jonas, and cast him into the sea; and the sea left raging. And the men feared the Lord exceedingly, doing sacrifices, and making vows unto the Lord.

Here see we two things: Jonas cast into the sea, and how the sea left thereupon his raging. Out of the first learneth every magistrate and king their office, to cast out of their commonwealth as many Jonases as they find stubborn, and will not amend their lives. If Jonas in the sea could not be saved, that offended but in neglecting of his duty, and yet confessed his fault, and converted the mariners, what may we think? Is it possible to sail or live quietly with so many obstinate Jonases? Nay, doubtless. What remedy then? Let them be cast all into the sea. But lest men should be too much offended with this severe punishment, as though I would all to be cast into the sea, I will bring the examination of the matter to the four sorts of people that I spake of before; and so appoint of every sort whom the king's majesty must cast into the sea, or send to the gallies.

First, let us speak of the bishops and priests. Their office was in the primitive and first church to be preachers of God's word, and ministers of Christ's sacraments; not to sacrifice for dead nor live, not to sing or mass, or any such like. Unto the first original must all these men (as they be called) of the holy church be called: else be they no shepherds, but ravening wolves to devour the sheep of God. And that this may the better be done, your majesty must begin with your chapel and chaplains; make them to serve the same souls that laboureth for their livings. If your grace do it not, ye shall put your own self in danger of God. And from henceforth make your chaplains men of the church, and let the chapel go. And when your majesty hath done this yourself, cause all noblemen of your realm to do the same. Then reform your colleges in the universities, and see honest men to have the leading and oversight of the youth. Such as will amend, let them tarry still in their offices; such as will not, your majesty must remove, if ever ye bring the ship to quietness. Unto the clerk from henceforth, as ye will answer unto it, give no benefice or spiritual promotions to none, but to such a one as can and will preach true doctrine, or else teach unto the youth the catechism, and help the people with some good counsel; or else cast them all into the sea, that is, put them out of their office, and put better in their places. And beware of this ungodly pity, wherewith all men for the most part be very much now-a-days cumbered withal, which will for pity rather let a fool or an evil man to enjoy his benefice[3], than a thousand souls to be brought to knowledge: this in no pity, but rather a cruelty and killing of the soul. Therefore if it should please the magistrates to make a law, that no man should have bishoprick, benefice, prebend, or other ecclesiastical vocation longer than he used himself according to his vocation, it were wonderful well[4].

The noblemen that buyeth their offices, and selleth again the justice and the law that is appointed to the office, must be admonished: in case they will not amend, into the sea with them! Put them out of their offices, and put better in. These gentlemen that liveth upon dicing, carding, idleness, or with other men's goods, must be also admonished: if they will not repent altogether, cast them into the sea. Foolish and preposterous pity hath brought both king and the laws, not only of this realm, but also of God, into contempt; and daily will more and more, if it be not foreseen. Now the laws that justly should be executed upon thieves and murderers is of foolish pity dispensed withal; and many judge it were better to save after his opinion, than to damn after the commandment of God. For they say, "O he is a tall fellow, and can do the king good service; it were pity he should be hanged." But in case they knew or God's laws or man's laws, and knew

---

[3 "Clerks" who favoured popery were allowed to retain their benefices; patrons also gave livings to ejected monks, thus saving the pensions they must otherwise have paid. See Burnet and Strype.]

[4 Hooper when translated to Worcester, held that see for life, "provided he behaved so long well."]

what maintaineth best a commonwealth, they would say, "Such a thief or murderer can never do the king's majesty better service than when he is hanged for his fault, that other men may fear to offend the law, by his example." Mark whereunto this preposterous and sinister pity hath brought the realm, to be pestered with more thieves than half Europe beside; insomuch that a man cannot travel surely by the way with twenty pound in his purse, though twenty men be together in a company: as it was seen by experience of late days, to the great shame of all the justices of the country, and to the slander of the whole law and the realm.

The fraud, guile, and covetousness of the lawyers must either be amended, either they themselves be cast into the sea. For unto this hath their craft and filthy lucre brought the law, that whereas at the beginning of it it was a succour and defence of the innocent, now be all honest men so afraid of it, that they had rather, yea, and it were better a man to lose half his right, than to complain and seek a remedy at the law. What may wise men think of that realm, where as the defence and sinews thereof is so weakened and corrupted? Doubtless, nothing but ruin and perdition.

The ocivity[1] and idleness, the impatiency and rebellion of the people must be punished and amended; or else they will cast the ship, the shipmaster, the king and his council, yea, and themselves withal, into the sea, and bring this realm to a desolation and utter destruction.

Even thus, as the king's majesty must do in his realm, so should every man do in his own household. When there cometh poverty, pestilence, war, hunger, and such like, he must diligently search whether there be any Jonas within his house, that is to say, any idle and unoccupied men, any thieves, adulterers, swearers, and such like; and the same to be amended or cast out of the house. Hereof your majesty must also take heed, that ye know the faith and conversation of your family; that whosoever of wit and knowledge enter your grace's court, may see the majesty of a godly house, and perceive by the order of your family that God dwelleth in the court and realm. But, (the more

[1 Ocivity: sloth.]

to be pitied!) it is so now, that whosoever enter and mark the conditions of many men in the court, he shall find in the most part of the house hangings of God's wounds, his flesh and his blood, with such blasphemous oaths as the devil himself, if he were incarnate, would tremble to speak. And great wonder it is there falleth not fire from heaven to burn them, and the house they tarry in. Likewise, whereas God's laws forbiddeth dice and cards, and also the common statutes of this realm, (the more shame it is,) it is used daily and hourly in the king's majesty's house; whereas not only the majesty of God is offended, but many an honest man undone in the year. That dicehouse must be cast into the sea: if it be not, God will cast the maintainers thereof at length into hell. What and if all men follow this godly counsel of Jonas; what will follow? This that is in the text:

The sea shall leave his raging.

As long as Jonas was in the ship, there was no quietness; now, being in the sea, all is at peace: so shall it be with us, if we amend, and cease from evil doings, as it is written, Hieremy ii. vi. vii. And this is easy to be proved by example, that no commonwealth can be pacified, except evil doers be punished. 2 Par. xvii., Josaphat, before he could bring his commonwealth to any good point, restored good judges to the civil state of his realm, and true doctors to the ecclesiastical state of his realm, chap. xix. The same may we see in David, 2 Sam. viii. 2 Par. xxii. xxiii. So did Artaxerces, that sent Esdras to the Jews, Esdras viii. *Jer. ii. vi. vii.* *2 Chron. xvii.* *2 Chron. xix.* *2 Chron. xxii. xxiii.* *Ezra viii.*

The same order took Cambyses[2], Cyrus's son, though he was an idle man. He caused the skin of a corrupt judge to be pulled over his head, and to be nailed in the place of judgment, to put other men in fear how they corrupted justice. For the keeping of all men in an order, it were well if men would think upon the law of the

[[2] Jam Cambyses inusitatæ severitatis, qui mali cujusdam judicis ex corpore pellem detractam sellæ intendi, in eaque filium ejus judicaturum considere jussit. Ceterum et rex et barbarus atroci ac nova poena judicis, ne quis postea corrumpi judex posset, providit. Valer. Max. Lib. vi. Cap. iii. Sect. 3. Lugd. Bat. 1661, p. 550.]

Corinthes, which men may read in the adages of Erasmus[1]; (the adage is *Proterviam fecit:*) where as every man was bound to give account how he lived, and maintained himself. And the same law had Solon[2] at Athens.

When the magistrate by negligence or preposterous pity will not punish for sin, then God striketh; as ye may see by the universal flood, by the fire in Sodom and Gomorre. Give heed, therefore, most gracious lords, to punish these Jonases, and to put better into their place; or else God will punish either with an evil beast, either with sword, either with famine, either with pestilence, as it is written, Ezechiel xiv. But in case ye will do it, the sea will cease, as I pray God it may. Amen.

Ezek. xiv.

[1 Erat hoc religiosum in nonnullis etiam aliis hostiis, ne quid ex sacris epulis relinqueretur; aut si quid reliquum esset, id igni absumeretur: quemadmodum Moyses tradit de agno paschali. Porro id genus sacrificii Romani *proterviam* appellant; unde celebratur illud Catonis festiviter dictum in Albidium quendam, qui patrimonium universum luxu absumpserat unis exceptis ædibus quæ incendio conflagrarunt: *Proterviam* (inquit) *fecit*, propterea quod ea quæ comesse non potuerit quasi combussisset........Apud veteres erant leges sumptuariæ, atque adeo Corinthi, quæ civitas erat ceteris corruptior, tamen lex erat opposita sumptuosius quam pro rei familiaris modo viventibus. Erasmi Op. Lugd. Bat. 1703. Tom. II. Adagiorum Co. 349.]

[2 See Plutarchi Vitæ, in Solon.]

THE FOURTH SERMON UPON JONAS,

MADE BY JOHN HOPER, THE 5th OF MARCH.

☞ THE PREFACE.

SAINT PAUL saith, " It is a most true saying, and worthy 1 Tim. i. to be received of every part, that Christ Jesus came into this world to save sinners." 1 Timo. i. Unto the which saying agreeth the words of our Saviour Christ, Luke xix. " The Son of man came to seek and save that which was Luke xix. lost." Who is it among us all that would not joyfully at the hearing of so amiable and sweet a saying rejoice, seeing we be all miserable and cursed sinners by nature; and yet would, as full of misery and blindness as we be, be saved, wish ever to be out of pain? But in this is all the heed to be taken, lest we sinisterly understand these comfortable promises, which the devil aventureth to suade us unto. Where as he cannot altogether bereave and rob us of the promises, he would us to construe and understand the promises amiss. And whereas these promises appertaineth to none but unto repentant sinners, he dazeth[3] and deceiveth our affection and love we bear to ourselves, that he will bear us in hand God's promise appertaineth as well to the impenitent and never-minding sinner to amend, as unto the sorrowful, afflicted, believing sinner, and he that will study the amendment of life; against the which illusion and craft of the devil Christ speaketh, Matt. ix. Matt. ix. Luke v. " I came not to call the just, but sinners to repentance." Of the which repentance if we be destitute, nothing availeth us the promises of God, Luke xiii. " Except Luke xiii. ye repent, all shall perish." And the former promises were not so sweet, but these threatenings be as bitter; not unto all men, but unto such as be obstinately evil or desperate. Against whom crieth John Baptist, " Even now is the axe Luke iii. put unto the root of the tree. Every tree that bringeth forth no good fruit, is cut down and put into the fire," Luke iii.

[3 Dazeth: dazzleth.]

But a man might ask, to what purpose this thing is spoken of by me: doubtless to this end, to prosecute and follow my matter begun. I said that the authors of this unquietness in the realm, in the church, and in every household, were very Jonases, and those that troubled the ship; which ought either to be amended, or removed out of their office, or else the ship may never come to rest. But because these that be cast into the sea should not despair, there must be some remedy found to solace and comfort such as be fallen into danger of drowning. This is the way. If they take the admonitions and the admonitors gently, and rail not against them, neither wink at their own faults; but with a true repentance of the heart follow this our prophet Jonas, who confessed his fault, and humbly asked remission and pardon for the same; so shall every sinner be saved, as he was, according to the oath of God, Eze. xviii, "As truly as I live, saith the Lord, I will not the death of a sinner, but that he be converted and live." This counsel of the Lord except our troublous Jonases follow, they shall be drowned in the water of eternal damnation with Pharao.

<small>Ezek. xviii.</small>

But as heretofore ye have heard how Jonas for his disobedience was punished, so now out of the text ye shall hear how he, repenting his misbehaviour and offences, is preserved in his dangers; how he prayeth; and at last, how he is delivered. And that I may the better and more plainly teach and open the same, I will divide the text that followeth into four parts. The first part containeth the behaviour and doings of the shipmen after they had cast Jonas into the sea: the second part containeth how Jonas, being cast into the sea, was received into the belly of the whale: the third containeth the behaviour and doings of Jonas in the whale's belly: the fourth containeth the deliverance and casting out of Jonas from the belly of the whale.

The first: the text sayeth,

> Those men feared wonderfully the Lord, and sacrificed unto him, and made their vows.

The shipmen did these three things: they feared; they sacrificed; and vowed.

After they perceived, upon the execution of Jonas, the sea to leave his trouble, they neglected not the true religion which they learned in their trouble, but are better and more strengthened in the same; for they feared the Lord, and honoured him only. Of these shipmen let us learn constancy and perseverance in the true knowledge of God; and when we be delivered out of danger, let us not give ourselves to liberty and folly of life, as naturally we be inclined and propense to do. Thus admonished Moses diligently the children, Deut. vi. and viii. that when they had Deut. vi. viii. received the abundant benefits of the Lord, they should not, in their saturity and abundance, be unmindful of the Lord that brought them out of the land of Egypt, and the penury and scarcity of the desert.

The thankfulness of these mariners shall be laid against us at the day of our examination for our unthankfulness. For God hath not only quieted the sea for us, but also abundantly given us the use and commodity both of sea and land; and not only that for the rest and quietness of the body, but also he hath appeased the sea of great displeasure and damnation eternal, by casting of his only beloved Son Christ Jesus upon the cross, to cease and appease the ire and displeasure between us and him: and yet we neither fear nor love him, but with continual hatred and despite contemn both him and his holy word.

They do sacrifice.

They thought it not enough inwardly to honour the Lord, but did outward sacrifice, to protest and declare unto the world the good judgment, faith, and knowledge they had in the Lord. So should we do: not only know God and fear him inwardly, but also outwardly, with prayer, thanksgiving, and other good works commanded by God, to declare the same, as they did by their sacrifices, before the coming of Christ into our flesh; the which were types and significations of Christ to come, that could not take away the sin of the world, as Saint Paul saith, Hebrews x.: Heb. x. "It is impossible that the blood of calves should take away sin. Christ's sacrifice, once offered for all, by that once satisfied for all sin." Heb. ix. "And where as is remission Heb. ix.

of sin, there needeth no more sacrifice." It is therefore an ungodly doctrine, that in this time of the new testament teacheth any other sacrifice for sin than the only death of Christ. If question now be asked, Is there then no sacrifices now left to be done of christian people? Yes, truly; but none other than such as ought to be done without altars. And they be of three sorts. The first is the sacrifices of thanksgiving, Psalms li. Amos the fourth and fifth, Hebrews the thirteenth, Oseas xiv.: the second is benevolence and liberality to the poor, Mich. vi. 1 Corinth. xvi. 2 Corinth. viii. and ix.: the third kind of sacrifice is the mortifying of our own bodies, and to die from sin, Rom. vi. Matt. xi. Luke xiv. If we study not daily to offer these sacrifices to God, we be no christian men.

Psal. l.
Amos iv. v.
Heb. xiii.
Hosea xiv.
Micah vi.
1 Cor. xvi.
2 Cor. viii. ix.
Rom. vi.
Matt. xi.
Luke xiv.

Seeing christian men have none other sacrifices than these, which may and ought to be done without altars, there should among Christians be no altars: and therefore it was not without the great wisdom and knowledge of God, that Christ, his apostles, and the primitive church, lacked altars; for they knew that the use of altars was taken away. It were well then, that it might please the magistrates to turn the altars into tables, according to the first institution of Christ, to take away the false persuasion of the people they have of sacrifices to be done upon the altars; for as long as the altars remain, both the ignorant people, and the ignorant and evil-persuaded priest, will dream always of sacrifice. Therefore were it best that the magistrates removed all the monuments and tokens of idolatry and superstition; then should the true religion of God the sooner take place.

They vow.

Most like they vowed to go to Hierusalem, there to manifest the mighty power of God to the people, and to give thanks unto the Lord, according to the law and manner of Moses' decrees. Lest we should err in the nature and condition of a vow, there be three things to be noted: to whom the vow is made; what is vowed; and who it is that maketh the vow. The vow should be made unto the Lord, as Esay the prophet saith, chapter xix. "They shall make their vows to the Lord." The thing vowed

Isai. xix

may not be contrary to any of the two tables within, Exodi xx. Deut. v. He that voweth must be such a one as is able to pay and satisfy his vow. So Saint Paul advised the younger widows to marry, perceiving how unruly and vehement the passions of young age was, that they were not apt to live sole, nor to keep their vow, if they should vow so to do. *Exod. xx. Deut. v.*

Now followeth the second member of the oration; how Jonas, being cast into the sea, was received of the whale: and it beginneth the second chapter of the prophet in this wise:

> But the Lord prepared a great fish that should devour Jonas. And Jonas was in the fish's belly three days and three nights.

The text containeth two things: first, that the fish prepared by the Lord swallowed up Jonas: the second, how long time Jonas was in the fish's belly. The things to be noted in the first member be also two in number. First is declared the wonderful pity and mercy of God, that can and will help the afflicted in the days of their afflictions. Jonas thought none other but to die, and so did the mariners; for they besought God not to require the innocent's blood at their hands: but the Lord, that is ready to help as many as call upon him, Psal. viii. and ix., left not his penitent and afflicted servant Jonas, but preserved his life, though it were with trouble. Thus will he do with all those that be the Jonases of this realm, in case they repent. Though they should be cast from all the honour and offices they have, better it were to lose them with the favour of God, than to keep them with God's displeasure: as Zacheus did, Luke xix.; Jacob, Gen. xxviii. *Psal. viii. ix.* *Luke xix. Gen xxviii.*

The means, how God saveth the afflicted, be unknown unto man, and man should not be curious to search too much for the knowledge of them, but commend them to God; for many times God useth those for life, that man judgeth should lead unto death. So was Jonas saved by the devouring mouth of the whale, which seemed unto Jonas' reason rather a present means unto death: so used he the crib of Moses, and the wonderful passage of the children of

Israel through the Red Sea. If we purge and cleanse our knowledge, religion and manners, the Lord will find means sufficient to save us; which we may not appoint to ourselves, but commend them to the providence of God. For by the same ways that we seek many times the favour of God and our commodity, we find his displeasure and our own destruction; as Saul did, 1 Regum xv. that sacrificed without the commandment of God, purchased the severe and just ire of God. The Israelites, that of good meaning and intention fasted, Zech. vii. and sought by that means God's good will, they found his displeasure. Caiaphas sought by counsel, John xi., to have oppressed the proceedings of Christ, and oppressed himself and the whole state of the commonwealth also. Cicero, Rome; Demosthenes, Athens, each put their commonwealth in danger by their best advised counsel for the preservation thereof: and so shall all the Jonases, extortioners, oppressors, deceivers, flatterers, and other of this realm, come into extreme poverty by the same means they seek riches; for the curse of God cannot suffer evil-gotten goods and possessions long to prosper.

margin: 1 Sam. xv.; Zech. vii.; John xi.

Now Jonas sayeth that he was in the belly of the whale three days and three nights. Of this we learn, that God helpeth not by and by the afflicted, but exerciseth them in their troubles. First, because he may the better humble them, and bring them to a true knowledge of their faults, whose greatness is so big that it cannot be perceived, whereas the pain for it is easy and light. But the Lord would us the better to judge of the fault by the greatness of the pain; and therefore the Lord is said to explorate and try his in affliction, as the gold is tried by the fire. Farther, his mighty power is the better declared, where as he helpeth such as be plain desperate of all other remedies and helps. Last of all, this time of Jonas being in the whale's body was a type and figure of Christ's being in the heart of the earth three days and three nights. Matt. xii.

margin: Matt. xii.

Now followeth it how this man behaved himself in the time of his trouble. When he perceived in the fish's belly some hope and sparkle of life, he fell unto prayer. But because prayer containeth in itself two things, the knowledge of the fault, and hope of forgiveness, I admonish all the Jonases of this realm, that they acknowledge and leave off from their faults, and beg pardon for them, except they will die eternally. The bishops and the priests, that hath either with false doctrine destroyed the church, either by negligence not builded it with the true word of God, let them acknowledge their faults, amend it, and ask remission betime, if they will not die in their sin. The noblemen and lawyers, that are secretly touched with the word of God, and their conscience condemneth them of wrongs, frauds, injuries and deceits, let them not indurate and harden their hearts; but pray to the Lord to take from them pride, arrogancy, blindness, and covetousness, lest they die in their sin, as Saul did. The people, let them pray unto God for knowledge and patience, that they may know and suffer all things, as true subjects ought to do; and that from henceforth they hate discord, dissension, treason, conspiracy, whoredom, adultery, idleness, hatred, envy, disdain, and such like, as provoketh God's ire, and leadeth to the destruction of a commonwealth.

But this prayer of Jonas is so acceptable, it might be thought of some men that the place where Jonas prayed in should have bettered it; as the foolish opinion of the world is at this time, that judgeth the prayer said at the high altar to be better than that which is said in the quire, that in the quire better than it that is said in the body of the church, that in the body of the church better than the prayer said in the field, or in a man's chamber. But our prophet sayeth, The Lord hath no respect to the place, but unto the heart and faith of him that prayeth: and that appeareth; for penitent Jonas prayeth out of the whale's belly, and miserable Job upon the dung-heap, Daniel in the cave of the lions, Hieremy in the clay-pit, the thief upon the cross, Saint Stephin under the stones. Wherefore the grace of God is to be prayed for in every place and every where, as our necessity shall have need and wanteth solace. Although I commend the prayer made to God in the name of Christ to be like in every place, because that our necessity requireth help in every place; yet I do not condemn the public place of prayer, where as God's word is preached, his holy sacraments used, and common prayer made unto God, but allow the same, and sorry it is no more frequented and haunted. But this I would wish, that the magistrates should put both the preacher, minister, and the people in one place, and shut up the partition called the chancel, that separateth the congregation of Christ one from the other, as though the veil and partition of the temple in the old law yet should remain in the church; where, indeed, all figures and types ended in Christ. And in case this were done, it should not only express the dignity and grace of the new testament, but also cause the people the better to understand the things read there by the minister; and also provoke the minister to a more study of the things that he readeth, lest he should be found by the judgment of the congregation not worthy neither to read nor to minister in the church. Farther, that such as would receive the holy communion of the precious body and blood of Christ, might both hear and see plainly what is done, as it was used in the primitive church, when as the abomination done upon altars was not known, nor the sacrifice of Christ's precious blood so conculcated and trodden under foot.

The third thing in this prayer is to be noted, lest in the port itself we make shipwreck, and offend God in praying: to whom we pray—unto him that only seeth the cogitations of our heart, and can and will do all things for us accordingly, help at need, and punish in due season; which only God can do. And unto him should we direct and make our prayer, after the examples of the patriarchs, prophets, and the apostles, who called always upon their God; for such as direct otherwise their prayers, they fail and err all the heavens wide. Against whom speaketh Esay lxv., Jer. ii. xv., Ezech. xiv. And the Lord is angry with his people, as Esay saith, chap. ix., "because they turned not unto him that strake them, nor unto the God of armour." And in the prophet Osee, chap. vii.: "They called not to me," sayeth the Lord, "in their hearts." And in the same place, a little after, sayeth the prophet, "They be returned, but not unto the Highest." So likewise are they no less to be blamed, that divide their hearts, part unto God, and part unto creatures; of whom speaketh Osee in the tenth chapter.

Isai. lxv.
Jer. ii. xv.
Ezek. xiv.
Isai. ix.

Hos. vii.

Hos. x.

If these three things that Jonas used in the whale's belly were used of the people that profess Christ's name in our temples, blessed were we. But it is all to the contrary: we know not what prayer is, nor yet will take the pains to learn it; the more is the pity, and the more is God stirred to vengeance and punishment, and the more cruel shall the pain be when it is executed by God.

As we know by the text he prayed, so may we know by the same how he prayed, and what was the form and manner of his prayer. That is very requisite to be known, marked, and borne away: the effect and sum thereof consisteth in three points. In two of the first verses he putteth forth briefly the abridgement and epitome of his prayer; then declareth he the greatness of his danger and jeopardy; thirdly, he setteth forth the pity and mercy of God. The first part:

From my troubles I have called upon the Lord, and he heard me: from the deepness of the deepest I cried, and thou heardest my voice.

Out of this first part we learn two doctrines: the one that we should not despair, nor clean cast off God in adversity; the other, that in adversity we should not fly, nor seek any forbidden or unlawful means of help. And these two things observed Jonas in this his trouble; and we should do the same according to the commandment of God. Psal. xcix. "Call upon me in the day of thy troubles, [Psal. l.] and I shall hear thee," as he did at all times. Psal. xcix. Psal. xcix. And this cry of Jonas to the Lord was rather the cry of his heart than the noise or sound of his mouth, as Moses' was, Exodi xiv., and the good woman's, 1 Samuel i. Exod. xiv. 1 Sam. i.

The circumstances of true prayer observed, the Lord heareth this faithful prayer according to his promises. Whereof all idololatrical bishops and priests may learn, if they will forsake their idololatry, and call unto the Lord, mercy is ready for them. And if the lascivious, avaricious, or covetous gentleman or lawyer will acknowledge his fault, and ask remission for it, it will be forgiven him. And so shall it be to the common sort of people, if they acknowledge their disobedience, rebellion, treason, pride, contempt of the superior powers, and ask mercy for it.

The second part of his prayer containeth a description of his dangers that he was in, after this sort:

Thou hast cast me down deep in the middest of the sea, and the flood compassed me about: yea, all the waves and rolls of water went over me: I thought I had been cast away out of thy sight; but I will yet again look toward thy holy temple. The waters compassed me even to my very life: the deep lay about me, and the weeds were wrapt about my head. I went down to the bottom of the hills, and was barred in with earth for ever.

It is the common sort of all holy men for the most part, in the holy scripture, to make mention in their prayers of their dangers, and to amplify them, that their greatness may be the better marked and known. And this is done for three causes: the one because, with the numbering and rehearsal of their great dangers, they may the more inflame themselves to ardent and earnest prayer; for the more a man feeleth his own grief, the more diligent he will be to seek a remedy. The other is to bring a man the more to a contempt and hatred of himself; for the greatness of the pain declareth the enormity and filthiness of the transgression and sin. The third is to set forth the power and good will of God, that can and will help in extreme and desperate evils, and save with superabundant mercy, where as he findeth iniquity and sin to abound. Romans v. And so, many times, the slavery and miserable state of the afflicted setteth forth the majesty and richness of God's mercy. Matt. viii. ix. John iv. ix.

Rom. v.

Matt. viii. ix.

This man of God noted and knew the displeasure of God against sin: but our Jonases sleep quietly in both ears, and feeleth not the pain of sin; and this security and insensibleness under the wrath of God cometh by the ignorancy that the whole world is lapped in almost, as touching the danger of their vocations. If the clergy, the bishops and priests would think upon this pain annexed unto their vocation, if they do it not truly, faithfully, and as they be commanded of God; *Sanguinem illorum de manu tua requiram*, that is to say, "I will require their blood at thy hand," Ezechiel iii. xxxiii.; they would serve the Lord and

Ezek. iii. xxxiii.

use more diligence in their vocation than they do. If the noblemen would think upon this text, "The Lord resisteth the proud;" and this text, Esay v., "Woe be unto you that join house to house, and field to field," &c.; and the lawyers and judges that is written, Proverbs xvii. and Matthew xxiii.; they would not sleep in great rest, nor use the place they be in with such partiality and falsehood as they do. In case the common people would think upon the third of Genesis, where as labour is commanded, and also 1 Thessalonians iv. 2 Thessalonians iii., they would not forsake labour, and seek weapon and strength to turn and alter the state and order that God hath appointed upon the earth. But this I say to every man of each of those degrees mentionated of: the less they feel the danger of eternal damnation, the nearer they be unto eternal pain, and have already one foot in hell, which shall never come again, but the whole body and soul shall follow, except they repent: for no man is farther from heaven than he that feareth not hell, nor no man farther from grace than he that feeleth not the danger of sin; as we see no man in more dangerous disease, than he that knoweth not himself to be sick, as those men be that are fallen into frenzy and madness. Let us learn with Jonas to know in what danger we be.

Isai. v.
Prov. xvii.
Matt. xxiii.
Gen. iii.
1 Thess. iv.
2 Thess. iii.

Yet is there another thing to be noted in Jonas' words, where as he sayeth: "Thou hast cast me down." Of these words should those that be damned by the magistrates acknowledge, that it is not the magistrate that putteth them to execution, but God, whose ministers they be; and ought to save such as God's word saveth, and damn those that God's word damneth. It is God that sendeth to hell, that hangeth for transgression upon the gallows, as Jonas knew in this his prayer: he accused not the mariners that cast him into the sea, but confessed the execution of the evil to be from God.

Let therefore from henceforth the bishop and parson, that is deprived of their vocations for their misbehaviour and false or negligent preaching in them, say, "The Lord hath cast me down." So let the noblemen and the lawyers say, when their ravine, covetousness, fraud, and deceit crieth vengeance before God, till they be displaced: "The

Lord hath cast me down." And the same let the traitorous subject, the thief, the murderer, and idle man say: "The Lord brought me to the gallows; the Lord would I should trouble the commonwealth no longer."

And I do here appeal and burden every subject's conscience of this realm of England. First, those that have the doings, receivings, occupyings and custody, oversight, rule, and office of the king's majesty's goods or lands. Then, their conscience, to whom the king and his council hath commended the teaching and instruction of his people in the knowledge and fear both of God and man. Finally, I appeal all the consciences of the subjects of this realm which meriteth, some for deceit, falsehood, and deceiving of the king, loss both of body and goods; some for preaching erroneous, seditious, and false doctrine, or for neglecting the preaching of the true doctrine, deserve most cruel punishment; some for false judgment merit the loss of their lives; the rest for rebellion, sedition and treason, deserve the sword and the gallows—whether, in suffering the pain appointed for such transgression, they can from their hearts say: "This suffer I worthily, and will the vengeance of God, because I have sinned against him and the law of my commonwealth." No, no, the Lord knoweth, every man extenuateth, yea, excuseth all things done against God and his order. But I will feign thee, thou thief and robber of the king and of the commonwealth, to be king, and the king thy officer and receiver: wouldest thou thy officer should deceive thee? Or, thou traitorous and false subject, if thou were king and the king thy subject, wouldest thou be contented that thy subject should conspire and imagine how to pluck thee out of thy realm? What if my lord bishop and master parson were kings, trow ye their majesties would be contented that their bishops and priests should whisper a tale of treason and sedition in auricular confession, or rather privy conventicles, to their subjects?[1]

Speak all ye that be feigned kings, and speak of your consciences: I dare say ye would not be thus handled. Why then do ye handle another so? Remember ye not

[1 This probably is in allusion to those of the clergy, who adhering to popery in their hearts, secretly promoted the rebellions against king Edward the sixth. See Burnet, Part I. Book 2.]

in this law of nature, *Quod tibi non vis fieri, alteri ne facias;* that is to say, "Do not to another that thou wouldest not another should do unto thee?" Amend therefore, every man, and be true and faithful unto the realm, to the king, and laws of him and his realm. And for the love of God, ye noblemen, gentlemen, justices and lawyers, the wholesome laws of the realm, the statutes and commissions that hath been made by the king and the council, for the preservation of the commonwealth and the help of the poor, which be both afflicted with your insatiable and never-contented covetousness—let them be faithfully executed, and uprightly interpretated, according to the mind and meaning of those that made them; for the evil construing and sinister taking of good laws, and godly meaning of godly magistrates, doth not only afflict the poor of this realm, but will sure at length cast the whole realm under the water. It cometh now into my mind, a practice of eviltaking the governor's word and commandment, how perilous and dangerous thing it is.

I was once in the Race of Britaine[2] with a fore wind and contrary flood, the seas in that place going both hollow, and that by reason of a multitude of rocks in the same place. The master of the ship, to conduct her the better, sat upon the main yard to see the seas aforehand, and cried to him that steered the stern, always upon which side he should steer the ship, to break best the danger of the sea. The wind blowing high, whereas the master cried a-larboard, he that steered mistook it, and steered a-starboard; and the once mistaking of the master's law had almost cast us under the water. Then thought I, It is not without cause that wise men compare a commonwealth to a ship; for one thing loseth and saveth them both. For in case the master's officer in the ship obey not his law, the ship will of force drown. So shall this commonwealth and every other, that when the king and his council shall make laws to help and save the poor, such as steer the hinder part of the ship behind the king's back, follow not that he is bid to do, but that that he listeth himself, and his own private commodity to do[3]; and thus putteth both the ship, the master,

[2 Probably the Race of Alderney.]
[3 To do, omitted in T.]

and all the mariners, in danger of drowning. Amend therefore every man betime; if ye do not, the Lord at length will cast ye out from all ye have, to the destruction of you and yours.

But of one thing I pray you all that be true and faithful subjects and friends unto the kingdom and the king's majesty—that ye will not impute, nor burden the king's majesty nor his council with the oppression, extortion, theft, injuries, deceits, falseheads, defrauds, cautelles[1], violences, and other wrongs, that those thieves and destroyers use towards you and the commonwealth: if their using might come to their knowledge, I doubt not but that your wrongs should be redressed by them. And this I know myself by experience in weighty matters, the king's majesty's council hath not only heard, but given accordingly sentence with the truth, and used me rather like fathers than like judges in such matters. If they had taken things spoken by me honestly, evil construed by mine accusers, there could have followed no less than my great undoing, and hinderance to all my labours and pains in the vineyard of the Lord. Therefore, pray to him that all good laws may be justly executed, and all other amended; which God grant!

There is one word more in the text which must not be neglected; where Jonas sayeth he shall see again the holy temple of the Lord: in the which words note two things: the one, how that in the most obscure and dark troubles of adversity God suffereth some spark of consolation to shine; the other, to what end a man being in trouble, should desire to be delivered—to extol and praise for ever the name of the Lord. Esay thirty and eight. But how this end of deliverance is practised in our days, the Lord knoweth. We use not to desire the Lord to be delivered, to glorify and laud his holy name, as this Jonas did, and David, Psal. li. cxviii.; but from sickness and adversity we turn ourself to all ungodliness and liberty of life; and where we were evil before trouble and sickness, we be worse after: therefore when God hath wasted one rod upon us in punishment, he beginneth to make another, more sharper than the first. And even as the fall again into a disease, before the first be quite past and overcome, bringeth the more danger

Isai xxxviii.

Psal. li. cxviii.

[1 Crafty proceedings.]

unto the patient; even so the relapse and fall again into the displeasure and judgment of God, not only doubleth the grief and pain of the punishment, but also endangereth the afflicted person with the horror and damnation of hell-fire; for every relapse aggravateth the pain for sin.

After this followeth the third part of Jonas' prayer, in the which is contained a commendation of God's mercy.

> But thou, O Lord my God, hast brought my life again out of corruption. When my soul fainted within me, I thought upon the Lord, and my prayer came in unto thee, even into thy holy temple.

In these verses is declared both the power of God and the truth of God: his power that saved his life, where was no likelihood but of death, yea, death itself; for he it is alone that bringeth to hell, and saveth from thence, 1 Sam. i.; his truth is declared, that whereas he saith, "Call upon me in the days of thy trouble, and I will hear thee," Psalm ninety and nine[2], here he performeth it in this afflicted Jonas; of whom we should learn both to fear his threatening justice, and to trust unto his promised mercy; for he can do both, punish the evil that will not repent, and save the afflicted that fleeth unto his mercy.

1 Sam. i.

> They that hold of vain vanities will forsake his mercy.

The people of God have a custom in their prayers, as they behold the true and saving health of the living God, so of the contrary part, to consider the false and deceitful help of the false gods; as David doth many times, and here also our Jonas. So do the true Christians at this day; in beholding the mercy of God in Christ, they behold and wonder at the fond and false hope, help and trust, that men put in vanity, error, and forbidden help of the mass, water, bread, salt, bough[3], candle, pardons and such like. And this note, christian reader, that the prophet calleth

[2 Psalm ninety and nine, omitted in T.]
[3 Bough: bowe, D. 1, bough, D. 2, boughe, T.]

false and vain religion vanity. So judge thou of every religion that is not contained within the word of God, to be nothing else than vanity, from whencesoever it cometh; though the world would bear thee in hand, it were as true as the gospel. But ask that true judge, the word of God, and it will shew thee it is superstition, beggary, and treachery unto the soul; and those do lose the benevolence and mercy, that God hath promised in Christ to as many as seek him in truth and in verity. Out of this text ye see the doctrine of Christ true, that is written Matthew vi., "No man can serve two masters," the true religion of God, and the superstition of man. Nor he can be saved that trusteth in Christ hanged upon the cross, and Christ offered in the mass: for the one is contrary plain unto the other; therefore Jonas confesseth what he will do—follow the one and forsake the other, as the text of his oration sayeth.

Matt. vi.

But I will do thee sacrifice with the voice of thanksgiving, and will pay that I have vowed.

Here Jonas eftsoons telleth, what he will do being delivered from his trouble: he will extol, magnify, and set forth the goodness of God. Then he will perform his vow made, that is to say, live obediently unto the commandment of God. The same must we do, and not use health and quietness as an occasion to sin, liberty, and filthiness of life. Jonas also amendeth the foolish opinion of the Jews, that trusted to have obtained remission of their sins, by the offering up of their[1] calves and other brute beasts: but Jonas declareth that the Lord delighteth in no sacrifice that man can do, saving in the sacrifice of thanksgiving; for only Christ is the sacrifice propitiatory, and he that alone meriteth before God the remission of sin. If then in the time of the shadow[2] Jonas knew the Lord to accept the sacrifice of the heart and mouth, that was endued with faith, above the sacrifice of the bloody calves, how much more now of us will he do the same, above the idololatrical sacrifice of the mass!

[1 Their, T., the, D. 1, 2.]
[2 "The law having a shadow of good things to come," &c. Heb. xi.]

Jonas, well trusting of God's mercy and promises, sheweth a reason, wherefore he will laud and praise the Lord, when he cometh out of trouble, and saith:

For salvation cometh of the Lord.

As though he had said, No man can give health of body or soul except God; as David saith almost in every psalm, and Esay xliii. xliv. If this doctrine were well printed into our heads, we would not go astray to every strange God, and superstition of man, as the world doth now-a-days more like heathens than Christians. Farther, we would the better sustain and endure adversity, seeing it can neither go nor come without the provision of God. Gracious king, and my lords of the council, remember this doctrine of Jonas; and then ye need not to fear to reform this church of England unto the primitive state and apostolical doctrine. Let the devil with all his ministers do what they will: if the judges remembered this doctrine, they would not fear to punish evil-doers; if the people knew this doctrine, they would not take armour and weapon against the magistrates, but seek help from God. Before all men let the preacher comfort himself with this word; for he is in danger of most displeasure, if he preach not truly. Also let the persecutors of God's word take heed of this doctrine: for in the Lord shall be their health, let them persecute what and how they will; though they burn, the Lord will quench; if they kill, the Lord will make alive; if they curse, the Lord will bless; if they damn to hell, the Lord will save in heaven. Blessed is then the man that trusteth in the Lord.

<small>Isai. xliii. xliv.</small>

Now followeth the conclusion of the chapter.

And the Lord spake unto the fish, and it cast out Jonas again upon the dry land.

Here ye may see the effect of a godly and earnest prayer—that it obtaineth deliverance from the danger. Of this in the whole we learn, that there is none so great danger, but that we may escape, if with penitence we return unto the Lord, and ask him mercy. As many Jonases therefore, as be in this realm, that hath and doth or

falsely use or negligently contemn their vocation, let them acknowledge their offence, and beg pardon; or else doubtless, where penitent Jonas was cast a dry land, they shall remain for ever in the pains of hell, as Saul doth. Let them see therefore, that be bishops and priests, in what danger they be, that neglect or abuse their vocation: if they amend, health cometh, as unto this miserable and penitent man. This I speak to the noblemen and to the lawyers, and also to the common people. I pray God all Jonases of this realm thus repent: in case all do not, yet that some follow this godly man, that they may be saved, as he is.
So be it.

THE FIFTH SERMON UPON JONAS,

MADE BY JOHN HOPER.

THE PREFACE.

THERE is no man that hath any respect or care at all of his health, that would not gladly his faith, knowledge, and faults should be approved and well taken of God: for he knoweth all labours and pains to be in vain and lost, that are not commended by him. Yet in this behalf men grievously offend and go out of the way, when the thing that God most esteemeth is of our parts most neglected, and the thing that God hateth and is displeased withal, we most diligently do and exercise ourselves in. Men be brought to this ignorancy and contempt of God and his word, that they judge every thing done of a good intention and well meaning should please the Lord; from whence sprung this infinite, dangerous, and superstitious number of sacrifices and other servings of God. But what thing, after the right judgment of the scripture, chiefly pleaseth God? Obedience: that is to say, when every man in his state and his vocation doth the thing he is commanded to do; as it is written, 1 Sam. xiii., "I desire obedience, and not sacrifice." Let no man therefore think he can do any thing acceptable unto the Lord, if he neglect the works necessary appointed unto his vocation.

_{1 Sam. xiii.}

Here may princes take heed they go not about with liberality to make other men good for them, learned for them, virtuous for them, wise for them, and they themselves neglect study, prayer, pains, and labour; but to know and do all things themselves, that is required to a princely office by the express word of God. Study, wisdom, knowledge, and exercise is required in the prince himself. Let the bishops and priests beware they go not about to please God with mass, dirige, pardons, rites and ceremonies invented by men. But let them do the works of their vocation, gravely study, diligently and truly preach the word of God, christianly minister the sacraments, and severely use discipline and correction of indurate men's faults. So let the councillor see what equity bindeth him to do, the honour of God, the obedience unto his prince, and the love of his country; and so judge and counsel for the glory of God, and wealth of the realm, and not for his own affection or profit; and think that the parson, bishop or priest is able to sing or say the remission or pardon for the neglecting of his duty; but he must do the works thereof himself. The common sort of people, let them learn to know and obey both God and man, and not trust to the pardon and remission of their ignorancy, and disobedient treason and sedition, at the parson's or vicar's hand; but they must know and fear both God and God's magistrate themselves.

How fair and religious, good and godly soever the good intention of man appear and shew itself to men, it is plain iniquity before God; as ye may see by Saul, that thought God would be pleased with the well-meant fat sacrifice of king Agag. 1 Sam. xiii. And also that he fought with the heathen before Samuel's coming, 1 Sam. xv. he was not only rebuked grievously for his fault, but disherited also of his kingdom for ever. I dare pronounce that all these mischiefs and troubles, that happen in this ship and commonwealth of England, spring out of this fountain. No man laboureth to do the works that God hath appointed to his vocation. And an example hereof we have seen in Jonas, whose disobedience and want of doing his vocation moved the winds in the air, the waters of the sea; so that it had like to have drowned himself, the ship, and as many as were within board. And seeing there is none of us but is culpable, from the highest to the lowest, in neglecting the works of our vocation, and thereby inobedient to the good will and commandment of God, let us repent and return to a better mind. He that erreth shall not perish, if, being admonished, he return home again. Ezech. xviii., Matt. xi., Joh. x. Let this glass and mirror of Jonas suffice us to behold another man's evil in, before we feel the like ourselves. We have seen the disobedience of Jonas and the pain thereof; we have seen his amendment and pensiveness, and the fruit thereof, his deliverance and salvation. Let us also now see how much he hath profited and learned in God's school under the rod of adversity, and let us learn to do the same. But before we come to the obedience that this man learned in adversity, we will pray unto God.

We be come so far as the text hath made mention of, the restitution of Jonas in life upon the dry ground. And now followeth his second legation and embassage to Ninive. But for the better understanding of all things that follow, I will divide the chapter into his parts, which are four.

The first containeth the commandment of God to Jonas: the second, Jonas' obedience: the third, the repentance of the Ninivites: the fourth, the mercy and compassion of God towards the penitent and sorrowful Ninivites.

THE FIRST PART.

The word of God came the second time to Jonas after this sort: Rise, go to Ninive, that great city, and preach in it the preaching that I have spoken unto thee of.

That Jonas goeth not to the city to preach of his own head, but tarrieth to be called unto it by God, we learn, no man should wish or desire for any office or vocation to a private commodity and his own lucre, but to tarry till God call him to it; chiefly the office of a bishop or preacher.

For that office hath so many difficulties, labours, and dangers, that in case the man that is in it be not well persuaded that he came to it by the calling of God, he shall never be able to endure the troubles annexed to the vocation: as the perfect man's tediousness and weariness therein declareth Jeremiah xx., who decreed with himself to have preached no more because of the malice

Jer. xx.

of the people, and for the contempt that followed him in doing of his vocation. Even so is the office of a good councillor and good magistrate; that in case he look not to come to his dignity and honour for ambition, pride, and private lucre, but cometh when he is called of God, he shall find so many labours and unquietness in his vocation, that doubtless, were it not for God, he could be glad to leave it to another man. For in case the magistrate do any thing contrary unto God, doubtless he shall fall into two evils; first, into God's displeasure, and then the thing he doth shall never prosper: as it is to be seen by the Israelites, that warred before they were commanded by God. Numb. xiv. Let no man therefore run into an office before the time God call him, neither buy himself into that office, as is now-a-days commonly used: for I know surely he that buyeth will sell, and never do God, the king, neither the subjects, good service, but dishonour the first, and rob the other.

<small>Numb. xiv.</small>

That Jonas is bid to rise and go to Ninive, in that is declared, that of all things in every vocation idleness and sloth must be chiefly avoided, and labours exercised, the which if we leave undone, being works annexed with our vocation, we declare ourselves unmeet for the room and vocation we be appointed unto. In case any man had a servant appointed to dress his meat in the kitchen, or to keep his horse in the stable, and yet would neglect the labours and pains that the offices ordinarily and of duty required, who gladly would be contented with such a servant, or desire he should be preferred to any office in his house? Therefore commandeth St Paul, "That he that will not labour should not eat." 1 Thess. iv.

<small>[2 Thess. iii.]</small>

The third doctrine of this first part declared, forasmuch as it behoveth every man to avoid idleness in his vocation, it might be demanded, what should a man do to satisfy his vocation? It is told Jonas in this place: "Preach," saith the text. He sayeth not, take the regiment and governance of the commonwealth; but preach. Of these words we learn, that every man is bound to do the works of the vocation he beareth the name of; and not to meddle with other men's labours. It is not the office of the bishop to play the king and lord, nor the king's part to play the bishop: for the king's office is enough for a king, and the bishop's office enough for a bishop. Let them do the best they can, and study each of them in their office. But let the king take heed he be able to judge, whether the bishop do true service to God in his vocation by the word of God: and let the bishop do the same; take heed whether the king or council would command him to do any thing contrary to the works of his vocation, which is to preach God's word: in case he do, with knowledge and soberness to admonish him, and to bring him to a better mind. If thou be a judge, remember thy name, and do the works of right judgment: if a justice, do according to thy name: if a merchant, buy and sell truly: if any other subject, do according to the name thou bearest, as our subjects of England of late did never a whit. For master parson and an old wife taught them to forget the duties of true and godly subjects, and would have made them all kings; but the Lord cast them into the sea. This duty of each man is handsomely set forth by certain pictures in the town-house at Basil, in this verse: *Tu supplex ora, tu regna, tuque labora*[1]. There be three images; the one of the pope, the other of the emperor, the third of a ploughman: and the verse teacheth all three their duties. He biddeth the pope "pray;" the emperor to "reign;" and the ploughman to "labour." Let therefore all bishops and priests know, their office is to preach and pray. This I say, God to record, of no hatred, but of love; for I am afraid of God's threatenings and vengeance toward them, if they amend not; for God saith he will require the blood of the people at the bishop's hand, Ezech. iii. xxxiii.; and Paul sayeth, "Woe be unto me if I preach not!" 1 Cor. ix.

Ezek. iii. xxxiii.
1 Cor. ix.

Here might the bishop or the parson, peradventure, partly excuse themselves, and say: "I know my fault, and would gladly amend it, if I could; but I am so old I cannot preach, nor never used myself thereunto." I would advise him, then, to follow the doings of Valerius, the bishop of Hipponensis, that in his old and latter days, perceiving his age could not satisfy the labours due unto his vocation, associated to himself a companion and co-

[1 Do thou pray, thou rule, and thou labour.]

adjutor, even Saint Augustine[1], as he testifieth, Epist. cxlviii. In the beginning of that epistle thus he writeth: "Before all things I would your godly prudence should think, in this our time, nothing to be more acceptable, facile, or more desired of men, than the office of a bishop, priest, or deacon, if their office be slightly and slenderly used; but with God nothing is more damnable, miserable, or sorrowful." The same knew Samuel: for in his age he instituted his sons to help and ease the intolerancy and importance of his office. So I would every bishop and parson, that for age or lack of learning cannot do his office, should institute and take unto him some wise and learned preacher to help him, and not a singer, as now is used.

If this counsel and doings of the godly men rehearsed before like them not, let them devise some other like; and all is one to me, so they eschew the ire of God: for, doubtless, it is horrible, to fall in this part into the hands of God; for what shall it avail them to win all the world, and lose their own souls? I would likewise pray and admonish the magistrates to see the schools better maintained; for the lack of them shall bring blindness into this church of England again. And such as be the patrons and givers of benefices, let them take heed they give and bestow them upon worthy men, and sell them not to asses and blind block-headed fellows; for if they bestow their benefices for lucre or affection to such as cannot, or will not, feed with the word of God the people of his cure, the patron shall die eternally for it, as well as his blind and naughty curate, parson, or vicar.

The fourth doctrine of this first part is very necessary. For when the bishops and priests hear their office is to preach, then think they, But what we preach, it is no matter, it lieth in our arbitrement and pleasure. Nay, sayeth the

[1 Augustinus Valerio episcopo suo, cui erat collega, præsertim in dispensando verbo Dei, &c. Ante omnia peto ut cogitet religiosa prudentia tua, nihil esse in hac vita, et maxime hoc tempore, facilius et lætius et hominibus acceptabilius episcopi aut presbyteri aut diaconi officio, si perfunctorie atque adulatorie res agatur; sed nihil apud Deum miserius et tristius et damnabilius. Aug. Op. Bas. 1541. Tom. II. Ep. cxlviii. col. 686.]

text, Preach that I bid thee; and so saith Saint Peter. 1 Pet. iv.
1 Pet. iv. Matt. xxviii.   Matt. xxviii.

In this vocation of preaching the preacher should so use himself, as he might say always, "My doctrine is not my doctrine, but his that hath sent me." For it is God's word and his law, that turneth the hearts of people to repentance. Psal. xix. cxix. For the word of God written Ps. xix. cxix. is as perfect as God himself, and is indeed able to make a man perfect in all things, 2 Tim. iii.: wherefore it needeth 2 Tim. iii. not that blasphemous and stinking help of the bishop of Rome, that durst say, The law of God is not of itself, but by his interpretation, wholesome and sufficient. But by this means he got authority over the scripture to bury it, and to stablish what he would, were it never so devilish and heretical. Therefore let such as be of God do as they have in commission from him, and not as they please themselves; for if they do, they be of the devil, and not of Christ.

THE OBEDIENCE OF JONAS.

Then Jonas arose, and went to Ninive, at the commandment of the Lord.

Jonas, now being an obedient servant, looketh no more for a ship to fly, but goeth the next way whither he is commanded, though the journey was painful and dangerous to the flesh. But the cross of trouble is not unprofitable to the Christians: it mortifieth the flesh, so that in the afflicted dwelleth the Spirit of God; it exerciseth the faith, and proveth obedience: as David saith, "Well it is with me that thou hast chastened me, Lord, that I may learn thy commandments." Both good and bad are afflicted in this world; but the good thereby is amended, and the evil is apeyred, and so they perish in their trouble. David was amended herewith. 2 Regum xii. xxiv. So was Eze- 2 Sam. xii. chias. Esay xxxviii. So was Daniel. Dan. ix. These and Isai. xxviii. like unto them be chastened *in* the world, because they Dan. ix. should not be damned *with* the world. The evil with affliction be not amended, but indurated and hardened through their own malice and obstinacy, as Saul and Pharao; and the pains and torments here be the beginning of the pains eternal. This diversity and contrary effect of persecution godly setteth forth the holy prophet David, Psalm lxxv.; wonderful godly. The which psalm I would all bishops should read, that knoweth the truth, and yet will take no pains to set it forth, but live idle; and such as have no learning to set it forth, or of malice whister[1] and secretly hindereth the setting forth of it: for, doubtless, at length they shall not only drink of the wine of adversity, but be compelled to drink dregs and all. So shall all these ravening and covetous noblemen, that with injuries and wrongs now afflict the poor; at length they shall be most afflicted themselves. So shall the avaricious judge, the covetous merchant, and the traitorous and seditious subject. But I rede you be wise in time; and as ye have followed this rebel Jonas in evil, so follow him in the good, and amend: if not, the king's majesty must cast you into the sea.

Psal. lxxv.

The obedience of Jonas is set forth and commended with many circumstances, and should therefore the better be noted. First, because he went the next way to Ninive, and hired none other, nor substituted his suffragan, nor went not into Samaria to ask counsel at his friends what was best to do, but went straightway himself. The second circumstance is worthy annotation: that he did all things as the Lord bad him. Wherein we are taught to be diligent we see all our doings, acts, and obedience to be according and as the word of God biddeth. There is put in, as though it were by a parenthesis, the description of Ninive.

And Ninive was a great city to the Lord, of three days' journey.

This description setteth forth the obedience of Jonas, that diligently preached thorough the whole city the pleasure of God, that it should be destroyed within forty days. The city is called great unto God, that is to say, a very great city, as the cedar of God, the mount of God, &c.: or else it is called the city of God, for the wonderful respect and pity that the Lord had in the saving of it. Whether the city were three days' journey about, or else three days'

[[1] Whister: probably silence, from *whist* or *hist*.]

space to visit all the streets thereof, it is not agreed yet upon among all writers; but this we know, it was a notable city, and among all cities in the east of most famous report.

Now it followeth what Jonas did after he entered into the city.

> When Jonas had entered the city one day's journey, he cried and said, Within this forty days Ninive shall be destroyed.

Of this text we learn, that Jonas lived not idle after he came to the place whither he was sent by God, but that he walked abroad and cried. So should every man that is called to the office of a bishop or pastor. It is not enough he go to his diocese or parsonage, but that he must walk abroad there, and cry out the commandment of the Lord; or else they be, with all their title, glory, pomp, and name, dumb dogs, subject unto the vengeance and plague of God. And this is the mark thou shouldest know a bishop and priest by; by his tongue, that soundeth the word of the Lord, and not by his cap or outward vesture. So should the judge go abroad in his country, and speak and declare everywhere justice: so should the provost, heads of colleges, masters of schools, go and teach the thing appertaineth to their place and vocation.

The text maketh mention of the sum and principal state of his sermon, that is, that the city should be destroyed within forty days; and that spake he simply and plainly without condition or gloss. Yet may we easily gather of the long time of forty days that was given unto it, that it was reversed unto penance[2] and amendment of life; and God would rather at this time fray them to make them amend, than to punish them and lose them for ever, and would pierce thus their minds, and bring them to a knowledge of their sins. And as subversion and destruction was threatened unto this Ninive, so is it to this whole realm. For there is among us as great and as many sins (God give grace there be no greater nor no more!) as were among them: we must, then, amend, or else we shall perish every each one, Luke xiii.; but what time, the Lord Luke xiii.

[2 Repentance.]

knoweth, and not I.—Now it followeth how the preaching of Jonas was accepted.

> And the people of Ninive believed God, and proclaimed fasting, and arrayed themselves in sackcloth, as well the great as the small of them.

Out of this text is first to be noted, how that the Ninivites resisted not the preaching of Jonas, when they had yet, if they would have excused their evil, many refuges and pretexts. Their obedience to the word of God condemneth both the Jews and us of obstinacy and malice.

First, they might have pretended, 'This Jonas is but one man; therefore not to be credited.' Second, 'He is a stranger, and speaketh it of hatred unto us, and of affection towards his own country.' Third, 'He is of a contrary religion to ours, and would deceive us from our fathers' faith.' Fourth, 'He is no king, but a man that seemeth to have little wit and less experience.' Fifth, 'He is one contemned of his own countrymen, and cannot be heard of them: and should we credit his words?' Sixth, 'He is a naughty liver, and one that God hateth and hath punished; and should we pass of his sayings?' But they remembered their own faults. At the preaching of one day they amended; they never looked for miracle. They pretended not the antiquity and ancientness of their city, that had stood almost from the time of the flood. Gen. x. They that heard him never desired[1] their amendment until such time as the king, the priests, and the other elders of the city, had agreed whether Jonas' doctrine were true or not. Of this facility and quickness of belief in the Ninivites we may see, that sooner believeth the very infidels the word of God, than such as beareth the name of God and be brought up in superstition: and that I think were easy to be seen, if experience should be taken to preach at Babylon or Constantinople, he should rather convert those cities than Rome. Farther, their promptness condemneth our obstinacy and hardness of heart, that daily hear the word of God preached, and yet nothing the better nor nearer to salvation.

[1] Desired. Perhaps, *deferred.*

It followeth, what the Ninivites do when they be converted. First, they believe in the Lord; second, they fast. A man ignorant of God offendeth two manner of ways, in body and in soul; and both these offences must be amended, if we will be reconciled unto God. By faith the mind is reconciled unto God; and by abstinence the body is kept in subjection, and the wantonness of concupiscence kept in obedience. But in this our miserable and cursed time of God for sin, is great question and controversy moved, not only concerning faith, but also fasting; of which two things I judge it meet somewhat to be spoken of. As touching faith, it is not an opinion and knowledge only, but a vehement, earnest, and certain persuasion of God's promises in Christ: and out of this faith springeth all godliness and virtuous works; and whatsoever springeth not hereof is sin. And this faith the almighty God confirmeth in his true and virtuous people two manner of ways, inwardly and outwardly: inwardly, by the Holy Ghost, who testifieth by his Spirit with our spirit, that we be the children of God; outwardly, by preaching of God's word, and ministration of the sacraments.

The preaching contain the innumerable benefits and promises of God made in the new testament and the old unto us in Christ, who is the seed that should and doth tread and break the head of the serpent. Gen. iii. John iii. Gen. iii. John iii.

The sacraments be as visible words offered unto the eyes and other senses, as the sweet sound of the word to the ear, and the Holy Ghost to the heart. The number of these sacraments in the public ministry of the church be two; one of baptism, and the other of the Lord's Supper; and both these teach and confirm none other thing than that the mercy of God saveth the faithful and believers.

Therefore is the bread in the holy supper called the body of Christ, and the wine the blood of Christ, because they be sacraments and seals of God's promises in Christ. This plain and simple doctrine of the sacraments were sufficient, if fraud, guile, treason, heresy, superstition, papistry, ignorancy, arrogancy, misery, and the malice of men would suffer it. But these evils afore rehearsed have called into question and controversy, whether carnally, corporally, and really, the precious body of Christ be present; and how the communion and sacrament of his body should be ministered and used: for the resolution and answering unto the which questions, I will sincerely and plainly shew my mind according to the word of God.

Of the presence of Christ's body in the sacrament.

I will not in this question say as much as I would or could, because of late days, in this place, it was godly and learnedly touched. But yet somewhat must I say, because the ignorance of it bringeth idolatry, idolatry bringeth eternal damnation, eternal damnation cometh not only to the ignorant, but also unto him that should in his vocation remove (or do his good will to remove) the ignorancy. I am appointed to remove ignorancy: thus therefore, I pray you, hear how ye may remove it. I will keep this order. First, I will shew by many arguments, that there is no corporal presence of Christ's body in the sacrament; then will I answer to the arguments of the adversaries that would have it here.

The first argument.

This I take of the name of Christ's body, which is like unto ours in all things except sin; Heb. ii. Esa. liii.; and in case it were not in all things like unto ours, (except sin and immortality,) Saint Paul's argument would prove nothing. 1 Cor. xv. But our bodies be, one to each one, measured certainly with quantity and quality, and occupy at one time one place; therefore so doeth and ever hath done Christ's body. And thus would Paul prove our resurrection, because our bodies be as Christ's is, that is risen, except sin and immortality. After that they say, Christ hath now a glorified body, and so we have not, it maketh nothing for their purpose: for when Christ made his supper, and instituted the sacrament of his death, he was a mortal and passible man, subject unto the tyranny and violence of his adversaries; yea, after his immortality he shewed manifest tokens and arguments of his pure, true, and sensible humanity, John xxi. 1 John i., for the apostles' fingers touched him. Farther, Saint Paul saith, he shall, Phil. iii.

that Christ shall make our bodies like unto his glorious body. Therefore they do destroy the true and very humanity of Christ's body, that say his body is in many places at one time, which robbeth his body of all the qualities, quantities, and properties of a true body. For the scripture of God confesseth that Christ's body is but in one place; and many of the popes' canons confirm the same. Thus it is written: *De consecrat.* distinct. ii. *Prima quidem. Donec sæculum finiatur, sursum Dominus est. Sed tamen hic nobiscum est veritas Domini. Corpus enim in quo resurrexit in uno loco esse oportet: veritas autem ejus ubique diffusa est*[1]: that is to say, "Till the world be ended, the Lord is above; but notwithstanding his truth is here with us. The body in which he rose must be in one place, and his verity is dispersed every where."

The second reason.

This is taken out of the nature and condition of a sacrament, which is this, That the thing that is remembered by the sacrament be itself absent, and yet the signs or sacraments take the name and nomination of the thing represented and signified by the signs, for a declaration of the thing that is done with the signs.

So is it in all the sacraments of the old testament and the new; therefore, also in this sacrament. The thing itself in this sacrament, that is, to wit, the precious body of Christ broken, and his innocent blood shed, be absent; yet be the bread and the wine called the body broken, and the blood-shedding, according to the nature of a sacrament, to set forth the better the thing done and signified by the sacrament. There is done in the sacrament the memory and remembrance of Christ's death, which was done on the cross, when his precious body and blood was rent and torn, shed and poured out for our sins.

With this agreeth the mind of Saint Augustine[2]: *Ad Bonifacium*, Epist. xxiii. *Si enim sacramenta quandam similitudinem earum rerum quarum sacramenta sunt non haberent, omnino sacramenta non essent*: that is to say, "If sacraments had not some proportion and likeness of the things whereof

[1 Corp. Jur. Can. Decr. 3 Pars. De consecrat. Dist. 2. c. 44., quoted from Aug.]

[2 Aug. Op. Basiliæ, 1541. Tom. ii. Ep. 23. col. 93.]

they be sacraments, they were no sacraments at all. And thus rather of the similitude and signification of the thing they represent and signify they take the name, and not that in deed they be as they be named."

So after this manner is the sacrament of Christ's body called Christ's body; and the sacraments of Christ's blood called Christ's blood; and the sacrament of faith is called faith. As Saint Augustine[1] learnedly and godly saith in the same argument, *Accedat verbum ad elementum, et fit sacramentum. Non ait, Tollat elementum, et fit sacramentum:* that is to say, " Let the word come unto the element, and then is made the sacrament." He sayeth not, Let the word change or transubstantiate the element, (that is to say, the substance and matter of the sacrament,) and then is made the sacrament.

The third reason.

If he were here in the sacrament bodily and corporally, he should every day suffer and shed his precious blood. For the scripture saith, "This is my body that is broken for you, and my blood that is shed for you:" Luke xxii. 1 Cor. xi. but this is not true that he daily suffereth pain and passion, Rom. vi.; no more is it true that he is in the sacrament bodily, for heaven keepeth him till the last day. Acts iii. Neither yet is the bread after consecration his very body, 1 Cor. xi. nor the wine his blood, Matt. xxvi.; but the bread remaineth still bread, and the wine still wine, after the word spoken, as they were before, concerning their substance, but the use of them be changed.

The fourth reason.

The scripture maketh no mention but of one ascension, and of two comings; one past, and the other we look for in the end of the world, at the latter judgment.

If their doctrine were true, there should be infinite ascensions, and infinite descensions. Farther, they cannot tell themselves, what is become of the body they feign to have in the sacrament, when the accidents and qualities corrupt and be consumed.

[[1] Augustine's words are, Accedit verbum ad elementum, et fit sacramentum etiam ipsum tanquam visibile verbum. Aug. Op. Basiliæ, 1541. Tom. ix. In Johan. Evang. cap. 15. Tr. 80. co. 445.]

Their gloss upon the canon, *Tribus gradibus*[2], *ait avolare in cœlum*[3]: that is to say, "It flieth into heaven"; but we say, he was there before. They dare not say it corrupteth, nor that it is turned into the substance of our bodies and souls: what is there then become of this body?

The fifth reason.

God had made, by this mean, his church in danger, and subject unto idololatry. For there be many chances and cases happen, that may let the priest to consecrate; and then should the people worship an idol for lack of the presence of Christ's body.

These dangers may chance three manner of ways: in the priest; in the words; and in the matter.

The priest, if he be not lawfully consecrated, if he be an heretic, one excommunicated, or a simoniac, he consecrateth not. Magister Sententiarum, Lib. IV. dist. xiii[4]. See the gloss *De consecrat.* dist. ii. cap. *Quid sit sanguis*[5].

[[2] Corp. Juris Canon. Decr. 3 Pars, De consecrat. Dist. 2. can. 23.]

[[3] In the ordinary gloss upon this canon these words occur: Certum est quod species quam cito dentibus teruntur, tam cito in cœlum rapitur corpus Christi. Decretum Gratiani, Antverpiæ, 1573, co. 2011. A.

Alcuinus, citante Gregorio, inquit: Uno, eodemque tempore ac momento in cœlo rapitur ministerio angelorum corpori Christi consociandum, et ante oculos sacerdotis in altari videtur. See Decreti 3 Pars, De Consecrat. Dist. 2. can. 73.]

[[4] Illi vero qui excommunicati sunt, vel de hæresi manifeste notati, non videntur hoc sacramentum posse conficere, licet sacerdotes sint * * * * Missa enim dicitur eo quod cœlestis nuncius ad consecrandum vivificum corpus adveniat, juxta dictum sacerdotis dicentis, Omnipotens Deus, jube hæc perferri per manus sancti angeli tui in sublime altare tuum, &c. Idcirco nisi angelus venerit, missa nequaquam jure vocari potest. Nunquid enim, si hoc mysterium hæreticus ausus fuerit usurpare, angelum de cœlo mittit Deus oblationem ejus consecrare? * * * Ex his colligitur, quod hæreticus a catholica ecclesia præcisus nequeat hoc sacramentum conficere; quia sancti angeli, qui hujus mysterii celebrationi assistunt, tunc non adsunt, quando hæreticus vel schismaticus hoc mysterium temerarie celebrare præsumit. Pet. Lombard. Lugduni, 1570. Lib. IV. Distinct. 13. fo. 317.]

[[5] In the canon *Quid sit sanguis,* it is written: "Calix enim quem sacerdos catholicus sacrificat," &c. the gloss upon which is, *Catholicus.* Hinc collige sacerdotem non catholicum corpus homini conficere non posse. Decretum Gratiani. Antv. 1573. co. 2043. A.]

In the words of consecration there is no less danger and doubt. First, many of their writers be ignorant with what words Christ consecrated. Johanes Duns[1] and Pope Innocent the third[2] (*Libro de Officio Missæ*, part iii. cap. vi. xiv.) do say the consecration to be comprehended in this word *Benedixit*. Comestor doubteth the gloss upon this canon, *Utrum sub figura*[3], where as the glossator interpreteth these words in the canon of the mass, *Jube hæc perferri ;* that is to say, "Command these things to be carried," as though they were the words of consecration. The which opinion the Master of the Sentence seemeth to favour in the place afore named: "If an heretic," saith he, "would take upon him to usurp this mystery, would God send an angel from

[[1] See Joh. Duns Scotus, Lib. iv. Distin. viii. Quæst. ii. fol. 41. &c. Parisiis, J. Granion.]

[[2] Quando Christus confecit, et qua sub forma. Cap. vi. Benedixit. Cum ad prolationem verborum istorum, Hoc est corpus meum, hic est sanguis meus, sacerdos conficiat, credibile judicatur, quod et Christus eadem verba dicendo confecit. Porro quidam dixerunt quod Christus confecit, cum benedixit, literam construentes hoc ordine: Accepit panem, benedixit; subaudiendum est, dicens, Hoc est corpus meum, et tunc fregit et dedit, et ait: Accipite et comedite; et iteravit, Hoc est corpus meum. Prius ergo protulit illa verba, ut eis vim conficiendi tribueret; deinde protulit eadem, ut Apostolos formam conficiendi doceret. Alii vero dixerunt quod et sacramentum confecit et formam instituit post benedictionem, cum dixit, Hoc est corpus meum; intelligentes illam benedictionem fuisse, vel aliquod signum quod super panem impressit, vel aliquod verbum quod super panem expressit. Quibus illud videtur obsistere, quod prius fregerit quam dixerit, Hoc est corpus meum. Nec etiam est credibile quod prius dederit quam confecerit. Sane dici potest, quod Christus virtute divina confecit, et postea formam expressit, sub qua posteri benedicerent. Ipse namque per se virtute propria benedixit; nos autem ex illa virtute quam indidit verbis.—Innoc. III. De Sacro. altaris mysterio. Antv. 1545. Lib. iv. cap. vi. fol. 166.]

[[3] The words in the canon are, "Jube, inquit, hoc perferri per manus angeli tui sancti in sublime altare tuum in conspectu divinæ majestatis tuæ." The gloss upon this is, "Perferri. id est transubstantiari; vel, perferri. id est, sursum efferri, id est, converti in sanctum altare tuum, id est, corpus tuum super choros angelorum exaltatum. Sed contra videtur quod oratio hæc sit superflua, quia hæc dicitur post verba quorum virtute conficitur corpus Christi, &c. Decretum Gratiani, Decret. 3 Pars, De Consecrat. Dist. 2. co. 2041.—See Comestor, Hist. Schol. fol. 237. Paris. 1518. See also Canon Missæ.]

heaven to consecrate his oblation?[4]" But howsoever they agree upon the words of consecration, there is yet another rule in their mass-books, that the words must be perfectly pronounced, or else they do nothing. How should this be known, when they speak them in silence?[5] Well, grant they would cry or sing them out, yet so might they else be vain; for there is also required the intention of him that will consecrate.

The matter must be such bread and such wine as the gloss[6] speaketh of, *De conse.* dist. ii. *Sicut non sanctificando*; the which properties if they be absent, nothing is consecrated.

The sixth reason.

If Christ be present corporally, then shall their sacrifices cease, as Saint Paul sayeth, 1 Cor. xi. "Ye shall shew the Lord's death till he come." He cometh after their belief and learning; then should they cease from sacrificing.

1 Cor. xi.

The seventh reason.

In case they could dissolve and answer to every one of these reasons, yet could not Christ's body be in the mass; for it lacketh the word of God, that is to say, the shewing of Christ's death. Farther, the mass destroyeth and dishonoureth the institution of Christ.

Solutions of their arguments.

These I will comprehend all in three points. First, they contend by the authority of the fathers. The second, by these words of Christ, "This is my body." The third, by the omnipotency of God.

[4 See Note 4, page 517.]

[5 This refers to the Romish method of performing certain parts of the service inaudibly.]

[6 Sicut non sanctificando. The words of the canon are: "Sic (or sicut) in sanctificando calicem Domini offerri sola aqua minime potest, quomodo nec vinum solum potest. Nam si," &c. The gloss upon which is: "Dicitur in hoc cap. quod in sacrificio non debet offerri vinum sine aqua nec aqua sine vino; sed simul illa duo, ut perfectum sit sacrificium; sicut corpus Christi non de farina solum, sed de pane perfecto debet confici." Decretum Gratiani. Antverpiæ, 1573. Decret. 3 Pars, De Consecrat. Dist. 2. col. 2001.]

Of the Fathers' authority.

When they be beaten by the authority of God's word, they flee for help at the fathers' authority. Let them make answer: Is this their opinion,—when the priest hath spoken these words, "This is my body;" by and by the substance of the bread to be changed, or the substance thereof to vanish away; (I ask the question, because yet they be not fully agreed thereupon;) and for it cometh the corporal body of Christ with the same quality and quantity he was born, lived, and died in? So that there hangs in the air, in the priest's hands, the accidents and qualities of bread, without any substance, and so thus to be honoured there of the people! In what apostle's writings find they this doctrine? Or in what man's writings that followed the apostles within one, two, three, four, five, six, yea, seven hundred years? If they can shew this in any authentical writer[1], in any work that hath not been doubted of, I will believe as they do. But that it may be known unto you that the fathers were not of their opinion, I will propound unto you certain conjectures.

First: We read not where there was ever any contention about the words of consecration, where they began and where they ended, neither any thing of the minister's intention, to be of such virtue they speak of.

The second: The elders never answered the Arian that denied the equality between God the Father and God the Son with this, 'Christ is God and equal with the Father, for we so honour him in the sacrament.' If the catholic church had so judged of Christ's bodily presence in the sacrament, as the new upstart church doth, and hath done of late years, there could not have been a stronger argument against Arius and his heresy.

The third: Neither did the Marcionists ever make such a reason, 'Though Christ seemed to have the qualities and conditions of a natural man; yet he had not them indeed: for in the sacrament of his body there seemeth to be the very qualities and conditions of bread and wine,

[1 Many editions of the fathers were so interpolated by the papists, as to be no longer "authentical." See James on the Corruptions, &c. and other writers.]

yet is there neither bread nor wine indeed.' If this opinion of the accidents, qualities, and sensual judgment[2] of the bread had been approved and taken in those days for Christianity and christian religion, how would this illusion and witchcraft have defended, I pray you, the Marcionist opinion[3]! Doubtless, nothing more. But Tertullian[4] against the Marcionists doth reason anotherwise, saying, "Christ of the bread that he took made his body, saying, 'This is my body,' that is to say, a figure of my body."

The fourth: They used chalices of wood and glass. De consecrat. dist. i. *Vasa in quibus*[5]. The wooden chalice could soak in the wine consecrated; the glassen chalices might soon have been broken: if any of them both had contained the precious blood of Christ, they would not so temorously[6] have used it.

The fifth: The sacrament was given to the children in their hands to bear it home with them[7]. Eccles. Hist. Lib. VII. cap. xxxiv.

The sixth: No scripture of God, neither doctor of the catholic faith, taught ever Christ to be honoured here in earth with candles and bowings of knees.

The seventh: In celebrating the supper, they said, "Lift up your hearts;" meaning not to have the mind affixed in the signs and elements of the sacraments, but in heaven. Whereof it may be easily gathered, that they never thought of a corporal presence here in the earth.

The eighth: Origen[8], upon the book of Leviticus, de-

[[2] Sensual judgment: judgment according to the senses.]

[[3] Viz.—That Christ had no real human nature.]

[[4] Acceptum panem et distributum discipulis corpus suum illum fecit, 'Hoc est corpus meum' dicendo, id est, figura corporis mei. Tertul. Adv. Marc. Paris. 1580. Lib. IV. cap. 40, p. 233. C.]

[[5] Quondam sacerdotes aurei ligneis calicibus utebantur; nunc e contrario lignei sacerdotes aureis utuntur calicibus.—Zepherinus xvi. Rom. Epis. patinis vitreis Missas celebrari constituit. Corp. Jur. Can. Decret. 3 pars, De conse. Dist. i. Can. 44.]

[[6] Rashly.]

[[7] βραχύ τι τῆς εὐχαριστίας ἐπέδωκεν τῷ παιδαρίῳ, κ. τ. λ. Euseb. Eccl. Hist. Lib. VI. cap. 44. Narratio Dionysii de Serapione, Moguntiæ, 1672, p. 246.]

[[8] Perhaps the author had in his mind the following passage, in which though no mention is made of burning the relics, yet in the verses under review (c. vii. 16, 17) the two circumstances of keeping the

clareth that the remanents and relics of the sacraments were not kept to be honoured, but they were burned. Who would handle his God so cruelly, I pray you, as to burn him like an heretic?

Also, there is a decree in the canon law[1], *Tribus gradibus*, the which commandeth the ministers to receive all the relics of the sacrament; and it is the rule of Clement III. that lived anno 1190.

In the mean time I speak no word of that followeth, I should say, wicked question, meet for jugglers, enchanters, and witches, and not for christian men, much less for divines and teachers of God's people: in what moment of time the bread is turned into the body, and the wine into the blood? when the priest speaketh these words, "This is my body;" if they grant at least these to be the words of consecration.

Gabriel Biel[2], lect. xlviii. sayeth that the body is not present whiles this oration is speaking, "This is my body;" *sed tota oratio est referenda ad ultimum instans ipsius orationis*, that is to say, "the whole oration must be referred unto the last instance of it." And with this opinion agreeth the gloss upon the canon law: De consecratione, distinct. ii. *Cum omne*, sayeth that the consecration is made only in the last letter[3].

And in another canon, *Ante benedictionem*[4], thus he

sacrifice and burning it with fire are connected together: "Nam et Dominus panem, quem discipulis dabat, et dicebat eis, Accipite et manducate, non distulit, nec servari jussit in crastinum." Orig. Hom. v. in Levit. c. vii.]

[1 Quod si remanserint, in crastinum non reserventur, sed cum timore et tremore clericorum diligentia consumantur. Corp. Jur. Can. Decret. 3 par. De consecrat. Dist. 2. can. 33.]

[2 Gab. Biel. super can. Missæ. Lugduni 1542. fol. 110. co. 3.]

[3 Sed nunquid verum est quod separatim consecratur corpus Christi et separatim sanguis? Dicunt quidam, quod non fit transubstantiatio nisi in ultima syllaba totius formæ prolata. Alii vero dicunt, &c. Sed ego dico quod si per copulativam duo dicuntur, tunc in prolatione hujus vocis, Hoc est corpus meum, transubstantiatur corpus, et in prolatione consequentis vocis sive locutionis transubstantiatur sanguis; sed si per copulativam tantum unum dicatur, tunc fiet tantum in ultima litera transubstantiatio. Decretum Gratiani. Antv. 1573. Decret. iii. Pars. De consecrat. Dist. ii. co. 2004.]

[4 The words of the canon are: "Ante benedictionem illa species

saith: *Licet verba successive proferantur, non tamen successive consecratio fit; sed in uno instanti corrumpitur panis, scilicet in ultimo instanti prolationis verborum:* that is to say, "Although the words be spoken one after another, yet is not the consecration made by a little and little; but in one instant, or point of time, the bread is altered, to say in the last moment of the words spoken." After this their wicked and idololatrical doctrine, this syllable (*um*) in this oration, *Hoc est corpus meum,* to say, "This is my body," hath all the strength and virtue to change and deify the bread! But I pray you, what syllable is it that changeth and deifieth the wine? for even with them these words seem to have more difficulty than the other. But let these illusions and crafts go, and let us cleave to the truth of God's word, and we shall be out of all danger.

A QUESTION.

Thus they say now: If this opinion be neither of the apostles, neither from the ancient doctors, how chanceth it to be so universally taken, and for so infallible and indoubted truth; yea, such a truth as in case men forsake all truth, and yet not contrary this truth, is accounted a man most christian and true?

ANSWER. Nothing is more expedient to answer directly unto the question, than to consider the time of our fathers. They thought it best to name the sacraments by the name of the thing was represented by the sacraments. Yet in many places of their writings they so interpretate themselves, that no man, except he will be wilfully blind, can say but they understood the sacrament to signify, and not to be the thing signified; to confirm, and not to exhibit grace; to help, and not to give faith; to seal, and not to win the promise of God, Rom. iv.; to shew what we Rom. iv. be before the use of them, and not to make us the thing we declare to be after them; to shew we are Christ's; to shew we be in grace, and not by them to be received

nominatur, post benedictionem corpus Christi significatur." The gloss upon this passage is: "Et licet verba successive proferantur, non tamen successive consecratio fit: sed in uno instanti corrumpitur panis, scilicet in ultimo instanti prolationis verborum; et licet panis sit corpus compositum, momentanea est tamen ejus corruptio." Decretum Gratiani. col. 2021.]

into grace; to shew we be saved, and not yet to be saved by them; to shew we be regenerated, and not to be regenerated by them: thus the old doctors meant.

But when all good learning, and the lesson of the holy scripture, were drowned by the Goths and Vandals in Europe, Asia, and Africa, and yet somewhat rescued and caught again by Charles the Great, anno 800, men not acquainted with the phrases and vein of the scripture accustomed themselves to the reading of doctors, and left the word of God. Whereof followed, among other evils, that in France, by certain Italians, this question to be very much and many times reasoned upon, as touching the corporal presence of Christ's body in the sacrament. Against the which error one John Scot[1], and one Bertram[2], wrote a book of the same matter to Charles the Great[3]. But the monks and the priests declined most unto the opinion of the carnal and corporal presence: whereupon, in the time of Leo the Ninth, a bishop of Rome, anno 1050, being a monk, called a council, named Vercellense; the which ruled, as chief president and great master, one Lancfranck[4], a monk, and afterward bishop of Canterbury. He damned Berengarius: but after that the same Berengarius had recanted, one Nicolaus[5], pope, assembled a

[1 John Scotus (Erigena), a native of Ireland, lived in the ninth century. He was one of the first writers against the newly received doctrine of transubstantiation and the real presence, and distinguished as a man of great genius and erudition. His chief work, a book against Paschasius Radbert, is not extant. It was condemned in several councils as heretical, and in the council at Rome, A.D. 1059, Berenger was required to burn it with his own hands. Scotus was the personal friend of Charles the Bald. See Mosheim's Eccles. Hist. cent. 9. part II. ch. i. sect. 7, and ch. iii. sect. 19. Full and interesting particulars of Berenger will be found in Soames's edition of Mosheim, Vol. II. p. 380—4.]

[2 Bertram, or Ratramnus, a celebrated monk of Corby, in the ninth century. "The Book of Bertram the Priest," a work written by him at the desire of Charles the Bald, on the body and blood of Christ, is said to have been mainly instrumental in convincing Bishop Ridley of the errors of the church of Rome. See Fabricii Biblioth. Lat. med. ævi. Vol. I. p. 1661; and Dr Glocester Ridley's Life of Bishop Ridley.]

[3 This is an error. It was Charles the Bald, and not Charles the Great: the same mistake was made by several of the Reformers. See Ridley's and Grindal's Works.]

[4 See Note 6, page 117 of this Vol.]

[5 See Concil. Omn. Col. Agrip. 1567. Tom. III. pp. 577, 589, and 600.]

council of the monks of Italy and priests, and so compelled Berengarius to a recantation, which ye may read. De consecrat. dist. ii. *Ego Berengarius*[6].

But here we will pause and deliberate awhile upon this recantation, and scan it a little. In this recantation, mark it, there is no mention made of transubstantiation, but the bread and the wine are called the body and blood of Christ; and that the same are touched with the hands of the priest, broken, and torn with the teeth of the faithful. This sentence is not admitted now-a-days among our scholastical divines; yea, the gloss upon the same canon saith, (read the place,) "There is more danger of

[[6] Confessio Berengarii. Ego Berengarius, indignus sancti Mauritii Andegavensis ecclesiæ Diaconus, cognoscens veram, catholicam et apostolicam fidem, anathematizo omnem hæresim, præcipue eam, de qua hactenus infamatus sum: quæ astruere conatur panem et vinum, quæ in altari ponuntur, post consecrationem solummodo sacramentum, et non verum corpus et sanguinem Domini nostri Jesu Christi esse; nec posse sensualiter, nisi in solo sacramento, manibus sacerdotum tractari, vel frangi, aut fidelium dentibus atteri. Consentio autem sanctæ Romanæ et apostolicæ sedi: et ore et corde profiteor de sacramentis Dominicæ mensæ, eamdem fidem me tenere, quam dominus et venerabilis Papa Nicolaus, et hæc sancta Synodus auctoritate evangelica et apostolica tenendam tradidit, mihique firmavit: scilicet panem et vinum, quæ in altari ponuntur, post consecrationem non solum sacramentum, sed etiam verum corpus et sanguinem Domini nostri Jesu Christi esse, et sensualiter, non solum sacramento, sed in veritate manibus sacerdotum tractari, frangi, et fidelium dentibus atteri; jurans per sanctam et homousion Trinitatem, et per hæc sacrosancta Christi evangelia. Eos vero, qui contra hanc fidem venerint, cum dogmatibus et sectatoribus suis æterno anathemate dignos esse pronuntio. Quod si ego ipse aliquando contra hæc aliquid sentire aut prædicare præsumpsero, subjaceam Canonum severitati.—Lecto et perlecto sponte subscripsi.

Hanc confessionem fidei de corpore et sanguine Domini nostri Jesu Christi a Berengario Romæ coram CXIII. episcopis factam misit Papa Nicolaus per urbes Italiæ, Germaniæ, Galliæ, et ad quæcumque loca fama pravitatis ejus pervenire ante potuit: ut ecclesiæ, quæ prius doluerant de averso atque perverso, postea gauderent de reverso atque converso. Corp. Jur. Can. Decret. III Pars. De consecr. Dist. 2. can. 42.—Berenger appears to have retained his first views, notwithstanding this forced retractation, which was followed by others. See Thesaur. Anecd. Vol. IV. and his reply to Lanfranc, noticed in Soames's Mosheim.]

heresy in Berengarius' words than was in Berengarius himself[1]."

That recantation of Berengarius sent the pope into all the cities of Italy, Germany, and France. But this religion could not be well accepted, nor judged to be good of all men, though Hildebrand[2], the monk and sorcerer, confirmed it, anno 1079. Wherefore they excogitated and dreamed out transubstantiation; the which opinion holp forth the monks of Benedict's order in their sermons. And because this new and wicked doctrine of transubstantiation could not be received and admitted of all men; after two hundred years almost, Innocentius the third confirmed it in the council of Laterane[3], anno 1215, sometime being a doctor of Paris. And that this wicked doctrine might take the sooner place, he bound men to auricular confession, wherein they persuaded men to what they pleased[4]. Immediately afterward began the begging friars, the self soldiers of antichrist, and meet persons to set forth such abomination. At the beginning of these monsters Honorius the third[5], bishop

[1 The gloss is, *Dentibus*. Nisi sane intelligas verba Berengarii, in majorem incides hæresim quam ipse habuit; et ideo omnia referas ad species ipsas, nam de Christi corpore partes non facimus. Decretum Gratiani, col. 2022. The gloss upon the canon, *Qui manducat*, says: Sacramentum per partes dividitur, sed non ipsum corpus. Ibid. col. 2044.]

[2 Hildebrand. In Regesto Gregorii VII. Lib. III. et VI. in Synodo An. Dom. 1079. Habetur alia ejusdem Berengarii abjuratio. Cui repetitioni quid causam dederit, exponitur in scholiis Conciliorum, quæ Coloniæ quatuor tomis sunt impressa. Corr. Rom. Corp. Jur. Civ. Paris. 1687, p. 458.]

[3 Jesus Christus, cujus corpus et sanguis in sacramento altaris sub speciebus panis et vini veraciter continentur, transubstantiatis pane in corpus et vino in sanguinem potestate divina, &c. Sac. Concil. Gen. Lateran. sub Innoc. III. cap. i. Innocent. Op. Colon. 1575, p. 461.]

[4 Omnis utriusque sexus fidelis, postquam ad annos discretionis pervenerit, omnia sua solus peccata confiteatur fideliter saltem semel in anno proprio sacerdoti, &c. Ibid. cap. xxi. p. 472.]

[5 Honorius III. an. 1212. Romæ. Sacerdos vero frequenter doceat plebem suam, ut cum in celebratione Missarum elevatur hostia salutaris, se reverenter inclinet, idem faciens cum eam defert presbyter ad infirmum. Quam in decenti habitu superposito mundo velamine ferat, et referat manifeste ac honorifice ante pectus cum omni reverentia et timore, semper lumine præcedente, &c. Decretal. Greg. IX. Lib. III. Tit. 41. cap. 10.]

of Rome, commanded this new bready god to be honoured, anno 1226. Lib. II. Decretal. Tit. De celebra. Missarum. And then began the pindfools[5] and cloisters to be made in the churches, to reserve their new God in. And when the monks had farther entered into the consciences of the people, and when they had more inculcated and beaten to men's heads more this new article of faith, for transubstantiation, than all the other of our belief in Christ, the pope began to excogitate more yet for the honour of this new God! For when they had brought Christ from heaven to earth again, and so concluded he should be honoured in the sacrament, he thought it injury to let him be without some solemn feast and day, wherein people might honour him according to their decrees; whereupon Urbanus the IV. instituted the feast that is called Corpus Christi, 1262.[6] Then increased the rabble and idololatrical number of private masses; and the honouring of this bread then was defended with sword and fire.

In the mean time many godly men were sore afflicted in their conscience, yet durst not declare their grief; partly for fear, partly because that sophistry had blinded part of their judgments. At length the Lord raised up godly men, yea, here in England John Wicliff, that resisted this new heretical doctrine, 1368. And now, (the Lord be praised!) children know the ungodliness thereof, and may see it plainly to be naught, if they will not be wilfully blind. How childishly they brag of the doctors, now ye may see; and even the same do they with the words, "This is my body;" and with the omnipotency of God, as ye shall hear in the next sermon.

[5 Pindfools: a ludicrous form of the word pinfolds; alluding to the pyxes. Ne propter incuriam sacerdotum divina indignatio gravius exardescat, districte præcipiendo mandamus, quatenus a sacerdotibus eucharistia in loco singulari mundo et signato semper honorifice collocata, devote ac fideliter conservetur. Ibid.]

[6 For an account of the institution of this feast, see Constitutiones Clementis Papæ V. Lib. III. Tit. xvi. cap. 1., in which the decree of Urban IV. is recited and confirmed by Clement V. at the Council of Vienne, an. 1312. Corp. Jur. Can. Parisiis, 1687. Tom. II. p. 367.]

THE SIXTH SERMON UPON JONAS,

MADE BY JOHN HOPER.

THEY object against the truth, as concerning the absence of Christ's body in the sacrament, the words of Christ, " This is my body." Unto the which we answer briefly. The words should be understanded according to the matter and purpose they be spoken for. But every man knoweth, the matter and purpose that Christ entreateth of, is to make and institute a sacrament: therefore ought every word to be taken sacramentally; which is to attribute unto the sacrament the name of the thing signified and represented by the sacrament: therefore they should not force nor constrain the sound of the words used in the sacrament to make of the sacrament an idol by false interpretation, whereas the true sense of the word maketh but a necessary ceremony and help to our infirm faith. In the canon law[1], Decreta. Lib. LI. De verbor. significat. tit. xl. cap. vi. *Non sermoni res, sed rei est sermo subjectus:* that is to say, " The matter should not be constrained to the word, but the word to serve the matter." Et cap. viii.[2] *Dum proprietas verborum attenditur, sensus veritatis amittitur:* that is to say, " When the nature of the word is forced, the meaning of the verity is lost." Farther, what should move them to deny us one trope in these words, when they themselves use a great many of tropes and figures, whereas we use but one; and the same one to be in the open word of God, and all theirs to be with-

[1 Decretal. Greg. IX. Lib. v. Tit. 40. cap. 6. Corp. Jur. Can. Parisiis, 1687. Tom. II. p. 278.]

[2 Ibid. cap. 8.]

out, and contrary to, the word of God? Note the words of Christ, *Hoc est corpus meum*, that is to say, "This is my body:" what they should make of this word, "This," they cannot tell, and hitherunto they have disputed of it; and yet not agreed. Read, I pray thee, Gabriel Biel[3], Ser. xliv. *Et glossam super Canonem*,[4] *Timorem docet*. "Is" they interpretate, "is made." The bread, they say, is the accidents of bread. But in the cup, they be constrained to use with us a figure: "This cup is the new testament in my blood;" for they say, the wine in the cup, and not the cup. They know themselves how fondly they interpretate these words; rather maliciously, obstinately, and falsely, than truly. We therefore thus take them: "This is my body," that is to say, the sacrament of my body, "broken and given for you." Either, "This is the new testament;" that is to say, the sign of the new testament, or the remission of sin obtained in the body of Christ, broken and torn for us. St Augustine[5], Lib. xx. *contra Faustum*, cap. 21, hath these words: *Hujus sacrificii caro et sanguis ante adventum Christi per victimas similitudinum promittebatur: in passione Christi per ipsam veritatem reddebatur: post ascensum Christi per sacramentum memoriæ celebratur:* that is to say, "The flesh and blood of this sacrifice before the coming of Christ was promised by the sacrifices of similitude: in the passion of Christ they were given in deed: after the ascension of Christ they be celebrated by a sacrament of memory." And the Gloss,[6] Dist. ii. *Tribus gradibus*, saith: *Certum est, quod species quam cito dentibus teruntur, tam cito in cœlum rapitur corpus Christi;* that is to say, "It is certain that as soon as the accidents and qualities of bread be broken with the teeth, straightway the body of Christ is taken into

[3 Gabriel Biel. Super Can. Missæ. Lugd. 1542. Lect. xliv. p. 96.]

[4 The gloss is, *Corpus*. Solet quæri quid demonstretur per hoc pronomen *hoc:* aut panis, aut corpus Christi? Panis non; quia ille non est corpus Christi. Item nec corpus; quia non videtur quod ante totius formæ prolationem fiat transubstantiatio. Ad hoc dico, quod per hanc dictionem *hoc* nihil demonstratur, nam, &c. Decretum Gratiani. Antv. 1573, Paris. De consecr. Distinc. 2. Can. 25. co. 2011.]

[5 Aug. Op. Basiliæ, 1542. Tom. vi. contra Faustum, Lib. xx. cap. 21. col. 376.]

[6 Decretum Gratiani. Antv. 1573, col. 2011.]

heaven." So that their own doctors do not believe, that the very body of Christ is received in the sacrament!

If a man should then ask: What faith and opinion should the Christian have concerning the presence or absence of Christ's body in the sacrament?

Answer.

The body of Christ should be considered two manner of ways: first, as it was born of the blessed virgin, being indeed our very natural brother; then, as it was offered upon the cross for the redemption of the world. And thus offered and put to his passion upon the cross, we consider him in the sacrament; for the bread there used is called the body of Christ broken, and the wine the blood-shedding. But the presence of Christ's natural body, or the opinion of his presence, they so little profit, that in very deed it doeth rather hurt and harm, as Christ said, "The flesh profiteth nothing," John vi.; and again, "It is expedient that I go away."

We must therefore lift up our minds into heaven, when we feel ourselves oppressed with the burden of sin, and there by faith apprehend and receive the body of Christ slain and killed, and his precious blood shed, for our offences: and so by faith apply the virtue, efficacy, and strength of the merits of Christ to our souls, and by that means quit ourselves from the danger, damnation, and curse of God. And thus to be partaker of the worthiness and deservings of Christ's passion, is to eat the body and to drink the blood: therefore doth Christ in the vi. of John take "eat" for "believe," and "believe" for "eat," so many times. And St Augustine[1] saith, *Ut quid paras dentem et ventrem? crede et manducasti:* "Why preparest thou the teeth and belly? Believe and thou hast eaten." And whosoever eateth after this sort the body of Christ, and drink his blood, hath everlasting life.

Then object they: If we may thus eat the body and blood of Christ without the sacrament, what availeth it to have any sacrament?

Answer.

Against these temptations of the devil the use of the sacraments were instituted in the church.

[[1] Aug. Op. Tom. ix. In Evan. Johan. Tract. 25. col. 218.]

The first temptation of the devil is, he would bear the Christian in hand, the promises of God's mercy to be false: therefore doth God confirm them unto us by his sacraments.

The second temptation. When the devil perceiveth we believe the promises of God to be true universally, yet would he make us doubt of them particularly, as though they appertained not unto the private or singular conscience afflicted. That doubt would God remove in us by his sacraments, and saith, they appertain to the private and particular conscience afflicted, even as every private man receiveth the sacraments of the promises.

The third temptation. The devil laboureth to take from us the knowledge of the means of our salvation; and how the promises of God be made ours,—by the free grace of God or by our merits. The sacraments therefore, which behold and represent only Christ, do teach us that the means of our salvation is only in Christ. And to put us out of doubt, wherewithal Christ hath merited for us the promises of God and this grace of our salvation, the sacrament sheweth us it was with and by his death and blood-shedding; and therefore hath he given the name of his body and blood to the signs and elements of the sacrament. So the bread is called the body broken, and the wine the blood shedden; admonishing thee that in the receiving of the sacrament thou shouldest not tarry, nor occupy thy meditations and contemplations in the bread and wine, but in the merits of the body broken and the blood shed. Whosoever mark and understand these things, eateth Christ: if he be ignorant hereof, he is in danger of eternal damnation.

Another objection.

They say: God can do all things, therefore it is not impossible for him to make his body present in the sacrament.

We be not so addict and given unto human ration[2], that we will believe nothing more than reason is able to account and give answer for: but we believe many things that directly reason sayeth we should not believe; as the in-

[2 Ration: reasoning.]

carnation of Christ, our resurrection, the making of the world, three persons in one Godhead and one essence; and these things we believe, because the express word of God commandeth to believe it: but the transelementation and alteration of the bread no place of the scripture commandeth us to believe, but many places forbid we should believe it. Neither do the papists agree among themselves, what should be the words of consecration; and if we had but that advantage of them only, it were enough to declare their transubstantiation to be no part of God's word.

It is a folly to object the omnipotency of God, without God's word: God nor doeth, nor cannot do, more than he will do. And as foolishly do they, making mention of a miraculous presence of Christ's body, and do declare themselves to be of antichrist by the same means; for he shall deceive the world, yea, the very elects, if it were possible, with new miracles. Matt. xxiv. 2 Thess. ii. The miracle of Christ's visible ascension, and other expressed in the scriptures of God, are sufficient for the catholic church. And the miracle of the invisible and miraculous presence, we leave to them that be deceived with the spirit of error. For they would have now Christ present, but in any case dumb and without speech; and whiles he lived and could speak, the members of the devil hanged him upon the cross.

Thus was the malice of the devil always great against our Saviour. Before he came into the flesh, he made many believe he was come, before the time appointed by the prophets was expired. When he was come in deed, then went he about to persuade he was not come, nor was not the Saviour of the world, and never left till he had killed him; because he would not deny but that the very true Saviour of the world was come. And now that in deed he is ascended and departed from us according to the scriptures, he goeth about all he can to prove him now to be here. So that neither before his coming into the world, nor at his being corporeally in the world, nor yet being out of the world, he cannot be in peace, sure and safe from the assaults and temptations of his and our mortal enemy, Satan.

But I know how the adversaries of the truth persuade

the people maliciously to give no credit to such as preach and teach the truth. They say, we condemn the holy sacrament, and make it of no estimation. But believe not their slanders and lies; but hear or read our opinion, knowledge, and godly estimation we have of the sacrament, and then judge and give sentence afterward. And here receive mine opinion as touching the form and manner to celebrate and use the sacraments.

The form and manner how to celebrate the Sacraments.

It were expedient to entreat this matter at length, if time would serve. But yet in few words I will say somewhat of the sacrament of the Lord's supper, and also of baptism.

Baptism consisteth in two parts; in the word, and the element. The word is the preaching of the good and merciful promises of God's goodness, accepting us into his favour and grace for the merits of Christ. The which promises be briefly comprehended in these words, Matt. xxviii. "I baptize thee in the name of the Father, and of the Son, and of the Holy Ghost." These words sheweth the form of baptism, and also, that only men, reasonable creatures, should be baptized. Mark xvi. So is condemned the gentility[1] and superstition that hath been used in the christening of bells[2]. The matter and element of this sacrament is pure water: whatsoever is added, oil, salt, cross, lights, and such other, be the inventions of men; and better it were they were abolished, than kept in the church: for they obscure the simplicity and perfectness of Christ our Saviour's institution. I pray the king's majesty and his most honourable council to prepare a ship, as soon as may be, to send them home again to their mother church, the bosom and breast of man.

The form how to celebrate the Lord's Supper.

Here must be marked two persons; the minister, and he that communicateth with the minister. These must come and assemble together, as Saint Paul saith, 1 Cor. xi.

[1 Gentility: gentilism.]
[2 See the service in the church of Rome for the Benediction of Bells.]

The duty and office of the Minister.

He doeth best his office, and is best instructed to minister the sacrament, if he in the ministration thereof go as near as is possible to the first institution of Christ and the apostles. For Christ was and is the Wisdom of the Father, and the apostles had received the Holy Ghost that brought them into all truth: therefore it must needs follow, their doings and ministration to be most perfect, holy, and religious.

How the Minister should prepare himself.

Inwardly and outwardly. The inward preparation is, if his mind and soul be instructed and furnished with godly doctrine, and a fervent spirit and zeal to teach his audience, to stablish them in the truth, and to exhort them to perpend and mark well the merits and deservings of Christ.

The outward preparation, the more simple it is, the better it is, and the nearer unto the institution of Christ and his apostles. If he have bread, wine, a table, and a fair table-cloth, let him not be solicitous nor careful for the rest, seeing they be no things brought in by Christ, but by popes; unto whom, if the king's majesty and his honourable council have good conscience, they must be restored again: and great shame it is for a noble king, emperor, or magistrate, contrary unto God's word to detain and keep from the devil or his minister any of their goods or treasure, as the candles, vestments, crosses, altars! For if they be kept in the church as things indifferent, at length they will be maintained as things necessary.

When the minister is thus well prepared with sound and godly doctrine, let him prepare himself to the distribution of the bread and wine; and as he giveth the bread, let him break it, after the example of Christ. He should give the bread, and not thrust it into the receiver's mouth: for the breaking of the bread hath a great mystery in it of the passion of Christ, in the which his body was broken for us; and that is signified in the breaking of the bread, which in no case should be admitted[1]: therefore let the minister break the

[[1] Admitted, should perhaps be *omitted*, or the old word *amitted*.]

round² bread; for broken it serveth as a sacrament, and not whole. Christ did break it, Matt. xxvi. Mark xiv. Luke xxii. And Saint Paul saith, "The bread that we break, is it not the communion of Christ's body?" 1 Cor. x. Thus should the perfection of Christ's institution be had in honour, and the memory of the dead left out³, and nothing done in this sacrament that had not God's word to bear it. But, alas! God is accounted a fool; for men can use the sacrament more religiously, devoutly, godly, and christianly, than Christ, God's Son, as it appeareth! For his form and manner is put out, and man's device and wisdom is accepted for it.

The duty and office of the people.

The duty of the receiver resteth in three parts: to say, what he should do before the receiving of the sacrament; what he should do in the receiving of it; and what after the receiving of it.

Before the receiving, he should prepare and make ready his mind, as the commandment of St Paul is: 1 Cor. xi. "Let the man prove and search himself," and so forth. And this may be done two manner of ways; first towards God, then towards man.

Towards God he should, from the bottom of his heart, confess his faults and sins, and acknowledge his just condemnation. Then should he persuade himself by true and lively faith, that God would be merciful unto him for the death of his dear beloved Son Jesus Christ, done in his body torn and in his blood shed. He should prepare himself towards his neighbour also. First, in case he hath hurt his neighbour in fame or goods, he should reconcile himself again with restitution of them both again. He that thus prepareth himself doth eat worthily the body of Christ; and he that doth not thus prepare himself, eateth nothing but the sacrament to his everlasting damnation.

[² In allusion to the form of the wafers, or bread, then and still used in the Romish church.]

[³ See the Canon Missæ, or Mass service, in which there is a prayer for the dead.]

I make no mention here of auricular confession, as though that were a thing necessary to be done before or after the receiving of the sacrament. For this confession is not of God, as their law doeth record: The gloss upon the decree of penance, *Distinct.* v. *In pœnitentia*[1].

In the receiving of this sacrament, there be things required both in the inward man, and also in the outward man. The inward preparation is, when the man receiving the bread and the wine, being subjects and matters under the judgment and censure of the senses, the mind is elevated and lift up into heaven; persuading himself by faith, that as truly appertaineth unto him the promises and grace of God, through the merits and death of Christ, as he sensibly and outwardly receiveth the sacrament and witness of God's promises; and doubt no more of an inward friendship, familiarity, concord, peace, love, atonement, and fatherly pity and compassion through Christ, by the means of faith, than he doubteth that his mouth outwardly doth receive the signs and sacraments of God's mercy[2]. To excitate in us this faith and belief in the merits of Christ, the bread is called the body, and the wine his blood, after the manner and phrase of the scripture.

The outward behaviour and gesture of the receiver should want all kind of suspicion, shew, or inclination of idololatry. Wherefore, seeing kneeling is a shew and external sign of honouring and worshipping, and heretofore hath grievous and damnable idolatry been committed by the honouring of the sacrament, I would wish it were commanded by the magistrates, that the communicators and receivers should do it standing or sitting. But sitting, in mine opinion, were best, for many considerations. The Paschal lamb was eaten standing, which signified Christ yet not to be come, that should give rest, peace, and

[[1] *In pœnitentia.*—Dicunt quidam institutam fuisse in Paradiso statim post peccatum dicente Domino ad Adam, Adam, ubi es?.........Alii dicunt quod sub lege fuit primo instituta, quando Josue præcepit Achor crimen suum confiteri.........Alii dicunt quod in novo testamento, a Jacobo dicente, Confitemini alterutrum peccata vestra, &c. Sed melius dicitur eam institutam fuisse a quadam universalis ecclesiæ traditione potius quam ex novi et veteris testamenti auctoritate. Et traditio ecclesiæ obligatoria est, &c. Decretum Gratiani. Antv. 1573, col. 1887.]

[[2] Mercies, D. 1, mercy, D. 2, T.]

quietness. Christ with his apostles used this sacrament, at the first, sitting; declaring that he was come that should quiet and put at rest both body and soul; and that the figure of the passover from thenceforth should be no more necessary; nor that men should travel no more to Jerusalem once in the year, to seek and use a sacrament of the Lamb to come, that should take away the sins of the world.

After the receiving of it, there should be thanksgiving of all the church for the benefits of Christ's death: there should be prayer made unto God, that they might persevere and continue in the grace of God received: they should help the poor with their alms. This form, me thinketh, is most like unto the form of Christ and the apostles.

How far the mass differeth from this, all men know.

I pray God the best may be taken, and the worst left, throughout all the world. And all such as be yet infirm, by reason of long custom and lack of knowledge, let them pray God, and search the scriptures without affection. Such as be perverse and obstinate, and will admit no reason, for them the ire and displeasure of God is ready and prest to punish them when he seeth time: as it is to be seen by the Corinthes, 1 Cor. xi., that for the abuse of the supper many of them fell sick and into diseases: so will he do with us, if we neglect his most perfect and godly institution. *1 Cor. xi.*

Let us repent therefore with the Ninivites from our former sins, and believe the remission of them for God's mercy in the deservings of Christ. Farther, let us submit ourselves, all our wisdom and learning, unto his word; and think, that Christ and his apostles have instituted and used, it can in no ways be bettered by us. And you, my gracious lord and king, restore the right use of the Supper of the Lord, as Josias did the right use of the Paschal lamb, 4 Regum xxiii. 2 Para. xxxv., after the word of God. *2 Kings xxiii. 2 Chron. xxxv.*

The text now followeth of the fast of the Ninivites.

OF FASTING.

There was a fasting proclaimed, and wearing of sackcloth, from the greatest to the smallest.

Here be two things to be noted in the fruits and signs of penitence: first, concerning the fast, and vileness of the apparel; the second, how they fasted from the greatest to the smallest.

Of fasting and sackcloth.

The hypocrites of the world, when they hear of this fasting and putting on of sackcloth, damn straightways the doctrine of faith, and teach that God saveth not only for Christ's sake, which only faith apprehendeth. As though faith could not only apprehend the mercy of God, and yet have fasting annexed with her. But this present text confoundeth this error; for it sayeth, The Ninivites first believed the Lord, and then fasted. But lest we should here err, I will speak a little of fasting; that we may love rather to fast well, than obstinately to defend a false fast.

What is fasting?

Fasting is a moderate use and taking of meat and drink, lest the flesh should, by abundance and too much of it, rebel and overcome the spirit. And this fast, either it is continually or at certain times used.

Continually, when as a christian man moderately feedeth his body with thanksgiving for necessary nutriment, and not for to abound or surfeit. This fasting and abstinence the scripture calleth sobriety. 1 Peter v.

1 Pet. v.

The fast done at certain times is, also, either private or public. Private, when any man, considering and weighing his own infirmities, bindeth himself from meats and drinks, to tame and overcome the vehement and lascivious inclinations thereof to the obedience and rule of the spirit. 1 Cor. vii.

1 Cor. vii.

A public fast is, when for a public and common calamity, trouble, or adversity, the magistrates command a solemn and public abstinence and fast.

But in both these fasts there must be used a circumspect and godly diligence, lest in the abuse of fasting we offend and provoke the ire and displeasure of God the more against us. We may offend, first, if we fast for any other purpose than to keep the body in subjection to the spirit: therefore it is to be taken heed of, that we fast not for merit or for custom. The second is, we offend if we fast in the honour of any creature. The third, if for one fasting day we make three glutton feasts, as the fashion is for the most part. I would wish therefore, that the true fast and abstinence were brought in again, and then the Lord would be pleased, I doubt not.

That they amend from the greatest to the smallest, we learn two things. First, of what great efficacy the sermon of Jonas was, that pleased all people, both great and small. The like hath not been seen; for it is easier for a cook to please an hundred mouths with one meat, than a preacher to order one sermon or oration to please ten heads. It were well in our time, if at every sermon were one of the magistrates and of the people converted; and at ten sermons one bishop and one priest.

The second, the facility and promptness of these Ninivites to believe, and amend their religion and conversation, doth condemn the ungodly obstinacy and frowardness of such as detract and prolong their amendment, and say they will believe when the king cometh to age. Thus the devil giveth them one occasion or other to defer their belief. If the king's majesty and his nobles should hate the truth, they would say, How can we believe the doctrine that our learned and wise magistrates detesteth? If the king's majesty and his nobles love and favour the best part, they excuse themselves upon the tender and young age of the king; as though his majesty's young age or old age could make any religion of God true or false; when, indeed, all ages and powers be, or ought to be, subject unto the religion and law made already, and given to be observed of and by all men, of what sort, condition, or state soever they be of.

> This thing came to the king of Ninive, who arose from his seat, doing off his apparel, clothed himself in sackcloth.

It is not without a singular counsel of the Holy Ghost, that this king is mentionated of so copiously.

Neither that his behaviour and doings after his conversion is so diligently manifested.

First, the text setteth forth the manner of his conversion, and sayeth, he returned unto God upon the fame and rumour of Jonas' preaching.

Wherefore we learn, how much the truth is worthy to be esteemed, seeing that a king, upon the bruit thereof made by his people, embraced, and resisted not, as now we see many times done by the greatest part of the world. Even so did Josias. As soon as he, being yet but a child, heard of the true book of God, he embraced it. 4 Regum xxii. So did David and Josaphat hear and grant to the admonitions of the prophets. All kings therefore and magistrates should hearken unto the truth, and learn it themselves out of the law, Deut. xvii. But this study and knowledge of God's law in princes and kings the bishops, priests, and other do let, bearing them in hand that it appertaineth nothing to their office to study and labour in the word of God, but the judgment and study thereof to be committed unto them: and so by the same means they persuade and cause princes many times to persecute the truth and verity by ignorance; as the kings of Israel did, that burned the writings of the prophets.

<small>2 Kings xxii.</small>

<small>Deut. xvii.</small>

But, most gracious king, and ye, my lords of his most honourable council, ye have not only heard the rumour and fame of God's word, but with your own ears have heard yourself the truth, and ye do credit and believe the same: therefore in all things express and declare it in fact.

And, most gracious king, take ye heed that the virtues ye learn and be brought up in in youth, ye practise and exercise them in age; and in case your majesty will so do, beware of one thing, the poison of flattery; the which your majesty may use as a good medicine, and not a poison, if ye take heed of it. It will be poison, if your grace think yourself to be at all times, as flatterers will bear your highness in hand to be: it shall be a medicine, if your majesty study to be the same in deed that flattery commendeth.

Your majesty may see an example hereof in king Jehoas, that in his youth favoured and set forth the truth, but in his elder days he fell from it by the means of flatterers, that deceived him.

But your majesty shall do best to follow this godly king of the Ninivites, and embrace continually the word of the living God: and thus shall your grace be the better able to do, in case your highness would have before you every Sunday one sermon, which should bring much knowledge and grace into your highness' court.

Now followeth the fruit of this godly king's penitence. First, he riseth from his seat, and putteth on sackcloth.

Of this we learn, that in faith and true repentance is no diversity between the king and a mean subject: and thus shall it be at the latter judgment; the rich, the poor, the king, the subject, the bishop, the priest, all shall appear naked before the throne of Christ, and be holpen nothing there by any title or name of glory. Here the honour and riches have their estimation and glory. Let all men therefore look to amend their faith and living here in this world.

As for this external doing on of sackcloth, it was the manner at that time so to do, and declared their repentance and amendment: and so I would it were now; he that offendeth in apparel, he would remove the pride thereof, and go soberly; he that in meat, would use more sobriety. Yet no man should think any holiness to be in the external vestment, nor yet any hurt or damnation in the meat; but the abuse of both displeaseth God. As for the vestments of the priest in the ministry, I would wish the magistrate to remove them; for they either shew or not shew virtue: if they shew not, they use them in vain; if they do declare and shew virtue, either the virtue is with them in deed, or absent. If he that weareth them have the virtue, why sheweth it he to the world? If he have not the virtue, then is he an hypocrite, whom God hateth.

The other fruit of penance of the king with his council, being converted to God: There was, as the text sayeth, a proclamation made through all the city of Ninive by the commandment of the king and his council.

In this proclamation, first, must be marked who be the authors of this proclamation; then what is contained in the proclamation. The persons be the king and the nobles of his realm. In these persons first note, that it is the king's offices, and the peers' of the realm, to purge their commonwealth from false religion by public and open proclamations.

So did Nabuchadnezer, Darius, and Cyrus, kings of most notable fame: therefore Christ calleth the princes the nurses of the church.

And so I doubt not, most gracious king, but your highness will, according to your title and style, purge this church of England to the purity and sincerity of God's word.

Farther, we learn how that the princes and councillors of a realm should help forth the godly purposes and statutes made for the glory of God within a realm.

So was this king's godly purpose holpen by his council; so David, so Josias. In that the king and his nobles do confirm the doings of his people, we learn that godly magistrates should not let, but further and confirm, all godly purposes and virtuous study of their people, when they study amendment of false religion: so did Josaphat, Ezechias, and Josias.

The sum of the proclamation.

It containeth the true and right form of repentance that pleaseth God, which is contained in four parts.

First, in outward signs of heaviness. Then, in calling upon the Lord. Thirdly, in leaving the wicked and accustomed evil life. Fourthly, in the trust and confidence of God's mercy.

Of these parts we will speak somewhat by order.

Of the external signs of a penitent heart.

Two notes of penance are here described: the one, abstinence from meat; the other, sordity and vileness of apparel; for after such sort, as natural men say, contraries are cured by contraries. He that is given to his body, cannot please God by penitence, except he come to a soberness; neither the proud and arrogant apparelled, except he remove the excess and abuse thereof.

I would, and exhort therefore, as many as do exceed and offend in these two, to return to penitence with the king and people of Ninive. If they would so do, they should not only find grace at God's hand, but also more health and soberness of body, more riches in the coffer, more plenty in the realm, more grace, wit, and soberness in their household.

That the beasts be tied up also from their meat, it declareth that the king and people had too much a delight in wanton and over-much gayness of their beasts; which, being kept out of their accustomed pride, should not allure them from their penitence, nor give them occasion to return again to the former evil.

Farther, it pleaseth so the Lord to punish the thing that allureth man's frail nature to sin, because the sin of man should the better be known: as we see by the killing of the Levitical beasts that never offended, God would preach unto man, that his sin deserved none other than present and sudden death. So did the Lord punish and curse the earth, that Adam and his posterity might know it was not a light thing, the transgression of God's commandment, Gen. iii. *Gen. iii.* So do all creatures weep and mourn, until the time of the revelation of the children of God. Rom. viii. And thus perished *Rom. viii.* he the beasts with man in the flood. Gen. viii. *Gen. viii.*

The second sign.

Lest men should think that the abstinence from meats, or the casting off of gay apparel for certain days, should deserve and merit this favour and mercy of God, it standeth in the proclamation that they called continually upon the Lord: that is to say, they asked fervently and continually help and favour of God.

Note in the conversion of this king, how that he commandeth not now to call upon strange gods, but upon one true and living God. Even so should we do in the days of our trouble, according to the commandment of God, and the example of all the patriarchs, prophets, and the apostles. But this is to be noted, that the text sayeth they should call strongly upon the Lord; that is to say, with a penitent heart, that is sorry for the evil, and willing to study for ever after to do good. We call earnestly upon the Lord two ways: the one, when we ask of God to turn and keep from us his ire and displeasure; the other, when we desire him to take from us, and give us grace to preserve away from us, the sins that provoked and merited his displeasure and wrath.

But we offend in this behalf two manner of ways: first, men call upon creatures; the second, they call coldly and unfaithfully, without an earnest mind to amend, and faith upon the promises of God for Christ's sake. So did Saul rather call to God to avoid pain, than for any love he had to virtue. For some, as soon as the pain is removed, they return again to their old iniquity, as Pharao. Exodi.

Exod.

The third note of penance.

Every man turned from his wicked ways, and from fraud and guile which they used before.

This is the third property of penance, without the which we be rather hypocrites than penitent Christians. And the property is this, to forsake all evil and fleshly studies, and apply himself to virtue and godliness.

Note first, that the text sayeth, "Every man turned." If the king offended, the council, the bishop, the parson, the parish priest, every one amended. So let us do, except we will perish.

And what shall we do to turn from us the ire of God, kindled and inflamed? Shall we by any man's merits and deservings? No, sayeth the text, but every man amend for himself; and so concludeth Esay, lviii. chapter. Jeremy vii. And because avarice, as St Paul saith, is the mother and root of all[1] evil, the proclamation of the king of Ninivites is, that they should leave their force, violence, and oppression, and so make restitution of the false-gotten goods. Here let all men learn how to be saved, that have gathered together, they care not whether with or against the law, with or against charity. Let them leave doing of this violence and oppression, and restore again all false-gotten goods, or else sure they will perish. So did Zacheus, Luke xix., and other godly men and rich men that repented. Let men look upon that wise saying of Salomon: Prov. xxii. "Spoil not the poor, because he is poor, neither oppress not the afflicted in the port: for the Lord will take upon him the defence of his cause."

Isai. lviii.
Jer. vii.

Luke xix.

Prov. xxii.

[1 All, wanting in D. 1.]

The fourth fruit of penitence.

Who can tell whether God will be converted, and moved with pity, turn from the fury of his wrath, that we perish not?

In this text we see, to turn and bow the anger and displeasure of God is a great matter; and that to afflict the body with fasting, to pray, and to change the old wicked life, is very expedient to win his favour: but all these things be in vain, except there' be likewise a confidence and true faith in the mercy of God. And this is the thing that God most delighteth in, when the sinner confesseth that he is merciful for his promises' sake in Christ, and not for the worthiness of his penance. So doth this king in the end of his proclamation set forth the mercy of God to his people, whereby both he and they be saved.

That it seemeth his oration to have a doubt in it, truly notwithstanding that he was very well[2] persuaded of God's mercy: for as Jonas proponed[3] nothing but God's ire, he maketh mention of his mercy.

The doubt he putteth, either to put away the sluggardness of his people, either to declare in himself the fight and battle that is always between the spirit and the flesh about God's promises. We may say also that in desiring worldly things of God we should ask them with a condition. Matt. viii.

We may learn here to put away despair, and trust to the Lord's mercy, although he threaten never so much our destruction.

Also, here princes may learn, what proclamations they should make in setting forth of religion; such as only extend to the glory and mercy of God in Christ.

How the people accepted this proclamation, I will shew in the next sermon.

FINIS.

[2 Well, D. 2, T, evil, D. 1.]
[3 Proponed: set before them.]

THE SEVENTH SERMON
UPON JONAS,
MADE BY JOHN HOPER.

THE TEXT.

And when God saw their works, how they turned from their wicked ways, he repented of the evil which he said he would do unto them, and did it not.

YE have heard how this mighty king, at the preaching of Jonas, corrected both his faith and manners; and how, by public proclamation, he willed all his subjects to do the same. Of this fact of the Ninivites we may learn, how that it is our office to obey unto all godly and virtuous commandments, proclamations, and decrees of princes, as many times as they command amendment of religion and manners. But our people, and especially the multitude of priests, be otherwise affected: for they do disobey both God and their king. It were a charitable way, if they have any thing to object against this reformation, that the king's majesty and the council godly intendeth, to bring forth arguments, and not force and violence of armour.

God therefore seeth, that is to say, approveth their works; not because they were clothed in sackcloth, but because they turned from their wicked ways; that they had changed their false religion, and restored the goods again they had by violence and extortion taken from their neighbours; and every man walked in his vocation. And even as the Lord pitied them, so will he do us if we amend our faith and conversation, and live in our vocation accordingly. Esay lviii. Ezech. xviii. But and if we hate not from the bottom of our hearts the evil we have committed, we tarry still in death.

Isai. lviii.
Ezek. xviii.

That God repenteth on the evil he purposed to do unto the Ninivites, we learn that all the threatenings of God be conditionally, that is to say, to fall upon us if we repent not of our evil deeds. That is godly shewed in these words, Jer. xviii: *Repente loquar adversum gentem et adversus regnum, ut era-* *dicem et destruam et disperdam illud: Si pœnitentiam egerit gens illa a malo suo, quod locutus sum adversus eam, ago et ego pœnitentiam super malo quod cogitavi ut facerem ei;* that is to say, "I will speak quickly against the people or kingdom, to waste and destroy them. If that people, against whom I have devised, convert from their wickedness, immediately I repent of the plague that I devised to bring upon them." The same may ye see, Ezech. xviii. Zach. i. "Turn unto me, saith the Lord, and I will turn unto you." Yet should not God be accounted inconstant, though he punish not as he threatened; for this is his nature that cannot be changed, to receive penitent sinners into grace. Ezech. xviii. Matt. xi. John iii. v. The heresy and false doctrine of the Catharones[1], that deny mercy and remission of sin to sinners, is damnable and naught.

<small>Jer. xviii.</small>

<small>Ezek. xviii.
Zech. i.</small>

<small>Ezek. xviii.
Matt. xi.
John iii. v.</small>

THE FOURTH CHAPTER OF JONAS.

The Argument.

The sum of this chapter is, that God will shew mercy unto penitent and sorrowful sinners, yea, though all the world would say nay. This mercy God declareth in this chapter, not only with words, but also with a metaphor and similitude of a tree.

The division of the Chapter.

It is divided into two parts. The one containeth how Jonas was angry for the mercy and compassion God took upon the penitent Ninivites, wherefore he is reprehended of God.

<small>[1 Catharones. Hooper appears to refer to the Cathari, and takes his view of their character from the Romish writers. Isidore of Seville thus describes them: Cathari propter munditiam ita se nominaverunt: gloriantes enim de suis meritis, negant pœnitentibus veniam peccatorum: viduas, si nupserint, tanquam adulteras damnant: mundiores se ceteris prædicant. Qui nomen suum si cognoscere vellent, mundanos se potius quam mundos vocarent. Isidori Etymolog. Lib. viii. cap. 5. Paris 1601.]</small>

The second part containeth, how Jonas, being in the fields, is taught of the Lord by a tree that suddenly growed up, and suddenly perished again, that he did naught to be angry with God's doings towards the Ninivites; and declareth farther, that he could do none other than save them.

> Therefore Jonas was sore discontent and angry; and he prayed unto the Lord, and said, "O Lord, was not this my saying, I pray thee, when I was yet in my country? Therefore I hasted to fly rather to Tharsis. For I know well enough that thou art a merciful God, full of compassion, long suffering, and of great kindness, and repentest when thou shouldest take punishment.

Of this text we learn, first, how horrible and wicked the perverseness of our nature is, seeing Jonas, I cannot tell upon what love towards himself, is angry; and not with man, but with God, that would favour of mercy the sorrowful Ninivites. Seeing there was such imperfection and infirmities in the holy saints, how much need have we to see what lieth in us miserable and wretched sinners!

Out of this text also we learn, what difficulty and hardness is in the office of preaching, if it be truly and well done. Continually, whether it happen and come to pass that he speaketh, or it come not to pass, the preacher standeth in danger of obloquy and contempt. We may see an example hereof in Jonas, that preached by the word of God the destruction of Ninive: which if it had come so to pass, they would have called Jonas a cruel tyrant and seeker of blood; and now that he seeth the city spared, he feareth least he should be accounted a false prophet, not only among his own countrymen the Israelites, but also among the gentiles; and then all his preaching should be taken for a mockery. This contempt so sore feareth Jonas, and he[1] is therewithal so troubled, that he offendeth God grievously. I may accommodate the same fortune unto myself and others right well, when we speak

[1 He, supplied from T.]

for a reformation of the church, schools, and policies. Into the church we wish to be put such ministers as can and would teach the doctrine of the apostles, and that they should not be known by their vestments and shavings, but by their doctrine: then such as would minister the sacraments gravely, religiously and simply, as Christ and his apostles did; in baptism nothing to be used but the word, and the simple and bare water; in the supper of the Lord to use the ceremonies and rites of Christ and his apostles, and all occasions of superstition to be avoided. But although this doctrine be as true as Christ and his apostles be, yet I perceive displeasure and great enmity rise hereupon to me and to other; yea, not only unto us that be subjects, but also to the king's majesty and his most honourable council. But the Lord keep us out of temptation, and give grace and strength to do all things to the glory of God, and to pray for our enemies! And as touching schools, specially the universities, they must be amended, and good heads and rulers appointed in the colleges; or else the word of God shall[2] be hindered always by such as ought most to set it forth. Such godly men as have wherewithal, should help and provide to have schools to bring up youth in everywhere through this realm; and then should godly and learned children occupy the place of superstitious and ignorant men, wherewithal this realm of England is sore and too much, (God amend it!) pestered and hurt withal. This might bishops in their dioceses help well, if they intended as much good as they bear the world in hand they do; and bestow some part of their excess upon the towardly youth of their dioceses. So might the nobility and our[3] worshipful men of the shire do: yea, so might every parson and curate do, either with his goods help forth the truth and old catholic faith of Christ, either with their goodwills animate them to learn the doctrine of the patriarchs, prophets, and the apostles: and such as have the talent of teaching might rather teach than play; help than hinder; build than pull down; help forth than draw back; promote God rather than the devil; favour Christ than antichrist; agree with the king than conspire with the pope. As concerning the policy and reformation thereof, I have said

[[2] Shall, D. 2, T, should, D. 1.]   [[3] Our: other, T.]

my mind before. The which God give grace it may be accepted and followed! if it be not, yet I have delivered my soul, and God shall require your bloods at your own hand. And in case any man be offended with me for my true saying, I had rather have displeasure of all the world, than of God, that is able to damn both my body and my soul.

In the third place, Jonas putteth an excellent description of God, the which we should well keep in mind, that he is a pitiful and merciful God, long suffering and of much clemency. This description of God agreeth with *Exod. xxxiv.* God's own words spoken to Moses, Exod. xxxiv.; the which encouraged Jonas, and should do the same to us, if we were of God. Great, doubtless, was the sin of Jonas, that took an occasion to be angry by God's favour and goodness towards this sorrowful city: even thus did the Pharisees, that were angry at Christ, because he kept company with sinners. Jonas was then as many men be now-a-days, that think wretched sinners should never find pardon for their sins before God.

Now followeth a farther description of Jonas' fault and impatiency.

And now, O Lord, take my life from me, I beseech thee; for I had rather die than live.

Of this text we learn two things: first, how sore and heinously this Jonas offended, that rather desired to die, than God should have pity upon these penitent people; by whose preservation he thought some shame and rebuke should happen unto him, because he did afore speak and threaten their perdition and loss. Much better, and more godly, did Moses and Paul, that wished rather their own harm than the loss of the people.

Also, this text declareth the weariness and impatiency of the flesh, that will not suffer the troubles annexed unto the vocation, but rather wisheth to die than *1 Kings xix.* to live: so did Elias desire death, 3 Reg. xix.: so that the text and experience daily sheweth, the best day that ever a true preacher shall see is the day of his death. But as the devil hath used the vocation of bishops and priests in this present time, there is no day so terrible nor fearful to them as the day of death. The cause thereof, methinketh, Saint Augustine[1], Episto. cxlviii. ad Valerium, sheweth right well: *Ante omnia, inquam, peto ut cogitet religiose prudentia tua nihil esse in hac vita, et maxime hoc tempore, facilius et lætius et hominibus acceptabilius episcopi aut presbyteri aut diaconi officio, si perfunctorie atque adulatorie res agatur; sed nihil apud Deum miserius et tristius et damnabilius:* that is to say, "Before all things I desire that your godly prudence would think nothing to be more light, facile, or joyful in this life, chiefly now this time, than the office of a bishop, priest, or deacon, if the thing be done lightly or hypocritically; but before God there is nothing more miserable, sorrowful, and damnable."

Now followeth the answer of God to this angry man.

God maketh answer to angry Jonas.

Then said the Lord: Art thou so angry?

Of this demand and question of the Lord we learn, how he, in a fume or hasty passion, (if a man may speak so of God,) will not cast away this infirm and weak Jonas; but with sufferance trained him to a better and more advised judgment.

So doth Esay report of God's nature, chap. xlii. "He will not put out the tow kindled." He did not only consider the weakness of the man, but also the dangers and trouble of his pastoral vocation. Pitifully therefore doth God bear with him, and schooleth him to a farther and better knowledge. Of this man we may learn how to beware of hasty and rash passions of ire; for if there be not in all our acts a moderation thereof, we shall never do nor judge things uprightly according to knowledge. If men would remember this demand of God towards Jonas, they would not be so angry when they be rebuked for their faults, but rather thank the admonitor for his good admonition and warning of God's displeasure.

Now followeth the second part of the chapter.

And Jonas gat him out of the city, and sat down on the east side thereof, and there made him a

[[1] Aug. Op. Basiliæ, 1541. Tom. II. col. 686.]

> booth, and sat under it in the shadow, till he might see what should chance unto the city.

When Jonas had no excuse to make why he was angry, nor would not confess his fault, (for he answereth now nothing to the question God demandeth of him,) he goeth himself out of the city to see the end; whether the Ninivites would persevere in their penance begun, or not. Of this we learn: if we be wrongfully angry and admonished, if we will not confess the fault, yet should we consider and weigh it the more deeply. In that he made himself a booth, we see with what simplicity the good man was contented withal, and likewise how he himself was content to labour to make his own couch. Our bishops and priests have all things prepared to their hands: God give them grace better to deserve it!

The text saith:

> The Lord God prepared a wild vine, which sprang up over Jonas, that he might have shadow above his head, to deliver him out of his pain.

The Lord here purposeth to help the infirmities of Jonas, and remove the sinister and false judgment he had of God's mercy, by the image of a young tree. He bringeth forth a young tree, that may give shadow to Jonas; whereof Jonas rejoiceth very much. But the Lord queeleth[1] it again straightway, and that maketh Jonas eftsoons angry. In the midst of his fumes cometh the Lord, and by a collation and similitude between the simple tree and the worthy city of Ninive he sheweth Jonas his fault, that was angry for the mercy shewed unto the city. But in these things be things to be marked, first in Jonas; then in God; thirdly in the tree.

In Jonas may be seen the image of a man that laboureth and is oppressed with many affections, and never contented with the doings of God. We should not follow this fault, but submit our judgments to his will; saying always, and in all God's works, "Thy will be done," whether thou send us mirth or sorrow, joy or pain; for every thing shall be to the best unto those that love the Lord. Jonas also, in

[1] Queeleth: quelleth, killeth.

this his perverse and froward opinion to withdraw the mercy of God from the Ninivites, expresseth the naughty opinion that saith, that sinners can never be received into grace, after they fall once from the Lord. They would abrogate the greatest work of God, to say[2] his mercy, that it should not work where it pleaseth him, but where as it pleaseth man's fancies to appoint it. The Lord doth not only favour and bear with Jonas' infirmities, but also covereth him from the burning and heat of the sun; and also teacheth him by the tree, that he is offended without cause. What tree this was, it is not agreed upon yet among writers: but it maketh no matter thereof; it is enough we know it was a tree with broad leaves, whereby the Lord would succour both the body and knowledge of the infirm Jonas. That it grew up suddenly, and withered away suddenly, it beareth therein the image and property of such honours, riches, and treasures as be in this world; which suddenly rise, and suddenly fall again. No man therefore should hazard or danger his soul for so brittle and frail things.

And by the withering away of this little tree God would shew Jonas, how uncharitable he was; angry that the great city of Ninive was saved: as though he had said, If it grieve thee so much for the loss of this little tree, should it not be a greater grief unto thee to see the destruction of so great a city? For the tree sprang up in one night, and the city had stand many hundred years. Again, for the tree Jonas laboured never a deal, but God builded Ninive. The tree is but one thing, the city had great number, both of men and cattle. And least Jonas might have said, Yea, but all men of the city be evil, therefore worthy to perish: but God addeth to the matter, and saith, there were in the city above a hundred and twenty thousand persons that knew not between the right hand and the left; that is to say, children and fools.

Of this dialogue between God and Jonas we may gather this general and universal doctrine, that God will save all penitent sinners, 1 Tim. ii.; for seeing he gave his only Son for us, whiles we were yet his enemies, how should it be he would not in him give us all things? Rom. viii. Matt. xi. But hereof cometh our loss and perdition, that we repent not from our evil, as the proclamation of the

1 Tim. ii.

Rom. viii.
Matt. xi.

[[2] i.e. that is to say.]

king of Ninive commanded the people and subjects thereof; that would not only men to amend their evil lives, but also they should restore again all false-gotten goods, and make restitution thereof, as well to God as to man.

Restitution towards God is, when all honour and glory is given unto him, as Saint Paul saith, 1 Tim. i. But this glory is and hath been taken from God by men of every sort, as well by those of the ecclesiastical policy as those of the civil policy.

_{1 Tim. i.}

Those of the ecclesiastical policy take away this honour and praise from God two ways; one by neglecting the true doctrine, the other by defending of false doctrine. By negligence offend such as know God and his ministry by the holy word of God, yet for private respects, either for lucre, or for fear of themselves, suffer many tokens, monuments, and ceremonies of superstition; as is the diversity of meats for religion's sake, (yet I approve the commandment of the magistrates, that for a civil policy cause certain days appointed to eat fish in[1];) images; forbidding of marriage in the Lent; the use of such vestiments or apparel, as obscure the ministry of Christ's church, and representeth the form and fashion of the Aaronical ministry of the old law, abrogated and ended in Christ; either else seldom or never teach the people, neither procure them to be taught. All those I exhort to restitution; or else doubtless their theft will bring them to damnation. Let them preach truly the word of God, and minister his sacraments after the institution of Christ; and then their harm done in time past shall not be thought upon.

There be another sort, that refuse not only to mock[2] this satisfaction, but also obstinately maintain and defend false doctrine, and study to oppress the true doctrine: of

[[1] It was lately enacted (1564) for the benefit and commodity of the realm, that the fish days in every week, as well those which were of ancient time by law allowed and continued, as also Wednesdays in every week, were now enjoyned to be observed and kept. Of this act, whereby Wednesday was made a fish day, Sir William Cecyl was the chief author, for the great benefit that wise man apprehended to be by spending much fish in the realm. But this was not well resented by the people, and but slenderly observed, the English nation being very much addicted to flesh meats, and not pleased to have more fish days imposed upon them. Strype, Life of Parker, p. 177. See also the Homily on fasting.]

[[2] Mock : make.]

this sort is no small number; but those I exhort also to leave their evil sayings, and to make restitution.

As many as be of the laity, as they be called, that is to say, not of the public ministry of the church, robbeth also God of his glory and honour: they seek remedy for sin by another means than through the death of Christ, as by the merchandise of masses, indulgences, invocation of saints, the pains of purgatory: but I advise them to give God that; for it appertaineth only unto him. Hearken unto the word of God, and call upon his name, as he teacheth, through Christ, in spirit and verity; and thank him for all his gifts he giveth both to your body and soul. At your death commend your souls to him for Christ, that died under Pontius Pilate, as Saint Steven did, Acts vii. Acts vii. And do not doubt of the dead, for they be at rest already, either in heaven, either in hell, John iii. v. 1 Cor. xv. 1 Thess. iv. Apoca. iv. Wherefore rather give thanks to God for them, than pray from[3] them.
John iii. v.
1 Cor. xv.
1 Thess. iv.
Rev. iv. [xiv.]

Of restitution to be made to man.

In external goods may a man offend three manner of ways: in evil getting of them; in evil keeping of them; and in evil spending of them.

They be evil-gotten many ways: first, when they be taken from another by murder, rape, violency, craft, or theft. Thus offended queen Jesabel in taking away Naboth's vineyard; 3 Reg. xxi. at length she was torn with dogs for her labour. Then be they evil-gotten by subtleties, frauds, corruption of laws, by lying, flattery, and such other. Let every man make restitution of goods thus gotten, or else he shall sure perish. Let the seditious, hurtful, and dangerous traitor, that contrary unto God's laws taketh weapon against his liege lord and king, restore both his heart and his goods again to the king's pleasure and commandment. Let all men cease from getting of their goods by this unlawful means; and the goods so gotten let them restore again, as Zachæus did. Luke xix. And that they may be the better fenced against this unlawful and ungodly getting together of goods, I pray them to read the canon of Saint Paul: 1 Tim. vi. "Such as will be rich," &c.
1 Kings xxi.
Luke xix.
1 Tim. vi.

[³ From: probably a misprint for *for*.]

Goods be evil-kept, first, if they exalt them unto arrogancy and pride, which bringeth the contempt of other: and then, if in the abundance of goods thou forget God: thirdly, if having goods thou cease from labour, and put thyself to ease, so that thou make thyself profitable neither to God neither to the commonwealth thou dwellest in. Here offend very sore and dangerously such as possess the goods of the church, and preach not; such as have stipends to teach, and teach not; wages to war, and war not; receive for a thousand soldiers, and serveth not with five hundred; such as enjoy hospitals, almoshouses, and the provision of the poor, to their own private commodity. To all these I say, repent ye, and make restitution.

Goods be evil-spent, first, if they be consumed in an evil cause[1]; as when they be applied to pride and excess in apparel; or meat and drink, to the oppression and hurt of the poor; either to find a great company of idle and loitering men.

Then if they be not used to a good use, to the edifying of Christ's church, the help of the poor, the prisoners and such like. For in the latter judgment the Lord shall ask what care and charge we had of the poor, Matt. xxv.; and we see the rich man damned, because he gave not to Lazarus. Luke xvi. Unto those also I say, Repent ye, and spend the gifts of God after knowledge and virtue; if ye will not, ye shall all perish, Luke xiii. God sleepeth not, but seeth all our acts and noteth our doings.

In case any of these men, whether they be of the ecclesiastical policy or the civil policy of this your realm, most gracious king, and you, my lords of his most honourable council, detract, and will not make restitution, nor use their goods well; for the office ye have taken from God ye be bound to compel them to do it. And first of all, because there is no man but sinneth, look first unto yourselves, and then, with the king of Ninive and the nobles of his realm, repent ye, and restore unto God that is God's, and unto man that which is for the comfort of your subjects—good laws, and diligent execution and usage of the same. Then compel both the spiritualty, as they be called, and also the temporalty, to make restitution both to God and man accordingly. And now the Lord

[¹ Case, D. 1, cause, D. 2, and T.]

hath given you peace, because ye might have leisure to do these things, as Paul saith, 1 Tim. ii.: do therefore as 1 Tim. ii. Salomon did, 3 Reg. viii.; abuse not the peace in playing 1 Kings viii. sports and pastime, but in the building of God's temple, which hath a long time lain desolate. Ye have an example, Numbers v.; and in any case let that example be followed. There be the gests[2] of Josaphat, the king, written 2 Chron. xvii. 2 Paral. xvii., in the which are three notable things.

First, he took away and removed from his people idololatry.

The second, he gave them true judges, whose godly conditions are written in the same book, chap. xix. that feared the Lord, accepted in judgment no persons; third, they received no bribes nor rewards.

The third, he placed and appointed priests, not in one place, but in all the cities of Juda; and not to the end they should play and pastime, but to teach, and not every thing, but the law of God. All these things must ye do, most gracious king, and you, my honourable lords of his high and wise council, if ye will live in peace and quietness. I do not exhort your majesty nor your most honourable council lightly, but upon great and weighty consideration, to remove all these things, that be either the devil's either man's invention.

For in the scripture I find that God many times is offended, when we give him but half honour. How well began Jehu, the king of Israel, 4 Reg. x.; but because 2 Kings x he remained in the sins of Hieroboam, his kingdom was not only afflicted, but at length destroyed also. Abolish therefore, godly king, all iniquity, and permit not mass, nor such abomination, to any man within your highness' realm; no, not to the strangers, which doubtless should be an occasion of slander to your realm and subjects. For Asa, the king of Juda, 3 Reg. xv., removed his mother from 1 Kings xv. the rule and governance of the realm, because she had an idol in a grove, the which her son the king brent. Then your majesty must institute true, faithful, and judges of good conscience: then send such priests through your realm, that have these two conditions, first, that they teach; then, that they teach the word of God. If your majesty do these things, then shall God send peace and quietness

[² Gests: *gesta*, deeds.]

to his pleasure. Farther, God shall make you a fear and terror to foreign and strange nations that know not the living God.

And this your majesty shall avoid the better, if ye beware of flatterers, and think, as Joada[1] in his youth favoured the truth of God, and in his age by flattery departed from it, 4 Reg. xii.; so the same evil and danger may corrupt your highness. Then, if it may please you to command more sundry times to have sermons before your majesty, it will not be a little help to you, if they be well made, well borne away, and well practised. And seeing there is in the year eight thousand seven hundred and sixty hours, it shall not be much for your highness, no, nor for all your household, to bestow of them fifty-two in the year to hear the sermon of God. If your majesty do these things, the blood of your people shall not be required at your hands. But I rede both king and council to be admonished, and to amend things amiss: if not, the king of Ninive with his people shall rise at the latter day, and condemn both king and council to death: for they converted at the preaching of one man, yea, at the preaching of a stranger; we have not only heard the same by the mouth of strangers, but also by the mouth of our own countrymen, and that many times. Let us, therefore, believe and amend, or else we must perish.

God preserve, for the death of Christ, the king's majesty, all his honourable council, with the whole realm! Amen.

marginal note: 2 Kings xii.

Τέλος.

Θεῷ δόξα.

Imprinted at London by Jhon Daye
dwellyng over Aldersgate, and
Wylliam Seres dwellinge
in Peter Colledge.

Cum privilegio ad imprimendum solum.

[1 Joada. It should be *Joash*.]

A FUNERAL SERMON,

ON REVELATION XIV. 13.

PREACHED JANUARY 13, 1549.

A funerall

oratyon made the xiiij. day
of January by John Hoper, the
yere of our saluation, 1549.
upon the texte wrytyne
in the Reuelatyone of
Sayncte Johne.
Ca. 14.

✠

1. Thessalo. 4.
Murne not as other do which
haue no hope.

A FUNERAL SERMON,

BY JOHN HOPER.

I heard a voice from heaven, saying unto me, Write, Blessed are the dead that die in the Lord straightway, so saith the Spirit, that they may rest from their labours, but their works follow them. [Rev. xiv. 13].

A PREFACE TO THE TEXT.

The death of a man's friend is painful for two considerations: the one, because he that liveth is forsaken and destitute of the familiarity and friendship of him that is dead; the other, that the living doubteth where the soul of his friend departed is become, whether it be in heaven or in hell. Both these ills may be redressed with one good; that is, to wit, if he that liveth be assured by the word of God, that his friend departed is by mortal death entered in Christ into eternal life. But now in this standeth all the doubt, how the living may know in what state the souls departed stand.

This doubt cannot the gentile dissolve, the wise men of the world, nor the common sort of such as beareth the name of Christianity; namely, for this: that they imagine their friends' souls to be broiled and roasted in the fire of purgatory: wherefore, even as they fear they wot not what, so seek they their remedy they know not how; with mass, dirige, and such other. This pains (by the living) presupposed of the dead, who can justly reprehend the misbelieving living for the state of the dead, that more than need is, paineth themselves, and more than profit is, redeemeth the prayers of other? But what may the truth conclude? Is there any certainty that putteth all out of doubt our friends' souls to depart from the earth straight unto eternal life? Truly, after the judgment of the flesh there is no such knowledge; for the flesh in this case either will plainly despair for the horror and greatness of sin, or else doubt of the means how it may be remedied. Only therefore the certainty is known by the scripture of God. Give therefore heed what in this case what the word of God certifieth us of the dead.

I heard a voice from heaven, saying unto me, Write, Blessed are the dead that die in the Lord straightway.

In a matter of doubt here behold the diversity between the learning of God and the learning of man. The learning of man without judgment, knowledge, and grace will compel and force them that live to believe their friends' souls departed to be broiled in purgatory. Desire them to give you a reason why: answer have they none; but that ye must so believe, or else be accounted for an heretic. So that rather they will force men with doubt to abide in sorrow, than with judgment of God's word happily to comfort them with joy. Blessed therefore be the God of mercy, that hath in this case put unto us an infallible truth and doctrine, to warrant the troubled mind of the living for the state of the dead! And among other places of most certain truth, here in this place he plainly sheweth them to be blessed that die in the Lord; that is to say, obtain the end that man was created unto, eternal felicity and joy everlasting. For a proof of the same against reason and man's doctrine, Saint John saith: "I heard a voice from heaven;" as though he had said, It is so true, it can be no way false, for it is from heaven. And because it should instruct the afflicted of our time, and ascertain us of the state and condition of the dead, as well as it did Saint John and them of his time, and for ever till the world's end, the angel bid Saint John write the same, saying, "Write, Blessed are the dead in the Lord." Although all men indifferently wish and covet to be blessed after their death, yet all men come not to the thing they most wish for, because they live contrary unto the will of God that solely giveth the bliss eternal, as Saint Paul saith, Ephe. v.; 1 Cor. vi. "No fornicator, covetous man, shall

Ephes. v.
Cor. vi.

have any heritage in the kingdom of Christ and God." And as Paul excludeth from heaven the doers of the fruits of infidelity; so doth Saint John exclude for infidelity itself, John iii. "He that believeth not the Son of God shall see no life, but the ire of God tarrieth upon him." True it is then, that all men obtain not this blessing of God after death. And even as the places before shew who shall miss of this joyful felicity, so Saint John in this place sheweth who shall come unto it, saying, "Blessed are they that die in the Lord." They only therefore be blessed that die in the Lord: and seeing a death in the Lord is the gate to eternal life, we will more at large declare what it is to die in the Lord. John iii.

To die in the Lord is to die in the faith of Christ, whom he sent into the world for the redemption thereof, John iii.: which is done when four things is observed. John iii.

First, if the sick man in his sickness call unto his remembrance what he hath done all his lifetime against the first and second table of the Lord's commandments: the second, if upon his examination he find his brother and neighbour hurt by him in goods or fame, he study unfeignedly to satisfy him as near as he can again in both: the third, that the sick man acknowledge unto the Lord as much as he hath offended against the commandments of the first table, with a detestation of them all: the fourth, that he ask of God, for the death of Christ, remission of them all.

But he that will assuredly trust to obtain this forgiveness had need to have ready and prompt many places of the scripture, that sheweth in Christ the Father of heaven to remit the sick man's offences, Gen. iii., Esa. liii., Matthew i. ii., Joh. i. iii. iv. v., Romano. iii. iv., 1 John i. ii. The assurance of faith by grace obtained, it is the sick man's part, and as many as be with him, religiously to pray for the perseverance of the same faith: and also to his power to help the needful with his alms, that they also may pray to the Lord for him. Then, thus commended himself unto God, let him commend all his likewise with some exhortation, that they diligently live in the fear of God, as the scripture teacheth. Gen. xlix. Deuter. xxxi., Josua xxiii. 3 Re. ii. Gen. iii.
Isai. liii.
Matt. i. ii.
John i. iii.
iv. v.
Rom. iii. iv.
1 John i. ii.

He that thus dieth, dieth in the Lord, and therefore blessed, as this text teacheth, and as it is taught in the fifth of Saint John: "Verily, verily, I say unto you, he that hear- Gen. xlix.
Deut. xxxi.
Josh. xxiii.
1 Kings ii.

eth my word, and believe in him that sent me, hath everlasting life, and shall not come into judgment, but pass from death to life." He cannot die a wicked death, that is blessed and sanctified in the blood of Christ; as he must needs be that in his sickness seeketh health by this medicine prescribed by Saint John; that by four words helpeth the greatest and damigerous[1] desperation, if credit and faith be given unto them. The first word is, "I heard a voice:" the second, "from heaven:" the third, "write:" the fourth, "Blessed be the dead that dieth in the Lord." If ye learn it well, it shall not only make you blessed at the hour of death, but also moderate the sorrows and mournings, which otherwise ye shall suffer while ye live here for your friends that die. Likewise it shall assure you of the state and condition of your friends departed, that they have the favour and presence of God, and better at ease in heaven with God than ye be in the earth with men. Learn to die well, therefore, by this lesson, ye mortal men; and leave not the medicine prescribed and taught by God the Father, made and tempered with the blood of Christ, ministered into the soul of man by the Holy Ghost, brought from heaven by an angel, written upon and to the people of the earth by holy Saint John, for the medicines appointed by man, as mass, dirige, peregrinations, pardons, other men's merits, when ye be gone; trentals, anniversaries, invocation and prayers of and to saints departed; auricular confession, and such other men's inventions, which cannot ease nor quiet the conscience of the poor sick man.

But the more of these trifles is promised unto the conscience of the afflicted man, the more (wretched creature) he desireth; as your conscience shall know at the time and hour of your sickness and danger. And then shall ye feel, when all other things be too little, that the precious blood of Christ is enough; and where as without doubt your own conscience shall bear you record (do you and all other men for you whatsoever may be done), ye are culpable and worthy death everlasting. So shall Christ's Spirit, if he be in you by faith, bear record with your spirit that ye are for Christ's sake only the heirs of eternal life. This is the only way to quiet every troubled

[[1] **Damigerous**: damnigerous, injurious; unless it should be *dangerous*.]

and afflicted conscience in the day of death, as Saint John saith: "Blessed are the dead that die in the Lord."

But seeing the devil cannot bear this doctrine, a man to be saved in Christ for the promise of God's sake, he goeth about to persuade this word of God to be false that saith, "He that dieth in the Lord is blessed;" and so with the most part of men he subverteth this godly consolation. Either he maketh the sick to despair of his salvation for the greatness of his sin: either causeth him to seek unsufficient and unlawful means to remove his sins. And that you and I be subject unto this temptation, read Matt. xxvii. Luke xxiii.; and see what the devil adventured to persuade unto Christ himself, and would have borne him in hand he was not the Son of God, neither that God cared for him, seeing he suffered his enemies thus to prevail against him: and the same temptation he burdened the holy prophet David withal. Psal. iii. If he could object and burden the Son of God with arguments, that he could not be blessed that died in the Lord, how much more doth he, yea, or may he not only suade and attempt, but also persuade and overcome our miserable and weak condition, ill prepared (God knoweth!) of a thousand sorts of temptation to sustain of them the least. Wherefore learn by time, or time deceive you, how to live without time. Of none ye may learn so well as by the life and death, and also the doctrine, of the patriarchs, prophets, Christ, and the apostles: whose example if ye follow not here, in case hereafter ye never come where they be, thank yourselves. And that ye take upon you to use another remedies (yea, and as many men saith, better) to warrant and stand at the time of death against the tyranny of sin, hell, the devil, and the world; if after your departure from hence it be worse with you than it is with them, blame none but yourselves. And the better blame-worthy be ye, so many times admonished, yet not a deal the better. Judge other men as they list, thus I believe. He that dieth as an apostle, shall hereafter live like an apostle. And he that believeth as an apostle shall be saved like an apostle. Understand what I say. It is of their doctrine and sufficient learning that I speak of, which is fully and sufficiently able to

Matt. xxvii. Luke xxiii.

Psal. iii.

lead a man into all truth. 2 Tim. iii. August.[1] Lib. Confess. vi. Cap. v. If any council, general or provincial, if any learning of man, could shew you how better to live and more godly to die, than the writings of the prophets and the apostles, in whose writings ye have a plate both of their life and also of their death, I would commend it unto you. But you know there is none: seeing ye be this persuaded of them, and allow so much their holiness and name, disable not their doctrine; lest peradventure those that ye now account to be your friends, hereafter shall be tests and records of your just damnation, because ye commend their name and persecute their blood in such as offereth you their doctrine.

The ignorancy of this true doctrine to teach men to live and die well, hath brought in that false and untrue opinion of feigned purgatory. The which induced four great ills: the first, it causeth the death of a man's friend to be more painful. The second, it abolisheth one of the chief articles of our belief, which is, "I believe the remission of sin." The third is, that it brought the works and deservings of men into greater estimation than the merits of Christ. The fourth, it causeth men to live in a greater security and liberty of life; because their opinion is, that their friends' doings for them after death shall help to their salvation. Beware therefore of this doctrine of purgatory, as of a most pestilent ill: and seeing all our salvation resteth in this, that we die in the Lord; whiles we be in health, let us learn this doctrine well, and exercise the same. It is not a Christian's part to sleep in sin, as an ill soldier, till the trump blow; neither yet to provide for weapon till his enemy be upon him: but to have it ready, that it serve as time and necessity requireth. And so we be admonished to do by the horrible example of the five foolish virgins in the xxv. chap. of Saint Matthew, that neglecting their own bound duty to know and live well, and trusting to the help of others, were shut out of the joy eternal. For whiles they were a buying other men's merits, they lost their own salvation.

The adversaries of the truth doth use to object

[1 Aug. Op. Basiliæ 1548. Tom. i. p. 110. The title of the chapter is, "De sacrorum librorum auctoritate et necessario usu."]

against this doctrine of God, that such as die in the Lord should straightway be blessed with him in heaven; and say, we deny not but they be blessed, but it is in hope to come, and not with present joy and felicity; for they must suffer the pains of purgatory, and so enter the place appointed. To the which objection Saint John in this place answereth, and denieth any deferring of time betwixt the death of a Christian and his acceptation into the fruition of God, and saith " by and by," not to go first into purgatory and then after into heaven. And so saith Christ himself, John v. The same teacheth us the parable of Lazarus' soul, straightway upon his death that was taken into Abraham's bosom. Luke xvi.; where as ye may learn the state of the souls departed. And here Saint John sheweth the cause why the souls that die be not drawn through purgatory, nor passeth through no such pains to come to heaven: "because," saith he, "they may rest from their labours," that is to say, from the pains due for sin, and from all other miseries of right annexed and laid upon men for sin. If the christian souls go into purgatory, they be not quit from their labours, but put unto more labours; from a hot fever into a hot fire, from pains tolerable to the pains that be (as their doctrine saith) as grievous as the pains of hell. So the death of man were not the end of his miseries, but the beginning. Neither were not death, as Saint Paul saith, 1 Cor. xv., the last enemy of man, but purgatory were. Neither were it true that he saith, Heb. ix. chap. "That man receiveth his judgment after his death;" but after he is first dead, and then sufficiently purged in purgatory. Whereof ye have no example in the New Testament nor in the Old: ye have neither any commandment to pray for the dead, nor yet promise that God will hear your prayer when ye pray. Who taught you to bring any religion into the church of God without God's commandment, and the decrees of the universal church, which is the church of the patriarchs, prophets, and the apostles, whose faith, life, death, and doctrine is and ought to be the ground and foundation of christian religion, as Saint Paul writeth, Ephes. ii.? Neither in the word of God is there any more mention than of two places, the right hand for the good in Christ, the left hand for

margin notes: John v. Luke xvi. 1 Cor. xv. Ephᵣ ii.

the ill: Abraham's bosom for the one, a place of joy; hell for the other, a place of pain. Let the adversaries of the truth shew by the scripture (which we esteem full sufficient to make a perfect man in all things) a third place, and then we will, as we be bound, give place unto them; but sure we be, the scripture canonical, which is sufficient, hath no such thing: but of this shall be more spoken hereafter. For in this text I mean to teach, and not to dispute.

Learn therefore here of Saint John to know that all miseries endeth with the Christians at their death; and seeing the word of God putteth them in joy, let not us put them in pain: nor those that the scriptures saveth, let not us condemn: if the scripture say they be "straightways blessed that die in Lord," let us not put them under the curse of the painful fire of purgatory. It is not the part of a good scholar to find fault at his master's doctrine, until such time as he be better learned than his master; neither before he hath or can learn the elements and principles of God's law, to add unto his master's rules; nor to better the thing that is perfectly good of itself with any wit of his, which is perfectly naught; nor to say his master's doctrine is not sufficient, when all the world knoweth the contrary. For the best learned men hath come out of his master's school, and yet never added neither diminished one iota to that their masters taught them. Behold the ancient stole of the patriarchs, prophets, and the apostles, which lived virtuously and died holily; yet never added to the souls any third place or pains of fire, but were contented with the two places that God had appointed; one for the good, the other for the ill. Wherefore it is my belief that the doctrine that sufficed them, sufficeth us, and the faith that saved them in Christ, saveth us; except God be changed, and hath made new ways to heaven since their death. Either they erred, and knew not what was sufficient to lead to eternal life, or these dreamers of purgatory err. For the one goeth as contrary in this article to the other as black is contrary unto white, and the catholic church of Christ to the smerm[1] and multitude of antichrist, and as far from the

[[1] Smerm, probably swarm.]

primitive church of the apostles, as God's word is from the superstition of man, and the doctrine and life of Saint Peter (that was but a record of Christ and his doctrine, Acts i.) from the life and doctrine of Boniface the Eighth, which is written *post Sextum Decretalium*.[2] Better therefore it is to believe with Saint John and the catholic church, that the dead be at rest, than with the school of the gentiles and multitude of men to judge them in pain. But let us hear what more the Holy Ghost saith unto Saint John.

Acts i.

Their works follow them.

By this text we learn two things: first, how these that die in the Lord be not nor cannot be hurt by the obloquy and slanderous report of ill speakers. Seeing the world for the most part accounted the very Christians of God to be heretics and seditious persons; therefore saith the Holy Ghost, "They depart hence with their own works:" which saying should cause us to bear strongly the perverse judgment of the world; for the judgment of God is just, and judgeth not after the face, but according to the truth. Let all us therefore lament and bewail our sins past, presently begin a better life, and hereafter beware in Christ of the like fall; then let the world say what it will.

The second doctrine here of Saint John repugneth and overthroweth the opinion of many ignorant and superstitious persons, that whiles they yet live here themselves passeth little what faith, religion, or works commanded by God they do; but in the time of death they think to redeem all their sins by other men's works after death, with mass, pilgrimage, pardons, and other. Foolish be they that sell this abomination; but more fools be the buyers, seeing Christ once cast such sellers out of the temple. But those hath the pope and his received in again with both hands. And as Christ beat them out with scourges, so the pope and his adherences with whip and fire beateth as many as call the people from this merchandise; and no marvel, for

[[2] Platina gives a very dark picture of the character of Boniface the Eighth, in his Lives of the Popes. The book of Decretals called "Sextus" was collected under his pontificate. See Platinæ Vit. Pontif. and Corp. Juris Canon.]

he is Christ's adversary. Because therefore this error hath so much availed in many men's consciences, that it is very difficult to remove it, (partly because they that sell wax rich by the means, partly because the merchandise seemeth good to the buyer, that trusteth to appease the ire of God with money,) I will rehearse testimonies of the scripture to prove that no man is the better for another man's works when he is dead. Christ, Matt. xxv., asketh, of the same he gave his talents unto, account of the same man again for the use of his talents, and thereunto constraineth each of his creditors. In the same chapter, sitting in the last judgment, as it were requireth account of such works as were done by them that shall be judged whiles they were yet alive: "I was an hungered, and ye gave me meat; athirst, and ye gave me drink;" and so forth: read the place. In the Old Testament and in the New is written many times, that the just God will give unto every man after his own works: so saith Saint Paul, Gal. vi., and to the Corinthians, "As he soweth, so shall he reap;" and that saith he also, 2 Cor. v. "Every man shall receive as he hath done in his body, be it good or ill." And be mindful of the five foolish virgins, that teach us how dangerous a thing it is to trust unto boughten merits. When they were waked out of the sleep to go meet the bridegroom, and had not oil sufficient in their lamps, they went unto their merchants to buy: but in the meantime, whiles they were agreeing upon the price, the gate was shut, and the miserable virgins excluded, and kept out from the eternal joys. After the same sort men, being ignorant of the truth of God's word, useth in the time of their sickness with the unlearned priests. Whiles the miserable and afflicted sick man is crucified and tormented with the fire of hell, in his agony and passion of death, asking counsel of his curate; when his curate should persuade the sick man to the restitution of his neighbour's goods and fame, if any such wrongs were committed, and then persuade him of Almighty God's mercy in Christ, in whose blood he forgiveth all offences, Gen. iii. Esa. liii. Ephes. ii. and maketh the sinner more whiter than the snow, Esa. i.; then the ungodly curate setteth forth his merchandise to sale; masses, ringing, lights, peregrinations, with other like. The wretched sick man, though his conscience beareth him record these things satisfy not, nor removeth the greatness of his temptation ; yet seeing he knoweth no better, and hath learned no farther than the opinion of man hath taught, he beginneth to entreat with the priest upon the price of his merchandise, and many times before they be fully at a point, the buyer and seller, the poor sick buyer dieth, and the gate of salvation is shut in : and thus for the lust of feigned purgatory, that the scripture of God feareth no man withal, he findeth unfeigned hell (eternal damnation), from whence neither the living, neither the dead, can release him. And thus I will yet add, in case there were any purgatory, yet could not the souls be delivered by these remedies that superstition hath prescribed, seeing their remedies for the most part be blasphemy against God : as the mass, a profanation of the Lord's supper, holy water, with other such like ; and other of their remedies be foolish and to be mocked at, as the ringing of bells, to ease the pain of the dead, with other.

I beseech you all, brethren, in the dear blood of Christ, to leave buying of God's grace, and the merits of men, that cannot merit enough for themselves : your own goods thus bestowed shall work your own damnation. Remember this saying of Saint John : " Their works follow them." Live hereafter virtuously, that ye may die godly. He fighteth not manfully, that is brought up always delicately. In the hour of death is like to be our hardest assault and greatest danger. The book of our conscience shall be opened. The devil will aggravate and give all the strength he can to our sin, and will (if God suffer him) either extenuate and diminish the mercy of God, or clean cause us to despair : hell then will gape and open his mouth upon us. Make ready, therefore, while ye have time, for yourselves in the blood of Christ, and study amendment of life. Besides the scripture, hear what Saint Augustine[1] saith, Tract. xlix. super Jo. *Unusquisque cum causa sua dormit, et cum causa sua resurget :* that is, " Every man sleepeth with his own cause, and shall

[[1] Sed quomodo interest in ipsis qui quotidie dormiunt et exsurgunt, quid quisque videat in somnis ; alii sentiunt læta somnia, alii torquentia, ita ut evigilans dormire timeat, ne ad ipsa iterum redeat : sic unusquisque hominum cum causa sua dormit, cum causa sua surgit. Aug. Op. Basiliæ 1542. Expos. in Joan. tr. 49. Tom. ix. col. 360.]

rise with his own cause." In our sickness let us therefore do these two things; reconcile ourselves to our neighbours: the second, let us cry unto the Lord in Christ, saying, " I believe remission of sin."

THE CONCLUSION.

If we will not lament the death of our friends, let us hear and read the scripture diligently, that saith, " They be blessed that die in the Lord." And we, if we purpose to die well, while we be in health, let us learn to know, to fear, and to put all our trust in the Lord, solely and only through Christ; and then in the trance and dangerous agony of death we shall overcome manfully, and say rather for our friends that die, " Blessed and thanked the Lord, who hath vouchsafed to take unto him his servant in the blood of Christ, from the miseries of this world, and the ills thereof;" rather than to say, (as the most part of men doth,) "God have mercy upon his soul !" which word includeth a very doubt of the state of the dead, and more spoken of custom than of knowledge. Let us therefore with the Holy Ghost say, " Blessed be the dead that dieth in the Lord." So be it.

FINIS.

☙ Imprinted at London by
Edwarde Whitechurch
at the signe of the
Sonne in flet
Strete.
1549.

Cum Privilegio ad Imprimendum solum.

INDEX.

A.

AARON and Moses fell, 23.
Abraham, his life as well as his faith is to be followed, 57.
Adelmannus, 118.
Adrastus, 184.
Adversity is sent to teach self-knowledge, 89; is an impediment that leadeth from God, 303; what thoughts follow, *ib.*; why God punisheth therewith, 304; the true church is more visited with than others, *ib.*; two good things in, 305; we should not despond in, 493; consolation from God shines in the deepest, 498.
Agathos, (Abbot,) 144.
Agrippa, Henry Cornelius, 327.
Algerus, 118.
Aloysius, 310, 457.
Altars, among Christians there should be none, 488; should be turned into tables, *ib.*; prayers said at high, are foolishly imagined better than in the quire, 491.
Amartian, 261.
Ambrose, 28; calleth the bread the thing that it representeth, 234; books *de sacramentis* are not his, *ib.*; calleth the cup the figure of the blood, 234; his division of the ten commandments, 349; on divorce, 385.
Amit, 534.
Anabaptists, 246.
Andrew, St, 314.
Anger, to beware of, 551.
Ansegisus, 228.
Answer to the bishop of Winchester's book, 97.
Anthropomorphitæ, 160.
Antilochus, 184.
Apethian, 261.
Apollinaris saith, there is no martyrdom where is not the truth of Christ, vii.
Apostles were not Christ's vicars, 22.
Apparel, excess in, is forbidden by the seventh commandment, 377.
Apuleius, 327.
Aquinas, Thomas, 193, 229, 291.
Aretinus, 118.
Aristides, v. vi.
Aristotle's authority with his scholars, 44; definition of invisible, 70; Politics, 78, 80; his school admits no accident without subject, 123; *de gen. et corrup.* 124; *Topic.*, 274; condemneth the act, when the mind consents not, 283, 297, 325, 351; saith religion is man's principal work, 352, 359, 361, 372.
Arius defended heresies by mistaking of scripture, 162, 282, 402; Christ's bodily presence in the sacrament was unknown in the church in his time, 520.
Arts, the fine, are not forbidden, 44.
Assemannus, 457.
Asthenean, 261.
Astrology, practice of, against the first commandment, 308.
Athanasius, *contra gentes*, denieth images to be laymen's books, 43; creed ascribed to, 125, 169.
Aubertin (Albertinus), 161.
Audius, 160.
Augustine, 118, 160, 193, 214, 226, 230, 231, 234, 282, 314, 320.
Augustine saith, that not the death but the cause maketh a martyr, vii.; erred, 28, 29; against images, 47; saith that Christ meant not to reign worldly, 79; expoundeth *Petra erat Christus*, 127; our faith is not grounded upon, *ib.*; his opinion of unbaptized infants, 132; allows appeal to scripture against himself, 132; writeth of certain heretics, 161; teacheth a godly way to understand scripture, 162; saith Christ's death was not of necessity, but of his own will, 168; saith Christ's body is in heaven, 192; declareth plainly no body can be, except it occupy space, 194; how he understands the words *diem meum*, 212; saith Christ was wholly in the womb, wholly on the cross, &c., 224; denies any miracle to be in the sacrament, 225; notes Tertullian's errors, 231; saith sacraments are food for the mind, not the mouth, 233; spiritually eaten, 235; writeth against those who say they worship not the image, but what it represents, 319; saith, images bring into error, *ib.*; condemns necromancy, 327; praises Regulus for keeping his oath, 336; on the rest of the sabbath, 339; saith, all are not glorified saints whose re-

lics are worshipped on earth, 345; quotes Seneca, 346; mentions only a few saints' days, 347; his division of the ten commandments, 349, 350; describes Paulinus as rich for the poor, 397; writeth of making restitution, 404; *De iis qui infamiam irrogant*, 406; against talebearers, 407; was coadjutor to Valerius, 508; saith sacraments take their name from a similitude to the thing they represent and signify, 515; saith the word comes to the element, and the sacrament is made, 516; calleth the Lord's supper a sacrament of memory, 529; saith, ' Believe, and thou hast eaten,' 530; describes the miserable state before God of unfaithful ministers, 551; on the authority and use of the scriptures, 565; saith that every man sleepeth and shall rise with his own cause, 571.

Augures, 327; various names of, 328.
Augustus, forbad necromancy, 329.
Auricular confession, 526.
Auxentius, 161.
Averroes, 70, 332.
Avicenna, 70, 332.

B.

Baptism, the external sacrament of, doth not cleanse us from sin, 74; penance and faith precede it, *ib.*; is twofold, *ib.*; explained by the ceremony of coronation, 75; is God's livery, *ib.*; why it is called a sacrament, 128; is a sign and seal of remission of sin already received by faith, *ib.*; infants are saved that have not received, 129, 132; is the confirmation of Christ's promise received before admission thereto, 130, 133; ought not to be omitted, 131; nor administered except by lawful ministers, *ib.*; of infants, 132; in what it consisteth, 533; of bells condemned, *ib.*

Barbara, St, 457.
Baronius, 376, 455.
Basil, St, 28; allowed monasticism, 29; was not author of private mass, 226.
Basyll (Basle), instructive pictures in the town-house of, 507.
Becon, 310.
Bede, 118; knew not of transubstantiation, or private mass, 227.
Bellarmine, 47.
Benedict, the order of, 227.
Benedixit, consecration in sacrament said to be in the word, 518.
Benno, cardinal, his life of Hildebrand, 123.

Berenger, written against by Lanfranc, &c., 118; denied the corporal presence, *ib.*; was an excellent and learned man, 124, 230; condemned, 524; his recantation, 525, 526.
Bernard, 28, 312.
Bertram, or Ratramnus, wrote against Paschasius on the eucharist, 118, 524.
Bevis, Sir, of Southampton, 77.
Bible, the, children should be taught, 32; was preserved miraculously, 138; were as well burned as rendered useless, 139; is made to serve a wicked purpose, 140; abused, *ib.*; is the best judge in controversy, 278. See *Scripture* and *Word of God.*
Biel, Gabriel, 522, 529.
Bishops, the first part of their office is to teach, 19; of Rome, arrogantly and wickedly claim to be Christ's vicars, 22; their ungodly lives prove them to be the first-begotten of antichrist, 23; succession of, a fallible token of true church, 82; the book of decrees no authority for the nature of a sacrament, 125; there are more of their decrees for the soul than of civil laws for the body, 142; should not make laws, *ib.*; how they should please God, 146; their laws are often changed, 154; laws of, pernicious, 284; office of, degenerated from scriptural original, 396; should be reasonably provided for, 398; and priests, their office in primitive church, 480; should retain their office only so long as they behaved well therein, 481; office very difficult, 505; those that cannot do their office should have coadjutors, 508; should be known by their tongue, and not by their cap or vesture, 511.
Blasphemy condemned, 476.
Body of Christ, the, is eaten spiritually by faith, and not otherwise, 55; Christ will have our senses judge of its verity, 63; is not invisibly in the sacrament, 68; is eaten spiritually, 69; the bread and wine are not changed into it by words of consecration, 119; cannot be *pantotopon*, 157; must occupy space, 158; is not in the sacrament by miracle, 164; is not corporally present in the sacrament, 514; the papists' own doctors believe not that the very body of Christ is received in the sacrament, 530; what our opinion should be concerning, *ib.*; may be eaten without the sacrament, *ib.* See *Sacraments* and *Supper.*
Bonaventura, 228, 229.
Boniface VIII., 568.
Bridget, St, saw wonders, 291.

Broided (broidered), 377.
Bucer, 246.
Buckstone, St Anne of, 40.
Budæus, 221, 237.
Bullayne, our Lady of, 455.
Burnet's Hist. Reform., xi., xii., 38, 41.

C.

Cambyses' punishment of a corrupt judge, 483.
Canon Missæ, 518, 535.
Canons: *Si Papa*, 284, 471, Cod. lib. IX. tit. xviii. cap. 5. 329, 330; cap. 2. 330; *Clericum per creaturas*, 478; *Si quis per creaturas*, ibid.; *Si aliqua causa*, ibid.; *Movet te iterum*, ibid.; gloss upon, ibid.; *Prima quidem*, 515; *Tribus gradibus*, 522; gloss upon, 517, 529; *Quid sit sanguis*, gloss, 517; *Utrum sub figura*, gloss upon, 518; *Sicut (Sic in) non sanctificando*, gloss upon, 519; *Vasa in quibus*, 521; *Cum omne*, gloss upon, 522; *Ante benedictionem*, gloss upon, 532; *Ego Berengarius*, 525; gloss upon, ibid.; *Qui manducat*, gloss upon, 526; *De celebra. Missarum*, ibid.; *De verbor. significat.* 528; *Timorem docet*, gloss upon, 529; *In pœnitentia*, gloss upon, 536; Sextus, 568.
Canterbury, idol of, 40.
Carthusians suffered death for denying king's supremacy, 202.
Catharenes, (Cathari), 169, 547.
Cato, precepts of, 284, 407.
Cave, 455.
Celsus, 273, 297.
Ceremonies, absurd, in churches at Easter, 46; augmented in sacraments by Bishops of Rome, 237.
Cerinthus, his heresy, 17.
Chalice, the, is transubstantiated, if the bread be, 122.
Charles the Bald, 118, 524.
Charles the Great, 47, 227, 228, 524.
Charterhouse monk, a, an arm of, found in a church, 202.
Chastity, wherein it consisteth, 375.
Chemnitius, 47.
Chiliastæ (millenarians), 161.
Christopher, Pope, 217.
Christian, a, his office, 15; what his office is when he is sanctified in Christ, 76; must live holily, 77, 93; is bound to obey the law, 94; to be one is difficult, 137; a science practive, not speculative, ib.; must leave man's word and cleave to God's, 139.
Christ, what he is, 16; light of light, ib.; becoming man retained his Godhead, 17; as God suffered not, ib.; raised his body by the power of his Godhead, 18; his might declared by creation, &c., his mercy by experience, &c., ib.; his title as omnipotent, ib.; his priesthood, 19; revealed all things necessary to salvation, 20; taught his disciples what to preach, ib.; though bodily absent, is spiritually present with his church, 21; admits of no vicar on earth, 24; always answered objections by the word of God, 25; his shadow is to be followed, rather than the body of councils, or doctors, ib.; his death is to be preached by the tongue of man from scripture, and not from decrees of bishops, 31; his intercession, 33; at God's right hand ministereth to saints, 34; Mediator of old and new testament, ib.; suffered for man's sin, as though himself a sinner, 48; made satisfaction by his death, ib.; his sacrifice once offered sufficeth, ib.; his death the only sufficient price and gage for sin, 50; the mean wherein we are justified, 51; his discourse with Nicodemus, 52; the cause, effect, and use of his incarnation, 54; how we eat his flesh and drink his blood, 62; is in his natural body in heaven, 67, 70; his office is to consecrate and sanctify believers, 71; prayed for his whole church, 72; his kingly office, 78; defendeth his church by his power and his laws, ib.; not by carnal weapons, 79; his kingdom spiritual, ib.; hath no body invisible, 112; the nature of his humanity, 113; his words, *hoc est corpus meum*, how to be taken, 115; is present in the sacrament at the contemplation of faith, 121; before his advent was eaten by the fathers in their sacraments, 127; his body was given to be slain, not eaten, 156; his body must occupy space, 158; is in heaven, and not out of heaven, 159, 192; his death the means of our reconciliation, 257; all the promises were made in and for, ib.; received our infirmities, but not the contempt of God and his law, 263; how God draweth unto, 265; hath fulfilled the law for us, 412; offered on the cross and in the mass, contrary to each other, 500; what it is to die in, 563.
Chrysostom interprets *de omnibus*, 106; how he understands *diem meum*, 212; saith, Christ is present in spirit unto faith, 224; on the Lord's day, 342; saith, the first degree of chastity is pure virginity, the second faithful matrimony, 375.

Church, the, is tied to the doctrine of Christ, 20; governed and protected by the Holy Ghost for ever, 21; as redeemed, so is defended by Christ, *ib.*; is not bound to a succession of bishops, 27, 138; is tied to the word of God, 27, 81, 138; is not to be taught by images, 30; is bound to scripture, and not to men's writings, 31; magistrates may make laws for, 31, 85; here shall always be in affliction, 80; the name of, abused, 83; true, is a small congregation, 84; discipline necessary in, and why, 91; of old testament is one with that of new, 127; they only belong to, who follow scripture, 139; there always have been in, such as followed the truth, 170; the discipline of, 183; its perpetuity and security, 201; what is the most pure, 343.

Cicero, *de Clar. Orat.* 27; *de Oratore*, 44, 214, 235; *de Legibus*, 273, 285; *de Nat. Deor.* 285; *Divin.*, 309; *de Repub.*, 327; *Tusc. Quæst.*, 329, 356; *De Offic.*, 336, 352, 378, 407; *De Repub.*, 390; *Ep. ad Var.*, ib.; *ad Heren.*, 408; endangered Rome, 490.

Claudius (Cæsar), abolished necromancy, 329.

Clement says, the water in sacramental cup is turned into phlegm, 168.

Clement III., Decrees of, 228, 522.

Clement V., Constitutions of, 527.

Cloyshe, or closh, a game, 393.

Cœnonia, (communion,) meaning of, 148.

Collier exposes the fraud of the blood of Hales, 41.

Comestor, (Peter the Eater,) held transubstantiation, 118, 518.

Commandments, the, should be daily explained, 144; are an epitome of scripture, *ib.*; Hooper's Declaration of the Ten Holy, 248; why they were given, 255; what they contain, *ib.*; the condition of, on God's behalf, and on man's, *ib.*; for whom made and given, 256; expounded by Christ and the apostles, 271; contain matter enough for every man to exercise himself in the exposition of, 272; he is not a Christian that knoweth not, 274; excuses for ignorance of, taken away, *ib.*; preparative rules unto, 286; seven preparatives, 287; first commandment, what it requires and forbids, 293; the foundation of all true religion, 294; the effect of, 296; sum of, 316; second commandment, the end of, *ib.*; the parts of, 317; third commandment, the design of, 322; the right use of, 323; can be kept only by a reconciled sinner, 324; works repugnant to, *ib.*; fourth commandment, why instituted, 337; persons rehearsed in, 339; what condemned in, 340; observance of, to be enforced, 341; ten, division of, 349; fifth commandment, who should be honoured, 355; how, 356; sixth commandment, God's purpose in, 367; what is forbidden by, 368; seventh commandment, the end of, 374; what it forbiddeth, 376; eighth commandment, the end of, 387; what it forbiddeth, 388; ninth commandment, what it requires and forbids, 405; three kinds of lies, *ib.*; tenth commandment, the purpose of, 409; declareth specially our weakness, 410; no man can fulfil it, *ib.*; self-love prevents its fulfilment, 411; was fulfilled for us by Christ, 412.

Commonwealths are preserved by force, and by law, 78; the devil is an enemy to, 80; should have only two governors, God and the prince, 142; how they are to be appeased when troubled, 459; the contempt of God's word is occasion of trouble to, 464; overmuch lenity in, is pestiferous, 473; compared to a ship, 497.

Compostella, St James at, 455.

Communion, the meaning of, 148, &c.; betwixt Christ's body and us, how made, 154; private, in what case it is lawful, 173.

Condemnation in man, the cause of, 264.

Conjurors break the third commandment, 326.

Consecration of Archbishops, &c., form of, 479.

Conscience is to be left free, 32; finds peace only in Christ, 50.

Consolation, what it rests in, 16; under bereavements, destroyed by doctrine of purgatory, 562.

Constantine V. condemned the use of images, 47.

Constantine, Edict of, 276, 278, 329, 352.

Constantinople, the church of, never acknowledged the supremacy of the Romish church, 226.

Conversion, ungodly doctrine and human tradition are a great hindrance to, 448.

Corporal presence, the, in the mass, is not to be believed till seen, 112; is disproved from the nature of Christ's humanity, 113; a late-invented doctrine, 125; arguments against, 147, 514, 528; when it began to be discussed, 524.

Corpus Christi, the feast of, how instituted, 527.
Corpus Juris Canonici : see Canons.
Corpus Juris Civilis : see Justinian.
Cranmer, archbishop, describes idolatry at Walsingham, &c., 40 ; his answer to Gardiner, 100 ; speaks of seditious priests, 461.
Creed, the, should be daily explained, 144.
Crœsus, 184.
Curiosity, an impediment to obedience to God's law, 419.
Cyprian, in his time the bread of the Lord's supper was given to children, 172; is not to be followed, but rather Christ's institution, 173; saith, the supper is a mystical eating, &c., 232; his advice respecting scripture, 238.
Cyril saith, Christ meant not to reign worldly, 79 ; quotes Pythagoras, 285.

D.

D'Acheri, 160.
Damascene calleth images laymen's books, 39.
Death of friends painful, 561 ; how the pain may be alleviated, *ib.*
Decree, *Si Papa*, horrible and wicked, 470.
Decretals contain marvels and mysteries, 291.
Decretum Gratiani, 478, 517, 518, 519, 522, 523, 526, 529, 536.
Demosthenes, 214, 490.
Denis, St, (Dionysius,) 313.
Desperation detracteth from God's mercy, 422 ; how men yield to it, *ib.*
Detection, A, of the devil's sophistry, title-page to, 99 ; preface to, 100 ; quoted, 213, 218, 220, 222, 223, 224, 225, 236, 239, 244, 245.
Devil, the, danger of being his servant, 107 ; to be avoided by conformity to God's word, 109 ; subtleties of, 294.
Diagoras, 297.
Diocesan, why so called, 143.
Dioclesian, 387.
Diodorus, 298.
Divorce, 378 ; what it is, 382 ; when lawful, *ib.*
Doctrine, false, the teaching thereof, a work against the fourth commandment, 345.
Documents of Edward VI.'s reign, 479.
Dugdale's Monasticon, 40.
Duns Scotus, 119, 167, 325, 518.
Duty, danger of flying from, 451.

E.

Ebion, his heresy, 17, 161.
Eckius, his argument for transubstantiation from Aaron's rod, 166.

Edward VI., 41 ; sermons on Jonas dedicated to, 435 ; his youthful age, no excuse for errors in religion, 439, 539 ; earnestly exhorted to virtue, 540 ; and to beware of flattery, *ib.* ; advised to hear one sermon every Sunday, 541 ; encouraged to purify the church, 542 ; exhorted to abolish the mass, &c., 557.
Election, the cause of man's, 264.
Ellis' early Eng. Met. Romances, 77.
Enthusiastæ, 245.
Epicureans, absurd notions respecting the sun, 222 ; blasphemous, 324.
Epiphanius, 28 ; would have images and pictures taken out of churches, 42 ; against women ministering, 132 ; 160, 161, 169; against Mariolatry, 206, 208.
Epitheton, 124.
Eras, St, (Erasmus), 309, 310.
Erasmus describes the evils of pilgrimages, &c., 40, 41 ; declares people should not be taught by images, 46 ; quoted, 240 ; on Lord's day, 342 ; adages of, *proterviam fecit*, 484.
Error, the best of men have fallen into, 28.
Est is expounded differently by papists to suit their purpose, 116 ; expounded *per (fit)*, 119, 529.
Eusebius referred to, vi, 83, 161, 169, 170, 172, 347, 383, 478, 521.
Eutyches, 64, 65.
Excommunication proper against open offenders, 90.
Exorcism, or conjuration of water, form of, 283.
Exuperius, Bishop of Tolosa, 233.

F.

Faith, true, is imperfect, 22 ; justifying, to be accompanied by repentance and honesty of life, 33 ; applies merits of Christ's death to us, 50 ; remission of sin is obtained only through, *ib.* ; Christ's righteousness is apprehended by, 51 ; is mistress in the soul, 78 ; required before receiving of the sacraments, 134 ; what it is, 145 ; the sole gift of God, 246 ; imperfect, how accepted of God, 261 ; for lack of it, we are called enemies of God, 262 ; lively, what it declares, 265 ; what it is, 513.
Fasting, an indifferent act, 32 ; false gloss on, 348 ; what it is, 538.
Fathers, the, allege the testimonies of the primitive church not to establish faith, but to shew in what sense the word of God was used, 169 ; of their authority, 520 ; interpolated by the

papists, 520; named the sacraments by the name of the thing represented by them, 523.
Fear, the first cause of idolatry, 453.
Feast-days, observance of, an indifferent act, 32.
Festival, the, 182.
Formosus, Pope, 217, 218.
Fredericus Suevus, emperor, 229.
Friars, begging, soldiers of antichrist, 526.
Frith, John, 245.
Fuchsius, Leonardus, 278.

G.

Galen, 278, 286, 297, 318, 333.
Gardiner, bishop: see Winchester.
Gellius, Aulus, 297, 329.
George, St, 313, 320.
Gilby, Anthony, his answer to Gardiner, 100.
Gloss, a fair, makes not good an evil thing, 30; upon canon: see Canons.
God, the great love of, in giving his Son, 17; a severe punisher of sin, 18; his ire against the impenitent, *ib.*; his people must hear Christ's voice, 19: slow to anger, but punishes heavily at length, 24; must be obeyed before all, 31; his glory, and majesty, and power seen in his creatures, 45; his mercy to Adam shewn in the fire descending on sacrifices, 48; declared his hatred of sin by death of Christ, 49; right hand of, means heaven, 66; also, it betokens power, 67; his mercy is the sole cause of the deliverance of Israel, 257; his justice intendeth to two diverse ends, 266; how we should love him, 299; in naming him, what is to be taken heed of, 322; his will must be known to be practised, 443; what his will is, 445; his mercy and pity, 489; mysterious in his deliverances, *ib.*; why he exerciseth the afflicted in their troubles, 490.
Gospel, holiness of, less welcome to some than its freeness, 59.
Gospellers, the, uphold an unholy religion, 58.
Gratianus, 239.
Gregory calleth images laymen's books, 29, 41; defendeth them, 47; his time overcharged with superstition, yet communion of both kinds used, 226, 227, 237; saw a child in the bread of the altar, 290.
Gregory VII, (Hildebrand), his life by Cardinal Bruno, 123; condemned Berenger, 526.
Gregory Nazianzen saith, it is not necessary to observe all things in the Lord's supper as Christ did, 241.
Guymundus, or Guitmundus, upheld transubstantiation, 118.

H.

Hales, the blood of, 40.
Health, six rules for preserving, 297.
Heaven, a particular place, 66; what it signifies in our own creed, 67; is a place of joy, *ib.*; Christ sits there in his natural body, *ib.*
Helvidius, 161.
Henry the Sixth, emperor, poisoned by the sacrament, 123.
Henry the Eighth, 37, 40, 41, 201, 438.
Hermias, 160.
Herodotus, 320, 417.
Hertford, earl of, the Declaration of Christ dedicated to, by Rosdell, v.
Hilarius, 235.
Hildebrand: see Gregory VII.
Hippocrates, v., 286, 297.
Hoc, the pronoun, referred to action of the whole supper, 116, 148; dispute upon, 529.
Hollingshed's Chronicles, 455.
Homer, 184, 298.
Honorius III. commanded a new bready God to be honoured, 526.
Hooper, account of his life, i., v.; notices, in letter to Bullinger, offer of a bishoprick, 434; his reasons for interpreting Jonah, 445; his reasons for being faithful, 468; marvels at the book for ordaining bishops, &c., 479; objects to the oath and the vestments, *ib.*; held his see during good behaviour, 481; wisheth chancels to be shut up, and minister and people to be in one place, 491; reflections in a storm in the Race of Britaine, 497; notices the enmity arising to himself from his faithful preaching, 549; would have the sacraments ministered simply, *ib.*
Horace, 356, 403, 418, 428, 430.
Hugo, 118; de St Victor, *ib.*; Lingonensis, 248.
Hypanis, viii.

I.

Idolatry, occasion of to be removed, 30, 37; continued, from God's word not being diligently preached, 201; what it is, 307; hath infected all the Latin church, 310; whereby it is to be examined, *ib.*; is committed in private masses, 311; inward, forbidden, 318; danger of, 457; all tokens of, should be removed, 488.
Ignorance, an impediment to obedience to God's law, 426.

Images have occasioned much harm to the church, 30; never used in the old or new testament church, *ib.*; against the use of, 36; the worship of, is destructive of many souls, 38; the temple of God dishonoured by, 39; called laymen's books, 39, 41; live long in churches, 40; excluded from the Greek church, *ib.*; having them in churches, idolatry, 85; what it is to honour, 317; not to be honoured, *ib.*; themselves to be avoided as well as the worship of, 320; not needed to shew God unto us, 321.
Imputed righteousness, Abraham and all the faithful saved by, 21.
Infants, dying unbaptized, saved, 129.
Innocentius III., 118, 123, 167, 168, 192; would prove transubstantiation by miracle, 225, 518.
Institutes: see Justinian.
Intercession of Christ, the, alone sufficient, 34; his church is bound thereto, *ib.*; the doctrine of, to be preached diligently, *ib.*
Invocation of saints, the, never practised by apostles, &c., 35; a derogation of God's honour, *ib.*; evils of, *ib.*; preferreth man's doctrine to God's word, 36; idolatry, 85; forbidden, 458.
Ippeswiche, our lady of, 40.
Irenæus quoted as to Christ's divine nature, 17, 83; interprets *diem meum*, 212; saith that two things are in the sacrament, one to the senses, the other to the spirit, 224; calleth bread of thanksgiving a creature of God, 227.
"Is," interpreted by the papists, " is made," 529.
Isidore of Seville, 547.

J.

Jerome saith, his time was darkness, 27; quoted, 41, 42; wrote against Helvidius, 161; calleth sacrament of Christ's body the body itself, 233, 237; mentions few saints' days, 347.
Jews, the, teach their children the scriptures early, 189; made not their sacrament their God, as Christians do, 211.
John X., 217.
John XI., 218.
John XIII., 218.
John XV., life of, 124.
Jonas, sermons on, when preached, 434.
Jonases, many to be found in the realm, 466; who they are, *ib.*, 469; ought to be cast out, 480.
Josephus referred to, ix., 249.
Julian, Emperor, 329.

Justice, divine, *correctivam* and *retributivam*, 267.
Justification by faith, meaning of, 49; two things to be observed in, 51; evils arising from denial of, 56; productive of holiness, 57.
Justinian, 78, 171, 273, 275, 334, 338, 352, 368, 376, 383, 386, 387, 390, 391, 392, 393, 394, 407, 408.
Justinus, 423.
Juvenal, 423.

K.

Keeling's Liturg. Brit. 479.
Kimchi saith, idols bring men into hatred with God, 43.
Kings, duty of, 360.
Knowledge should be practical, 152.

L.

Lactantius inveigheth against images, 43, 46; *de Resurrect.* 46; *de Opificio Dei*, 86; *de Orig. Err.* 318; on the Lord's day, 342.
Lanfranc, one of the inventors of transubstantiation, 117, 124; wrote against Berenger, 118; procured his condemnation as a heretic, 124, 524.
Lateran, the council of, 526.
Latimer exposes the abomination of the blood of Hales, 41.
Law of God, the, wherein it differs from man's, 26; delivereth not from sin, 92; believers delivered from curse of, by Christ, 94; believers bound to obey it, 95; perfection of, 105; why it was given, 256; for whom, *ib.*; what it is, 271; requires diligence and circumspection in interpreting it, *ib.*; expounded by Christ, *ib.*; what it teacheth, 272; what the word meaneth, 273; by it we come to the end of our profession, *ib.*; the difference of man's and God's, 274; God's law, every man must learn, *ib.*; Christ's law, many causes to provoke to study of, 275; man erreth from, many ways, *ib.*; erreth from ignorance, *ib.*; erreth from power of the world, 276; erreth from mistaking of the time, *ib.*; prescribed for a time, pernicious, *ib.*; in matter of faith, conscience of man bound only unto, 277; all realms are to be governed by, 280; use of, 281; corrupt nature cannot obey, *ib.*; prohibitory and primitive, 282; convicting and condemning, *ib.*; directing, *ib.*; the estimation of the, 290; the profit that it bringeth, *ib.*; the meaning thereof must be rightly understood, 291; is

to be interpreted by consent of other places and allegory of the letter, 292; not to be added to or taken from, *ib.*; our works cannot fulfil the, 411; Christ hath performed it for us, *ib.*; Moses' forcible persuasions to obey, 413; objections thereto soluted: (1) of time and place, *ib.*; (2) exception of persons, 414; obedience alike required of all, 415; (3) presumption, *ib.*; (4) curiosity, 419; (5) desperation, 422; (6) ignorance, 426.

Legenda Aurea, 182.
Leo III. condemned image-worship, 47.
Leo V., 217.
Leo IX., 118; condemned Berenger, 124, 524.
Lepidus, M., 297.
Lights (high) idolatrous, 317.
Livius, Titus, 327, 417.
Lombard, Peter, 118, 167, 168, 192, 193, 224, 228, 229, 350, 517, 518.
Loye, St (Eloi), 310.
Lucan, 328, 329.
Lucretia, 284.
Ludovicus, 228.
Lugd. (Lyons), council of, 347.
Lupus, Father, 376.
Luther pre-eminent in preaching justification, 29, 144, 246.
Lycurgus, 351.

M.

Magister Sententiarum: see Lombard.
Magistrates are bound to punish transgressors as well as to protect the innocent, 369, 475; godly, would all men to be saved, 472.
Maimonides, 350.
Malmsbury, William of, 291, 451.
Man, of the knowledge of, 86; what he is, 87; his misery, 89; it is increased by malice of the devil, 90; natural corruption and wilful malice joined in him, 304; perverseness of his nature, 548.
Manes, 65.
Manichees, 263.
Marcion, 28, 65, 70, 162, 168, 282, 520, 521.
Martial, 393.
Martin I. established image-worship, 47.
Mass, the, a profanation of Christ's supper, 31; a yesterday's bird, 112; nothing good in the form of, save the scripture, 140; to partake of it is idolatry, 152, 312; no ceremony of God's, 174; or of Christ's supper, 181; but a profanation thereof, *ib.*; the name of, when first used, 226; all the rites of should be taken away, 440; Christ offered in the, contrary to Christ on the cross, 500.
Matrimony, definition of, 380; ends of, 381; not to be avoided for poverty, or any such cause, *ib.*; christian and approved, *ib.*; offence in, *ib.*; remedies against offences in, 382; when the faith of it may be broken, 385; true, forbids plurality of wives, 386.
Maximianus, 387.
Maximinus, 169.
Medea, 138.
Mediator, Christ the only, 34; mediators, vain distinction of, 35.
Meletius, bishop of Lycopolis, sowed a false doctrine, 169.
Memoria, two things to be noted in the word, 209.
Mene (Menna), archbishop, 171.
Menno, 246.
Mercy of God, the only source of Israel's blessings, 257.
Metaphrastes, Simeon, 457.
Minhah, meaning of, 241.
Ministers, how to be esteemed, 20; how far to be followed, 21: not Christ's vicars, 22; are tied to the word of God alone, *ib.*; the office of a good, 26; to be believed only as preaching God's word, 28.
Miracles, strange, are sent of God to call men to repentance, 417.
Missah, meaning of, 241.
Missale Romanum, 283, 284.
Mosheim, 47, 246, 263, 375, 524.
Mould engendered in the consecrated bread, 123, 224.
Mucktar, meaning of, 241.
Multitude, the, not always to be followed, 84.
Munzer, 246.
Murder may be of the heart, 372; or tongue, 373; how committed, 474.

N.

Nations, law of, to be respected, 289.
Nero, 284.
Nestorius, 64, 65.
Nice, council of, 64, 276, 376.
Nicolaus, pope, 193, 524.
Novatians, 169.
Numa Pompilius, forbad images, 284, 352.

O.

Oaths lawful, 324; if needless, sinful, 335; two kinds of, 476; swearing by creatures is unlawful, 477.
Obedience to God's law is required alike of all, 415.
Onkelos, 351.

Oration, a fair and well-ordered, very persuasive, 102.
Orators, custom and manner of, 413.
Orestes, 184.
Origen, 160, 340, 521.
Ovid quoted, 58, 120, 138, 278, 407.

P.

Pantotopon : Christ's body would be, if Christ's words in the sacrament be not figurative, 157.
Paphnutius, 376.
Papistry, all remains of, should be taken away, 438; to buy the ministry of the church, a common practice in, 447.
Parents, duty of, 360.
Paschasius, one of the authors of the doctrine of transubstantiation, 118, 524.
Patrick, St, his purgatory, 290.
Paulinus, bishop of Nola, 397.
Pelagius, 263.
Peleus, 184.
Penitent, pardon for the, 486, 493; external signs of the, 542; God will save all the, 533.
Pesah, (Passover), 125, 172, 190.
Peter, bishop of Alexandria, 169.
Phocas first declared church of Rome to be head of Greeks and Latins, 226.
Phœnix, 184.
Physiognomy, 329.
Pighius preferreth adultery before wedlock, 32.
Pindfools, the word applied to pyxes, 527.
Pinkey, the battle of, xi.
Platina, 47, 125, 217, 225, 276, 291, 451, 569.
Plato, 351.
Pliny, 297, 328, 359, 365, 393.
Ploughman, a, instructed in the resurrection by corn sown, better than by a crucifix, 45.
Plutarch, 297, 484.
Poison administered in the sacrament, 123; in the cup, 451.
Pole, Cardinal, 37.
Polycarp, vi., 28, 39, 83, 347; refused to swear by Cæsar's fortune, 478.
Polycreta, 297.
Pope, the, not Christ's vicar, 22; is the beast in the Apocalypse, 24; his doctrine of the eucharist is opposed to Christ's, 120; he breaks the third commandment, 325.
Powers, superior, how to be honoured and obeyed, 357.
Prayer, the tenor of David's, in 51st Psalm, 57; a difficult work, 144; its efficacy, 184; the Lord's prayer, a compendium of all the Psalms and prayers in scripture, 428; duty of, 458; place of, God hath not respect to, but to the heart and faith, 491.
Preachers of human imaginations break the third commandment, 325; of God's word must be called, ordinarily or extraordinarily, 447; how hard and difficult it is to be, 450; should always be able to say, 'my doctrine is not mine, but his that sent me,' 508.
Preaching, to abolish, against the fourth commandment, 345; hardness in the office of, 549.
Presence, a real, in sacrament, reasons against, 62, 115, 119, 155, 158, 400, 514.
Presumption, the occasion of continuance in sin, 416; original cause of, *ib.*; how nourished, *ib.*
Priest, his office, 183; it is not necessary that he wear a shaven crown and long gown, 245; should be known by his tongue, preaching God's word, and not by cap or vesture, 511.
Priesthood of Christ, 19, 48.
Princes, the most godly the most opposed, 80; shall sustain God's ire if they suffer ungodly preachers to rule over the conscience, 140; they sustain wrongs from usurping bishops, 141; are to have neither more nor less honour than God's word allows, 288; to be honoured and obeyed, 356; the duty of, 360; their noblest work is to promote religion, 435.
Promise, the, made in and for Christ, 258; is co-extensive with the curse, *ib.*; howbeit within certain limits, 259; was made to faith, 261; that is made to all, how we are excluded from, 263; made to the penitent, *ib.*
Prosperity, how to behave in, 301; Moses' rule therein, *ib.*; two precepts in his rule, 302.
Purgatory, St Patrick's, 290; belief in, is a cause of doubt to survivors, 561; how such doubts are removed, 562; evils arising from the doctrine of, 567; is a most pestilent ill, 566.
Pythagoras, 285.

Q.

Quintilian, 221.

R.

Race of Britaine, (Alderney), 497.
Radbert, Paschasius, 291, 524.
Rainbow, a sacrament of God's promise to Noah, 134.
Reformation to be according to God's word, 29.

Regulus shameth christian men, 336.
Religion, the foundation of, 294; first point of, is the fear of God, 298; second, faith and confidence in his word, ib.; third, love, 299; what is the fountain and origin of all true, 306.
Restitution to God, 554; to man, 555.
Restoration of man, means prepared by God for, 15.
Ridley, 524.
Rituale Romanum, 345, 533.
Robin Hood, gestes of, 77.
Roch, St, 457.
Romanus I., pope, 217.
Rome, the see of, is a tyranny of body and soul, 23; the council of, 117; the seat of, is the nest of abomination, 447.
Rosdell, Christopher, iv., v.
Rutherius, 160.
Rutilius, P., 297.

S.

Sabbath, how far the observation of extendeth, 339; the observance of, to be enforced, 341; is not man's precept, 342; is broken by any common work unnecessarily done, 349.
Sabellicus, referred to, v.
Sabellius, 161.
Sackcloth, 538.
Sacrament, a, the nature and use of, 127, 147; it maketh not, but ratifieth our peace, 127; the attributing salvation unto, is an ungodly opinion, 131; carnal presence in the, not supported by John vi., 155; a memory of Christ's death, 156, 190; what ceremony should be in the church, before the use of, 177; preaches penitence and faith, 178; how Christ administered it, 180; is not a bare sign or picture, 190, 199; is a seal to confirm and declare, 191; there is no miracle in, 225; in both kinds was not formerly forbidden, 229; is a memory of Christ's passion in the flesh, and not a distribution of flesh, 402; of Christ's corporal presence in, 514; when the corporal presence began to be maintained, 524.
Sacraments, spoken of sacramentally, 62, 528; to be used holily, yet not to have Christ's office given to them, 76; of old and new testament in effect are one, 126, 190, 200; Christ to come was eaten in, by the ancient Fathers, 127; they give not Christ, ib.; are not to be administered by women, 133; to what end given, ib.; what is required before their being received, 134; are unavailing where faith is not, 135, 146; are witnesses to God's promise, 136; when not rightly used, are abhorred by God, 146; however misused they are not to be contemned, 175; are *Sphragides*, signs and confirmations, 194; illustrated by a banner of an army, 195, the keys of a city, ib., bells, 197, also by the crowing of a cock, 197; two kinds of, 198; of the old and new testament churches compared, 200; in both churches received by faith, ib.; not to be honoured for God, nor for the things they represent, 208; they do nothing but signify and confirm the things that they represent, ib.; are testimonies of God's good will to man, 211; the manner of observance to be decided by word of God, 213; that the true use of is not to be known by the unlearned, is a false opinion, 214; every man is bound to know it, 216; it is to be known by scripture, 218; they should be administered only as God commandeth, 236; to depravate the use of, is a breach of the fourth commandment, 345; to add too much to, or take from, is sacrilege, 399; too much taken from, when they are said to be but external signs, ib.; too much is added to, when as much is attributed to them, as unto the grace and promise that they confirm, ib.; of the old testament were confirmations of, and not the things they were called, 403; are as visible words offered to the senses, 513; Christ is not corporally present in, 514; what it availeth to have, 530; the form and manner of celebrating, 533.
Sallust, 353.
Salvation, means of, when and to whom revealed, 15.
Samosata, Paul of, condemned in the council of Nice, 64; his heresy, 83.
Sanctification, the nature of, 71; is through Christ's blood, 72; is not by the bishop of Rome, or by holy water, &c., 73.
Sardanapalus, 422, 423.
Satisfaction for sin, false gloss on, 348.
Scipio, 365.
Scotland, occasion of war with, xii.
Scott, John, wrote against Paschasius, 118; wrote against the corporal presence in the sacrament, 524.
Scripture, the, teacheth what Christ is, also man, heaven, and hell, 26; how to be interpreted, 28, 84; is to be for holiness as well as for wisdom, 77; the knowledge of, is practical, 95;

is alone sufficient for doctrine and practice, 105, 111; all heresies and false doctrines may be confuted by, 111; is its own best interpreter, 271; two things are to be marked in doubtful texts of, 292; the meaning of, and not the words only to be taken, 401. See *Bible* and *Word of God.*
Seleuciani, 160.
Self-knowledge, how attained, 88, 89.
Seneca to Lucilius, 285; *contra superstitiones,* 346.
Serenus was reprehended for breaking images, 41.
Sergius, II., private masses were not known prior to, 228.
Sergius, III., 218.
Sermon, a, should be preached before the holy supper, 177, 178; it must not be heard only, but followed, *ib.*
Serpent, the brasen, cause of its erection, effect, and use, 54.
Sextus, Decret., 568.
Sextus, Pompeius, 329.
Sign, a, should be known what it is, 195; is not the thing signified, 196.
Similitudes, and not images, are used by Christ for instruction, 45.
Sin, all Christians should beware of, 73; insensibility to, is dangerous, 87; flourishes where there is no correction for it, 90; God's judgment against, is not to be extenuated, 92; the principal remedy against, is to believe Christ's gospel, 109; the servitude of, how called, 261; is the cause of all trouble, 459; will be known at length, *ib.*
Sion House, formerly a Monastery of St Bridget, 291.
Sloth and idleness to be avoided, 506.
Socrates, 169, 376.
Solinus quoted, vi.
Solon, 351, 484.
Somerset, duke of, Declaration of Christ dedicated to, by Hooper, xi.
Sons of God, how the faithful are, 16.
Sophocles, 285.
Sorcery, 308.
Sozomen, 376.
Sphragizo, meaning of, 133.
Spirit, the Holy, the power of, 21.
Spirits, evil, to seek intercourse with, is a breach of the third commandment, 326.
Stephen, VI., 217.
Stoic, 263.
Storck, 246.
Stubner, 246.
Sufferings of Christ, 60.
Superiors, the duty of, 360.
Superstition is to be avoided, 85; all monuments and tokens of, should be removed, 488; persons brought up in, are more slow to believe God's word than infidels, 512.
Supper, the Lord's, the true use of, is to be learned from the doctrine of justification, 60; the abuse of it is the conculcation of Christ's blood, 61; how rightly to use it, 61, 182; how Christ is present in it, 121; is the banner of Christ, 154; is not to be received alone, 170; was not celebrated in private houses for the sick by the apostles, 170; was commanded by St Paul to be done in the church, 171; the definition of, 175; the right use of, very profitable, 186; a law requiring all to partake of, once a year, 228; was simply used by apostles, 237; the form of celebration, 533; the office of minister in, 544; how he should prepare himself for, 534; the office of people in, 535; what is required in receiving, 536. See *Sacrament.*
Suspire, meaning of, illustrated from *Rituale Romanum,* 345.
Sylvester, 278.

T.

Tarquinius Sextus, 284.
Tatian, 375.
Temperance, on, 349.
Temptations of the devil, respecting the sacraments, 530.
Terence, 370.
Termin (Thermopylæ), 356.
Tertullian, 29; *de corona militis,* condemneth images, 43, 160; saith, *Deum posse, velle est,* 168; calleth the bread of thanksgiving a creature of God, 227; expoundeth *Hoc est corpus meum,* 231, 521; denieth the bread to be Christ's body, 232, 282.
Theft, what it is, 391; greatest of all, sacrilege, 395.
Theodore II., pope, 217.
Theodoret, 169, 242.
Theodosius, perhaps Theodorus I., defends images, 47.
Theophylact, 237.
Theostygas, contemners of God, 262.
Thomas of Canterbury, (à Becket), 40, 41.
Tradition is a fallible token of a true church, 82; the mass falsely supported by, 236.
Transubstantiation, whether it be a doctrine of Christ, 112; Rome is its mother, 117; illegitimate, *ib.*; by whom it was introduced into the church, 118; the words of consecration make nothing for, 120; absurdity of its doctrine shewn, 122; arguments

against, 147; is not to be proved from the words, *Hoc est corpus meum*, 162; defenders of, are not agreed in themselves, 167; is not to be proved from God's power, 168; a new term, 210; not to be stablished from the nature of faith, 220; disproved by mould in the bread, 224; antiquity is against it, 235; a new and wicked doctrine, 526.
Travise, (traverse) and play between conscience and law, 89.
Tribbechovius, 47.
Tripartita Historia, makes no mention of saints' days, 347.
Tritemius, J., 327.
Triveth, Nic., 314.
Trope, a, the words of Christ are not to be taken without, 115; papists deny, but use, 121, 528.
Trophonius' cave, 290.
Trouble, profitable to Christians, 509.
Truth, the, always assaulted by Satan, 26; darkened by man's wisdom, 27.
Turner's History of Henry VIII., 38.
Tyndall, 245.

V.

Valentinian, 65.
Valerius (bishop), associated Augustine with himself, 507.
Valerius Maximus, 24, 297, 298, 327, 328, 336, 357, 417, 483.
Valesius, 376.
Valla, Laurentius, 221.
Valois, Tho., 314.
Varenius, viii.
Varro, 27.
Vatablus, 242.
Vercelli, council of, transubstantiation unknown until after, 118, 524.
Vestments, Hooper's opinion upon, 479, 554.
Vicars, Christ's, the apostles assumed not to be, 21, 22.
Victor III., poisoned by the sacrament, 123, 451.
Virgil, ix., 353, 365, 393.
Virgil (Polydore), 239.
Vitæ (Vitas) Patrum, 144, 291.

Vitruvius, viii.
Vocation, danger of transgressing, 456.

U.

Union between Christ and his church, not by eating his body corporally, but by the Spirit of God received by faith, 153.
Urban IV., 527.

W.

War, in what case it may be lawful, 475.
White, St, 320.
Wickliff, resisted the popish doctrine of the mass, 527.
Will of man opposed to virtue, 152.
William of Malmsbury, 291, 451.
Winchester, (Gardiner) bishop of, his book on the sacrament, 99; answer to, 98; Hooper's dedication to, 101; his arguments answered, 213.
Word of God, the truth of, is darkened by man's wisdom, 27; is the judge of the doctors' writings, 30; the knowledge of, leadeth to virtue, 109; glosses and false interpretations of, are to be avoided, 110; the true preaching of, needs to be restored, 205; is to be read believingly, 287; obediently, 289; forsaken for the writings of doctors in ninth century, 524. See *Scripture* and *Bible*.
Works, the imperfection of our, 51; deserve not remission of sin, 56.
Wormius, 161.
Worms are sometimes in consecrated bread, 123.

X.

Xenophon saith, that a good prince differeth nothing from a good father, 361.
Xerxes, 417.

Z.

Zeloten, force of the word, 94.
Zilam (*umbra*), 104.
Zurich, viii.

www.ingramcontent.com/pod-product-compliance
Lightning Source LLC
Chambersburg PA
CBHW071230300426
44116CB00008B/983